W9-AOH-671

American Short-Fiction Criticism
and Scholarship

American and British Literature
Reference Works from Swallow Press

The English Novel: *Twentieth Century Criticism*

Volume I: Defoe Through Hardy
edited by Richard J. Dunn

Volume II: Twentieth Century Novelists
edited by Paul Schlueter and
June Schlueter

Articles on American and British Literature

an Index to Selected
Periodicals, 1950-1977
edited by Larry B. and Sandra Corse

American Short-Fiction Criticism and Scholarship

1959-1977, A Checklist
edited by Joe Weixlmann

Fourth Directory of Periodicals

Publishing Articles on English
and American Literature and Language
edited by Donna Gerstenberger and
George Hendrick

American
Short-Fiction Criticism
and Scholarship, 1959–1977
A Checklist

Joe Weixlmann

Swallow Press
Ohio University Press
Chicago   Athens, Ohio   London

Swallow Press Books
are published by
Ohio University Press
Athens, Ohio 45701

Library of Congress Cataloging in Publication Data

Weixlmann, Joseph.
   American short fiction criticism and scholarship, 1959-1977.

   1. American fiction—History and criticism—Bibliography. 2. Short
stories, American—History and criticism—Bibliography. I. Title.
Z1231.F4W43   [PS374.85]   016.813′01′09   81-11208
ISBN 0-8040-0381-5   AACR2

023537

For My Parents

CONTENTS

INTRODUCTION AND USAGE GUIDE

More than 500 authors are treated in this volume, which will, I hope, be serviceable to all American short-fiction students—casual or committed, lay or professional. The genesis of the book owes a great deal to the publication by Alan Swallow in 1960 of Jarvis Thurston, O. B. Emerson, Carl Hartman, and Elizabeth V. Wright's *Short Fiction Criticism: A Checklist of Interpretation since 1925 of Stories and Novelettes (American, British, Continental), 1800-1958.* But begun simply to update the portion of that volume devoted to the literature of the United States, *American Short-Fiction Criticism and Scholarship, 1959-1977* soon grew beyond its predecessor in terms of coverage—and sheer bulk. Far from sharing the New Critical bias which led Thurston and his fellow compilers to exclude mention of those books and articles dealing solely with "the 'environmental' circumstances of literature (biography, genesis, source, etc.)," the present volume includes not only works of all critical and scholarly persuasions but also interviews and bibliographies, primary as well as secondary. This is not to say, of course, that this checklist is exhaustive, but its exclusions (outlined below) are not based on the once-popular belief that textual explication is superior to all other modes of literary investigation.

In compiling this volume, I have examined approximately 5,000 books as well as all of the relevant instructor's manuals I was able to locate,[1] and I have indexed more than 325 serial publications. The serials, which are listed at the end of the book, include many journals with a "minority" emphasis. Their incorporation helps to lend a definite multiethnic flavor to this volume, although it bears noting, in this regard, that because editorial restrictions prevented the inclusion of non-English language items from the checklist, it was difficult for me to do justice to Chicano literary criticism, much of which is in Spanish. Those interested in this body of writing will, however, be well-served by Julio Martínez's recent *Chicano Scholars and Writers: A Bio-Bibliographical Dictionary* (Scarecrow, 1979). Other noteworthy exclusions include general histories of American literature, most introductions to anthologies (as opposed to prefaces to single-author collections, which are cited), book reviews, serial bibliographies *not* devoted to individual authors, and reprints. In general, only the initial publication of an article or book is given, exceptions being made for recent English translations of foreign-language criticism (including that first printed prior to 1959). I have chosen to terminate coverage with the year 1977 because it is the last date through which I could be assured that my canvassing would be relatively complete.[2] The annual bibliographies published by the Modern Language Association and the Modern Humanities Research Association, in particular, should be consulted for newer items and for items beyond the purview of my research.

Among the more difficult tasks facing anyone compiling a bibliography such as this one, is deciding which works to treat individually, which are, in fact, pieces of short fiction. To use pagination to distinguish the point at which a novella becomes a novel (150 pages is a frequently employed guideline) is not wholly satisfactory: A novella such as John Barth's "Bellerophoniad" is nearly twice the length of Richard Brautigan's *Trout Fishing in America* or Nathanael West's *Miss Lonelyhearts*, both of which are regarded as novels. So I have attempted to solve the novella/novel issue on an individual (and, admittedly, somewhat subjective) basis. In those cases in which I adjudged a work to be a novel and in which my judgment was substantiated by the inclusion of the work in the companion volume to mine, Donna L. Gerstenberger and George Hendrick's *The American Novel: A Checklist of Twentieth Century Criticism* (Swallow, 1961, 1970), I have not covered that work. There remains some overlapping in coverage between Gerstenberger and Hendrick's bibliography and my own—e.g., James's "Daisy Miller" and Melville's "Billy Budd"—, but, to my knowledge, no lacunae exist. I have, moreover, provided individual coverage for some short-story collections frequently considered as novels (Anderson's *Winesburg, Ohio*, for instance) and a pair of dramatic works, Hemingway's "Today Is Friday" and Toomer's "Kabnis," commonly treated as stories. Parts of novels (such as Cather's "Tom Outland's Story" and Hawthorne's "The Custom-House") dealt with by Gerstenberger and Hendrick are customarily omitted from consideration here.

With the exception of the interviews and bibliographies, some pertinent theoretical and biographical studies, and a few brief notes devoted to a particular piece of short fiction, each item in the checklist includes a discussion of *at least one full page* on a given story (or short-fiction canon). Because of space limitations, specific pagination within books has not been provided, and an extensive cross-indexing system, using reference numbers, has been employed. When an item labeled "general" has a minimum of one full page given over to a specific work, a *"See . . . "* or *"See also . . . "* notation ordinarily directs the user to that critique; unexpanded or partially expanded "general" items are prefaced by an asterisk (*). If the user is looking for a substantial critique of an individual work and that work does not appear in the author listing, the "general" author section should be examined for an asterisk-prefaced item and that item, if present, consulted.[3] The large general sections which begin the bibliography, as well as the appropriate general section in the author lists, should be scanned by those seeking to establish a theoretical framework in which to understand an indi-vidual work or those wishing to locate cursory treatments of an individual work. The interview sections in the author listings should also be useful to those attempting to construct a theoretical backdrop against which a particular work or body of works can be understood. And the general and author bibliographies will permit many needing even more information to find it. To limit confu-sion, referencing has also been provided for those writers who have changed their names or are listed in the checklist by a *nom de plume*.

In the more than five years it has taken me to compile this check-list, many personal debts have accrued, the more significant of which I would like to acknowledge. A grant from the Indiana State University Research Fund allowed me to do some very necessary travel, and I am most grateful to two former chairpersons, Marion C. Michael of Texas Tech University and James B. Misenheimer of Indiana State, for the financial support which permitted me, at times, to hire student assistants. To those assistants—Rick Brown, Joel Ford, Donna Michalik, Sylvia Phegley, and, especially, Nan-cy Benson Carroll and Sylvia Clough—I am deeply obliged. My thanks also go out to Carol Chapman, Karen Chittick, and Mary Ann Phillips of the interlibrary-loan staff of Indiana State; to edi-tors Larry Evers (*Sun Tracks: An American Indian Literary Quarter-ly*) and Daniel Walden (*Studies in American Jewish Literature*), who provided me with copies of their journals; and to my former col-league Warren Walker, who gave me access to his extensive collec-tion of instructor's manuals in addition to sharing some hints that made recording my data simple, yet exacting. And let me not fail to mention the many students who, by turns, supported me and bore with me as I saw the book through to completion.

Joe Weixlmann
Terre Haute, Indiana

---

[1]Although instructor's manuals can be devilishly hard to obtain, I thought it preferable to include references to the many I could secure rath-er than to ignore them all. The most extensive checklist of the critical material to be found in manuals appears in Landon C. Burns and Janet P. Alwang's "Cross-Referenced Index of Short Fiction Anthologies and

Author-Title Listing," *Studies in Short Fiction*, 7 (1970), 1–218; 8 (1971), 353–409; 13 (1976), 113–276; 14 (1977), 205–32; 15 (1978), 215–52; 16 (1979), 93–170; and continuing annually. Users of this "Index" should be aware that many of the items cited are brief.

[2]As this book goes to press, four of the journals selected for indexing—*American Speech*, *Literature East & West*, *Southwestern American Literature*, and *Studies in American Humor*—have yet to publish all of their "1977" issues.

[3]In a few cases—e.g., Ronald L. Baker's book on Rowland E. Robinson (item 6435)—numerous stories that no one else has examined are given extensive treatment. To list each would be excessively space-consumptive, and the method arrived at to resolve this dilemma should, I trust, cause the user of the bibliography little inconvenience. This expedient has been utilized only with "minor" authors, and no more than one item per author is so treated.

GENERAL

GENERAL STUDIES
(EIGHTEENTH/NINETEENTH CENTURIES)

1. ADAMS, ROBERT MARTIN. *Nil: Episodes in the Literary Conquest of Void during the Nineteenth Century.* New York: Oxford Univ. Press, 1966.
2. ALTENBERND, LYNN, AND LESLIE L. LEWIS. *A Handbook for the Study of Fiction.* New York: Macmillan, 1966.
3. ANDERSON, JOHN Q., ED. WITH INTROS. *With the Bark On: Popular Humor of the Old South.* Nashville, TN: Vanderbilt Univ. Press, 1967.
4. AUSTIN, JAMES C. "American Humor in France." *Papers on Language & Literature,* 5 (1969), 100–09.
5. BARNETT, LOUISE K. *The Ignoble Savage: American Literary Racism, 1790–1890.* Westport, CT: Greenwood, 1975.
6. BENDER, BERT. "The Lyrical Short Fiction of Dunbar and Chesnutt." In *A Singer in the Dawn: Reinterpretations of Paul Laurence Dunbar.* Ed. Jay Martin. New York: Dodd, Mead, 1975. pp. 208–22.
7. BICKLEY, R. BRUCE, JR. "The Minor Fiction of Hawthorne and Melville." *American Transcendental Quarterly,* no. 14 (1972), pp. 149–52.
8. BIRDSALL, RICHARD D. *Berkshire County: A Cultural History.* New Haven, CT: Yale Univ. Press, 1959.
9. BREINIG, HELMBRECHT. "The Destruction of Fairyland: Melville's 'Piazza' in the Tradition of the American Imagination." *ELH,* 35 (1968), 254–83.
10. BRODHEAD, RICHARD H. *Hawthorne, Melville, and the Novel.* Chicago: Univ. of Chicago Press, 1976.
11. CADY, EDWIN H. *The Light of Common Day: Realism in American Fiction.* Bloomington: Indiana Univ. Press, 1971.
12. CALLOW, JAMES T. *Kindred Spirits: Knickerbocker Writers and American Artists, 1807–1855.* Chapel Hill: Univ. of North Carolina Press, 1967.
13. CARTER, EVERETT. *The American Idea: The Literary Response to American Optimism.* Chapel Hill: Univ. of North Carolina Press, 1977.
14. CHARVAT, WILLIAM. *Literary Publishing in America 1790–1850.* Philadelphia: Univ. of Pennsylvania Press, 1959.
15. _____. *The Profession of Authorship in America, 1800–1870: The Papers of William Charvat.* Ed. Matthew J. Bruccoli. Columbus: Ohio State Univ. Press, 1968.

16. COHEN, HENNIG. "A Comic Mode of the Romantic Imagination: Poe, Hawthorne, Melville." In *The Comic Imagination in American Literature*. Ed. Louis D. Rubin, Jr. New Brunswick, NJ: Rutgers Univ. Press, 1973. pp. 85–99.

17. COHN, JAN. "The Civil War in Magazine Fiction of the 1860's." *Journal of Popular Culture*, 4 (1970), 355–82.

18. _____. "The Negro Character in Northern Magazine Fiction of the 1860's." *The New England Quarterly*, 43 (1970), 572–92.

19. COX, JAMES M. "Humor and America: The Southwestern Bear Hunt, Mrs. Stowe, and Mark Twain." *The Sewanee Review*, 83 (1975), 573–601.

20. _____. "Humor of the Old Southwest." In *The Comic Imagination in American Literature*. Ed. Louis D. Rubin, Jr. New Brunswick, NJ: Rutgers Univ. Press, 1973. pp. 101–12.

21. CURRENT-GARCIA, EUGENE. "Soundings and Alarums: The Beginnings of Short Fiction in America." *The Midwest Quarterly*, 17 (1976), 311–28.

22. CURRY, JANE. "The Ring-Tailed Roarers Rarely Sang Soprano." *Frontiers*, 2, no. 3 (1977), 129–40.

23. DANNER, RICHARD. "The Poe-Matthews Theory of the American Short Story." *Ball State University Forum*, 8, no. 1 (1967), 45–50.

24. DAVIS, RICHARD BEALE. "The Americanness of American Literature: Folk and Historic Themes and Materials in Formal Writing." *The Literary Criterion*, 3, no. 4 (1959), 10–22.

25. DIETRICHSON, JAN W. *The Image of Money in the American Novel of the Gilded Age*. Oslo: Universitetsforlaget, 1969.

26. DOUBLEDAY, NEAL FRANK. *Variety of Attempt: British and American Fiction in the Early Nineteenth Century*. Lincoln: Univ. of Nebraska Press, 1976.

27. DUCKETT, MARGARET. *Mark Twain and Bret Harte*. Norman: Univ. of Oklahoma Press, 1964.

28. EAKIN, JOHN PAUL. *The New England Girl: Cultural Ideals in Hawthorne, Stowe, Howells and James*. Athens: Univ. of Georgia Press, 1976.

29. EATON, CLEMENT. *The Mind of the Old South*. Baton Rouge: Louisiana State Univ. Press, 1964.

30. EBY, CECIL D. "Faulkner and the Southwestern Humorists." *Shenandoah*, 11, no. 1 (1959), 13–21.

31. ELLISON, GEORGE R. "William Tappan Thompson and the *Southern Miscellany*, 1842–1844." *The Mississippi Quarterly*, 23, (1970), 155–68.

32. FALK, ROBERT. "The Search for Reality: Writers and Their

Literature." In *The Gilded Age: A Reappraisal.* Ed. H. Wayne Morgan. Syracuse, NY: Syracuse Univ. Press, 1963. pp. 196–220.

33. **FLANAGAN, JOHN T.** "Native Themes in Early Nineteenth-Century American Fiction." In *Popular Literature in America: A Symposium in Honor of Lyon N. Richardson.* Ed. James C. Austin and Donald A. Koch. Bowling Green, OH: Bowling Green Univ. Popular Press, 1972. pp. 53–69.

34. **FOSTER, EDWARD HALSEY.** *The Civilized Wilderness: Backgrounds to American Romantic Literature, 1817–1860.* New York: Free Press, 1975.

35. **FRANKLIN, H. BRUCE.** *Future Perfect: American Science Fiction of the Nineteenth Century.* New York: Oxford Univ. Press, 1966.

36. **FREDERICK, JOHN T.** *The Darkened Sky: Nineteenth-Century American Novelists and Religion.* Notre Dame, IN: Univ. of Notre Dame Press, 1969.

37. **FRYER, JUDITH.** *The Faces of Eve: Women in the Nineteenth Century American Novel.* New York: Oxford Univ. Press, 1976.

38. **FUSSELL, EDWIN.** *Frontier: American Literature and the American West.* Princeton, NJ: Princeton Univ. Press, 1965.

39. **GIBSON, WILLIAM M.** "The American Literary Scene, 1815–1860." In *Washington Irving: A Tribute.* Ed. Andrew B. Myers. Tarrytown, NY: Sleepy Hollow Restorations, 1972. pp. 77–82.

40. **GILMORE, MICHAEL T.** *The Middle Way: Puritanism and Ideology in American Romantic Fiction.* New Brunswick, NJ: Rutgers Univ. Press, 1977.

41. **GRADE, ARNOLD E.** *The Merrill Guide to Early Juvenile Literature.* Columbus, OH: Merrill, 1970.

42. **GREEN, CLAUD B.** "The Rise and Fall of Local Color in Southern Literature." *The Mississippi Quarterly,* 18 (1965), 1–6.

43. **HAFLEY, JAMES.** "Malice in Wonderland." *The Arizona Quarterly,* 15 (1959), 5–12.

44. **HALL, WADE H.** *Reflections of the Civil War in Southern Humor.* Gainesville: Univ. of Florida Press, 1962.

45. **HANCOCK, CARLA.** *Seven Founders of American Literature.* Winston-Salem, NC: John F. Blair, 1976.

46. **HARAP, LOUIS.** *The Image of the Jew in American Literature: From Early Republic to Mass Immigration.* Philadelphia, PA: Jewish Publication Society of America, 1974.

47. **HOFFMAN, DANIEL G.** *Form and Fable in American Fiction.* New York: Oxford Univ. Press, 1961.

48. **HOLLIS, C. CARROLL.** "Rural Humor of the Late Nineteenth Century." In *The Comic Imagination in American Literature.* Ed. Louis D. Rubin, Jr. New Brunswick, NJ: Rutgers Univ. Press, 1973. pp. 165–77.

49.   HOLMAN, [C.] HUGH, ET AL. "Nineteenth-Century Southern Literature." In *Southern Literary Study: Problems and Possibilities.* Ed. Louis D. Rubin, Jr., and C. Hugh Holman. Chapel Hill: Univ. of North Carolina Press, 1975. pp. 102-32.

50.   HONIG, EDWIN. *Dark Conceit: The Making of Allegory.* Evanston, IL: Northwestern Univ. Press, 1959.

51.   INGE, M. THOMAS. "Introduction." In *The Frontier Humorists: Critical Views.* Ed. M. Thomas Inge. Hamden, CT: Archon Books, 1975. pp. 1-11.

52.   _____. "William Dean Howells on Southern Literature." *The Mississippi Quarterly*, 21 (1968), 291-304.

53.   KAPLAN, HAROLD. *Democratic Humanism and American Literature.* Chicago: Univ. of Chicago Press, 1972.

54.   KAUL, A. N. *The American Vision: Actual and Ideal Society in Nineteenth-Century American Fiction.* New Haven, CT: Yale Univ. Press, 1963.

55.   KENNEDY, J. GERALD. "The Magazine Tales of the 1830's." *American Transcendental Quarterly*, no. 24, Supplement Two (1974), pp. 23-28.

56.   KERR, HOWARD. *Mediums, and Spirit-Rappers, and Roaring Radicals: Spiritualism in American Literature, 1850-1900.* Urbana: Univ. of Illinois Press, 1972.

57.   KING, KIMBALL. "Local Color and the Rise of the American Magazine." In *Essays Mostly on Periodical Publishing in America: A Collection in Honor of Clarence Gohdes.* Ed. James Woodress, et al. Durham, NC: Duke Univ. Press, 1973. pp. 121-33.

58.   KOLB, HAROLD H., JR. *The Illusion of Life: American Realism as a Literary Form.* Charlottesville: Univ. Press of Virginia, 1969.

59.   _____. "In Search of Definition: American Literary Realism and the Clichés." *American Literary Realism, 1870-1910*, 2 (1969), 165-73.

60.   KUHLMANN, SUSAN. *Knave, Fool, and Genius: The Confidence Man As He Appears in Nineteenth-Century American Fiction.* Chapel Hill: Univ. of North Carolina Press, 1973.

61.   KWIAT, JOSEPH J. "Stephen Crane and Frank Norris: The Magazine and the 'Revolt' in American Literature of the 1890s." *Western Humanities Review*, 30 (1976), 309-22.

62.   LINNEMAN, WILLIAM R. "Immigrant Stereotypes: 1880-1900." *Studies in American Humor*, 1 (1974), 28-39.

63.   LYNEN, JOHN F. *The Design of the Present: Essays on Time and Form in American Literature.* New Haven, CT: Yale Univ. Press, 1969.

64.   LYNN, KENNETH S. *Mark Twain and Southwestern Humor.* Boston, MA: Little, Brown, 1959.

65. _____. "Violence in American Literature and Folklore." In *Visions of America: Eleven Literary Historical Essays*. Westport, CT: Greenwood, 1973. pp. 189–205.

66. MacLeod, Anne Scott. *A Moral Tale: Children's Fiction and American Culture, 1820–1860*. Hamden, CT: Archon Books, 1975.

67. Malin, Irving. "American Gothic Images." *Mosaic*, 6, no. 3 (1973), 145–71.

68. _____. "The Authoritarian Family in American Fiction." *Mosaic*, 4, no. 3 (1971), 153–73.

69. Marder, Daniel. "Exiles at Home in American Literature." *Mosaic*, 8, no. 3 (1975), 49–75.

70. Marler, Robert F. "From Tale to Short Story: The Emergence of a New Genre in the 1850's." *American Literature*, 46 (1974), 153–69.

71. Martin, Terence. *The Instructed Vision: Scottish Common Sense Philosophy and the Origin of American Fiction*. Bloomington: Indiana Univ. Press, 1961.

72. Meserole, Harrison T. "Some Notes on Early American Fiction: Kelroy Was There." *Studies in American Fiction*, 5 (1977), 1–12.

73. Moore, Jack B. "Images of the Negro in Early American Short Fiction." *The Mississippi Quarterly*, 22 (1969), 47–57.

74. Moss, Sidney. "Hawthorne and Melville: An Inquiry into Their Art and the Mystery of Their Friendship." *Literary Monographs*, no. 7 (1975), pp. 45–84.

75. Parks, Edd Winfield. *Ante-Bellum Southern Literary Criticism*. Athens: Univ. of Georgia Press, 1962.

76. _____. "The Intent of the Ante-Bellum Southern Humorists." *The Mississippi Quarterly*, 13 (1960), 163–68.

77. Pauly, Thomas H. "The Literary Sketch in Nineteenth-Century America." *Texas Studies in Literature and Language*, 17 (1975), 489–503.

78. Penrod, James H. "Characteristic Endings of Southwestern Yarns." *The Mississippi Quarterly*, 15 (1962), 27–35.

79. Pizer, Donald. *Realism and Naturalism in Nineteenth-Century American Literature*. Carbondale and Edwardsville: Southern Illinois Univ. Press, 1966.

80. Plumstead, A. W. "Puritanism and Nineteenth Century American Literature." *Queen's Quarterly*, 70 (1963), 209–22.

81. Porte, Joel. *The Romance in America: Studies in Cooper, Poe, Hawthorne, Melville, and James*. Middletown, CT: Wesleyan Univ. Press, 1969.

82. REYNOLDS, ALBERT E., II. "The California Gold Rush as a Basis for Literature." In *Americana-Austriaca: Beiträge zur Amerikakunde*, Vol. 2. Ed. Klaus Lanzinger. Vienna: Braumüller, 1970. pp. 61–80.

83. RHODE, ROBERT D. *Setting in the American Short Story of Local Color, 1865–1900*. The Hague: Mouton, 1975.

84. RICKELS, MILTON. "Inexpressibles in Southwestern Humor." *Studies in American Humor*, 3 (1976), 76–83.

85. RIESE, T. A. "The Idea of Evil in American and European Literature." In *Diverging Parallels: A Comparison of American and European Thought and Action*. Ed. A. N. J. den Hollander. Leiden: Brill, 1971. pp. 185–201.

86. RUBIN, LOUIS D., JR. "Southern Local Color and The Black Man." *The Southern Review*, NS 6 (1970), 1011–30.

87. SCHMITZ, NEIL. "Tall Tale, Tall Talk: Pursuing the Lie in Jacksonian Literature." *American Literature*, 48 (1977), 471–91.

88. SEDERBERG, NANCY B. "Antebellum Southern Humor in the *Camden Journal*: 1826–1840." *The Mississippi Quarterly*, 27 (1974), 41–74.

89. SIMPSON, CLAUDE M. "Introduction." In *The Local Colorists: American Short Stories, 1857–1900*. New York: Harper, 1960. pp. 1–20.

90. SLOTKIN, RICHARD. *Regeneration through Violence: The Mythology of the American Frontier, 1600–1860*. Middletown, CT: Wesleyan Univ. Press, 1973.

91. SMITH, HERBERT F. *Richard Watson Gilder*. New York: Twayne, 1970.

92. SPENGEMANN, WILLIAM C. *The Adventurous Muse: The Poetics of American Fiction, 1789–1900*. New Haven, CT: Yale Univ. Press, 1977.

93. STOUT, JANIS P. *Sodoms in Eden: The City in American Fiction before 1860*. Westport, CT: Greenwood, 1976.

94. SUVIN, DARKO. "Radical Rhapsody and Romantic Recoil in the Age of Anticipation: A Chapter in the History of SF." *Science-Fiction Studies*, 1 (1974), 255–69.

95. TOTH, SUSAN ALLEN. " 'The Rarest and Most Peculiar Grape': Versions of the New England Woman in 19th-Century Local Color Literature." *The Kate Chopin Newsletter*, 2, no. 2 (1976), 38–45.

96. _____. "Sarah Orne Jewett and Friends: A Community of Interest." *Studies in Short Fiction*, 9 (1972), 233–41.

97. TURNER, ARLIN. "Comedy and Reality in Local Color Fiction, 1865–1900." In *The Comic Imagination in American Literature*. Ed. Louis D. Rubin, Jr. New Brunswick, NJ: Rutgers Univ. Press, 1973. pp. 157–64.

98. _____. "Dim Pages in Literary History: The South since the Civil War." In *Southern Literary Study: Problems and Possibilities*. Ed. Louis D. Rubin, Jr., and C. Hugh Holman. Chapel Hill: Univ. of North Carolina Press, 1975, pp. 36-47.

99. _____. "Realism and Fantasy in Southern Humor." *The Georgia Review*, 12 (1958), 451-57.

100. _____. "The Uncertainties of Authorship in the South after the Civil War." In *Popular Literature in America: A Symposium in Honor of Lyon N. Richardson*. Ed. James C. Austin and Donald A. Koch. Bowling Green, OH: Bowling Green Univ. Popular Press, 1972. pp. 184-98.

101. WASSERSTROM, WILLIAM. "The Spirit of Myrrha." *American Imago*, 13 (1956), 455-72.

102. WATSON, HAROLD FRANCIS. *Coasts of Treasure Island: A Study of the Backgrounds and Sources for Robert Louis Stevenson's Romance of the Sea*. San Antonio, TX: Naylor, 1969.

103. WEBNER, HELENE L. "Hawthorne, Melville and Lowell: *The Old Glory*." RE: *Arts & Letters*, 4, no. 1 (1970), 1-17.

104. WEST, JAMES L. W., III. "Early Backwoods Humor in the Greenville *Mountaineer*, 1826-1840." *The Mississippi Quarterly*, 25 (1972), 69-82.

105. WILSON, EDMUND. *Patriotic Gore: Studies in the Literature of the American Civil War*. New York: Oxford Univ. Press, 1962.

106. WILSON, JAMES D. "Incest and American Romantic Fiction." *Studies in the Literary Imagination*, 7, no. 1 (1974), 31-50.

107. WRIGHT, NATHALIA. *American Novelists in Italy, The Discoverers: Allston to James*. Philadelphia: Univ. of Pennsylvania Press, 1965.

108. ZIFF, LARNER. *The American 1890's: Life and Times of a Lost Generation*. New York: Viking, 1966.

109. ZIPES, JACK D. *The Great Refusal: Studies of the Romantic Hero in German and American Literature*. Bad Homburg: Athenäum, 1970.

GENERAL STUDIES (TWENTIETH CENTURY)

110. ADAMS, ROBERT MARTIN. *After Joyce: Studies in Fiction after Ulysses*. New York: Oxford Univ. Press, 1977.

111. ALLEN, MARY. *The Necessary Blankness: Women in Major American Fiction of the Sixties*. Urbana: Univ. of Illinois Press, 1976.

112. ALLEN, WALTER. *Tradition and Dream: The English and American Novel from the Twenties to Our Time*. London: Phoenix House, 1964.

113. **ALTER, ROBERT.** "Jewish Humor and the Domestication of Myth." In *Veins of Humor*. Ed. Harry Levin. Cambridge, MA: Harvard Univ. Press, 1972. pp. 255–67.

114. **AMIS, KINGSLEY.** *New Maps of Hell: A Survey of Science Fiction*. New York: Harcourt, Brace & World, 1960.

115. **ANON.** "The Characteristic Form: A Distinct Predilection for the Short Story." *The Times* (London) *Literary Supplement*, 6 Nov. 1959, p. xv.

116. **AUSTEN, ROGER.** *Playing the Game: The Homosexual Novel in America*. Indianapolis, IN: Bobbs-Merrill, 1977.

117. **BALDESHWILER, EILEEN.** "The Lyrical Short Story: The Sketch of a History." *Studies in Short Fiction*, 6 (1969), 443–53.

118. **BARTHELME, DONALD, WILLIAM GASS, GRACE PALEY, AND WALKER PERCY.** "A Symposium on Fiction." *Shenandoah*, 27, no. 2 (1976), 3–31.

119. **BARTON, REBECCA CHALMERS.** *Black Voices in American Fiction, 1900–1930*. Oakdale, NY: Dowling College Press, 1976.

120. **BEACH, SYLVIA.** *Shakespeare and Company*. New York: Harcourt, Brace, 1959.

121. **BELLAMY, JOE DAVID.** "Fiction in the Age of Excess." *Saturday Review*, 2 (23 Aug. 1975), 40–41.

122. **BELLOW, SAUL.** "Some Notes on Recent American Fiction." *Encounter*, 21, no. 5 (1963), 22–29.

123. **BENNETT, STEPHEN B., AND WILLIAM W. NICHOLS.** "Violence in Afro-American Fiction: An Hypothesis." *Modern Fiction Studies*, 17 (1971), 221–28.

124. **BERGER, ALBERT I.** "The Triumph of Prophecy: Science Fiction and Nuclear Power in the Post-Hiroshima Period." *Science-Fiction Studies*, 3 (1976), 143–50.

125. **BERGONZI, BERNARD.** "An Appendix on the Short Story." In *The Situation of the Novel*. London: Macmillan, 1970. pp. 214–18.

126. **BILLINGSLEY, RONALD G.** "The Burden of the Hero in Modern Afro-American Fiction." *Black World*, 25, no. 2 (1975), 38–45, 66–73.

127. **BORDEN, CAROLINE.** "Characterization in Revolutionary Chinese and Reactionary American Short Stories." *Literature & Ideology*, no. 12 (1972), pp. 9–16.

128. **BOUCHER, ANTHONY.** "There Was No Mystery in What the Crime Editor Was After." *The New York Times Book Review*, 26 Feb. 1961, pp. 4–5, 50.

129. **BOURJAILY, VANCE.** "That Stories Should Not Be Their Own Reward." *The New York Times Book Review*, 5 Aug. 1973, p. 27.

130. BOVA, BENJAMIN. *Through Eyes of Wonder: Science Fiction and Science.* Reading, MA: Addison-Wesley, 1975.

131. BRADBURY, JOHN M. *Renaissance in the South: A Critical History of the Literature, 1920-1960.* Chapel Hill: Univ. of North Carolina Press, 1963.

132. BRETNOR, REGINALD. "Science Fiction in the Age of Space." In *Science Fiction, Today and Tomorrow.* Ed. Reginald Bretnor. New York: Harper & Row, 1974. pp. 150-78.

133. BROOKS, CLEANTH. *The Hidden God: Studies in Hemingway, Faulkner, Yeats, Eliot, and Warren.* New Haven, CT: Yale Univ. Press, 1963.

134. _____. "Southern Literature: The Wellsprings of Its Vitality." *The Georgia Review*, 16 (1962), 238-53.

135. BRUCE-NOVOA, JUAN. "Round Table on Chicano Literature." *The Journal of Ethnic Studies*, 3, no. 1 (1975), 99-103.

136. _____. "The Space of Chicano Literature." *De Colores*, 1, no. 4 (1975), 22-42.

137. BRUCK, PETER. "Black American Short Fiction in the 20th Century: Problems of Audience, and the Evolution of Artistic Stances and Themes." In *The Black American Short Story in the 20th Century: A Collection of Critical Essays.* Ed. Peter Bruck. Amsterdam: B. R. Grüner, 1977. pp. 1-19.

138. BUCHEN, IRVING H. "Jewish-American Writers As a Literary Group." *Renascence*, 19 (1967), 142-50.

139. BURNETT, HALLIE. "Personal Recollections of a *STORY* Editor." *The Connecticut Review*, 6, no. 2 (1973), 5-12.

140. CARTER, PAUL A. *The Creation of Tomorrow: Fifty Years of Magazine Science Fiction.* New York: Columbia Univ. Press, 1977.

141. _____. "Extravagant Fiction Today—Cold Fact Tomorrow: A Rationale for the First American Science-Fiction Magazines." *Journal of Popular Culture*, 5 (1972), 842-57.

142. _____. "Rockets to the Moon, 1919-1944: A Dialogue between Fiction and Reality." *American Studies*, 15, no. 1 (1974), 31-46.

143. CLARESON, THOMAS D. "Many Futures, Many Worlds." In *Many Futures, Many Worlds: Theme and Form in Science Fiction.* Ed. Thomas D. Clareson. Kent, OH: Kent State Univ. Press, 1977. pp. 14-26.

144. CLEMENT, HAL. "Hard Sciences and Tough Technologies." In *The Craft of Science Fiction.* Ed. Reginald Bretnor. New York: Harper & Row, 1976. pp. 37-52.

145. COOK, BRUCE. "New Faces in Faulkner Country." *Saturday Review*, 3 (4 Sept. 1976), 39-41.

146. COOK, SYLVIA JENKINS. *From Tobacco Road to Route 66: The Southern Poor White in Fiction.* Chapel Hill: Univ. of North Carolina Press, 1976.

147. COOPERMAN, STANLEY. *World War I and the American Novel.* Baltimore, MD: Johns Hopkins Univ. Press, 1967.

148. COVELLI, PASQUALE. "Cheever vs. Barthelme." *Fiction*, no. 8 (1974), pp. 98, 100.

149. COWLEY, MALCOLM. *A Second Flowering: Works and Days of the Lost Generation.* New York: Viking, 1973.

150. DAVIS, ARTHUR P. *From the Dark Tower: Afro-American Writers 1900 to 1960.* Washington, DC: Howard Univ. Press, 1974.

151. DEKLE, BERNARD. *Profiles of Modern American Authors.* Rutland, VT: Charles E. Tuttle, 1969.

152. DEMBO, L. S. "Dissent and Dissent: A Look at Fiedler and Trilling." In *Contemporary American-Jewish Literature.* Ed. Irving Malin. Bloomington: Indiana Univ. Press, 1973. pp. 134–55.

153. DeMOTT, BENJAMIN. "Jewish Writers in America: A Place in the Establishment." *Commentary*, 31 (1961), 127–34.

154. DETWEILER, ROBERT. "The Moment of Death in Modern Fiction." *Contemporary Literature*, 12 (1971), 269–94.

155. DICKSTEIN, MORRIS. "Fiction Hot and Kool: Dilemmas of the Experimental Writer." *TriQuarterly*, no. 33 (1975), pp. 257–72.

156. ———. *Gates of Eden: American Culture in the Sixties.* New York: Basic Books, 1977.

157. DIETRICH, R. F., AND ROGER H. SUNDELL. *Instructor's Manual for "The Art of Fiction."* New York: Holt, Reinhart and Winston, 1967.

158. DISCH, THOMAS M. "The Embarrassments of Science Fiction." In *Science Fiction at Large: A Collection of Essays, by Various Hands, about the Interface between Science Fiction and Reality.* Ed. Peter Nicholls. New York: Harper & Row, 1976. pp. 141–55.

159. DONOVAN, FRANK P. "Mystery Rides the Rails—Part II: Railroad Short Stories of Detection and Mystery in America." *The Armchair Detective*, 2 (1968), 46–48.

160. DOTY, WILLIAM G. "The Stories of Our Times." In *Religion as Story.* Ed. James B. Wiggins. New York: Harper & Row, 1975. pp. 93–121.

161. DURHAM, PHILIP. "The *Black Mask* School." In *Tough Guy Writers of the Thirties.* Ed. David Madden. Carbondale and Edwardsville: Southern Illinois Univ. Press, 1968. pp. 51–79.

162. EISINGER, CHESTER E. *Fiction of the Forties.* Chicago: Univ. of Chicago Press, 1963.

163. EMANUEL, JAMES A. "The Challenge of Black Literature: Notes on Interpretation." In *The Black Writer in Africa and the*

Americas. Ed. Lloyd W. Brown. Los Angeles, CA: Hennessey & Ingalls, 1973. pp. 85-100.

164. **FEDERMAN, RAYMOND.** "Surfiction—Four Propositions in Form of an Introduction." In *Surfiction: Fiction Now . . . and Tomorrow*. Ed. Raymond Federman. Chicago: Swallow, 1975. pp. 5-15.

165. _____, **JOSEPH HYNES,** and **MAS'UD ZAVARZADEH.** "Tri(y)-log." *Chicago Review*, 28, no. 2 (1976), 93-109.

166. **FELHEIM, MARVIN.** "Eudora Welty and Carson McCullers." In *Contemporary American Novelists*. Ed. Harry T. Moore. Carbondale: Southern Illinois Univ. Press, 1964. pp. 41-53.

167. **FEUSER, WILLFRIED F.** "The Men Who Lived Underground: Richard Wright and Ralph Ellison." In *A Celebration of Black and African Writing*. Ed. Bruce King and Kolawole Ogungbesan. Zaria: Ahmadu Bello Univ. Press, 1975. pp. 87-101.

168. **FIEDLER, LESLIE A.** *The Jew in the American Novel*. New York: Herzl Institute, 1959.

169. **FINKELSTEIN, SIDNEY.** *Existentialism and Alienation in American Literature*. New York: International, 1965.

170. **FITZ GERALD, GREGORY.** "Character Typology in Satiric Short Stories." *Satire Newsletter*, 7 (1969), 100-03.

171. **FOGLE, RICHARD HARTER.** "Illusion, Point of View, and Modern Novel-Criticism." In *The Theory of the Novel: New Essays*. Ed. John Halperin. New York: Oxford Univ. Press, 1974. pp. 338-52.

172. **FORD, HUGH.** *Published in Paris: American and British Writers, Printers, and Publishers in Paris, 1920-1939*. New York: Macmillan, 1975.

173. **FOX, HUGH.** "Standards: Some Subjectivities on Fiction." *Southern Humanities Review*, 7 (1973), 183-90.

174. **FREDERICKS, S. C.** "Revivals of Ancient Mythologies in Current Science Fiction and Fantasy." In *Many Futures, Many Worlds: Theme and Form in Science Fiction*. Ed. Thomas D. Clareson. Kent, OH: Kent State Univ. Press, 1977. pp. 50-65.

175. **FRENCH, WARREN.** *The Social Novel at the End of an Era*. Carbondale and Edwardsville: Southern Illinois Univ. Press, 1966.

176. **FRIEDMAN, MELVIN J.** "Dislocations of Setting and Word: Notes on American Fiction Since 1950." *Studies in American Fiction*, 5 (1977), 79-98.

177. **GARDNER, JOHN.** "The Way We Write Now." *The New York Times Book Review*, 9 July 1972, pp. 2, 32-33.

178. **GLAZIER, TERESA FERSTER.** *Instructor's Manual for "Short Stories for Insight."* New York: Harcourt, Brace & World, 1967.

179. GLICKSBERG, CHARLES I. *The Sexual Revolution in Modern American Literature*. The Hague: Martinus Nijhoff, 1971.

180. GOLLIN, RITA K. "Understanding Fathers in American Jewish Fiction." *The Centennial Review*, 18 (1974), 273-87.

181. GOSSETT, LOUISE Y. *Violence in Recent Southern Fiction*. Durham, NC: Duke Univ. Press, 1965.

182. GRABER, RALPH S. Baseball in American Fiction." *English Journal*, 56 (1967), 1107-14.

183. GRAFF, GERALD. "Babbitt at the Abyss: The Social Context of Postmodern American Fiction." *TriQuarterly*, no. 33 (1975), pp. 305-37.

184. GRAHAM, DON. "Is Dallas Burning? Notes on Recent Texas Fiction." *Southwestern American Literature*, 4 (1974), 68-73.

185. GRAY, RICHARD. *The Literature of Memory: Modern Writers of the American South*. Baltimore, MD: Johns Hopkins Univ. Press, 1977.

186. GREENMAN, MYRON. "Understanding New Fiction." *Modern Fiction Studies*, 20 (1974), 307-16.

187. GUERARD, ALBERT J. "Notes on the Rhetoric of Anti-Realist Fiction." *TriQuarterly*, no. 30 (1974), 3-50.

188. GULLASON, THOMAS A. "Revelation and Evolution: A Neglected Dimension of the Short Story." *Studies in Short Fiction*, 10 (1973), 347-56.

189. GUNN, JAMES. "Science Fiction and the Mainstream." In *Science Fiction, Today and Tomorrow*. Ed. Reginald Bretnor. New York: Harper & Row, 1974. pp. 183-214.

190. GUTTMANN, ALLEN. "The Conversions of the Jews." In *The Cry of Home: Cultural Nationalism and the Modern Writer*. Ed. H. Ernest Lewald. Knoxville: Univ. of Tennessee Press, 1972. pp. 245-67.

191. ————. "Jewish Humor." In *The Comic Imagination in American Literature*. Ed. Louis D. Rubin, Jr. New Brunswick, NJ: Rutgers Univ. Press, 1973. pp. 329-38.

192. GYSIN, FRITZ. *The Grotesque in American Negro Fiction: Jean Toomer, Richard Wright, and Ralph Ellison*. Bern: Francke, 1975.

193. HANSEN, ARLEN J. "The Celebration of Solipsism: A New Trend in American Fiction." *Modern Fiction Studies*, 19 (1973), 5-15.

194. HARDY, JOHN EDWARD. *Commentaries on Five Modern American Short Stories*. Frankfurt: Diesterweg, 1963.

195. HARPER, HOWARD M., JR. *Desperate Faith: A Study of Bellow, Salinger, Mailer, Baldwin, and Updike*. Chapel Hill: Univ. of North Carolina Press, 1967.

196. HARRIS, TRUDIER. "Ceremonial Fagots: Lynching and

Burning Rituals in Black Literature." *Southern Humanities Review*, 10 (1976), 235–47.

197. HARTMAN, CARL, AND HAZARD ADAMS. *Teacher's Manual for* "Fiction as Process." New York: Dodd, Mead, 1968.

198. HASSAN, IHAB. "Fiction." In *Contemporary American Literature, 1945-1972: An Introduction*. New York: Ungar, 1973. pp. 22–87.

199. _____. "Fiction and Future: An Extravaganza for Voice and Tape." In *Liberations: New Essays on the Humanities in Revolution*. Ed. Ihab Hassan. Middletown, CT: Wesleyan Univ. Press, 1971. pp. 176–96.

200. _____. *Radical Innocence: Studies in the Contemporary American Novel*. Princeton, NJ: Princeton Univ. Press, 1961.

201. HAYS, R. W. "The Clue of the Dying Message." *The Armchair Detective*, 7 (1973), 1–3.

202. HICKS, GRANVILLE. "Generations of the Fifties: Malamud, Gold, and Updike." In *The Creative Present: Notes on Contemporary American Fiction*. Ed. Nona Balakian and Charles Simmons. Garden City, NY: Doubleday, 1963. pp. 217–37.

203. HILFER, ANTHONY CHANNELL. *The Revolt from the Village, 1915-1930*. Chapel Hill: Univ. of North Carolina Press, 1969.

204. HILL, HAMLIN. "Black Humor and the Mass Audience." In *American Humor: Essays Presented to John C. Gerber*. Ed. O. M. Brack, Jr. Scottsdale, AZ: Arete, 1977. pp. 1–11.

205. HINOJOSA, ROLANDO. "Mexican-American Literature: Toward an Identification." *Books Abroad*, 49 (1975), 422–30.

206. HOFFMAN, FREDERICK J. *The Art of Southern Fiction: A Study of Some Modern Novelists*. Carbondale and Edwardsville: Southern Illinois Univ. Press, 1967.

207. _____. *The Twenties: American Writing in the Postwar Decade*. Rev. ed. New York: Collier Books, 1962.

208. HOLMAN, C. HUGH. "Anodyne for the Village Virus." In *The Comic Imagination in American Literature*. Ed. Louis D. Rubin, Jr. New Brunswick, NJ: Rutgers Univ. Press, 1973. pp. 247–58.

209. HOWARD, DANIEL F. *Manual to Accompany* "The Modern Tradition: Short Stories," Second Edition. Boston, MA: Little, Brown, 1972.

210. HUGGINS, NATHAN IRVIN. *Harlem Renaissance*. New York: Oxford Univ. Press, 1971.

211. INGRAM, FORREST L., S. J. "The Dynamics of Short Story Cycles." *The New Orleans Review*, 2 (1970), 7–12.

212. _____. *Representative Short Story Cycles of the Twentieth Century: Studies in a Literary Genre*. The Hague: Mouton, 1971.

213. **JOHNSON, JAMES WILLIAM.** "The Adolescent Hero: A Trend in Modern Fiction." *Twentieth Century Literature*, 5 (1959), 3-11.

214. **JONES, HARRY L.** "Black Humor and the American Way of Life." *Satire Newsletter*, 7 (1969), 1-4.

215. **JOSELYN, SISTER M., O.S.B.** "Edward Joseph O'Brien and the American Short Story." *Studies in Short Fiction*, 3 (1965), 1-15.

216. **KAFKA, JANET.** "Why Science Fiction?" *English Journal*, 64 (1975), 46-53.

217. **KAGLE, STEVEN.** "Science Fiction as Simulation Game." In *Many Futures, Many Worlds: Theme and Form in Science Fiction.* Ed. Thomas D. Clareson. Kent, OH: Kent State Univ. Press, 1977. pp. 224-36.

218. **KAZIN, ALFRED.** *Bright Book of Life: American Novelists and Storytellers from Hemingway to Mailer.* Boston, MA: Little, Brown, 1973.

219. **KELLOG, GENE.** *The Vital Tradition: The Catholic Novel in a Period of Convergence.* Chicago: Loyola Univ. Press, 1970.

220. **KENNER, HUGH.** *A Homemade World: American Modernist Writing.* New York: Knopf, 1975.

221. **KING, J. NORMAN.** "Theology, Science Fiction, and Man's Future Orientation." In *Many Futures, Many Worlds: Theme and Form in Science Fiction.* Ed. Thomas D. Clareson. Kent, OH: Kent State Univ. Press, 1977. pp. 237-59.

222. **KLEIN, MARCUS.** *After Alienation: American Novels in Mid-Century.* Cleveland, OH: World, 1964.

223. **KLINKOWITZ, JEROME.** *The Life of Fiction.* Urbana: Univ. of Illinois Press, 1977.

224. _____. *Literary Disruptions: The Making of a Post-Contemporary American Fiction.* Urbana: Univ. of Illinois Press, 1975.

225. **KLOTMAN, PHYLLIS RAUCH.** *Another Man Gone: The Black Runner in Contemporary Afro-American Literature.* Port Washington, NY: Kennikat, 1977.

226. **KNIGHT, DAMON.** *In Search of Wonder: Essays on Modern Science Fiction.* 2nd ed. Chicago: Advent, 1967.

227. **KORT, WESLEY A.** *Shriven Selves: Religious Problems in Recent American Fiction.* Philadelphia, PA: Fortress Press, 1972.

228. **KOSTELANETZ, RICHARD.** *The End of Intelligent Writing: Literary Politics in America.* New York: Sheed and Ward, 1974.

229. _____. " 'New American Fiction' Reconsidered." *TriQuarterly*, no. 8 (1967), pp. 279-86.

230. _____. "New Fiction in America." *The University of Denver Quarterly*, 8, no. 3 (1973), 1-17.

231. _____. "Notes on the American Short Story Today." *The Minnesota Review*, 5 (1965), 214-21.

232. **KRISHNAMURTHI, M. G.** "The Distaff Faulknerians." *The Literary Criterion*, 8, no. 1 (1967), 69–78.

233. **KROITOR, HARRY P.** "The Special Demands of Point of View in Science Fiction." *Extrapolation*, 17 (1976), 153–59.

234. **KRUEGER, JOHN R.** "Names and Nomenclatures in Science-Fiction." *Names*, 14 (1966), 203–14.

235. **LACHMANN, MARVIN.** "The American Regional Mystery: Southern California." *The Armchair Detective*, 10 (1977), 294–306.

236. ———. "Forgotten Men." *The Armchair Detective*, 2 (1969), 217–23.

237. ———. "Sports and the Mystery Story." *The Armchair Detective*, 6 (1972), 1–6; 6 (1973), 83–85, 243–45; 7 (1974), 195–97, 261–62, 269; 8 (1975), 108–10.

238. **LARSON, CHARLES R.** "Keeping the Short Story Alive." *The Nation*, 222 (1976), 629–31.

239. **LEE, L. L.** " 'What's New in Fiction, If It's Possible?' " *Style*, 9 (1975), 335–52.

240. **LEHAN, RICHARD.** *A Dangerous Crossing: French Literary Existentialism and the Modern American Novel*. Carbondale and Edwardsville: Southern Illinois Univ. Press, 1973.

241. **LEM, STANISLAW.** "The Time-Travel Story and Related Matters of SF Structuring." Trans. Thomas H. Hoisington and Darko Suvin. *Science-Fiction Studies*, 1 (1974), 143–54.

242. **LESSER, M. X., AND JOHN N. MORRIS.** *Teacher's Manual to Accompany* "Modern Short Stories: The Fiction of Experience." New York: McGraw-Hill, 1964.

243. **LE VOT, ANDRE.** "Disjunctive and Conjunctive Modes in Contemporary American Fiction." *Forum* (University of Houston), 14, no. 1 (1976), 44–55.

244. **LEWIS, STUART A.** "The Jewish Author Looks at the Black." *The Colorado Quarterly*, 21 (1973), 317–30.

245. **LISCA, PETER.** "Steinbeck and Hemingway: Suggestions for a Comparative Study." In *Steinbeck's Literary Dimension: A Guide to Comparative Studies*. Ed. Tetsumaro Hayashi. Metuchen, NJ: Scarecrow, 1973. pp. 46–54.

246. **LYTLE, ANDREW, ET AL.** "The Writer's Sense of Place: A Symposium and Commentaries." *South Dakota Review*, 13, no. 3 (1975), 1–139.

247. **McCAFFREY, ANNE.** "Hitch Your Dragon to a Star: Romance and Glamour in Science Fiction." In *Science Fiction, Today and Tomorrow*. Ed. Reginald Bretnor. New York: Harper & Row, 1974. pp. 278–92.

248. **McCLINTOCK, MICHAEL W.** "Some Preliminaries to the Criticism of Science Fiction." *Extrapolation*, 15 (1973), 17–24.

249. McCormick, John. *Fiction as Knowledge: The Post-Romantic Novel*. New Brunswick, NJ: Rutgers Univ. Press, 1975.

250. ———. *The Middle Distance: A Comparative History of American Imaginative Literature, 1919-1932*. New York: Free Press, 1971.

251. McKenzie, James. "Pole-Vaulting in Top Hats: A Public Conversation with John Barth, William Gass, and Ishmael Reed." *Modern Fiction Studies*, 22 (1976), 131-51.

252. McSherry, Frank D., Jr. "The Amateurs' Hour." *The Armchair Detective*, 3 (1969), 14-22.

253. ———. "The Golden Road to Samarkand: The Arabian Nights in Detective Fiction." *The Armchair Detective*, 7 (1974), 77-94.

254. ———. "The Shape of Crimes to Come." In *The Mystery Writer's Art*. Ed. Francis M. Nevins, Jr. Bowling Green, OH: Bowling Green Univ. Popular Press, 1970. pp. 326-38.

255. Malin, Irving. "Introduction." In *Contemporary American-Jewish Literature*. Ed. Irving Malin. Bloomington: Indiana Univ. Press, 1973, pp. 3-9.

256. ———. *Jews and Americans*. Carbondale and Edwardsville: Southern Illinois Univ. Press, 1965.

257. ———. *New American Gothic*. Carbondale: Southern Illinois Univ. Press, 1962.

258. Margolies, Edward. *Native Sons: A Critical Study of Twentieth-Century Negro American Authors*. Philadelphia, PA: Lippincott, 1968.

259. Martin, Robert A. "Primitivism in Stories by Willa Cather and Sherwood Anderson." *Midamerica*, 3 (1976), 39-45.

260. Mathews, Richard. "Intermedia Fictions and the Critical Consciousness." *Style*, 9 (1975), 353-71.

261. Meese, Elizabeth A. "Telling It All: Literary Standards and Narratives by Southern Women." *Frontiers*, 2, no. 2 (1977), 63-67.

262. Mellard, James M. "Racism, Formula, and Popular Fiction." *Journal of Popular Culture*, 5 (1971), 10-37.

263. ———. "Solipsism, Symbolism, and Demonism: The Lyrical Mode in Fiction." *Southern Humanities Review*, 8 (1974), 37-52.

264. Meyers, Walter E. "The Future History and Development of the English Language." *Science-Fiction Studies*, 3 (1976), 130-42.

265. M[ilton], J[ohn] R., et al. "The Western Novel—A Symposium." *South Dakota Review*, 2, no. 1 (1964), 3-36.

266. Minot, Stephen, and Robley Wilson, Jr. *Teacher's*

Manual—"Three Stances of Modern Fiction: A Critical Anthology of the Short Story." Cambridge, MA: Winthrop, 1972.

267. MIZENER, ARTHUR. *A Handbook of Analyses, Questions, and a Discussion of Technique for Use with* "Modern Short Stories: The Uses of Imagination," Revised Edition. New York: Norton, 1966.

268. _____. *A Handbook of Analyses, Questions, and a Discussion of Technique for Use with* "Modern Short Stories: The Uses of Imagination," Third Edition. New York: Norton, 1971.

269. _____. *The Sense of Life in the Modern Novel*. Boston, MA: Houghton Mifflin, 1964.

270. MOLYNEUX, THOMAS. "The Affirming Balance of Voice." *Shenandoah*, 25, no. 2 (1974), 27–43.

271. MORGAN, H. WAYNE. *Writers in Transition: Seven Americans*. New York: Hill and Wang, 1963.

272. MOSKOWITZ, SAM. *Seekers of Tomorrow: Masters of Modern Science Fiction*. Cleveland, OH: World, 1966.

273. NOWER, JOYCE. "Foolin Master." *Satire Newsletter*, 7 (1969), 5–10.

274. O'CONNOR, FRANK. *The Lonely Voice: A Study of the Short Story*. Cleveland, OH: World, 1963.

275. O'CONNOR, WILLIAM VAN. "The Grotesque: An American Genre." In *The Grotesque: An American Genre and Other Essays*. Carbondale: Southern Illinois Univ. Press, 1962. pp. 3–19.

276. PANSHIN, ALEXEI AND CORY. "A New Worldview." In *SF in Dimension: A Book of Explorations*. Chicago: Advent Publishers, 1976. pp. 247–83.

277. PEDEN, WILLIAM. *The American Short Story: Continuity and Change, 1940–1975*. Boston, MA: Houghton Mifflin, 1975.

278. _____. *The American Short Story: Front Line in the National Defense of Literature*. Boston, MA: Houghton Mifflin, 1964.

279. _____. "The American Short Story during the Twenties." *Studies in Short Fiction*, 10 (1973), 367–71.

280. _____. "The Black Explosion." *Studies in Short Fiction*, 12 (1975), 231–41.

281. _____. "Publishers, Publishing, and the Recent American Short Story." *Studies in Short Fiction*, 1 (1963), 33–44.

282. PEREBINOSSOFF, PHILIPPE. "What Does a Kiss Mean? The Love Comic Formula and the Creation of the Ideal Teen-age Girl." *Journal of Popular Culture*, 8 (1975), 825–35.

283. PERRY, MARGARET. *Silence to the Drums: A Survey of the Literature of the Harlem Renaissance*. Westport, CT: Greenwood Press, 1976.

284. PHILLIPS, ELIZABETH C. "American Negro Literature in the High School." *Interpretations*, 2 (1969), 1–9.

285. PINSKER, SANFORD. "Isaac Bashevis Singer and Joyce Carol Oates: Some Versions of Gothic." *The Southern Review*, NS 9 (1973), 895–908.

286. _____. *The Schlemiel as Metaphor: Studies in the Yiddish and American Jewish Novel*. Carbondale and Edwardsville: Southern Illinois Univ. Press, 1971.

287. POHL, FREDERICK. "The Publishing of Science Fiction." In *Science Fiction, Today and Tomorrow*. Ed. Reginald Bretnor. New York: Harper & Row, 1974. pp. 17–44.

288. PORTER, KATHERINE ANNE, ET AL. *Recent Southern Fiction: A Panel Discussion*. Macon, GA: Wesleyan College, 1961.

289. REIGELMAN, MILTON M. The Midland: *A Venture in Literary Regionalism*. Iowa City: Univ. of Iowa Press, 1975.

290. RHODES, CAROLYN. "Tyranny by Computer: Automated Data Processing and Oppressive Government in Science Fiction." In *Many Futures, Many Worlds: Theme and Form in Science Fiction*. Ed. Thomas D. Clareson. Kent, OH: Kent State Univ. Press, 1977. pp. 66–93.

291. ROBINSON, CLAYTON. "Faulkner and Welty and the Mississippi Baptists." *Interpretations*, 5 (1973), 51–54.

292. _____. "Memphis in Fiction: Rural Values in an Urban Setting." In *Myths and Realities: Conflicting Values in America*. Ed. Berkley Kalin and Clayton Robinson. Memphis, TN: Memphis State Univ., 1972. pp. 29–38.

293. ROSE, LOIS AND STEPHEN. *The Shattered Ring: Science Fiction and the Quest for Making*. Richmond, VA: John Knox Press, 1970.

294. ROSEN, KENNETH. "Introduction." In *The Man to Send Rain Clouds: Contemporary Stories by American Indians*. New York: Viking, 1974. pp. ix–xiv.

295. ROSENBLATT, ROGER. "Black as the Color of Chaos." In *The Interpretation of Narrative: Theory and Practice*. Ed. Morton W. Bloomfield. Cambridge, MA: Harvard Univ. Press, 1970. pp. 249–61.

296. _____. *Black Fiction*. Cambridge, MA: Harvard Univ. Press, 1974.

297. ROTHER, JAMES. "Parafiction: The Adjacent Universe of Barth, Barthelme, Pynchon, and Nabokov." *boundary 2*, 5 (1976), 21–43.

298. RUPP, RICHARD H. *Celebration in Postwar American Fiction, 1945-1967*. Coral Gables, FL: Univ. of Miami Press, 1970.

299. SARGENT, PAMELA, ET AL. " 'Dear *Frontiers*': Letters from

Women Fantasy and Science Fiction Writers." *Frontiers*, 2, no. 3 (1977), 62–78.

300. **SCHATT, STANLEY.** *Understanding Modern American Literature: Cultural and Historical Perspectives.* Tokyo: Bunka Hyoron, 1977.

301. **SCHEVILL, JAMES.** "Notes on the Grotesque: Anderson, Brecht, and Williams." *Twentieth Century Literature*, 23 (1977), 229–38.

302. **SCHOLES, ROBERT.** "Metafiction." *The Iowa Review*, 1, no. 4 (1970), 100–15.

303. _____. *Structural Fabulation: An Essay on Fiction of the Future.* Notre Dame, IN: Univ. of Notre Dame Press, 1975.

304. **SCHORER, MARK.** "McCullers and Capote: Basic Patterns." In *The Creative Present: Notes on Contemporary American Fiction.* Ed. Nona Balakian and Charles Simmons. Garden City, NY: Doubleday, 1963. pp. 83–107.

305. _____. "Sherwood Anderson, F. Scott Fitzgerald, Ernest Hemingway." In *Major Writers of America.* Ed. Perry Miller. 2 vols. New York: Harcourt, Brace & World, 1962. II, 671–84.

306. **SCHULZ, MAX F.** *Black Humor Fiction of the Sixties: A Pluralistic Definition of Man and His World.* Athens: Ohio Univ. Press, 1973.

307. _____. "Characters (Contra Characterization) in the Contemporary Novel." In *The Theory of the Novel: New Essays.* Ed. John Halperin. New York: Oxford Univ. Press, 1974. pp. 141–54.

308. _____. *Radical Sophistication: Studies in Contemporary Jewish-American Novelists.* Athens: Ohio Univ. Press, 1969.

309. **SCHWARTZ, SHEILA.** "Science Fiction: Bridge Between the Two Cultures." *English Journal*, 60 (1971), 1043–51.

310. **SHARMA, P. P.** "William Faulkner's South and the Other South." *Indian Journal of American Studies*, 7, no. 1 (1977), 79–93.

311. **SIMMEN, EDWARD.** " 'We Must Make This Beginning': The Chicano Leader Image in the Short Story." *Southwest Review*, 57 (1972), 126–33.

312. **SIMON, J. D.** "Reading the American Proletarian Fiction of the Thirties." *Literature & Ideology*, no. 18 (1974), pp. 25–32.

313. **SKAGGS, CALVIN.** "Introduction." In *The American Short Story.* Ed. Calvin Skaggs. New York: Dell, 1977. pp. 11–18.

314. **SPRINGER, ANNE M.** *The American Novel in Germany: A Study of the Critical Reception of Eight American Novelists between the Two World Wars.* Hamburg: Cram, de Gruyter, 1960.

315. **SPRINGER, MARY DOYLE.** *Forms of the Modern Novella.* Chicago: Univ. of Chicago Press, 1975.

316. **STEINLEY, GARY.** "The Contemporary American Novella: An Existential Approach." *English Journal,* 59 (1970), 52–58.

317. **STEVICK, PHILIP.** "Lies, Fictions, and Mock-Facts." *Western Humanities Review,* 30 (1976), 1–12.

318. ———. "Scheherazade Runs Out of Plots, Goes on Talking; The King, Puzzled, Listens: An Essay on New Fiction." *TriQuarterly,* no. 26 (1973), pp. 332–62.

319. **STOVER, LEON.** "Science Fiction, The Research Revolution, and John Campbell." *Extrapolation,* 14 (1973), 129–46.

320. **STRAUMANN, HEINRICH.** *American Literature in the Twentieth Century.* 3rd rev. ed. New York: Harper & Row, 1965.

321. **SUKENICK, RONALD.** "Fiction in the Seventies: Ten Digressions on Ten Digressions." *Studies in American Fiction,* 5 (1977), 99–108.

322. ———. "The New Tradition in Fiction." In *Surfiction: Fiction Now . . . and Tomorrow.* Ed. Raymond Federman. Chicago: Swallow, 1975. pp. 35–45.

323. **SULLIVAN, WALTER.** "The Continuing Renascence: Southern Fiction in the Fifties." In *South: Modern Southern Literature and Its Cultural Setting.* Ed. Louis D. Rubin, Jr., and Robert D. Jacobs. Garden City, NY: Dolphin Books, 1961. pp. 376–91.

324. ———. *Death by Melancholy: Essays on Modern Southern Fiction.* Baton Rouge: Louisiana State Univ. Press, 1972.

325. ———. *A Requiem for the Renascence: The State of Fiction in the Modern South.* Athens: Univ. of Georgia Press, 1976.

326. **SWADOS, HARVEY.** "More Short Stories, Fewer Short Stories." *The New York Times Book Review,* 21 Jan. 1973, p. 35.

327. **TANNER, TONY.** *City of Words: American Fiction 1950–1970.* New York: Harper & Row, 1971.

328. ———. "My Life in American Literature." *TriQuarterly,* no. 30 (1974), pp. 83–108.

329. **TATUM, CHARLES M.** "Contemporary Chicano Prose Fiction: Its Ties to Mexican Literature." *Books Abroad,* 49 (1975), 431–38.

330. **THORP, WILLARD.** *American Writing in the Twentieth Century.* Cambridge, MA: Harvard Univ. Press, 1960.

331. ———. "The Newest American Fiction." *The Literary Criterion,* 5, no. 1 (1961), 94–107.

332. ———. "Whit Burnett and *Story* Magazine." *The Princeton University Library Chronicle,* 27 (1965), 107–12.

333. **TIMKO, MICHAEL.** *Instructor's Manual for "29 Short Stories: An Introductory Anthology."* New York: Knopf, 1975.

334. **TRESSIN, DEANNA.** "Toward Understanding." *English Journal,* 55 (1966), 1170–74.

335. TUCKER, CYNTHIA G. "The Teacher's Problems of Obsceni-
ty and Race: Killing Two Birds with One Stone." *Interpretations*, 4 (1972), 40–49.
336. TUGUSHEVA, A. "The Most American Genre." In *20th Century American Literature: A Soviet View*. Trans. Ronald Vroom.
Moscow: Progress, 1976. pp. 121–42.
337. TURPIN, WATERS E. "Four Short Fiction Writers of the Harlem Renaissance—Their Legacy of Achievement." *CLA Journal*, 11 (1967), 59–72.
338. ULANOV, BARRY. "The Short Story." In *The Two Worlds of
American Art: The Private and the Popular*. New York: Macmillan, 1965. pp. 190–208.
339. WAGNER, LINDA W. "Sherwood, Stein, the Sentence, and
Grape Sugar and Oranges." In *Sherwood Anderson: Dimensions of
His Literary Art: A Collection of Critical Essays*. Ed. David D.
Anderson. East Lansing: Michigan State Univ. Press, 1976. pp.
75–89.
340. WASHINGTON, MARY HELEN. "Introduction." In *Black-Eyed
Susans: Classic Stories by and about Black Women*. Garden City,
NY: Anchor Books, 1975. pp. ix–xxxii.
341. WATKINS, FLOYD C. *The Flesh and the Word: Eliot, Hemingway, Faulkner*. Nashville, TN: Vanderbilt Univ. Press, 1971.
342. WEALES, GERALD. "Not for the Old Lady in Dubuque." In
The Comic Imagination in American Literature. Ed. Louis D. Rubin, Jr. New Brunswick, NJ: Rutgers Univ. Press, 1973. pp.
231–46.
343. WEBER, BROM. "The Mode of 'Black Humor.'" In *The
Comic Imagination in American Literature*. Ed. Louis D. Rubin,
Jr. New Brunswick, NJ: Rutgers Univ. Press, 1973. pp. 361–71.
344. WEBER, RONALD. "The Literature of Reduction." In *America in Change: Reflections on the 60's and 70's*. Ed. Ronald Weber.
Notre Dame, IN: Univ. of Notre Dame Press, 1972. pp. 220–38.
345. WEINBERG, HELEN. *The New Novel in America: The Kafkan
Mode in Contemporary Fiction*. Ithaca, NY: Cornell Univ. Press,
1970.
346. WEINKAUF, MARY S. "Aesthetics and Overpopulation." *Extrapolation*, 13 (1972), 152–64.
347. WEST, PAUL. "Part Three: The United States." In *The Modern Novel*. 2 vols. London: Hutchinson, 1963. II, 219–315.
348. WHALEY, CHARLOTTE T. "Black and Bright Humor: Comic
Vision in the Modern Short Story." *Southwest Review*, 61 (1976),
370–83.
349. WICKES, GEORGE. *Americans in Paris*. Garden City, NY:
Doubleday, 1969.

350. **WILLIAMS, SHERLEY ANNE.** *Give Birth to Brightness: A Thematic Study in Neo-Black Literature.* New York: Dial, 1972.
351. **WILLIAMSON, JACK.** "Short Stories and Novelettes." In *The Craft of Science Fiction.* Ed. Reginald Bretnor. New York: Harper & Row, 1976. pp. 195–213.
352. ———. "The Years of Wonder." In *Voices for the Future: Essays on Major Science Fiction Writers.* Ed. Thomas D. Clareson. Bowling Green, OH: Bowling Green Univ. Popular Press, 1976. pp. 1–13.
353. **WOLFE, GARY K.** "The Known and the Unknown: Structure and Image in Science Fiction." In *Many Futures, Many Worlds: Theme and Form in Science Fiction.* Ed. Thomas D. Clareson. Kent, OH: Kent State Univ. Press, 1977. pp. 94–116.
354. **WOLLHEIM, DONALD A.** *The Universe Makers: Science Fiction Today.* New York: Harper & Row, 1971.
355. **WOOD, TOM.** "The Short Story Genius." *Lost Generation Journal,* 1, no. 2 (1973), 18–22.
356. **WRIGHT, AUSTIN MCGIFFERT.** *The American Short Story in the Twenties.* Chicago: Univ. of Chicago Press, 1961.
357. **WYMER, THOMAS L.** "Perception and Value in Science Fiction." *Extrapolation,* 16 (1975), 103–12.
358. **YATES, NORRIS W.** *The American Humorist: Conscience of the Twentieth Century.* Ames: Iowa State Univ. Press, 1964.

GENERAL STUDIES (GENERAL)

359. **AARON, DANIEL.** *The Unwritten War: American Writers and the Civil War.* New York: Knopf, 1973.
360. **ABCARIAN, RICHARD, AND MARVIN KLOTZ.** *Instructor's Manual To Accompany* "Literature: The Human Experience." New York: St. Martin's Press, 1973.
361. **ADAMS, RICHARD P.** "Permutations of American Romanticism." *Studies in Romanticism,* 9 (1970), 249–68.
362. **ALDISS, BRIAN.** *Billion Year Spree: The True History of Science Fiction.* Garden City, NY: Doubleday, 1973.
363. **ALLEN, WALTER.** *The Urgent West: The American Dream and Modern Man.* New York: Dutton, 1969.
364. **ANDERSON, POUL.** "The Creation of Imaginary Worlds: The World Builder's Handbook and Pocket Companion." In *Science Fiction, Today and Tomorrow.* Ed. Reginald Bretnor. New York: Harper & Row, 1974. pp. 235–57.
365. **ASH, BRIAN.** *Faces of the Future: The Lessons of Science Fiction.* New York: Taplinger, 1975.
366. **AUCHINCLOSS, LOUIS.** *Pioneers & Caretakers: A Study of 9*

American Women Novelists. Minneapolis: Univ. of Minnesota Press, 1965.

367. **BAKER, CARLOS.** "The Place of the Bible in American Fiction." In *Religion in American Life.* Vol. II of *Religious Perspectives in American Culture.* Ed. James Ward Smith and A. Leland Jamison. Princeton, NJ: Princeton Univ. Press, 1961. pp. 243-72.

368. **BALLOU, BARBARA.** "Exercises Building Toward the Short Story." *English Journal,* 49 (1960), 345-46.

369. **BARNES, DANIEL R.** "The Bosom Serpent: A Legend in American Literature and Culture." *Journal of American Folklore,* 85 (1972), 111-22.

370. **BARNES, MELVYN.** *Best Detective Fiction: A Guide from Godwin to the Present.* London: Clive Bingley, 1975.

371. **BARZUN, JACQUES.** "A Critical Vocabulary for Crime Fiction." *The Armchair Detective,* 4 (1971), 75-78.

372. _____, and Wendell Hertig Taylor. *A Catalogue of Crime.* New York: Harper & Row, 1971.

373. **BEACHCROFT, T. O.** *The Modest Art: A Survey of the Short Story in English.* London: Oxford Univ. Press, 1968.

374. **BENS, JOHN H.** *Instructor's Manual and Objective Quizzes for* "A Search for Awareness." New York: Holt, Rinehart and Winston, 1966.

375. **BENTON, RICHARD P.** "The Problems of Literary Gothicism." *ESQ,* 18 (1972), 5-9.

376. **BERTHOFF, WARNER.** *The Ferment of Realism: American Literature, 1884-1919.* New York: Free Press, 1965.

377. **BEWLEY, MARCUS.** *The Eccentric Design: Form in the Classic American Novel.* New York: Columbia Univ. Press, 1959.

378. **BIER, JESSE.** *The Rise and Fall of American Humor.* New York: Holt, Rinehart and Winston, 1968.

379. _____. "The Romantic Coordinates of American Literature." *Bucknell Review,* 18, no. 2 (1970), 16-33.

380. **BLACKER, IRWIN R.** "Notes for a Preface." In *The Old West in Fiction.* New York: Ivan Obolensky, 1961. pp. ix-xvi.

381. **BLACKMUR, R. P.** "Introduction." In *American Short Novels.* New York: Crowell, 1960. pp. 1-17.

382. **BLAIR, WALTER.** " 'A Man's Voice, Speaking': A Continuum in American Humor." In *Veins of Humor.* Ed. Harry Levin. Cambridge, MA: Harvard Univ. Press, 1972. pp. 185-204.

383. _____. *Native American Humor.* 2nd ed. San Francisco, CA: Chandler, 1960.

384. **BONAZZA, BLAZE O., AND EMIL ROY.** *Instructor's Manual to Accompany* "Studies in Fiction." New York: Harper & Row, 1965.

385. _____, AND _____. *Instructor's Manual to Accompany* Studies in Fiction," Second Edition. New York: Harper & Row, 1971.

386. BONE, ROBERT. *Down Home: A History of Afro-American Short Fiction from Its Beginnings to the End of the Harlem Renaissance.* New York: Putnam's, 1975.

387. _____. *The Negro Novel in America.* Rev. ed. New Haven, CT: Yale Univ. Press, 1965.

388. BONTEMPS, ARNA. "The Black Contribution to American Letters: Part I." In *The Black American Reference Book.* Ed. Mabel M. Smythe. Englewood Cliffs, NJ: Prentice-Hall, 1976. pp. 741–66.

389. BOOTH, WAYNE C. *The Rhetoric of Fiction.* Chicago: Univ. of Chicago Press, 1961.

390. BOULTON, MARJORIE. *The Anatomy of the Novel.* London: Routledge & Kegan Paul, 1975.

391. BOVA, BEN. "The Role of Science Fiction." In *Science Fiction, Today and Tomorrow.* Ed. Reginald Bretnor. New York: Harper & Row, 1974. pp. 3–14.

392. BRACE, GERALD WARNER. *The Stuff of Fiction.* New York: Norton, 1969.

393. BRIDGMAN, RICHARD. *The Colloquial Style in America.* New York: Oxford Univ. Press, 1966.

394. BROOKS, CLEANTH, AND ROBERT PENN WARREN. *Understanding Fiction.* 2nd ed. New York: Appleton-Century-Crofts, 1959.

395. BROWN, DEMING. *Soviet Attitudes toward American Writing.* Princeton: NJ: Princeton Univ. Press, 1962.

396. BROWN, STERLING A. "A Century of Negro Portraiture in American Literature." *The Massachusetts Review,* 7 (1966), 73–96.

397. BUCHEN, IRVING H. "The Modern Visionary Tradition and Romanticism." *Western Humanities Review,* 21 (1967), 21–29.

398. BUKOSKI, ANTHONY. "The Lady and Her Business of Love in Selected Southern Fictions." *Studies in the Humanities,* 5, no. 1 (1976), 14–18.

399. CASSILL, R. V. "The Norton Anthology of Short Fiction": *Instructor's Handbook for the Complete and Shorter Editions.* New York: Norton, 1977.

400. CHAMETZKY, JULES. "Our Decentralized Literature: A Consideration of Regional, Ethnic, Racial, and Sexual Factors." *Jahrbuch für Amerikastudien,* 17 (1972), 56–72.

401. CHAMPIGNY, ROBERT. "Implicitness in Narrative Fiction." *PMLA,* 85 (1970), 988–91.

402. _____. *Ontology of the Narrative.* The Hague: Mouton, 1972.

403. _____. *What Will Have Happened: A Philosophical and Technical Essay on Mystery Stories*. Bloomington: Indiana Univ. Press, 1977.

404. CHAPMAN, ARNOLD. *The Spanish American Reception of United States Fiction, 1920–1940*. Berkeley: Univ. of California Press, 1966.

405. CHATMAN, SEYMOUR. "The Structure of Narrative Transmission." In *Style and Structure in Literature: Essays in the New Stylistics*. Ed. Roger Fowler. Ithaca, NY: Cornell Univ. Press, 1975. pp. 213–57.

406. CLARESON, THOMAS D. "The Other Side of Realism." In *SF—The Other Side of Realism: Essays on Modern Fantasy and Science Fiction*. Ed. Thomas D. Clareson. Bowling Green, OH: Bowling Green Univ. Popular Press, 1971. pp. 1–28.

407. CLARKE, JOHN HENRIK. "The Origin and Growth of Afro-American Literature." *Negro Digest*, 17, no. 2 (1967), 54–67.

408. CLEMENT, HAL. "The Creation of Imaginary Beings." In *Science Fiction, Today and Tomorrow*. Ed. Reginald Bretnor. New York: Harper & Row, 1974. pp. 259–75.

409. COHEN, HENNIG. "The American as Involved and Dropout: An Afterword." In *Landmarks of American Writing*. Ed. Hennig Cohen. New York: Basic Books, 1969. pp. 379–89.

410. _____. "American Literature and American Folklore." In *Our Living Traditions: An Introduction to American Folklore*. Ed. Tristram Potter Coffin. New York: Basic Books, 1968. pp. 238–47.

411. COOK, ALBERT. *The Meaning of Fiction*. Detroit, MI: Wayne State Univ. Press, 1960.

412. COX, MARTHA HEASLEY. *Student Guide*—"Image and Value: An Invitation to Literature." New York: Harcourt, Brace & World, 1967.

413. CULLER, JONATHAN. "Defining Narrative Units." In *Style and Structure in Literature: Essays in the New Stylistics*. Ed. Roger Fowler. Ithaca, NY: Cornell Univ. Press, 1975. pp. 123–42.

414. DE CAMP, L. SPRAGUE, AND CATHERINE CROOK DE CAMP. *Science Fiction Handbook, Revised*. Philadelphia, PA: Owlswick Press, 1975.

415. DETWEILER, ROBERT. "Games and Play in Modern American Fiction." *Contemporary Literature*, 17 (1976), 44–62.

416. DICKINSON, LEON T. *Suggestions for Teachers of* "Introduction to Literature," Fifth Edition, Edited by Locke, Gibson, and Arms. New York: Holt, Rinehart and Winston, 1967.

417. DICKSON, GORDON R. "Plausibility in Science Fiction." In *Science Fiction, Today and Tomorrow*. Ed. Reginald Bretnor. New York: Harper & Row, 1974. pp. 295–306.

418. **DILLINGHAM, WILLIAM B.** "Days of the Tall Tale." *The Southern Review*, NS 4 (1968), 569–77.

419. **DOLEŽEL, LUBOMÍR.** "Toward a Structural Theory of Content in Prose Fiction." In *Literary Style: A Symposium*. Ed. Seymour Chatman. London: Oxford Univ. Press, 1971. pp. 95–110.

420. **DUFFEY, BERNARD.** "Humor, Chicago Style." In *The Comic Imagination in American Literature*. Ed. Louis D. Rubin, Jr. New Brunswick, NJ: Rutgers Univ. Press, 1973. pp. 207–16.

421. **DURHAM, PHILIP, AND TAUNO F. MUSTANOJA.** *American Fiction in Finland: An Essay and Bibliography*. Helsinki: Société Néophilologique, 1960.

422. **EARNEST, ERNEST.** *The American Eve in Fact and Fiction, 1775–1914*. Urbana: Univ. of Illinois Press, 1974.

423. _____. *Expatriates and Patriots: American Artists, Scholars, and Writers in Europe*. Durham, NC: Duke Univ. Press, 1968.

424. **EASTMAN, RICHARD M.** *A Guide to the Novel*. San Francisco, CA: Chandler, 1965.

425. **ECKLEY, WILTON.** "Hear the Guns Roar: The Feud in Southern Mountain Fiction." In *Popular Literature in America: A Symposium in Honor of Lyon N. Richardson*. Ed. James C. Austin and Donald A. Koch. Bowling Green, OH: Bowling Green Univ. Popular Press, 1972. pp. 42–52.

426. **EMANUEL, JAMES A.** "America Before 1950: Black Writers' Views." *Negro Digest*, 18, no. 10 (1969), 26–34, 67–69.

427. _____. "The Invisible Men of American Literature." *Books Abroad*, 37 (1963), 391–94.

428. **EVERSON, WILLIAM.** "Archetype West." In *Regional Perspectives: An Examination of America's Literary Heritage*. Ed. John G. Burke. Chicago: American Library Association, 1973. pp. 207–306.

429. _____. *Archetype West: The Pacific Coast as a Literary Region*. Berkeley, CA: Oyez, 1976.

430. **EZELL, JOHN SAMUEL.** "The Southern Literary Renaissance." In *The South since 1865*. New York: Macmillan, 1963. pp. 277–95.

431. **FELHEIM, MARVIN.** "Recent Anthologies of the Novella." *Genre*, 2 (1969), 21–27.

432. **FERRARA, FERNANDO.** "Theory and Model for the Structural Analysis of Fiction." *New Literary History*, 5 (1974), 245–68.

433. **FIEDLER, LESLIE A.** *Love and Death in the American Novel*. New York: Criterion Books, 1960.

434. _____. *Love and Death in the American Novel*. Rev. ed. New York: Stein and Day, 1966.

435. _____. *The Return of the Vanishing American*. New York: Stein and Day, 1968.

436. **FINE, DAVID M.** *The City, The Immigrant and American Fiction, 1880–1920*. Metuchen, NJ: Scarecrow, 1977.
437. **FITZGERALD, GREGORY.** "The Satiric Short Story: A Definition." *Studies in Short Fiction*, 5 (1968), 349–54.
438. **FOLEY, MARTHA.** "Introduction." In *200 Years of Great American Short Stories*. Boston, MA: Houghton Mifflin, 1975. pp. 1–23.
439. **FOLSOM, JAMES K.** *The American Western Novel*. New Haven, CT: College & University Press, 1966.
440. **FOSTER, RUEL E.** "Kentucky Humor: Salt River Roarer to Ol' Dog Ring." *The Mississippi Quarterly*, 20 (1967), 224–30.
441. **FRIEDMAN, ALAN WARREN.** "The Modern Multivalent Novel: Form and Function." In *The Theory of the Novel: New Essays*. Ed. John Halperin. New York: Oxford Univ. Press, 1974. pp. 121–40.
442. **FURNESS, EDNA L.** "Image of the Schoolteacher in Western Literature." *The Arizona Quarterly*, 18 (1962), 346–57.
443. **GAYLE, ADDISON, JR.** *The Way of the New World: The Black Novel in America*. Garden City, NY: Anchor Books, 1976.
444. **GINSBERG, ELAINE.** "The Female Initiation Theme in American Fiction." *Studies in American Fiction*, 3 (1975), 27–37.
445. **GOING, WILLIAM T.** "Alabama in the Short Story: Notes for an Anthology." In *Essays on Alabama Literature*. University: Univ. of Alabama Press, 1975. pp. 39–60.
446. **GROSS, THEODORE L.** *The Heroic Ideal in American Literature*. New York: Free Press, 1971.
447. **GUERIN, WILFRED L., EARLE LABOR, LEE MORGAN, AND JOHN R. WILLINGHAM.** *Instructor's Manual to Accompany* "Mandala: Literature for Critical Analysis." New York: Harper & Row, 1970.
448. **GULLASON, THOMAS A.** "The Short Story: An Underrated Art." *Studies in Short Fiction*, 2 (1964), 13–31.
449. **GUNN, DREWEY WAYNE.** *American and British Writers in Mexico, 1556–1973*. Austin: Univ. of Texas Press, 1974.
450. **GUNN, JAMES.** *Alternate Worlds: The Illustrated History of Science Fiction*. Englewood Cliffs, NJ: Prentice-Hall, 1975.
451. ———. "Heroes, Heroines, Villains: The Characters in Science Fiction." In *The Craft of Science Fiction*. Ed. Reginald Bretnor. New York: Harper & Row, 1976. pp. 161–75.
452. **GUTTMANN, ALLEN.** *The Conservative Tradition in America*. New York: Oxford Univ. Press, 1967.
453. ———. *The Jewish Writer in America: Assimilation and the Crisis of Identity*. New York: Oxford Univ. Press, 1971.
454. **HAGOPIAN, JOHN V., ET AL.** *Insight I: Analyses of American Literature*. Frankfurt am Main: Hirschgraben, 1962.

455. **HALE, NANCY.** *The Realities of Fiction: A Book about Writing.* Boston, MA: Little, Brown, 1962.

456. **HALL, JAMES B.** *Teacher's Manual for* "The Realm of Fiction: 61 Short Stories." New York: McGraw-Hill, 1965.

457. **HALL, WADE.** *The Smiling Phoenix: Southern Humor from 1865 to 1914.* Gainesville: Univ. of Florida Press, 1965.

458. **HARPER, RALPH.** *The World of the Thriller.* Cleveland, OH: Press of Case Western Reserve Univ., 1969.

459. **HARRISON, HARRY.** "Worlds Beside Worlds." In *Science Fiction at Large: A Collection of Essays, by Various Hands, about the Interface between Science Fiction and Reality.* Ed. Peter Nicholls. New York: Harper & Row, 1976. pp. 107–14.

460. **HAUCK, RICHARD BOYD.** *A Cheerful Nihilism: Confidence and "The Absurd" in American Humorous Fiction.* Bloomington: Indiana Univ. Press, 1971.

461. **HAYS, PETER L.** "Runaways on a One-Way Ticket, or Dropouts in Literature." *The Arizona Quarterly,* 31 (1975), 301–10.

462. **HEINLEIN, ROBERT A.** "Science Fiction: Its Nature, Faults and Virtues." In *The Science Fiction Novel: Imagination and Social Criticism.* Chicago: Advent, 1959. pp. 17–63.

463. **HENDERSON, HARRY B., III.** *Versions of the Past: The Historical Imagination in American Fiction.* New York: Oxford Univ. Press, 1974.

464. **HOLMAN, C. HUGH.** "Detective Fiction as American Realism." In *Popular Literature in America: A Symposium in Honor of Lyon N. Richardson.* Ed. James C. Austin and Donald A. Koch. Bowling Green, OH: Bowling Green Univ. Popular Press, 1972. pp. 30–41.

465. ———. "The Southerner as American Writer." In *The Southerner as American.* Ed. Charles Grier Sellers, Jr. Chapel Hill: Univ. of North Carolina Press, 1960. pp. 180–99.

466. **HOUK, ANNELLE S., AND CARLOTTA L. BOGART.** *Understanding the Short Story.* New York: Odyssey Press, 1969.

467. **HOWARD, DANIEL F.** *Manual to Accompany* "The Modern Tradition: An Anthology of Short Stories." Boston, MA: Little, Brown, 1968.

468. ———, **AND WILLIAM PLUMMER.** *Instructor's Manual to Accompany* "The Modern Tradition," Third Edition. Boston, MA: Little, Brown, 1976.

469. **HOWARD, LEON.** *Literature and the American Tradition.* Garden City, NY: Doubleday, 1960.

470. **HOWE, IRVING.** "Anarchy and Authority in American Literature." *The University of Denver Quarterly,* 2, no. 3 (1967), 5–30.

471. **HUBBELL, JAY B.** *Southern Life in Fiction.* Athens: Univ. of Georgia Press, 1960.

472. _____. *Who Are the Major American Writers?: A Study of the Changing Literary Canon.* Durham, NC: Duke Univ. Press, 1972.

473. HUTCHINSON, W. H. "Theseus in Leather Leggins." *Fiction*, no. 9 (1976), pp. 62–64, 71.

474. IRWIN, W. R. *The Game of the Impossible: A Rhetoric of Fantasy.* Urbana: Univ. of Illinois Press, 1976.

475. JAMES, CHARLES L. *Notes for Teaching* "From the Roots: Short Stories by Black Americans." New York: Dodd, Mead, 1970.

476. JONES, HOWARD MUMFORD. *Jeffersonianism and the American Novel.* New York: Teachers College Press, 1966.

477. KAMINSKY, ALICE R. "On Literary Realism." In *The Theory of the Novel: New Essays.* Ed. John Halperin. New York: Oxford Univ. Press, 1974. pp. 213–32.

478. KANE, THOMAS S., AND LEONARD J. PETERS. *Some Suggestions for Using* "The Short Story and the Reader: Discovering Narrative Techniques." New York: Oxford Univ. Press, 1976.

479. KAPLAN, MILTON A. "Style *Is* Content." *English Journal*, 57 (1968), 1330–34.

480. KATZ, JOSEPH. "Eroticism in American Literary Realism." *Studies in American Fiction*, 5 (1977), 35–50.

481. KENNEDY, X. J. *Instructor's Manual to Accompany* "An Introduction to Fiction." Boston, MA: Little, Brown, 1976.

482. KETTERER, DAVID. *New Worlds for Old: The Apocalyptic Imagination, Science Fiction, and American Literature.* Garden City, NY: Anchor Books, 1974.

483. KIMMEY, JOHN L. *Instructor's Manual for* "Experience and Expression: Reading and Responding to Short Fiction." Glenview, IL: Scott, Foresman, 1976.

484. KLOTZ, MARVIN, AND RICHARD ABCARIAN. *Instructor's Manual to Accompany* "The Experience of Fiction." New York: St. Martin's Press, 1975.

485. KNOEPFLE, JOHN. "Crossing the Midwest." In *Regional Perspectives: An Examination of America's Literary Heritage.* Ed. John G. Burke. Chicago: American Library Association, 1973. pp. 77–174.

486. KNOLL, ROBERT E. *Instructor's Manual for* "Contrasts," Second Edition. New York: Harcourt, Brace, 1959.

487. KOLODNY, ANNETTE. *The Lay of the Land: Metaphor as Experience and History in American Life and Letters.* Chapel Hill: Univ. of North Carolina Press, 1975.

488. KOSTELANETZ, RICHARD. "Constructivist Fiction." *Chicago Review*, 28, no. 2 (1976), 138–42.

489. LA COUR, TAGE, AND HARALD MORGENSEN. *The Murder Book: An Illustrated History of the Detective Story.* Trans. Roy Duffell. London: George Allen and Unwin, 1971.

490. LEE, HECTOR H. "Tales and Legends in Western American Literature." *Western American Literature*, 9 (1975), 239–54.

491. LEE, ROBERT EDSON. *From West to East: Studies in the Literature of the American West.* Urbana: Univ. of Illinois Press, 1966.

492. LEIBOWITZ, JUDITH. *Narrative Purpose in the Novella.* The Hague: Mouton, 1974.

493. LEVIN, GERALD. *Teacher's Manual for* "Prose and Criticism," Edited by John McCallum. New York: Harcourt, Brace & World, 1966.

494. LITTLEJOHN, DAVID. *Black on White: A Critical Survey of Writing by American Negroes.* New York: Grossman, 1966.

495. LITZ, A. WALTON. Introductions. In *Major American Short Stories.* New York: Oxford Univ. Press, 1975. pp. 3–21, 383–91, 443–59, 715–19.

496. MACLACHLAN, JOHN M. "Southern Humor as a Vehicle of Social Evaluation." *The Mississippi Quarterly*, 13 (1960), 157–62.

497. MACLEAN, KATHERINE. "Alien Minds and Nonhuman Intelligences." In *The Craft of Science Fiction.* Ed. Reginald Bretnor. New York: Harper & Row, 1976. pp. 136–57.

498. MCSHERRY, FRANK D., JR. "The Smallest Sub-Genre." *The Armchair Detective*, 10 (1977), 267–70.

499. MCWILLIAMS, WILSON CAREY. *The Idea of Fraternity in America.* Berkeley: Univ. of California Press, 1973.

500. MAGALANER, MARVIN, AND EDMOND L. VOLPE. *Teacher's Manual To Accompany* "Twelve Short Stories." New York: Macmillan, 1961.

501. MAJOR, MABEL, AND T. M. PEARCE. *Southwest Heritage: A Literary History with Bibliographies.* 3rd ed. Albuquerque: Univ. of New Mexico Press, 1972.

502. MALE, ROY R. "The Story of the Mysterious Stranger in American Fiction." *Criticism*, 3 (1961), 281–94.

503. MALIN, IRVING. "The Compulsive Design." In *American Dreams, American Nightmares.* Ed. David Madden. Carbondale and Edwardsville: Southern Illinois Univ. Press, 1970. pp. 58–75.

504. MARCOTTE, EDWARD. "Intersticed Prose." *Chicago Review*, 26, no. 4 (1975), 31–36.

505. MARLER, ROBERT F. " 'Bartleby, the Scrivener' and the American Short Story." *Genre*, 6 (1973), 428–47.

506. MAROVITZ, SANFORD E. "Romance or Realism? Western Periodical Literature: 1893–1902." *Western American Literature*, 10 (1975), 45–58.

507. **MARTIN, JAY.** *Harvests of Change: American Literature 1865-1914.* Englewood Cliffs, NJ: Prentice-Hall, 1967.

508. **MARX, LEO.** *The Machine and the Garden: Technology and the Pastoral Ideal in America.* New York: Oxford Univ. Press, 1964.

509. **MAXWELL, D. E. S.** *American Fiction: The Intellectual Background.* London: Routledge and Kegan Paul, 1963.

510. **MAY, CHARLES E.** "The Unique Effect of the Short Story: A Reconsideration and an Example." *Studies in Short Fiction*, 13 (1976), 289-97.

511. **MELLARD, JAMES M.** *Instructor's Manual—*"Four Modes: A Rhetoric of Modern Fiction." New York: Macmillan, 1973.

512. _____. "Prolegomena to a Study of the Popular Mode in Narrative." *Journal of Popular Culture*, 6 (1972), 1-19.

513. **MEYER, ROY W.** *The Middle Western Farm Novel in the Twentieth Century.* Lincoln: Univ. of Nebraska Press, 1965.

514. **MILES, ELTON.** *Southwest Humorists.* Austin, TX: Steck-Vaughn, 1969.

515. **MILLER, JAMES E., JR., AND BERNICE SLOTE.** *Notes for Teaching* "The Dimensions of Literature: A Critical Anthology." New York: Dodd, Mead, 1967.

516. _____, AND _____. *Notes for Teaching* "The Dimensions of the Short Story." New York: Dodd, Mead, 1964.

517. **MINOT, STEPHEN.** "The Writing of Fiction." In *Three Genres: The Writing of Fiction, Poetry, and Drama.* Englewood Cliffs, NJ: Prentice-Hall, 1965. pp. 3-111.

518. _____. "The Writing of Fiction." In *Three Genres: The Writing of Poetry, Fiction, and Drama.* 2nd ed. Englewood Cliffs, NJ: Prentice-Hall, 1971. pp. 125-253.

519. **MONTGOMERY, MARION.** "Dangers of Form and Theory: A Postscript to Stories Past." *The Georgia Review*, 14 (1960), 165-71.

520. _____. "The Sense of Violation: Notes toward a Definition of 'Southern' Fiction." *The Georgia Review*, 19 (1965), 278-87.

521. **MOONEY, JOAN M.** "Best-Selling American Detective Fiction." *The Armchair Detective*, 3 (1970), 98-114, 141-60, 215-39; 4 (1970), 12-29; 4 (1971), 87-103.

522. **MORGAN, H. WAYNE.** *American Writers in Rebellion: From Mark Twain to Dreiser.* New York: Hill and Wang, 1965.

523. **MORRIS, WRIGHT.** *About Fiction: Reverent Reflections on the Nature of Fiction with Irreverent Observations on Writers, Readers, & Other Abuses.* New York: Harper & Row, 1975.

524. **MOSKOWITZ, SAM.** *Explorers of the Infinite: Shapers of Science Fiction.* Cleveland, OH: World, 1963.

525. _____. *Strange Horizons: The Spectrum of Science Fiction.* New York: Scribner's, 1976.

526. **NICHOLLS, PETER.** "Science Fiction: The Monsters and the Critics." In *Science Fiction at Large: A Collection of Essays, by Various Hands, about the Interface between Science Fiction and Reality.* Ed. Peter Nicholls. New York: Harper & Row, 1976. pp. 160–83.

527. **NIVEN, LARRY.** "The Words of Science Fiction." In *The Craft of Science Fiction.* Ed. Reginald Bretnor. New York: Harper & Row, 1976. pp. 178–93.

528. **NOURSE, ALAN E.** "Science Fiction and Man's Adaptation to Change." In *Science Fiction, Today and Tomorrow.* Ed. Reginald Bretnor. New York: Harper & Row, 1974. pp. 116–32.

529. **OATES, JOYCE CAROL.** "The Short Story." *Southern Humanities Review*, 5 (1971), 213–14.

530. **OPPEL, HORST.** "American Literature in Postwar Germany: Impact or Alienation?" *Die Neueren Sprachen*, 61 (1962), 1–10.

531. **OREL, HAROLD.** "The American Detective-Hero." *Journal of Popular Culture*, 2 (1968), 395–403.

532. **OSBORNE, WILLIAM.** "Form and Value in Four Short Stories: Some Critical Approaches." *Interpretations*, 1 (1968), 22–27.

533. **PANSHIN, ALEXEI AND CORY.** "Fiction and Human Development." In *SF in Dimension: A Book of Explorations.* Chicago: Advent Publishers, 1976. pp. 215–20.

534. ———. "Science Fiction: New Trends and Old." In *Science Fiction, Today and Tomorrow.* Ed. Reginald Bretnor. New York: Harper & Row, 1974. pp. 217–33.

535. **PERRINE, LAURENCE.** *Instructor's Manual for* "Story and Structure," Fourth Edition. New York: Harcourt Brace Jovanovich, 1974.

536. **PICKERING, JAMES H.** *Instructor's Manual—*"Fiction 100: An Anthology of Short Stories." New York: Macmillan, 1974.

537. **POIRIER, RICHARD.** *A World Elsewhere: The Place of Style in American Literature.* New York: Oxford Univ. Press, 1966.

538. **POLLIN, BURTON R.** "Poe and Hemingway on Violence and Death." *English Studies*, 57 (1976), 139–42.

539. **POURNELLE, JERRY.** "The Construction of Believable Societies." In *The Craft of Science Fiction.* Ed. Reginald Bretnor. New York: Harper & Row, 1976. pp. 104–19.

540. **PRICE, LAWRENCE MARSDEN.** *The Reception of United States Literature in Germany.* Chapel Hill: Univ. of North Carolina Press, 1966.

541. **QUANTIC, DIANE DUFVA.** "The Revolt from the Village and Middle Western Fiction 1870–1915." *Kansas Quarterly*, 5, no. 4 (1973), 5–16.

542. **RABAN, JONATHAN.** *The Technique of Modern Fiction: Essays in Practical Criticism.* London: Edward Arnold, 1968.

543. REES, ROBERT A., AND BARRY MENIKOFF. *A Manual to Accompany "The Short Story: An Introductory Anthology."* Boston, MA: Little, Brown, 1969.

544. RIDEOUT, WALTER B. *Instructor's Manual for "The Experience of Prose."* New York: Crowell, 1960.

545. ROBERTS, THOMAS J. *When Is Something Fiction?* Carbondale and Edwardsville: Southern Illinois Univ. Press, 1972.

546. ROBINSON, CECIL. *With the Ears of Strangers: The Mexican in American Literature.* Tucson: Univ. of Arizona Press, 1963.

547. ROCKWELL, F. A. *Modern Fiction Techniques.* Boston, MA: The Writer, 1962.

548. ROHRBERGER, MARY. *Hawthorne and the Modern Short Story: A Study in Genre.* The Hague: Mouton, 1966.

549. ROSE, ALAN HENRY. *Demonic Vision: Racial Fantasy and Southern Fiction.* Hamden, CT: Archon Books, 1976.

550. ROSS, DANFORTH. *The American Short Story.* Minneapolis: Univ. of Minnesota Press, 1961.

551. ROTTENSTEINER, FRANZ. *The Science Fiction Book: An Illustrated History.* New York: Seabury Press, 1975.

552. RUBIN, LOUIS D., JR. "Introduction: 'The Great American Joke.' " In *The Comic Imagination in American Literature.* Ed. Louis D. Rubin, Jr. New Brunswick, NJ: Rutgers Univ. Press, 1973. pp. 3-15.

553. _____. "Southern Literature and Southern Society: Notes on a Clouded Relationship." In *Southern Literary Study: Problems and Possibilities.* Ed. Louis D. Rubin, Jr., and C. Hugh Holman. Chapel Hill: Univ. of North Carolina Press, 1975. pp. 3-20.

554. _____. *The Writer in the South: Studies in Literary Continuity.* Athens: Univ. of Georgia Press, 1972.

555. RUEHLMANN, WILLIAM. *Saint with a Gun: The Unlawful American Private Eye.* New York: New York Univ. Press, 1974.

556. RUSS, JOANNA. "Dream Literature and Science Fiction." *Extrapolation*, 11 (1969), 6-14.

557. RUTHROF, H. G. "Aspects of a Phenomenological View of Narrative." *The Journal of Narrative Technique*, 4 (1974), 87-99.

558. SCHMIDT, STANLEY. "The Science in Science Fiction." In *Many Futures, Many Worlds: Theme and Form in Science Fiction.* Ed. Thomas D. Clareson. Kent, OH: Kent State Univ. Press, 1977. pp. 27-49.

559. SCHNEIDER, ROBERT W. *Five Novelists of the Progressive Era.* New York: Columbia Univ. Press, 1965.

560. SCHOLES, ROBERT. "The Contributions of Formalism and Structuralism to the Theory of Fiction." *Novel*, 6 (1973), 134-51.

561. _____, AND ERIC S. RABKIN. *Science Fiction: History • Science • Vision*. New York: Oxford Univ. Press, 1977.

562. SCHOLZ, BERNHARD F., AND ROBERT CHAMPIGNY. "Implicitness in Narrative Fiction." *PMLA*, 86 (1971), 1026–28.

563. SCORTIA, THOMAS N. "Science Fiction as the Imaginary Experiment." In *Science Fiction, Today and Tomorrow*. Ed. Reginald Bretnor. New York: Harper & Row, 1974. pp. 135–47.

564. SCOTT, VIRGIL. *Instructor's Manual for* "Studies in the Short Story," Alternate Edition. New York: Holt, Rinehart and Winston, 1971.

565. _____. *Instructor's Manual to Accompany* "Studies in the Short Story," Third Edition. New York: Holt, Rinehart and Winston, 1968.

566. SHRODES, CAROLINE, JUSTINE VAN GUNDY, AND JOEL DORIUS. *Instructor's Manual*—"Reading for Understanding: Fiction, Drama, Poetry." New York: Macmillan, 1968.

567. SHUMAKER, ARTHUR W. *A History of Indiana Literature, with Emphasis on the Authors of Imaginative Works Who Commenced Writing Prior to World War II*. Indianapolis: Indiana Historical Society, 1962.

568. SIEGEL, ROSLYN. "The Black Man and the Macabre in American Literature." *Black American Literature Forum*, 10 (1976), 133–36.

569. SIMONSON, HAROLD P. *Instructor's Manual to Accompany* "Trio: A Book of Stories, Plays and Poems," Third Edition. New York: Harper & Row, 1970.

571. SKAGGS, MERRILL MAGUIRE. *The Folk in Southern Fiction*. Athens: Univ. of Georgia Press, 1972.

572. SMITH, DAVID E. "The English Pilgrimage of Man: Metamorphosis of a Theme in American Literature." *Ball State University Forum*, 7, no. 2 (1966), 65–72.

573. SMITH, GOLDIE CAPERS. "*The Overland Monthly*: Landmark in American Literature." *New Mexico Quarterly*, 33 (1963), 333–40.

574. SMITH, LEVERETT T., JR. *The American Dream and the National Game*. Bowling Green, OH: Bowling Green Univ. Popular Press, 1975.

575. SPINRAD, NORMAN. "Rubber Sciences." In *The Craft of Science Fiction*. Ed. Reginald Bretnor. New York: Harper & Row, 1976. pp. 54–69.

576. STARKE, CATHERINE JUANITA. *Black Portraiture in American Fiction*. New York: Basic Books, 1971.

577. STEAD, CHRISTINA, HERBERT GOLD, ET AL. "The International Symposium on the Short Story." *The Kenyon Review*, 30 (1968), 443–90; 31 (1969), 57–94, 449–503; 32 (1970), 77–108.

578. **STEGNER, WALLACE.** *Teaching the Short Story.* Davis Publications in English, No. 2. Davis: Dept. of English, Univ. of California, 1965.

579. **STEIN, AARON MARC.** "The Mystery Story in Cultural Perspective." In *The Mystery Story.* Ed. John Ball. Del Mar, CA: Publishers Inc., 1976. pp. 29–59.

580. **STEINBRUNNER, CHRIS, ET AL., ED.** *Encyclopedia of Mystery and Detection.* New York: McGraw-Hill, 1976.

581. **STERNBERG, MEIR.** "What Is Exposition? An Essay in Temporal Delimitation." In *The Theory of the Novel: New Essays.* Ed. John Halperin. New York: Oxford Univ. Press, 1974. pp. 25–70.

582. **STEWART, RANDALL.** "Tidewater and Frontier." *The Georgia Review,* 13 (1959), 296–307.

583. **STONE, EDWARD.** *A Certain Morbidness: A View of American Literature.* Carbondale and Edwardsville: Southern Illinois Univ. Press, 1969.

584. ———. "Usher, Poquelin, and Miss Emily: The Progress of Southern Gothic." *The Georgia Review,* 14 (1960), 433–43.

585. ———. *Voices of Despair: Four Motifs in American Literature.* Athens: Ohio Univ. Press, 1966.

586. **STROUT, CUSHING.** *The American Image of the Old World.* New York: Harper & Row, 1963.

587. **STURGEON, THEODORE.** "Science Fiction, Morals, and Religion." In *Science Fiction, Today and Tomorrow.* Ed. Reginald Bretnor. New York: Harper & Row, 1974. pp. 98–113.

588. **SYMONS, JULIAN.** *Mortal Consequences: A History—From the Detective Story to the Crime Novel.* New York: Harper & Row, 1972.

589. **TANNER, TONY.** *The Reign of Wonder: Naivety and Reality in American Literature.* Cambridge: Cambridge Univ. Press, 1965.

590. **TAYLOR, J. GOLDEN.** "The Western Short Story." *South Dakota Review,* 2, no. 1 (1964), 37–55.

591. **THORP, WILLARD.** *American Humorists.* Minneapolis: Univ. of Minnesota Press, 1964.

592. ———. "Suggs and Sut in Modern Dress: The Latest Chapter in Southern Humor." *The Mississippi Quarterly,* 13 (1960), 169–75.

593. **TISCHLER, NANCY M.** *Black Masks: Negro Characters in Modern Southern Fiction.* University Park: Pennsylvania State Univ. Press, 1969.

594. **TOLIVER, HAROLD.** *Animate Illusions: Explorations of Narrative Structure.* Lincoln: Univ. of Nebraska Press, 1974.

595. **TRILLING, LIONEL, ED.** *The Experience of Literature.* New York: Holt, Rinehart and Winston, 1967.

596. **VAN NOSTRAND, A. D.** *Everyman His Own Poet: Romantic Gospels in American Literature*. New York: McGraw-Hill, 1968.

597. **VOSS, ARTHUR.** *The American Short Story: A Critical Survey*. Norman: Univ. of Oklahoma Press, 1973.

598. **WADLINGTON, WARWICK.** *The Confidence Game in American Literature*. Princeton, NJ: Princeton Univ. Press, 1975.

599. **WALCUTT, CHARLES CHILD.** *Man's Changing Mask: Modes and Methods of Characterization in Fiction*. Minneapolis: Univ. of Minnesota Press, 1966.

600. **WALKER, DON D.** "The Mountain Man as Literary Hero." *Western American Literature*, 1 (1966), 15–25.

601. **WARREN, AUSTIN.** *The New England Conscience*. Ann Arbor: Univ. of Michigan Press, 1966.

602. **WARRICK, PATRICIA.** "Images of the Man-Machine Intelligence Relationship in Science Fiction." In *Many Futures, Many Worlds: Theme and Form in Science Fiction*. Ed. Thomas D. Clareson. Kent, OH: Kent State Univ. Press, 1977. pp. 182–223.

603. **WASHINGTON, MARY HELEN.** "Teaching *Black-Eyed Susans*: An Approach to the Study of Black Women Writers." *Black American Literature Forum*, 11 (1977), 20–24.

604. **WASSERSTROM, WILLIAM.** *Heiress of All the Ages: Sex and Sentiment in the Genteel Tradition*. Minneapolis: Univ. of Minnesota Press, 1959.

605. **WAUGH, HILLARY.** "The Mystery versus the Novel." In *The Mystery Story*. Ed. John Ball. Del Mar, CA: Publishers Inc., 1976. pp. 61–80.

606. **WEAVER, RICHARD M.** "Realism and the Local Color Interlude." Ed. George Core. *The Georgia Review*, 22 (1968), 301–05.

607. **WEIMANN, ROBERT.** "Point of View in Fiction." In *Preserve and Create: Essays in Marxist Literary Criticism*. Ed. Gaylord C. LeRoy and Ursula Beitz. New York: Humanities Press, 1973. pp. 54–75.

608. **WEIMER, DAVID R.** *The City as Metaphor*. New York: Random House, 1966.

609. **WEST, RAY B., JR.** "Introduction." In *American Short Stories*. New York: Crowell, 1959. pp. 1–11.

610. **WHITE, MORTON AND LUCIA.** *The Intellectual versus the City: From Thomas Jefferson to Frank Lloyd Wright*. Cambridge, MA: Harvard Univ. Press and M. I. T. Press, 1962.

611. **WHITLOW, ROGER.** *Black American Literature: A Critical History*. Chicago: Nelson-Hall, 1973.

612. **WILCOX, EARL J., AND DAVID L. RANKIN.** *Fundamentals of Fiction*. Boston, MA: Allyn and Bacon, 1975.

613. **WILKINSON, JEAN, AND MURIEL BLATT.** *Teacher's Manual to*

Accompany "Reader's Choice: Essays, Stories, Poems." San Francisco CA: Canfield Press, 1970.

614. **WILLIAMS, CECIL B.** "Regionalism in American Culture." In *Geist einer freien Gesellschaft: Festschrift zu Ehren von Senator William Fulbright aus Anlass des zehnjährigen Bestehens des deutschen Fulbright-Programms.* Ed. Lewis Hammond, Dieter Sattler, and Emil Lehnartz. Heidelberg: Quelle & Meyer, 1962. pp. 331-87.

615. **WILLIAMS, KENNY J.** *They Also Spoke: An Essay on Negro Literature in America, 1787-1930.* Nashville, TN: Townsend Press, 1970.

616. **WILLIAMS, ROBERT.** "Three Short Stories for Eighth Graders." *Interpretations,* 1 (1968), 28-36.

617. **WILLIAMSON, JACK.** "Science Fiction, Teaching and Criticism." In *Science Fiction, Today and Tomorrow.* Ed. Reginald Bretnor. New York: Harper & Row, 1974. pp. 309-28.

618. **WINTERICH, JOHN T.** *Writers in America, 1842-1967.* Jersey City, NJ: Davey, 1968.

619. **WOOD, ANN DOUGLAS.** "The Literature of Impoverishment: The Women Local Colorists in America 1865-1914." *Women's Studies,* 1 (1972), 3-45.

620. **WOODS, JOHN.** *The Logic of Fiction: A Philosophical Sounding of Deviant Logic.* The Hague: Mouton, 1974.

621. **WRIGHT, WALTER F.** "Tone in Fiction." In *The Theory of the Novel: New Essays.* Ed. John Halperin. New York: Oxford Univ. Press, 1974. pp. 297-304.

622. **YODER, R. A.** "The Equilibrist Perspective: Toward a Theory of American Romanticism." *Studies in Romanticism,* 12 (1973), 705-40.

623. **ZACHARIAS, LEE.** "Point of View and the Nature of Truth in Detective Fiction." In *Proceedings of the Fifth National Convention of the Popular Culture Association, St. Louis, Missouri, March 20-22, 1975.* Ed. Michael T. Marsden. Bowling Green, OH: Bowling Green Univ. Popular Press, 1975. pp. 667-83.

624. **ZEMACH, EDDY M.** "Intention, Attention, and the Nature of Fiction." *The Hebrew University Studies in Literature,* 5 (1977), 135-54.

GENERAL BIBLIOGRAPHIES

625. **ANDERSON, JOHN Q.** "Scholarship in Southwestern Humor—Past and Present." *The Mississippi Quarterly,* 17 (1964), 67-86.

626. **BAIRD, NEWTON D., AND ROBERT GREENWOOD.** *An Annotat-*

ed Bibliography of California Fiction, 1664-1970. Georgetown, CA: Talisman Literary Research, 1971.

627. BARRON, NEIL, ED. *Anatomy of Wonder: Science Fiction.* New York: Bowker, 1976.

628. BENNETT, J. R. "Style in Twentieth Century British and American Fiction: A Bibliography." *West Coast Review,* 2, no. 3 (1968), 43–51.

629. BRINEY, ROBERT E. "The Literature of the Subject: An Annotated Bibliography." In *The Mystery Story.* Ed. John Ball. Del Mar, CA: Publishers Inc., 1976. pp. 365–90.

630. BRYER, JACKSON R. "Contemporary American-Jewish Literature: A Selected Checklist of Criticism." In *Contemporary American-Jewish Literature.* Ed. Irving Malin. Bloomington: Indiana Univ. Press, 1973. pp. 270–300.

631. CLARESON, THOMAS. *Science Fiction Criticism: An Annotated Checklist.* Kent, OH: Kent State Univ. Press, 1972.

632. CORRIGAN, ROBERT A. "Afro-American Fiction: A Checklist, 1853-1970." *Midcontinent American Studies Journal,* 11, no. 2 (1970), 114–35.

633. _____. "Afro-American Fiction: Errata and Additions." *American Studies,* 12, no. 1 (1971), 69–73.

634. _____. "Afro-American Fiction Since 1970." *American Studies,* 14, no. 2 (1973), 85–90.

635. _____. "Bibliography of Afro-American Fiction: 1853-1970." *Studies in Black Literature,* 1, no. 2 (1970), 51–86.

636. COX, JAMES T., MARGARET PUTNAM, AND MARVIN WILLIAMS. "Textual Studies in the Novel: A Selected Checklist, 1950-74." *Studies in the Novel,* 7 (1975), 445–71.

637. DAVIS, CHARLES E., AND MARTHA B. HUDSON. "Humor of the Old Southwest: A Checklist of Criticism." In *The Frontier Humorists: Critical Views.* Ed. M. Thomas Inge. Hamden, CT: Archon Books, 1975. pp. 303–23.

638. EICHELBERGER, CLAYTON, ET AL. *A Guide to Critical Reviews of United States Fiction, 1870-1910.* 2 vols. Metuchen, NJ: Scarecrow, 1971-74.

639. ETULAIN, RICHARD W. *Western American Literature: A Bibliography of Interpretative Books and Articles.* Vermillion, SD: Dakota Press, 1972.

640. FINE, DAVID M. "Immigrant Ghetto Fiction, 1885-1918: An Annotated Bibliography." *American Literary Realism, 1870-1910,* 6 (1973), 169–95.

641. FISHER, BENJAMIN FRANKLIN, IV. "Ancilla to the Gothic Tradition: A Supplementary Bibliography." *American Transcendental Quarterly,* no. 30, Part Two (1976), pp. 22–36.

642. FREE, WILLIAM J. "American Fiction in the *Columbian Magazine*, 1786-1792: An Annotated Checklist." *Bulletin of Bibliography and Magazine Notes*, 25 (1968), 150-51.

643. GIBSON, MICHAEL D. "The Western: A Selective Bibliography." *Journal of Popular Culture*, 7 (1973), 743-48.

644. GOHDES, CLARENCE. *Bibliographical Guide to the Study of the Literature of the U. S. A.* 4th ed. Durham, NC: Duke Univ. Press, 1976. [3rd ed., 1970; 2nd ed., 1963; 1st ed., 1959]

645. HAGEN, ORDEAN A. *Who Done It?: A Guide to Detective, Mystery, and Suspense Fiction.* New York: Bowker, 1969.

646. HALPERIN, JOHN. "Approaches to Fiction: A Select Descriptive Bibliography." In *The Theory of the Novel: New Essays.* Ed. John Halperin. New York: Oxford Univ. Press, 1974. pp. 389-92.

647. HARPER, HOWARD. "General Studies of Recent American Fiction: A Selected Checklist." *Modern Fiction Studies*, 19 (1973), 127-33.

648. JACOBSON, ANGELINE. *Contemporary Native American Literature: A Selected & Partially Annotated Bibliography.* Metuchen, NJ: Scarecrow, 1977.

649. KING, FRANCES. "Treatment of the Mental Retarded Character in Modern American Fiction." *Bulletin of Bibliography and Magazine Notes*, 32 (1975), 106-14, 131.

650. KIRBY, DAVID K. *American Fiction to 1900: A Guide to Information Sources.* Detroit, MI: Gale, 1975.

651. LEARY, LEWIS, AND JOHN AUCHARD. *American Literature: A Study and Research Guide.* New York: St. Martin's Press, 1976.

652. LOMELÍ, FRANCISCO A., AND DONALDO W. URIOSTE. *Chicano Perspectives in Literature: A Critical and Annotated Bibliography.* Albuquerque, NM: Pajarito Publications, 1976.

653. McDOWELL, ROBERT E., AND GEORGE FORTENBERRY. "A Checklist of Books and Essays about American Negro Novelists." *Studies in the Novel*, 3 (1971), 219-36.

654. [MAY, CHARLES E.] "A Selected, Annotated Bibliography of the Short Story." In *Short Story Theories.* Ed. Charles E. May. Athens: Ohio Univ. Press, 1976. pp. 226-51.

655. MESSERLI, DOUGLAS, AND HOWARD N. FOX. *Index to Periodical Fiction in English, 1965-1969.* Metuchen, NJ: Scarecrow, 1977.

656. METCALF, NORM. *The Index of Science Fiction Magazines, 1951-1965.* El Cerrito, CA: J. Ben Stark, 1968.

657. MUNDELL, E. H., JR., AND G. JAY RAUSCH. *The Detective Short Story: A Bibliography and Index.* Manhattan: Kansas State Univ. Library, 1974.

658. NAGEL, JAMES. "An Annotated Bibliography of Selected Recent Books on American Fiction." *Studies in American Fiction*, I (1973), 76–91.

659. PALUKA, FRANK. *Iowa Authors: A Bio-Bibliography of Sixty Native Writers*. Iowa City: Friends of the Univ. of Iowa Libraries, 1967.

660. PICKERING, JAMES H. "Bibliography of Short Fiction Criticism." In *Instructor's Manual—"Fiction 100: An Anthology of Short Stories."* New York: Macmillan, 1974. pp. 67–115.

661. ROSA, ALBERT F., AND PAUL A. ESCHHOLZ. *Contemporary Fiction in America and England, 1950–1970: A Guide to Information Sources*. Detroit, MI: Gale, 1976.

662. RUBIN, LOUIS D., JR., ED. *A Bibliographical Guide to the Study of Southern Literature*. Baton Rouge: Louisiana State Univ. Press, 1969.

663. RUSH, THERESSA GUNNELS, CAROL FAIRBANKS MYERS, AND ESTHER SPRING ARATA. *Black American Writers, Past and Present: A Biographical and Bibliographical Dictionary*. 2 vols. Metuchen, NJ: Scarecrow, 1975.

664. SMITH FRANK R. "Periodical Articles on the American Short Story: A Selected, Annotated Bibliography." *Bulletin of Bibliography and Magazine Notes*, 23 (1960–61), 9–13, 46–48, 69–72, 95–96.

665. SPILLER, ROBERT E., ET AL., ED. *Literary History of the United States: Bibliography*. 4th ed. New York: Macmillan, 1974. [3rd ed., 1963; Supplement to 1st ed., 1959]

666. STRONKS, JAMES B. "Addenda to the Bibliographies of Stephen Crane, Dreiser, Frederic, Fuller, Garland, Herne, Howells, London, and Norris." *The Papers of the Bibliographical Society of America*, 71 (1977), 362–69.

667. THURSTON, JARVIS, ET AL. *Short Fiction Criticism: A Checklist of Interpretation since 1925 of Stories and Novelettes (American, British, Continental), 1800–1958*. Denver, CO: Swallow, 1960.

668. TYMN, MARSHALL B., ET AL. *A Research Guide to Science Fiction Studies: An Annotated Checklist of Primary and Secondary Sources for Fantasy and Science Fiction*. New York: Garland, 1977.

669. WALKER, WARREN S. *Twentieth-Century Short Story Explication: Interpretations, 1900–1975, of Short Fiction since 1800*. 3rd ed. Hamden, CT: Shoe String Press, 1977. [Supplements to 2nd ed., 1973, 1970; 2nd ed., 1967; Supplements to 1st ed., 1965, 1963; 1st ed., 1961]

670. WHITE, BARBARA A. *American Women Writers: An Annotated Bibliography of Criticism*. New York: Garland, 1977.

671. **WOODRESS, JAMES.** *American Fiction, 1900–1950: A Guide to Information Sources.* Detroit, MI: Gale, 1974.

672. **WRIGHT, LYLE H.** *American Fiction, 1774–1850: A Contribution toward a Bibliography.* 2nd ed. San Marino, CA: Huntington Library, 1969.

673. ———. *American Fiction, 1876–1900: A Contribution toward a Bibliography.* San Marino, CA: Huntington Library, 1966.

AUTHORS

ABISH, WALTER

"Minds Meet"

See 223.

Interviews

674. **KLINKOWITZ, JEROME**. "Walter Abish: An Interview." *fiction international*, nos. 4–5 (1975), pp. 93–100.

ADAMS, ANDY

"The Corporal Segundo"

See 675.

"The Passing of Peg-Leg"

See 675.

General Studies

675. **HUDSON, WILSON M**. *Andy Adams: His Life and Writings.* Dallas, TX: Southern Methodist Univ. Press, 1964.
676. _____. *Andy Adams: Storyteller and Novelist of the Great Plains.* Austin, TX: Steck-Vaughn, 1967.

ADE, GEORGE

"Effie Whittlesy"

See 680.

"The Two Mandolin Players and the Willing Performer"

677. **SALZMAN, JACK**. "Dreiser and Ade: A Note on the Text of *Sister Carrie*." *American Literature*, 40 (1969), 544–48.

General Studies

678. **BLEILER, E. F**. "Introduction." In *Fables in Slang and More Fables in Slang*, by George Ade. New York: Dover, 1960. pp. v–xii.
679. **BRENNER, JACK**. "Howells and Ade." *American Literature*, 38 (1966), 198–207.
680. **COYLE, LEE**. *George Ade*. New York: Twayne, 1964.
681. **DANIELS, R. BALFOUR**. "George Ade as Social Critic." *The Mississippi Quarterly*, 12 (1959), 194–204.

682. **MATSON, LOWELL.** "Ade—Who Needed None." *The Literary Review*, 5 (1961), 99–114.
683. **MEINE, FRANKLIN J.** "Introduction." In *Chicago Stories*, by George Ade. Chicago: Henry Regnery, 1963. pp. ix–xxx.
684. **SHEPHERD, JEAN.** "Introduction." In *The America of George Ade (1866–1944): Fables, Short Stories, Essays*. New York: Putnam's, 1961. pp. 9–22.

Bibliography

685. **KOLB, HAROLD H., JR.** "George Ade (1866–1944)." *American Literary Realism, 1870–1910*, 4 (1971), 157–69.

AGEE, JAMES

"Boys Will Be Brutes"

See 695.

"Death in the Desert"

See 690, 695.

"Dedication Day"

See 690.

"Dream Sequence"

See 690.

"The Morning Watch"

686. **BROUGHTON, GEORGE, AND PANTHEA REID BROUGHTON.** "Agee and Autonomy." *Southern Humanities Review*, 4 (1970), 101–11.
687. **DA PONTE, DURANT.** "James Agee: The Quest for Identity." *Tennessee Studies In Literature*, 8 (1963), 25–37.
688. **OHLIN, PETER H.** *Agee.* New York: Ivan Obolensky, 1966.
689. **SEIB, KENNETH.** *James Agee: Promise and Fulfillment.* Pittsburgh, PA: Univ. of Pittsburgh Press, 1968.
See also 691, 693, 695.

"A Mother's Tale"

See 686, 688–691, 693, 695.

"1928 Story"

See 690–692.

"They That Sow in Sorrow Shall Reap"

See 690, 695.

"The Waiting"

See 267.

"A Walk Before Mass"

See 693, 695.

General Studies

690. **BARSON, ALFRED T.** *A Way of Seeing: A Critical Study of James Agee.* Amherst: Univ. of Massachusetts Press, 1972.

691. **KRAMER, VICTOR A.** *James Agee.* Boston, MA: Twayne, 1975.

692. _____, **ED.** "Agee in the Forties: Unpublished Poetry and Fiction." *The Texas Quarterly*, 11, no. 1 (1968), 9–55.

693. **LARSEN, ERLING.** *James Agee.* Minneapolis: Univ. of Minnesota Press, 1971.

694. **MADDEN, DAVID, ED.** *Remembering James Agee.* Baton Rouge: Louisiana State Univ. Press, 1974.

695. **MOUREAU, GENEVIÈVE.** *The Restless Journey of James Agee.* Trans. Miriam Kleiger and Morty Schiff. New York: Morrow, 1977.

Bibliography

696. **FABRE, GENEVIÈVE.** "A Bibliography of the Works of James Agee." *Bulletin of Bibliography and Magazine Notes*, 24 (1965), 145–48, 163–66.

AIKEN, CONRAD

"Gehenna"

See 706.

"Impulse"

697. **HANDA, CAROLYN.** " 'Impulse': Calculated Artistry in Conrad Aiken." *Studies in Short Fiction*, 12 (1975), 375–80.

"The Last Visit"

See 705.

"Life Isn't a Short Story"

See 704-706.

"Mr. Arcularis"

698. **TUTTLETON, JAMES W.** "Aiken's 'Mr. Arcularis': Psychic Regression and the Death Instinct." *American Imago*, 20 (1963), 295–314.

See also 704.

"Silent Snow, Secret Snow"

699. **GOSSMAN, ANN.** " 'Silent Snow, Secret Snow': The Child as Artist." *Studies in Short Fiction*, 1 (1964), 123–28.
700. **GRAHAM, BALLEW.** " 'Silent Snow, Secret Snow': The Short Story as Poem." *English Journal*, 57 (1968), 693–95.
701. **JONES, WILLIAM M.** "Aiken's 'Silent Snow, Secret Snow.' " *The Explicator*, 18 (1960), item 34.
702. **PERKINS, GEORGE.** "Aiken's 'Silent Snow, Secret Snow.' " *The Explicator*, 21 (1962), item 26.
See also 263, 334, 585, 704.

"Spider, Spider"

See 704.

"Strange Moonlight"

See 704.

General Studies

703. **BROWN, CALVIN S.** "The Achievement of Conrad Aiken." *The Georgia Review*, 27 (1973), 477–88.
704. **HOFFMAN, FREDERICK J.** *Conrad Aiken*. New York: Twayne, 1962.
705. **MARTIN, JAY.** *Conrad Aiken: A Life of His Art*. Princeton, NJ: Princeton Univ. Press, 1962.
706. **SCHORER, MARK.** "Preface." In *The Collected Short Stories of Conrad Aiken*. Cleveland, OH: World, 1960. pp. vii–xiv.

Interviews

707. **HUTCHENS, JOHN K.** "One Thing and Another." *Saturday Review*, 52 (20 Dec. 1969), 24–25.

Bibliography

708. **HARRIS, M. CATHERINE.** "Conrad Aiken: Critical Recognition, 1914–1976." *Bulletin of Bibliography and Magazine Notes*, 34 (1977), 29–34, 137–40, 156.

ALCOTT, LOUISA MAY

"Behind a Mask, or a Woman's Power"

See 711.

"An Hour"

See 18.

"M. L."

See 709.

"My Contraband"

See 18, 709.

"Pauline's Passion and Punishment"

See 710, 711.

General Studies

709. HAMBLEN, ABIGAIL ANN. "Louisa May Alcott and The Racial Question." *The University Review* (Kansas City), 37 (1971), 307–13.
710. SAXTON, MARTHA. *Louisa May: A Modern Biography of Louisa May Alcott*. Boston, MA: Houghton Mifflin, 1977.
711. STERN, MADELEINE. "Introduction." In *Behind a Mask: The Unknown Thrillers of Louisa May Alcott*. New York: Morrow, 1975. pp. vii–xxxiii.

Bibliography

712. PAYNE, ALMA J. "Louisa May Alcott (1832–1888)." *American Literary Realism, 1870–1910*, 6 (1973), 27–43.

ALDRICH, THOMAS BAILEY

"Marjorie Daw"

See 101.

General Studies

*713. SAMUELS, CHARLES E. *Thomas Bailey Aldrich*. New York: Twayne, 1965.

ALGER, HORATIO, JR.

"A Fancy of Hers"

See 716.

"Five Hundred Dollars"

See 716.

"Little Floy"

See 717.

"Lost and Found"

See 717.

"A Race up the Hill"

See 717.

"The Veiled Mirror"

See 717.

General Studies

714. **GARDNER, RALPH D.** *Horatio Alger, or the American Hero Era.* Mendota, IL: Wayside Press, 1964.
715. **HOYT, EDWIN P.** *Horatio's Boys: The Life and Works of Horatio Alger, Jr.* Radnor, PA: Chilton, 1974.
716. **SCHARNHORST, GARY F.** "The Boudoir Tales of Horatio Alger, Jr." *Journal of Popular Culture*, 10 (1976), 215–26.
717. **TEBBEL, JOHN.** *From Rags to Riches: Horatio Alger, Jr., and the American Dream.* New York: Macmillan, 1963.

Bibliography

718. **GARDNER, RALPH D.** *Road to Success: The Bibliography of the Works of Horatio Alger.* Rev. ed. Mendota, IL: Wayside Press, 1971.

ALGREN, NELSON

"A Bottle of Milk for Mother"

719. **LID, R. W.** "A World Imagines: The Art of Nelson Algren." In *American Literary Naturalism: A Reassessment.* Ed. Yoshinobu Hakutani and Lewis Fried. Heidelberg: Carl Winter, 1975. pp. 176–96.
720. **SILKOWSKI, DANIEL R.** "Alienation and Isolation in Nelson Algren's 'A Bottle of Milk for Mother.' " *English Journal*, 60 (1971), 724–27.
See also 721.

"Design for Departure"

See 721.

"How the Devil Came Down Division Street"

See 721.

"So Help Me"

See 721.

General Studies

721. **COX, MARTHA HEASLEY, AND WAYNE CHATTERTON.** *Nelson Algren.* Boston, MA: Twayne, 1975.

Interviews

722. **[CORRINGTON, JOHN WILLIAM.]** "Nelson Algren Talks

With *NOR's* Editor-at-Large." *The New Orleans Review*, 1 (1969), 130–32.
723. **DONOHUE, H. E. F.** *Conversations with Nelson Algren.* New York: Hill & Wang, 1964.
724. ———. "Nelson Algren at Fifty-Five." *The Atlantic Monthly*, 214, no. 4 (1964), 79–80, 83–85.

Bibliography

725. **McCOLLUM, KENNETH G.** *Nelson Algren: A Checklist.* Detroit, MI: Gale, 1973.
726. **STUDING, RICHARD.** "A Nelson Algren Checklist." *Twentieth Century Literature*, 19 (1973), 27–39.

ALLEN, JAMES LANE
"Sister Dolorosa"
See 83, 728.

"Summer in Arcady"
See 83, 728.

"Two Gentlemen of Kentucky"
See 83, 728.

General Studies

727. **BOTTORFF, WILLIAM K.** "Introduction." In *A Kentucky Cardinal, Aftermath, and Other Selected Works*, by James Lane Allen. New Haven, CT: College & University Press, 1967. pp. 7–15.
*728. ———. *James Lane Allen.* New York: Twayne, 1964.

Bibliography

729. **BOTTORFF, WILLIAM K.** "James Lane Allen (1849–1925)." *American Literary Realism, 1870–1910*, 2 (1969), 121–24.

ANDERSON, POUL
"Goat Song"
See 276.

"Sam Hall"
See 290.

ANDERSON, SHERWOOD
"Adventure"
See 212, 511, 832.

"An Awakening"

See 212, 356, 761.

"The Book of the Grotesque"

730. **ALSEN, EBERHARD.** "The Futile Pursuit of Truth in Twain's 'What Is Man?' and Anderson's 'The Book of the Grotesque.' " *Mark Twain Journal*, 17, no. 3 (1975), 12–14.
731. **PHILLIPS, WILLIAM L.** "Emerson in Anderson." *American Notes & Queries*, 15 (1976), 4–5.
See also 212, 761, 763, 768, 784, 832.

"Brother Death"

See 801, 832.

"A Chicago Hamlet"

See 805.

"Death"

See 212, 768.

"Death in the Woods"

732. **GUERIN, WILFRED L.** " 'Death in the Woods': Sherwood Anderson's 'Cold Pastoral.' " *The CEA Critic*, 30, no. 8 (1968), 4–5.
733. **HEPBURN, JAMES G.** "Disarming and Uncanny Visions: Freud's 'The Uncanny' with Regard to Form and Content in Stories by Sherwood Anderson and D. H. Lawrence." *Literature and Psychology*, 9 (1959), 9–12.
734. **JOSELYN, SISTER MARY, O.S.B.** "Some Artistic Dimensions of Sherwood Anderson's 'Death in the Woods.' " *Studies in Short Fiction*, 4 (1967), 252–59.
735. **LAWRY, JON S.** " 'Death in the Woods' and the Artist's Self in Sherwood Anderson." *PMLA*, 74 (1959), 306–11.
736. **ROBINSON, ELEANOR M.** "A Study of 'Death in the Woods.' " *The CEA Critic*, 30, no. 4 (1968), 6.
737. **ROHRBERGER, MARY.** "The Man, the Boy, and the Myth: Sherwood Anderson's 'Death in the Woods.' " *Midcontinent American Studies Journal*, 3, no. 2 (1962), 48–54.
738. **SCHEICK, WILLIAM J.** "Compulsion toward Repetition: Sherwood Anderson's 'Death in the Woods.' " *Studies in Short Fiction*, 11 (1974), 141–46.
See also 259, 339, 399, 447, 548, 597, 805, 813, 832, 833.

"Departure"

See 212, 758, 761, 777.

"Drink"

See 790.

"The Dumb Man"

See 832.

"The Egg"

739. **Joseph, Gerhard.** "The American Triumph of the Egg: Anderson's 'The Egg' and Fitzgerald's 'The Great Gatsby.' " *Criticism*, 7 (1965), 131–40.
740. **Kingsbury, Stewart A.** "A Structural Semantic Analysis of the 'Punch Line' of Sherwood Anderson's Short Story, 'The Egg.' " In *Papers from the Michigan Linguistic Society Meeting, October 3, 1970.* Ed. David Lawton. Mt. Pleasant: Dept. of English, Central Michigan Univ., 1971. pp. 52–61.
741. **West, Michael D.** "Sherwood Anderson's Triumph: 'The Egg.' " *American Quarterly*, 20 (1968), 675–93.
See also 267, 356, 399, 454, 791, 801, 814, 832.

"Godliness"

742. **Laughlin, Rosemary M.** "Godliness and the American Dream in Winesburg, Ohio." *Twentieth Century Literature*, 13 (1967), 97–103.
743. **O'Neill, John.** "Anderson Writ Large: 'Godliness' in *Winesburg, Ohio.*" *Twentieth Century Literature*, 23 (1977), 67–83.
See also 758, 762, 776, 805, 832.

"Hands"

See 116, 212, 356, 597, 768, 777, 804, 805.

"I Want to Know Why"

744. **Gross, Seymour L.** "Sherwood Anderson's Debt to Huckleberry Finn." *The Mark Twain Journal*, 11, no. 2 (1960), 3–5, 24.
745. **Lawry, Jon S.** "Love and Betrayal in Sherwood Anderson's 'I Want to Know Why.' " *Shenandoah*, 13, no. 3 (1962), 46–54.
746. **Naugle, Helen H.** "The Name 'Bildad.' " *Modern Fiction Studies*, 22 (1977), 591–94.
747. **Ringe, Donald A.** "Point of View and Theme In 'I Want to Know Why.' " *Critique*, 3, no. 1 (1959), 24–29.
748. **Smith, Anneliese H.** "Part of the Problem: Student Responses to Sherwood Anderson's 'I Want to Know Why.' " *Negro American Literature Forum*, 7 (1973), 28–31.
See also 178, 374, 394, 801, 805, 813, 816, 3431.

"I'm a Fool"

749. **PECILE, JORDON.** "On Sherwood Anderson and 'I'm a Fool.'" In *The American Short Story.* Ed. Calvin Skaggs. New York: Dell, 1977. pp. 145–49.
See also 157, 404, 535, 801, 805, 832.

"Loneliness"

See 212.

"The Man Who Became a Woman"

750. **BABB, HOWARD S.** "A Reading of Sherwood Anderson's 'The Man Who Became a Woman.'" *PMLA*, 80 (1965), 432–35.
See also 801, 805, 809, 832.

"A Meeting South"

751. **FEIBLEMAN, JAMES K.** "Literary New Orleans between World Wars." *The Southern Review*, NS 1 (1965), 702–19.
752. **RICHARDSON, H. EDWARD.** "Anderson and Faulkner." *American Literature*, 36 (1964), 298–314.
See also 805, 2058.

"The New Englander"

See 832.

"An Ohio Pagan"

753. **RIDEOUT, WALTER B.** "A Borrowing from Borrow." In *Sherwood Anderson: Centennial Studies.* Ed. Hilbert H. Campbell and Charles E. Modlin. Troy, NY: Whitston, 1976. pp. 162–74.

"Out of Nowhere into Nothing"

See 805.

"Paper Pills"

See 393, 762, 768, 832.

"The Philosopher"

754. **ZLOTNICK, JOAN.** "Dubliners in Winesburg, Ohio: A Note on Joyce's 'The Sisters' and Anderson's 'The Philosopher.'" *Studies in Short Fiction*, 12 (1975), 405–07.
See also 790.

" 'Queer' "

See 212, 832.

"The Sad Horn-Blowers"

755. **LUCOW, BEN.** "Mature Identity in Sherwood Anderson's 'The Sad Horn-Blowers.' " *Studies in Short Fiction*, 2 (1965), 291–93.
See also 833.

"Seeds"

756. **SUTTON, WILLIAM A.** *The Revision of "Seeds."* Muncie, IN: Ball State Univ., 1976.
See also 597, 805.

"Sophistication"

See 212, 758, 763, 774, 777.

"The Strength of God"

See 179, 212, 765.

"The Teacher"

See 356, 765.

"There She Is—She Is Taking Her Bath"

See 828.

"The Thinker"

See 356, 804, 812.

"The Triumph of a Modern or, Send for the Lawyer"

See 828.

"Unlighted Lamps"

See 805, 832.

"The Untold Lie"

757. **RIDEOUT, WALTER B.** " 'The Tale of Perfect Balance': Sherwood Anderson's 'The Untold Lie.' " *The Newberry Library Bulletin*, 6 (1971), 243–50.
See also 770.

"Unused"

See 832.

"Winesburg, Ohio"

758. **ABCARIAN, RICHARD.** "Innocence and Experience in *Winesburg, Ohio*." *The University Review* (Kansas City), 35 (1968), 95–105.

759. ANDERSON, DAVID D. "Anderson and Myth." In *Sherwood Anderson: Dimensions of His Literary Art: A Collection of Critical Essays*. Ed. David D. Anderson. East Lansing: Michigan State Univ. Press, 1976. pp. 118–41.

760. BAKER, CARLOS. "Sherwood Anderson's Winesburg: A Reprise." *The Virginia Quarterly Review*, 48 (1972), 568–79.

761. BLUEFARB, SAM. "George Willard: Death and Resurrection." In *The Escape Motif in the American Novel: Mark Twain to Richard Wright*. Columbus: Ohio State Univ. Press, 1972. pp. 42–58.

762. BORT, BARRY D. "*Winesburg, Ohio*: The Escape from Isolation." *The Midwest Quarterly*, 11 (1970), 443–56.

763. BOWDEN, EDWIN T. *The Dungeon of the Heart: Human Isolation and the American Novel*. New York: Macmillan, 1961.

764. BRADY, JOHN. "When Sherwood Anderson's Mudguards Were Dented." *The American Book Collector*, 19, no. 10 (1969), 20–22.

765. BROWNING, CHRIS. "Kate Swift: Sherwood Anderson's Creative Eros." *Tennessee Studies In Literature*, 13 (1968), 141–48.

766. BUDD, LOUIS J. "The Grotesques of Anderson and Wolfe." *Modern Fiction Studies*, 5 (1959), 304–10.

767. BUNGE, NANCY. "Women as Social Critics in *Sister Carrie*, *Winesburg, Ohio*, and *Main Street*." *Midamerica*, 3 (1976), 46–55.

768. CIANCIO, RALPH. " 'The Sweetness of the Twisted Apples': Unity of Vision in *Winesburg, Ohio*." *PMLA*, 87 (1972), 994–1006.

769. CLARK, EDWARD. "*Winesburg, Ohio*: An Interpretation." *Die Neueren Sprachen*, 58 (1959), 547–52.

770. COWLEY, MALCOLM. "Introduction." In *Winesburg, Ohio*, by Sherwood Anderson. New York: Viking, 1960. pp. 1–15.

771. _____. "The Living Dead—IX: Sherwood Anderson's Epiphanies." *The London Magazine*, 7, no. 7 (1960), 61–66.

772. FERRES, JOHN H. "The Nostalgia of *Winesburg, Ohio*." *The Newberry Library Bulletin*, 6 (1971), 235–42.

773. FERTIG, MARTIN J. " 'A Great Deal of Wonder in Me': Inspiration and Transformation in *Winesburg, Ohio*." *The Markham Review*, 6 (Summer 1977), 65–70.

774. FUSSELL, EDWIN. " 'Winesburg, Ohio': Art and Isolation." *Modern Fiction Studies*, 6 (1960), 106–14.

775. HOWE, IRVING. "Sherwood Anderson, *Winesburg, Ohio*." In *The American Novel: From James Fenimore Cooper to William Faulkner*. Ed. Wallace Stegner. New York: Basic Books, 1965. pp. 154–65.

776. LORCH, THOMAS M. "The Choreographic Structure of *Winesburg, Ohio*." *CLA Journal*, 12 (1968), 56–65.

777. LOVE, GLEN A. "*Winesburg, Ohio* and the Rhetoric of Silence." *American Literature*, 40 (1968), 38–57.

778. MCDONALD, WALTER R. "*Winesburg, Ohio*: Tales of Isolation." *The University Review* (Kansas City), 35 (1969), 237–40.

779. MARESCA, CAROL J. "Gestures as Meaning in Sherwood Anderson's *Winesburg, Ohio*." *CLA Journal*, 9 (1966), 279–83.

780. MELLARD, JAMES M. "Narrative Forms in *Winesburg, Ohio*." *PMLA*, 83 (1968), 1304–12.

781. MILLICHAP, JOSEPH R. "Distorted Matter and Disjunctive Forms: The Grotesque as Modernist Genre." *The Arizona Quarterly*, 33 (1977), 339–47.

782. MUELLER, G. H. S. "Hans Erich Nossack and Sherwood Anderson's *Winesburg, Ohio*." *The Winesburg Eagle*, 3, no. 1 (1977), 7.

783. MURPHY, GEORGE D. "The Theme of Sublimation in Anderson's *Winesburg, Ohio*." *Modern Fiction Studies*, 13 (1967), 237–46.

784. PARK, MARTHA M. "How Far from Emerson's Man of One Idea to Anderson's Grotesques?" *CLA Journal*, 20 (1977), 374–79.

785. PHILLIPS, WILLIAM L. "The Eclectic Dr. Reefy." *American Notes & Queries*, 15 (1976), 2–4.

786. PICKERING, SAMUEL. "*Winesburg, Ohio*: A Portrait of the Artist as a Young Man." *The Southern Quarterly*, 16 (1977), 27–38.

787. RIDEOUT, WALTER B. "The Simplicity of *Winesburg, Ohio*." *Shenandoah*, 13, no. 3 (1962), 20–31.

788. ———. "Talbot Whittingham and Anderson: A Passage to *Winesburg, Ohio*." In *Sherwood Anderson: Dimensions of His Literary Art: A Collection of Critical Essays*. Ed. David D. Anderson. East Lansing: Michigan State Univ. Press, 1976. pp. 41–60.

789. ROGERS, DOUGLAS G. "Development of the Artist in *Winesburg, Ohio*." *Studies in the Twentieth Century*, no. 10 (1972), pp. 91–99.

790. SAN JUAN, EPIFANIO, JR. "Vision and Reality: A Reconsideration of Sherwood Anderson's *Winesburg, Ohio*." *American Literature*, 35 (1963), 137–55.

791. STEWART, MAAJA A. "Scepticism and Belief in Chekhov and Anderson." *Studies in Short Fiction*, 9 (1972), 29–40.

792. STOUCK, DAVID. "*Winesburg, Ohio* and the Failure of Art." *Twentieth Century Literature*, 15 (1969), 145–51.

793. ———. "*Winesburg, Ohio* As a Dance of Death." *American Literature*, 48 (1977), 525–42.

794. SULLIVAN, JOHN H. "Winesburg Revisited." *The Antioch Review*, 20 (1960), 213–21.

795. **WHITE, RAY LEWIS.** *"Winesburg, Ohio:* A Lost Chicago Review." *The Winesburg Eagle,* 2, no. 2 (1977), 2.

796. **WILSON, GIL.** "A Mural Portrait of Sherwood Anderson." *The Winesburg Eagle,* 1, no. 2 (1976), 1–4; 2, no. 1 (1976), 5–7; 2, no. 2 (1977), 1, 6–8.

797. **WRENN, JOHN H., AND MARGARET M. WRENN.** " 'T. M.': The Forgotten Muse of Sherwood Anderson and Edgar Lee Masters." In *Sherwood Anderson: Centennial Studies.* Ed. Hilbert H. Campbell and Charles E. Modlin. Troy, NY: Whitston, 1976. pp. 175–83.

798. **ZLOTNICK, JOAN.** "Of Dubliners and Ohioans: A Comparative Study of Two Works." *Ball State University Forum,* 17, no. 4 (1976), 33–36.

See also 151, 179, 203, 212, 250, 271, 275, 305, 338, 356, 363, 404, 589, 597, 801, 805, 811, 812, 814, 815, 830, 832–836, 850, 5110, 6708.

"The Yellow Gown"

See 828.

General Studies

799. **ANDERSON, DAVID D.** "Chicago as Metaphor." *The Great Lakes Review,* 1, no. 1 (1974), 3–15.

800. _____. "The Search for a Living Past." In *Sherwood Anderson: Centennial Studies.* Ed. Hilbert H. Campbell and Charles E. Modlin. Troy, NY: Whitston, 1976. pp. 212–23.

801. _____. *Sherwood Anderson: An Introduction and Interpretation.* New York: Barnes & Noble, 1967.

802. _____. "Sherwood Anderson After 20 Years." *The Midwest Quarterly,* 3 (1962), 119–32.

803. _____. "Sherwood Anderson, Virginia Journalist." *The Newberry Library Bulletin,* 6 (1971), 251–62.

804. **BALDESHWILER, EILEEN.** "Sherwood Anderson and the Lyric Story." In *The Twenties: Fiction, Poetry, Drama.* Ed. Warren French. Deland, FL: Everett/Edwards, 1975. pp. 65–74.

805. **BURBANK, REX.** *Sherwood Anderson.* New York: Twayne, 1964.

806. **COWLEY, MALCOLM.** "Anderson's Last Days of Innocence." *The New Republic,* 142, no. 7 (1960), 16–18.

807. **CURRY, MARTHA MULROY.** "Anderson's Theories on Writing Fiction." In *Sherwood Anderson: Dimensions of His Literary Art: A Collection of Critical Essays.* Ed. David D. Anderson. East Lansing: Michigan State Univ. Press, 1976. pp. 90–109.

808. **DURHAM, JOHN.** "Did the 'Lionel Trilling Syndicate' Murder Sherwood Anderson?" *Forum* (University of Houston), 4, no. 3 (1964), 11–14.

809. **GEISMAR, MAXWELL.** "Introduction." In *Sherwood Anderson: Short Stories*. New York: Hill and Wang, 1962. pp. ix–xxiii.

810. **GREGORY, HORACE.** "On Sherwood Anderson." In *Talks with Authors*. Ed. Charles F. Madden. Carbondale and Edwardsville: Southern Illinois Univ. Press, 1968. pp. 12–22.

811. **HOFFMAN, FREDERICK J.** "The Voice of Sherwood Anderson." *Shenandoah*, 13, no. 3 (1962), 5–19.

812. **JOSELYN, SISTER M., O.S.B.** "Sherwood Anderson and the Lyric Story." In *The Twenties, Poetry and Prose: 20 Critical Essays*. Ed. Richard E. Langford and William E. Taylor. Deland, FL: Everett/Edwards, 1966. pp. 70–73.

813. **LAWRY, JON S.** "The Artist in America: The Case of Sherwood Anderson." *Ball State University Forum*, 7, no. 2 (1966), 15–26.

814. _____. "The Arts of Winesburg and Bidwell, Ohio." *Twentieth Century Literature*, 23 (1977), 53–66.

815. **LEARY, LEWIS.** "Sherwood Anderson: *The Man Who Became a Boy Again*." In *Literatur und Sprache der Vereinigten Staaten: Aufsätze zu Ehren von Hans Galinsky*. Heidelberg: Carl Winter, 1969. pp. 135–43.

816. **LOVE, GLEN A.** "Horses or Men: Primitive and Pastoral Elements in Sherwood Anderson." In *Sherwood Anderson: Centennial Studies*. Ed. Hilbert H. Campbell and Charles E. Modlin. Troy, NY: Whitston, 1976. pp. 235–48.

817. **LOVETT, ROBERT MORSS.** "Sherwood Anderson." In *After the Genteel Tradition: American Writers 1910–1930*. Rev. ed. Ed. Malcolm Cowley. Carbondale: Southern Illinois Univ. Press, 1964. pp. 74–82.

818. **MERIWETHER, JAMES B.** "Faulkner's Essays on Anderson." In *Faulkner: Fifty Years After* The Marble Faun. Ed. George H. Wolfe. University: Univ. of Alabama Press, 1976. pp. 159–81.

819. **MILLER, WILLIAM V.** "Earth-Mothers, Succubi, and Other Ectoplasmic Spirits: The Women in Sherwood Anderson's Short Stories." *Midamerica*, 1 (1974), 64–81.

820. _____. "In Defense of Mountaineers: Sherwood Anderson's Hill Stories." *Ball State University Forum*, 15, no. 2 (1974), 51–58.

821. _____. "Portraits of the Artist: Anderson's Fictional Storytellers." In *Sherwood Anderson: Dimensions of His Literary Art: A Collection of Critical Essays*. Ed. David D. Anderson. East Lansing: Michigan State Univ. Press, 1976. pp. 1–23.

822. OHASHI, KICHINOSUKI. "Sherwood Anderson in Japan: The Early Period." *Twentieth Century Literature*, 23 (1977), 115-39.

823. PAVESE, CESARE. "Sherwood Anderson." In *American Literature: Essays and Opinions*. Trans. Edwin Fussell. Berkeley: Univ. of California Press, 1970. pp. 30-41.

824. RIDEOUT, WALTER B. "Introduction." In *Sherwood Anderson: A Collection of Critical Essays*. Englewood Cliffs, NJ: Prentice-Hall, 1974. pp. 1-11.

825. ———. "Why Sherwood Anderson Employed Buck Fever." *The Georgia Review*, 13 (1959), 76-85.

826. SCHRIBER, MARY SUE. "Sherwood Anderson in France: 1919-1939." *Twentieth Century Literature*, 23 (1977), 140-53.

827. SOMERS, PAUL P., JR. "Anderson's Twisted Apples and Hemingway's Crips." *Midamerica*, 1 (1974), 82-97.

828. ———. "Sherwood Anderson's Mastery of Narrative Distance." *Twentieth Century Literature*, 23 (1977), 84-93.

829. SPENCER, BENJAMIN F. "Sherwood Anderson: American Mythopoeist." *American Literature*, 41 (1969), 1-18.

830. SUTTON, WILLIAM A. *The Road to Winesburg: A Mosaic of the Imaginative Life of Sherwood Anderson*. Metuchen, NJ: Scarecrow, 1972.

831. TAYLOR, WELFORD DUNAWAY. "Anderson and the Problem of Belonging." In *Sherwood Anderson: Dimensions of His Literary Art: A Collection of Critical Essays*. Ed. David D. Anderson. East Lansing: Michigan State Univ. Press, 1976. pp. 61-74.

832. ———. *Sherwood Anderson*. New York: Ungar, 1977.

833. WAY, BRIAN. "Sherwood Anderson." In *The American Novel and the Nineteen Twenties*. Ed. Malcolm Bradbury and David Palmer. London: Edward Arnold, 1971. pp. 107-26.

834. WEBER, BROM. *Sherwood Anderson*. Minneapolis: Univ. of Minnesota Press, 1964.

835. ———. "Sherwood Anderson." In *Seven Novelists in the American Naturalist Tradition: An Introduction*. Ed. Charles Child Walcutt. Minneapolis: Univ. of Minnesota Press, 1974. pp. 168-204.

836. WHITE, RAY LEWIS. "Introduction." In *The Achievement of Sherwood Anderson: Essays in Criticism*. Chapel Hill: Univ. of North Carolina Press, 1966. pp. 1-18.

837. WINTHER, S. K. "The Aura of Loneliness in Sherwood Anderson." *Modern Fiction Studies*, 5 (1959), 145-52.

Interviews

838. DERLETH, AUGUST. "Sherwood Anderson." In *Three Literary Men: A Memoir of Sinclair Lewis, Sherwood Anderson, Edgar Lee Masters*. New York: Candlelight Press, 1963. pp. 31-36.

Bibliography

839.   **PHILLIPS, WILLIAM L.** "The Editions of *Winesburg, Ohio.*"
In *Sherwood Anderson: Centennial Studies.* Ed. Hilbert H. Campbell and Charles E. Modlin. Troy, NY: Whitston, 1976. pp.
151-55.

840.   **RIDEOUT, WALTER B.** "Sherwood Anderson." In *Fifteen
Modern American Authors: A Survey of Research and Criticism.* Ed.
Jackson R. Bryer. Durham, NC: Duke Univ. Press, 1969. pp.
3-22.

841.   _____. "Sherwood Anderson." In *Sixteen Modern American
Authors: A Survey of Research and Criticism.* Ed. Jackson R. Bryer. Durham, NC: Duke Univ. Press, 1974. pp. 3-28.

842.   **ROGERS, DOUGLAS G.** *Sherwood Anderson: A Selective, Annotated Bibliography.* Metuchen, NJ: Scarecrow, 1976.

843.   **SHEEHY, EUGENE P., AND KENNETH A. LOHF.** *Sherwood Anderson: A Bibliography.* Los Gatos, CA: Talisman Press, 1960.

844.   **TANSELLE, G. THOMAS.** "Addenda to Sheehy and Lohf's
Sherwood Anderson: Copyright Information and Later Printings." In *Sherwood Anderson: Centennial Studies.* Ed. Hilbert H.
Campbell and Charles E. Modlin. Troy, NY: Whitston, 1976.
pp. 145-50.

845.   _____. "Additional Reviews of Sherwood Anderson's
Work." *The Papers of the Bibliographical Society of America,* 56
(1962), 358-65.

846.   **WHITE, RAY LEWIS.** "A Checklist of Sherwood Anderson
Studies, 1959-1969." *The Newberry Library Bulletin,* 6 (1971),
288-302.

847.   _____. *The Merrill Checklist of Sherwood Anderson.* Columbus, OH: Merrill, 1969.

848.   _____. *Sherwood Anderson: A Reference Guide.* Boston, MA:
G. K. Hall, 1977.

849.   _____. "A Sherwood Anderson Checklist." *The Winesburg
Eagle,* 1, no. 1 (1975), 4-5; 1, no. 2 (1976), 7-8; 2, no. 1 (1976), 4.

850.   _____. "*Winesburg, Ohio*: First Impression Errors." *The
Papers of the Bibliographical Society of America,* 71 (1977), 222-23.

851.   _____, AND DIANA HASKELL. "Anderson in Chicago Newspapers: A Supplementary List." *The Winesburg Eagle,* 3, no. 1
(1977), 3-5.

852.   _____, AND DOUGLAS G. ROGERS. "Sherwood Anderson in
Print." *The Winesburg Eagle,* 2, no. 2 (1977), 3-4.

[ANONYMOUS]

"*The Child of Snow*"

853.   **MOORE, JACK B.** "Black Humor in an Early American Short

Story." *Early American Literature Newsletter*, 1, no. 2 (1966), 7–8.
854. **SANDERLIN, R. REED.** "A Variant Version of 'The Child of Snow.' " *Early American Literature Newsletter*, 2, no. 2 (1967), 22–25.

"The Desperate Negroe"
See 73.

"Joseph and Sophia"
See 21.

"Metaphysics of Bear Hunting"
855. **MULQUEEN, JAMES E.** "Foreshadowing of Melville & Faulkner." *American Notes & Queries*, 6 (1968), 102.

"The Negro"
See 73.

"Singular Recovery from Death"
See 5420.

"Something Unaccountable"
856. **MOORE, JACK B.** "A Neglected Early American Short Story." *American Notes & Queries*, 4 (1966), 84–86.

"The Story of the Captain's Wife, and An Aged Woman"
857. **MOORE, JACK B.** " 'The Captain's Wife': A Native Short-Story Before Irving." *Studies in Short Fiction*, 1 (1964), 103–06.
See also 21.

"Taillah"
See 73.

ARIAS, RON[ALD]

Interviews
858. **BRUCE-NOVOA, [JUAN].** "Interview with Ron Arias." *The Journal of Ethnic Studies*, 3, no. 4 (1976), 70–73.

ARNOW, HARRIETTE

General Studies
*859. **ECKLEY, WILTON.** *Harriette Arnow.* New York: Twayne, 1974.

ARP, BILL
General Studies
860. AUSTIN, JAMES C. *Bill Arp*. New York: Twayne, 1969.

ASIMOV, ISAAC
"The Bicentennial Man"
See 871.

"The Evitable Conflict"
See 864, 868.

"Galley Slave"
See 365.

"The Key"
See 868, 869

"Mirror Image"
See 869.

"Nightfall"
861. STANTON, MICHAEL N. "The Startled Muse: Emerson and
Science Fiction." *Extrapolation*, 16 (1974), 64–66.
See also 248, 357, 867, 868.

"The Resublimated Properties of Endochronic Thiotimoline"
See 867.

"Robbie"
See 868, 871.

General Studies
862. ASIMOV, ISAAC. "Asimov's Guide to Asimov." In *Isaac
Asimov*. Ed. Joseph D. Olander and Martin Harry Greenberg.
New York: Taplinger, 1977. pp. 201–06.
863. MCSHERRY, FRANK D., JR. "Under Two Flags: The Detective Story in Science Fiction." *The Armchair Detective*, 2 (1969),
171–73.
864. MILLER, MARJORIE MITHOFF. "The Social Science Fiction of
Isaac Asimov." In *Isaac Asimov*. Ed. Joseph D. Olander and
Martin Harry Greenberg. New York: Taplinger, 1977. pp.
13–31.
865. MILMAN, FERN. "Human Reactions to Technological

Change in Asimov's Fiction." In *Isaac Asimov*. Ed. Joseph D. Olander and Martin Harry Greenberg. New York: Taplinger, 1977. pp. 120–34.

866. **MOORE, MAXINE.** "Asimov, Calvin, and Moses." In *Voices for the Future: Essays on Major Science Fiction Writers*. Ed. Thomas D. Clareson. Bowling Green, OH: Bowling Green Univ. Popular Press, 1976. pp. 88–103.

867. ———. "The Use of Technical Metaphors in Asimov's Fiction." In *Isaac Asimov*. Ed. Joseph D. Olander and Martin Harry Greenberg. New York: Taplinger, 1977. pp. 59–96.

*868. **PATROUCH, JOSEPH F., JR.** *The Science Fiction of Isaac Asimov*. Garden City, NY: Doubleday, 1974.

869. **PIERCE, HAZEL.** " 'Elementary, My Dear . . . ': Asimov's Science Fiction Mysteries." In *Isaac Asimov*. Ed. Joseph D. Olander and Martin Harry Greenberg. New York: Taplinger, 1977. pp. 32–58.

870. **WAGES, JACK D.** "Isaac Asimov's Debt to Edgar Allan Poe." *Poe Studies*, 6 (1973), 29.

871. **WARRICK, PATRICIA S.** "Ethical Evolving Artificial Intelligence: Asimov's Computers and Robots." In *Isaac Asimov*. Ed. Joseph D. Olander and Martin Harry Greenberg. New York: Taplinger, 1977. pp. 174–200.

872. **WATT, DONALD.** "A Galaxy Full of People: Characterization in Asimov's Major Fiction." In *Isaac Asimov*. Ed. Joseph D. Olander and Martin Harry Greenberg. New York: Taplinger, 1977. pp. 135–58.

Interviews

873. **NICHOLS, LEWIS.** "Isaac Asimov: Man of 7,560,000 Words." *The New York Times Book Review*, 3 Aug. 1969, pp. 8, 28.

Bibliography

874. **COX, DAVID M., AND GARY R. LIBBY.** "A Bibliography of Isaac Asimov's Major Science Fiction Works through 1976." In *Isaac Asimov*. Ed. Joseph D. Olander and Martin Harry Greenberg. New York: Taplinger, 1977. pp. 217–33.

875. **MILLER, MARJORIE M.** *Isaac Asimov: A Checklist of Works Published in the United States, March 1939–May 1972*. Kent, OH: Kent State Univ. Press, 1972.

ATHERTON, GERTRUDE

General Studies

876. **McCLURE, CHARLOTTE S.** *Gertrude Atherton*. Boise, ID: Boise State Univ., 1976.

Bibliography

877. McCLURE, CHARLOTTE S. "A Checklist of the Writings of and about Gertrude Atherton." *American Literary Realism, 1870–1910,* 9 (1976), 103–62.
878. _____. "Gertrude Atherton (1857–1948)." *American Literary Realism, 1870–1910,* 9 (1976), 95–101.

AUSTIN, MARY [HUNTER]

"Papago Wedding"

See 883.

"The Walking Woman"

See 880.

"The Woman at the Eighteen-Mile"

See 880.

General Studies

879. BERRY, J. WILKES. "Characterization in Mary Austin's Southwest Works." *Southwestern American Literature,* 2 (1972), 119–24.
880. GURIAN, JAY. "Style in the Literary Desert: Mary Austin." In *Western American Writing: Tradition and Promise.* Deland, FL: Everett/Edwards, 1975. pp. 71–80.
881. JOHNSON, LEE ANN. "Western Literary Realism: The California Tales of Norris and Austin." *American Literary Realism, 1870–1910,* 7 (1974), 278–80.
882. LYDAY, JO W. *Mary Austin: The Southwest Works.* Austin, TX: Steck-Vaughn, 1968.
883. PEARCE, T. M. *Mary Hunter Austin.* New York: Twayne, 1965.

Bibliography

884. BERRY, J. WILKES. "Mary Hunter Austin (1868–1934)." *American Literary Realism, 1870–1910,* 2 (1969), 125–31.

AUSTIN, WILLIAM

"The Man with the Cloaks"

See 2648.

"Some Account of Peter Rugg, The Missing Man, Late of Boston, New-England"

885. YOUNG, PHILIP. "The Story of the Missing Man." In *Direc-*

tions in Literary Criticism: Contemporary Approaches to Literature.
Ed. Stanley Weintraub and Philip Young. University Park:
Pennsylvania State Univ. Press, 1973. pp. 143-59.
See also 26, 2871.

AVALLONE, MICHAEL

Bibliography

886. **MERTZ, STEPHEN.** "Michael Avallone: A Checklist." *The
Armchair Detective*, 9 (1976), 132-34.

BALDWIN, JAMES

"Going to Meet the Man"

887. **FREESE, PETER.** "James Baldwin, 'Going to Meet the Man'
(1965)." In *The Black American Short Story in the 20th Century: A
Collection of Critical Essays.* Ed. Peter Bruck. Amsterdam: B. R.
Grüner, 1977. pp. 171-85.
888. **WHITLOW, ROGER.** "Baldwin's *Going to Meet the Man*: Racial Brutality and Sexual Gratification." *American Imago*, 34
(1977), 351-56.
See also 196, 258, 360, 484.

"Previous Condition"

889. **BLUEFARB, SAM.** "James Baldwin's 'Previous Condition': A
Problem of Identification." *Negro American Literature Forum*, 3
(1969), 26-29.

"Sonny's Blues"

890. **GOLDMAN, SUZY BERNSTEIN.** "James Baldwin's 'Sonny's
Blues': A Message in Music." *Negro American Literature Forum*,
8 (1974), 231-33.
891. **INGE, M. THOMAS.** "James Baldwin's Blues." *Notes on Contemporary Literature*, 2, no. 4 (1972), 8-11.
892. **MURRAY, DONALD C.** "James Baldwin's 'Sonny's Blues':
Complicated and Simple." *Studies in Short Fiction*, 14 (1977),
353-57.
893. **OGNIBENE, ELAINE R.** "Black Literature Revisited: 'Sonny's
Blues.' " *English Journal*, 60 (1971), 36-37.
894. **REILLY, JOHN M.** " 'Sonny's Blues': James Baldwin's Image
of Black Community." *Negro American Literature Forum*, 4
(1970), 56-60.
See also 222, 333, 399.

"This Morning, This Evening, So Soon"

895. **HAGOPIAN, JOHN V.** "James Baldwin: The Black and the Red-White-and-Blue." *CLA Journal*, 7 (1963), 133–40. *See also* 454, 483, 564.

General Studies

896. **ECKMAN, FERN MARJA.** *The Furious Passage of James Baldwin.* New York: M. Evans, 1966.
897. **MOORE, JOHN REES.** "An Embarrassment of Riches: Baldwin's *Going to Meet the Man*." *The Hollins Critic*, 2, no. 5 (1965), 1–12.
898. **WEATHERBY, W. J.** *Squaring Off: Mailer vs. Baldwin.* New York: Mason/Charter, 1977.

Interviews

899. **ANON.** "*The Black Scholar* Interviews James Baldwin." *The Black Scholar*, 5, no. 4 (1974), 33–42.
900. **COLES, ROBERT.** "James Baldwin Back Home." *The New York Times Book Review*, 31 July 1977, pp. 1, 22–24.

Bibliography

901. **FISCHER, RUSSELL G.** "James Baldwin: A Bibliography, 1947–1962." *Bulletin of Bibliography and Magazine Notes*, 24 (1965), 127–30.
902. **KINDT, KATHLEEN A.** "James Baldwin: A Checklist, 1947–1962." *Bulletin of Bibliography and Magazine Notes*, 24 (1965), 123–26.
903. **STANDLEY, FRED L.** "James Baldwin: A Checklist, 1963–1967." *Bulletin of Bibliography and Magazine Notes*, 25 (1968), 135–37, 160.

BALDWIN, JOSEPH GLOVER

"Samuel Hele, Esq."

See 64, 549.

"Simon Suggs, Jr., Esq."

904. **RUBIN, LOUIS D., JR.** "The Great American Joke." *The South Atlantic Quarterly*, 72 (1973), 82–94. *See also* 552.

General Studies

905. **AMACHER, RICHARD E., AND GEORGE W. POLHEMUS.** "Introduction." In *The Flush Times of California*, by Joseph Glover Baldwin. Athens: Univ. of Georgia Press, 1966. pp. 1–10.

BANKS, RUSSELL

Interviews

906. ROOKE, CONSTANCE. "Russell Banks: An Interview." *fiction international*, nos. 6-7 (1976), pp. 37-45.

BARAKA, AMIRI

"The Alternative"

907. WAKEFIELD, JOHN. "Amiri Baraka (LeRoi Jones), 'The Alternative' (1965)." In *The Black American Short Story in the 20th Century: A Collection of Critical Essays*. Ed. Peter Bruck. Amsterdam: B. R. Grüner, 1977. pp. 187-204.
See also 224, 911.

"A Chase (Alighieri's Dream)"

908. O'BRIEN, JOHN. "Racial Nightmares and the Search for Self: An Explication of Leroi Jones' 'A Chase (Alighieri's Dream).' " *Negro American Literature Forum*, 7 (1973), 89-90.
See also 224, 225.

"The Death of Horatio Alger"

909. LHAMON, W. T. "Baraka and the Bourgeois Figure." *Studies in Black Literature*, 6, no. 1 (1975), 18-21.
See also 911.

"Words"

See 911.

General Studies

910. BROWN, CECIL. "About LeRoi Jones." *Evergreen Review*, 14 (Feb. 1970), 65-70.
911. COLEMAN, LARRY G. "LeRoi Jones' *Tales*: Sketches of the Artist as a Young Man Moving toward a Blacker Art." *Black Lines*, 1, no. 2 (1970), 17-26.
912. HUDSON, THEODORE R. *From LeRoi Jones to Amiri Baraka: The Literary Works*. Durham, NC: Duke Univ. Press, 1973.

Interviews

913. ANON. "*Black Books Bulletin* Interviews Imamu Amiri Baraka." *Black Books Bulletin*, 2, no. 2 (1974), 33-37, 40-43.
914. WATKINS, MEL. "Talk with LeRoi Jones." *The New York Times Book Review*, 27 June 1971, pp. 4, 24, 26-27.
915. X, MARVIN, AND FARUK. "Islam and Black Art: An Interview With LeRoi Jones." *Negro Digest*, 18, no. 3 (1969), 4-10, 77-80.

Bibliography

916. **DACE, LETITIA.** *LeRoi Jones (Imamu Amiri Baraka): A Checklist of Works by and about Him.* London: Nether Press, 1971.

917. **HUDSON, THEODORE.** "An Imamu Amiri Baraka (LeRoi Jones) Bibliography: A Keyed Guide to Selected Works By and About Him." *Black Books Bulletin*, 2, no. 2 (1974), 70–79.

918. ———. *A LeRoi Jones (Amiri Baraka) Bibliography: A Keyed Research Guide to Works by LeRoi Jones and to Writing about Him and His Works.* Washington, DC: Privately printed, 1971.

919. **SCHATT, STANLEY.** "LeRoi Jones: A Checklist to Primary and Secondary Sources." *Bulletin of Bibliography and Magazine Notes*, 28 (1971), 55–57.

BARNES, DJUNA

"Aller et Retour"

See 921–923.

"Cassation"

See 922, 923.

"The Doctors"

See 921–923.

"The Grand Malade"

See 923.

"Indian Summer"

See 923.

"Ladies Almanack"

See 922, 923.

"The Nigger"

See 923.

"A Night Among the Horses"

See 921–923.

"No-Man's Mare"

See 923.

"The Passion"

See 922.

"The Perfect Murder"

See 922.

"The Rabbit"

See 921–923.

"The Robin's House"

See 923.

"Spillway"

See 921–923.

General Studies

920.   BAIRD, JAMES. "Djuna Barnes and Surrealism: 'Backward Grief.' " In *Individual and Community: Variations on a Theme in American Fiction*. Ed. Kenneth H. Baldwin and David K. Kirby. Durham, NC: Duke Univ. Press, 1975. pp. 160–81.

921.   FERGUSON, SUZANNE C. "Djuna Barnes's Short Stories: An Estrangement of the Heart." *The Southern Review*, NS 5 (1969), 26–41.

922.   KANNENSTINE, LOUIS F. *The Art of Djuna Barnes: Duality and Damnation*. New York: New York Univ. Press, 1977.

923.   SCOTT, JAMES B. *Djuna Barnes*. Boston, MA: Twayne, 1976.

Bibliography

924.   HIPKISS, ROBERT A. "Djuna Barnes (1892–   )—A Bibliography." *Twentieth Century Literature*, 14 (1968), 161–63.

925.   MESSERLI, DOUGLAS. *Djuna Barnes: A Bibliography*. New York: David Lewis, 1975.

BARNES, MARGARET AYER

General Studies

*926.   TAYLOR, LLOYD C., JR. *Margaret Ayer Barnes*. New York: Twayne, 1974.

BARTH, JOHN

"Ambrose His Mark"

927.   STUBBS, JOHN C. "John Barth As a Novelist of Ideas: The Themes of Value and Identity." *Critique*, 8, no. 2 (1966), 101–16. *See also* 937, 942.

"Anonymiad"

928.   JONES, D. ALLAN. "John Barth's 'Anonymiad.' " *Studies in Short Fiction*, 11 (1974), 361–66.

See also 306, 327, 594, 937, 941, 947, 952, 960.

"Autobiography: A Self-Recorded Fiction"
See 942, 955.

"Bellerophoniad"
See 930–932, 955, 960.

Chimera
929. **DAVIS, CYNTHIA.** " 'The Key to the Treasure': Narrative Movements and Effects in *Chimera*." *The Journal of Narrative Technique*, 5 (1975), 105–15.
930. **MACKENZIE, URSULA.** "John Barth's *Chimera* and the Strictures of Reality." *Journal of American Studies*, 10 (1976), 91–101.
931. **POWELL, JERRY.** "John Barth's *Chimera*: A Creative Response to the Literature of Exhaustion." *Critique*, 18, no. 2 (1976), 59–72.
932. **WARRICK, PATRICIA.** "The Circuitous Journey in Barth's *Chimera*." *Critique*, 18, no. 2 (1976), 73–85.
See also 224, 954, 955, 957, 960.

"Dunyazadiad"
See 929–932, 955, 957.

"Echo"
See 306, 937, 942, 955, 960.

"Frame-Tale"
See 947.

"Glossolalia"
933. **KOELB, CLAYTON.** "John Barth's 'Glossolalia.' " *Comparative Literature*, 26 (1974), 334–45.
934. **STREHLE, SUSAN.** "John Barth's Narrative Guile in 'Glossolalia.' " *Notes on Contemporary Literature*, 6, no. 2 (1976), 13–15.

"Life-Story"
See 937, 941.

"Lost in the Funhouse"
935. **BIENSTOCK, BEVERLY GRAY.** "Lingering on the Autognostic Verge: John Barth's *Lost in the Funhouse*." *Modern Fiction Studies*, 19 (1973), 69–78.
936. **GILLESPIE, GERALD.** "Barth's 'Lost in the Funhouse': Short

Story Text in Its Cyclic Context." *Studies in Short Fiction*, 12 (1975), 223-30.

937. HARRIS, CHARLES B. "A Continuing, Strange Love Letter: Sex and Language in 'Lost in the Funhouse.' " *Psychocultural Review*, 1 (1977), 338-55.

938. HINDEN, MICHAEL. "*Lost in the Funhouse*: Barth's Use of the Recent Past." *Twentieth Century Literature*, 19 (1973), 107-18.

939. JOSEPH, GERHARD. *John Barth*. Minneapolis: Univ. of Minnesota Press, 1970.

940. KIERNAN, ROBERT F. "John Barth's Artist in the Fun House." *Studies in Short Fiction*, 10 (1973), 373-80.

941. KRIER, WILLIAM J. "*Lost in the Funhouse*: 'A Continuing, Strange Love Letter.' " *boundary 2*, 5 (1976), 103-16.

942. KYLE, CAROL A. "The Unity of Anatomy: The Structure of Barth's *Lost in the Funhouse*." *Critique*, 13, no. 3 (1972), 31-43.

943. LE CLAIR, THOMAS. "John Barth's *The Floating Opera*: Death and the Craft of Fiction." *Texas Studies in Literature and Language*, 14 (1973), 711-30.

944. MORRIS, CHRISTOPHER D. "Barth and Lacan: The World of the Moebius Strip." *Critique*, 17, no. 1 (1975), 69-77.

945. PINSKER, SANFORD. "John Barth: The Teller Who Swallowed His Tale." *Studies in the Twentieth Century*, no. 10 (1972), pp. 55-68.

946. SLETHAUG, GORDON E. "Barth's Refutation of the Idea of Progress." *Critique*, 13, no. 3 (1972), 11-29.

947. VITANZA, VICTOR J. "The Novelist as Topologist: John Barth's *Lost in the Funhouse*." *Texas Studies in Literature and Language*, 19 (1977), 83-97.

See also 110, 111, 224, 240, 277, 302, 306, 307, 327, 460, 952, 954, 955, 957, 960, 988.

948. FIRTH, JOHN. "Lost in the Funhouse." In *Instructor's Manual for* "The Art of Fiction," Second Edition. Ed. R. F. Dietrich and Roger H. Sundell. New York: Holt, Rinehart and Winston, 1974. pp. 131-34.

949. KNAPP, EDGAR H. "Found in the Barthhouse: Novelist As Savior." *Modern Fiction Studies*, 14 (1968), 446-51.

See also 306, 327, 483, 935, 936, 942, 944, 955, 960.

"Menelaiad"

See 306, 935, 937, 938, 941, 945, 947, 952, 954, 957, 960.

"Night-Sea Journey"

See 460, 511, 594, 938, 942, 960.

"Perseid"

950. **RABINOWITZ, NANCY S.** "Medusa's Head: Myth, Impotence and John Barth's *Chimera.*" In *Proceedings of the Sixth National Convention of the Popular Culture Association, Chicago, Illinois, April 22-24, 1976.* Ed. Michael T. Marsden. Bowling Green, OH: Bowling Green Univ. Popular Press, 1976. pp. 1125-33.
See also 930-932, 957.

"Petition"

See 955, 957.

"Title"

See 955.

General Studies

951. **BARTH, JOHN.** "The Literature of Exhaustion." *The Atlantic Monthly*, 220, no. 2 (1967), 29-34.
952. **FARWELL, HAROLD.** "John Barth's Tenuous Affirmation: 'The Absurd, Unending Possibility of Love.' " *The Georgia Review*, 28 (1974), 290-306.
953. **McCONNELL, FRANK.** "The Corpse of the Dragon: Notes on Postromantic Fiction." *TriQuarterly*, no. 33 (1975), pp. 273-303.
954. _____. *Four Postwar American Novelists: Bellow, Mailer, Barth and Pynchon.* Chicago: Univ. of Chicago Press, 1977.
955. **MORRELL, DAVID.** *John Barth: An Introduction.* University Park: Pennsylvania State Univ. Press, 1976.
956. **SCHOLES, ROBERT.** "The Allegory of Exhaustion." *fiction international*, no. 1 (1973), pp. 106-08.
957. **STARK, JOHN O.** *The Literature of Exhaustion: Borges, Nabokov, and Barth.* Durham, NC: Duke Univ. Press, 1974.
958. **TATHAM, CAMPBELL.** "Correspondences/Notes/Etceteras." *Chicago Review*, 26, no. 4 (1975), 112-32.
959. _____. "Message [Concerning the *Felt* Ultimacies of One John Barth]." *boundary 2*, 3 (1975), 259-87.
960. **THARPE, JAC.** *John Barth: The Comic Sublimity of Paradox.* Carbondale and Edwardsville: Southern Illinois Univ. Press, 1974.

Interviews

961. **BELLAMY, JOE DAVID.** "Having It Both Ways: A Conversation between John Barth and Joe David Bellamy." *New American Review*, no. 15 (1972), pp. 134-50.

962. ENCK, JOHN J. "John Barth: An Interview." *Wisconsin Studies in Contemporary Literature*, 6 (1965), 3–14.
963. GADO, FRANK. "John Barth." In *First Person: Conversations on Writers & Writing*. Ed. Frank Gado. Schenectady, NY: Union College Press, 1973. pp. 110–41.
964. LE REBELLER, ANNIE. "A Spectatorial Skeptic: An Interview with John Barth." *Caliban* (University of Toulouse), no. 12 (1975), pp. 93–110.
965. MERAS, PHYLLIS. "John Barth: A Truffle No Longer." *The New York Times Book Review*, 7 Aug. 1966, p. 22.
966. SHENKER, ISRAEL. "Complicated Simple Things." *The New York Times Book Review*, 24 Sept. 1972, pp. 35–38.

Bibliography

967. BRYER, JACKSON R. "Two Bibliographies." *Critique*, 6, no. 2 (1963), 86–94.
968. VINE, RICHARD. *John Barth: An Annotated Bibliography*. Metuchen, NJ: Scarecrow, 1976.
969. WALSH, THOMAS P. *John Barth: Jerzy Kosinski, and Thomas Pynchon: A Reference Guide*. Boston, MA: G. K. Hall, 1977.
970. WEIXLMANN, JOSEPH N. "John Barth: A Bibliography." *Critique*, 13, no. 3 (1972), 45–55.
971. _____. *John Barth: A Descriptive Primary and Annotated Secondary Bibliography, including a Descriptive Catalog of Manuscript Holdings in United States Libraries*. New York: Garland, 1976.

BARTHELME, DONALD

"The Balloon"

972. DERVIN, DANIEL A. "Breast Fantasy in Barthelme, Swift, and Philip Roth: Creativity and Psychoanalytic Structure." *American Imago*, 33 (1976), 102–22.

"City Life"

See 483.

"Daumier"

See 980.

"The Dolt"

See 979, 989, 990.

"Engineer-Private Paul Klee Misplaces an Aircraft Between Milbertshofen and Cambrai, March 1916"

See 992.

"A Film"

See 979.

"The Glass Mountain"

See 982.

"The Great Hug"

973. **O'CONNELL, SHAUN.** "Zone of Remission: Current American Fiction." *The Massachusetts Review*, 18 (1977), 357–72.

"The Indian Uprising"

974. **BOCOCK, MACLIN.** " 'The Indian Uprising' or Donald Barthelme's Strange Object Covered with Fur." *fiction international*, nos. 4–5 (1975), pp. 134–46.
See also 481, 981, 988.

"Kierkegaard Unfair to Schlegel"

See 193, 982, 992, 1345.

"Magellan"

975. **LIPPMAN, BERT.** "Literature and Life." *The Georgia Review*, 25 (1971), 145–58.

"The Party"

976. **WHALEN, TOM.** "Wonderful Elegance: Barthelme's 'The Party.' " *Critique*, 16, no. 3 (1975), 44–48.

"Robert Kennedy Saved from Drowning"

977. **GILES, JAMES R.** "The 'Marivaudian Being' Drowns His Children: Dehumanization in Donald Barthelme's 'Robert Kennedy Saved from Drowning' and Joyce Carol Oates' *Wonderland*." *Southern Humanities Review*, 9 (1975), 63–75.
See also 224, 984, 990.

"The Sandman"

See 992.

"Sentence"

See 218.

"A Shower of Gold"

See 183.

"That Cosmopolitan Girl"

See 348.

"Views of My Father Weeping"

978. **DOXEY, W. S.** "Donald Barthelme's 'Views of My Father Weeping': A Modern View of Oedipus." *Notes on Contemporary Literature*, 3, no. 2 (1973), 14–15.
See also 224, 318, 981.

"The Wound"

See 980.

General Studies

979. **DAVIS, ROBERT MURRAY.** "Donald Barthelme's Textual Revisions." *Resources for American Literary Study*, 7 (1977), 182–91.
980. **DITSKY, JOHN M.** " 'With Ingenuity and Hard Work, Distracted': The Narrative Style of Donald Barthelme." *Style*, 9 (1975), 388–400.
981. **GILLEN, FRANCIS.** "Donald Barthelme's City: A Guide." *Twentieth Century Literature*, 18 (1972), 37–44.
982. **JOHNSON, R. E., JR.** " 'Bees Barking in the Night': The End and Beginning of Donald Barthelme's Narrative." *boundary 2*, 5 (1976), 71–92.
983. **KLINKOWITZ, JEROME.** "Donald Barthelme's SuperFiction." *Critique*, 16, no. 3 (1975), 5–18.
984. _____. "Literary Disruptions; or, What's Become of American Fiction?" *Partisan Review*, 40 (1973), 433–44.
985. **KRUPNICK, MARK L.** "Notes from the Funhouse." *Modern Occasions*, 1 (1970), 108–12.
986. **LELAND, JOHN.** "Remarks Re-marked: Barthelme, What Curios of Signs!" *boundary 2*, 5 (1977), 795–811.
987. **MORAN, CHARLES.** "Barthelme The Trash-Man: The Uses Of Junk In The Classroom." *The CEA Critic*, 36, no. 4 (1974), 32–33.
988. **SCHMITZ, NEIL.** "Donald Barthelme and the Emergence of Modern Satire." *The Minnesota Review*, NRP no. 1 (1971), pp. 109–18.
989. **SPIVAK, GAYATRI CHAKRAVORTY.** "Thoughts on the Principle of Allegory." *Genre*, 5 (1972), 327–52.
990. **STOTT, WILLIAM.** "Donald Barthelme and the Death of Fiction." *Prospects*, no. 1 (1975), pp. 369–86.
991. **WICKES, GEORGE.** "From Breton to Barthelme: Westward the Course of Surrealism." In *Proceedings: Pacific Northwest Conference on Foreign Languages*, Vol. 22. Ed. Walter C. Kraft. Corvallis: Oregon State Univ., 1971. pp. 208–14.
992. **WILDE, ALAN.** "Barthelme Unfair to Kierkegaard: Some Thoughts on Modern and Postmodern Irony." *boundary 2*, 5 (1976), 45–70.

Interviews

993. **KLINKOWITZ, JEROME**. "Donald Barthelme." In *The New Fiction: Interviews with Innovative American Writers*. Ed. Joe David Bellamy. Urbana: Univ. of Illinois Press, 1974. pp. 45–54.

Bibliography

994. **KLINKOWITZ, JEROME**. "Donald Barthelme: A Checklist, 1957–1974." *Critique*, 16, no. 3 (1975), 49–58.

995. ———, **ASA PIERATT, AND ROBERT MURRAY DAVIS**. *Donald Barthelme: A Comprehensive Bibliography and Annotated Secondary Checklist*. Hamden, CT: Archon Books, 1977.

996. **MCCAFFERY, LARRY**. "A Donald Barthelme Checklist." *Bulletin of Bibliography and Magazine Notes*, 31 (1974), 101–02, 106.

BASSING, ROBERT

"Lullaby"

See 197.

BEALE, MRS. O. A. S.

"Shadow in the House"

See 66.

BELLAMY, EDWARD

Bibliography

997. **BOWMAN, SYLVIA E**. "Edward Bellamy (1850–1898)." *American Literary Realism, 1870–1910*, 1, no. 1 (1967), 7–12.

BELLOW, SAUL

"Address by Gooley MacDowell to the Hasbeens Club of Chicago"
See 1015.

"By the Rock Wall"

See 1012.

"A Father-To-Be"

998. **DIETRICH, R. F**. "A Father-to-Be." In *Instructor's Manual* for "The Art of Fiction," Second Edition. Ed. R. F. Dietrich and Roger H. Sundell. New York: Holt, Rinehart and Winston, 1974. pp. 108–16.
See also 385, 1002, 1009, 1011.

"The Gonzaga Manuscripts"

999. GALLOWAY, DAVID. "Saul Bellow, 'The Gonzaga Manuscripts' (1956)." In *Die amerikanische Short Story der Gegenwart:
Interpretationen.* Ed. Peter Freese. Berlin: Erich Schmidt, 1976.
pp. 168–74.
See also 1009.

"Leaving the Yellow House"

1000. LIPPIT, NORIKO M. "A Perennial Survivor: Saul Bellow's
Heroine in the Desert." *Studies in Short Fiction,* 12 (1975), 281–83.
1001. ROOKE, CONSTANCE. "Saul Bellow's 'Leaving the Yellow
House': The Trouble with Women." *Studies in Short Fiction,* 14
(1977), 184–87.
See also 399.

"Looking for Mr. Green"

1002. DEMAREST, DAVID P., JR. "The Theme of Discontinuity in
Saul Bellow's Fiction: 'Looking for Mr. Green' and 'A Father-
to-Be.' " *Studies in Short Fiction,* 6 (1969), 175–86.
1003. RODRIGUES, EUSEBIO L. "Koheleth in Chicago: The Quest
for the Real in 'Looking for Mr. Green.' " *Studies in Short Fiction,* 11 (1974), 387–93.
See also 1009, 1012.

"The Old System"

See 327.

"Trip To Galena"

See 1012.

"Two Morning Monologues"

See 1012, 1015.

General Studies

1004. BELLOW, SAUL. "Deep Readers of the World, Beware."
The New York Times Book Review, 15 Feb. 1959, pp. 1, 34.
1005. ———. "Facts That Put Fancy to Flight." *The New York
Times Book Review,* 11 Feb. 1962, pp. 1, 28.
1006. ———. "The Sealed Treasure." *The Times* (London) *Literary Supplement,* 1 July 1960, p. 414.
1007. ———. "The Thinking Man's Waste Land." *Saturday
Review,* 48 (3 Apr. 1956), 20.
1008. ———. "Where Do We Go From Here: The Future of
Fiction." In *To the Young Writer: Hopwood Lectures, Second Series.*
Ed. A. L. Bader. Ann Arbor: Univ. of Michigan Press, 1965. pp.
136–46.

1009. **Clayton, John Jacob.** *Saul Bellow: In Defense of Man.* Bloomington: Indiana Univ. Press, 1968.

1010. **Detweiler, Robert.** *Saul Bellow: A Critical Essay.* Grand Rapids, MI: Eerdmans, 1967.

1011. **Malin, Irving.** *Saul Bellow's Fiction.* Carbondale and Edwardsville: Southern Illinois Univ. Press, 1969.

1012. **Opdahl, Keith Michael.** *The Novels of Saul Bellow: An Introduction.* University Park: Pennsylvania State Univ. Press, 1967.

1013. **Rovit, Earl.** *Saul Bellow.* Minneapolis: Univ. of Minnesota Press, 1967.

1014. **Scheer-Schäzler, Brigitte.** *Saul Bellow.* New York: Ungar, 1972.

1015. **Tanner, Tony.** *Saul Bellow.* Edinburgh: Oliver and Boyd, 1965.

Interviews

1016. **Bellow, Saul.** "The Art of Fiction XXXVII." With Gordon Lloyd Harper. *The Paris Review*, no. 36 (1966), pp. 49–73.

1017. ———. "An Interview with Myself." *The New Review*, 2, no. 18 (1975), 53–56.

1018. **Brans, Jo.** "Common Needs, Common Preoccupations: An Interview with Saul Bellow." *Southwest Review*, 62 (1977), 1–19.

1019. **Enck, John J.** "Saul Bellow: An Interview." *Wisconsin Studies in Contemporary Literature*, 6 (1965), 156–60.

1020. **Epstein, Joseph.** "Saul Bellow of Chicago." *The New York Times Book Review*, 9 May 1971, pp. 4, 12, 14, 16.

1021. ———. "A Talk with Saul Bellow." *The New York Times Book Review*, 5 Dec. 1976, pp. 3, 92–93.

1022. **Gutwillig, Robert.** "Talk with Saul Bellow." *The New York Times Book Review*, 20 Sept. 1964, p. 42.

1023. **Kulshrestha, Chirantan.** "A Conversation with Saul Bellow." *Chicago Review*, 23, no. 4–24, no. 1 (1972), 7–15.

Bibliography

1024. **Galloway, David D.** "A Saul Bellow Checklist." In *The Absurd Hero in American Fiction: Updike, Styron, Bellow, Salinger.* Austin: Univ. of Texas Press, 1966. pp. 210–26.

1025. ———. "A Saul Bellow Checklist." In *The Absurd Hero in American Fiction: Updike, Styron, Bellow, Salinger.* Rev. ed. Austin: Univ. of Texas Press, 1970. pp. 220–39.

1026. **Lercangée, F.** *Saul Bellow: A Bibliography of Secondary Sources.* Brussels: Center for American Studies, 1977.

1027. **Nault, Marianne.** *Saul Bellow, His Works and His Critics:*

An Annotated International Bibliography. New York: Garland, 1977.

1028. **SCHNEIDER, HAROLD W.** "Two Bibliographies: Saul Bellow/William Styron." *Critique*, 3, no. 3 (1960), 71–91.

1029. **SOKOLOFF, B. A., AND MARK E. POSNER.** *Saul Bellow: A Comprehensive Bibliography*. Folcroft, PA: Folcroft Press, 1971.

BENEFIELD, [JOHN] BARRY

General Studies

1030. **HATLEY, DONALD W.** "Folklore in the Fiction of Barry Benefield." *The Mississippi Quarterly*, 21 (1968), 63–70.

BENÉT, STEPHEN VINCENT

"The Devil and Daniel Webster"

See 454, 1032, 5696.

"Freedom's A Hard-Bought Thing"

See 178, 1032.

General Studies

1031. **ABBE, GEORGE, ED.** *Stephen Vincent Benét on Writing: A Great Writer's Letters of Advice to a Young Beginner*. Brattleboro, VT: Stephen Greene Press, 1964.

*1032. **STROUD, PARRY.** *Stephen Vincent Benét*. New York: Twayne, 1962.

BENSON, MILDRED WIRT

General Studies

1033. **BENSON, MILDRED WIRT.** "The Ghost of Ladora." *Books at Iowa*, no. 19 (1973), pp. 24–29.

BERNE, STANLEY

General Studies

1034. **BERNE, STANLEY.** "Prefaces to *The Unconscious Victorious and Other Stories*." *South Dakota Review*, 4, no. 3 (1966), 14–27.

Interviews

1035. **ZEKOWSKI, ARLENE, AND STANLEY BERNE.** "The Revolution of the Word: New Influences on the Novel." With Warren Bower. *South Dakota Review*, 6, no. 2 (1968), 56–65.

BESTER, ALFRED
"The Push of a Finger"
See 140.

BETTS, DORIS
"The Mandarin"
1036. EVANS, ELIZABETH. "The Mandarin and the Lady: Doris Betts' Debt to Amy Lowell." *Notes on Contemporary Literature*, 6, no. 5 (1976), 2–5.

General Studies
*1037. EVANS, ELIZABETH. "Negro Characters in the Fiction of Doris Betts." *Critique*, 17, no. 2 (1975), 59–76.

Interviews
1038. BETTS, DORIS. "Interview." *Story Quarterly*, no. 1 (1975), pp. 67–72.

BIERCE, AMBROSE
"An Affair at Coulter's Notch"
See 1050.

"An Affair of Outposts"
See 1056.

"A Baby Tramp"
See 1060.

"Chickamauga"
See 1056, 1058, 1060.

"The Coup de Grâce"
See 1060.

"The Death of Halpin Frayser"
1039. MCLEAN, ROBERT C. "The Deaths in Ambrose Bierce's 'Halpin Frayser.' " *Papers on Language & Literature*, 10 (1974), 394–402.
1040. STEIN, WILLIAM BYSSHE. "Bierce's 'The Death of Halpin Frayser': The Poetics of Gothic Consciousness." *ESQ*, 18 (1972), 115–22.
See also 1050.

"The Famous Gilson Bequest"

See 1050.

"Häita the Shepherd"

See 1050, 1060.

"A Horseman in the Sky"

See 356, 483, 1050.

"Jupiter Doke, Brigadier-General"

See 1050.

"Killed at Resaca"

See 1049, 1055.

"The Man and the Snake"

See 1060.

"The Mocking-Bird"

See 1060.

"Moxon's Master"

See 1054.

"My Favorite Murder"

See 1060.

"An Occurrence at Owl Creek Bridge"

1041. FRASER, HOWARD M. "Points South: Ambrose Bierce, Jorge Louis Borges, and the Fantastic." *Studies in Twentieth Century Literature*, 1 (1977), 173–81.

1042. LOGAN, F. J. "The Wry Seriousness of 'Owl Creek Bridge.'" *American Literary Realism, 1870-1910*, 10 (1977), 101–13.

1043. PALMER, JAMES W. "From Owl Creek to *La Riviere du Hibou*: The Film Adaptation of Bierce's 'An Occurrence at Owl Creek Bridge.'" *Southern Humanities Review*, 11 (1977), 363–71.

1044. STEINMANN, THEO. "The Second Death of Nunez in 'The Country of the Blind.'" *Studies in Short Fiction*, 9 (1972), 157–63.

See also 356, 360, 399, 454, 484, 1058, 1060, 3254.

"Oil of Dog"

See 1048.

"One Kind of Officer"

See 356.

"One of the Missing"
See 1054, 1060.

"One Officer, One Man"
See 1060.

"Parker Adderson, Philosopher"
1045. KAZIN, ALFRED. "On Ambrose Bierce and 'Parker Adderson, Philosopher.' " In *The American Short Story.* Ed. Calvin Skaggs. New York: Dell, 1977. pp. 31-34. *See also* 1050, 1060.

"A Resumed Identity"
See 1050.

"A Son of the Gods"
See 1050, 1056, 1060.

"The Suitable Surroundings"
See 1050.

"A Tough Tussle"
See 1050, 1060.

"A Watcher by the Dead"
See 1050.

General Studies
1046. AARON, DANIEL. "Ambrose Bierce and the American Civil War." In *Uses of Literature.* Ed. Monroe Engel. Cambridge, MA: Harvard Univ. Press, 1973. pp. 115-31.
1047. ANDREWS, WILLIAM L. "Some New Ambrose Bierce Fables." *American Literary Realism, 1870-1910,* 8 (1975), 349-52.
1048. BAHR, HOWARD W. "Ambrose Bierce and Realism." *The Southern Quarterly,* 1 (1963), 309-31.
1049. FIELD, B. S., JR. "Ambrose Bierce as a Comic." *Western Humanities Review,* 31 (1977), 173-80.
1050. GRENANDER, M. E. *Ambrose Bierce.* New York: Twayne, 1971.
1051. _____. "Ambrose Bierce and *In the Midst of Life.*" *The Book Collector,* 20 (1971), 321-31.
1052. _____. "Ambrose Bierce, John Camden Hotten, *The Fiend's Delight,* and *Nuggets and Dust.*" *The Huntington Library Quarterly,* 28 (1965), 353-71.

1053. MARTIN, JAY. "Ambrose Bierce." In *The Comic Imagination in American Literature*. Ed. Louis D. Rubin, Jr. New Brunswick, NJ: Rutgers Univ. Press, 1973. pp. 195-205.

1054. O'CONNOR, RICHARD. *Ambrose Bierce: A Biography*. Boston, MA: Little, Brown, 1967.

1055. ROTH, RUSSELL. "Ambrose Bierce's 'Detestable Creature.' " *Western American Literature*, 9 (1974), 169-76.

1056. SOLOMON, ERIC. "The Bitterness of Battle: Ambrose Bierce's War Fiction." *The Midwest Quarterly*, 5 (1964), 147-65.

1057. WAGENKNECHT, EDWARD. "Introduction." In *The Stories and Fables of Ambrose Bierce*. Owings Mills, MD: Stemmer House, 1977. pp. xi-xxiv.

1058. WIGGINS, ROBERT A. *Ambrose Bierce*. Minneapolis: Univ. of Minnesota Press, 1964.

1059. ———. "Ambrose Bierce: A Romantic in an Age of Realism." *American Literary Realism, 1870-1910*, 4 (1971), 1-10.

1060. WOODRUFF, STUART C. *The Short Stories of Ambrose Bierce: A Study in Polarity*. Pittsburgh, PA: Univ. of Pittsburgh Press, 1964.

Bibliography

1061. FATOUT, PAUL. "Ambrose Bierce (1842-1914)." *American Literary Realism, 1870-1910*, 1, no. 1 (1967), 13-19.

1062. FORTENBERRY, GEORGE E. "Ambrose Bierce (1842-1914?): A Critical Bibliography of Secondary Comment." *American Literary Realism, 1870-1910*, 4 (1971), 11-56.

1063. MONTEIRO, GEORGE. "Addenda to Gaer: Bierce in *The Anti-Philistine*." *The Papers of the Bibliographical Society of America*, 66 (1972), 71-72.

1064. ———. "Addenda to Gaer: Reprintings of Bierce's Stories." *The Papers of the Bibliographical Society of America*, 68 (1974), 330-31.

1065. STUBBS, JOHN C. "Ambrose Bierce's Contributions to *Cosmopolitan*: An Annotated Bibliography." *American Literary Realism, 1870-1910*, 4 (1971), 57-59.

BILLINGS, JOSH

General Studies

1066. KESTERSON, DAVID B. *Josh Billings (Henry Wheeler Shaw)*. New York: Twayne, 1973.

BIRD, ROBERT MONTGOMERY

General Studies

1067. **DAHL, CURTIS.** *Robert Montgomery Bird.* New York: Twayne, 1963.

BISHOP, JOHN PEALE

"If Only: 1867–1900"

See 1068, 1069.

General Studies

1068. **ELBY, CECIL D., JR.** "The Fiction of John Peale Bishop." *Twentieth Century Literature*, 7 (1961), 3–9.
*1069. **WHITE, ROBERT L.** *John Peale Bishop.* New York: Twayne, 1966.

BISSELL, RICHARD

General Studies

1070. **ANDERSON, FRANK J.** "The View from the River: Richard Bissell's Satirical Humor." *The Midwest Quarterly*, 5 (1964), 311–22.

BLOCH, ROBERT

"The Shambler from the Stars"

See 4278.

BLUE, CECIL

"The 'Flyer' "

See 283.

BOLES, ROBERT

"The Engagement Party"

See 126.

BONNER, SHERWOOD

"The Gentlemen of Sarsar"

See 571, 1071.

General Studies

*1071. FRANK, WILLIAM L. *Sherwood Bonner (Catherine Mc-Dowell)*. Boston, MA: Twayne, 1976.

1072. MOORE, RAYBURN S. "Sherwood Bonner's Contributions to Lippincott's Magazine and Harper's New Monthly." *The Mississippi Quarterly*, 17 (1964), 226–30.

1073. SIMMS, L. MOODY, JR. "Sherwood Bonner: A Contemporary Appreciation." *Notes on Mississippi Writers*, 2 (1969), 25–33.

Bibliography

1074. BIGLANE, JEAN NOSSER. "Sherwood Bonner: A Bibliography of Primary and Secondary Materials." *American Literary Realism, 1870–1910*, 5 (1972), 39–60.

BONTEMPS, ARNA

"Boy Blue"

See 386.

"A Summer Tragedy"

See 123, 386.

"3 Pennies for Luck"

See 386.

Interviews

1075. O'BRIEN, JOHN. "Arna Bontemps." In *Interviews with Black Writers*. Ed. John O'Brien. New York: Liveright, 1973. pp. 3–15.

BOUCHER, ANTHONY

General Studies

1076. OFFORD, LENORE GLEN. "A Boucher Portrait: Anthony Boucher as Seen by His Friends and Colleagues." *The Armchair Detective*, 2 (1969), 69–76.

Bibliography

1077. CHRISTOPHER, J. R., WITH D. W. DICKENSHEET AND R. E. BRINEY. "A. Boucher Bibliography." *The Armchair Detective*, 2 (1969), 77–85, 143–55, 263–73.

BOWLES, PAUL

"A Distant Episode"

See 564.

General Studies

1078. **EVANS, OLIVER.** "Paul Bowles and The 'Natural' Man." *Critique*, 3, no. 1 (1959), 43–59.

Interviews

1079. **HALPERN, DANIEL.** "Interview with Paul Bowles." *Tri-Quarterly*, no. 33 (1975), pp. 159–77.

1080. **RUMBOLD, RICHARD.** "An Evening with Paul Bowles." *The London Magazine*, 7, no. 11 (1960), 65–73.

BOYD, JAMES

"The Flat Town"

See 1081.

"Old Pines"

See 1081.

General Studies

1081. **WHISNANT, DAVID E.** *James Boyd.* New York: Twayne, 1972.

BOYESEN, HJALMAR HJORTH

"The Man Who Lost His Name"

See 1082.

"Swart Among the Buckeyes"

See 1082.

General Studies

1082. **GLASRUD, CLARENCE A.** *Hjalmar Hjorth Boyesen.* Northfield, MN: Norwegian-American Historical Association, 1963.

BOYLE, KAY

"The Astronomer's Wife"

See 564.

"The Bridegroom's Body"

See 1083.

"The Crazy Hunter"

See 1083.

"Effigy of War"

See 564.

"Rest Cure"

See 399.

"The White Horses of Vienna"

See 384.

General Studies

1083. **CARPENTER, RICHARD C.** "Kay Boyle: The Figure in the Carpet." *Critique*, 7, no. 2 (1965), 65–78.

Interviews

1084. **DREW, KATHY.** "Kay Boyle Dedicates Self to Human Dignity." *Lost Generation Journal*, 4, no. 1 (1976), 14, 22–23.

1085. **MADDEN, CHARLES F., ED.** "Kay Boyle." In *Talks with Authors*. Carbondale and Edwardsville: Southern Illinois Univ. Press, 1968. pp. 215–36.

1086. **TOOKER, DAN, AND ROGER HOFHEINS.** "Kay Boyle." In *Fiction!: Interviews with Northern California Novelists*. New York: Harcourt Brace Jovanovich, 1976. pp. 15–35.

BRACKENBRIDGE, HUGH HENRY

"The Cave of Vanhest"

See 1087.

"The Trial of Mamachtaga"

See 1087.

General Studies

1087. **MARDER, DANIEL.** *Hugh Henry Brackenbridge*. New York: Twayne, 1967.

BRADBURY, RAY

"And the Rock Cried Out"

See 565.

"The Exiles"

See 399.

"Sun and Shadow"

See 374.

General Studies

1088. **DIMEO, STEVEN.** "Man and Apollo: A Look at Religion in the Science Fantasies of Ray Bradbury." *Journal of Popular Culture*, 5 (1972), 970–78.

1089. **McNELLY, WILLIS E.** "Bradbury Revisited." *The CEA Critic*, 31, no. 6 (1969), 4, 6.

1090. ———. "Ray Bradbury—Past, Present, and Future." In *Voices for the Future: Essays on Major Science Fiction Writers*. Ed. Thomas D. Clareson. Bowling Green, OH: Bowling Green Univ. Popular Press, 1976. pp. 167–75.

*1091. **SLUSSER, GEORGE EDGAR.** *The Bradbury Chronicles*. San Bernardino, CA: Borgo Press, 1977.

1092. **STUPPLE, A. JAMES.** "The Past, the Future, and Ray Bradbury." In *Voices for the Future: Essays on Major Science Fiction Writers*. Ed. Thomas D. Clareson. Bowling Green OH: Bowling Green Univ. Popular Press, 1976. pp. 175–84.

1093. **SULLIVAN, ANITA T.** "Ray Bradbury and Fantasy." *English Journal*, 61 (1972), 1309–14.

Bibliography

1094. **NOLAN, WILLIAM F.** "The Crime/Suspense Fiction of Ray Bradbury: A Listing." *The Armchair Detective*, 4 (1971), 155.

1095. ———. *The Ray Bradbury Companion: A Life and Career History, Photolog, and Comprehensive Checklist of Writings with Facsimiles from Ray Bradbury's Unpublished and Uncollected Work in All Media*. Detroit, MI: Gale, 1975.

BRAUTIGAN, RICHARD

"The World War I Los Angeles Airplane"

1096. **GALLOWAY, DAVID.** "Richard Brautigan, 'The World War I Los Angeles Airplane' (1971)." In *Die amerikanische Short Story der Gegenwart: Interpretationen*. Ed. Peter Freese. Berlin: Erich Schmidt, 1976. pp. 333–39.

See also 318.

General Studies

1097. **WALKER, CHERYL.** "Richard Brautigan: Youth Fishing in America." *Modern Occasions*, 2 (1972), 308–13.

Bibliography

1098. JONES, STEPHEN R. "Richard Brautigan: A Bibliography."
Bulletin of Bibliography and Magazine Notes, 33 (1976), 53–59.
1099. WANLESS, JAMES, AND CHRISTINE KOLODZIEJ. "Richard
Brautigan: A Working Checklist." *Critique*, 16, no. 1 (1974),
41–52.

BROMFIELD, LOUIS
General Studies

1100. ANDERSON, DAVID D. *Louis Bromfield*. New York:
Twayne, 1964.
1101. GELD, ELLEN BROMFIELD. *The Heritage: A Daughter's Memories of Louis Bromfield*. New York: Harper, 1962.

BROWN, ALICE
"Farmer Eli's Vacation"

See 1102, 1103.

"A Sea Change"

See 1102, 1103.

"A Second Marriage"

See 1102, 1103.

General Studies

1102. TOTH, SUSAN ALLEN. "A Forgotten View from Beacon
Hill: Alice Brown's New England Short Stories." *Colby Library
Quarterly*, 10 (1973), 1–17.
*1103. WALKER, DOROTHEA. *Alice Brown*. New York: Twayne,
1974.

Bibliography

1104. TOTH, SUSAN ALLEN. "Alice Brown (1857–1948)." *American Literary Realism, 1870–1910*, 5 (1972), 134–43.

BROWN, CHARLES BROCKDEN
"Insanity: A Fragment"

1105. HEMENWAY, ROBERT. "Brockden Brown's Twice Told Insanity Tale." *American Literature*, 40 (1968), 211–15.

"Portrait of an Emigrant"

1106. **BENNETT, CHARLES E.** "Charles Brockden Brown's 'Portrait of an Emigrant.' " *CLA Journal*, 14 (1970), 87–90.

"The Story of Julius"

1107. **BROWN, HERBERT.** "Charles Brockden Brown's 'The Story of Julius': Rousseau and Richardson 'Improved.' " In *Essays Mostly on Periodical Publishing in America: A Collection in Honor of Clarence Gohdes*. Ed. James Woodress, et al. Durham, NC: Duke Univ. Press, 1973. pp. 35–53.

Bibliography

1108. **HEMENWAY, ROBERT E.** "Charles Brockden Brown, America's First Important Novelist: A Check List of Biography and Criticism." *The Papers of the Bibliographical Society of America*, 60 (1966), 349–62.

1109. **KRAUSE, SYDNEY J., AND JANE NIESET.** "A Census of the Works of Charles Brockden Brown." *The Serif*, 3, no. 4 (1966), 27–55.

1110. **WITHERINGTON, PAUL.** "Charles Brockden Brown: A Bibliographical Essay." *Early American Literature*, 9 (1974), 164–87.

BROWN, FREDERIC

General Studies

1111. **BAIRD, NEWTON.** "Paradox and Plot: The Fiction of Frederic Brown." *The Armchair Detective*, 9 (1976), 282–88; 10 (1977), 33–38, 85–87, 151–59, 249–60.

Bibliography

1112. **BAIRD, NEWTON.** "Paradox and Plot: A Frederic Brown Checklist." *The Armchair Detective*, 10 (1977), 370–75; 11 (1978), 86–91, 102.

BROWNE, CHARLES FARRAR (See WARD, ARTEMUS)

BUCK, PEARL S.

"East Wind"

See 1114.

General Studies

1113. **Doyle, Paul A.** "Pearl S. Buck's Short Stories: A Survey." *English Journal*, 55 (1966), 62–68.
1114. **Harris, Theodore F.** *Pearl S. Buck: A Biography.* New York: John Day, 1969.

BUMPUS, JERRY

General Studies

1115. **Murray, G. E.** "Unmapped Places." *fiction international*, nos. 6–7 (1976), pp. 141–46.

BUNCH, DAVID R.

"For Tomorrow, Daphalene"

1116. **Colquitt, Betsy.** "Editorial: Satire and 'For Tomorrow, Daphalene.' " *Descant*, 5, no. 3 (1961), 2–3.

BUNNER, H[ENRY] C[UYLER]

"The Love-Letters of Smith"

1117. **Stronks, James B.** "Frank Norris's *McTeague*: A Possible Source in H. C. Bunner." *Nineteenth-Century Fiction*, 25 (1971), 474–78.

BURKE, KENNETH

General Studies

*1118. **Frank, Armin Paul.** *Kenneth Burke.* New York: Twayne, 1969.
1119. **Rueckert, William H.** *Kenneth Burke and the Drama of Human Relations.* Minneapolis: Univ. of Minnesota Press, 1963.

Bibliography

1120. **Frank, Armin Paul, and Mechthild Frank.** "The Writings of Kenneth Burke." In *Critical Responses to Kenneth Burke, 1924–1966.* Ed. William H. Rueckert. Minneapolis: Univ. of Minnesota Press, 1969. pp. 495–512.
1121. **Rueckert, William H.** "Works about Kenneth Burke." In *Critical Responses to Kenneth Burke, 1924–1966.* Ed. William H. Rueckert. Minneapolis: Univ. of Minnesota Press, 1969. pp. 515–21.

BURNETT, FRANCES HODGSON

Bibliography

1122. MOLSON, FRANCIS J. "Frances Hodgson Burnett (1848–1924)." *American Literary Realism, 1870–1910*, 8 (1975), 35–41.

BURROUGHS, EDGAR RICE

General Studies

1123. LUPOFF, RICHARD A. *Edgar Rice Burroughs: Master of Adventure*. New York: Canaveral Press, 1965.

1124. ———. *Edgar Rice Burroughs: Master of Adventure*. Rev. ed. New York: Ace, 1968.

Bibliography

1125. HEINS, HENRY HARDY. *A Golden Anniversary Bibliography of Edgar Rice Burroughs*. West Kingston, RI: Donald M. Grant, 1964.

BURROUGHS, WILLIAM S.

General Studies

1126. BURROUGHS, W. S. "The Literary Techniques of Lady Sutton-Smith." *The Times* (London) *Literary Supplement*, 6 Aug. 1964, pp. 682–83.

Interviews

1127. BOCKRIS, VICTOR. "Information about the Operation: A Portrait of William Burroughs." *The New Review*, 3, no. 25 (1976), 37–46.

1128. BURROUGHS, WILLIAM. "The Art of Fiction XXXVI." With Conrad Knickerbocker. *The Paris Review*, no. 35 (1965), pp. 13–49.

1129. GOODMAN, RICHARD, JR. "An Evening with William Burroughs." *The Michigan Quarterly Review*, 13 (1974), 18–24.

1130. ODIER, DANIEL. *The Job: Interviews with William S. Burroughs*. New York: Grove Press, 1970.

1131. ———. *The Job: Interviews with William S. Burroughs*. Rev. ed. New York: Grove Press, 1974.

1132. ———. "Journey through Time-Space: An Interview with William S. Burroughs." *Evergreen Review*, no. 67 (1969), pp. 39–41, 78–89.

Bibliography

1133. GOODMAN, MICHAEL B. *William S. Burroughs: An Annotated Bibliography of His Works and Criticism.* New York: Garland, 1975.
1134. RUSHING, LYNDA LEE. "William S. Burroughs: A Bibliography." *Bulletin of Bibliography and Magazine Notes*, 29 (1972), 87–92.
1135. SKERL, JENNIE. "A William S. Burroughs Bibliography." *The Serif*, 11, no. 2 (1974), 12–20.

CABELL, JAMES BRANCH

"Balthazar's Daughter"

1136. BLISH, JAMES. "Cabell as Playwright." *Kalki*, 5 (1971), 35–37.

"The Choices"

See 1144.

"In Necessity's Mortar"

See 1144.

"In the Second April"

See 1144.

"Porcelain Cups"

See 1139.

"The Sestina"

See 1144.

"The Tenson"

See 1144.

General Studies

1137. BLISH, JAMES. "The Stallion's Other Members." *Kalki*, 4 (1970), 67–69.
1138. CANARY, ROBERT H. *The Cabell Scene.* New York: Revisionist Press, 1977.
1139. DAVIS, JOE LEE. *James Branch Cabell.* New York: Twayne, 1962.
1140. DUKE, MAURICE. "The Baroque Waste Land of James Branch Cabell." In *The Twenties: Fiction, Poetry, Drama.* Ed. Warren French. Deland, FL: Everett/Edwards, 1975. pp. 75–86.

1141. _____. "The Ornate Wasteland of James Branch Cabell." *Kalki*, 6 (1974), 79–89.
1142. JAMES, EDWARD M. "Cabellian Economics: The Uses of the Short Stories." *Kalki*, 2 (1968), 101–02.
1143. MACDONALD, EDGAR. "Cabell's Game of Hide and Seek." *The Cabellian*, 4 (1971), 9–16.
1144. TARRANT, DESMOND. *James Branch Cabell: The Dream and the Reality*. Norman: Univ. of Oklahoma Press, 1967.
1145. WELLS, ARVIN R. *Jesting Moses: A Study in Cabellian Comedy*. Gainesville: Univ. of Florida Press, 1962.

Bibliography

1146. DAVIS, JOE LEE. "Recent Cabell Criticism." *The Cabellian*, 1 (1968), 1–12.
1147. HALL, JAMES N. *James Branch Cabell: A Complete Bibliography*. New York: Revisionist Press, 1974.

CABLE, GEORGE WASHINGTON

"The Adventures of Françoise and Suzanne"

See 1152.

"The Angel of the Lord"

See 1153.

"Attalie Brouillard"

See 1153.

"Belles Demoiselles Plantation"

1148. FULWEILER, HOWARD W. "Of Time and the River: 'Ancestral Nonesense' vs. Inherited Guilt in Cable's 'Belles Demoiselles Plantation.' " *Midcontinent American Studies Journal*, 7, no. 2 (1966), 53–59.
1149. RINGE, DONALD A. "The Moral World of Cable's 'Belles Demoiselles Plantation.' " *The Mississippi Quarterly*, 29 (1976), 83–90.
See also 571, 1153, 1155–1157.

"Bras Coupé"

See 576.

"Caranco"

See 83.

"The Entomologist"

See 1153.

"The 'Haunted House' in Royal Street"

See 1152, 1154.

"Jean-Ah Poquelin"

1150. **EGAN, JOSEPH J.** " 'Jean-Ah Poquelin': George Washington Cable as Social Critic and Mythic Artist." *The Markham Review*, 2, no. 3 (1970), 46–47.
1151. **HOWELL, ELMO.** "Cable and the Creoles: A Note on 'Jean-Ah Poquelin.' " *Xavier University Studies*, 9, no. 3 (1970), 9–15.
See also 584, 1152, 1155, 1157.

"Madame Déliceuse"

See 1157.

"Madame Delphine"

See 83, 1152, 1154.

"Père Raphaël"

See 83.

"Posson Jane"

See 1157.

"Salome Miller, The White Slave"

See 1152.

" 'Sieur George"

See 1153, 1156, 1157.

"The Solitary"

See 1153.

"The Taxidermist"

See 1153.

" 'Tite Poulette"

See 1152–1154, 1157.

General Studies

1152. **BUTCHER, PHILIP.** *George W. Cable: The Northampton Years.* New York: Columbia Univ. Press, 1959.

1153. _____. *George Washington Cable*. New York: Twayne, 1962.

1154. CLARK, WILLIAM BEDFORD. "Cable and the Theme of Miscegenation in *Old Creole Days* and *The Grandissimes*." *The Mississippi Quarterly*, 30 (1977), 597-609.

1155. CLEMAN, JOHN. "College Girl Wilderness: Nature in the Work of George W. Cable." *The Markham Review*, 5 (1976), 24-31.

1156. DOWNS, ROBERT B. "Romantic New Orleans: George W. Cable's *Old Creole Days*." In *Books That Changed the South*. Chapel Hill: Univ. of North Carolina Press, 1977. pp. 148-55.

1157. RUBIN, LOUIS D., JR. *George W. Cable: The Life and Times of a Southern Heretic*. New York: Pegasus, 1969.

1158. TROTMAN, C. JAMES. "George W. Cable and Tradition." *The Texas Quarterly*, 19, no. 3 (1976), 51-58.

1159. TURNER, ARLIN. *George W. Cable*. Austin, TX: Steck-Vaughn, 1969.

1160. _____. "Introduction." In *Creoles and Cajuns: Stories of Old Louisiana*, by George W. Cable. Garden City, NY: Doubleday, 1959. pp. 1-19.

Bibliography

1161. BUTCHER, PHILIP. "George Washington Cable (1844-1925)." *American Literary Realism, 1870-1910*, 1, no. 1 (1967), 20-25.

1162. PUGH, GRIFFITH T. "George Washington Cable." *The Mississippi Quarterly*, 20 (1967), 69-76.

CAHAN, ABRAHAM

"The Apostate of Chego-Chegg"

See 46, 1163.

"The Imported Bridegroom"

See 46, 436, 1163.

General Studies

*1163. CHAMETZKY, JULES. *From the Ghetto: The Fiction of Abraham Cahan*. Amherst: Univ. of Massachusetts Press, 1977.

1164. MAROVITZ, SANFORD E. "The Lonely New Americans of Abraham Cahan." *American Quarterly*, 20 (1968), 196-210.

Bibliography

1165. MAROWITZ, SANFORD E., AND LEWIS FRIED. "Abraham Cahan (1860-1951): An Annotated Bibliography." *American Literary Realism, 1870-1910*, 3 (1970), 197-243.

CAIN, JAMES M.

General Studies

1166. **MADDEN, DAVID.** *James M. Cain.* New York: Twayne, 1970.

Bibliography

1167. **HAGEMANN, E. R., AND PHILIP C. DURHAM.** "James M. Cain, 1922-1958: A Selected Checklist." *Bulletin of Bibliography and Magazine Notes*, 23 (1960), 57-61.

CALDWELL, ERSKINE

"Kneel to the Rising Sun"
See 146.

"Saturday Afternoon"

1168. **RENEK, MORRIS.** "Rediscovering Erskine Caldwell." *The Nation*, 220 (1975), 758.
See also 1796.

General Studies

1169. **CALDWELL, ERSKINE.** "The Art, Craft, and Personality of Writing." *The Texas Quarterly*, 7, no. 1 (1964), 37-43.
1170. **COLLINS, CARVEL.** "Introduction." In *Erskine Caldwell's Men and Women*. Boston, MA: Little, Brown, 1961. pp. 3-9.
1171. **KORGES, JAMES.** *Erskine Caldwell*. Minneapolis: Univ. of Minnesota Press, 1969.
*1172. **MACDONALD, SCOTT.** "Repetition as Technique in the Short Stories of Erskine Caldwell." *Studies in American Fiction*, 5 (1977), 213-25.

Interviews

1173. **CALDWELL, ERSKINE.** "An Interview in Florida with Erskine Caldwell." *Studies in the Novel*, 3 (1971), 316-31.
1174. **FRANKEL, HASKEL.** "Fathers, Lovers, and Fiction." *Saturday Review*, 48 (6 Feb. 1965), 26-27.
1175. **NEWQUIST, ROY.** "Erskine Caldwell." In *Counterpoint*. Chicago: Rand McNally, 1964. pp. 66-73.

CALISHER, HORTENSE
"Heartburn"
See 369.

Interviews
1176. **NEWQUIST, ROY.** "Hortense Calisher." In *Conversations*. New York: Rand McNally, 1967. pp. 62–70.

CAMPBELL, JOHN W.
"Twilight"
See 357.

General Studies
1177. **BERGER, ALBERT I.** "The Magic That Works: John W. Campbell and the American Response to Technology." *Journal of Popular Culture*, 5 (1972), 867–943.

Bibliography
1178. **STOVER, LEON.** "Checklist of John Campbell's Fiction." *Extrapolation*, 14 (1973), 147–48.

CAMPBELL, WILLIAM EDWARD MARSH
(See MARCH, WILLIAM)

CAPOTE, TRUMAN
"Among the Paths to Eden"
See 1183.

"Children on Their Birthdays"
1179. **ZACHARIAS, LEE.** "Living the American Dream: 'Children on Their Birthdays.' " *Studies in Short Fiction*, 12 (1975), 343–50. See also 1180, 1183.

"A Diamond Guitar"
See 194, 1183.

"The Duke in His Domain"
See 1183.

"The Headless Hawk"
See 200, 257, 564, 1180.

"House of Flowers"

See 1183.

"A House on the Heights"

See 1183.

"Master Misery"

See 257, 1180, 1183.

"Miriam"

See 1180, 1183.

"Shut a Final Door"

See 257, 1183.

"A Tree of Night"

See 399, 1180, 1183.

General Studies

1180. GOAD, CRAIG M. "Daylight and Darkness, Dream and Delusion: The Works of Truman Capote." *The Emporia State Research Studies*, 16, no. 1 (1967), 5–57.

1181. HASSAN, IHAB H. "The Daydream and Nightmare of Narcissus." *Wisconsin Studies in Contemporary Literature*, 1, no. 2 (1960), 5–21.

1182. NAKA, MICHIKO. "Truman Capote: Negation of Differentiation." In *American Literature in the 1940's*. Annual Report, 1975. Tokyo: Tokyo Chapter, American Literary Society of Japan, 1976. pp. 75–91.

1183. NANCE, WILLIAM L. *The Worlds of Truman Capote*. New York: Stein and Day, 1970.

1184. SCHORER, MARK. "Introduction." In *Selected Writings*, by Truman Capote. New York: Random House, 1963. pp. vii–xii.

Interviews

1185. FRANKEL, HASKEL. Interview with Truman Capote. *Saturday Review*, 49 (22 Jan. 1966), 36–37.

1186. NEWQUIST, ROY. "Truman Capote." In *Counterpoint*. Chicago: Rand McNally, 1964. pp. 76–83.

Bibliography

1187. VANDERWERKEN, DAVID L. "Truman Capote, 1943–1968: A Critical Bibliography." *Bulletin of Bibliography and Magazine Notes*, 27 (1970), 57–60, 71.

1188. **WALL, RICHARD J., AND CARL L. CRAYCRAFT.** "A Checklist of Works about Truman Capote." *Bulletin of The New York Public Library*, 71 (1967), 165–72.

CARPENTER, DON[ALD]

Interviews

1189. **TOOKER, DAN, AND ROGER HOFHEINS.** "Don Carpenter." In *Fiction!: Interviews with Northern California Novelists*. New York: Harcourt Brace Jovanovich, 1976. pp. 37–53.

CASEY, BILL

General Studies

1190. **TURNER, STEVE.** "Bill Casey: Jottings before a Journey." *Southwestern American Literature*, 1 (1971), 80–86.

CASSILL, R[ONALD] V[ERLIN]

"And in My Heart"

See 1192.

"The Biggest Band"

1191. **CASSILL, R. V.** Introduction to "The Biggest Band." In *Writer's Choice*. Ed. Rust Hills. New York: McKay, 1974. pp. 69–70.

"The Happy Marriage"

See 456, 511.

"The Outer Island"

See 197.

"The Puzzle Factory"

See 197.

"This Hand, These Talons"

See 197, 1192.

General Studies

1192. **ROBERTS, DAVID.** "The Short Fiction of R. V. Cassill." *Critique*, 9, no. 1 (1966), 56–70.

CATHER, WILLA

"Before Breakfast"

See 1213, 1224.

"The Best Years"

1193. **BUSH, SARGENT, JR.** " 'The Best Years': Willa Cather's Last Story and its Relation to Her Canon." *Studies in Short Fiction*, 5 (1968), 269–74.

1194. **SCHNEIDER, SISTER LUCY, C.S.J.** "Willa Cather's 'The Best Years': The Essence of Her 'Land-Philosophy.' " *The Midwest Quarterly*, 15 (1973), 61–69.

See also 1213.

"The Bohemian Girl"

See 1212, 1219, 1224, 1229.

"The Clemency of the Court"

See 1207, 1219.

"Coming, Aphrodite!"

See 1211, 1212, 1224.

"The Count of the Crow's Nest"

See 1212.

"A Death in the Desert"

See 1212, 1224, 1229.

"The Diamond Mine"

See 1215.

"Double Birthday"

See 1224.

"The Elopement of Allen Poole"

See 1221.

"Eric Hermannson's Soul"

See 1212, 1219, 1224.

"Flavia and Her Artists"

See 1212.

"The Garden Lodge"

See 1212.

"A Gold Slipper"

See 1212.

"Jack-A-Boy"

See 1212.

"The Joy of Nelly Deane"

See 1212.

"Lou, The Prophet"

See 1219.

"Nanette: An Aside"

See 1212.

"Neighbour Rosicky"

1195. ANDES, CYNTHIA J. "The Bohemian Folk Practice in 'Neighbour Rosicky.' " *Western American Literature*, 7 (1972), 63–64.

1196. HINZ, EVELYN J. "Willa Cather's Technique and the Ideology of Populism." *Western American Literature*, 7 (1972), 47–61.

1197. SCHNEIDER, SISTER LUCY, C.S.J. " 'Land' Relevance in 'Neighbour Rosicky.' " *Kansas Quarterly*, 1 (1968), 105–10.

See also 259, 454, 513, 1212, 1213, 1215, 1216, 1224, 1229.

"The Old Beauty"

See 399, 1213, 1215, 1224.

"Old Mrs. Harris"

See 1212, 1213, 1215, 1216, 1224, 1225, 1229.

"On the Divide"

See 1200, 1212, 1215, 1219.

"On the Gull's Road"

See 1229.

"Paul's Case"

1198. RUBIN, LARRY. "The Homosexual Motif in Willa Cather's 'Paul's Case.' " *Studies in Short Fiction*, 12 (1975), 127–31.

See also 334, 356, 491, 1211, 1212, 1215, 1227, 1229.

"Peter"

See 1212.

"The Prodigies"

See 1212.

"Scandal"

See 1212.

"The Sculptor's Funeral"

1199. CARY, RICHARD. "The Sculptor and the Spinster: Jewett's 'Influence' on Cather." *Colby Library Quarterly*, 10 (1973), 168–78. *See also* 203, 1200, 1215, 1224, 1229.

"Tommy, The Unsentimental"

See 1200, 1224.

"The Treasure of Far Island"

See 1212.

"Uncle Valentine"

See 1224.

"A Wagner Matinée"

See 1200, 1212, 1215, 1219, 1229.

General Studies

1200. BAKER, BRUCE, II. "Nebraska Regionalism in Selected Works of Willa Cather." *Western American Literature*, 3 (1968), 19–35.

1201. BENNETT, MILDRED R. "How Willa Cather Chose Her Names." *Names*, 10 (1962), 29–37.

1202. _____. "Introduction." In *Willa Cather's Collected Short Fiction, 1892–1912*. Lincoln: Univ. of Nebraska Press, 1965. pp. xiii–xli.

1203. _____. "Willa Cather in Pittsburgh." *Prairie Schooner*, 33 (1959), 64–76.

1204. _____. *The World of Willa Cather*. Rev. ed. Lincoln: Univ. of Nebraska Press, 1961.

1205. BLOOM, LILLIAN D., AND EDWARD A. BLOOM. "The Poetics of Willa Cather." In *Five Essays on Willa Cather: The Merrimack Symposium*. Ed. John J. Murphy. North Andover, MA: Merrimack College, 1974. pp. 97–119.

1206. _____, AND _____. *Willa Cather's Gift of Sympathy*. Carbondale: Southern Illinois Univ. Press, 1962.

1207. **BOHLKE, L. BRENT.** "Beginnings: Willa Cather and 'The Clemency of the Court.' " *Prairie Schooner*, 48 (1974), 134–44.

1208. **BONHAM, BARBARA.** *Willa Cather.* Philadelphia, PA: Chilton, 1970.

1209. **BRENNAN, JOSEPH X.** "Willa Cather and Music." *The University Review* (Kansas City), 31 (1965), 175–83.

1210. **EDEL, LEON.** *Willa Cather: The Paradox of Success.* Washington, DC: Reference Department, Library of Congress, 1960.

1211. **GERBER, PHILIP.** *Willa Cather.* Boston, MA: Twayne, 1975.

1212. **GIANNONE, RICHARD.** *Music in Willa Cather's Fiction.* Lincoln: Univ. of Nebraska Press, 1968.

1213. **McFARLAND, DOROTHY TUCK.** *Willa Cather.* New York: Ungar, 1972.

1214. **PERS, MONA.** *Willa Cather's Children.* Stockholm: Almqvist & Wiksell, 1975.

1215. **RANDALL, JOHN H., III.** *The Landscape and the Looking Glass: Willa Cather's Search for Value.* Boston, MA: Houghton Mifflin, 1960.

1216. ———. "Willa Cather: The Middle West Revisited." *New Mexico Quarterly*, 31 (1961), 25–36.

1217. **SCHNEIDER, SISTER LUCY, C.S.J.** "Artistry and Instinct: Willa Cather's 'Land-Philosophy.' " *CLA Journal*, 16 (1973), 485–504.

1218. ———. "Artistry and Intuition: Willa Cather's 'Land-Philosophy.' " *South Dakota Review*, 6, no. 4 (1969), 53–64.

1219. ———. "Willa Cather's Early Stories in the Light of Her 'Land-Philosophy.' " *The Midwest Quarterly*, 9 (1967), 75–94.

1220. **SCHROETER, JAMES.** "Willa Cather and the Professor's House." *The Yale Review*, 54 (1965), 494–512.

1221. **SLOTE, BERNICE.** "The Kingdom of Art." In *The Kingdom of Art: Willa Cather's First Principles and Critical Statements, 1893-1896.* Ed. Bernice Slote. Lincoln: Univ. of Nebraska Press, 1966. pp. 31–112.

1222. ———. "Willa Cather as a Regional Writer." *Kansas Quarterly*, 2, no. 2 (1970), 7–15.

1223. ———. "Writer in Nebraska." In *The Kingdom of Art: Willa Cather's First Principles and Critical Statements, 1893-1896.* Ed. Bernice Slote. Lincoln: Univ. of Nebraska Press, 1966. pp. 3–29.

1224. **STOUCK, DAVID.** *Willa Cather's Imagination.* Lincoln: Univ. of Nebraska Press, 1975.

1225. ———. "Willa Cather's Last Four Books." *Novel*, 7 (1973), 41–53.

1226. TOLER, SISTER COLETTE, S.C. "Willa Cather's Vision of the Artist." *The Personalist*, 45 (1964), 503-23.
1227. VAN GHENT, DOROTHY. *Willa Cather*. Minneapolis: Univ. of Minnesota Press, 1964.
1228. WELTY, EUDORA. "The House of Willa Cather." In *The Art of Willa Cather*. Ed. Bernice Slote and Virginia Faulkner. Lincoln: Univ. of Nebraska Press, 1974. pp. 3-20, 259.
1229. WOODRESS, JAMES. *Willa Cather: Her Life and Art*. New York: Pegasus, 1970.

Bibliography

1230. LATHROP, JOANNA. *Willa Cather: A Checklist of Her Published Writing*. Lincoln: Univ. of Nebraska Press, 1975.
1231. SLOTE, BERNICE. "Willa Cather." In *Fifteen Modern American Authors: A Survey of Research and Criticism*. Ed. Jackson R. Bryer. Durham, NC: Duke Univ. Press, 1969. pp. 23-62.
1232. ———. "Willa Cather." In *Sixteen Modern American Authors: A Survey of Research and Criticism*. Ed. Jackson R. Bryer. Durham, NC: Duke Univ. Press, 1974. pp. 29-73.

CHANDLER, RAYMOND

General Studies

1233. BEEKMAN, E. M. "Raymond Chandler & an American Genre." *The Massachusetts Review*, 14 (1973), 149-73.
*1234. DURHAM, PHILIP. *Down These Mean Streets a Man Must Go: Raymond Chandler's Knight*. Chapel Hill: Univ. of North Carolina Press, 1963.

Bibliography

1235. BRUCCOLI, MATTHEW J. *Raymond Chandler: A Checklist*. Kent, OH: Kent State Univ. Press, 1968.

CHASE, MARY ELLEN

General Studies

1236. WESTBROOK, PERRY D. *Mary Ellen Chase*. New York: Twayne, 1965.

Bibliography

1237. CARY, RICHARD. "A Bibliography of the Published Writings of Mary Ellen Chase." *Colby Library Quarterly*, 6 (1962), 34-45.

CHEEVER, JOHN

"The Angel of the Bridge"

See 1248.

"The Common Day"

See 1248.

"The Country Husband"

See 270, 384, 478, 564, 1248.

"The Death of Justina"

See 1248.

"The Embarkment for Cythera"

See 1244.

"The Enormous Radio"

1238. **KENDLE, BURTON**. "Cheever's Use of Mythology in 'The Enormous Radio.'" *Studies in Short Fiction*, 4 (1967), 262–64.

1239. **SIZEMORE, CHRISTINE W.** "The Sweeney Allusion in John Cheever's 'Enormous Radio.'" *Notes on Contemporary Literature*, 7, no. 4 (1977), 9.

1240. **TEN HARMSEL, HENRIETTA**. "'Young Goodman Brown' and 'The Enormous Radio.'" *Studies in Short Fiction*, 9 (1972), 407–08.

See also 277, 1248.

"Expelled"

See 1248.

"The Fourth Alarm"

See 399.

"Goodbye, My Brother"

1241. **CHEEVER, JOHN**. "What Happened." In *Understanding Fiction*. 2nd ed. Ed. Cleanth Brooks and Robert Penn Warren. New York: Appleton-Century-Crofts, 1959. pp. 570–72.

See also 565, 1245, 1248.

"The Housebreaker of Shady Hill"

See 1247, 1248.

"The Music Teacher"

See 1248.

"O Youth and Beauty!"

See 1248, 1251.

"The Scarlet Moving Van"

See 1248, 1251.

"The Seaside Houses"

See 1248.

"The Swimmer"

1242. **AUSER, CORTLAND P.** "John Cheever's Myth of Man and Time: 'The Swimmer.' " *The CEA Critic*, 29, no. 6 (1967), 18–19.
1243. **GRAVES, NORA CALHOUN.** "The Dominant Color in John Cheever's 'The Swimmer.' " *Notes on Contemporary Literature*, 4, no. 2 (1974), 4–5.
See also 1247, 1248, 1251.

"A Vision of the World"

See 1248.

"A World of Apples"

See 1248.

"The Wrysons"

See 1248.

General Studies

1244. **BRACHER, FREDERICK.** "John Cheever: A Vision of the World." *Claremont Quarterly*, 11, no. 2 (1964), 47–57.
1245. ———. "John Cheever and Comedy." *Critique*, 6, no. 1 (1963), 66–77.
1246. **BURHANS, CLINTON S., JR.** "John Cheever and the Grave of Social Coherence." *Twentieth Century Literature*, 14 (1969), 187–98.
1247. **CHESNICK, EUGENE.** "The Domesticated Stroke of John Cheever." *The New England Quarterly*, 44 (1971), 531–52.
1248. **COALE, SAMUEL.** *John Cheever.* New York: Ungar, 1977.
1249. **DONALDSON, SCOTT.** "The Machines in Cheever's Garden." In *The Changing Face of the Suburbs.* Ed. Barry Schwartz. Chicago: Univ. of Chicago Press, 1976. pp. 309–22.
1250. **GARRETT, GEORGE.** "John Cheever and the Charms of Innocence: The Craft of *The Wapshot Scandal*." *The Hollins Critic*, 1, no. 2 (1964), 1–4, 6–12.
1251. **MOORE, STEPHEN C.** "The Hero on the 5:42: John Cheever's Short Fiction." *Western Humanities Review*, 30 (1976), 147–52.

Interviews

1252. **BAURES, MARY.** "Interview with John Cheever." *Fiction*,
no. 8 (1974), pp. 14–15, 93.

1253. **CHEEVER, JOHN.** "The Art of Fiction LXII." With Annette Grant. *The Paris Review*, no. 67 (1976), pp. 39–66.

1254. **FIRTH, JOHN.** "Talking with John Cheever." *Saturday Review*, 4 (2 Apr. 1977), 22–23.

1255. **HERSEY, JOHN.** "Talk with John Cheever." *The New York
Times Book Review*, 6 Mar. 1977, pp. 1, 24, 26–28.

1256. **LEHMANN-HAUPT, CHRISTOPHER.** "Talk with John Cheever." *The New York Times Book Review*, 27 Apr. 1969, pp. 42–44.

1257. **NICHOLS, LEWIS.** "A Visit with John Cheever." *The New
York Times Book Review*, 5 Jan. 1964, p. 28.

CHESNUTT, CHARLES W[ADDELL]

"Baxter's Procrustes"

1258. **ANDREWS, WILLIAM L.** " 'Baxter's Procrustes': Some
More Light on the Biographical Connection." *Black American
Literature Forum*, 11 (1977), 75–78, 89.

1259. **HEMENWAY, ROBERT.** " 'Baxter's Procrustes': Irony and
Protest." *CLA Journal*, 18 (1974), 172–85.
See also 386.

"The Conjurer's Revenge"

See 386, 1267.

"Dave's Neckliss"

See 1266.

"The Goophered Grapevine"

1260. **HOVET, THEODORE R.** "Chesnutt's 'The Goophered Grapevine' as Social Criticism." *Negro American Literature Forum*, 7
(1973), 86–88.
See also 386, 576, 1266–1268, 1271.

"The Gray Wolf's Ha'nt"

See 386.

"The March of Progress"

See 1277.

"Mars Jeems's Nightmare"

See 1267.

"A Matter of Principle"

See 386.

"The Origin of the Hatchet Story"

See 1277.

"Po' Sandy"

See 1267, 1268, 1273.

"Rena"

1261. SEDLACK, ROBERT P. "The Evolution of Charles Chesnutt's *The House Behind the Cedars*." *CLA Journal*, 19 (1975), 125–35.

"The Sheriff's Children"

1262. HASLAM, GERALD W. " 'The Sheriff's Children': Chesnutt's Tragic Racial Parable." *Negro American Literature Forum*, 2 (1968), 21–26.

1263. SELKE, HARTMUT K. "Charles Waddell Chesnutt, 'The Sheriff's Children' (1889)." In *The Black American Short Story in the 20th Century: A Collection of Critical Essays*. Ed. Peter Bruck. Amsterdam: B. R. Grüner, 1977. pp. 21–38.

1264. WALCOTT, RONALD. "Chesnutt's 'The Sheriff's Children' as Parable." *Negro American Literature Forum*, 7 (1973), 83–85.

See also 386, 1272.

"Sis' Becky's Pickaninny"

See 386, 1268, 1271.

"Uncle Peter's House"

See 1277.

"The Web of Circumstance"

See 1277.

"The Wife of His Youth"

See 386, 1272.

General Studies

1265. ANDREWS, WILLIAM L. "A Reconsideration of *Charles Waddell Chesnutt: Pioneer of the Color Line*." *CLA Journal*, 19 (1975), 136–51.

1266. ———. "The Significance of Charles W. Chesnutt's 'Conjure Stories.' " *The Southern Literary Journal*, 7, no. 1 (1974), 78–99.

1267. **BALDWIN, RICHARD E.** "The Art of *The Conjure Woman*." *American Literature*, 43 (1971), 385-98.

1268. **BRITT, DAVID D.** "Chesnutt's Conjure Tales: What You See Is What You Get." *CLA Journal*, 15 (1972), 269-83.

1269. **CHAMETZKY, JULES.** "Regional Literature and Ethnic Realities." *The Antioch Review*, 31 (1971), 385-96.

1270. **CUNNINGHAM, JOAN.** "The Uncollected Short Stories of Charles Waddell Chesnutt." *Negro American Literature Forum*, 9 (1975), 57-58.

1271. **DIXON, MELVIN.** "The Teller as Folk Trickster in Chesnutt's *The Conjure Woman*." *CLA Journal*, 18 (1974), 186-97.

1272. **FARNSWORTH, ROBERT M.** "Charles Chesnutt and the Color Line." In *Minor American Novelists*. Ed. Charles Alva Hoyt. Carbondale and Edwardsville: Southern Illinois Univ. Press, 1970. pp. 28-40, 139.

1273. _____. "Introduction." In *The Conjure Woman*, by Charles W. Chesnutt. Ann Arbor: Univ. of Michigan Press, 1969. pp. v-xix.

1274. **FOSTER, CHARLES W.** "The Phonology of the Conjure Tales of Charles W. Chesnutt." *Publication of the American Dialect Society*, no. 55 (1971), 1-43.

1275. **GARTNER, CAROL B.** "Charles W. Chesnutt: Novelist of a Cause." *The Markham Review*, 1, no. 3 (1968), 5-12.

1276. **GILES, JAMES R.** "Chesnutt's Primus and Annie: A Contemporary View of *The Conjure Woman*." *The Markham Review*, 3 (1972), 46-49.

1277. **HEERMANCE, J. NOEL.** *Charles W. Chesnutt: America's First Great Black Novelist*. Hamden, CT: Archon Books, 1974.

1278. **HEMENWAY, ROBERT.** "Gothic Sociology: Charles Chesnutt and the Gothic Mode." *Studies in the Literary Imagination*, 7, no. 1 (1974), 101-19.

1279. **JACKSON, WENDELL.** "Charles W. Chesnutt's Outrageous Fortune." *CLA Journal*, 20 (1976), 195-204.

1280. **MASON, JULIAN D., JR.** "Charles W. Chesnutt as Southern Author." *The Mississippi Quarterly*, 20 (1967), 77-89.

1281. **MIXON, WAYNE.** "The Unfulfilled Dream: Charles W. Chesnutt and the New South Movement." *Southern Humanities Review*, Bicentennial Issue (1976), 23-33.

1282. **OGUNYEMI, CHIKWENYE OKONJO.** "The Africanness of *The Conjure Woman* and *Feather of the Jungle*." *Ariel*, 8, no. 2 (1977), 17-30.

1283. **RENDER, SYLVIA LYONS.** "Introduction." In *The Short Fiction of Charles W. Chesnutt*. Washington, DC: Howard Univ. Press, 1974. pp. 3-56.

1284. _____. "Tar Heela in Chesnutt." *CLA Journal*, 9 (1965), 39–50.

1285. **SMITH, ROBERT A.** "A Note on the Folktales of Charles W. Chesnutt." *CLA Journal*, 5 (1962), 229–32.

1286. **SOCKEN, JUNE.** "Charles Waddell Chesnutt and the Solution to the Race Problem." *Negro American Literature Forum*, 3 (1969), 52–56.

1287. **TAXEL, JOEL.** "Charles Waddell Chesnutt's Sambo: Myth and Reality." *Negro American Literature Forum*, 9 (1975), 105–08.

1288. **TELLER, WALTER.** "Charles W. Chesnutt's Conjuring and Color-Line Stories." *The American Scholar*, 42 (1973), 125–27.

Bibliography

1289. **ANDREWS, WILLIAM L.** "Charles Waddell Chesnutt: An Essay in Bibliography." *Resources for American Literary Study*, 6 (1976), 3–22.

1290. _____. "The Works of Charles W. Chesnutt: A Checklist." *Bulletin of Bibliography and Magazine Notes*, 33 (1976), 45–47, 52.

1291. **CUNNINGHAM, JOAN.** "Secondary Studies on the Fiction of Charles W. Chesnutt." *Bulletin of Bibliography and Magazine Notes*, 33 (1976), 48–52.

1292. **ELLISON, CURTIS W., AND E. W. METCALF, JR.** *Charles W. Chesnutt: A Reference Guide*. Boston, MA: G. K. Hall, 1977.

1293. **KELLER, DEAN H.** "Charles Waddell Chesnutt (1858–1932)." *American Literary Realism, 1870–1910*, 1, no. 3 (1968), 1–4.

CHILD, LYDIA MARIA
"Jumbo and Zairee"
See 66.

General Studies

1294. **BAER, HELENE G.** *The Heart is Like Heaven: The Life of Lydia Maria Child*. Philadelphia: Univ. of Pennsylvania Press, 1964.

CHOPIN, KATE
"At the 'Cadian Ball"
See 1301.

"Athénaïse"
See 1302, 1310.

"Beyond the Bayou"

1295.   ROWE, ANNE. "A Note on 'Beyond the Bayou.' " *The Kate Chopin Newsletter*, 1, no. 2 (1975), 7–9.

"Désirée's Baby"

1296.   ARNER, ROBERT D. "Pride and Prejudice: Kate Chopin's 'Désirée's Baby.' " *The Mississippi Quarterly*, 25 (1972), 131–40.

"The Maid of Saint Philippe"

See 1304.

"A No-Account Creole"

See 1310.

"Ozéme's Holiday"

See 1310.

"A Point At Issue"

See 1310.

"Regret"

See 1310.

"A Sentimental Soul"

1297.   TOTH, EMILY. "The Cult of Domesticity and 'A Sentimental Soul.' " *The Kate Chopin Newsletter*, 1, no. 2 (1975), 9–16.

"The Storm"

1298.   GAUDÉ, PAMELA. "Kate Chopin's 'The Storm': A Study of Maupassant's Influence." *The Kate Chopin Newsletter*, 1, no. 2 (1975), 1–6.
See also 422, 1301, 1302, 1310.

"The Story of an Hour"

See 1310.

"Vagabonds"

1299.   ARNER, ROBERT D. "Characterization and the Colloquial Style in Kate Chopin's 'Vagabonds.' " *The Markham Review*, 2 (1971), 110–12.

"A Vocation and A Voice"

See 1302.

"Wiser Than a God"

See 1310.

General Studies

1300. **ARMS, GEORGE.** "Kate Chopin's *The Awakening* in the Perspective of Her Literary Career." In *Essays on American Literature in Honor of Jay B. Hubbell.* Ed. Clarence Gohdes. Durham, NC: Duke Univ. Press, 1967. pp. 215–28.

1301. **ARNER, ROBERT D.** "Kate Chopin's Realism: 'At the 'Canadian Ball' and 'The Storm.' " *The Markham Review*, 2, no. 2 (1970), 21–24.

1302. **BENDER, BERT.** "Kate Chopin's Lyrical Short Stories." *Studies in Short Fiction*, 11 (1974), 257–66.

1303. **BONNER, THOMAS, JR.** "Kate Chopin's European Consciousness." *American Literary Realism, 1870–1910,* 8 (1975), 281–84.

1304. **LADENSON, JOYCE RUDDEL.** "The Return of St. Louis' Prodigal Daughter: Kate Chopin After Seventy Years." *Midamerica*, 2 (1975), 24–34.

1305. **LEARY, LEWIS.** "Introduction." In *The Awakening and Other Stories*, by Kate Chopin. New York: Holt, Rinehart, and Winston, 1970. pp. iii–xviii.

1306. **O'BRIEN, SHARON.** "Sentiment, Local Color, and the New Woman Writer: Kate Chopin and Willa Cather." *The Kate Chopin Newsletter*, 2, no. 3 (1977), 16–24.

1307. **RINGE, DONALD A.** "Cane River World: Kate Chopin's *At Fault* and Related Stories." *Studies in American Fiction*, 3 (1975), 157–66.

1308. **SEYERSTED, PER.** "Introduction." In *The Complete Works of Kate Chopin.* 2 vols. Baton Rouge: Louisiana State Univ. Press, 1969. I, 21–33.

1309. ———. "Introduction." In *The Storm and Other Stories, by Kate Chopin, with The Awakening.* Old Westbury, NY: Feminist Press, 1974. pp. 7–18.

1310. ———. *Kate Chopin: A Critical Biography.* Baton Rouge: Louisiana State Univ. Press, 1969.

1311. **TOTH, EMILY.** "The Independent Woman and 'Free' Love." *The Massachusetts Review*, 16 (1975), 647–64.

Bibliography

1312. **BONNER, THOMAS, JR.** "Kate Chopin: An Annotated Bibliography." *Bulletin of Bibliography and Magazine Notes*, 32 (1975), 101–05.

1313. **SEYERSTED, PER.** "Kate Chopin (1851–1904)." *American Literary Realism, 1870–1910,* 3 (1970), 153–59.

1314. **SPRINGER, MARLENE.** *Edith Wharton and Kate Chopin: A Reference Guide.* Boston, MA: G. K. Hall, 1976.

1315. [**TOTH, EMILY**]. "Kate Chopin: Forthcoming Works and Works in Progress." *The Kate Chopin Newsletter,* 1, no. 1 (1975), 14–16.

1316. _____. "Kate Chopin Bibliography." *The Kate Chopin Newsletter,* 1, no. 2 (1975), 35–40; 1, no. 3 (1976), 32–38; 2, no. 1 (1976), 28–34; 2, no. 2 (1976), 47–48; *Regionalism and the Female Imagination,* 3, no. 1 (1977), 45–48.

CHURCHILL, WINSTON

"By Order of the Admiral"

See 1317.

General Studies

1317. **TITUS, WARREN I.** *Winston Churchill.* New York: Twayne, 1963.

CLARK, WALTER VAN TILBURG

"The Buck in the Hills"

See 486.

"The Indian Well"

1318. **HOUGHTON, DONALD E.** "Man and Animals in 'The Indian Well.' " *Western American Literature,* 6 (1971), 215–18.

"The Portable Phonograph"

1319. **COHEN, EDWARD H.** "Clark's 'The Portable Phonograph.' " *The Explicator,* 28 (1970), item 69.
See also 565.

"The Watchful Gods"

See 1323–1325.

"The Wind and the Snow of Winter"

1320. **WEST, RAY B., JR.** "The Use of Setting in 'The Wind and the Snow of Winter.' " In *The Art of Writing Fiction.* Ed. Ray B. West, Jr. New York: Crowell, 1968. pp. 181–87.

General Studies

1321. EISINGER, CHESTER E. "The Fiction of Walter Van Tilburg Clark: Man and Nature in the West." *Southwest Review*, 44 (1959), 214-26.

1322. HERRMANN, JOHN. "The Death of the Artist as Hero." *South Dakota Review*, 4, no. 2 (1966), 51-55.

1323. LEE, L. L. *Walter Van Tilburg Clark*. Boise, ID: Boise State College, 1973.

1324. MILTON, JOHN R. "The Western Attitude: Walter Van Tilburg Clark." *Critique*, 2, no. 3 (1959), 57-73.

1325. WESTBROOK, MAX. *Walter Van Tilburg Clark*. New York: Twayne, 1969.

Interviews

1326. MILTON, [JOHN R.]. "Conversation with Walter Van Tilburg Clark." *South Dakota Review*, 9, no. 1 (1971), 27-38.

Bibliography

1327. ETULAIN, RICHARD. "Walter Van Tilburg Clark: A Bibliography." *South Dakota Review*, 3, no. 1 (1965), 73-77.

CLARKE, JOHN HENRIK

"Santa Claus is a White Man"

See 475.

CLEMENS, SAMUEL LANGHORNE (See TWAIN, MARK)

COBB, JOSEPH B.

General Studies

*1328. ROGERS, TOMMY W. "The Folk Humor of Joseph B. Cobb." *Notes on Mississippi Writers*, 3 (1970), 13-35.

1329. ————. "Joseph B. Cobb: Antebellum Humorist and Critic." *The Mississippi Quarterly*, 22 (1969), 131-46.

COLLIER, JOHN

"De Mortuis"

See 565.

"Wet Saturday"

See 478.

COLTER, CYRUS
General Studies

1330. O'BRIEN, JOHN. "Forms of Determinism in the Fiction of Cyrus Colter." *Studies in Black Literature*, 4, no. 2 (1973), 24–28.

Interviews

1331. FARNSWORTH, ROBERT M. "Conversation with Cyrus Colter." *New Letters*, 39, no. 3 (1973), 17–39.
1332. O'BRIEN, JOHN. "Cyrus Colter." In *Interviews with Black Writers*. Ed. John O'Brien. New York: Liveright, 1973. pp. 17–33.

CONNELL, EVAN S., JR.
"The Condor and the Guests"

See 511.

General Studies

1333. BLAISDELL, GUS. "After Ground Zero: The Writings of Evan S. Connell, Jr." *New Mexico Quarterly*, 36 (1966), 181–207.

Interviews

1334. BENSKY, LAWRENCE M. "Meet Evan Connell, Friend of Mr. and Mrs. Bridge." *The New York Times Book Review*, 20 Apr. 1969, p. 2.
1334a. TOOKER, DAN, AND ROGER HOFHEINS. "Evan S. Connell, Jr." In *Fiction!: Interviews with Northern California Novelists.* New York: Harcourt Brace Jovanovich, 1976. pp. 55–69.

CONROY, JACK
"The Siren"

1335. LARSEN, ERLING. "Jack Conroy's *The Disinherited*; or, The Way It Was." In *Proletarian Writers of the Thirties*. Ed. David Madden. Carbondale and Edwardsville: Southern Illinois Univ. Press, 1968. pp. 85–95.

Interviews

1335a. FRIED, LEWIS. "Conversation with Jack Conroy." *New Letters*, 39, no. 1 (1972), 41–56.

Bibliography

1335b. BURKE, JOHN GORDON. "A Preliminary Checklist of the

Writings of Jack Conroy." *The American Book Collector*, 21, no. 8
(1971), 20–24.

COOKE, ROSE TERRY

"How Celia Changed Her Mind"

See 1336.

"Polly Mariner, Tailoress"

See 1336.

General Studies

1336.   TOTH, SUSAN ALLEN. "Character Studies in Rose Terry
Cooke: New Faces for the Short Story." *The Kate Chopin Newsletter*, 2, no. 1 (1976), 19–26.

Bibliography

1337.   TOTH, SUSAN ALLEN. "Rose Terry Cooke (1827–1892)."
American Literary Realism, 1870–1910, 4 (1971), 170–76.

COOPER, JAMES FENIMORE

"Heart"

See 1338.

"Imagination"

1338.   BEARD, JAMES FRANKLIN. "Introduction." In *Tales for Fifteen (1823)*, by James Fenimore Cooper. Gainesville, FL: Scholars' Facsimiles & Reprints, 1959. pp. v–xii.

Bibliography

1339.   BEARD, JAMES FRANKLIN. "James Fenimore Cooper." In
*Fifteen American Authors before 1900: Bibliographic Essays on Re-
search and Criticism*. Ed. Robert A. Rees and Earl N. Harbert.
Madison: Univ. of Wisconsin Press, 1971. pp. 63–96.

COOVER, ROBERT

"The Babysitter"

1340.   WEINSTOCK, E. B. "Robert Coover — 'The Babysitter': An
Observation on Experimental Writing." *Style*, 9 (1975), 378–87.
See also 399.

"The Leper's Helix"

1341.   COPE, JACKSON I. "Robert Coover's Fictions." *The Iowa
Review*, 2, no. 4 (1971), 94–110.

"The Magic Poker"

See 1347.

"A Pedestrian Accident"

1342. ROSA, ALFRED F. "Mrs. Grundy Finally Appears in Robert Coover's 'The Pedestrian Accident.'" *Notes on Contemporary Literature*, 2, no. 5 (1972), 2–3.

1343. WOODWARD, ROBERT H. "An Ancestor of Robert Coover's Mrs. Grundy." *Notes on Contemporary Literature*, 3, no. 1 (1973), 11–12.

See also 318.

General Studies

1344. DILLARD, R. H. W. "The Wisdom of The Beast: The Fictions of Robert Coover." *The Hollins Critic*, 7, no. 2 (1970), 1–11.

1345. HECKARD, MARGARET. "Robert Coover, Metafiction, and Freedom." *Twentieth Century Literature*, 22 (1976), 210–27.

1346. MCCAFFERY, LARRY. "The Magic of Fiction-Making." *fiction international*, nos. 4–5 (1975), pp. 147–53.

1347. SCHMITZ, NEIL. "Robert Coover and the Hazards of Metafiction." *Novel*, 7 (1974), 210–19.

Interviews

1348. GADO, FRANK. "Robert Coover." In *First Person: Conversations on Writers & Writing*. Ed. Frank Gado. Schenectady, NY: Union College Press, 1973. pp. 142–59.

1349. HERTZEL, LEO J. "An Interview With Robert Coover." *Critique*, 11, no. 3 (1969), 25–29.

Bibliography

1350. BLACHOWITZ, CAMILLE. "Robert Coover." *The Great Lakes Review*, 3, no. 1 (1976), 69–73.

1351. HERTZEL, LEO J. "A Coover Checklist (1968)." *Critique*, 11, no. 3 (1969), 23–24.

1352. MCCAFFERY, LARRY. "A Robert Coover Checklist." *Bulletin of Bibliography and Magazine Notes*, 31 (1974), 103–04.

CORMIER, ROBERT

Interviews

1353. JANECZKO, PAUL. "An Interview with Robert Cormier." *English Journal*, 66, no. 6 (1977), 10–11.

COSTELLO, MARK

"Murphy's Xmas"

See 399.

Interviews

1354. FIELDS, JENNIE. "Mark Costello Interview." *Story Quarterly*, no. 4 (1976), pp. 31–36.

COXE, GEORGE HARMON

General Studies

1355. COX, J. RANDOLPH. "Mystery Master: A Survey and Appreciation of the Fiction of George Harmon Coxe." *The Armchair Detective*, 6 (1973), 63–74, 160–66, 232–41; 7 (1973), 11–24.

COZZENS, JAMES GOULD

"Eyes to See"

1356. SHEPHERD, ALLEN. " 'The New Aquist of Incredible Experience': Point of View and Theme in James Gould Cozzens' 'Eyes to See.' " *Studies in Short Fiction*, 13 (1976), 378–81.
See also 1359.

General Studies

1357. BRACHER, FREDERICK. *The Novels of James Gould Cozzens.* New York: Harcourt, Brace, 1959.
1358. HICKS, GRANVILLE. *James Gould Cozzens.* Minneapolis: Univ. of Minnesota Press, 1966.
1359. MICHEL, PIERRE. *James Gould Cozzens.* New York: Twayne, 1974.

Bibliography

1360. MERIWETHER, JAMES B. *James Gould Cozzens: A Checklist.* Detroit, MI: Gale, 1973.
1361. MICHEL, PIERRE. *James Gould Cozzens: An Annotated Checklist.* Kent, OH: Kent State Univ. Press, 1971.

CRADDOCK, CHARLES EGBERT

"A-Playin' of Old Sledge at the Settlement"

See 82.

"The Bushwacker"

See 83.

"Drifting Down Lost Creek"

See 571, 1362.

"The 'Harnt' That Walks Chilhowee"

See 83.

"Over on T'Other Mounting"

See 83.

General Studies

*1362. CARY, RICHARD. *Mary N. Murfree*. New York: Twayne, 1967.

1363. NILLES, MARY. "Craddock's Girls: A Look at Some Unliberated Women." *The Markham Review*, 3 (1972), 74–77.

Bibliography

1364. CARLTON, REESE M. "Mary Noailles Murfree (1850–1922): An Annotated Bibliography." *American Literary Realism, 1870–1910*, 7 (1974), 293–378.

1365. CARY, RICHARD. "Mary Noailles Murfree (1850–1922)." *American Literary Realism, 1870–1910*, 1, no. 1 (1967), 79–83.

CRANE, JONATHAN TOWNLEY

General Studies

*1366. GULLASON, THOMAS A. "The Fiction of the Reverend Jonathan Townley Crane, D.D." *American Literature*, 43 (1971), 263–73.

CRANE, STEPHEN

"The Angel-Child"

See 1512, 1519.

"Apache Crossing"

1367. STALLMAN, R. W., ED. WITH A NOTE. "Stephen Crane's 'Apache Crossing': The Text of an Unfinished Story." *Prairie Schooner*, 43 (1969), 184–86.

"Art in Kansas City"

1368. [KATZ, JOSEPH], ED. WITH AN INTRO. " 'Art in Kansas

City': A New 'Uncle Clarence' Story." *Stephen Crane Newsletter*, 2, no. 1 (1967), 3–4.
See also 1412.

"Billy Atkins Went to Omaha"

See 1508.

"The Black Dog"

See 1488.

"The Blue Hotel"

1369. DAVIDSON, RICHARD ALLAN. "Crane's 'Blue Hotel' Revisited: The Illusion of Fate." *Modern Fiction Studies*, 15 (1969), 537–39.

1370. DILLINGHAM, WILLIAM B. " 'The Blue Hotel' and the Gentle Reader." *Studies in Short Fiction*, 1 (1964), 224–26.

1371. ELLIS, JAMES. "The Game of High-Five in 'The Blue Hotel.' " *American Literature*, 49 (1977), 440–42.

1372. GIBSON, DONALD B. " 'The Blue Hotel' and the Ideal of Human Courage." *Texas Studies in Literature and Language*, 6 (1964), 388–97.

1373. GLECKNER, ROBERT F. "Stephen Crane and the Wonder of Man's Conceit." *Modern Fiction Studies*, 5 (1959), 271–81.

1374. GRENBERG, BRUCE L. "Metaphysic of Despair: Stephen Crane's 'The Blue Hotel.' " *Modern Fiction Studies*, 14 (1968), 203–13.

1375. HOUGH, ROBERT L. "Crane on Herons." *Notes and Queries*, 9 (1962), 108–09.

1376. [KATZ, JOSEPH]. "An Early Draft of 'The Blue Hotel.' " *Stephen Crane Newsletter*, 3, no. 1 (1968), 1–2, 3.

1377. ———. "Introduction." In *Stephen Crane: The Blue Hotel*. Columbus, OH: Merrill, 1969. pp. 1–4.

1378. KAZIN, ALFRED. "On Stephen Crane and 'The Blue Hotel.' " In *The American Short Story*. Ed. Calvin Skaggs. New York: Dell, 1977. pp. 77–81.

1379. KINNAMON, JON M. "Henry James, The Bartender in Stephen Crane's 'The Blue Hotel.' " *The Arizona Quarterly*, 30 (1974), 160–63.

1380. KLOTZ, MARVIN. "Stephen Crane—Tragedian or Comedian: 'The Blue Hotel.' " *The University of Kansas City Review*, 27 (1961), 170–74.

1381. MACLEAN, HUGH N. "The Two Worlds of 'The Blue Hotel.' " *Modern Fiction Studies*, 5 (1959), 260–70.

1382. NARVESON, ROBERT. " 'Conceit' in 'The Blue Hotel.' "
Prairie Schooner, 43 (1969), 187–91.

1383. OSBORN, NEAL J. "Crane's *The Monster* and 'The Blue
Hotel.' " *The Explicator*, 23 (1964), item 10.

1384. PILGRIM, TIM A. "Repetition as a Nihilistic Device in Stephen Crane's 'The Blue Hotel.' " *Studies in Short Fiction*, 11
(1974), 125–29.

1385. ROOKE, CONSTANCE. "Another Visitor to 'The Blue Hotel.' " *South Dakota Review*, 14, no. 4 (1977), 50–56.

1386. SLOTE, BERNICE. "Stephen Crane in Nebraska." *Prairie
Schooner*, 43 (1969), 192–99.

1387. STARR, ALVIN. "The Concept of Fear in the Works of Stephen Crane and Richard Wright." *Studies in Black Literature*, 6,
no. 2 (1975), 6–10.

1388. VANDERBEETS, RICHARD. "Character as Structure: Ironic
Parallel and Transformation in 'The Blue Hotel.' " *Studies in
Short Fiction*, 5 (1968), 294–95.

1389. WARD, J. A. " 'The Blue Hotel' and 'The Killers.' " *The
CEA Critic*, 21, no. 6 (1959), 1, 7–8.

1390. WEINIG, SISTER MARY ANTHONY. "Heroic Convention in
'The Blue Hotel.' " *Stephen Crane Newsletter*, 2, no. 3 (1968), 6–7.

1391. WOLFORD, CHESTER L. "The Eagle and the Crow: High
Tragedy and the Epic in 'The Blue Hotel.' " *Prairie Schooner*, 51
(1977), 260–74.

1392. WYCHERLEY, H. ALAN. "Crane's 'The Blue Hotel': How
Many Collaborators?" *American Notes & Queries*, 4 (1966), 88.

See also 376, 399, 507, 559, 564, 583, 597, 695, 1436, 1471, 1475,
1477, 1482, 1488, 1490, 1500, 1502, 1506, 1508, 1511, 1519,
1520, 1524, 1526, 1533, 1535.

"The Bride Comes to Yellow Sky"

1393. COOK, ROBERT G. "Stephen Crane's 'The Bride Comes to
Yellow Sky.' " *Studies in Short Fiction*, 2 (1965), 368–69.

1394. FERGUSON, S. C. "Crane's 'The Bride Comes to Yellow
Sky.' " *The Explicator*, 21 (1963), item 59.

1395. JAMES, OVERTON PHILIP. "The 'Game' in 'The Bride
Comes to Yellow Sky.' " *Xavier University Studies*, 4 (1965), 3–11.

1396. MAROVITZ, SANFORD E. "Scratchy the Demon in 'The
Bride Comes to Yellow Sky.' " *Tennessee Studies In Literature*, 16
(1971), 137–40.

1397. MONTEIRO, GEORGE. "Stephen Crane's 'The Bride Comes
to Yellow Sky.' " In *Approaches to the Short Story*. Ed. Neil D.
Isaacs and Louis H. Leiter. San Francisco, CA: Chandler, 1963.
pp. 221–37.

1398. **TIBBETTS, A. M.** "Stephen Crane's 'The Bride Comes to Yellow Sky.'" *English Journal*, 54 (1965), 314–16.

1399. **WEST, RAY B., JR.** "The Use of Action in 'The Bride Comes to Yellow Sky.'" In *The Art of Writing Fiction*. Ed. Ray B. West, Jr. New York: Crowell, 1968. pp. 134–40.

Also see 360, 384, 439, 478, 484, 507, 511, 597, 1427, 1471, 1488, 1500, 1508, 1511, 1519, 1522, 1524, 1526, 1531, 1533.

"The Clan of No-Name"

1400. **OSBORN, NEAL J.** "The Riddle in 'The Clan': A Key to Crane's Major Fiction?" *Bulletin of The New York Public Library*, 69 (1965), 247–58.

See also 1488, 1500, 1519.

"Dan Emmonds"

1401. **GILKES, LILLIAN B.** "No Hoax: A Reply to Mr. Stallman." *Studies in Short Fiction*, 2 (1964), 77–83.

1402. ———. "Stephen Crane's 'Dan Emmonds': A Pig in a Storm." *Studies in Short Fiction*, 2 (1964), 66–71.

1403. **MONTEIRO, GEORGE.** "Stephen Crane's Dan Emmonds: A Case Reargued." *The Serif*, 6, no. 1 (1969), 32–36.

1404. **STALLMAN, R. W.** "Was Crane's Sketch of the Fleet off Crete a Journalistic Hoax? A Reply to Miss Gilkes." *Studies in Short Fiction*, 2 (1964), 72–76.

1405. ———, **ED. WITH AN INTRO.** "New Short Fiction by Stephen Crane: I—Dan Emmonds." *Studies in Short Fiction*, 1 (1963), 1–7.

See also 1489, 1519, 1524.

"The Dark Brown Dog"

See 1488.

"Death and the Child"

1406. **[KATZ, JOSEPH].** "An Early Draft of 'Death and the Child.'" *Stephen Crane Newsletter*, 3, no. 3 (1969), 1, 2.

See also 559, 1488, 1500, 1508, 1511, 1517, 1519, 1521, 1524.

"A Desertion"

See 1501.

"A Duel Between an Alarm Clock and a Suicidal Purpose"

See 1524.

"The Duel That Was Not Fought"

See 1488.

"An Episode of War"

See 510, 1488, 1508.

"An Experiment in Luxury"

See 1470, 1471, 1508, 1529.

"An Experiment in Misery"

1407. BASSAN, MAURICE. "The Design of Stephen Crane's Bowery 'Experiment.' " *Studies in Short Fiction*, 1 (1964), 129–32.
1408. BONNER, THOMAS, JR. "Crane's 'An Experiment in Misery.' " *The Explicator*, 34 (1976), item 56.
1409. JOHNSON, CLARENCE O. "Crane's 'Experiment in Misery.' " *The Explicator*, 35, no. 4 (1977), 20–21.
1410. NAGEL, JAMES. "Structure and Theme in Crane's 'An Experiment in Misery.' " *Studies in Short Fiction*, 10 (1973), 169–74.
See also 1470, 1471, 1487, 1500, 1508, 1524, 1529.

"An Explosion of Seven Babes"

See 1488.

"The Fight"

See 1519.

"The Five White Mice"

See 1471, 1488, 1511, 1519, 1524, 1526.

"Flanagan and His Short Filibustering Adventure"

See 1457, 1511, 1519.

"Four Men in a Cave"

See 1488, 1508.

"A Ghoul's Accountant"

See 1488.

"God Rest Ye, Merry Gentlemen"

See 1524.

"Great Bugs at Onondaga"

See 1524.

"His New Mittens"

See 1500, 1512, 1536.

"The Holler Tree"

See 1488.

"Horses—One Dash"

See 1511, 1516, 1519, 1531.

"How the Ocean Was Formed"

1411. ANDREWS, WILLIAM L. "A New Stephen Crane Fable." *American Literature*, 47 (1975), 113–14.

"In the Country of Rhymers and Writers"

1412. STALLMAN, R. W., ED. WITH INTROS. "New Short Fiction by Stephen Crane: II." *Studies in Short Fiction*, 1 (1964), 147–52.

"In the Tenderloin"

See 1519.

"Killing His Bear"

See 1471, 1474, 1488, 1508, 1523.

"A Little Pilgrimage"

1413. MONTEIRO, GEORGE. "Whilomville as Judah: Crane's 'A Little Pilgrimage.' " *Renascence*, 19 (1967), 184–89.
See also 1519.

"The Little Regiment"

1414. IVES, C. B. " 'The Little Regiment' of Stephen Crane at the Battle of Fredericksburg." *The Midwest Quarterly*, 8 (1967), 247–60.
See also 1481.

"The Lover and the Tell-Tale"

See 1512, 1519.

"Lynx-Hunting"

See 1512, 1519.

"A Man And—Some Others"

See 1471, 1483, 1488, 1511, 1516, 1519, 1524, 1531.

"The Men in the Storm"

1415. KATZ, JOSEPH. "Theodore Dreiser and Stephen Crane: Studies in a Literary Relationship." In *Stephen Crane in Transition: Centenary Essays*. Ed. Joseph Katz. DeKalb: Northern Illinois Univ. Press, 1972. pp. 174–204.

1416. **MONTEIRO, GEORGE.** "Society and Nature in Stephen Crane's 'The Men in the Storm.' " *Prairie Schooner*, 45 (1971), 13–17.
See also 1488, 1508, 1524, 1529.

"The Mesmeric Mountain"

See 1488, 1508.

"The Monster"

1417. **ANDERSON, MARGARET P.** "A Note on 'John Twelve' in Stephen Crane's *The Monster*." *American Notes & Queries*, 15 (1976), 23–24.
1418. **COOLEY, JOHN R.** " 'The Monster'—Stephen Crane's 'Invisible Man.' " *The Markham Review*, 5 (1975), 10–14.
1419. **FOSTER, MALCOLM.** "The Black Crepe Veil: The Significance of Stephen Crane's *The Monster*." *The International Fiction Review*, 3 (1976), 87–91.
1420. **HAFLEY, JAMES.** " 'The Monster' and the Art of Stephen Crane." *Accent*, 19 (1959), 159–65.
1421. **IVES, C. B.** "Symmetrical Design in Four of Stephen Crane's Stories." *Ball State University Forum*, 10, no. 1 (1969), 17–26.
1422. **KAHN, SY.** "Stephen Crane and the Giant Voice in the Night: An Explication of 'The Monster.' " In *Essays in Modern American Literature*. Ed. Richard E. Langford, et al. Deland, FL: Stetson Univ. Press, 1963. pp. 35–45.
1423. **MODLIN, CHARLES E., AND JOHN R. BYERS, JR.** "Stephen Crane's 'The Monster' as Christian Allegory." *The Markham Review*, 3 (1973), 110–13.
1424. **MONTEIRO, GEORGE.** "Stephen Crane and the Antinomies of Christian Charity." *The Centennial Review*, 16 (1972), 91–104.
1425. **TENENBAUM, RUTH BETSY.** "The Artful Monstrosity of Crane's *Monster*." *Studies in Short Fiction*, 14 (1977), 403–05.
See also 203, 559, 576, 1475, 1488, 1489, 1498, 1500, 1506, 1508, 1512, 1519, 1524, 1526, 1536.

"Moonlight on the Snow"

1426. **[KATZ, JOSEPH].** "An Early Draft of 'Moonlight on the Snow.' " *Stephen Crane Newsletter*, 3, no. 4 (1969), 1–2.
1427. **MONTEIRO, GEORGE.** "Stephen Crane's 'Yellow Sky' Sequel." *The Arizona Quarterly*, 30 (1974), 119–26.
See also 1500, 1511, 1519.

"A Mystery of Heroism"

1428. **WITHERINGTON, PAUL.** "Stephen Crane's 'A Mystery of

Heroism': Some Redefinitions." *English Journal*, 58 (1969), 201–04, 218.
See also 1481, 1508, 1519, 1521, 1526.

"Ol' Bennet and the Indians"

See 1488.

"The Open Boat"

1429. **AUTREY, MAX L.** "The Word Out of the Sea: A View of Crane's 'The Open Boat.' " *The Arizona Quarterly*, 30 (1974), 101–110.

1430. **BRENNAN, JOSEPH X.** "Stephen Crane and the Limits of Irony." *Criticism*, 11 (1969), 183–200.

1431. **BROER, LAWRENCE.** "The Open Boat." In *Instructor's Manual for* "The Art of Fiction," Second Edition. Ed. R. F. Dietrich and Roger H. Sundell. New York: Holt, Rinehart and Winston, 1974. pp. 116–24.

1432. **BUITENHUIS, PETER.** "The Essentials of Life: 'The Open Boat' as Existentialist Fiction." *Modern Fiction Studies*, 5 (1959), 243–50.

1433. **BURNS, LANDON C., JR.** "On 'The Open Boat.' " *Studies in Short Fiction*, 3 (1966), 455–57.

1434. **COLVERT, JAMES B.** "Style and Meaning in Stephen Crane: *The Open Boat.*" *Texas Studies in English*, 37 (1958), 34–45.

1435. **DENDINGER, LLOYD N.** "Stephen Crane's Inverted Use of Key Images of 'The Rime of the Ancient Mariner.' " *Studies in Short Fiction*, 5 (1968), 192–94.

1436. **DICKERSON, LYNN C., II.** "Stephen Crane and the Dispossessed Character." In *A* Festschrift *for Professor Marguerite Roberts, on the Occasion of Her Retirement from Westhampton College, University of Richmond, Virginia.* Ed. Frieda Elaine Penninger. Richmond, VA: Univ. of Richmond, 1976. pp. 188–204.

1437. **DOW, EDDY.** "Cigars, Matches, and Men in 'The Open Boat.' " *RE: Artes Liberales*, 2, no. 1 (1975), 47–49.

1438. **FREDERICK, JOHN T.** "The Fifth Man in 'The Open Boat.' " *The CEA Critic*, 30, no. 8 (1968), 1, 12–14.

1439. **FULLER, MARY ELBIN.** "The Subtle Metaphor." *English Journal*, 57 (1968), 708–09.

1440. **GERSTENBERGER, DONNA.** " 'The Open Boat': Additional Perspective." *Modern Fiction Studies*, 17 (1971), 557–61.

1441. **GOING, WILLIAM T.** "William Higgins and Crane's 'The Open Boat': A Note about Fact and Fiction." *Papers on English Language & Literature*, 1 (1965), 79–82.

1442. **GULLASON, THOMAS A.** "The New Criticism and the Older

Ones: Another Ride in 'The Open Boat.' " *The CEA Critic*, 31, no. 9 (1969), 8.

1443. HAGEMANN, E. R. " 'Sadder than the End': Another Look at 'The Open Boat.' " In *Stephen Crane in Transition: Centenary Essays*. Ed. Joseph Katz. DeKalb: Northern Illinois Univ. Press, 1972. pp. 66–85.

1444. KATZ, JOSEPH. "Stephen Crane, 'Samuel Carlton,' and a Recovered Letter." *Nineteenth-Century Fiction*, 23 (1968), 220–25.

1445. LYTLE, ANDREW. " 'The Open Boat': A Pagan Tale." In *The Hero with the Private Parts*. Baton Rouge: Louisiana State Univ. Press, 1966. pp. 60–75.

1446. MARCUS, MORDECAI. "The Three-Fold View of Nature in 'The Open Boat.' " *Philological Quarterly*, 41 (1962), 511–15.

1447. METZGER, CHARLES R. "Realistic Devices in Stephen Crane's 'The Open Boat.' " *The Midwest Quarterly*, 4 (1962), 47–54.

1448. MEYERS, ROBERT. "Crane's 'The Open Boat.' " *The Explicator*, 21 (1963), item 60.

1449. MONTEIRO, GEORGE. "The Logic Beneath 'The Open Boat.' " *The Georgia Review*, 26 (1972), 326–35.

1450. NAPIER, JAMES J. "Indifference of Nature in Crane and Camus." *The CEA Critic*, 28, no. 5 (1966), 11–12.

1451. _____. "Land Imagery in 'The Open Boat.' " *The CEA Critic*, 29, no. 7 (1967), 15.

1452. _____. "Touché." *The CEA Critic*, 30, no. 8 (1968), 15.

1453. RANDEL, WILLIAM. "The Cook in 'The Open Boat.' " *American Literature*, 34 (1962), 405–11.

1454. _____. "From Slate to Emerald Green: More Light on Crane's Jacksonville Visit." *Nineteenth-Century Fiction*, 19 (1965), 357–68.

1455. _____. "Stephen Crane's Jacksonville." *The South Atlantic Quarterly*, 62 (1963), 268–74.

1456. REED, KENNETH T. " 'The Open Boat' and Dante's *Inferno*: Some Undiscovered Analogues." *Stephen Crane Newsletter*, 4, no. 4 (1970), 1–3.

1457. SKERRETT, JOSEPH T., JR. "Changing Seats in the Open Boat: Alternative Attitudes in Two Stories by Stephen Crane." *Studies in the Humanities*, 4, no. 1 (1974), 22–27.

1458. SMITH, LEVERETT T., JR. "Stephen Crane's Calvinism." *The Canadian Review of American Studies*, 2 (1971), 13–25.

1459. STALLMAN, R. W. "Journalist Crane in that Dinghy." *Bulletin of The New York Public Library*, 72 (1968), 261–77.

1460. _____. "The Land-Sea Irony in 'The Open Boat.' " *The CEA Critic*, 30, no. 8 (1968), 15.

1461. STAPPENBECK, HERB. "Crane's 'The Open Boat.'" *The Explicator*, 34 (1976), item 41.

1462. WHITE, W. M. "The Crane-Hemingway Code: A Reevaluation." *Ball State University Forum*, 10, no. 2 (1969), 15–20.

See also 2, 356, 399, 447, 454, 479, 481, 493, 559, 565, 597, 1471, 1475, 1477, 1478, 1488, 1490, 1500, 1508, 1511, 1518–1520, 1522, 1524, 1526, 1528, 1533, 1534.

"The Pace of Youth"

1463. SCHELLHORN, G. C. "Stephen Crane's 'The Pace of Youth.'" *The Arizona Quarterly*, 25 (1969), 334–42.

See also 1508, 1511.

"A Poker Game"

See 1511.

"The Price of the Harness"

See 1519, 1521, 1524.

"A Self-Made Man"

See 1519.

"Shame"

See 1500.

"The Silver Pageant"

1464. OSBORN, NEAL J. "Optograms, George Moore, and Crane's 'Silver Pageant.'" *American Notes & Queries*, 4 (1965), 39–40.

"The Stove"

See 1519.

"A Tale of Mere Chance"

See 1501.

"Three Miraculous Soldiers"

1465. MAYER, CHARLES W. "Stephen Crane and the Realistic Tradition: 'Three Miraculous Soldiers.'" *The Arizona Quarterly*, 30 (1974), 127–34.

"Twelve O'Clock"

See 1511, 1519.

"Uncle Jake and the Bell-Handle"

1466. HOFFMAN, DANIEL G. "Stephen Crane's First Story." *Bulletin of The New York Public Library*, 64 (1960), 273–78.

"The Upturned Face"

1467. WITHERINGTON, PAUL. "Public and Private Order in Stephen Crane's 'The Upturned Face.' " *The Markham Review*, 6 (Summer 1977), 70–71.
See also 374, 1488, 1500, 1508.

"The Veteran"
See 1488, 1500.

"War Memories"
See 1500, 1508.

"When Every One is Panic-Stricken"
See 1471, 1524.

"Why did the Young Clerk Swear? Or, the Unsatisfactory French"
See 480, 1519.

"The Wise Men: A Detail of American Life in Mexico"
See 1511, 1531.

General Studies

1468. ARNOLD, HANS. "Stephen Crane's 'Wyoming Valley Tales': Their Source and their Place in the Author's War Fiction." *Jahrbuch für Amerikastudien*, 4 (1959), 161–69.
1469. BASSAN, MAURICE. "Introduction." In *Stephen Crane: A Collection of Critical Essays*. Englewood Cliffs, NJ: Prentice-Hall, 1967. pp. 1–11.
1470. ———. "Stephen Crane and 'The Eternal Mystery of Social Condition.' " *Nineteenth-Century Fiction*, 19 (1965), 387–94.
1471. BERGON, FRANK. *Stephen Crane's Artistry*. New York: Columbia Univ. Press, 1975.
1472. BROWN, ELLEN A. "Stephen Crane's *Whilomville Stories*: A Backward Glance." *The Markham Review*, 3 (1973), 105–09.
1473. BRUCCOLI, MATTHEW J., AND JOSEPH KATZ. "Scholarship and Mere Artifacts: The British and Empire Publications of Stephen Crane." *Studies in Bibliography*, 22 (1969), 277–87.
1474. CADY, EDWIN H. "Introduction." In *Tales, Sketches, and Reports*, by Stephen Crane. Ed. Fredson Bowers. Charlottesville: Univ. Press of Virginia, 1973. pp. xxi–xli.

1475. _____. *Stephen Crane*. New York: Twayne, 1962.

1476. _____. "Stephen Crane and the Strenuous Life." *ELH*, 28 (1961), 376–82.

1477. CAZEMAJOU, JEAN. *Stephen Crane*. Minneapolis: Univ. of Minnesota Press, 1969.

1478. _____. "Stephen Crane." In *Seven Novelists in the American Naturalist Tradition: An Introduction*. Ed. Charles Child Walcutt. Minneapolis: Univ. of Minnesota Press, 1974. pp. 21–54.

1479. CHASE, RICHARD. "Introduction." In *The Red Badge of Courage and Other Writings*, by Stephen Crane. Boston, MA: Houghton Mifflin, 1960. pp. vii–xxi.

1480. COLVERT, JAMES B. "Introduction." In *Tales of War*, by Stephen Crane. Ed. Fredson Bowers. Charlottesville: Univ. Press of Virginia, 1970. pp. xi–xxxvi.

1481. _____. "Stephen Crane: Style as Invention." In *Stephen Crane in Transition: Centenary Essays*. Ed. Joseph Katz. DeKalb: Northern Illinois Univ. Press, 1972. pp. 127–52.

1482. _____. "Structure and Theme in Stephen Crane's Fiction." *Modern Fiction Studies*, 5 (1959), 199–208.

1483. DEAMER, ROBERT GLEN. "Stephen Crane and The Western Myth." *Western American Literature*, 7 (1972), 111–23.

1484. DEAN, JAMES L. "The Wests of Howells and Crane." *American Literary Realism, 1870–1910*, 10 (1977), 254–66.

1485. EDWARDS, FOREST CAROLL. "Decorum: Its Genesis and Function in Stephen Crane." *The Texas Quarterly*, 18, no. 2 (1975), 131–43.

1486. FOX, AUSTIN McC. "Introduction: The Gossip and the Legends." In *Maggie and Other Stories*, by Stephen Crane. New York: Washington Square Press, 1960. pp. v–xviii.

1487. FRYCKSTEDT, OLOV W. "Introduction." In *Stephen Crane: Uncollected Writings*. Stockholm: Almqvist & Wiksell, 1963, pp. xvii–lxvii.

1488. GIBSON, DONALD B. *The Fiction of Stephen Crane*. Carbondale and Edwardsville: Southern Illinois Univ. Press, 1968.

1489. GILKES, LILLIAN. "Stephen Crane and the Biographical Fallacy: The Cora Influence." *Modern Fiction Studies*, 16 (1970), 441–61.

1490. GRIFFITH, CLARK. "Stephen Crane and the Ironic Last Word." *Philological Quarterly*, 47 (1968), 83–91.

1491. GULLASON, THOMAS A. "Introduction." In *The Complete Short Stories & Sketches of Stephen Crane*. Garden City, NY: Doubleday, 1963. pp. 19–45.

1492. _____. "The Significance of 'Wounds in the Rain.' " *Modern Fiction Studies*, 5 (1959), 235–42.

1493. _____. "Stephen Crane: In Nature's Bosom." In *American Literary Naturalism: A Reassessment*. Ed. Yoshinobu Hakutani and Lewis Fried. Heidelberg: Carl Winter, 1975. pp. 37–56.

1494. _____. "Stephen Crane and the *Arena*: Three 'Lost' Reviews." *The Papers of the Bibliographical Society of America*, 65 (1971), 297–99.

1495. _____. "Stephen Crane as Short-Story Writer: An Introduction." In *Stephen Crane's Career: Perspectives and Evaluations*. Ed. Thomas A. Gullason. New York: New York Univ. Press, 1972. pp. 407–09.

1496. _____. "A Stephen Crane Find: Nine Newspaper Sketches." *Southern Humanities Review*, 2 (1968), 1–37.

1497. _____. "Stephen Crane's Private War on Yellow Journalism." *The Huntington Library Quarterly*, 22 (1959), 201–08.

1498. _____. "Stephen Crane's Short Stories: The True Road." In *Stephen Crane's Career: Perspectives and Evaluations*. Ed. Thomas A. Gullason. New York: New York Univ. Press, 1972. pp. 470–85.

1499. HALLAM, GEORGE W. "Some New Stephen Crane Items." *Studies in Bibliography*, 20 (1967), 263–66.

1500. HOLTON, MILNE. *Cylinder of Vision: The Fiction and Journalistic Writing of Stephen Crane*. Baton Rouge: Louisiana State Univ. Press, 1972.

1501. ITABASHI, YOSHIE. "New York City Sketches—Crane's Creed and Art." *Studies in English Literature* (Tokyo), 48 (1972), 243–58.

1502. JOHNSON, GEORGE W. "Stephen Crane's Metaphor of Decorum." *PMLA*, 78 (1963), 250–56.

1503. KARLEN, ARNO. "The Craft of Stephen Crane." *The Georgia Review*, 28 (1974), 470–84.

1504. [KATZ, JOSEPH]. "*The Open Boat and Other Stories*: Dedication and Contents." *Stephen Crane Newsletter*, 3, no. 4 (1969), 9, 10.

1505. KAZIN, ALFRED. "The Scholar Cornered: A Procession of Children." *The American Scholar*, 33 (1964), 171–73, 176–78, 180–83.

1506. KNAPP, DANIEL. "Son of Thunder: Stephen Crane and the Fourth Evangelist." *Nineteenth-Century Fiction*, 24 (1969), 253–91.

1507. LAFRANCE, MARSTON. "The Ironic Parallel in Stephen Crane's 1892 Newspaper Correspondence." *Studies in Short Fiction*, 6 (1968), 101–03.

1508. _____. *A Reading of Stephen Crane*. Oxford: Clarendon Press, 1971.

1509. _____. "Stephen Crane in Our Time." In *The Chief Glory of Every People: Essays on Classic American Writers*. Ed. Matthew J. Bruccoli. Carbondale and Edwardsville: Southern Illinois Univ. Press, 1973. pp. 25-51.

1510. LEAVER, FLORENCE. "Isolation in the Work of Stephen Crane." *The South Atlantic Quarterly*, 61 (1962), 521-32.

1511. LEVENSON, J. C. "Introduction." In *Tales of Adventure*, by Stephen Crane. Ed. Fredson Bowers. Charlottesville: Univ. Press of Virginia, 1970. pp. xv-cxxxii.

1512. _____. "Introduction." In *Tales of Whilomville*, by Stephen Crane. Ed. Fredson Bowers. Charlottesville: Univ. Press of Virginia, 1969. pp. xi-lx.

1513. _____. "Stephen Crane." In *Major Writers of America*. Ed. Perry Miller. 2 vols. New York: Harcourt, Brace & World, 1962. II, 383-97.

1514. MILNE, W. GORDON. "Stephen Crane: Pioneer in Technique." *Die Neueren Sprachen*, 58 (1959), 297-303.

1515. ØVERLAND, ORM. "The Impressionism of Stephen Crane: A Study in Style and Technique." In *Americana Norvegica: Norwegian Contributions to American Studies*, Vol. 1. Ed. Sigmund Skard and Henry H. Wasser. Oslo: Gyldendal Norsk, 1966. pp. 239-85.

1516. PARADES, RAYMUND A. "Stephen Crane and The Mexican." *Western American Literature*, 6 (1971), 31-38.

1517. ROGERS, RODNEY O. "Stephen Crane and Impressionism." *Nineteenth-Century Fiction*, 24 (1969), 292-304.

1518. SCHNEIDER, ROBERT W. "Stephen Crane and the Drama of Transition." *Midcontinent American Studies Journal*, 2, no. 1 (1961), 1-16.

1519. SOLOMON, ERIC. *Stephen Crane: From Parody to Realism*. Cambridge, MA: Harvard Univ. Press, 1966.

1520. _____. *Stephen Crane in England: A Portrait of the Artist*. Columbus: Ohio State Univ. Press, 1964.

1521. _____. "Stephen Crane's War Stories." *Texas Studies in Literature and Language*, 3 (1961), 67-80.

1522. STALLMAN, R. W. "Crane's Short Stories." In *The Houses That James Built and Other Literary Studies*. East Lansing: Michigan State Univ. Press, 1961. pp. 103-10.

1523. _____. "Introduction." In *Stephen Crane: Sullivan County Tales and Sketches*. Ames: Iowa State Univ. Press, 1968. pp. 3-24.

1524. _____. *Stephen Crane: A Biography*. New York: Braziller, 1968.

1525. _____, AND E. R. HAGEMANN. "Preface." In *The New*

York City Sketches of Stephen Crane and Related Pieces. New York: New York Univ. Press, 1966. pp. ix–xvi.

1526. STEIN, WILLIAM BYSSHE. "Stephen Crane's *Homo Absurdus.*" *Bucknell Review*, 8 (1959), 168–88.

1527. STRONKS, JAMES B. "Stephen Crane's English Years: The Legend Corrected." *The Papers of the Bibliographical Society of America*, 57 (1963), 340–49.

1528. TANNER, TONY. "Stephen Crane's Long Dream of War." *London Magazine*, NS 8, no. 9 (1968), 5–19.

1529. TRACHTENBERG, ALAN. "Experiments in Another Country: Stephen Crane's City Sketches." *The Southern Review*, NS 10 (1974), 265–85.

1530. VANOUSE, DONALD. "Popular Culture in the Writings of Stephen Crane." *Journal of Popular Culture*, 10 (1976), 424–30.

1531. VORPAHL, BEN MERCHANT. "Murder by the Minute: Old and New in 'The Bride Comes to Yellow Sky.' " *Nineteenth-Century Fiction*, 26 (1971), 196–218.

1532. WEATHERFORD, RICHARD M. "Introduction." In *Stephen Crane: The Critical Heritage.* London: Routledge & Kegan Paul, 1973. pp. 1–34.

1533. WEST, RAY B., JR. "Stephen Crane: Author in Transition." *American Literature*, 34 (1962), 215–28.

1534. WESTBROOK, MAX. "Stephen Crane: The Pattern of Affirmation." *Nineteenth-Century Fiction*, 14 (1959), 219–29.

1535. ———. "Stephen Crane's Social Ethic." *American Quarterly*, 14 (1962), 587–96.

1536. ———. "Whilomville: The Coherence of Radical Language." In *Stephen Crane in Transition: Centenary Essays.* Ed. Joseph Katz. DeKalb: Northern Illinois Univ. Press, 1972. pp. 86–105.

Bibliography

1537. BEEBE, MAURICE, AND THOMAS A. GULLASON. "Criticism of Stephen Crane: A Selected Checklist with an Index to Studies of Separate Works." *Modern Fiction Studies*, 5 (1959), 282–91.

1538. BRAUNSTEIN, SIMEON. "A Checklist of Writings by and about Stephen Crane in *The Fra.*" *Stephen Crane Newsletter*, 3, no. 2 (1968), 8.

1539. COPPA, JOSEPH. "Stephen Crane Bibliography." *Thoth*, 13, no. 3 (1973), 45–46.

1540. DENNIS, SCOTT A. "Stephen Crane Bibliography." *Thoth*, 11, no. 3 (1971), 33–34.

1541. ENGLE, JAMES D. "Stephen Crane Bibliography." *Thoth*, 15, no. 3 (1975), 27–28.

1542. FERSTEL, JOHN W. "Stephen Crane Bibliography." *Thoth*, 12, no. 3 (1972), 39–40.

1543. FORSTER, IMOGENE, ED. "The *Thoth* Annual Bibliography of Stephen Crane Scholarship." *Thoth*, 10, no. 2 (1969), 25–27.

1544. FRASER, ROBERT S., ED. "The *Thoth* Annual Bibliography of Stephen Crane Scholarship." *Thoth*, 9 (1968), 58–61.

1545. GROSS, THEODORE L., AND STANLEY WERTHEIM. *Hawthorne, Melville, Stephen Crane: A Critical Bibliography*. New York: Free Press, 1971.

1546. [GULLASON, THOMAS A.] "Selected Bibliography: Stephen Crane and His Writings." In *Stephen Crane's Career: Perspectives and Evaluations*. Ed. Thomas A. Gullason. New York: New York Univ. Press, 1972. pp. 496–532.

1547. HAGEMANN, E. R. "Stephen Crane and *The Argonaut*: 1895–1901." *Stephen Crane Newsletter*, 5, no. 1 (1970), 8–11.

1548. ———. "Stephen Crane in the Pages of *Life* (1896–1901): A Checklist." *Stephen Crane Newsletter*, 3, no. 3 (1969), 1, 3–5.

1549. HUDSPETH, ROBERT N., ED. "A Bibliography of Stephen Crane Scholarship: 1893–1962." *Thoth*, 4 (1963), 30–58.

1550. ———, ED. "The *Thoth* Annual Bibliography of Stephen Crane Scholarship." *Thoth*, 5 (1964), 85–87; 6 (1965), 31–33; 7 (1966), 76–77; 8 (1967), 98–99.

1551. ———, ET AL. "A Bibliography of Stephen Crane Scholarship: 1893–1969." *Thoth*, Special Supplement (Fall 1970), pp. 3–38.

1552. KATZ, JOSEPH. "Afterword: Resources for the Study of Stephen Crane." In *Stephen Crane in Transition: Centenary Essays*. Ed. Joseph Katz. DeKalb: Northern Illinois Univ. Press, 1972. pp. 205–31.

1553. ———. *The Merrill Checklist of Stephen Crane*. Columbus, OH: Merrill, 1969.

1554. ———. "Quarterly Checklist of Stephen Crane Scholarship." *Stephen Crane Newsletter*, 1, no. 1 (1966), 4–6; 1, no. 2 (1966), 6–8; 1, no. 3 (1967), 6–7; 1, no. 4 (1967), 7–8; 2, no. 1 (1967), 11–12; 2, no. 2 (1967), 10–12; 2, no. 3 (1968), 12; 2, no. 4 (1968), 11–12; 3, no. 1 (1968), 12; 3, no. 2 (1968), 11–12; 3, no. 3 (1969), 12; 3, no. 4 (1969), 11–12; 4, no. 1 (1969), 6, 8; 4, no. 2 (1969), 11–12; 4, no. 3 (1970), 12; 4, no. 4 (1970), 12; 5, no. 1 (1970), 12.

1555. LAFRANCE, MARSTON. "Stephen Crane Scholarship Today and Tomorrow." *American Literary Realism, 1870–1910*, 7 (1974), 125–35.

1556. MAY, CANDACE. "Stephen Crane Bibliography." *Thoth*, 14, nos. 2–3 (1974), 53–55.

1557. MONTEIRO, GEORGE. "Stephen Crane and *Public Opinion*:

An Annotated Checklist, an Unrecorded Parody, and a Review of *The O'Ruddy.*" *Stephen Crane Newsletter*, 5, no. 1 (1970), 5–8.
1558. PIZER, DONALD. "Stephen Crane." In *Fifteen American Authors before 1900: Bibliographic Essays on Research and Criticism.* Ed. Robert A. Rees and Earl N. Harbert. Madison: Univ. of Wisconsin Press, 1971. pp. 97–137.
1559. SLOTE, BERNICE. "Stephen Crane in the Nebraska *State Journal,* 1894–1896." *Stephen Crane Newsletter*, 3, no. 4 (1969), 4–5.
1560. STALLMAN, R. W. *Stephen Crane: A Critical Bibliography.* Ames: Iowa State Univ. Press, 1972.
1561. WEATHERFORD, RICHARD M. "Stephen Crane in *The Lotus* and *Chips.*" *Stephen Crane Newsletter*, 4, no. 3 (1970), 2–3.

CRAWFORD, FRANCIS MARION

Bibliography

1562. MORAN, JOHN C. "An F. Marion Crawford Miscellany." *The Papers of the Bibliographical Society of America*, 71 (1977), 369–73.
1563. PILKINGTON, JOHN, JR. "A Crawford Bibliography." *The University of Mississippi Studies in English*, 4 (1963), 1–20.
1564. ———. "Francis Marion Crawford (1854–1909)." *American Literary Realism, 1870–1910*, 4 (1971), 177–82.

CREELEY, ROBERT

"The Dress"

See 1565.

General Studies

1565. HAMMOND, JOHN G. "Solipsism and the Sexual Imagination in Robert Creeley's Fiction." *Critique*, 16, no. 3 (1975), 59–69.

Bibliography

1566. JOHNSON, LEE ANN. "Robert Creeley: A Checklist, 1946–1970." *Twentieth Century Literature*, 17 (1971), 181–98.
1567. NOVIK, MARY. *Robert Creeley: An Inventory, 1945–1970.* Kent, OH: Kent State Univ. Press, 1973.
1568. ———, AND DOUGLAS CALHOUN. "Robert Creeley: A Critical Checklist." *West Coast Review*, 6, no. 3 (1972), 51–71.

CUOMO, GEORGE

"A Part of the Bargain"

See 1569.

"Sing, Choir of Angels"

See 1569.

General Studies

1569. **BRYANT, JERRY H.** "The Fiction of George Cuomo." *The Arizona Quarterly*, 30 (1974), 253–72.

CURLEY, DANIEL

"The Manhunt"

See 565.

CURWOOD, JAMES OLIVER

"The Match"

1570. **SCHLOTTMAN, DAVID HENRY.** "To Build Yet Another Fire." *Jack London Newsletter*, 8 (1975), 11–14.

DALY, CARROLL JOHN

General Studies

1571. **NOLAN, WILLIAM F.** "Carroll John Daly: The Forgotten Pioneer of the Private Eye." *The Armchair Detective*, 4 (1970), 1–4.

DANA, RICHARD HENRY, SR.

"Paul Felton"

1572. **RINGE, DONALD A.** "Early American Gothic: Brown, Dana and Allston." *American Transcendental Quarterly*, no. 19 (1973), pp. 3–8.

DARROW, CLARENCE

General Studies

*1573. **RAVITZ, ABE C.** *Clarence Darrow and the American Literary Tradition*. Cleveland, OH: Press of Western Reserve Univ., 1962.

DAVENPORT, GUY
"The Dawn in Erewhon"
See 1574.

"Tatlin!"
See 1574.

General Studies
1574. **DAVENPORT, GUY.** "Ernst Machs Max Ernst." *New Literary History*, 9 (1977), 137–48.

DAVIS, H[AROLD] L[ENOIR]
"Open Winter"
1575. **BRYANT, PAUL T.** "H. L. Davis: Viable Uses for the Past." *Western American Literature*, 3 (1968), 3–18.

Bibliography
1576. **ETULAIN, RICHARD W.** "H. L. Davis: A Bibliographical Addendum." *Western American Literature*, 5 (1970), 129–35.
1577. **KELLOGG, GEORGE.** "H. L. Davis, 1896–1960: A Bibliography." *Texas Studies in Literature and Language*, 5 (1963), 294–303.

DAVIS, REBECCA HARDING
"John Lamar"
See 18.

"Life in the Iron-Mills"
1578. **HESFORD, WALTER.** "Literary Contexts of 'Life in the Iron-Mills.'" *American Literature*, 49 (1977), 70–85.
1579. **ROSEN, NORMA.** "The Ordeal of Rebecca Harding." *The New York Times Book Review*, 15 Apr. 1973, p. 39.

"The Wife's Story"
See 5225.

General Studies
1580. **AUSTIN, JAMES C.** "Success and Failure of Rebecca Harding Davis." *Midcontinent American Studies Journal*, 3, no. 1 (1962), 44–49.

1581. **LANGFORD, GERALD.** *The Richard Harding Davis Years: A Biography of a Mother and Son.* New York: Holt, Rinehart and Winston, 1971.

DAVIS, RICHARD HARDING

"The Deserter"

1582. **SHEPHERD, ALLEN.** " 'The Best War Story [Richard Harding Davis] Ever Knew': 'The Deserter' Concluded." *The Markham Review*, 5 (1976), 39–40.

"The Nature Faker"

1583. **SOLENSTEN, JOHN.** "Richard Harding Davis' Rejection of 'The Call of the Wild.' " *Jack London Newsletter*, 4 (1971), 122–23.

General Studies

1584. **LANGFORD, GERALD.** *The Richard Harding Davis Years: A Biography of a Mother and Son.* New York: Holt, Rinehart and Winston, 1971.

1585. **OSBORN, SCOTT C.** "Richard Harding Davis: Critical Battleground." *American Quarterly*, 12 (1960), 84–92.

1586. **SOLENSTEN, JOHN.** "The Gibson Boy: A Reassessment." *American Literary Realism, 1870–1910*, 4 (1971), 303–12.

Bibliography

1587. **EICHELBERGER, CLAYTON L., AND ANN M. McDONALD.** "Richard Harding Davis (1864–1916): A Check List of Secondary Comment." *American Literary Realism, 1870–1910*, 4 (1971), 313–89.

1588. **SOLENSTEN, JOHN M.** "Richard Harding Davis (1864–1916)." *American Literary Realism, 1870–1910*, 3 (1970), 160–66.

DE FOREST, JOHN WILLIAM

"A Gentleman of the Old School"

See 18.

"Yesebel"

See 1591.

General Studies

1589. **BERGMANN, FRANK.** "Mark Twain and the Literary Misfortunes of John William DeForest." *Jahrbuch für Amerikastudien*, 13 (1968), 249–52.

1590. **HAGEMANN, E. R.** "John William DeForest Faces *The Nation.*" *American Literary Realism, 1870-1910*, 1, no. 4 (1968), 65-75.
1591. **LIGHT, JAMES F.** *John William DeForest.* New York: Twayne, 1965.

Bibliography

1592. **EICHELBERGER, CLAYTON L., ET AL.** "John William DeForest (1826-1906): A Critical Bibliography of Secondary Comment." *American Literary Realism, 1870-1910*, 1, no. 4 (1968), 1-56.
1593. **HAGEMANN, E. R.** "A John William DeForest Supplement, 1970." *American Literary Realism, 1870-1910*, 3 (1970), 148-152.
1594. **LIGHT, JAMES F.** "John William DeForest (1826-1906)." *American Literary Realism, 1870-1910*, 1, no. 1 (1967), 32-35.

DELL, FLOYD

"Jessica Screams"

1595. **TANSELLE, G. THOMAS.** "Ezra Pound and a Story of Floyd Dell's." *Notes and Queries*, NS 8 (1961), 350-52.

General Studies

1596. **HART, JOHN E.** *Floyd Dell.* New York: Twayne, 1971.

DEMBY, WILLIAM

Interviews

1597. **JOHNSON, JOE.** "Interview With William Demby." *Black Creation*, 3, no. 3 (1972), 18-21.

DENT, LESTER

General Studies

1598. **BLOSSER, FRED.** "The Man from Miami—Lester Dent's Oscar Sail." *The Armchair Detective*, 5 (1972), 93.

DE VRIES, PETER

General Studies

1599. **JELLEMA, RODERICK.** *Peter De Vries: A Critical Essay.* Grand Rapids, MI: Eerdmans, 1966.

Interviews

1600. **DAVIS, DOUGLAS M.** "An Interview with Peter De Vries." *College English*, 28 (1967), 524–28.

1601. **DE VRIES, PETER.** "An Interview in New York with Peter De Vries." *Studies in the Novel*, 1 (1969), 364–69.

1602. **NEWQUIST, ROY.** "Peter De Vries." In *Counterpoint*. Chicago: Rand McNally, 1964. pp. 146–54.

Bibliography

1603. **BOWDEN, EDWIN T.** "Peter De Vries—The First Thirty Years: A Bibliography, 1934–1964." *Texas Studies in Literature and Language*, 6 (1965), 545–70.

DICK, PHILIP K.

General Studies

1604. **DICK, PHILIP K.** "[Unpublished] Foreword to *The Preserving Machine.*" *Science-Fiction Studies*, 2 (1975), 22–23.

1605. **SUVIN, DARKO.** "P. K. Dick's Opus: Artifice as Refuge and World View (Introductory Remarks)." *Science-Fiction Studies*, 2 (1975), 8–22.

Bibliography

1606. **McNELLY, WILLIS E., AND R. D. MULLEN.** "Philip K. Dick: Manuscripts and Books." *Science-Fiction Studies*, 2 (1975), 4–8.

DOBIE, J[AMES] FRANK

General Studies

1607. **ABERNETHY, FRANCIS EDWARD.** *J. Frank Dobie.* Austin, TX: Steck-Vaughn, 1967.

1608. **BODE, WINSTON.** *J. Frank Dobie: A Portrait of Pancho.* Austin, TX: Steck-Vaughn, 1968.

1609. **CAMPBELL, JEFF H.** "Pancho at College—Toga or Sombrero?" *Southwestern American Literature*, 1 (1971), 149–55.

Bibliography

1610. **McVICKER, MARY LOUISE.** *The Writings of J. Frank Dobie: A Bibliography.* Lawton, OK: Museum of the Great Plains, 1968.

DODGE, MARY

"Our Contraband"

See 18.

DODSON, OWEN

"Come Home Early, Chile"

See 494.

DONLEAVY, J[AMES] P[ATRICK]

"The Saddest Summer of Samuel S"

1611. MASINTON, CHARLES G. "*The Saddest Summer of Samuel S.*" In *J. P. Donleavy: The Style of His Sadness and Humor.* Bowling Green, OH: Bowling Green Univ. Popular Press, 1975. pp. 45–51.

Interviews

1612. DONLEAVY, J. P. "The Art of Fiction LIII." With Molly McKaughan. *The Paris Review*, no. 63 (1975), pp. 123–66.

D[OOLITTLE], H[ILDA]

"Hipparchia"

See 1614, 1616–1618.

"Murex"

See 1614, 1616–1618.

"Secret Name"

See 1614, 1616–1618.

General Studies

1613. BRUCCOLI, MATTHEW J. "A Note on the Text." In *Palimpsest*, by H. D. Carbondale and Edwardsville: Southern Illinois Univ. Press, 1968. pp. 245–68.

1614. DUNCAN, ROBERT. "Two Chapters from *H. D.*." *TriQuarterly*, no. 12 (1968), pp. 67–98.

1615. McALMON, ROBERT. "Forewarned as regards H. D.'s Prose." In *Palimpsest*, by H. D. Carbondale and Edwardsville: Southern Illinois Univ. Press, 1968. pp. 241–44.

1616. QUINN, VINCENT. *Hilda Doolittle (H. D.).* New York: Twayne, 1967.

1617. SWANN, THOMAS BURNETT. *The Classical World of H. D.* Lincoln: Univ. of Nebraska Press, 1962.

1618. WEATHERHEAD, A. KINGSLEY. "Style in H. D.'s Novels." *Contemporary Literature*, 10 (1969), 537–56.

Bibliography

1619.   BRYER, JACKSON R., AND PAMELA ROBLYER. "H. D.: A Preliminary Checklist." *Contemporary Literature*, 10 (1969), 632-75.

DOS PASSOS, JOHN

General Studies

1620.   LANDSBERG, MELVIN. *Dos Passos' Path to* U.S.A.: *A Political Biography*. Boulder: Colorado Associated Univ. Press, 1972.
1621.   WRENN, JOHN H. *John Dos Passos*. New York: Twayne, 1961.

Interviews

1622.   DOS PASSOS, JOHN. "The Art of Fiction XLIV." With David Sanders. *The Paris Review*, no. 46 (1969), pp. 147-72.
1623.   GADO, FRANK. "John Dos Passos." In *First Person: Conversations on Writers & Writing*. Ed. Frank Gado. Schenectady, NY: Union College Press, 1973. pp. 31-62.
1624.   MADDEN, CHARLES F., ED. "John Dos Passos." In *Talks with Authors*. Carbondale and Edwardsville: Southern Illinois Univ. Press, 1968. pp. 3-11.
1625.   SANDERS, DAVID. "Interview with John Dos Passos." *Claremont Quarterly*, 11, no. 3 (1964), 89-100.

Bibliography

1626.   REINHART, VIRGINIA S. "John Dos Passos 1950-1966: Bibliography." *Twentieth Century Literature*, 13 (1967), 167-78.

DOWNING, J[OHN] HYATT

General Studies

1627.   WADDEN, ANTHONY T. "Late to the Harvest: The Fiction of J. Hyatt Downing." *Western American Literature*, 6 (1971), 203-14.

DREISER, THEODORE

"Butcher Rogaum's Door"

See 1637.

"Chains"

See 1633.

"Convention"

See 1633.

"The Cruise of the 'Idlewild' "

1628. **GRAHAM, D[ON] B.** " 'The Cruise of the "Idlewild" ': Dreiser's Revisions of a 'Rather Light' Story." *American Literary Realism, 1870–1910*, 8 (1975), 1–11.

"Free"

See 1633, 1639.

"Fulfillment"

See 1633.

"The Hand"

See 1633.

"Her Boy"

See 1637.

"The Lost Phoebe"

See 356, 1639.

"Marriage—For One"

See 1633.

"Married"

See 1633.

"The 'Mercy' of God"

See 1633.

"Nigger Jeff"

1629. **PIZER, DONALD.** "Theodore Dreiser's 'Nigger Jeff': The Development of an Aesthetic." *American Literature*, 41 (1969), 331–41.
See also 1633, 1637, 1639.

"The Old Neighborhood"

See 1633.

"Old Rogaum and His Theresa"

See 1633.

"Phantom Gold"

See 1633.

"The Prince Who Was a Thief"

See 1633.

"St. Columba and the River"

See 1633.

"The Shining Slave Makers"

1630. GRAHAM, D[ON] B. "Dreiser and Thoreau: An Early Influence." *The Dreiser Newsletter*, 7, no. 1 (1976), 1–4.
1631. ———. "Dreiser's Ant Tragedy: The Revision of 'The Shining Slave Makers.' " *Studies in Short Fiction*, 14 (1977), 41–48.
See also 1635, 1637, 1638.

"When the Old Century Was New"

See 1637, 1638.

General Studies

1632. ELIAS, ROBERT H. *Theodore Dreiser: Apostle of Nature.* Emended ed. Ithaca, NY: Cornell Univ. Press, 1970.
1633. GERBER, PHILIP L. *Plots and Characters in the Fiction of Theodore Dreiser.* Hamden, CT: Archon Books, 1977.
1634. ———. *Theodore Dreiser.* New York: Twayne, 1964.
1635. MOERS, ELLEN. *Two Dreisers.* New York: Viking, 1969.
1636. MOOKERJEE, R. N. *Theodore Dreiser: His Thought and Social Criticism.* Delhi: National, 1974.
1637. PIZER, DONALD. *The Novels of Theodore Dreiser: A Critical Study.* Minneapolis: Univ. of Minnesota Press, 1976.
1638. ———. "A Summer at Maumee: Theodore Dreiser Writes Four Stories." In *Essays Mostly on Periodical Publishing in America: A Collection in Honor of Clarence Gohdes.* Ed. James Woodress, et al. Durham, NC: Duke Univ. Press, 1973. pp. 193–204.
1639. Shapiro, Charles. *Theodore Dreiser: Our Bitter Patriot.* Carbondale: Southern Illinois Univ. Press, 1962.
1640. SWANBERG, W. A. *Dreiser.* New York: Scribner's, 1965.

Bibliography

1641. ATKINSON, HUGH C. *The Merrill Checklist of Theodore Dreiser.* Columbus, OH: Merrill, 1969.
1642. ———. *Theodore Dreiser: A Checklist.* Kent, OH: Kent State Univ. Press, 1971.

1643. **DOWELL, RICHARD W.** "Checklist: Dreiser Studies, 1969." *The Dreiser Newsletter*, 1, no. 2 (1970), 14–18.

1644. ———, **AND FREDERIC E. RUSCH.** "A Dreiser Checklist, 1970." *The Dreiser Newsletter*, 3, no. 1 (1972), 13–21.

1645. **ELIAS, ROBERT H.** "Theodore Dreiser." In *Fifteen Modern American Authors: A Survey of Research and Criticism.* Ed. Jackson R. Bryer. Durham, NC: Duke Univ. Press, 1969. pp. 101–38.

1646. ———. "Theodore Dreiser." In *Sixteen Modern American Authors: A Survey of Research and Criticism.* Ed. Jackson R. Bryer. Durham, NC: Duke Univ. Press, 1974. pp. 123–79.

1647. **PIZER, DONALD.** "The Publications of Theodore Dreiser: A Checklist." *Proof,* 1 (1971), 247–92.

1648. ———, **RICHARD W. DOWELL, AND FREDERIC E. RUSCH.** *Theodore Dreiser: A Primary and Secondary Bibliography.* Boston, MA: G. K. Hall, 1975.

1649. **RUSCH, FREDERIC E.** "A Dreiser Checklist." *The Dreiser Newsletter,* 3, no. 2 (1972), 12–19; 4, no. 1 (1973), 5–11; 4, no. 2 (1973), 12–23; 5, no. 2 (1974), 12–20; 6, no. 2 (1975), 17–24; 7, no. 2 (1976), 10–16; 8, no. 2 (1977), 9–18.

1650. **SALZMAN, JACK.** "Criticism of Theodore Dreiser: A Selected Checklist." *Modern Fiction Studies,* 23 (1977), 473–87.

1651. ———. "Theodore Dreiser (1871–1945)." *American Literary Realism, 1870–1910,* 2 (1969), 132–38.

DU BOIS, W[ILLIAM] E[DWARD] B[URGHARDT]

"Of the Coming of John"

See 1652.

General Studies

1652. **RAMPERSAD, ARNOLD.** *The Art and Imagination of W. E. B. Du Bois.* Cambridge, MA: Harvard Univ. Press, 1976.

Bibliography

1653. **PARTINGTON, PAUL G.** *W. E. B. DuBois: A Bibliography of His Published Writings.* Whittier, CA: Paul G. Partington, 1977.

DUNBAR, PAUL LAURENCE

"Anner 'Lizer's Stumblin' Block"

See 6.

"The Lynching of Jube Benson"

See 6.

"The Scapegoat"

1654. **WAKEFIELD, JOHN.** "Paul Laurence Dunbar, 'The Scapegoat' (1904)." In *The Black American Short Story in the 20th Century: A Collection of Critical Essays.* Ed. Peter Bruck. Amsterdam: B. R. Grüner, 1977. pp. 39–51.
See also 576.

General Studies

1655. **LEE, A. ROBERT.** "The Fiction of Paul Laurence Dunbar." *Negro American Literature Forum,* 8 (1974), 166–72.
1656. **MARTIN, JAY, AND GOSSIE H. HUDSON.** "Introduction to the Short Stories." In *The Paul Laurence Dunbar Reader.* Ed. Jay Martin and Gossie H. Hudson. New York: Dodd, Mead, 1975. pp. 63–66.

Bibliography

1657. **METCALF, E. W., JR.** *Paul Laurence Dunbar: A Bibliography.* Metuchen, NJ: Scarecrow, 1975.

DUNBAR-NELSON, ALICE RUTH [MOORE]

Bibliography

1658. **WILLIAMS, ORA.** "Works by and about Alice Ruth (Moore) Dunbar-Nelson: A Bibliography." *CLA Journal,* 19 (1976), 322–26.

DUNLAP, WILLIAM

"It Might Have Been Better! It Might Have Been Worse"
See 72.

DUVAL, JOHN C.

General Studies

1659. **ANDERSON, JOHN Q.** *John C. Duval: First Texas Man of Letters.* Austin, TX: Steck-Vaughn, 1967.

EAST, CHARLES

Interviews

1660. **WEAVER, GORDON.** "An Interview with Charles East." *Notes on Mississippi Writers,* 4 (1972), 87–108.

EASTLAKE, WILLIAM

General Studies

1661. **HASLAM, GERALD W.** *William Eastlake.* Austin, TX: Steck-Vaughn, 1970.

EASTMAN, CHARLES ALEXANDER

General Studies

1662. **STENSLAND, ANNA LEE.** "Charles Alexander Eastman: Sioux Storyteller and Historian." *American Indian Quarterly*, 3 (1977), 199–208.

EASTMAN, HAROLD

"The Mockingbird"

See 197.

EDWARDS, HARRY STILLWELL

"Elder Brown's Backslide"

See 571.

"His Defense"

See 571.

EGGLESTON, EDWARD

"The Gunpowder Plot"

See 83.

"Uncle Sim's Boy"

See 1663.

General Studies

1663. **RANDEL, WILLIAM.** *Edward Eggleston.* New York: Twayne, 1963.

Bibliography

1664. **RANDEL, WILLIAM.** "Edward Eggleston (1837–1902)." *American Literary Realism, 1870–1910,* 1, no. 1 (1967), 36–38.

ELKIN, STANLEY

"The Bailbondsman"

See 1667.

"I Look Out for Ed Wolfe"

1665. ELKIN, STANLEY. Introduction to "I Look Out for Ed Wolfe." In *Writer's Choice*. Ed. Rust Hills. New York: McKay, 1974. pp. 125-26.

General Studies

1666. LeClair, Thomas. "The Obsessional Fiction of Stanley Elkin." *Contemporary Literature*, 16 (1975), 146-62.
1667. Olderman, Raymond M. "The Politics of Vitality." *fiction international*, nos. 2-3 (1974), pp. 140-44.

Interviews

1668. Duncan, Jeffrey L. "A Conversation with Stanley Elkin and William H. Gass." *The Iowa Review*, 7, no. 1 (1976), 48-77.
1669. Elkin, Stanley. "The Art of Fiction LXI." With Thomas LeClair. *The Paris Review*, no. 66 (1976), pp. 55-86.
1670. _____. "Stanley Elkin on Fiction: An Interview." With Phyllis and Joseph Brent. *Prairie Schooner*, 50 (1976), 14-25.
1671. Leonard, John. "Stanley Elkin, Nice Guy." *The New York Times Book Review*, 15 Oct. 1967, p. 40.
1672. Sanders, Scott. "An Interview with Stanley Elkin." *Contemporary Literature*, 16 (1975), 131-45.

Bibliography

1673. McCaffery, Larry. "Stanley Elkin: A Bibliography, 1957-1977." *Bulletin of Bibliography and Magazine Notes*, 34 (1977), 73-76.

ELLIOTT, GEORGE P.

"Children of Ruth"

1674. Elliott, George P. Introduction to "Children of Ruth." In *Writer's Choice*. Ed. Rust Hills. New York: McKay, 1974. pp. 153-54.

"The NRACP"

See 399.

General Studies

1675. **GELFANT, BLANCHE H.** "Beyond Nihilism: The Fiction of George P. Elliott." *The Hollins Critic*, 5, no. 5 (1968), 1–6, 8–12.

ELLISON, HARLAN

"A Boy and His Dog"

1676. **CROW, JOHN, AND RICHARD ERLICH.** "Mythic Patterns in Ellison's *A Boy and His Dog.*" *Extrapolation*, 18 (1977), 162–66. *See also* 1678.

"I Have No Mouth, and I Must Scream"

See 233, 1678.

" 'Repent, Harlequin!' Said the Ticktockman"

1677. **WHITE, MICHAEL D.** "Ellison's Harlequin: Irrational Moral Action in Static Time." *Science-Fiction Studies*, 4 (1977), 161–65. *See also* 360, 484.

General Studies

*1678. **SLUSSER, GEORGE EDGAR.** *Harlan Ellison: Unrepentant Harlequin.* San Bernardino, CA: Borgo Press, 1977.

Bibliography

1679. **SWIGART, LESLIE KAY.** *Harlan Ellison: A Bibliographical Checklist.* Dallas, TX: Williams, 1973.

ELLISON, RALPH

"Battle Royal"

See 268, 483.

"Flying Home"

1680. **TRIMMER, JOSEPH F.** "Ralph Ellison's 'Flying Home.' " *Studies in Short Fiction*, 9 (1972), 175–82. *See also* 126, 333, 481, 1686, 1687.

"In a Strange Country"

See 1687.

"King of the Bingo Game"

1681. **CHAFFEE, PATRICIA.** "Slippery Ground: Ralph Ellison's Bingo Player." *Negro American Literature Forum*, 10 (1976), 23–24.

1682. **GVERESCHI, EDWARD.** "Anticipations of *Invisible Man*: Ralph Ellison's 'King of the Bingo Game.' " *Negro American Literature Forum*, 6 (1972), 122–24.

1683. **REAL, WILLI.** "Ralph Ellison, 'King of the Bingo Game' (1944)." In *The Black American Short Story in the 20th Century: A Collection of Critical Essays*. Ed. Peter Bruck. Amsterdam: B. R. Grüner, 1977. pp. 111–27.

1684. **SAUNDERS, PEARL I.** "Symbolism in Ralph Ellison's 'King of the Bingo Game.' " *CLA Journal*, 20 (1976), 35–39.

See also 399, 446.

"That I Had Wings"

See 1687.

General Studies

1685. **BONE, ROBERT.** "Ralph Ellison and the Uses of Imagination." In *Anger, and Beyond: The Negro Writer in the United States*. Ed. Herbert Hill. New York: Harper & Row, 1966. pp. 86–111.

1686. **DEUTSCH, LEONARD J.** "Ellison's Early Fiction." *Negro American Literature Forum*, 7 (1973), 53–59.

1687. **DOYLE, MARY ELLEN, S.C.N.** "In Need of Folk: The Alienated Protagonists of Ralph Ellison's Short Fiction." *CLA Journal*, 19 (1975), 165–72.

Interviews

1688. **CARSON, DAVID L.** "Ralph Ellison: Twenty Years After." *Studies in American Fiction*, 1 (1973), 1–23.

1689. **ELLISON, RALPH, AND JAMES ALAN MCPHERSON.** "Indivisible Man." *The Atlantic Monthly*, 226, no. 6 (1970), 45–60.

1690. **HARPER, MICHAEL, AND ROBERT STEPTO.** "Study & Experience: An Interview with Ralph Ellison." *The Massachusetts Review*, 18 (1977), 417–35.

1691. **HERSEY, JOHN.** "Introduction: 'A Completion of Personality'—A Talk with Ralph Ellison." In *Ralph Ellison: A Collection of Critical Essays*. Ed. John Hersey. Englewood Cliffs, NJ: Prentice-Hall, 1974. pp. 1–19.

1692. **O'BRIEN, JOHN.** "Ralph Ellison." In *Interviews with Black Writers*. Ed. John O'Brien. New York: Liveright, 1973. pp. 63–77.

1693. **REED, ISHMAEL, QUINCY TROUPE, AND STEVE CANNON.** "The Essential Ellison." *Y'bird*, 1, no. 1 (1977), 126–59.

1694. **THOMPSON, JAMES, LENNOX RAPHAEL, AND STEVE CANNON.** " 'A Very Stern Discipline': An Interview with Ralph Ellison." *Harper's Magazine*, 234 (Mar. 1967), 76–80, 83–86, 88, 90, 93–95.

Bibliography

1695. BENOIT, BERNARD, AND MICHEL FABRE. "A Bibliography of Ralph Ellison's Published Writings." *Studies in Black Literature*, 2, no. 3 (1971), 25–28.

1696. COVO, JACQUELINE. *The Blinking Eye: Ralph Waldo Ellison and His American, French, German and Italian Critics, 1952–1971: Bibliographic Essays and a Checklist*. Metuchen, NJ: Scarecrow, 1974.

1697. ———. "Ralph Waldo Ellison: Bibliographical Essays and Finding List of American Criticism, 1952–1964." *CLA Journal*, 15 (1971), 171–96.

1698. LILLARD, R. S. "A Ralph Waldo Ellison Bibliography (1914–1967)." *The American Book Collector*, 19, no. 3 (1968), 18–22.

1699. MOORER, FRANK E., AND LUGENE BAILEY. "A Selected Check List of Material by and about Ralph Ellison." *Black World*, 20, no. 2 (1970), 126–30.

1700. POLSGROVE, CAROL. "Addenda to 'A Ralph Waldo Ellison Bibliography,' 1914–1968." *The American Book Collector*, 20, no. 3 (1969), 11–12.

ERDMAN, LOULA GRACE

Interviews

1701. SEWELL, ERNESTINE. "An Interview with Loula Grace Erdman." *Southwestern American Literature*, 2 (1972), 33–41.

EVANS, MAX

Interviews

1702. M[ILTON], J[OHN] R. "Interview: Max Evans." *South Dakota Review*, 5, no. 2 (1967), 77–87.

1703. ———. "Max Evans." In *Three West: Conversations with Vardis Fisher, Max Evans, Michael Straight*. Vermillion, SD: Dakota Press, 1970. pp. 47–112.

EWER, FERDINAND C.

"The Eventful Nights of August 20th and 21st, 1854"

See 56.

FARMER, PHILIP JOSÉ

General Studies

1704. LETSON, RUSSELL. "The Worlds of Philip José Farmer." *Extrapolation*, 18 (1977), 124–30.

Bibliography

1705. **WYMER, THOMAS.** "Speculative Fiction, Bibliographies, & Philip José Farmer." *Extrapolation*, 18 (1976), 59–72.

FARRELL, JAMES T.

"Helen, I Love You"

See 1707.

General Studies

1706. **BRANCH, EDGAR M.** *James T. Farrell*. Minneapolis: Univ. of Minnesota Press, 1963.
1707. ———. *James T. Farrell*. New York: Twayne, 1971.
1708. ———, "James T. Farrell." In *Seven Novelists in the American Naturalist Tradition: An Introduction*. Ed. Charles Child Walcutt. Minneapolis: Univ. of Minnesota Press, 1974. pp. 245–89.
1709. ———. "The 1930's in James T. Farrell's Fiction." *The American Book Collector*, 21, no. 6 (1971), 9–12.
1710. **O'CONNELL, BARRY.** "The Lost World of James T. Farrell's Short Stories." *Twentieth Century Literature*, 22 (1976), 36–51.
1711. **WALLENSTEIN, BARRY.** "James T. Farrell: Critic of Naturalism." In *American Literary Naturalism: A Reassessment*. Ed. Yoshinobu Hakutani and Lewis Fried. Heidelberg: Carl Winter, 1975. pp. 154–75.

Interviews

1712. **FLYNN, DENNIS, AND JACK SALZMAN.** "An Interview with James T. Farrell." *Twentieth Century Literature*, 22 (1976), 1–10.
1713. **MADDEN, CHARLES F., ED.** "James T. Farrell." In *Talks with Authors*. Carbondale and Edwardsville: Southern Illinois Univ. Press, 1968. pp. 89–102.

Bibliography

1714. **BRANCH, EDGAR M.** "Bibliography of James T. Farrell: A Supplement." *The American Book Collector*, 17, no. 9 (1967), 9–19.
1715. ———. "Bibliography of James T. Farrell: January, 1967–August, 1970—A Supplement." *The American Book Collector*, 21, no. 6 (1971), 13–18.
1716. ———. "Bibliography of James T. Farrell, September 1970–February 1975: A Supplement." *The American Book Collector*, 26, no. 3 (1976), 17–22.
1717. ———. *A Bibliography of James T. Farrell's Writings, 1921–1957*. Philadelphia: Univ. of Pennsylvania Press, 1959.

1718. _____. "A Supplement to the Bibliography of James T. Farrell's Writings." *The American Book Collector*, 11, no. 10 (1961), 42–48.

1719. SALZMAN, JACK. "James T. Farrell: An Essay in Bibliography." *Resources for American Literary Study*, 6 (1976), 131–63.

1720. WESTLAKE, NEDA M. "The James T. Farrell Collection at the University of Pennsylvania." *The American Book Collector*, 11, no. 10 (1961), 21–23.

FAULKNER, JOHN
Bibliography

1721. WHITE, HELEN, AND REDDING S. SUGGS, JR. "John Faulkner: An Annotated Check List of His Published Works and of His Papers." *Studies in Bibliography*, 23 (1970), 217–29.

FAULKNER, WILLIAM
"An Absolution"

See 1983.

"Ad Astra"

1722. MOSES, W. R. "Victory in Defeat: 'Ad Astra' and *A Farewell to Arms.*" *The Mississippi Quarterly*, 19 (1966), 85–89.
See also 1986, 2020, 2032.

"Afternoon of a Cow"

See 2007.

"All the Dead Pilots"

See 356, 1960, 1986, 2032.

"Ambuscade"

See 212, 1960, 1983, 2007, 2068.

"Artist at Home"

See 2056.

"Barn Burning"

1723. BROER, LAWRENCE. "'Barn Burning' (Faulkner)." In *Instructor's Manual to Accompany* "The Realities of Literature." Ed. R. F. Dietrich. Waltham, MA: Xerox Publishing, 1971. pp. 65–72.

1724. FISHER, MARVIN. "The World of Faulkner's Children." *The University of Kansas City Review*, 27 (1960), 13–18.

1725. FRANKLIN, PHYLLIS. "Sarty Snopes and 'Barn Burning.'"
The Mississippi Quarterly, 21 (1968), 189–93.

1726. JOHNSTON, KENNETH G. "Time of Decline: Pickett's
Charge and the Broken Clock in Faulkner's 'Barn Burning.'"
Studies in Short Fiction, 11 (1974), 434–36.

1727. MITCHELL, CHARLES. "The Wounded Will of Faulkner's
Barn Burner." *Modern Fiction Studies*, 11 (1965), 185–89.

1728. NICOLET, WILLIAM P. "Faulkner's 'Barn Burning.'" *The
Explicator*, 34 (1975), item 25.

1729. WILSON, GAYLE EDWARD. "'Being Pulled Two Ways': The
Nature of Sarty's Choice in 'Barn Burning.'" *The Mississippi
Quarterly*, 24 (1971), 279–88.

See also 146, 399, 416, 481, 566, 595, 1957, 1983, 2007, 2044, 2056,
2069.

"The Bear"

1730. ACKERMAN, R. D. "The Immolation of Isaac McCaslin."
Texas Studies in Literature and Language, 16 (1974), 557–65.

1731. ADAMS, RICHARD P. "Focus on William Faulkner's 'The
Bear': Moses and the Wilderness." In *American Dreams, American Nightmares*. Ed. David Madden. Carbondale and Edwardsville: Southern Illinois Univ. Press, 1970. pp. 129–35.

1732. ANON. "*The Bear* and *Huckleberry Finn*: Heroic Quests for
Moral Liberation." *The Mark Twain Journal*, 12, no. 1 (1963),
12–13, 21.

1733. BACKMAN, MELVIN. "The Wilderness and the Negro in
Faulkner's 'The Bear.'" *PMLA*, 76 (1961), 595–600.

1734. [BARTH, J. ROBERT, S.J.] "Commentary." In *Religious
Perspectives in Faulkner's Fiction*. Ed. J. Robert Barth, S.J. Notre
Dame, IN: Univ. of Notre Dame Press, 1972. pp. 199–201.

1735. BAUMGARTEN, MURRAY. "The Language of Faulkner's
The Bear." *Western Humanities Review*, 15 (1961), 180–82.

1736. BEAUCHAMP, GORMAN. "The Rite of Initiation in Faulkner's *The Bear*." *The Arizona Quarterly*, 28 (1972), 319–25.

1737. BELL, H. H., JR. "A Footnote to Faulkner's 'The Bear.'"
College English, 24 (1962), 179–83.

1738. BRADFORD, M. E. "The Gum Tree Scene: Observations on
the Structure of 'The Bear.'" *Southern Humanities Review*, 1
(1967), 141–50.

1739. BROCKI, SISTER MARY DAMASCENE, CSSJ. "Faulkner and
Hemingway: Values in a Modern World." *The Mark Twain
Journal*, 11, no. 4 (1962), 5–9, 15.

1740. BROGUNER, JOSEPH. "A Source for the Commissary Entries
in *Go Down, Moses*." *Texas Studies in Literature and Language*, 14
(1972), 545–54.

1741. CARPENTER, THOMAS P. "A Gun for Faulkner's Old Ben."
American Notes & Queries, 5 (1967), 133–34.
1742. CHAPMAN, ARNOLD. "Pampas and Big Woods: Heroic Initia:ion in Güiraldes and Faulkner." *Comparative Literature*, 11
(1959), 61–77.
1743. CONNOLLY, THOMAS E. "Fate and 'the Agony of Will': Determinism in Some Works of William Faulkner." In *Essays on Determinism in American Literature*. Ed. Sydney J. Krause. Kent, OH: Kent State Univ. Press, 1964. pp. 36–52.
1744. DORSCH, ROBERT L. "An Interpretation of the Central Themes in the Work of William Faulkner." *The Emporia State Research Studies*, 11, no. 1 (1962), 5–42.
1745. EDINGER, HARRY G. "Episodes in the History of the Literary Bear." *Mosaic*, 4, no. 1 (1970), 1–12.
1746. FISHER, RICHARD E. "The Wilderness, the Commissary, and the Bedroom: Faulkner's Ike McCaslin as Hero in a Vacuum." *English Studies*, 44 (1963), 19–28.
1747. FRANK, YAKIRA H. "Correlating Language and Literature." *English Journal*, 61 (1972), 239–45.
1748. GELFANT, BLANCHE H. "Faulkner and Keats: The Ideality of Art in 'The Bear.'" *The Southern Literary Journal*, 2, no. 1 (1969), 43–65.
1749. GILLEY, LEONARD. "The Wilderness Theme in Faulkner's 'The Bear.'" *The Midwest Quarterly*, 6 (1965), 379–85.
1750. HARRISON, ROBERT. "Faulkner's 'The Bear': Some Notes on Form." *The Georgia Review*, 20 (1966), 318–27.
1751. HART, JOHN A. "That Not Impossible He: Faulkner's Third-Person Narrator." In *Studies in Faulkner*. Ed. Neal Woodruff, Jr. Pittsburgh, PA: Carnegie Institute of Technology, 1961. pp. 29–41.
1752. HARTT, JULIAN N. "The Dream of Innocence Shattered." In *The Lost Image of Man*. Baton Rouge: Louisiana State Univ. Press, 1963. pp. 38–54.
1753. HIERS, JOHN T. "Faulkner's Lord-to-God Bird in 'The Bear.'" *American Literature*, 47 (1976), 636–37.
1754. HOFFMAN, DANIEL. "William Faulkner: 'The Bear.'" In *Landmarks of American Writing*. Ed. Hennig Cohen. New York: Basic Books, 1969. pp. 341–52.
1755. HOGAN, PATRICK G., JR. 'Faulkner's 'Female Line': 'Callina' McCaslin." *Studies in Short Fiction*, 1 (1963), 63–65.
1756. HOWELL, ELMO. "Faulkner's Elegy: An Approach to 'The Bear.'" *The Arlington Quarterly*, 2, no. 3 (1970), 122–32.
1757. ———. "William Faulkner and the Chickasaw Funeral." *American Literature*, 36 (1965), 523–25.

1758. HUTCHISON, E. R. "A Footnote to the Gum Tree Scene." *College English*, 24 (1963), 564-65.

1759. JENSEN, ERIC G., S.J. "The Play Element in Faulkner's 'The Bear.'" *Texas Studies in Literature and Language*, 6 (1964), 170-87.

1760. KERN, ALEXANDER C. "Myth and Symbol in Criticism of Faulkner's 'The Bear.'" In *Myth and Symbol: Critical Approaches and Applications*. Ed. Bernice Slote. Lincoln: Univ. of Nebraska Press, 1963. pp. 152-61.

1761. KNIGHT, KARL F. "'Spintrius' in Faulkner's 'The Bear.'" *Studies in Short Fiction*, 12, (1975), 31-32.

1762. KORENMAN, JOAN S. "Faulkner's Grecian Urn." *The Southern Literary Journal*, 7, no. 1 (1974), 3-23.

1763. LEHAN, RICHARD. "Faulkner's Poetic Prose: Style and Meaning in *The Bear*." *College English*, 27 (1965), 243-47.

1764. LEWIS, R. W. B. *The Picaresque Saint: Representative Figures in Contemporary Fiction*. Philadelphia, PA: Lippincott, 1959.

1765. McDONALD, WALTER R. "Faulkner's 'The Bear': Part IV." *The CEA Critic*, 34, no. 2 (1972), 31-32.

1766. MAINI, D. S. "The Rhetoric of William Faulkner." *The Indian Journal of English Studies*, 16 (1976), 29-43.

1767. MAUD, RALPH. "Faulkner, Mailer, and Yogi Bear." *The Canadian Review of American Studies*, 2 (1971), 69-75.

1768. NAGEL, JAMES. "*Huck Finn* and *The Bear*: The Wilderness and Moral Freedom." *English Studies in Africa*, 12 (1969), 59-63.

1769. NESTRICK, WILLIAM V. "The Function of Form in *The Bear*, Section IV." *Twentieth Century Literature*, 12 (1966), 131-37.

1770. O'CONNOR, WILLIAM VAN. "The Wilderness Theme in Faulkner's 'The Bear.'" In *William Faulkner: Three Decades of Criticism*. Ed. Frederick J. Hoffman and Olga W. Vickery. East Lansing: Michigan State Univ. Press, 1960. pp. 322-30.

1771. OTTEN, TERRY. "Faulkner's Use of the Past: A Comment." *Renascence*, 20 (1968), 198-207, 214.

1772. PERLUCK, HERBERT A. "'The Heart's Driving Complexity': An Unromantic Reading of Faulkner's 'The Bear.'" *Accent*, 20 (1960), 23-46.

1773. PRASAD, V. R. N. "The Pilgrim and the Picaro: A Study of Faulkner's *The Bear* and *The Reivers*." In *Indian Essays in American Literature: Papers in Honour of Robert E. Spiller*. Ed. Sujit Mukherjee and D. V. K. Raghavacharyulu. Bombay: Popular Prakashan, 1969. pp. 209-21.

1774. RAINES, CHARLES A. "Faulkner and Human Freedom." *Forum* (University of Houston), 3, no. 3 (1959), 50-53.

1775. **RINALDI, NICHOLAS M.** "Game Imagery and Game-Consciousness in Faulkner's Fiction." *Twentieth Century Literature*, 10 (1964), 108–18.

1776. **SACHS, VIOLA.** "*The Bear.*" In *The Myth of America: Essays in the Structures of Literary Imagination*. The Hague: Mouton, 1973. pp. 125–42, 159–62.

1777. **SCHAMBERGER, J. EDWARD.** "Renaming Percival Brownlee in Faulkner's *Bear.*" *College Literature*, 4 (1977), 92–94.

1778. **SIMPSON, LEWIS P.** "Isaac McCaslin and Temple Drake: The Tale of the New World Man." In *Nine Essays in Modern Literature*. Ed. Donald E. Stanford. Baton Rouge: Louisiana State Univ. Press, 1965. pp. 88–106, 186.

1779. **STEPHENS, ROSEMARY.** "Ike's Gun and Too Many Novembers." *The Mississippi Quarterly*, 23 (1970), 279–87.

1780. **STONE, EDWARD.** "More on *Moby-Dick* and 'The Bear.'" *Notes on Modern American Literature*, 1 (1977), item 13.

1781. **STONE, WILLIAM B.** "Ike McCaslin and the Grecian Urn." *Studies in Short Fiction*, 10 (1973), 93–94.

1782. **STONESIFER, RICHARD J.** "Faulkner's 'The Bear': A Note on Structure." *College English*, 23 (1961), 219–23.

1783. **TAYLOR, WALTER.** "The Freedman in *Go Down, Moses:* Historical Fact and Imaginative Failure." *Ball State University Forum*, 8, no. 1 (1967), 3–7.

1784. **WALTON, GERALD W.** "Tennie's Jim and Lucas Beauchamp." *American Notes & Queries*, 8 (1969), 23–24.

1785. **WARREN, JOYCE W.** "The Role of Lion in Faulkner's 'The Bear': Key to a Better Understanding." *The Arizona Quarterly*, 24 (1968), 252–60.

1786. **WERTENBAKER, THOMAS J., JR.** "Faulkner's Point of View and The Chronicle of Ike McCaslin." *College English*, 24 (1962), 169–78.

1787. **WILNER, HERBERT.** "Aspects of American Fiction: A Whale, a Bear, and a Marlin." In *Americana-Austriaca: Festschrift des Amerika-Instituts der Universität Innsbruck anlässlich seines zehnjährigen Bestehens*. Ed. Klaus Lanzinger. Vienna: Braumüller, 1966. pp. 229–46.

1788. **WOODRUFF, NEAL, JR.** "'The Bear' and Faulkner's Moral Vision." In *Studies in Faulkner*. Ed. Neal Woodruff, Jr. Pittsburgh, PA: Carnegie Institute of Technology, 1961. pp. 43–67.

See also 218, 240, 341, 487, 493, 532, 537, 596, 597, 1806–1808, 1811, 1813–1817, 1821, 1822, 1827–1830, 1834, 1837, 1838, 1841, 1843, 1845, 1948, 1950, 1951, 1956, 1960, 1969, 1975–1977, 1980, 1982–1984, 1992, 1998, 1999, 2001, 2002, 2004, 2005, 2007–2010, 2014, 2015, 2019, 2023, 2029–2031,

2037–2039, 2041, 2048, 2049, 2056, 2059, 2070, 2073–2077, 2079, 2080, 2084, 2091.

"A Bear Hunt"

See 1984, 2031, 2044, 2056, 2069.

"The Big Shot"

1789. LANG, BÉATRICE. "An Unpublished Faulkner Story: 'The Big Shot.'" *The Mississippi Quarterly*, 26 (1973), 312–24.

"Black Music"

See 2092.

"The Brooch"

1790. GARRISON, JOSEPH M., JR. "Faulkner's 'The Brooch': A Story for Teaching." *College English*, 36 (1974), 51–57.
1791. HULT, SHARON SMITH. "William Faulkner's 'The Brooch': The Journey to the Riolama." *The Mississippi Quarterly*, 27 (1974), 291–305.

"By the People"

See 1983, 2007.

"Centaur in Brass"

See 1983, 2007, 2069.

"A Courtship"

1792. CANTRELL, FRANK. "Faulkner's 'A Courtship.'" *The Mississippi Quarterly*, 24 (1971), 289–95.
1793. HOWELL, ELMO. "Inversion and the 'Female' Principle: William Faulkner's 'A Courtship.'" *Studies in Short Fiction*, 4 (1967), 308–14.
See also 1984, 2013, 2031.

"Death Drag"

See 454, 2032.

"Delta Autumn"

1794. HARTER, CAROL CLANCEY. "The Winter of Isaac McCaslin: Revisions and Irony in Faulkner's 'Delta Autumn.'" *Journal of Modern Literature*, 1 (1970), 209–25.
See also 487, 1730, 1731, 1806–1808, 1814, 1816, 1822, 1827–1830, 1834, 1837, 1841, 1843, 1951, 1956, 1957, 1969, 1975, 1982, 1983, 2007, 2015, 2019, 2031, 2038, 2039, 2041, 2056, 2076, 2077, 2079, 2084, 2091.

"Dry September"

1795. **FAULKNER, HOWARD.** "The Stricken World of 'Dry September.'" *Studies in Short Fiction*, 10 (1973), 47–50.

1796. **JOHNSON, IRA.** "Faulkner's 'Dry September' and Caldwell's 'Saturday Afternoon': An Exercise in Practical Criticism." In *Tradition et innovation—littérature et paralittérature: Actes du Congrès de Nancy (1972)*. Paris: Marcel Didier, 1975. pp. 269–78.

1797. **McDERMOTT, JOHN V.** "Faulkner's Cry for a Healing Measure: 'Dry September.'" *The Arizona Quarterly*, 32 (1976), 31–34.

1798. **VICKERY, JOHN B.** "Ritual and Theme in Faulkner's *Dry September*." *The Arizona Quarterly*, 18 (1962), 5–14.

1799. **WINSLOW, JOAN D.** "Language and Destruction in Faulkner's 'Dry September.'" *CLA Journal*, 20 (1977), 380–86.

1800. **WOLFE, RALPH HAVEN, AND EDGAR F. DANIELS.** "Beneath the Dust of 'Dry September.'" *Studies in Short Fiction*, 1 (1964), 158–59.

See also 360, 484, 544, 2007, 2023, 2052, 2056, 2080.

"Elly"

1801. **BRADFORD, M. E.** "Faulkner's 'Elly': An Exposé." *The Mississippi Quarterly*, 21 (1968), 179–87.

See also 2052.

"An Error in Chemistry"

1802. **HUNT, JOEL A.** "Thomas Mann and Faulkner: Portrait of a Magician." *Wisconsin Studies in Contemporary Literature*, 8 (1967), 431–36.

See also 1997, 2026.

"Evangeline"

See 2062.

"Father Abraham"

See 1983.

"The Fire and the Hearth"

1803. **CREIGHTON, JOANNE VANISH.** "Revision and Craftsmanship in Faulkner's 'The Fire and the Hearth.'" *Studies in Short Fiction*, 11 (1974), 161–72.

1804. **MILLGATE, JANE.** "Short Story into Novel: Faulkner's Reworking of 'Gold is not Always.'" *English Studies*, 45 (1964), 310–17.

1805. **Smithey, Robert A.** "Faulkner and the Status Quo." *CLA Journal*, 11 (1967), 109-16.
See also 267, 1807, 1811, 1828, 1830, 1834, 1845, 1948, 1951, 1960, 1969, 1983, 2007, 2019, 2056, 2074, 2076, 2077, 2079, 2084.

"Fool About a Horse"
See 1983, 2007.

"Go Down, Moses"
1806. **Adamowski, T. H.** "Isaac McCaslin and the Wilderness of the Imagination." *The Centennial Review*, 17 (1973), 92-112.
1807. **Beck, Warren.** *"Go Down, Moses."* In *Faulkner: Essays.* Madison: Univ. of Wisconsin Press, 1976. pp. 334-582.
1808. **Benert, Annette.** "The Four Fathers of Isaac McCaslin." *Southern Humanities Review*, 9 (1975), 423-33.
1809. **Brissenden, R. F.** "Outrage, Impotence and Honour in the World of William Faulkner." *The Melbourne Critical Review*, no. 3 (1960), pp. 31-40.
1810. **Brumm, Ursula.** "Forms and Functions of History in the Novels of William Faulkner." *Archiv für das Studium der Neueren Sprachen und Literaturen*, 209 (1972), 43-56.
1811. **Butler, Robert.** "Images of Contraction and Expansion in *Go Down, Moses.*" *Notre Dame English Journal*, NS 1, no. 2 (1966), 6-27.
1812. **Cowley, Malcolm.** "The Etiology of Faulkner's Art." *The Southern Review*, NS 13 (1977), 83-95.
1813. **Creighton, Joanne Vanish.** "Revision and Craftsmanship in the Hunting Trilogy of *Go Down, Moses.*" *Texas Studies in Literature and Language*, 15 (1973), 577-92.
1814. **Culley, Margaret M.** "Judgment in Yoknapatawpha Fiction." *Renascence*, 28 (1976), 59-70.
1815. **Devlin, Albert J.** "Faulknerian Chronology: Puzzles and Games." *Notes on Mississippi Writers*, 5 (1973), 98-101.
1816. _____. "'How Much It Takes to Compound a Man': A Neglected Scene in *Go Down, Moses.*" *The Midwest Quarterly*, 14 (1973), 408-21.
1817. **Dussinger, Gloria R.** "Faulkner's Isaac McCaslin as Romantic Hero *Manqué.*" *The South Atlantic Quarterly*, 68 (1969), 377-85.
1818. **Eigner, Edwin M.** "Faulkner's Isaac and the American Ishmael." *Jahrbuch für Amerikastudien*, 14 (1969), 107-15.
1819. **Eschliman, Herbert R.** "Francis Christensen in Yoknapatawpha County." *The University Review* (Kansas City), 37 (1971), 232-39.

1820. FOOTE, SHELBY, DARWIN T. TURNER, AND EVANS HARRINGTON. "Faulkner and Race." In *The South and Faulkner's Yoknapatawpha: The Actual and the Apocryphal*. Ed. Evans Harrington and Ann J. Abadie. Jackson: Univ. Press of Mississippi, 1977. pp. 86-103.

1821. HAMILTON, GARY D. "The Past in the Present: A Reading of *Go Down, Moses*." *Southern Humanities Review*, 5 (1971), 171-81.

1822. HOCHBERG, MARK R. "The Unity of *Go Down, Moses*." *Tennessee Studies In Literature*, 21 (1976), 58-65.

1823. HOGAN, PATRICK G., JR., DALE A. MYERS, AND JOHN E. TURNER. "Muste's 'Failure of Love' in Faulkner's *Go Down, Moses*." *Modern Fiction Studies*, 12 (1966), 267-70.

1824. INGRASCI, HUGH J. "Strategic Withdrawal or Retreat: Deliverance from Racial Oppression in Kelley's *A Different Drummer* and Faulkner's *Go Down, Moses*." *Studies in Black Literature*, 6, no. 3 (1975), 1-6.

1825. JAMES, STUART. "'I Lay My Hand on My Mouth': Religion in Yoknapatawpha County." *Illinois Quarterly*, 40, no. 1 (1977), 38-53.

1826. KENT, GEORGE. "Faulkner and the Heritage of White Racial Consciousness: Notes on White Nationalism in Literature." In *Blackness and the Adventure of Western Culture*. Chicago: Third World Press, 1972. pp. 164-83.

1827. KINNEY, ARTHUR F. "Faulkner and the Possibilities for Heroism." *The Southern Review*, NS 6 (1970), 1110-25.

1828. KLOTZ, MARVIN. "Procrustean Revision in Faulkner's *Go Down, Moses*." *American Literature*, 37 (1965), 1-16.

1829. KOLODNY, ANNETTE. "'Stript, shorne and made deformed': Images of the Southern Landscape." *The South Atlantic Quarterly*, 75 (1976), 55-73.

1830. MELLARD, JAMES M. "The Biblical Rhythm of *Go Down, Moses*." *The Mississippi Quarterly*, 20 (1967), 135-47.

1831. MERIWETHER, JAMES B. "A Proposal for a CEAA Edition of William Faulkner." In *Editing Twentieth Century Texts*. Ed. Frances G. Halpenny. Toronto: Univ. of Toronto Press, 1972. pp. 12-27.

1832. MILLGATE, MICHAEL. "Faulkner and the South: Some Reflections." In *The South and Faulkner's Yoknapatawpha: The Actual and the Apocryphal*. Ed. Evans Harrington and Ann J. Abadie. Jackson: Univ. Press of Mississippi, 1977. pp. 195-210.

1833. ———. "'The Firmament of Man's History': Faulkner's Treatment of the Past." *The Mississippi Quarterly*, 25, Special Supplement (1972), 25-35.

1834. **MUSTE, JOHN M.** "The Failure of Love in *Go Down, Moses.*" *Modern Fiction Studies*, 10 (1964), 366–78.

1835. **PEARCE, RICHARD.** "Norman Mailer's *Why Are We in Vietnam?*: A Radical Critique of Frontier Values." *Modern Fiction Studies*, 17 (1971), 409–14.

1836. **PETESCH, DONALD A.** "Some Notes on the Family in Faulkner's Fiction." *Notes on Mississippi Writers*, 10 (1977), 11–18.

1837. **PILKINGTON, JOHN.** "Nature's Legacy to William Faulkner." In *The South and Faulkner's Yoknapatawpha: The Actual and the Apocryphal.* Ed. Evans Harrington and Ann J. Abadie. Jackson: Univ. Press of Mississippi, 1977. pp. 104–27.

1838. **SAMS, LARRY MARSHALL.** "Isaac McCaslin and Keats's 'Ode on a Grecian Urn.'" *The Southern Review*, NS 12 (1976), 632–39.

1839. **SIMPSON, LEWIS P.** "Faulkner and the Southern Symbolism of Pastoral." *The Mississippi Quarterly*, 28 (1975), 401–15.

1840. **STEWART, DAVID H.** "The Purpose of Faulkner's Ike." *Criticism*, 3 (1961), 333–42.

1841. **SULTAN, STANLEY.** "Call Me Ishmael: The Hagiography of Isaac McCaslin." *Texas Studies in Literature and Language*, 3 (1961), 50–66.

1842. **TAYLOR, WALTER.** "Faulkner: Social Commitment and the Artistic Temperament." *The Southern Review*, NS 6 (1970), 1075–92.

1843. ———. "Let My People Go: The White Man's Heritage in *Go Down, Moses.*" *The South Atlantic Quarterly*, 58 (1959), 20–32.

1844. **TICK, STANLEY.** "The Unity of *Go Down, Moses.*" *Twentieth Century Literature*, 8 (1962), 67–73.

1845. **VINSON, AUDREY L.** "Miscegenation and Its Meaning in *Go Down, Moses.*" *CLA Journal*, 14 (1970), 143–55.

1846. **WAGNER, LINDA.** "Codes and Codicils: Faulkner's Last Novels." In *Itinerary 3: Criticism.* Ed. Frank Baldanza. Bowling Green, OH: Bowling Green Univ. Press, 1977. pp. 1–9.

1847. **WALTON, GERALD W.** "Some Southern Farm Terms in Faulkner's *Go Down, Moses.*" *Publication of the American Dialect Society*, no. 47 (1967), pp. 23–29.

1848. **WATKINS, FLOYD C.** "The Gentle Reader and Mr. Faulkner's Morals." *The Georgia Review*, 13 (1959), 68–75.

See also 341, 549, 597, 1869, 1948, 1951, 1956, 1957, 1960, 1969, 1971, 1975, 1983, 1984, 1987, 1998, 1999, 2004, 2005, 2007–2010, 2014, 2015, 2019, 2021, 2023, 2030, 2031, 2039-2041. 2048, 2049, 2052, 2056, 2066, 2070, 2072-2077, 2079, 2087.

"Go Down, Moses"

See 269, 1807, 1830, 1845, 1948, 1969, 1983, 2019, 2079.

"Gold Is Not Always"

See 1983.

"The Golden Land"

1849. **BRADFORD M. E.** "Escaping Westward: Faulkner's 'Golden Land.'" *The Georgia Review*, 19 (1965), 72–76.
See also 399.

"Hair"

See 2056.

"Hand Upon the Waters"

See 2026.

"The Hill"

1850. **GRESSET, MICHEL.** "Faulkner's 'The Hill.'" *The Southern Literary Journal*, 6, no. 2 (1974), 3–18.
1851. **MOMBERGER, PHILIP.** "A Reading of Faulkner's 'The Hill.'" *The Southern Literary Journal*, 9, no. 2 (1977), 16–29.
See also 1948, 2019, 2058.

"Hog Pawn"

See 1983.

"Hong Li"

1852. **POLK, NOEL.** "'Hong Li' and *Royal Street*: The New Orleans Sketches in Manuscript." *The Mississippi Quarterly*, 26 (1973), 394–95.

"Honor"

See 2032.

"The Horseswap"

See 2019.

"The Hound"

See 1983, 2007, 2088.

"A Justice"

1853. **CLARK, WILLIAM BEDFORD.** "A Tale of Two Chiefs: William Faulkner's Ikkemotubbe and Washington Irving's Blackbird." *Western American Literature*, 12 (1977), 223–25.

1854. HOWELL, ELMO. "Sam Fathers: A Note on Faulkner's 'A Justice.'" *Tennessee Studies In Literature*, 12 (1967), 149–53.
See also 1984, 2007, 2013.

"The Kingdom of God"

1855. PEAVY, CHARLES D. "An Early Casting of Benjy: Faulkner's 'The Kingdom of God.'" *Studies in Short Fiction*, 3 (1966), 347–48.
1856. ———. "The Eyes of Innocence: Faulkner's 'The Kingdom of God.'" *Papers on Language & Literature*, 2 (1966), 178–82.

"Knight's Gambit"

1857. DUNLAP, MARY MONTGOMERY. "William Faulkner's 'Knight's Gambit' and Gavin Stevens." *The Mississippi Quarterly*, 23 (1970), 223–39.
1858. GROSSMAN, JOEL M. "The Source of Faulkner's 'Less Oft Is Peace.'" *American Literature*, 47 (1975), 436–38.
1859. SMITH, BEVERLEY E. "A Note on Faulkner's 'Greenbury Hotel.'" *The Mississippi Quarterly*, 24 (1971), 297–98.
See also 1960, 1997, 2026, 2039.

"Lion"

See 1770, 1807, 1813, 1983, 2007.

"Lizards in Jamshyd's Courtyard"

See 1960, 1983, 2007, 2088.

"Lo!"

See 1984, 2013.

"Miss Zilphia Gant"

1860. MORELL, GILIANE. "Prisoners of the Inner World: Mother and Daughter in *Miss Zilphia Gant*." *The Mississippi Quarterly*, 28 (1975), 299–305.
1861. PITAVY, FRANÇOIS L. "A Forgotten Faulkner Story: 'Miss Zilphia Gant.'" *Studies in Short Fiction*, 9 (1972), 131–42.
See also 1960, 2007, 2052.

"Mr. Acarius"

See 1945.

"Mistral"

1862. CLARK, CHARLES C. "'Mistral': A Study in Human Tempering." *The Mississippi Quarterly*, 21 (1968), 195–204.
See also 1908, 2062.

"Monk"

See 1997, 2026.

"Mule in the Yard"

See 1983, 2007, 2056.

"Notes on a Horsethief"

See 2007.

"Nympholepsy"

1863. M[ERIWETHER], J[AMES] B., ED. "Nympholepsy." *The Mississippi Quarterly*, 26 (1973), 403-09.

"An Odor of Verbena"

1864. BACKMAN, MELVIN. "Faulkner's 'An Odor of Verbena': Dissent from the South." *College English*, 22 (1961), 253-56.
See also 133, 212, 341, 1951, 1960, 1967, 1969, 1983, 1999, 2007, 2033, 2039, 2041, 2079, 2083.

"The Old Man"

1865. McHANEY, THOMAS L. *William Faulkner's* The Wild Palms: *A Study*. Jackson: Univ. of Mississippi Press, 1975.
See also 315, 341, 1946, 1951, 1958, 1960, 1975, 2009, 2010, 2015, 2018, 2030, 2031, 2037, 2039, 2041, 2059, 2066, 2070, 2074, 2076, 2077, 2079, 2080.

"The Old People"

1866. CAMBON, GLAUCO. "Faulkner's 'The Old People': The Numen-Engendering Style." *The Southern Review*, NS 1 (1965), 94-107.
See also 1770, 1806, 1807, 1811, 1813, 1828, 1830, 1837, 1948, 1960, 1975, 1983, 1984, 2007, 2015, 2039, 2079, 2080.

"Out of Nazareth"

See 2065.

"Pantaloon in Black"

1867. ALSEN, EBERHARD. "An Existentialist Reading of Faulkner's 'Pantaloon in Black.'" *Studies in Short Fiction*, 14 (1977), 169-78.
1868. BLANCHARD, LEONARD A. "The Failure of the Natural Man: Faulkner's 'Pantaloon in Black.'" *Notes on Mississippi Writers*, 8 (1975), 28-32.
1869. CLEMAN, JOHN L. "'Pantaloon in Black': Its Place in *Go Down, Moses*." *Tennessee Studies In Literature*, 22 (1977), 170-81.

1870. **NOBLE, DONALD R.** "Faulkner's 'Pantaloon in Black': An Aristotelian Reading." *Ball State University Forum*, 14, no. 3 (1973), 16–19.

1871. **STEPHENS, ROSEMARY.** "Mythical Elements of 'Pantaloon in Black.'" *The University of Mississippi Studies in English*, 11 (1971), 45–51.

1872. **STONEBACK, H. R.** "Faulkner's Blues: 'Pantaloon in Black.'" *Modern Fiction Studies*, 21 (1975), 241–45.

1873. **TAYLOR, WALTER.** "Faulkner's Pantaloon: The Negro Anomaly at the Heart of *Go Down, Moses.*" *American Literature*, 44 (1972), 430–44.

See also 341, 549, 1807, 1811, 1830, 1834, 1960, 1969, 1983, 2007, 2019, 2023.

"A Point of Law"

See 1983, 2007.

"Portrait of Elmer Hodge"

See 2039.

"The Priest"

1874. **M[ERIWETHER], J[AMES] B., ED.** "The Priest." *The Mississippi Quarterly*, 29 (1976), 445–50.

"Race at Morning"

1875. **BRADFORD, M. E.** "The Winding Horn: Hunting and the Making of Men in Faulkner's 'Race at Morning.'" *Papers on English Language & Literature*, 1 (1965), 272–78.

"Raid"

See 212, 267, 1983, 2007, 2068, 2079.

"Red Leaves"

1876. **BIEDLER, PETER G.** "A Darwinian Source for Faulkner's Indians in 'Red Leaves.'" *Studies in Short Fiction*, 10 (1973), 421–23.

1877. **FUNK, ROBERT W.** "Satire and Existentialism in Faulkner's 'Red Leaves.'" *The Mississippi Quarterly*, 25 (1972), 339–48.

1878. **HOWELL, ELMO.** "William Faulkner's Chickasaw Legacy: A Note on 'Red Leaves.'" *The Arizona Quarterly*, 26 (1970), 293–303.

1879. **LANGFORD, BEVERLY YOUNG.** "History and Legend in William Faulkner's 'Red Leaves.'" *Notes on Mississippi Writers*, 6 (1973), 19–24.

1880. **MILUM, RICHARD A.** "The Title of Faulkner's 'Red Leaves.'" *American Notes & Queries*, 13 (1974), 58–59.

1881. **MULLER, GILBERT H.** "The Descent of the Gods: Faulkner's 'Red Leaves' and the Garden of the South." *Studies in Short Fiction*, 11 (1974), 243–49.

1882. **PRYSE, MARJORIE.** "Race: Faulkner's 'Red Leaves.' " *Studies in Short Fiction*, 12 (1975), 133–38.

1883. **VOLPE, EDMOND L.** "Faulkner's 'Red Leaves': The Deciduation of Nature." *Studies in American Fiction*, 3 (1975), 121–31.

See also 549, 564, 1960, 1984, 2007, 2013, 2056, 2075.

"Retreat"

See 212, 1960, 1983, 2068.

"Riposte in Tertio"

See 212, 2079.

"A Rose for Emily"

1884. **BARBER, MARION.** "The Two Emilys: A Ransom Suggestion to Faulkner?" *Notes on Mississippi Writers*, 5 (1973), 103–05.

1885. **BARNES, DANIEL R.** "Faulkner's Miss Emily and Hawthorne's Old Maid." *Studies in Short Fiction*, 9 (1972), 373–77.

1886. **BRIDE, SISTER MARY, O.P.** "Faulkner's 'A Rose for Emily.'" *The Explicator*, 20 (1962), item 78.

1887. **CLEMENTS, ARTHUR L.** "Faulkner's 'A Rose for Emily.' " *The Explicator*, 20 (1962), item 78.

1888. **DAVIS, WILLIAM V.** "Another Flower for Faulkner's Bouquet: Theme and Structure in 'A Rose for Emily.'" *Notes on Mississippi Writers*, 7 (1974), 34–38.

1889. **EDWARDS, C. HINES, JR.** "Three Literary Parallels to Faulkner's 'A Rose for Emily.'" *Notes on Mississippi Writers*, 7 (1974), 21–25.

1890. **HAGOPIAN, JOHN V., AND MARTIN DOLCH.** "Faulkner's 'A Rose for Emily.'" *The Explicator*, 22 (1964), item 68.

1891. **HELLER, TERRY.** "The Telltale Hair: A Critical Study of William Faulkner's 'A Rose for Emily.'" *The Arizona Quarterly*, 28 (1972), 301–18.

1892. **HOLLAND, NORMAN N.** "Fantasy and Defense in Faulkner's 'A Rose for Emily.'" *Hartford Studies in Literature*, 4 (1972), 1–35.

1893. **HOWELL, ELMO.** "Faulkner's 'A Rose for Emily.' " *The Explicator*, 19 (1961), item 26.

1894. ———. "A Note on Faulkner's Emily as a Tragic Heroine." *The Serif*, 3, no. 3 (1966), 13–15.

1895. **KOBLER, J. F.** "Faulkner's 'A Rose for Emily.'" *The Explicator*, 32 (1974), item 65.

1896. **LEVITT, PAUL.** "An Analogue for Faulkner's 'A Rose for Emily.'" *Papers on Language & Literature*, 9 (1973), 91–94.

1897. **McGLYNN, PAUL D.** "The Chronology of 'A Rose for Emily.'" *Studies in Short Fiction*, 6 (1969), 461–62.

1898. **MULLER, GIL.** "Faulkner's 'A Rose for Emily.'" *The Explicator*, 33 (1975), item 79.

1899. **NEBEKER, HELEN E.** "Chronology Revised." *Studies in Short Fiction*, 8 (1971), 471–73.

1900. **STAFFORD, T. J.** "Tobe's Significance in 'A Rose for Emily.'" *Modern Fiction Studies*, 14 (1968), 451–53.

1901. **STRONKS, JAMES.** "A Poe Source for Faulkner? 'To Helen' and 'A Rose for Emily.'" *Poe Newsletter*, 1 (1968), 11.

1902. **SULLIVAN, RUTH.** "The Narrator in 'A Rose for Emily.'" *The Journal of Narrative Technique*, 1 (1971), 159–78.

1903. **WEST, RAY B., JR.** "The Use of Atmosphere in 'A Rose for Emily.'" In *The Art of Writing Fiction*. Ed. Ray B. West, Jr. New York: Crowell, 1968. pp. 197–203.

1904. **WILSON, G. R., JR.** "The Chronology of Faulkner's 'A Rose for Emily' Again." *Notes on Mississippi Writers*, 5 (1972), 44, 56, 58–62.

See also 356, 374, 384, 394, 399, 447, 454, 584, 2039, 2052, 2056, 2063.

"Shall Not Perish"

1905. **BRADFORD, M. E.** "Faulkner and the Jeffersonian Dream: Nationalism in 'Two Soldiers' and 'Shall Not Perish.'" *The Mississippi Quarterly*, 18 (1965), 94–100.

See also 2056.

"Shingles for the Lord"

1906. **HOWELL, ELMO.** "Faulkner's Country Church: A Note on 'Shingles for the Lord.'" *The Mississippi Quarterly*, 21 (1968), 205–10.

See also 194, 2031, 2044.

"Skirmish at Sartoris"

1907. **MERIWETHER, JAMES B.** "Faulkner and the South." In *The Dilemma of the Southern Writer: Institute of Southern Culture Lectures, Longwood College, 1961*. Ed. Richard K. Meeker. Farmville, VA: Longwood College, 1961. pp. 143–63.

See also 212, 2033.

"Smoke"

See 1997, 2026.

"Snow"

1908. **CANTRELL, FRANK.** "An Unpublished Faulkner Story: 'Snow.' " *The Mississippi Quarterly*, 26 (1973), 325–30.
See also 2062.

"Spotted Horses"

1909. **GARDNER, JOHN, AND LENNIS DUNLAP.** "Analysis." In *The Forms of Fiction*. New York: Random House, 1962. pp. 108–12.
1910. **GREINER, DONALD J.** "Universal Snopesism: The Significance of 'Spotted Horses.' " *English Journal*, 57 (1968), 1133–37.
1911. **HEALD, WILLIAM F.** "Morality in 'Spotted Horses.' " *The Mississippi Quarterly*, 15 (1962), 85–91.
1912. **HOUGHTON, DONALD E.** "Whores and Horses in Faulkner's 'Spotted Horses.' " *The Midwest Quarterly*, 11 (1970), 361–69.
1913. **SANDERSON, JAMES L.** " 'Spotted Horses' and the Theme of Social Evil." *English Journal*, 57 (1968), 700–04.
1914. **WELTY, EUDORA.** "Place in Fiction." *The South Atlantic Quarterly*, 76 (1977), 438–53.
See also 315, 511, 1977, 1983, 2007, 2019, 2039, 2052, 2088, 2092, 2466.

"Sunset"

See 2007.

"The Tall Men"

1915. **BRADFORD, M. E.** "Faulkner's 'Tall Men.' " *The South Atlantic Quarterly*, 61 (1962), 29–39.
1916. **HOWELL, ELMO.** "William Faulkner and the New Deal." *The Midwest Quarterly*, 5 (1964), 323–32.
See also 146.

"That Evening Sun"

1917. **BETHEA, SALLY.** "Further Thoughts on Racial Implications in Faulkner's 'That Evening Sun.' " *Notes on Mississippi Writers*, 6 (1974), 87–92.
1918. **BRADFORD, MEL E.** "Faulkner's 'That Evening Sun.' " *The CEA Critic*, 28, no. 8 (1966), 1, 3.
1919. **BROWN, MAY CAMERON.** "Voice in 'That Evening Sun': A Study of Quentin Compson." *The Mississippi Quarterly*, 29 (1976), 347–60.

1920. **DAVIS, SCOTTIE.** "Faulkner's Nancy: Racial Implications in 'That Evening Sun.' " *Notes on Mississippi Writers*, 5 (1972), 30–32.

1921. **GARRISON, JOSEPH M., JR.** "The Past and the Present in 'That Evening Sun.' " *Studies in Short Fiction*, 13 (1976), 371–73.

1922. **HERMANN, JOHN.** "Faulkner's Heart's Darling in 'That Evening Sun.' " *Studies in Short Fiction*, 7 (1970), 320–23.

1923. **HOGAN, PATRICK G., JR.** "Faulkner: A Rejoinder." *The CEA Critic*, 28, no. 8 (1966), 3.

1924. **JOHNSTON, KENNETH G.** "The Year of Jubilee: Faulkner's 'That Evening Sun.' " *American Literature*, 46 (1974), 93–100.

1925. **MANGLAVITI, LEO M. J.** "Faulkner's 'That Evening-Sun' and Mencken's 'Best Editorial Judgment.' " *American Literature*, 43 (1972), 649–54.

1926. **SANDERS, BARRY.** "Faulkner's Fire Imagery in 'That Evening Sun.' " *Studies in Short Fiction*, 5 (1967), 69–71.

1927. **SLABEY, ROBERT M.** "Quentin Compson's 'Lost Childhood.' " *Studies in Short Fiction*, 1 (1964), 173–83.

1928. **TOOLE, WILLIAM B., III.** "Faulkner's 'That Evening Sun.' " *The Explicator*, 21 (1963), item 52.

See also 169, 454, 455, 535, 565, 569, 1724, 1957, 2056.

"That Will Be Fine"

See 2056.

"There Was a Queen"

1929. **BELL, HANEY H., JR.** "A Reading of Faulkner's *Sartoris* and 'There Was a Queen.' " *Forum* (University of Houston), 4, no. 8 (1965), 23–26.

1930. **CASTILLE, PHILIP.** " 'There Was a Queen' and Faulkner's Narcissa Sartoris." *The Mississippi Quarterly*, 28 (1975), 307–15.

1931. **WAGNER, LINDA WELSHIMER, VICTORIA FIELDEN BLACK, AND EVANS HARRINGTON.** "Faulkner and Women." In *The South and Faulkner's Yoknapatawpha: The Actual and the Apocryphal*. Ed. Evans Harrington and Ann J. Abadie. Jackson: Univ. Press of Mississippi, 1977. pp. 147–51.

See also 1964.

"Tomorrow"

1932. **BRADFORD, M. E.** "Faulkner's 'Tomorrow' and the Plain People." *Studies in Short Fiction*, 2 (1965), 235–40.

1933. **HOWELL, ELMO.** "Faulkner's Enveloping Sense of History: A Note on 'Tomorrow.' " *Notes on Contemporary Literature*, 3, no. 2 (1973), 5–6.

See also 1997, 2020, 2026.

"Turnabout"

1934. BENSON, WARREN B. "Faulkner for the High School: 'Turnabout.' " *English Journal*, 55 (1966), 867–69, 874.
See also 1986.

"Twilight"

See 1960.

"Two Soldiers"

See 1905, 2056.

"Uncle Willy"

See 291, 2056, 2069.

"The Unvanquished"

See 212, 2007, 2068, 2081.

"Vendée"

See 212, 2007, 2068, 2079.

"Victory"

1935. SMITH, RALEIGH W., JR. "Faulkner's 'Victory': The Plain People of Clydebank." *The Mississippi Quarterly*, 23 (1970), 241–49.

"Was"

1936. BRADFORD, MELVIN. "All the Daughters of Eve: 'Was' and the Unity of *Go Down, Moses.*" *The Arlington Quarterly*, 1, no. 1 (1967), 28–37.
1937. DABNEY, LEWIS M. " 'Was': Faulkner's Classic Comedy of the Frontier." *The Southern Review*, NS 8 (1972), 736–48.
1938. TAYLOR, WALTER. "Horror and Nostalgia: The Double Perspective of Faulkner's 'Was.' " *Southern Humanities Review*, 8 (1974), 74–84.
1939. WALTERS, THOMAS N. "On Teaching William Faulkner's 'Was.' " *English Journal*, 55 (1966), 182–88.
1940. ZENDER, KARL F. "A Hand of Poker: Game and Ritual in Faulkner's 'Was.' " *Studies in Short Fiction*, 11 (1974), 53–60.
See also 1807, 1828, 1834, 1969, 1972, 1983, 1993, 2019, 2031, 2056, 2080, 2092.

"Wash"

1941. HOWELL, ELMO. "Faulkner's Wash Jones and the Southern Poor White." *Ball State University Forum*, 8, no. 1 (1967), 8–12.

1942. ISAACS, NEIL D. "Götterdämmerung in Yoknapatawpha." *Tennessee Studies In Literature*, 8 (1963), 47–55.

1943. STEWART, JACK F. "Apotheosis and Apocalypse in Faulkner's 'Wash.' " *Studies in Short Fiction*, 6 (1969), 586–600.

1944. TUSO, JOSEPH F. "Faulkner's 'Wash.' " *The Explicator*, 27 (1968), item 17.

See also 146, 478, 548, 1983, 2007, 2020, 2062.

"Weekend Revisited"

1945. GRESSET, MICHEL. "Weekend, Lost and Revisited." *The Mississippi Quarterly*, 21 (1968), 173–78.

"The Wild Palms"

1946. MOLDENHAUER, JOSEPH J. "Unity of Theme and Structure in *The Wild Palms.*" In *William Faulkner: Three Decades of Criticism.* Ed. Frederick J. Hoffman and Olga W. Vickery. East Lansing: Michigan State Univ. Press, 1960. pp. 305–22.

See also 179, 341, 1865, 1951, 1958, 1960, 1975, 2009, 2010, 2015, 2018, 2030, 2037, 2039, 2041, 2048, 2049, 2052, 2059, 2066, 2070, 2074, 2076, 2077, 2079, 2080.

General Studies

1947. ADAMS, RICHARD P. "The Apprenticeship of William Faulkner." *Tulane Studies in English*, 12 (1962), 113–56.

1948. _____. *Faulkner: Myth and Motion.* Princeton, NJ: Princeton Univ. Press, 1968.

1949. ANDERSON, HILTON. "Two Possible Sources for Faulkner's Drusilla Hawk." *Notes on Mississippi Writers*, 3 (1971), 108–10.

1950. AYTÜR, NECLA. "Faulkner in Turkish." In *William Faulkner: Prevailing Verities and World Literature.* Proceedings of the Comparative Literature Symposium, Vol. 6. Ed. Wolodymyr T. Zyla and Wendell M. Aycock. Lubbock: Interdepartmental Committee on Comparative Literature, Texas Tech Univ., 1973. pp. 25–39.

1951. BACKMAN, MELVIN. *Faulkner, The Major Years: A Critical Study.* Bloomington: Indiana Univ. Press, 1966.

1952. BASSETT, JOHN. "Introduction." In *William Faulkner: The Critical Heritage.* London: Routledge & Kegan Paul, 1975. pp. 1–46.

1953. BEAUCHAMP, GORMAN. "*The Unvanquished*: Faulkner's Oresteia." *The Mississippi Quarterly*, 23 (1970), 273–77.

1954. BECK, WARREN. "Faulkner after 1940." In *Faulkner: Essays.* Madison: Univ. of Wisconsin Press, 1976. pp. 55–102.

1955. _____. "Fictional Entities and the Artist's *Oeuvre*." In *Faulkner: Essays*. Madison: Univ. of Wisconsin Press, 1976. pp. 103–21.

1956. _____. "Good and Evil." In *Faulkner: Essays*. Madison: Univ. of Wisconsin Press, 1976. pp. 122–43.

1957. _____. "Short Stories into Novels." In *Faulkner: Essays*. Madison: Univ. of Wisconsin Press, 1976. pp. 275–333.

1958. BEDELL, GEORGE C. *Kierkegaard and Faulkner: Modalities of Existence*. Baton Rouge: Louisiana State Univ. Press, 1972.

1959. BLOTNER, JOSEPH. "The Faulkners and the Fictional Families." *The Georgia Review*, 30 (1976), 572–92.

1960. _____. *Faulkner: A Biography*. 2 vols. New York: Random House, 1974.

1961. _____. "The Sole Owner and Proprietor." In *Faulkner: Fifty Years After* The Marble Faun. Ed. George H. Wolfe. University: Univ. of Alabama Press, 1976. pp. 1–20.

1962. BOSWELL, GEORGE W. "Picturesque Faulknerisms." *The University of Mississippi Studies in English*, 9 (1968), 47–56.

1963. _____. "Traditional Verse and Music Influence in Faulkner." *Notes on Mississippi Writers*, 1 (1968), 23–31.

1964. BRADFORD, MELVIN E. A. "Certain Ladies of Quality: Faulkner's View of Women and the Evidence of 'There Was a Queen.'" *The Arlington Quarterly*, 1, no. 2 (1968), 106–39.

1965. BROOKS, CLEANTH. "The British Reception of Faulkner's Work." In *William Faulkner: Prevailing Verities and World Literature*. Proceedings of the Comparative Literature Symposium, Vol. 6. Ed. Wolodymyr T. Zyla and Wendell M. Aycock. Lubbock: Interdepartmental Committee on Comparative Literature, Texas Tech Univ., 1973. pp. 41–55.

1966. _____. "Faulkner and History." *The Mississippi Quarterly*, 25, Special Supplement (1972), 3–14.

1967. _____. "Faulkner's Vision of Good and Evil." *The Massachusetts Review*, 3 (1962), 692–712.

1968. _____. "A Note on Faulkner's Early Attempts at the Short Story." *Studies in Short Fiction*, 10 (1973), 381–88.

1969. _____. *William Faulkner: The Yoknapatawpha Country*. New Haven, CT: Yale Univ. Press, 1963.

1970. _____. "William Faulkner and William Butler Yeats: Parallels and Affinities." In *Faulkner: Fifty Years After* The Marble Faun. Ed. George H. Wolfe. University: Univ. of Alabama Press, 1976. pp. 139–58.

1971. BROUGHTON, PANTHEA REID. *William Faulkner: The Abstract and the Actual*. Baton Rouge: Louisiana State Univ. Press, 1974.

1972. BROWN, CALVIN S. "Faulkner's Manhunts." *The Georgia Review*, 20 (1966), 388–95.

1973. ———. "Faulkner's Use of the Oral Tradition." *The Georgia Review*, 22 (1968), 160–69.

1974. ———. *A Glossary of Faulkner's South*. New Haven, CT: Yale Univ. Press, 1976.

1975. BRYLOWSKI, WALTER. *Faulkner's Olympian Laugh: Myth in the Novels*. Detroit, MI: Wayne State Univ. Press, 1968.

1976. CHURCH, MARGARET. "William Faulkner: Myth and Duration." In *Time and Reality: Studies in Contemporary Fiction*. Chapel Hill: Univ. of North Carolina Press, 1963. pp. 227–50.

1977. COLE, HUNTER MCKELVA. "Welty on Faulkner." *Notes on Mississippi Writers*, 9 (1976), 28–49.

1978. COLLINS, CARVEL. "Faulkner at the University of Mississippi." In *William Faulkner: Early Prose and Poetry*. Boston, MA: Little, Brown, 1962. pp. 3–33.

1979. ———. "Introduction." In *New Orleans Sketches*, by William Faulkner. New York: Random House, 1968. pp. xi–xxxiv.

1980. ———. "On William Faulkner." In *Talks with Authors*. Ed. Charles F. Madden. Carbondale and Edwardsville: Southern Illinois Univ. Press, 1968. pp. 39–55.

1981. COOLEY, THOMAS W., JR. "Faulkner Draws The Long Bow." *Twentieth Century Literature*, 16 (1970), 268–77.

1982. COWLEY, MALCOLM. "Ike McCaslin and the Wilderness." *The University of Mississippi Studies in English*, 14 (1976), 89–97.

1983. CREIGHTON, JOANNE V. *William Faulkner's Craft of Revision: The Snopes Trilogy*, The Unvanquished, *and* Go Down, Moses. Detroit, MI: Wayne State Univ. Press, 1977.

1984. DABNEY, LEWIS M. *The Indians of Yoknapatawpha: A Study in Literature and History*. Baton Rouge: Louisiana State Univ. Press, 1974.

1985. DANIEL, BRADFORD. "William Faulkner and the Southern Quest for Freedom" In *Black, White and Gray: Twenty-one Points of View on the Race Question*. Ed. Bradford Daniel. New York: Sheed and Ward, 1964. pp. 291–308.

1986. DAY, DOUGLAS. "The War Stories of William Faulkner." *The Georgia Review*, 15 (1961), 385–94.

1987. DICKERSON, MARY JEAN. " 'The Magician's Wand': Faulkner's Compson Appendix." *The Mississippi Quarterly*, 28 (1975), 317–37.

1988. DOYLE, CHARLES. "The Moral World of Faulkner." *Renascence*, 19 (1966), 3–12.

1989. EITNER, WALTER H. "The Aristoi of Yoknapatawpha County." *Notes on Contemporary Literature*, 7, no. 4 (1977), 10–11.

1990. EMERSON, O. B. "Prophet Next Door." In *Reality and Myth: Essays in American Literature in Memory of Richmond Croom Beatty*. Ed. William E. Walker and Robert L. Welker. Nashville, TN: Vanderbilt Univ. Press, 1964. pp. 237–74.

1991. FALKNER, MURRY C. *The Falkners of Mississippi: A Memoir*. With a foreword by Lewis P. Simpson. Baton Rouge: Louisiana State Univ. Press, 1967.

1992. FLANAGAN, JOHN T. "Folklore in Faulkner's Fiction." *Papers on Language & Literature*, 5 (1969), 119–44.

1993. FLYNN, PEGGY. "The Sister Figure and 'Little Sister Death' in the Fiction of William Faulkner." *The University of Mississippi Studies in English*, 14 (1976), 99–117.

1994. FOOTE, SHELBY. "Faulkner's Depiction of the Planter Aristocracy." In *The South and Faulkner's Yoknapatawpha: The Actual and the Apocryphal*. Ed. Evans Harrington and Ann J. Abadie. Jackson: Univ. Press of Mississippi, 1977. pp. 40–61.

1995. FORD, MARGARET PATRICIA, AND SUZANNE KINCAID. *Who's Who in Faulkner*. Baton Rouge: Louisiana State Univ. Press, 1963.

1996. GAGE, DUANE. "William Faulkner's Indians." *American Indian Quarterly*, 1 (1974), 27–33.

1997. GIDLEY, MARK. "Elements of the Detective Story in William Faulkner's Fiction." *Journal of Popular Culture*, 7 (1973), 97–123.

1998. GOLD, JOSEPH. *William Faulkner: A Study in Humanities, From Metaphor to Discourse*. Norman: Univ. of Oklahoma Press, 1966.

1999. GOLDMAN, ARNOLD. "Faulkner and the Revision of Yoknapatawpha History." In *The American Novel and the Nineteen Twenties*. Ed. Malcolm Bradbury and David Palmer. London: Edward Arnold, 1971. pp. 165–95.

2000. GORMAN, THOMAS R. "Faulkner's Ethical Point of View." *The CEA Critic*, 28, no. 8 (1966), 5–6.

2001. GUERARD, ALBERT J. *The Triumph of the Novel: Dickens, Dostoevsky, Faulkner*. New York: Oxford Univ. Press, 1976.

2002. GUETTI, JAMES. *The Limits of Metaphor: A Study of Melville, Conrad, and Faulkner*. Ithaca, NY: Cornell Univ. Press, 1967.

2003. HAWKINS, E. O., JR. "Jane Cook and Ceclia Farmer." *The Mississippi Quarterly*, 18 (1965), 248–51.

2004. HOFFMAN, FREDERICK J. *William Faulkner*. New York: Twayne, 1961.

2005. _____. *William Faulkner*. 2nd ed. New York: Twayne, 1966.

2006. HOGAN, PATRICK G., JR. "Faulkner Scholarship and the CEA." *The CEA Critic*, 26, no. 1 (1963), 1, 5, 7–8, 12.

2007. HOLMES, EDWARD M. *Faulkner's Twice-Told Tales: His Re-Use of His Material*. The Hague: Mouton, 1966.

2008. HOWE, IRVING. "William Faulkner." In *Major Writers of America*. Ed. Perry Miller. 2 vols. New York: Harcourt, Brace & World, 1962. II, 825–41.

2009. ———. *William Faulkner: A Critical Study*. 2nd ed. New York: Random House, 1962.

2010. ———. *William Faulkner: A Critical Study*. 3rd ed. Chicago: Univ. of Chicago Press, 1975.

2011. ———. "Yoknapatawpha County Was a World That Was Complete in Itself." *The New York Times Book Review*, 22 July 1962, pp. 6–7, 24.

2012. HOWELL, ELMO. "Faulkner and Scott and the Legacy of the Lost Cause." *The Georgia Review*, 26 (1972), 314–25.

2013. ———. "William Faulkner and the Mississippi Indians." *The Georgia Review*, 21 (1967), 386–96.

2014. HUNT, JOHN W. *William Faulkner: Art in Theological Tension*. Syracuse, NY: Syracuse Univ. Press, 1965.

2015. HUNTER, EDWIN R. *William Faulkner: Narrative Practice and Prose Style*. Washington, DC: Windhover Press, 1973.

2016. IRWIN, JOHN T. *Doubling and Incest/Repetition and Revenge: A Speculative Reading of Faulkner*. Baltimore, MD: Johns Hopkins Univ. Press, 1975.

2017. JACOBS, ROBERT D. "William Faulkner: The Passion and the Penance." In *South: Modern Southern Literature and Its Cultural Setting*. Ed. Louis D. Rubin, Jr., and Robert D. Jacobs. Garden City, NY: Dolphin Books, 1961. pp. 142–76.

2018. JARRETT-KERR, MARTIN. *William Faulkner: A Critical Essay*. Grand Rapids, MI: Eerdmans, 1970.

2019. JEHLEN, MYRA. *Class and Character in Faulkner's South*. New York: Columbia Univ. Press, 1976.

2020. KAWIN, BRUCE F. *Faulkner and Film*. New York: Ungar, 1977.

2021. KERR, ELIZABETH. "The Evolution of Yoknapatawpha." *The University of Mississippi Studies in English*, 14 (1976), 23–62.

2022. ———. "William Faulkner and the Southern Concept of Woman." *The Mississippi Quarterly*, 15 (1962), 1–16.

2023. ———. *Yoknapatawpha: Faulkner's "Little Postage Stamp of Native Soil."* New York: Fordham Univ. Press, 1969.

2024. KIBLER, JAMES E., JR. "A Possible Source in Ariosto for Drusilla." *The Mississippi Quarterly*, 23 (1970), 321–22.

2025. **KIRK, ROBERT W., AND MARVIN KLOTZ.** *Faulkner's People: A Complete Guide and Index to Characters in the Fiction of William Faulkner.* Berkeley: Univ. of California Press, 1963.

2026. **KLINKOWITZ, JEROME F.** "The Thematic Unity of *Knight's Gambit.*" *Critique*, 11, no. 2 (1969), 81–100.

2027. **KNIEGER, BERNARD.** "Faulkner's 'Mountain Victory,' 'Doctor Martino,' and 'There Was a Queen.' " *The Explicator*, 30 (1972), item 45.

2028. **KULSETH, LEONARD I.** "Cincinnatus Among the Snopses: The Role of Gavin Stevens." *Ball State University Forum*, 10, no. 1 (1969), 28–34.

2029. **LEARY, LEWIS.** *William Faulkner of Yoknapatawpha County.* New York: Crowell, 1973.

2030. **LEVINS, LYNN GARTRELL.** *Faulkner's Heroic Design: The Yoknapatawpha Novels.* Athens: Univ. of Georgia Press, 1976.

2031. **LONGLEY, JOHN LEWIS, JR.** *The Tragic Mask: A Study of Faulkner's Heroes.* Chapel Hill: Univ. of North Carolina Press, 1963.

2032. **MACMILLAN, DUANE.** "*Pylon*: From Short Stories to Major Work." *Mosaic*, 7, no. 1 (1973), 185–212.

2033. **MEMMOTT, A. JAMES.** "Sartoris *Ludens*: The Play Element in *The Unvanquished.*" *The Mississippi Quarterly*, 29 (1976), 375–87.

2034. **MERIWETHER, JAMES B.** "Faulkner's Correspondence with *The Saturday Evening Post.*" *The Mississippi Quarterly*, 30 (1977), 461–75.

2035. ———. "A Source in Balzac for *The Unvanquished.*" *The Mississippi Quarterly*, 20 (1967), 165–66.

2036. ———. "The Text of Faulkner's Books: An Introduction and Some Notes." *Modern Fiction Studies*, 9 (1963), 159–70.

2037. **MERTON, THOMAS.** " 'Baptism in the Forest': Wisdom and Initiation in William Faulkner." In *Mansions of the Spirit: Essays in Literature and Religion.* Ed. George A. Panichas. New York: Hawthorn Books, 1967. pp. 17–44.

2038. **MICHEL, LAURENCE.** "Faulkner: Saying No to Death." In *The Thing Contained: Theory of the Tragic.* Bloomington: Indiana Univ. Press, 1970. pp. 107–30, 172–77.

2039. **MILLGATE, MICHAEL.** *The Achievement of William Faulkner.* New York: Random House, 1966.

2040. ———. "Faulkner and History." In *The South and Faulkner's Yoknapatawpha: The Actual and the Apocryphal.* Ed. Evans Harrington and Ann J. Abadie. Jackson: Univ. Press of Mississippi, 1977. pp. 22–39.

2041. ———. *William Faulkner.* Edinburgh: Oliver & Boyd, 1961.

2042. _____. "William Faulkner: The Problem of Point of View." In *Patterns of Commitment in American Literature*. Ed. Marston LaFrance. Toronto: Univ. of Toronto Press, 1967. pp. 181–92.

2043. MILUM, RICHARD A. "Ikkemotubbe and the Spanish Conspiracy." *American Literature*, 46 (1974), 389–91.

2044. MOMBERGER, PHILIP. "Faulkner's 'Country' as Ideal Community." In *Individual and Community: Variations on a Theme in American Fiction*. Ed. Kenneth H. Baldwin and David K. Kirby. Durham, NC: Duke Univ. Press, 1975. pp. 112–36.

2045. MURRAY, D. M. "Faulkner, the Silent Comedies, and the Animated Cartoon." *Southern Humanities Review*, 9 (1975), 241–57.

2046. O'BRIEN, MATTHEW C. "A Note on Faulkner's Civil War Women." *Notes on Mississippi Writers*, 1 (1968), 56–63.

2047. O'CONNOR, WILLIAM VAN. "Faulkner, Hemingway, and the 1920's." In *The Twenties, Poetry and Prose: 20 Critical Essays*. Ed. Richard E. Langford and William E. Taylor. Deland, FL: Everett/Edwards, 1966. pp. 95–98.

2048. _____. *William Faulkner*. Minneapolis: Univ. of Minnesota Press, 1959.

2049. _____. *William Faulkner*. Rev. ed. Minneapolis: Univ. of Minnesota Press, 1964.

2050. O'DEA, RICHARD J. "Faulkner's Vestigal Christianity." *Renascence*, 21 (1968), 44–54.

2051. PAGE, SALLY R. "Faulkner's Sense of the Sacred." In *Faulkner: Fifty Years After The Marble Faun*. Ed. George H. Wolfe. University: Univ. of Alabama Press, 1976. pp. 101–21.

2052. _____. *Faulkner's Women: Characterization and Meaning*. Deland, FL: Everett/Edwards, 1972.

2053. PRICE-STEPHENS, GORDON. "The British Reception of William Faulkner, 1929–1962." *The Mississippi Quarterly*, 18 (1965), 119–200.

2054. PUTZEL, MAX. "Evolution of Two Characters in Faulkner's Early and Unpublished Fiction." *The Southern Literary Journal*, 5, no. 2 (1973), 47–63.

2055. _____. "Faulkner's Short Story Sending Schedule." *The Papers of the Bibliographical Society of America*, 71 (1977), 98–105.

2056. REED, JOSEPH W., JR. *Faulkner's Narrative*. New Haven, CT: Yale Univ. Press, 1973.

2057. REED, RICHARD. "The Role of Chronology in Faulkner's Yoknapatawpha Fiction." *The Southern Literary Journal*, 7, no. 1 (1974), 24–48.

2058.   RICHARDSON, H. EDWARD. *William Faulkner: The Journey to Self-Discovery*. Columbia: Univ. of Missouri Press, 1969.

2059.   RICHARDSON, KENNETH E. *Force and Faith in the Novels of William Faulkner*. The Hague: Mouton, 1967.

2060.   RUNYAN, HARRY. *A Faulkner Glossary*. New York: Citadel Press, 1964.

2061.   RUOFF, GENE W. "Faulkner: The Way Out of the Waste Land." In *The Twenties: Fiction, Poetry, Drama*. Ed. Warren French. Deland, FL: Everett/Edwards, 1975. pp. 235–48.

2062.   SCHOENBERG, ESTELLA. *Old Tales and Talking: Quentin Compson in William Faulkner's* Absalom, Absalom! *and Related Works*. Jackson: Univ. Press of Mississippi, 1977.

2063.   SEYPPEL, JOACHIM. *William Faulkner*. New York: Ungar, 1971.

2064.   SHOWETT, H. K. "A Note on Faulkner's Title, *These Thirteen*." *Notes on Mississippi Writers*, 9 (1976), 120–22.

2065.   SIMPSON, LEWIS P. "Faulkner and the Legend of the Artist." In *Faulkner: Fifty Years After* The Marble Faun. Ed. George H. Wolfe. University: Univ. of Alabama Press, 1976. pp. 69–100.

2066.   SLATOFF, WALTER J. *Quest for Failure: A Study of William Faulkner*. Ithaca, NY: Cornell Univ. Press, 1960.

2067.   SPIVEY, HERMAN E. "Faulkner and the Adamic Myth: Faulkner's Moral Vision." *Modern Fiction Studies*, 19 (1973), 497–505.

2068.   STONE, EDWARD. "William Faulkner's Two Little Confederates." *The Ohio University Review*, 4 (1962), 5–18.

2069.   STROZIER, ROBERT. "Some Versions of Faulkner's Pastoral." *Forum* (University of Houston), 5, no. 1 (1967), 35–40.

2070.   SWIGGART, PETER. *The Art of Faulkner's Novels*. Austin: Univ. of Texas Press, 1962.

2071.   SWINK, HELEN. "William Faulkner: The Novelist as Oral Narrator." *The Georgia Review*, 26 (1972), 183–209.

2072.   TAYLOR, WALTER. "Faulkner: Nineteenth-Century Notions of Racial Mixture and the Twentieth-Century Imagination." *The South Carolina Review*, 10, no. 1 (1977), 57–68.

2073.   THOMPSON, LAWRANCE. *William Faulkner: An Introduction and Interpretation*. New York: Barnes & Noble, 1963.

2074.   TUCK, DOROTHY. *Crowell's Handbook of Faulkner*. New York: Crowell, 1964.

2075.   TURNER, DARWIN T. "Faulkner and Slavery." In *The South and Faulkner's Yoknapatawpha: The Actual and the Apocryphal*. Ed. Evans Harrington and Ann J. Abadie. Jackson: Univ. Press of Mississippi, 1977. pp. 62–85.

2076. **VICKERY, OLGA W.** *The Novels of William Faulkner: A Critical Interpretation.* Baton Rouge: Louisiana State Univ. Press, 1959.

2077. _____. *The Novels of William Faulkner: A Critical Interpretation.* Rev. ed. Baton Rouge: Louisiana State Univ. Press, 1964.

2078. _____. "William Faulkner and the Figure in the Carpet." *The South Atlantic Quarterly*, 63 (1964), 318–35.

2079. **VOLPE, EDMOND L.** *A Reader's Guide to William Faulkner.* New York: Noonday Press, 1964.

2080. **WAGGONER, HYATT H.** *William Faulkner: From Jefferson to the World.* Lexington: Univ. of Kentucky Press, 1959.

2081. **WAGNER, LINDA WELSHIMER.** "Faulkner and (Southern) Women." In *The South and Faulkner's Yoknapatawpha: The Actual and the Apocryphal.* Ed. Evans Harrington and Ann J. Abadie. Jackson: Univ. Press of Mississippi, 1977. pp. 128–46.

2082. _____. *Hemingway and Faulkner: Inventors/Masters.* Metuchen, NJ: Scarecrow, 1975.

2083. **WALKER, WILLIAM E.** "*The Unvanquished*: The Restoration of Tradition." In *Reality and Myth: Essays in American Literature in Memory of Richmond Croom Beatty.* Ed. William E. Walker and Robert L. Welker. Nashville, TN: Vanderbilt Univ. Press, 1964. pp. 275–97.

2084. **WARREN, ROBERT PENN.** "Faulkner: The South and the Negro." *The Southern Review*, 1 (1965), 501–29.

2085. _____. "Introduction: Faulkner—Past and Future." In *Faulkner: A Collection of Critical Essays.* Englewood Cliffs, NJ: Prentice-Hall, 1966. pp. 1–22.

2086. **WATKINS, FLOYD C.** "Faulkner and His Critics." *Texas Studies in Literature and Language*, 10 (1968), 317–29.

2087. _____. "Habet: Faulkner and the Ownership of Property." In *Faulkner: Fifty Years After The Marble Faun.* Ed. George H. Wolfe. University: Univ. of Alabama Press, 1976. pp. 123–37.

2088. _____, AND **THOMAS DANIEL YOUNG.** "Revisions of Style in Faulkner's 'The Hamlet.'" *Modern Fiction Studies*, 5 (1959), 327–36.

2089. **WEBB, JAMES W., AND A. WIGFALL GREEN, ED.** *William Faulkner of Oxford.* Baton Rouge: Louisiana State Univ. Press, 1965.

2090. **WETHERBY, H. L.** "Sutpen's Garden." *The Georgia Review*, 21 (1967), 354–69.

2091. **WHEELER, OTIS B.** "Faulkner's Wilderness." *American Literature*, 31 (1959), 127–36.

2092. _____. "Some Uses of Folk Humor by Faulkner." *The Mississippi Quarterly*, 17 (1964), 107–22.

2093. ZELLEFROW, KEN. "Faulkner's Flying Tales: A View of the Past." *Descant*, 16, no. 4 (1972), 42–48.

Interviews

2094. BOUVARD, LOIC. "Conversation with William Faulkner." *Modern Fiction Studies*, 5 (1959), 361–64.

2095. FANT, JOSEPH L., III, AND ROBERT ASHLEY, ED. *Faulkner at West Point*. New York: Random House, 1964.

2096. GWYNN, FREDERICK L., AND JOSEPH L. BLOTNER, ED. *Faulkner in the University: Class Conferences at the University of Virginia 1957–1958*. Charlottesville: Univ. of Virginia Press, 1959.

2097. MARKOVIĆ, VIDA. "Interview with Faulkner." *Texas Studies in Literature and Language*, 5 (1964), 463–66.

2098. MERIWETHER, JAMES B., AND MICHAEL MILLGATE, ED. *Lion in the Garden: Interviews with William Faulkner, 1926–1962*. New York: Random House, 1968.

Bibliography

2099. BASSETT, JOHN. *William Faulkner: An Annotated Checklist of Criticism*. New York: David Lewis, 1972.

2100. BEEBE, MAURICE. "Criticism of William Faulkner: A Selected Checklist." *Modern Fiction Studies*, 13 (1967), 115–61.

2101. EMERSON, O. B. "Faulkner and His Bibliographers." *Bulletin of Bibliography and Magazine Notes*, 30 (1973), 90–92.

2102. HAGOPIAN, JOHN V. "The Adyt and the Maze: Ten Years of Faulkner Studies in America." *Jahrbuch für Amerikastudien*, 6 (1961), 134–51.

2103. HOFFMAN, FREDERICK J. "Introduction." In *William Faulkner: Three Decades of Criticism*. Ed. Frederick J. Hoffman and Olga W. Vickery. East Lansing: Michigan State Univ. Press, 1960. pp. 1–50.

2104. LLOYD, JAMES BARLOW. "An Annotated Bibliography of William Faulkner, 1967–1970." *The University of Mississippi Studies in English*, 12 (1971), 1–57.

2105. McDONALD, W. U., JR. "Bassett's Checklist of Faulkner Criticism: Some 'Local' Addenda." *Bulletin of Bibliography and Magazine Notes*, 32 (1975), 76.

2106. McHANEY, THOMAS L. *William Faulkner: A Reference Guide*. Boston, MA: G. K. Hall, 1976.

2107. MERIWETHER, JAMES B. "The Books of William Faulkner: A Guide for Students and Scholars." *The Mississippi Quarterly*, 30 (1977), 417–28.

2108. ———. *The Literary Career of William Faulkner: A Bibliographical Study*. Princeton, NJ: Princeton Univ. Press, 1961.

2109. _____. *The Merrill Checklist of William Faulkner*. Columbus, OH: Merrill, 1970.

2110. _____. "The Short Fiction of William Faulkner: A Bibliography." *Proof*, 1 (1971), 293–329.

2111. _____. "William Faulkner." In *Fifteen Modern American Authors: A Survey of Research and Criticism*. Ed. Jackson R. Bryer. Durham, NC: Duke Univ. Press, 1969. pp. 175–210.

2112. _____. "William Faulkner." In *Sixteen Modern American Authors: A Survey of Research and Criticism*. Ed. Jackson R. Bryer. Durham, NC: Duke Univ. Press, 1974. pp. 223–75.

2113. SLEETH, IRENE LYNN. *William Faulkner: A Bibliography of Criticism*. Denver, CO: Swallow, 1963.

2114. _____. "William Faulkner: A Bibliography of Criticism." *Twentieth Century Literature*, 8 (1962), 18–43.

2115. VICKERY, OLGA W. "A Selective Bibliography." In *William Faulkner: Three Decades of Criticism*. Ed. Frederick J. Hoffman and Olga W. Vickery. East Lansing: Michigan State Univ. Press, 1960. pp. 393–428.

FAUSET, ARTHUR HUFF

"Symphonesque"

See 283.

FAUST, IRVIN

"Roar Lion Roar"

See 399.

FEIKEMA, FEIKE (See MANFRED, FREDERICK)

FELSEN, [HENRY] GREGOR

"First Skirmish"

See 374.

FERBER, EDNA

"An Etude For Emma"

See 2116.

General Studies

2116. SHAUGHNESSY, MARY ROSE. *Women and Success in American*

Society in the Works of Edna Ferber. New York: Gordon Press, 1977.

FERGUSSON, ERNA

"Justice As Interpreted"

2117. **REMLEY, DAVID A.** *Erna Fergusson.* Austin, TX: Steck-Vaughn, 1969.

FIEDLER, LESLIE A.

"The First Spade in the West"

See 308, 2119.

"The Last Jew in America"

See 2119.

"The Last WASP in the World"

See 2119.

"Nude Croquet"

2118. **CURRAN, RONALD.** " 'Fallen King' as Scapegoat in Fiedler's 'Nude Croquet.' " *Notes on Contemporary Literature*, 4, no. 1 (1974), 8–13.

General Studies

2119. **BLUEFARB, SAM.** "Pictures of the Anti-Stereotype: Leslie Fiedler's Triptych, *The Last Jew in America.*" *CLA Journal*, 18 (1975), 412–21.

2120. **DAVIS, ROBERT GORHAM.** "Leslie Fiedler's Fictions." *Commentary*, 43, no. 1 (1967), 73–77.

2121. **KOSTELANETZ, RICHARD.** "Leslie Fiedler (1965)." *Studies in the Twentieth Century*, no. 13 (1974), pp. 21–38.

2122. **SCHULZ, MAX F.** "Leslie A. Fiedler and the Hieroglyphs of Life." *Twentieth Century Literature*, 14 (1968), 24–34.

Interviews

2123. **KANNAN, LAKSHMI.** "The Contemporary Jewish-American Writer: A Conversation with Leslie A. Fiedler." *Indian Journal of American Studies*, 5, nos. 1–2 (1975), 76–81.

2124. **MERAS, PHYLLIS.** Interview with Leslie Fiedler. *Saturday Review*, 49 (30 July 1966), 32.

FISHER, DOROTHY CANFIELD

General Studies

2125. SMITH, BRADFORD. "Dorothy Canfield Fisher." *The Atlantic Monthly*, 204, no. 2 (1959), 73–77.

FISHER, RUDOLPH

"The City of Refuge"

See 283, 475.

"Common Meter"

2126. FRIEDMANN, THOMAS. "The Good Guys in the Black Hats: Color Coding in Rudolf Fisher's 'Common Meter.' " *Studies in Black Literature*, 7, no. 2 (1976), 8–9.
See also 386.

"Miss Cynthie"

See 283, 337, 386.

FISHER, VARDIS

General Studies

2127. CHATTERTON, WAYNE. *Vardis Fisher: The Frontier and Regional Works*. Boise, ID: Boise State College, 1972.
2128. FLORA, JOSEPH M. *Vardis Fisher*. New York: Twayne, 1965.
2129. GROVER, DORYS C. "Fisher's Theory of Art and Artists." In *A Solitary Voice—Vardis Fisher: A Collection of Essays*. New York: Revisionist Press, 1973. pp. 28–42, 59–60.

Interviews

2130. MILTON, JOHN R. "Vardis Fisher." In *Three West: Conversations with Vardis Fisher, Max Evans, Michael Straight*. Vermillion, SD: Dakota Press, 1970. pp. 1–45.

Bibliography

2131. KELLOGG, GEORGE. *Vardis Fisher: A Bibliography*. Moscow: Univ. of Idaho Library, 1961.
2132. _____. "Vardis Fisher: A Bibliography." *The American Book Collector*, 14, no. 1 (1963), 37–39.
2133. _____. "Vardis Fisher: A Bibliography." *Western American Literature*, 5 (1970), 45–64.

FITZGERALD, F[RANCIS] SCOTT

"Absolution"

2134. MORSE, J. I. "Fitzgerald's *Sagitta Volante in Dei*: An Emendation and a Possible Source." *Fitzgerald/Hemingway Annual 1972*, pp. 321–22.

2135. STEWART, LAWRENCE D. " 'Absolution' and *The Great Gatsby*." *Fitzgerald/Hemingway Annual 1973*, pp. 181–87.
See also 565, 2175, 2181–2183, 2187, 2199, 2206.

"The Adjuster"

See 2185.

"Author's House"

See 2203.

"Babes in the Woods"

See 2206.

"Babylon Revisited"

2136. EDENBAUM, ROBERT I. " 'Babylon Revisited': A Psychological Note on F. Scott Fitzgerald." *Literature and Psychology*, 18 (1968), 27–29.

2137. GRIFFITH, RICHARD R. "A Note on Fitzgerald's 'Babylon Revisited.' " *American Literature*, 35 (1963), 236–39.

2138. GROSS, SEYMOUR L. "Fitzgerald's 'Babylon Revisited.' " *College English*, 25 (1963), 128–35.

2139. HAGOPIAN, JOHN V. "A Prince in Babylon." *Fitzgerald Newsletter*, no. 19 (1962), pp. 99–101.

2140. LINDFORS, BERNTH. "Paris Revisited." *Fitzgerald Newsletter*, no. 16 (1962), pp. 77–78.

2141. McCOLLUM, KENNETH. " 'Babylon Revisited' Revisited." *Fitzgerald/Hemingway Annual 1971*, pp. 314–16.

2142. MALE, ROY R. " 'Babylon Revisited': A Story of the Exile's Return." *Studies in Short Fiction*, 2 (1965), 270–77.

2143. OSBORNE, WILLIAM R. "The Wounds of Charlie Wales in Fitzgerald's 'Babylon Revisited.' " *Studies in Short Fiction*, 2 (1964), 86–87.

2144. SLATTERY, SISTER MARGARET PATRICE. "The Function of Time in [*The*] G[*reat*] G[*atsby*] and 'Babylon.' " *Fitzgerald Newsletter*, no. 39 (1967), pp. 279–82.

2145. STALEY, THOMAS F. "Time and Structure in Fitzgerald's 'Babylon Revisited.' " *Modern Fiction Studies*, 10 (1964), 386–88.

2146. **TOOR, DAVID.** "Guilt and Retribution in 'Babylon Revisited.' " *Fitzgerald/Hemingway Annual 1973*, pp. 155–64.

2147. **WHITE, WILLIAM.** "The Text of 'Babylon Revisited.' " *Fitzgerald Newsletter*, no. 28 (1965), pp. 169–71.

2148. _____. "Two Versions of F. Scott Fitzgerald's 'Babylon Revisited': A Textual and Bibliographical Study." *The Papers of the Bibliographical Society of America*, 60 (1966), 439–52.

See also 207, 267, 399, 454, 2183, 2187, 2191, 2194, 2196, 2200, 2205, 2206, 2213.

"Basil and Cleopatra"

See 493, 2181, 2182.

"Bernice Bobs Her Hair"

2149. **BRUCCOLI, MATTHEW J.** "On F. Scott Fitzgerald and 'Bernice Bobs Her Hair.' " In *The American Short Story*. Ed. Calvin Skaggs. New York: Dell, 1977. pp. 219–22.

See also 2182, 2187.

"The Boy Who Killed His Mother"

See 2206.

"The Camel's Back"

2150. **MARGOLIES, ALAN.** " 'The Camel's Back' and *Conductor 1492.*" *Fitzgerald/Hemingway Annual 1974*, pp. 87–88.

"The Count of Darkness"

See 2197.

"Crazy Sunday"

See 2169, 2183, 2187, 2190, 2194, 2205, 2206.

"The Cut Glass Bowl"

See 2173.

"Cyclone in Silent Land"

See 2170.

"Dearly Beloved"

2151. **MANGUM, BRYANT.** "The Reception of *Dearly Beloved.*" *Fitzgerald/Hemingway Annual 1970*, pp. 241–44.

2152. **WEST, JAMES L. W., III.** "F. Scott Fitzgerald to Arnold Gingrich: A Composition Date for 'Dearly Beloved.' " *The Papers of the Bibliographical Society of America*, 67 (1973), 452–54.

"The Debutante"

See 2187.

"The Diamond as Big as the Ritz"

2153.   **KELLEY, DAVID J. F.** "The Polishing of 'Diamond.' " *Fitzgerald Newsletter*, no. 40 (1968), pp. 301–02.
See also 377, 2175, 2181–2183, 2187, 2190, 2199, 2205, 2206, 2213.

"Diamond Dick and the First Law of Woman"

See 2187.

"Dice, Brass Knuckles and Guitar"

See 2187.

"Emotional Bankruptcy"

See 2180, 2187.

"Family in the Wind"

See 2187.

"The Fiend"

See 2187.

"Flight and Pursuit"

See 2178.

"Forging Ahead"

See 2183.

"The Freshest Boy"

See 334, 2183.

"A Full Life"

See 2209.

"Fun in an Artist's Studio"

See 2210.

"Gods of Darkness"

See 2197.

"Gretchen's Forty Winks"

See 2187.

"He Thinks He's Wonderful"

See 2183.

"The I.O.U."

See 2170.

"The Ice Palace"

2154. MOSES, EDWIN. "F. Scott Fitzgerald And The Quest To
The Ice Palace." *The CEA Critic*, 36, no. 2 (1974), 11–14.
See also 511, 2181–2183, 2187.

"I'd Die for You"

See 2170.

"In the Darkest Hour"

See 2197.

"Jacob's Ladder"

See 2169, 2187.

"The Jelly-Bean"

See 2187, 2206, 2213.

"Jemima, The Mountain Girl"

See 2176.

"John Jackson's Arcady"

2155. EBLE, KENNETH. " 'John Jackson's Arcady' and [*The*]
G[*reat*] G[*atsby*]." *Fitzgerald Newsletter*, no. 21 (1963), pp. 117–18.
See also 2187.

"The Kingdom in the Dark"

See 2197.

"The Last of the Belles"

See 2187, 2205.

"The Lees of Happiness"

See 2187, 2213.

"Lo, The Poor Peacock!"

2156. ATKINSON, JENNIFER McCABE. "Indeed, 'Lo, The Poor
Peacock!' " *Fitzgerald/Hemingway Annual 1972*, pp. 283–85.
See also 2209.

"The Long Way Out"

2157. B[RUCCOLI], M[ATTHEW] J. "A Source for 'The Long Way
Out.' " *Fitzgerald Newsletter*, no. 34 (1966), p. 229.

"Love in the Night"

See 2187.

"Magnetism"

See 2187, 2194.

"Make Yourself at Home"

See 2170.

"May Day"

2158. **CASS, COLIN S.** "Fitzgerald's Second Thoughts About 'May Day': A Collation and Study." *Fitzgerald/Hemingway Annual 1970*, pp. 69–95.

2159. **GRUBER, MICHAEL PAUL.** "Fitzgerald's 'May Day': A Prelude to Triumph." *Essays in Literature* (Univ. of Denver), 2, no. 1 (1974), 20–35.

2160. **MAZZELLA, ANTHONY J.** "The Tension of Opposites in Fitzgerald's 'May Day.'" *Studies in Short Fiction*, 14 (1977), 379–85.

See also 2175, 2187, 2199, 2200, 2205, 2206, 2213.

"News of Paris—Fifteen Years Ago"

See 2187.

"A Night at the Fair"

See 2183.

"No Harm Trying"

See 2177.

" 'O Russet Witch!' "

See 2187.

"The Offshore Pirate"

2161. **ATKINSON, JENNIFER MCCABE.** "The Discarded Ending of 'The Offshore Pirate.'" *Fitzgerald/Hemingway Annual 1974*, pp. 47–49.

See also 2185, 2187, 2213.

"Offside Play"

See 2170, 2209.

"One Trip Abroad"

See 2200.

"The Ordeal"

See 2213.

"Outside the Cabinet-Maker's"

See 269, 2187, 2203.

"Pat Hobby's Christmas Wish"

See 2177.

"A Patriotic Short"

See 2177.

"The Pearl and the Fur"

See 2170, 2209.

"The Pierian Springs and the Last Straw"

See 2187, 2198, 2213.

"The Popular Girl"

See 2187.

"The Rich Boy"

2162. **KATZ, JOSEPH.** "The Narrator and 'The Rich Boy.' " *Fitzgerald Newsletter*, no. 32 (1966), pp. 208–10.

2163. **STEIN, WILLIAM BYSSHE.** "Two Notes on 'The Rich Boy.' " *Fitzgerald Newsletter*, no. 14 (1961), pp. 59–60.

2164. **WEST, JAMES L. W., III, AND J. BARCLAY INGE.** "F. Scott Fitzgerald's Revision of 'The Rich Boy.' " *Proof*, 5 (1977), 127–46.

See also 384, 2175, 2181, 2187, 2188, 2190, 2200, 2205, 2206, 2213, 3078.

"Salute to Lucie and Elsie"

See 2209.

" 'The Sensible Thing' "

See 2187.

"Sentiment—And the Use of Rouge"

See 2213.

"A Short Trip Home"

See 2181, 2182, 2187.

"Six of One—"

See 2213.

"The Swimmers"

See 2213.

"Temperature"

See 2170.

"They Never Grow Older"

See 2170.

"Three Acts of Music"

See 2208.

"Too Cute for Words"

See 2178.

"Two for a Cent"

See 2187.

"Two Old-Timers"

See 2177, 2210.

"Two Wrongs"

See 2181, 2182, 2187, 2190.

"What To Do About It"

See 2170.

"Winter Dreams"

2165. **BOGGAN, J. R.** "A Note on 'Winter Dreams.' " *Fitzgerald Newsletter*, no. 13 (1961), pp. 53–54.

2166. **BURHANS, CLINTON S., JR.** " 'Magnificently Attune to Life': The Value of 'Winter Dreams.' " *Studies in Short Fiction*, 6 (1969), 401–12.

2167. **DANIELS, THOMAS E.** "The Texts of 'Winter Dreams.' " *Fitzgerald/Hemingway Annual 1977*, pp. 77–100.

See also 356, 564, 2181–2183, 2185, 2187, 2190, 2199, 2200, 2213.

"Women in the House"

See 2209.

General Studies

2168. **ALLEN, JOAN M.** "The Better Fathers: The Priests in Fitzgerald's Life." *Fitzgerald/Hemingway Annual 1974*, pp. 29–39.

2169. **ARNOLD, EDWIN T.** "The Motion Picture as Metaphor in the Works of F. Scott Fitzgerald." *Fitzgerald/Hemingway Annual 1977*, pp. 43-60.

2170. **ATKINSON, JENNIFER MCCABE.** "Lost and Unpublished Stories by F. Scott Fitzgerald." *Fitzgerald/Hemingway Annual 1971*, pp. 32-63.

2171. **BERRY, LINDA.** "The Text of *Bits of Paradise.*" *Fitzgerald/Hemingway Annual 1975*, pp. 141-45.

2172. **BRYER, JACKSON R., AND JOHN KUEHL.** "Introduction." In *The Basil and Josephine Stories*, by F. Scott Fitzgerald. New York: Scribner's, 1973. pp. vii-xxix.

2173. **CASTY, ALAN.** " 'I and It' in the Stories of F. Scott Fitzgerald." *Studies in Short Fiction*, 9 (1972), 47-58.

2174. **CONSUELA, SISTER MARY, R.D.C.** "Babylon and All-American Boys: A Study of the Dream in Slow Motion." *Notre Dame English Journal*, 1, no. 2 (1962), 12-13, 19.

2175. **CROSS, K. G. W.** *Scott Fitzgerald.* Edinburgh: Oliver and Boyd, 1964.

2176. **CURRY, RALPH, AND JANET LEWIS.** "Stephen Leacock: An Early Influence on F. Scott Fitzgerald." *The Canadian Review of American Studies*, 7 (1976), 5-14.

2177. **DANIELS, THOMAS E.** "Pat Hobby: Anti-Hero." *Fitzgerald/Hemingway Annual 1973*, pp. 131-39.

2178. _____. "Toward a Definitive Edition of F. Scott Fitzgerald's Short Stories." *The Papers of the Bibliographical Society of America*, 71 (1977), 295-310.

2179. **DONALDSON, SCOTT.** "Scott Fitzgerald's Romance with the South." *The Southern Literary Journal*, 5, no. 2 (1973), 3-17.

2180. **DRAKE, CONSTANCE.** "Josephine And Emotional Bankruptcy." *Fitzgerald/Hemingway Annual 1969*, pp. 5-13.

2181. **EBLE, KENNETH.** *F. Scott Fitzgerald.* New York: Twayne, 1963.

2182. _____. *F. Scott Fitzgerald.* Rev. ed. Boston, MA: Twayne, 1977.

2183. **FAHEY, WILLIAM A.** *F. Scott Fitzgerald and the American Dream.* New York: Crowell, 1973.

2184. **GINGRICH, ARNOLD.** "Introduction." In *The Pat Hobby Stories*, by F. Scott Fitzgerald. New York: Scribner's, 1962. pp. ix-xxiii.

2185. **GOLDHURST, WILLIAM.** *F. Scott Fitzgerald and His Contemporaries.* Cleveland, OH: World, 1963.

2186. **GREENFELD, HOWARD.** *F. Scott Fitzgerald.* New York: Crown, 1974.

2187. **HIGGINS, JOHN A.** *F. Scott Fitzgerald: A Study of the Stories.* Jamaica, NY: St. John's Univ. Press, 1971.

2188. **HINDUS, MILTON.** *F. Scott Fitzgerald: An Introduction and Interpretation.* New York: Barnes & Noble, 1968.

2189. **HUNT, JAN, AND JOHN M. SUAREZ.** "The Evasion of Adult Love in Fitzgerald's Fiction." *The Centennial Review*, 17 (1973), 152–69.

2190. **KOENIGSBERG, RICHARD A.** "F. Scott Fitzgerald: Literature and the Work of Mourning." *American Imago*, 24 (1967), 248–70.

2191. **KREUTER, KENT AND GRETCHEN.** "The Moralism of the Later Fitzgerald." *Modern Fiction Studies*, 7 (1961), 71–81.

2192. **KUEHL, JOHN.** "Introduction." In *The Apprentice Fiction of F. Scott Fitzgerald.* New Brunswick, NJ: Rutgers Univ. Press, 1965. pp. 3–16.

2193. **LaGATES, CHARLOTTE.** "Dual-Perspective Irony and the Fitzgerald Short Story." *Iowa English Bulletin: Yearbook*, 26, no. 7 (1977), 18–20.

2194. **LANAHAN, FRANCES FITZGERALD.** "Introduction." In *Six Tales of the Jazz Age and Other Stories.* New York: Scribner's, 1960. pp. 5–11.

2195. **LATHAM, AARON.** *Crazy Sundays: F. Scott Fitzgerald in Hollywood.* New York: Viking, 1971.

2196. **LEHAN, RICHARD D.** *F. Scott Fitzgerald and the Craft of Fiction.* Carbondale and Edwardsville: Southern Illinois Univ. Press, 1966.

2197. **LEWIS, JANET.** "Fitzgerald's 'Philippe, Count of Darkness.'" *Fitzgerald/Hemingway Annual 1975*, pp. 7–32.

2198. **MILFORD, NANCY.** *Zelda: A Biography.* New York: Harper & Row, 1970.

2199. **MILLER, JAMES E., JR.** *F. Scott Fitzgerald: His Art and His Technique.* New York: New York Univ. Press, 1964.

2200. **MIZENER, ARTHUR.** *The Far Side of Paradise: A Biography of F. Scott Fitzgerald.* Rev. ed. Boston, MA: Houghton Mifflin, 1965.

2201. ———. "Introduction." In *The Fitzgerald Reader.* New York: Scribner's 1963. pp. xv–xxvii.

2202. ———. "Introductory Essay." In *Flappers and Philosophers*, by F. Scott Fitzgerald. New York: Scribner's, 1959. pp. 11–16.

2203. ———. "The Maturity of Scott Fitzgerald." *The Sewanee Review*, 67 (1959), 658–75.

2204. **MOERS, ELLEN.** "F. Scott Fitzgerald: Reveille at Taps." *Commentary*, 34 (1962), 526–30.

2205. **PEROSA, SERGIO.** *The Art of F. Scott Fitzgerald.* Trans. Charles Matz and Sergio Perosa. Ann Arbor: Univ. of Michigan Press, 1965.

2206. **PIPER, HENRY DAN.** *F. Scott Fitzgerald: A Critical Portrait.* New York: Holt, Rinehart and Winston, 1965.

2207. **PRIGOZY, RUTH.** "Gatsby's Guest List and Fitzgerald's Technique of Naming." *Fitzgerald/Hemingway Annual 1972*, pp. 99–112.

2208. ———. " 'Poor Butterfly': F. Scott Fitzgerald and Popular Music." *Prospects*, 2 (1976), 41–67.

2209. ———. "The Unpublished Stories: Fitzgerald in His Final Stage." *Twentieth Century Literature*, 20 (1974), 69–90.

2210. **REES, JOHN O.** "Fitzgerald's Pat Hobby Stories." *The Colorado Quarterly*, 23 (1975), 553–62.

2211. **ROBILLARD, DOUGLAS.** "The Paradises of Scott Fitzgerald." *Essays in Arts and Sciences*, 4 (1975), 64–73.

2212. **SHAIN, CHARLES E.** *F. Scott Fitzgerald.* Minneapolis: Univ. of Minnesota Press, 1961.

2213. **SKLAR, ROBERT.** *F. Scott Fitzgerald: The Last Laocöon.* New York: Oxford Univ. Press, 1967.

2214. **TAMKE, ALEXANDER R.** "Basil Duke Lee: The Confederate F. Scott Fitzgerald." *The Mississippi Quarterly*, 20 (1967), 231–33.

2215. **TURNBULL, ANDREW.** *Scott Fitzgerald.* New York: Scribner's, 1962.

2216. **WELLS, WALTER.** "The Hero and the Hack." In *Tycoons and Locusts: A Regional Look at Hollywood Fiction of the 1930s.* Carbondale and Edwardsville: Southern Illinois Univ. Press, 1973. pp. 103–21.

2217. **WYCHERLEY, H. ALAN.** "Fitzgerald Revisited." *Texas Studies in Literature and Language*, 8 (1966), 277–83.

Interviews

2218. **FITZGERALD, F. SCOTT.** "An Interview with F. Scott Fitzgerald." *Saturday Review*, 43 (5 Nov. 1960), 26, 56.

Bibliography

2219. **ANON.** "Checklist." *Fitzgerald Newsletter*, no. 4 (1959), pp. 14–15; no. 5 (1959), pp. 18–19; no. 6 (1959), pp. 22–23; no. 7 (1959), p. 28; no. 8 (1960), pp. 32–33; no. 9 (1960), pp. 37–38; no. 10 (1960), p. 43; no. 12 (1961), pp. 50–51; no. 13 (1961), pp. 56–57; no. 14 (1961), pp. 61–63; no. 15 (1961), pp. 71–73; no. 16 (1962), pp. 80–81; no. 17 (1962), pp. 89–91; no. 18 (1962), pp. 96–98; no. 19 (1962), pp. 103–04; no. 20 (1963), pp. 109–11; no. 21 (1963), pp. 121–23; no. 22 (1963), pp. 126–27;

no. 23 (1963), pp. 132–34; no. 24 (1964), pp. 139–42; no. 25 (1964), pp. 150–52; no. 26 (1964), pp. 160–61; no. 27 (1964), pp. 164–66; no. 28 (1965), pp. 172–76; no. 29 (1965), pp. 184–86; no. 30 (1965), pp. 192–94; no. 31 (1965), pp. 203–05; no. 32 (1966), pp. 214–16; no. 33 (1966), pp. 223–25; no. 34 (1966), pp. 231–33; no. 35 (1966), pp. 242–43; no. 36 (1967), pp. 254–55; no. 37 (1967), pp. 263–65; no. 38 (1967), pp. 272–76; no. 39 (1967), pp. 294–95; no. 40 (1968), pp. 314–18.

2220. ANON. "Checklist: F. Scott Fitzgerald." *Fitzgerald/Hemingway Annual 1970*, pp. 272–73.

2221. ANON. "Fitzgerald Checklist." *Fitzgerald/Hemingway Annual 1971*, pp. 366–73; *1972*, pp. 341–46.

2222. BEEBE, MAURICE, AND JACKSON R. BRYER. "Criticism of F. Scott Fitzgerald: A Selected Checklist." *Modern Fiction Studies*, 7 (1961), 82–94.

2223. B[RUCCOLI], M[ATTHEW] J. "Bruccoli Addenda." *Fitzgerald/Hemingway Annual 1973*, pp. 339–46; *1974*, pp. 275–83; *1975*, pp. 337–39; *1976*, pp. 251–53; *1977*, pp. 247–49.

2224. _____. *F. Scott Fitzgerald: A Descriptive Bibliography.* Pittsburgh, PA: Univ. of Pittsburgh Press, 1972.

2225. _____. *F. Scott Fitzgerald: Collector's Handlist.* Columbus, OH: Fitzgerald Newsletter, 1964.

2226. _____. *The Merrill Checklist of F. Scott Fitzgerald.* Columbus, OH: Merrill, 1970.

2227. BRYER, JACKSON R. *The Critical Reputation of F. Scott Fitzgerald: A Bibliographical Study.* Hamden, CT: Archon Books, 1967.

2228. _____. "F. Scott Fitzgerald." In *Fifteen Modern American Authors: A Survey of Research and Criticism.* Ed. Jackson R. Bryer. Durham, NC: Duke Univ. Press, 1969. pp. 211–38.

2229. _____. "F. Scott Fitzgerald." In *Sixteen Modern American Authors: A Survey of Research and Criticism.* Ed. Jackson R. Bryer. Durham, NC: Duke Univ. Press, 1974. pp. 277–321.

2230. _____. "F. Scott Fitzgerald: A Review of Research and Scholarship." *Texas Studies in Literature and Language*, 5 (1963), 147–63.

2231. _____. "F. Scott Fitzgerald and His Critics: A Bibliographical Record." *Bulletin of Bibliography and Magazine Notes*, 23 (1962), 155–58, 180–83, 201–08.

2232. DANIELS, THOMAS E. "English Periodical Publications of Fitzgerald's Short Stories: A Correction of the Record." *Fitzgerald/Hemingway Annual 1976*, pp. 124–29.

2233. DUGGAN, MARGARET M. "Fitzgerald Checklist." *Fitzgerald/Hemingway Annual 1973*, pp. 349–56; *1974*, pp. 317–22; *1975*, pp. 341–50; *1976*, pp. 254–59; *1977*, pp. 250–54.

2234. _____. "Reprintings of Fitzgerald." *Fitzgerald/Hemingway Annual 1974*, pp. 285–311.

2235. PORTER, BERNARD H. "The First Publications of F. Scott Fitzgerald." *Twentieth Century Literature*, 5 (1960), 176–82.

FITZGERALD, ZELDA [SAYRE]

"A Couple of Nuts"

See 2236, 2238.

"A Millionaire's Girl"

See 2236.

"Miss Ella"

See 2236, 2238.

"Our Own Movie Queen"

See 2236.

General Studies

2236. ANDERSON, W. R. "Rivalry and Partnership: The Short Fiction of Zelda Sayre Fitzgerald." *Fitzgerald/Hemingway Annual 1977*, pp. 19–42.

2237. GOING, WILLIAM T. "Zelda Sayre Fitzgerald and Sara Haardt Mencken." In *Essays on Alabama Literature*. University: Univ. of Alabama Press, 1975. pp. 114–41.

2238. MILFORD, NANCY. *Zelda: A Biography*. New York: Harper & Row, 1970.

FLINT, TIMOTHY

General Studies

*2239. FOLSOM, JAMES K. *Timothy Flint*. New York: Twayne, 1965.

FOOTE, MARY HALLOCK

"The Maid's Progress"

See 2240.

General Studies

2240. MAGUIRE, JAMES H. *Mary Hallock Foote*. Boise, ID: Boise State College, 1972.

Bibliography

2241. ETULAIN, RICHARD. "Mary Hallock Foote: A Checklist." *Western American Literature*, 10 (1975), 59–65.

2242. ———. "Mary Hallock Foote (1847–1938)." *American Literary Realism, 1870–1910*, 5 (1972), 145–50.

FOOTE, SHELBY

"Child by Fever"

See 2245.

"Rain Down Home"

2243. VAUTHIER, SIMONE. "Fiction and Fictions in Shelby Foote's 'Rain Down Home.' " *Notes on Mississippi Writers*, 8 (1975), 35–50.

General Studies

2244. FOOTE, SHELBY. "The Novelist's View of History." *The Mississippi Quarterly*, 17 (1964), 219–25.

2245. LANDESS, THOMAS H. "Southern History and Manhood: Major Themes in the Works of Shelby Foote." *The Mississippi Quarterly*, 24 (1971), 321–47.

Interviews

2246. [GRAHAM, JOHN]. "Talking with Shelby Foote—June 1970." *The Mississippi Quarterly*, 24 (1971), 405–27.

2247. HARRINGTON, EVANS. "Interview with Shelby Foote." *The Mississippi Quarterly*, 24 (1971), 349–77.

Bibliography

2248. KIBLER, JAMES E., JR. "Shelby Foote: A Bibliography." *The Mississippi Quarterly*, 24 (1971), 437–65.

FORD, JESSE HILL

Interviews

2249. NEWQUIST, ROY. "Jesse Hill Ford." In *Conversations*. New York: Rand McNally, 1967. pp. 119–20.

Bibliography

2250. WHITE, HELEN. *Jesse Hill Ford: An Annotated Check List of His Published Works and of His Papers*. Memphis, TN: John Willard Brister Library, Memphis State Univ., 1969.

FORT, KEITH

"The Coal Shoveller"

2251. BROER, LAWRENCE. "The Coal Shoveller." In *Instructor's Manual for* "The Art of Fiction," Second Edition. Ed. R. F. Dietrich and Roger H. Sundell. New York: Holt, Rinehart and Winston, 1974. pp. 125-31.

FOX, JOHN, JR.

"Grayson's Baby"

See 571.

General Studies

*2252. TITUS, WARREN I. *John Fox, Jr.* New York: Twayne, 1971.

Bibliography

2253. TITUS, WARREN I. "John Fox, Jr. (1862-1919)." *American Literary Realism, 1870-1910*, i, no. 3 (1968), 5-8.

FOX, WILLIAM PRICE

Interviews

2254. BRUCCOLI, MATTHEW J. "William Price Fox." In *Conversations with Writers*, Vol. I. Detroit, MI: Gale, 1977. pp. 47-80.

FRANK, WALDO

General Studies

*2255. CARTER, PAUL J. *Waldo Frank.* New York: Twayne, 1967.

FREDERIC, HAROLD

"Cordelia and the Moon"

2256. BLACKALL, JEAN FRANTZ. "Harold Frederic: A Provocative Revision." *Notes and Queries*, NS 20 (1973), 257-60.

"In the Shadow of Gabriel"

See 2261.

"The Martyrdom of Maev"

2257. GARNER, STANTON. "More Notes on Harold Frederic in Ireland." *American Literature*, 39 (1968), 560-62.

"The Path of Murtogh"

See 2261.

"The Truce of the Bishop"

See 2261.

"The Two Rochards"

2258. O'DONNELL, THOMAS F. "An Addition to the HF Bibliography: 'The Two Rochards,' by 'Edgar.' " *The Frederic Herald*, 1, no. 2 (1967), 4.

"The War Widow"

See 2260.

"The Wooing of Teige"

See 2261.

General Studies

2259. BRIGGS, AUSTIN, JR. *The Novels of Harold Frederic*. Ithaca, NY: Cornell Univ. Press, 1969.
2260. GARNER, STANTON. *Harold Frederic*. Minneapolis: Univ. of Minnesota Press, 1969.
2261. ———. "Some Notes on Harold Frederic in Ireland." *American Literature*, 39 (1967), 60–74.
2262. O'DONNELL, THOMAS F. *Frederic in the Mohawk Valley*. Utica, NY: Occasional Papers from Utica College, 1968.
2263. ———, AND HOYT C. FRANCHERE. *Harold Frederic*. New York: Twayne, 1961.
2264. WILSON, EDMUND. "Introduction." In *Harold Frederic's Stories of York State*. Ed. with a preface by Thomas F. O'Donnell. Syracuse, NY: Syracuse Univ. Press, 1966. pp. xi–xvi.
2265. WOODWARD, ROBERT H. "Harold Frederic and the Yorker's Image of New England." *The Emerson Society Quarterly*, no. 27 (1962), pp. 36–37.

Bibliography

2266. EICHELBERGER, CLAYTON L., ET AL. "Harold Frederic (1856–1898): A Critical Bibliography of Secondary Comment." *American Literary Realism, 1870–1910*, 1, no. 2 (1968), 1–70.
2267. GARNER, STANTON B. "A Harold Frederic First." *Studies in Bibliography*, 15 (1962), 268–69.
2268. MONTEIRO, GEORGE. "Harold Frederic: An Unrecorded Story." *The Papers of the Bibliographical Society of America*, 59 (1965), 327.

2269. O'DONNELL, THOMAS F. "Harold Frederic (1856–1898)." *American Literary Realism, 1870–1910*, 1, no. 1 (1967), 39–44.

2270. _____. *The Merrill Checklist of Harold Frederic.* Columbus, OH: Merrill, 1969.

2271. _____, STANTON GARNER, AND ROBERT H. WOODWARD. *A Bibliography of Writings by and about Harold Frederic.* Boston, MA: G. K. Hall, 1975.

2272. WOODWARD, ROBERT H. "The Frederic Bibliographies: Errata." *The Frederic Herald*, 3, no. 1 (1969), 3–4.

2273. _____. "Harold Frederic: A Bibliography." *Studies in Bibliography*, 13 (1960), 247–57.

2274. _____. "Harold Frederic: Supplemental Critical Bibliography of Secondary Comment." *American Literary Realism, 1870–1910*, 3 (1970), 95–147.

2275. _____, AND STANTON GARNER. "Frederic's Short Fiction: A Checklist." *American Literary Realism, 1870–1910*, 1, no. 2 (1968), 73–76.

FREEMAN, MARY E[LEANOR] WILKINS

"Amanda and Love"

2276. CROWLEY, JOHN W. "Freeman's Yankee Tragedy: 'Amanda and Love.'" *The Markham Review*, 5 (1976), 58–60.

"The Apple Tree"

See 2281.

"Arethusa"

See 2284.

"The Bar Lighthouse"

See 2282.

"A Conflict Ended"

See 2281, 2282, 2285.

"A Conquest of Humility"

See 2281, 2285.

"Coronation"

See 2281.

"Gentian"

See 601, 2281.

"A Humble Romance"

See 2285.

"An Independent Thinker"

See 2284.

"Life Everlastin' "

See 2282.

"A New England Nun"

2277. HIRSCH, DAVID H. "Subdued Meaning in 'A New England Nun.' " *Studies in Short Fiction*, 2 (1965), 124–36. *See also* 356.

"A New England Prophet"

See 2285.

"An Object of Love"

See 2285.

"Old Woman Magoun"

See 2281.

"A Poetess"

See 2285.

"The Revolt of 'Mother' "

2278. GALLAGHER, EDWARD J. "Freeman's 'The Revolt of "Mother." ' " *The Explicator*, 27 (1969), item 48. *See also* 2281.

"Sister Liddy"

See 2285.

"A Solitary"

See 601, 2285.

"The Three Old Sisters and The Old Bean"

2279. TOTH, SUSAN ALLEN. "Mary Wilkins Freeman's Parable of Wasted Life." *American Literature*, 42 (1971), 564–67.

"Two Old Lovers"

See 2281.

"A Village Lear"

See 356.

"A Village Singer"

2280. **FORTENBERRY, GEORGE.** "Proper Names in Frederic (4): *Candace.*" *The Frederic Herald*, 2, no. 1 (1968), 5.
See also 356, 2284, 2285.

"A Wayfaring Couple"
See 356.

General Studies

2281. **BRAND, ALICE GLARDEN.** "Mary Wilkins Freeman: Misanthropy as Propaganda." *The New England Quarterly*, 50 (1977), 83–100.
2282. **HAMBLEN, ABIGAIL ANN.** *The New England Art of Mary E. Wilkins Freeman.* Amherst, MA: Green Knight Press, 1966.
2283. **QUNIA, JAMES H., JR.** "Character Types in the Fiction of Mary Wilkins Freeman." *Colby Library Quarterly*, 9 (1971), 432–39.
2284. **TOTH, SUSAN ALLEN.** "Defiant Light: A Positive View of Mary Wilkins Freeman." *The New England Quarterly*, 46 (1973), 82–93.
2285. **WESTBROOK, PERRY D.** *Mary Wilkins Freeman.* New York: Twayne, 1967.

Bibliography

2286. **WESTBROOK, PERRY D.** "Mary E. Wilkins Freeman (1852–1930)." *American Literary Realism, 1870–1910*, 2 (1969), 139–42.

FRENCH, ALICE (See *THANET, OCTAVE*)

FRIEDMAN, BRUCE JAY

General Studies

2287. **LEWIS, STUART.** "Myth and Ritual in The Short Fiction of Bruce Jay Friedman." *Studies in Short Fiction*, 10 (1973), 415–16.
*2288. **SCHULZ, MAX F.** *Bruce Jay Friedman.* New York: Twayne, 1974.

FRIEDRICH, OTTO

"Freedom of the Press"
See 374.

FROST, ROBERT

General Studies

*2289. GEYER, C. W. "A Poulterer's Pleasure: Robert Frost as Prose Humorist." *Studies in Short Fiction*, 8 (1971), 589-99.

FULLER, HENRY BLAKE

"Dr. Gowdy and the Squash"

See 2292.

"The Downfall of Abner Joyce"

2290. PILKINGTON, JOHN. "Henry Blake Fuller's Satire on Hamlin Garland." *The University of Mississippi Studies in English*, 8 (1967), 1-6.
See also 2292.

"The Greatest of These"

See 2291.

"Little O'Grady vs. The Grindstone"

See 2291, 2292.

"Pasquale's Picture"

See 2291.

General Studies

2291. BOWRON, BERNARD R., JR. *Henry B. Fuller of Chicago: The Ordeal of a Genteel Realist in Ungenteel America*. Westport, CT: Greenwood Press, 1974.
2292. PILKINGTON, JOHN. "Fuller, Garland, Taft, and the Art of the West." *Papers on Language & Literature*, 8, Supplement (1972), 39-56.
2293. ———. *Henry Blake Fuller*. New York: Twayne, 1970.

Bibliography

2294. SWANSON, JEFFREY. "A Checklist of the Writings of Henry Blake Fuller (1857-1929)." *American Literary Realism, 1870-1910*, 7 (1974), 211-43.
2295. WILLIAMS, KENNY JACKSON. "Henry Blake Fuller (1857-1929)." *American Literary Realism, 1870-1910*, 1, no. 3 (1968), 9-13.

FUTRELLE, JACQUES

"The Problem of Cell 13"

2296. **GILBERT, ELLIOT L.** "Murder Without Air: Jacques Futrelle." *The New Republic*, 177, no. 5 (1977), 33–34.

GAINES, ERNEST J.

"Bloodline"

See 2299, 2302.

"Just Like A Tree"

See 2299, 2300.

"A Long Day in November"

2297. **PUSCHMANN-NALENZ, BARBARA.** "Ernest J. Gaines, 'A Long Day in November' (1963)." In *The Black American Short Story in the 20th Century: A Collection of Critical Essays.* Ed. Peter Bruck. Amsterdam: B. R. Grüner, 1977. pp. 157–69. *See also* 2299, 2302.

"The Sky Is Gray"

See 268, 535, 2299, 2302.

"Three Men"

See 2299, 2302.

General Studies

2298. **BRYANT, JERRY H.** "From Death to Life: The Fiction of Ernest J. Gaines." *The Iowa Review*, 3, no. 1 (1972), 106–20.

2299. **BURKE, WILLIAM.** "*Bloodline*: A Black Man's South." *CLA Journal*, 19 (1976), 545–58.

2300. **HICKS, JACK.** "To Make These Bones Live: History and Community in Ernest Gaines's Fiction." *Black American Literature Forum*, 11 (1977), 9–19.

2301. **McDONALD, WALTER R.** " 'You Not a Bum, You a Man': Ernest J. Gaines's *Bloodline*." *Negro American Literature Forum*, 9 (1975), 47–49.

2302. **SHELTON, FRANK W.** "Ambiguous Manhood in Ernest J. Gaines's *Bloodline*." *CLA Journal*, 19 (1975), 200–09.

Interviews

2303. **BEAUFORD, FRED.** "A Conversation With Ernest J. Gaines." *Black Creation*, 4, no. 1 (1972), 16–18.

2304. **Fitz Gerald, Gregory.** "An Interview: Ernest J. Gaines." *The New Orleans Review*, 1 (1969), 331–35.

2305. **Ingram, Forrest, and Barbara Steinberg.** "On the Verge: An Interview with Ernest J. Gaines." *The New Orleans Review*, 3 (1973), 339–44.

2306. **Laney, Ruth.** "A Conversation with Ernest Gaines." *The Southern Review*, NS 10 (1974), 1–14.

2307. **O'Brien, John.** "Ernest J. Gaines." In *Interviews with Black Writers.* Ed. John O'Brien. New York: Liveright, 1973. pp. 79–93.

2308. **Tooker, Dan, and Roger Hofheins.** "Ernest J. Gaines." In *Fiction!: Interviews with Northern California Novelists.* New York: Harcourt Brace Jovanovich, 1976. pp. 87–99.

GALE, ZONA

"Bridal Pond"

See 2309.

"The Story of Jeffro"

See 2309.

General Studies

2309. **Simonson, Harold P.** *Zona Gale.* New York: Twayne, 1962.

Bibliography

2310. **Simonson, Harold P.** "Zona Gale (1874–1938)." *American Literary Realism, 1870–1910*, 1, no. 3 (1968), 14–17.

GALLICO, PAUL

General Studies

2311. **Rao, V. V. B. Rama.** "The Achievement of Paul Gallico." *Indian Journal of American Studies*, 4, nos. 1–2 (1974), 78–87.

GARDNER, ERLE STANLEY

"It's the McCoy"

See 2312.

General Studies

2312. **Nevins, Francis M., Jr.** "Notes on Some Uncollected Gardners." *Journal of Popular Culture*, 21 (1968), 488–92.

Bibliography

2313. **MUNDELL, E. H.** *Erle Stanley Gardner: A Checklist*. Kent, OH: Kent State Univ. Press, 1968.

GARDNER, JOHN

Interviews

2314. **CLARK, C. E. FRAZER, JR.** "John Gardner." In *Conversations with Writers*, Vol. I. Detroit, MI: Gale, 1977. pp. 83–103.

2315. **ENSWORTH, PAT, AND JOE DAVID BELLAMY.** "John Gardner: An Interview." *fiction international*, nos. 2–3 (1974), pp. 33–49.

Bibliography

2316. **DILLON, DAVID D.** "John C. Gardner: A Bibliography." *Bulletin of Bibliography and Magazine Notes*, 34 (1977), 86–89, 104.

GARLAND, [HANNIBAL] HAMLIN

"Among the Corn Rows"

See 356.

"A Branch-Road"

See 203, 597, 2328.

"A Common Case"

See 2328.

"Delmar of Pima"

See 311.

"A Girl of Modern Tyre"

See 91.

"John Boyle's Conclusion"

2317. **PIZER, DONALD.** " 'John Boyle's Conclusion': An Unpublished Middle Border Story by Hamlin Garland." *American Literature*, 31 (1959), 59–75.
See also 2328.

"The Land of the Straddle-Bug"

See 2328.

"The Moccasin Ranch"

2318. **REAMER, OWEN J.** "Hamlin Garland: Literary Freedom Crusader Manqué." *The Markham Review*, 5 (1976), 47–52.

"The Return of a Private"

2319. IRSFELD, JOHN H. "The Use of Military Language in Hamlin Garland's 'The Return of a Private.' " *Western American Literature*, 7 (1972), 145–47.
See also 597.

"Rising Wolf—Ghost Dancer"
See 439.

"The Silent Eaters"
See 439, 2322, 2326, 2330.

"The Story of Howling Wolf"
See 439.

"Ten Years Dead"
See 2328.

"Under the Lion's Paw"
See 356.

"Up The Coulé"
See 597, 2320.

General Studies

2320. EVANS, T. JEFF. "The Return Motif as a Function of Realism in *Main-Travelled Roads.*" *Kansas Quarterly*, 5, no. 4 (1973), 33–40.
2321. FULLER, DANIEL J. "Mark Twain and Hamlin Garland: Contrarieties in Regionalism." *Mark Twain Journal*, 17, no. 1 (1974), 14–18.
2322. GISH, ROBERT. *Hamlin Garland: The Far West.* Boise, ID: Boise State Univ., 1976.
2323. HARRISON, STANLEY R. "Hamlin Garland and the Double Vision of Naturalism." *Studies in Short Fiction*, 6 (1969), 548–56.
2324. HOLLOWAY, JEAN. *Hamlin Garland: A Biography.* Austin: Univ. of Texas Press, 1960.
2325. MARTINEC, BARBARA. "Hamlin Garland's Revisions of *Main-Travelled Roads.*" *American Literary Realism, 1870-1910*, 5 (1972), 167–72.
2326. MEYER, ROY W. "Hamlin Garland and The American Indian." *Western American Literature*, 2 (1967), 109–25.
2327. MILLER, CHARLES T. "Hamlin Garland's Retreat from Realism." *Western American Literature*, 1 (1966), 119–29.

2328. **Pizer, Donald**. *Hamlin Garland's Early Work and Career.* Berkeley: Univ. of California Press, 1960.

2329. ———. "Introduction." In *Main-Travelled Roads*, by Hamlin Garland. Columbus, OH: Merrill, 1970. pp. v–xviii.

2330. **Reamer, Owen J.** "Garland and the Indians." *New Mexico Quarterly*, 34 (1964), 257–80.

2331. **Saum, Lewis O.** "Hamlin Garland and Reform." *South Dakota Review*, 10, no. 4 (1972), 36–62.

2332. **Underhill, Lonnie E.** "Hamlin Garland and the Indian." *American Indian Quarterly*, 1 (1974), 103–13.

2333. **Whitford, Kathryn.** "Crusader without a Cause: An Examination of Hamlin Garland's Middle Border." *Midcontinent American Studies Journal*, 6, no. 1 (1965), 61–72.

Bibliography

2334. **Arvidson, Lloyd A., ed.** *Hamlin Garland: Centennial Tributes and A Checklist of the Hamlin Garland Papers in the University of Southern California Library.* Los Angeles: Univ. of Southern California Library, 1962.

2335. **Bryer, Jackson R., and Eugene Harding.** "Hamlin Garland (1860–1940): A Bibliography of Secondary Comment." *American Literary Realism, 1870–1910*, 3 (1970), 290–387.

2336. ———, and ———. "Hamlin Garland: Reviews and Notices of His Work." *American Literary Realism, 1870–1910*, 4 (1971), 103–56.

2337. ———, ———, and **Robert A. Rees**. *Hamlin Garland and the Critics: An Annotated Bibliography.* Troy, NY: Whitston, 1973.

2338. **Pizer, Donald.** "Hamlin Garland (1860–1940)." *American Literary Realism, 1870–1910*, 1, no. 1 (1967), 45–51.

2339. **Silet, Charles L. P., and Robert E. Welch.** "Further Additions to *Hamlin Garland and the Critics.*" *American Literary Realism, 1870–1910*, 9 (1976), 268–75.

2340. **Stronks, James.** "A Supplement to Bryer & Harding's *Hamlin Garland and the Critics: An Annotated Bibliography.*" *American Literary Realism, 1870–1910*, 9 (1976), 261–67.

GARRETT, GEORGE

Interviews

2341. **Israel, Charles.** "Interview: George Garrett." *The South Carolina Review*, 6, no. 1 (1973), 43–48.

GASS, WILLIAM H.

"Icicles"

2342. KANE, PATRICIA. "A Point of Law in William Gass's 'Icicles.' " *Notes on Contemporary Literature*, 1, no. 2 (1971), 7–8.
See also 2349.

"In the Heart of the Heart of the Country"

2343. BUSCH, FREDERICK. "But This Is What It Is to Live in Hell: William Gass's 'In the Heart of the Heart of the Country.' " *Modern Fiction Studies*, 19 (1973), 97–108.
2344. SCHOLES, ROBERT. "The Fictional Heart of the Country: From Rølvaag to Gass." In *Ole Rølvaag: Artist and Cultural Leader*. Ed. Gerald Thorson. Northfield, MN: St. Olaf College Press, 1975. pp. 1–13.
See also 511, 2349.

"Mrs. Mean"

See 2349.

"The Pederson Kid"

2345. KANE, PATRICIA. "The Sun Burned on the Snow: Gass's 'The Pedersen Kid.' " *Critique*, 14, no. 2 (1972), 89–96.
See also 2349.

"Willie Masters' Lonesome Wife"

2346. BLAU, MARION. " 'How I Would Brood Upon You': The Lonesome Wife of William Gass." *The Great Lakes Review*, 2, no. 1 (1975), 40–50.
2347. McCAFFERY, LARRY. "The Art of Metafiction: William Gass's *William Masters' Lonesome Wife*." *Critique*, 18, no. 1 (1976), 21–35.
2348. MERRILL, REED B. "The Grotesque as Structure: 'Willie Masters' Lonesome Wife.' " *Criticism*, 18 (1976), 305–16.

General Studies

2349. BASSOFF, BRUCE. "The Sacrificial World of William Gass: *In the Heart of the Heart of the Country*." *Critique*, 18, no. 1 (1976), 36–58.
2350. FRENCH, NED. "Against the Grain: Theory and Practice in the Work of William H. Gass." *The Iowa Review*, 7, no. 1 (1976), 96–107.

Interviews

2351. DUNCAN, JEFFREY L. "A Conversation with Stanley Elkin and William H. Gass." *The Iowa Review*, 7, no. 1 (1976), 48–77.

2352. **GASS, WILLIAM.** "The Art of Fiction LXV." With Thomas LeClair. *The Paris Review*, no. 70 (1977), pp. 61–94.
2353. **McCAULEY, CAROLE SPEARIN.** "William H. Gass." In *The New Fiction: Interviews with Innovative American Writers*. Ed. Joe David Bellamy. Urbana: Univ. of Illinois Press, 1974. pp. 32–44.

Bibliography

2354. **McCAFFERY, LARRY.** "A William H. Gass Bibliography." *Critique*, 18, no. 1 (1976), 59–66.
2355. ———. "A William H. Gass Checklist." *Bulletin of Bibliography and Magazine Notes*, 31 (1974), 104–06.

GEROULD, KATHERINE FULLERTON

"The Great Tradition"

See 356.

"Wesendonck"

See 356.

GILL, BRENDAN

Interviews

2356. **BAKER, JOHN.** "Brendan Gill." In *Conversations with Writers*, Vol. 1. Detroit, MI: Gale, 1977. pp. 105–24.

GILMAN, CHARLOTTE PERKINS

"The Yellow Wallpaper"

2357. **HEDGES, ELAINE R.** "Afterword." In *The Yellow Wallpaper*, by Charlotte Perkins Gilman. Old Westbury, NY: Feminist Press, 1973. pp. 37–63.
2358. **MacPIKE, LORALEE.** "Environment as Psychopathological Symbolism in 'The Yellow Wallpaper.'" *American Literary Realism, 1870–1910*, 8 (1975), 286–88.
2359. ———. "Metaphors of Madness." *Moving Out*, 7, no. 1 (1977), 21–24.
2360. **SCHÖPP-SCHILLING, BEATE.** " 'The Yellow Wallpaper': A Rediscovered 'Realistic' Story." *American Literary Realism, 1870–1910*, 8 (1975), 284–86.

GIPSON, FRED
General Studies

2361. **HENDERSON, SAM H.** *Fred Gipson*. Austin, TX: Steck-Vaughn, 1967.

GLASGOW, ELLEN
"Between Two Shores"

See 2366, 2367.

"Dare's Gift"

See 2368.

"The Difference"

See 2368.

"Jordan's End"

See 2366–2368.

"The Past"

2362. **DILLARD, R. H. W.** "The Writer's Best Solace: Textual Revisions in Ellen Glasgow's 'The Past.' " *Studies in Bibliography*, 19 (1966), 245–50.

"A Point in Morals"

See 2369.

"The Professional Instinct"

2363. **KELLY, WILLIAM W., ED. WITH AN INTRO.** " 'The Professional Instinct': An Unpublished Short Story by Ellen Glasgow." *Western Humanities Review*, 16 (1962), 301–17.
See also 2368.

"Romance and Sally Byrd"

See 2368.

"The Shadowy Third"

See 2368.

"Thinking Makes It So"

See 2368.

"Whispering Leaves"

See 2368.

General Studies

2364. **GODBOLD, E. STANLEY, JR.** *Ellen Glasgow and the Woman Within*. Baton Rouge: Louisiana State Univ. Press, 1972.

2365. **McDOWELL, FREDERICK P. W.** *Ellen Glasgow and the Ironic Art of Fiction*. Madison: Univ. of Wisconsin Press, 1960.

2366. **MEEKER, RICHARD K.** "Introduction." In *The Collected Stories of Ellen Glasgow*. Baton Rouge: Louisiana State Univ. Press, 1963. pp. 3-23.

2367. ———. "The Shadowy Stories of Ellen Glasgow." In *The Dilemma of the Southern Writer: Institute of Southern Culture Lectures, Longwood College, 1961*. Ed. Richard K. Meeker. Farmville, VA: Longwood College, 1961. pp. 95-117.

2368. **RAPER, JULIUS ROWAN.** "Invisible Things: The Short Stories of Ellen Glasgow." *The Southern Literary Journal*, 9, no. 2 (1977), 66-90.

2369. ———. *Without Shelter: The Early Career of Ellen Glasgow*. Baton Rouge: Louisiana State Univ. Press, 1971.

2370. **RICHARDS, MARION K.** *Ellen Glasgow's Development as a Novelist*. The Hague: Mouton, 1971.

2371. **ROUSE, BLAIR.** *Ellen Glasgow*. New York: Twayne, 1962.

Bibliography

2372. **KELLEY, WILLIAM W.** *Ellen Glasgow: A Bibliography*. Charlottesville: Univ. Press of Virginia, 1964.

2373. **MacDONALD, EDGAR E.** "Ellen Glasgow: An Essay in Bibliography." *Resources for American Literary Study*, 2 (1972), 131-56.

2374. ———. "An Essay in Bibliography." In *Ellen Glasgow: Centennial Essays*. Ed. M. Thomas Inge. Charlottesville: Univ. Press of Virginia, 1976. pp. 191-224.

2375. **QUESENBERY, W. D., JR.** "Ellen Glasgow: A Critical Bibliography." *Bulletin of Bibliography and Magazine Notes*, 22 (1959), 201-06, 230-36.

GLASPELL, SUSAN

"A Jury of Her Peers"

See 535.

Bibliography

2376. **NOE, MARCIA.** "A Susan Glaspell Checklist." *Books at Iowa*, no. 27 (1977), pp. 14-20.

2377. **WATERMAN, ARTHUR E.** "Susan Glaspell (1882?-1948)." *American Literary Realism, 1870-1910*, 4 (1971), 183-91.

GODWIN, GAIL

"A Sorrowful Woman"

2378. **GARDINER, JUDITH K.** " 'A Sorrowful Woman': Gail Godwin's Feminist Parable." *Studies in Short Fiction*, 12 (1975), 287–90.

GOLD, HERBERT

"The Heart of the Artichoke"

See 202, 2380.

"The Witch"

2379. **KRUPP, KATHLEEN McCOY.** "Psychological Tripling in 'The Witch.' " In *The Process of Fiction: Contemporary Stories and Criticism.* Ed. Barbara McKenzie. New York: Harcourt, Brace & World, 1969. pp. 161–67.

General Studies

2380. **GOLD, HERBERT.** "Postface." In *Love & Like.* New York: Dial, 1960. pp. 301–07.
2381. **MOORE, HARRY T.** "The Fiction of Herbert Gold." In *Contemporary American Novelists.* Ed. Harry T. Moore. Carbondale: Southern Illinois Univ. Press, 1964. pp. 170–81.

Interviews

2382. **NEWQUIST, ROY.** "Herbert Gold." In *Counterpoint.* Chicago: Rand McNally, 1964. pp. 280–88.
2383. **TOOKER, DAN, AND ROGER HOFHEINS.** "Herbert Gold." In *Fiction!: Interviews with Northern California Novelists.* New York: Harcourt Brace Jovanovich, 1976. pp. 111–23.

GOLD, MICHAEL

"Love on a Garbage Dump"

See 2384.

General Studies

2384. **FOLSOM, MICHAEL BREWSTER.** "The Education of Michael Gold." In *Proletarian Writers of the Thirties.* Ed. David Madden. Carbondale and Edwardsville: Southern Illinois Univ. Press, 1968. pp. 222–51.

GOODMAN, PAUL

"The Architect from New York"

2385. SMITH, HADLEY ANNE. "The Measure of Larry Hodges." In *The Process of Fiction: Contemporary Stories and Criticism.* Ed. Barbara McKenzie. New York: Harcourt, Brace & World, 1969. pp. 280-85.

General Studies

2386. GARDNER, GEOFFREY. "Citizen of the World, Animal of Nowhere." *New Letters*, 42, nos. 2-3 (1976), 216-27.

2387. STOEHR, TAYLOR. "Introduction." *New Letters*, 42, nos. 2-3 (1976), 8-12.

2388. TRUE, MICHAEL. "Paul Goodman and the Triumph of American Prose Style." *New Letters*, 42, nos. 2-3 (1976), 228-36.

Bibliography

2389. GLASSHEIM, ELIOT. "Paul Goodman: A Checklist, 1931-1971." *Bulletin of Bibliography and Magazine Notes*, 29 (1972), 61-72.

2390. NICELY, TOM. "Notes toward a Bibliography: The Chief References & a Checklist of the Published Stories." *New Letters*, 42, nos. 2-3 (1976), 246-53.

GOODRICH, SAMUEL GRISWOLD

General Studies

2391. ROSELLE, DANIEL. *Samuel Griswold Goodrich, Creator of Peter Parley: A Study of His Life and Work.* Albany: State Univ. of New York Press, 1968.

GORDON, CAROLINE

"All Lovers Love the Spring"

See 2396.

"The Brilliant Leaves"

See 2396, 2405.

"The Burning Eyes"

See 2398.

"The Captive"

2392. BROWNE, JANE GIBSON. "Woman in Nature: A Study of Caroline Gordon's 'The Captive.' " In *The Short Fiction of Caroline Gordon: A Critical Symposium*. Ed. Thomas H. Landess. Dallas, TX: Univ. of Dallas Press, 1972. pp. 75–84.

2393. ROBB, KENNETH. "Self-Preservation in Caroline Gordon's 'The Captive.' " In *Itinerary 3: Criticism*. Ed. Frank Baldanza. Bowling Green, OH: Bowling Green Univ. Press, 1977. pp. 137–47.

2394. RUBIN, LARRY. "Christian Allegory in Caroline Gordon's 'The Captive.' " *Studies in Short Fiction*, 5 (1968), 283–89.

See also 2407.

"Emmanuele! Emmanuele!"

2395. DUPREE, ROBERT S. "Caroline Gordon's 'Constants' of Fiction." In *The Short Fiction of Caroline Gordon: A Critical Symposium*. Ed. Thomas H. Landess. Dallas, TX: Univ. of Dallas Press, 1972. pp. 33–51.

See also 2405, 2406.

"The Enemies"

See 2396, 2406.

"The Forest of the South"

See 2397.

"Hear the Nightingale Sing"

See 2397.

"Her Quaint Honor"

See 2400.

"The Ice House"

See 2397, 2406.

"The Last Day in the Field"

See 565, 2398, 2406.

"The Long Day"

See 2400.

"Mr. Powers"

See 2400.

"Old Red"

See 267, 394, 564, 2398, 2405, 2406.

"The Olive Garden"

See 2395.

"One Against Thebes"

See 2396, 2398, 2406.

"One More Time"

See 2406.

"The Petrified Woman"

See 2396.

"The Presence"

See 2398, 2406.

"Summer Dust"

See 2396, 2406.

"Tom Rivers"

See 2396, 2400.

General Studies

2396. ALVIS, JOHN E. "The Idea of Nature and the Sexual Role in Caroline Gordon's Early Short Stories of Love." In *The Short Fiction of Caroline Gordon: A Critical Symposium.* Ed. Thomas H. Landess. Dallas, TX: Univ. of Dallas Press, 1972. pp. 85–111.

2397. BRADFORD, M. E. "The High Cost of 'Union': Caroline Gordon's Civil War Stories." In *The Short Fiction of Caroline Gordon: A Critical Symposium.* Ed. Thomas H. Landess. Dallas, TX: Univ. of Dallas Press, 1972. pp. 113–29.

2398. COWAN, LOUISE. "Aleck Maury, Epic Hero and Pilgrim." In *The Short Fiction of Caroline Gordon: A Critical Symposium.* Ed. Thomas H. Landess, Dallas, TX: Univ. of Dallas Press, 1972. pp. 7–31.

2399. FLETCHER, MARIE. "The Fate of Women in a Changing South: A Persistent Theme in the Fiction of Caroline Gordon." *The Mississippi Quarterly,* 21 (1968), 17–28.

2400. LANDESS, THOMAS H. "Caroline Gordon's Ontological Stories." In *The Short Fiction of Caroline Gordon: A Critical Symposium.* Ed. Thomas H. Landess. Dallas, TX: Univ. of Dallas Press, 1972. pp. 53–73.

2401. _____. "Introduction." In *The Short Fiction of Caroline Gordon: A Critical Symposium*. Ed. Thomas H. Landess. Dallas, TX: Univ. of Dallas Press, 1972. pp. 1–5.

2402. McDowell, Frederick P. W. *Caroline Gordon*. Minneapolis: Univ. of Minnesota Press, 1966.

2403. O'Connor, William Van. "Art and Miss Gordon." In *South: Modern Southern Literature and Its Cultural Setting*. Ed. Louis D. Rubin, Jr., and Robert D. Jacobs. Garden City, NY: Dolphin Books, 1961. pp. 314–22.

2404. Rocks, James E. "The Mind and Art of Caroline Gordon." *The Mississippi Quarterly*, 21 (1968), 1–16.

2405. _____. "The Short Fiction of Caroline Gordon." *Tulane Studies in English*, 18 (1970), 115–35.

2406. Stuckey, W. J. *Caroline Gordon*. New York: Twayne, 1972.

Interviews

2407. Baum, Catherine B., and Floyd C. Watkins. "Caroline Gordon and 'The Captive': An Interview." *The Southern Review*, NS 7 (1971), 447–62.

Bibliography

2408. Bradford, M. E. "Caroline Gordon: A Working Bibliography, 1957–1972." In *The Short Fiction of Caroline Gordon: A Critical Symposium*. Ed. Thomas H. Landess. Dallas, TX: Univ. of Dallas Press, 1972. pp. 130–33.

2409. Golden, Robert E., and Mary C. Sullivan. *Flannery O'Connor and Caroline Gordon: A Reference Guide*. Boston, MA: G. K. Hall, 1977.

GOYEN, WILLIAM

"The Enchanted Nurse"

See 2411.

"The Rescue"

See 2411.

"The White Rooster"

2410. Phillips, Robert. "Samuels and Samson: Theme and Legend in 'The White Rooster.' " *Studies in Short Fiction*, 6 (1969), 331–33.

General Studies

2411. Paul, Jay S. " 'Marvelous Reciprocity': The Fiction of William Goyen." *Critique*, 19, no. 2 (1977), 77–91.

Interviews

2412. **GOYEN, WILLIAM.** "The Art of Fiction LXIII." With Robert Phillips. *The Paris Review*, no. 68 (1976), pp. 59–100.

GRANICH, IRWIN (See GOLD, MICHAEL)

GRAU, SHIRLEY ANN

"The Black Prince"

See 181.

"Eight O'Clock One Morning"

See 374.

General Studies

2413. **BERLAND, ALWYN.** "The Fiction of Shirley Ann Grau." *Critique*, 6, no. 1 (1963), 78–84.
2414. **PEARSON, ANN.** "Shirley Ann Grau: Nature is the Vision." *Critique*, 17, no. 2 (1975), 47–58.

Bibliography

2415. **GRISSOM, MARGARET S.** "Shirley Ann Grau: A Checklist." *Bulletin of Bibliography and Magazine Notes*, 28 (1971), 76–78.

GREENLEE, SAM

Interviews

2416. **BURRELL, WALTER.** "Rappin With Sam Greenlee." *Black World*, 20, no. 9 (1971), 42–47.

GREY, ZANE

General Studies

2417. **GRUBER, FRANK.** *Zane Grey.* Cleveland, OH: World, 1970.
2418. **JACKSON, CARLTON.** *Zane Grey.* Boston, MA: Twayne, 1973.

GUTHRIE, A[LFRED] B[ERTRAM], JR.

"Mountain Medicine"

2419. **TODD, EDGELEY W.** "A Note on 'The Mountain Man as Literary Hero.'" *Western American Literature*, 1 (1966), 219–21.
See also 600.

General Studies

2420. FORD, THOMAS W. *A. B. Guthrie, Jr.* Austin, TX: Steck-Vaughn, 1968.

Bibliography

2421. ETULAIN, RICHARD W. "A. B. Guthrie: A Bibliography." *Western American Literature*, 4 (1969), 133–38.

HALE, EDWARD EVERETT

"*A Man Without a Country*"

See 616.

General Studies

2422. ADAMS, JOHN R. *Edward Everett Hale.* Boston, MA: Twayne, 1977.

HALE, NANCY

"*A Summer's Long Dream*"

See 455.

HALE, SARAH JOSEPHA

"*The Silver Mine*"

See 2423.

General Studies

2423. TAYLOR, WILLIAM R. *Cavalier and Yankee: The Old South and American National Character.* New York: Braziller, 1961.

HALL, JAMES

"*The Backwoodsman*"

See 90.

HALL, JAMES NORMAN

General Studies

2424. BRIAND, PAUL L., JR. *In Search of Paradise: The Nordhoff-Hall Story.* New York: Duell, Sloan & Pearce, 1966.

HALL, OAKLEY
"The Crown"
See 197.

"The Retaining Wall"
See 197.

HALLET, RICHARD MATTHEWS
Bibliography
2425. CARY, RICHARD. "A Bibliography of Richard Matthews Hallet." *Colby Library Quarterly*, 7 (1967), 453–63.

HAMMETT, [SAMUEL] DASHIELL
"The Big Knockover"
See 2427.

General Studies
2426. BLAIR, WALTER. "Dashiell Hammett: Themes and Techniques." In *Essays on American Literature in Honor of Jay B. Hubbell*. Ed. Clarence Gohdes. Durham, NC: Duke Univ. Press, 1967. pp. 295–306.
2427. NOLAN, WILLIAM F. *Dashiell Hammett: A Casebook*. Santa Barbara, CA: McNally & Loftin, 1969.

Bibliography
2428. FLOWER, DESMOND. "A Dashiell Hammett Omnibus." *The Book Collector*, 11 (1962), 217.
2429. MUNDELL, E. H. *A List of Original Appearances of Dashiell Hammett's Magazine Work*. Kent, OH: Kent State Univ. Press, 1968.
2430. NOLAN, WILLIAM F. "The Hammett Checklist Revisited." *The Armchair Detective*, 6 (1973), 249–54.
2431. _____. "Revisiting the Revisited Hammett Checklist." *The Armchair Detective*, 9 (1976), 292–95, 324–29.
2432. _____. "Shadowing the Continental Op." *The Armchair Detective*, 8 (1975), 121–23.
2433. SANDOE, JAMES. "The Hardboiled Dick: A Personal Checklist." *The Armchair Detective*, 1 (1968), 38–42.
2434. STODDARD, ROGER E. "Some Uncollected Authors XXXI: Dashiell Hammett, 1894–1961." *The Book Collector*, 11 (1962), 71–78.

HANNAH, BARRY

"Behold the Husband in His Perfect Agony"

See 2435.

General Studies

2435. **HILL, ROBERT W.** "Barry Hannah." *The South Carolina Review*, 9, no. 1 (1976), 25–29.

HARBEN, WILL[IAM] N.

General Studies

2436. **BUSH, ROBERT.** "Will N. Harben's Northern Georgia Fiction." *The Mississippi Quarterly*, 20 (1967), 103–17.

HARRIS, CORRA

General Studies

2437. **TALMADGE, JOHN E.** *Corra Harris: Lady of Purpose.* Athens: Univ. of Georgia Press, 1968.

HARRIS, GEORGE WASHINGTON

"Bill Ainsworth's Quarter Race"

2438. **BLAIR, WALTER.** "Harris' Best: Bill Ainsworth's Quarter Race." *The Lovingood Papers 1965*, pp. 16–25.

"Dad's Dog School"

See 2457, 2469.

"Frustrating a Funeral"

See 549.

"How Sut Love[n]good Dosed His Dog"

2439. **BUNGERT, HANS.** "How Sut Lovegood [*sic*] Dosed His Dog." *The Lovingood Papers 1963*, pp. 32–34.

"The Knob Dance"

See 2469.

"Mrs. Yardley's Quilting"

2440. **McCLARY, BEN HARRIS.** "On Quilts." *The Lovingood Papers 1965*, pp. 61–62.

"Old Skissim's Middle Boy"

See 549.

"Playing Old Sledge for the Presidency"

2441. **WEBER, BROM.** "Playing Old Sledge for the Presidency: Dream of Sut Lovengood's." *The Lovingood Papers 1962*, pp. 25-29.

"Rare Ripe Garden Seed"

See 2469.

"A Snake-Bit Irishman"

See 2469.

"Sut Lovengood at Bull's Gap"

2442. **MILLER, F. DeWOLFE.** "Sut Lovengood at Bull's Gap." *The Lovingood Papers 1962*, pp. 36-46.

"Sut Lovengood Blown Up"

See 2469.

"Sut Lovengood Escapes Assassination"

See 2444.

"Sut Lovengood, on the Puritan Yankee"

2443. **BUNGERT, HANS.** "Sut Lovengood, on the Puritan Yankee." *The Lovingood Papers 1963*, pp. 57-60.
See also 2469.

"Sut Lovengood Reports What Bob Dawson Said,
After Marrying a Substitute"

See 2454.

"Sut Lovengood Travels with Old Abe"

See 2469.

"Sut Lovengood's Adventures in New York"

2444. **DAY, DONALD.** "Sut Lovengood's Adventures in New York." *The Lovingood Papers 1964*, pp. 10-21.

"Sut Lovengood's Big Dinner Story"

2445. **PARKS, EDD WINFIELD.** "Sut Lovengood's Big Dinner Story." *The Lovingood Papers 1963*, pp. 49-56.

"Sut Lovengood's Big Music Box Story"

2446. McCLARY, BEN HARRIS. "Sut Lovingood's Big Music Box Story." *The Lovingood Papers 1964*, pp. 30–34.

"Sut Lovengood's Chest Story"

2447. MILLER, F. DeWOLFE. "Sut Lovengood's Chest Story." *The Lovingood Papers 1962*, pp. 30–35.
See also 2469.

"Sut Lovengood's Daddy 'Acting Horse'"

See 2469.

"Sut Lovengood's Hark from the Tombs Story"

2448. FOLMSBEE, STANLEY J., AND THOMAS C. SCHRODT. "Sut Lovengood's Hark from the Tombs Story." *The Lovingood Papers 1964*, pp. 35–39.

"Sut Lovengood's Shirt"

See 2469.

"Sut Lovingood Allegory"

See 2463.

"Sut Lovingood Come to Life"

2449. RICKELS, MILTON. "Sut Lovingood Come to Life." *The Lovingood Papers 1963*, pp. 42–47.
See also 2463, 2469.

"Sut Lovingood's Dream: Tartarus, and What He Saw There"

2450. HILL, HAMLIN. "Sut Lovingood's Dream: Tartarus, and What He Saw There." *The Lovingood Papers 1963*, pp. 61–64.
See also 2469.

"Sut Lovingood's Hog Ride"

2451. INGE, M. THOMAS. "Sut Lovingood's Hog Ride." *The Lovingood Papers 1963*, pp. 35–41.

*"Sut Lovingood's Love-Feast of Varmints Held at Nashville,
March 28th and 29th"*

2452. GRAF, LeROY P. "Sut Lovingood's Love-Feast of Varmints Held at Nashville, March 28th and 29th." *The Lovingood Papers 1963*, pp. 13–31.
See also 2463.

"Well! Dad's Dead"

See 2469.

General Studies

2453. BOYKIN, CAROL. "Sut's Speech: The Dialect of a 'Nat'ral Borned' Mountaineer." *The Lovingood Papers 1965*, pp. 36–42.

2454. BROWNE, RAY B. "Marrying a Substitute." *The Lovingood Papers 1964*, pp. 22–29.

2455. BURT, JESSE C., AND GILBERT GOVAN. "Sut's Dedicatory." *The Lovingood Papers 1962*, pp. 11–17.

2456. COHEN, HENNIG. "Mark Twain's Sut Lovingood." *The Lovingood Papers 1962*, pp. 19–24.

2457. CURRENT-GARCIA, EUGENE. "Sut Lovingood's Rare Ripe Southern Garden." *Studies in Short Fiction*, 9 (1972), 117–29.

2458. DAY, DONALD. "Searching for Sut: A Chapter from His Autobiography." *The Lovingood Papers 1965*, pp. 9–15.

2459. HOWELL, ELMO. "Timon in Tennessee: The Moral Fever of George Washington Harris." *The Georgia Review*, 24 (1970), 311–19.

2460. INGE, M. THOMAS. "Introduction." In *High Times and Hard Times: Sketches and Tales by George Washington Harris*. Nashville, TN: Vanderbilt Univ. Press, 1967. pp. 3–8.

2461. _____. "Introduction." In *Sut Lovingood's Yarns*, by George Washington Harris. New Haven, CT: College and University Press, 1966. pp. 9–24.

2462. _____. "A Personal Encounter with George W. Harris." *The Lovingood Papers 1963*, pp. 9–12.

2463. _____. "The Satiric Artistry of George W. Harris." *Satire Newsletter*, 4 (1967), 63–72.

2464. _____. "Sut and His Contemporary Reviewers." *The Lovingood Papers 1965*, pp. 55–56.

2465. _____. "Sut and His Illustrations." *The Lovingood Papers 1965*, pp. 26–35.

2466. _____. "William Faulkner and George Washington Harris: In the Tradition of Southwestern Humor." *Tennessee Studies In Literature*, 7 (1962), 47–59.

2467. KNIGHT, DONALD R. "Sut's Dog Imagery." *The Lovingood Papers 1965*, pp. 59–60.

2468. LEARY, LEWIS. "The Lovingoods: Notes Toward a Genealogy." In *Southern Excursions: Essays on Mark Twain and Others*. Baton Rouge: Louisiana State Univ. Press, 1971. pp. 111–30.

2469. RICKELS, MILTON. *George Washington Harris*. New York: Twayne, 1965.

2470. _____. "The Imagery of George Washington Harris."
American Literature, 31 (1959), 173–87.

2471. ROSS, STEPHEN M. "Jason Compson and Sut Lovingood:
Southwestern Humor as Stream of Consciousness." *Studies in the
Novel*, 8 (1976), 278–90.

2472. WEBER, BROM. "A Note on Edmund Wilson and George
Washington Harris." *The Lovingood Papers 1962*, pp. 47–53.

Bibliography

2473. MCCLARY, BEN HARRIS. "George and Sut: A Working Bibliography." *The Lovingood Papers 1962*, pp. 5–9.

HARRIS, JOEL CHANDLER

"At Teague Poteet's"

See 91, 2475.

"Azalia"

See 91.

"The Comedy of War"

See 457.

"Free Joe and the Rest of the World"

See 2475.

"A Ghost Story"

See 6408.

"Little Compton"

See 571.

"Mingo"

See 571, 2475.

"Mr. Rabbit Grossly Deceives Mr. Fox"

See 86.

"Mombi: Her Friends and Her Enemies"

See 576.

"A Story about the Little Rabbits"

See 386.

"Tar-Baby"

2474. **REID, JOHN T.** "From India to America through Spain." *The Literary Half-Yearly*, 2, no. 1 (1961), 83–84.

General Studies

2475. **COUSINS, PAUL M.** *Joel Chandler Harris: A Biography*. Baton Rouge: Louisiana State Univ. Press, 1968.

2476. **DAVID, BEVERLY R.** "Visions of the South: Joel Chandler Harris and His Illustrators." *American Literary Realism, 1870–1910*, 9 (1976), 189–206.

2477. **DOWNS, ROBERT B.** "Black Folktales: Joel Chandler Harris's *Uncle Remus: His Songs and His Sayings*." In *Books That Changed the South*. Chapel Hill: Univ. of North Carolina Press, 1977. pp. 156–64.

2478. **ENGLISH, THOMAS H.** "The Other Uncle Remus." *The Georgia Review*, 21 (1967), 210–17.

2479. **FLUSCHE, MICHAEL.** "Joel Chandler Harris and the Folklore of Slavery." *Journal of American Studies*, 9 (1975), 347–63.

2480. _____. "Underlying Despair in the Fiction of Joel Chandler Harris." *The Mississippi Quarterly*, 29 (1976), 91–103.

2481. **LIGHT, KATHLEEN.** "Uncle Remus and the Folklorists." *The Southern Literary Journal*, 7, no. 2 (1975), 88–104.

2482. **RUBIN, LOUIS D., JR.** "Uncle Remus and the Ubiquitous Rabbit." *The Southern Review*, NS 10 (1974), 787–804.

2483. **TURNER, DARWIN T.** "Daddy Joel Harris and His Old-Time Darkies." *The Southern Literary Journal*, 1, no. 1 (1968), 20–41.

2484. **WOODS, GEORGE A.** "In Uncle Remus Land." *The New York Times Book Review*, 17 Dec. 1967, p. 18.

Bibliography

2485. **STRICKLAND, WILLIAM BRADLEY.** "A Check List of the Periodical Contributions of Joel Chandler Harris (1848–1908)." *American Literary Realism, 1870–1910*, 9 (1976), 207–29.

2486. **TURNER, ARLIN.** "Joel Chandler Harris (1848–1908)." *American Literary Realism, 1870–1910*, 1, no. 3 (1968), 18–23.

HARRIS, MARILYN

Interviews

2487. **SMITH, NORMAN, AND FRED WOODRUFF.** "An Interview with Marilyn Harris." *Cimarron Review*, no. 40 (1977), pp. 27–36.

HARRIS, MARK

Interviews

2488. **ENCK, JOHN J.** "Mark Harris: An Interview." *Wisconsin Studies in Contemporary Literature*, 6 (1965), 15–26.

HARTE, [FRANCIS] BRET[T]

"High-Water Mark"

See 83.

"In the Carquinez Woods"

See 2496.

"An Ingénue of the Sierras"

2489. **McKEITHAN, D. M.** "Bret Harte's Yuba Bill Meets The Ingenue." *The Mark Twain Journal*, 14, no. 1 (1968), 1–7.
See also 60, 2502.

"The Judgment of Bolinas Plain"

See 2504.

"The Luck of Roaring Camp"

2490. **BOGGAN, J. R.** "The Regeneration of 'Roaring Camp.'" *Nineteenth-Century Fiction*, 22 (1967), 271–80.
See also 27, 82, 83, 439, 454, 597, 2497, 2499, 2501, 2502.

"The Mystery of the Hacienda"

See 2504.

"The Outcasts of Poker Flat"

See 83, 2502.

"The Passing of Enríquez"

See 546.

"The Right Eye of the Commander"

See 2499.

"The Story of a Mine"

See 60.

"Tennessee's Partner"

2491. **HUTCHINSON, E. R.** "Harte's 'Tennessee's Partner.'" *The Explicator*, 22 (1963), item 10.

2492. **MAY, CHARLES E.** "Bret Harte's 'Tennessee's Partner': The Reader Euchred." *South Dakota Review*, 15, no. 1 (1977), 109–17.
See also 394, 2497.

"Thankful Blossom"
See 2502.

"What Happened at the Fonda"
See 2504.

General Studies

2493. **BUCKLAND, ROSCOE L.** "Jack Hamlin: Bret Harte's Romantic Rogue." *Western American Literature*, 8 (1973), 111–22.

2494. **CLARK, GEORGE PIERCE.** "Mark Twain on Bret Harte." *The Mark Twain Journal*, 10, no. 4 (1958), 12–13.

2495. **GARDNER, JOSEPH H.** "Bret Harte and the Dickensian Mode in America." *The Canadian Review of American Studies*, 2 (1971), 89–101.

2496. **GLOVER, DONALD E.** "A Reconsideration of Bret Harte's Later Work." *Western American Literature*, 8 (1973), 143–51.

2497. **KRAUSE, SYDNEY J.** "Bret Harte: The Grumbling Realist's Friend and Foe." In *Mark Twain as Critic*. Baltimore, MD: Johns Hopkins Press, 1967. pp. 190–224.

2498. **LAUTERBACH, EDWARD S.** "Tom Hood Discovers Bret Harte." *American Literature*, 34 (1962), 285–87.

2499. **MORROW, PATRICK.** *Bret Harte*. Boise, ID: Boise State College, 1972.

2500. _____. "Bret Harte, Popular Fiction, and the Local Color Movement." *Western American Literature*, 8 (1973), 123–31.

2501. _____. "The Predicament of Bret Harte." *American Literary Realism, 1870–1910*, 5 (1972), 181–88.

2502. **O'CONNOR, RICHARD.** *Bret Harte: A Biography*. Boston, MA: Little, Brown, 1966.

2503. **STEGNER, WALLACE.** "Introduction." In *The Outcasts of Poker Flat and Other Tales*, by Bret Harte. New York: New American Library, 1961. pp. vii–xvi.

2504. **THOMAS, JEFFREY F.** "Bret Harte and the Power of Sex." *Western American Literature*, 8 (1973), 91–109.

Bibliography

2505. **BARNETT, LINDA D.** "Bret Harte: An Annotated Bibliography of Secondary Comment." *American Literary Realism, 1870–1910*, 5 (1972), 189–320, 331–484.

2506. **MORROW, PATRICK.** "Bret Harte (1836–1902)." *American Literary Realism, 1870–1910,* 3 (1970), 167–77.

HAWES, WILLIAM P.
"A Bear Story and No Mistake!"
See 460.

"A Shark Story"
See 460.

HAWKES, JOHN
"Charivari"

2507. **FRAKES, JAMES R.** "The 'Undramatized Narrator' in John Hawkes: Who Says?" In *A John Hawkes Symposium: Design and Debris.* Ed. Anthony C. Santore and Michael Pocalyko. New York: New Directions, 1977. pp. 27–37.

2508. **GREEN, JAMES L.** "Nightmare and Fairy Tale in Hawkes' 'Charivari.'" *Critique,* 13, no. 1 (1971), 83–95.

2509. **SCHOLES, ROBERT.** *The Fabulators.* New York: Oxford Univ. Press, 1967.
See also 257, 2512, 2513.

"Death of an Airman"

2510. **LeCLAIR, THOMAS.** "John Hawkes's 'Death of an Airman' and *Second Skin*." *Notes on Contemporary Literature,* 4, no. 1 (1974), 2–3.

"The Goose on the Grave"
See 257, 2512, 2513, 2515.

"The Owl"

2511. **SCHOLES, ROBERT.** "John Hawkes as Novelist: The Example of the Owl." *The Hollins Critic,* 14, no. 3 (1977), 1–10.
See also 257, 2512, 2513, 2515, 2516.

"The Traveler"
See 2519.

General Studies

2512. **BUSCH, FREDERICK.** *Hawkes: A Guide to His Fictions.* Syracuse, NY: Syracuse Univ. Press, 1973.

2513. **GREINER, DONALD J.** *Comic Terror: The Novels of John Hawkes.* Memphis, TN: Memphis State Univ. Press, 1973.

2514. **KLEIN, MARCUS.** "John Hawkes' Experimental Compositions." In *Surfiction: Fiction Now . . . and Tomorrow.* Ed. Raymond Federman. Chicago: Swallow, 1975. pp. 203–14.

2515. **KUEHL, JOHN.** *John Hawkes and the Craft of Conflict.* New Brunswick, NJ: Rutgers Univ. Press, 1975.

2516. **MATTHEWS, CHARLES.** "The Destructive Vision of John Hawkes." *Critique*, 6, no. 2 (1963), 38–52.

2517. **ROVIT, EARL.** "The Fiction of John Hawkes: An Introductory View." *Modern Fiction Studies*, 10 (1964), 150–62.

2518. **SCHOTT, WEBSTER.** "John Hawkes, American Original." *The New York Times Book Review*, 29 May 1966, pp. 4, 24–25.

2519. **STEINER, ROBERT.** "Form and the Bourgeois Traveler." In *A John Hawkes Symposium: Design and Debris.* Ed. Anthony C. Santore and Michael Pocalyko. New York: New Directions, 1977. pp. 109–41.

2520. **TRACHTENBERG, ALAN.** "Barth and Hawkes: Two Fabulists." *Critique*, 6, no. 2 (1963), 4–29.

Interviews

2521. **DUNN, DOUGLAS.** "Profile 11: John Hawkes." *The New Review*, 1, no. 12 (1975), 23–28.

2522. **EMMETT, PAUL, AND RICHARD VINE.** "A Conversation with John Hawkes." *Chicago Review*, 28, no. 2 (1976), 163–71.

2523. **ENCK, JOHN J.** "John Hawkes: An Interview." *Wisconsin Studies in Contemporary Literature*, 6 (1965), 141–55.

2524. **FRANKEL, HASKEL.** "Professors to Ping Pong Players." *Saturday Review*, 47 (25 July 1964), 22–23.

2525. **GRAHAM, JOHN.** "John Hawkes: On His Novels." *The Massachusetts Review*, 7 (1966), 449–61.

2526. **KUEHL, JOHN.** "Interview." In *John Hawkes and the Craft of Conflict.* New Brunswick, NJ: Rutgers Univ. Press, 1975. pp. 155–83.

2527. **LEVINE, NANCY.** "An Interview with John Hawkes." In *A John Hawkes Symposium: Design and Debris.* Ed. Anthony C. Santore and Michael Pocalyko. New York: New Directions, 1977. pp. 91–108.

2528. **SANTORE, ANTHONY C., AND MICHAEL POCALYKO.** "'A Trap to Catch Little Birds With': An Interview with John Hawkes." In *A John Hawkes Symposium: Design and Debris.* Ed. Anthony C. Santore and Michael Pocalyko. New York: New Directions, 1977. pp. 165–84.

2529. _____, AND _____, ED. "John Hawkes and Albert Guerard in Dialogue." In *A John Hawkes Symposium: Design and Debris*. Ed. Anthony C. Santore and Michael Pocalyko. New York:
New Directions, 1977. pp. 14–26.

Bibliography

2530. BRYER, JACKSON R. "Two Bibliographies." *Critique*, 6, no.
2 (1963), 86–94.
2531. PLUNG, DANIEL. "John Hawkes: A Selected Bibliography,
1943–1975." *Critique*, 17, no. 3 (1976), 53–63.
2532. SCOTTO, ROBERT M. *Three Contemporary Novelists: An Annotated Bibliography of Works by and about John Hawkes, Joseph
Heller, and Thomas Pynchon*. New York: Garland, 1977.

HAWTHORNE, JULIAN

"The Minister's Oath"

See 2533.

General Studies

2533. BASSAN, MAURICE. *Hawthorne's Son: The Life and Literary
Career of Julian Hawthorne*. Columbus: Ohio State Univ. Press,
1970.

Bibliography

2534. BASSAN, MAURICE. "The Literary Career of Julian Hawthorne: A Selected Check List." *Bulletin of Bibliography and
Magazine Notes*, 24 (1965), 157–62.
2535. MONTEIRO, GEORGE. "Additions to the Bibliography of Julian Hawthorne." *Bulletin of Bibliography and Magazine Notes*, 25
(1967), 64.
2536. _____. "Further Additions to the Bibliography of Julian
Hawthorne." *Bulletin of Bibliography and Magazine Notes*, 27
(1970), 6–7.

HAWTHORNE, NATHANIEL

"Alice Doane's Appeal"

2537. BAYM, NINA. "Hawthorne's Gothic Discards: *Fanshawe*
and 'Alice Doane.'" *The Nathaniel Hawthorne Journal 1974*, pp.
105–15.
2538. BRODWIN, STANLEY. "Hawthorne and the Function of
History: A Reading of 'Alice Doane's Appeal.'" *The Nathaniel
Hawthorne Journal 1974*, pp. 116–28.

2539. **COFFEY, DENNIS G.** "Hawthorne's 'Alice Doane's Appeal': The Artist Absolved." *ESQ*, 21 (1975), 230–40.

2540. **ELIAS, HELEN L.** "Alice Doane's Innocence: The Wizard Absolved." *ESQ*, no. 62 (1971), pp. 28–32.

2541. **FOSSUM, ROBERT H.** "The Summons of the Past: Hawthorne's 'Alice Doane's Appeal.' " *Nineteenth-Century Fiction*, 23 (1968), 294–303.

2542. **SCHROEDER, JOHN.** "Alice Doane's Story: An Essay on Hawthorne and Spenser." *The Nathaniel Hawthorne Journal 1974*, pp. 129–34.

2543. **SWANN, CHARLES.** "'Alice Doane's Appeal': or, How to Tell a Story." *Literature and History*, no. 5 (1977), pp. 4–25.

See also 106, 2841, 2860, 2893, 2898, 2916, 2961, 2968, 3002, 3006, 3021.

"The Ambitious Guest"

2544. **D'AVANZO, MARIO L.** "The Ambitious Guest at the Hands of an Angry God." *English Language Notes*, 14 (1976), 38–42.

2545. **DEVLIN, JAMES E.** "A German Analogue for 'The Ambitious Guest.'" *American Transcendental Quarterly*, no. 17 (1973), pp. 71–74.

2546. **GROSSMAN, JAMES.** "Vanzetti and Hawthorne." *American Quarterly*, 22 (1970), 902–07.

2547. **MOSS, SIDNEY P.** "The Mountain God of Hawthorne's *The Ambitious Guest*." *The Emerson Society Quarterly*, no. 47 (1967), pp. 74–75.

See also 2842, 2871.

"The Antique Ring"

2548. **McDONALD, JOHN J.** "Longfellow in Hawthorne's 'The Antique Ring.'" *The New England Quarterly*, 46 (1973), 622–26.

See also 2892.

"The Artist of the Beautiful"

2549. **BILLY, TED.** "Time and Transformation in 'The Artist of the Beautiful.'" *American Transcendental Quarterly*, no. 29 (1976), pp. 33–35.

2550. **BRILL, LESLEY W.** "Conflict and Accommodation in Hawthorne's 'The Artist of the Beautiful.'" *Studies in Short Fiction*, 12 (1975), 381–86.

2551. **CUDDY, LOIS A.** "Symbolic Identification of Whitman with Hawthorne." *American Notes & Queries*, 15 (1977), 71–72.

2552. **CURRAN, RONALD T.** "Irony: Another Thematic Dimension to 'The Artist of the Beautiful.'" *Studies in Romanticism*, 6 (1966), 34–45.

2553. **DELAUNE, HENRY M.** "The Beautiful in 'The Artist of the Beautiful.'" *Xavier University Studies*, 1 (1961), 94–99.

2554. **DETTLAFF, SHIRLEY M.** "The Concept of Beauty in 'The Artist of the Beautiful' and Hugh Blair's Rhetoric." *Studies in Short Fiction*, 13 (1976), 512–15.

2555. **GARGANO, JAMES W.** "Hawthorne's 'The Artist of the Beautiful.'" *American Literature*, 35 (1963), 225–30.

2556. **LEWIS, PAUL.** "Victor Frankenstein and Owen Warland: The Artist as Satan and as God." *Studies in Short Fiction*, 14 (1977), 279–82.

2557. **LIEBMAN, SHELDON W.** "Hawthorne's Romanticism: 'The Artist of the Beautiful.'" *ESQ*, 22 (1976), 85–95.

2558. **McCULLEN, J. T., JR.** "Influences on Hawthorne's 'The Artist of the Beautiful.'" *The Emerson Society Quarterly*, no. 50, Supplement (1968), pp. 43–46.

2559. **MOORE, L. HUGH, JR.** "Hawthorne's Ideal Artist as Presumptuous Intellectual." *Studies in Short Fiction*, 2 (1965), 278–83.

2560. **MOYER, PATRICIA.** "Time and the Artist in Kafka and Hawthorne." *Modern Fiction Studies*, 4 (1958), 295–306.

2561. **SANDERS, CHARLES.** "A Note on Metamorphosis in Hawthorne's 'The Artist of the Beautiful.'" *Studies in Short Fiction*, 4 (1966), 82–83.

2562. **SCHRIBER, MARY SUE.** "Emerson, Hawthorne, and 'The Artist of the Beautiful.'" *Studies in Short Fiction*, 8 (1971), 607–16.

2563. **STEIN, WILLIAM BYSSHE.** "'The Artist of the Beautiful': Narcissus and the Thimble." *American Imago*, 18 (1961), 35–44.

2564. **TRAVIS, MILDRED K.** "Of 'Hawthorne's "The Artist of the Beautiful" and Spenser's "Muiopotmos." ' " *Philological Quarterly*, 54 (1975), 537.

2565. **WEST, HARRY C.** "The Sources for Hawthorne's 'The Artist of the Beautiful.'" *Nineteenth-Century Fiction*, 30 (1975), 105–11.

2566. **WOODWARD, ROBERT H.** "Automata in Hawthorne's 'Artist of the Beautiful' and Taylor's 'Meditation 56.'" *The Emerson Society Quarterly*, no. 31 (1963), pp. 63–66.

2567. **ZIVLEY, SHERRY.** "Hawthorne's 'The Artist of the Beautiful' and Spenser's 'Muiopotmos.'" *Philological Quarterly*, 48 (1969), 134–37.

See also 11, 35, 54, 109, 377, 503, 597, 2569, 2589, 2821, 2833, 2835, 2842, 2843, 2860, 2863, 2865, 2879, 2880, 2882, 2889, 2892, 2893, 2896, 2898, 2912, 2917, 2921, 2946, 2949, 2961, 2995, 3020.

"The Battle-Omen"

See 47.

"The Birth-Mark"

2568. **ARNER, ROBERT D.** "The Legend of Pygmalion in 'The Birthmark.'" *American Transcendental Quarterly*, no. 14 (1972), pp. 168-71.

2569. **BAXTER, DAVID J.** "'The Birthmark' in Perspective." *The Nathaniel Hawthorne Journal 1975*, pp. 232-40.

2570. **CHAMBERS, JANE.** "Two Legends of Temperance: Spenser's and Hawthorne's." *ESQ*, 20 (1974), 275-79.

2571. **COLSON, THEODORE.** "Analogues of Faulkner's *The Wild Palms* and Hawthorne's 'The Birthmark.'" *Dalhousie Review*, 56 (1976), 510-18.

2572. **FRANKLIN, H. BRUCE.** "Science Fiction as an Index to Popular Attitudes toward Science: A Danger, Some Problems, and Two Possible Paths." *Extrapolation*, 6 (1965), 23-31.

2573. **HORNE, LEWIS B.** "The Heart, the Hand and 'The Birthmark.'" *American Transcendental Quarterly*, no. 1 (1969), pp. 38-41.

2574. **REID, ALFRED S.** "Hawthorne's Humanism: 'The Birthmark' and Sir Kenelm Digby." *American Literature*, 38 (1966), 337-51.

2575. **SCHEER, THOMAS F.** "Aylmer's Divine Roles in 'The Birthmark.'" *American Transcendental Quarterly*, no. 22 (1974), p. 108.

2576. **VAN LEER, DAVID M.** "Aylmer's Library: Transcendental Alchemy in Hawthorne's 'The Birthmark.'" *ESQ*, 22 (1976), 211-20.

2577. **VAN WINKLE, EDWARD S.** "Aminadab, the Unwitting 'Bad Anima.'" *American Notes & Queries*, 8 (1970), 131-33.

2578. **WALSH, THOMAS F., JR.** "Character Complexity in Hawthorne's 'The Birthmark.'" *The Emerson Society Quarterly*, no. 23 (1961), pp. 12-15.

2579. **WENTERSDORF, KARL P.** "The Genesis of Hawthorne's 'The Birthmark.'" *Jahrbuch für Amerikastudien*, 8 (1963), 171-86.

2580. **WEST, HARRY C.** "The Evolution of Hawthorne's 'The Birth-mark': From Source to Artifact." *The Nathaniel Hawthorne Journal 1976*, pp. 240-56.

See also 35, 399, 566, 2821, 2834, 2835, 2840, 2842, 2843, 2860, 2882, 2889, 2892, 2893, 2896, 2898, 2940, 2948, 2949, 2961, 2987, 2991, 3013, 3015, 3017, 5042.

"A Book of Autographs"

See 2978.

"The Canterbury Pilgrims"

2581.   LEVY, LEO B. "Hawthorne's 'Middle Ground.'" *Studies in Short Fiction*, 2 (1964), 56–60.
2582.   SECOR, ROBERT. "Hawthorne's 'The Canterbury Pilgrims.'" *The Explicator*, 22 (1963), item 8.
See also 2871, 2893, 3006.

"The Celestial Rail-Road"

2583.   BRUCCOLI, MATTHEW J. "Negative Evidence About 'The Celestial Rail-Road.'" *The Papers of the Bibliographical Society of America*, 58 (1964), 290–92.
2584.   PATTISON, JOSEPH C. "'The Celestial Railroad' as Dream-Tale." *American Quarterly*, 20 (1968), 224–36.
2585.   WOOD, CLIFFORD A. "Teaching Hawthorne's 'The Celestial Railroad.'" *The English Journal*, 54 (1965), 601–05.
See also 13, 2821, 2824, 2842, 2879, 2892, 2893, 2898, 3006.

"The Chimaera"

See 2956.

"Chippings with a Chisel"

See 2922.

"The Christmas Banquet"

See 2835, 2842, 2892, 2898, 2922.

"Circe's Palace"

See 2956.

"David Swan"

See 2892.

"The Devil in Manuscript"

See 2842, 2860, 2863, 2865.

"Dr. Heidegger's Experiment"

2586.   BLAIR, WILLIAM T. "'Dr. Heidegger's Experiment': An Allegory of Sin." *The Nathaniel Hawthorne Journal 1976*, pp. 286–91.
2587.   SCANLON, LAWRENCE E. "That Very Singular Man, Dr. Heidegger." *Nineteenth-Century Fiction*, 17 (1962), 253–63.
See also 509, 2842, 2871, 2882, 2892.

"Drowne's Wooden Image"

2588.   DAVIS, SARAH I. "Hawthorne and the Revision of American Art History." *The Nathaniel Hawthorne Journal 1977*, pp. 125-36.

2589. **TRIPATHY, BIYOT K.** "Hawthorne, Art and The Artist: A Study of 'Drowne's Wooden Image' and 'The Artist of the Beautiful.'" *Indian Journal of American Studies*, 1, no. 4 (1971), 63-71.
See also 377, 2833, 2841-2843, 2863, 2871, 2892, 2898, 2955, 2991.

"Earth's Holocaust"

2590. **HOSTETLER, NORMAN H.** "'Earth's Holocaust': Hawthorne's Parable of the Imaginative Process." *Kansas Quarterly*, 7, no. 4 (1975), 85-89.
See also 36, 2842, 2893, 2898, 3006.

"Edward Randolph's Portrait"

See 2825, 2843, 2865, 2871, 2893, 2895, 2898, 2989.

"Egotism; or, The Bosom-Serpent"

2591. **ARNER, ROBERT D.** "Hawthorne and Jones Very: Two Dimensions of Satire in 'Egotism; or, The Bosom Serpent.'" *The New England Quarterly*, 42 (1969), 267-75.

2592. **BARNES, DANIEL R.** "'Physical Fact' and Folklore : Hawthorne's 'Egotism; or the Bosom Serpent.'" *American Literature*, 43 (1971), 117-21.

2593. **BOSWELL, JACKSON CAMPBELL.** "Bosom Serpents before Hawthorne: Origin of a Symbol." *English Language Notes*, 12 (1975), 279-87.

2594. **BUSH, SARGENT, JR.** "Bosom Serpents before Hawthorne: The Origins of a Symbol." *American Literature*, 43 (1971), 181-99.

2595. **HARDING, WALTER.** "Another Source for Hawthorne's 'Egotism; or the Bosom Serpent.'" *American Literature*, 40 (1969), 537-38.

2596. **HILDEBRAND, ANNE.** "Incomplete Metamorphosis in 'Allegories of the Heart.'" *American Transcendental Quarterly*, no. 13 (1972), pp. 28-31.

2597. **MARKS, ALFRED H.** "Two Rodericks and Two Worms: 'Egotism; or, The Bosom Serpent' as Personal Satire." *PMLA*, 74 (1959), 607-12.

2598. **MONTEIRO, GEORGE.** "Hawthorne's Emblematic Serpent." *The Nathaniel Hawthorne Journal 1973*, pp. 134-42.

2599. _____. "A Nonliterary Source for Hawthorne's 'Egotism; or the Bosom Serpent.'" *American Literature*, 41 (1970), 575-77.

2600. **ROSS, MORTON L.** "Hawthorne's Bosom Serpent and Mather's *Magnalia*." *The Emerson Society Quarterly*, no. 47 (1967), p. 13.

2601. SCHROEDER, JOHN W. "Hawthorne's 'Egotism; or, The Bosom Serpent' and Its Source." *American Literature*, 31 (1959), 150–62.

2602. WERGE, THOMAS. "Thomas Shepard and Crèvecoeur: Two Uses of the Bosom Serpent before Hawthorne." *The Nathaniel Hawthorne Journal 1974*, pp. 236–39.

See also 54, 369, 2821, 2835, 2842, 2892, 3010, 3790.

"Endicott and the Red Cross"

2603. BERCOVITCH, SACVAN. "Endicott's Breastplate: Symbolism and Typology in 'Endicott and the Red Cross.'" *Studies in Short Fiction*, 4 (1967), 289–99.

2604. GALLAGHER, EDWARD J. "History in 'Endicott and the Red Cross.'" *The Emerson Society Quarterly*, no. 50, Supplement (1968), pp. 62–65.

2605. HALLIGAN, JOHN. "Hawthorne on Democracy: 'Endicott and the Red Cross.'" *Studies in Short Fiction*, 8 (1971), 301–07.

2606. NEWBERRY, FREDERICK. "The Demonic in 'Endicott and the Red Cross.'" *Papers on Language & Literature*, 13 (1977), 251–59.

2607. WILSON, ROD. "Further Spenserian Parallels in Hawthorne." *The Nathaniel Hawthorne Journal 1972*, pp. 195–201.

See also 103, 2841, 2860, 2871, 2889, 2893, 2894, 2961, 2986.

"Ethan Brand"

2608. DAVIDSON, RICHARD ALLAN. "The Villagers and 'Ethan Brand.'" *Studies in Short Fiction*, 4 (1967), 260–62.

2609. EISIMINGER, STERLING. "The Legend of Shelley's Heart and Hawthorne's 'Ethan Brand.'" *The Nathaniel Hawthorne Society Newsletter*, 2, no. 2 (1976), 3–4.

2610. HENNELLY, MARK. "Hawthorne's *Opus Alchymicum*: 'Ethan Brand.'" *ESQ*, 22 (1976), 96–106.

2611. HERNDON, JERRY A., AND SIDNEY P. MOSS. "The Identity and Significance of the German Jewish Showman in Hawthorne's 'Ethan Brand.'" *College English*, 23 (1962), 362–63.

2612. JOSEPH, BROTHER. "Art and Event in 'Ethan Brand.'" *Nineteenth-Century Fiction*, 15 (1960), 249–57.

2613. KELLY, RICHARD. "Hawthorne's 'Ethan Brand.'" *The Explicator*, 28 (1970), item 47.

2614. LEVY, ALFRED J. "'Ethan Brand' and the Unpardonable Sin." *Boston University Studies in English*, 5 (1961), 185–90.

2615. LIEBMAN, SHELDON W. "Ethan Brand and the Unpardonable Sin." *American Transcendental Quarterly*, no. 24, Supplement Two (1974), pp. 9–14.

2616. McELROY, JOHN. "The Brand Metaphor in 'Ethan Brand.'" *American Literature*, 43 (1972), 633–37.

2617. SCHULZ, DIETER. "'Ethan Brand' and the Structure of the American Quest Romance." *Genre*, 7 (1974), 233–49.

2618. SCHWARTZ, JOSEPH. "'Ethan Brand' and the Natural Goodness of Man: A Phenomenological Inquiry." *The Emerson Society Quarterly*, no. 39 (1965), pp. 78–81.

2619. STOCK, ELY. "The Biblical Context of 'Ethan Brand.'" *American Literature*, 37 (1965), 115–34.

2620. VANDERBILT, KERMIT. "The Unity of Hawthorne's 'Ethan Brand.' " *College English*, 24 (1963), 453–56.

2621. WHITE, WILLIAM M. "Hawthorne's Eighteen-Year Cycle: Ethan Brand and Reuben Bourne." *Studies in Short Fiction*, 6 (1969), 215–18.

See also 54, 109, 508, 2834, 2835, 2840–2843, 2863, 2875, 2876, 2879, 2882, 2886, 2889, 2892, 2898, 2912, 2924, 2934, 2945, 2952, 2961, 2966, 2970, 2973, 2996, 3002, 5701.

"Fancy's Shadow Box"

See 2841, 2863, 2871, 2892, 3006.

"Feathertop"

2622. ESTRIN, MARK W. "Narrative Ambivalence in Hawthorne's 'Feathertop.'" *The Journal of Narrative Technique*, 5 (1975), 164–73.

See also 2833, 2835, 2842, 2892, 3019.

"Fragments from the Journal of a Solitary Man"

2623. PANCOST, DAVID W. "Evidence of Editorial Additions to Hawthorne's 'Fragments from the Journal of a Solitary Man.'" *The Nathaniel Hawthorne Journal 1975*, pp. 210–26.

See also 2835, 2843, 2863, 2898.

"The Gentle Boy"

2624. DUBAN, JAMES. "Hawthorne's Debt to Edmund Spenser and Charles Chauncy in 'The Gentle Boy.' " *The Nathaniel Hawthorne Journal 1976*, pp. 189–95.

2625. TREMBLAY, WILLIAM A. "A Reading of Nathaniel Hawthorne's 'The Gentle Boy.'" *Massachusetts Studies in English*, 2 (1970), 80–87.

2626. TURNER, ARLIN. "Park Benjamin on the Author and the Illustrator of 'The Gentle Boy.'" *The Nathaniel Hawthorne Journal 1974*, pp. 85–91.

2627. **WHITE, PETER.** "The Monstrous Birth and 'The Gentle Boy': Hawthorne's Use of the Past." *The Nathaniel Hawthorne Journal 1976*, pp. 173–88.
See also 463, 597, 2824, 2842, 2843, 2860, 2871, 2879, 2892, 2893, 2898, 2919, 2927, 2938, 2961, 2972, 2984, 3012.

"The Golden Fleece"

See 2898, 2956.

"The Golden Touch"

See 2892.

"The Gorgon's Head"

See 2892, 2956.

"Graves and Goblins"

2628. **BEZANSON, WALTER. E.** "The Hawthorne Game: 'Graves and Goblins.'" *ESQ*, no. 54 (1969), pp. 73–77.

"The Gray Champion"

2629. **DAVIS, JOSEPH A.** "The Oldest Puritan: A Study of the Angel of Hadley Legend in Hawthorne's 'The Gray Champion.'" *Rackham Literary Studies*, no. 4 (1973), pp. 25–43.
2630. **NEWBERRY, FREDERICK.** "'The Gray Champion': Hawthorne's Ironic Criticism of Puritan Rebellion." *Studies in Short Fiction*, 13 (1976), 363–70.
2631. **PANDEYA, P. K.** "Pangs of Democracy: A Study of Hawthorne's 'The Gray Champion.'" *The Indian Journal of English Studies*, 15 (1974), 38–46.
See also 2860, 2865, 2871, 2893, 2894, 2917, 2969, 2978, 2986.

"The Great Carbuncle"

2632. **LUEDTKE, LUTHER S.** "Hawthorne's Doctor Cacaphodel: The Significance of a Name." *The Nathaniel Hawthorne Journal 1977*, pp. 167–72.
2633. **MORROW, PATRICK.** "A Writer's Workshop: Hawthorne's 'The Great Carbuncle.'" *Studies in Short Fiction*, 6 (1969), 157–64.
See also 38, 377, 2842, 2863, 2871, 2945.

"The Great Stone Face"

2634. **LITZINGER, BOYD.** "Mythmaking in America: 'The Great Stone Face' and *Raintree County*." *Tennessee Studies In Literature*, 8 (1963), 81–84.
2635. **LYNCH, JAMES J.** "Structure and Allegory in 'The Great Stone Face.'" *Nineteenth-Century Fiction*, 15 (1960), 137–46.

2636. **MURPHY, MORRIS.** "Wordsworthian Concepts in 'The Great Stone Face.'" *College English*, 23 (1962), 364–65.
See also 2842, 2898, 2945.

"The Hall of Fantasy"

2637. **JONES, BUFORD.** "'The Hall of Fantasy' and the Early Hawthorne-Thoreau Relationship." *PMLA*, 83 (1968), 1429–38.
See also 2821, 2842, 2890, 2892.

"The Haunted Mind"

2638. **ST. ARMAND, BARTON LEVI.** "Hawthorne's 'Haunted Mind': A Subterranean Drama of the Self." *Criticism*, 13 (1971), 1–25.
See also 38, 71, 2841, 2883, 2897, 2961, 2965, 3006.

"The Hollow of the Three Hills"

2639. **BURHANS, CLINTON S., JR.** "Hawthorne's Mind and Art in 'The Hollow of the Three Hills.'" *Journal of English and Germanic Philosophy*, 60 (1961), 286–95.
2640. **McCALL, DAN.** " 'I Felt a Funeral in My Brain' and 'The Hollow of the Three Hills.'" *The New England Quarterly*, 42 (1969), 432–35.
2641. **PANDEYA, PRABHAT K.** "The Drama of Evil in 'The Hollow of the Three Hills.'" *The Nathaniel Hawthorne Journal 1975*, pp. 177–81.
2642. **STOCK, ELY.** "Witchcraft in 'The Hollow of the Three Hills.'" *American Transcendental Quarterly*, no. 14 (1972), pp. 31–33.
See also 377, 466, 2863, 2865, 2960, 2961, 2991, 3002, 3006.

"Howe's Masquerade"

2643. **ANO, FUMIO.** "The Mischianza Ball and Hawthorne's 'Howe's Masquerade.'" *The Nathaniel Hawthorne Journal 1974*, pp. 231–35.
See also 2825, 2865, 2871, 2893, 2895, 2958, 2986, 2989, 5388, 5559.

"The Intelligence Office"
See 2842.

"The Interrupted Nuptials"

2644. **CLARK, C. E. FRAZER, JR.** "'The Interrupted Nuptials': A Question of Attribution." *The Nathaniel Hawthorne Journal 1971*, pp. 49–66.

"John Inglefield's Thanksgiving"

See 2991.

"Lady Eleanore's Mantle"

2645. CLAYTON, LAWRENCE. "'Lady Eleanore's Mantle': A Metaphorical Key to Hawthorne's 'Legends of the Province House.'" *English Language Notes*, 9 (1971), 49–51.
2646. LIEBMAN, SHELDON W. "Ambiguity in 'Lady Eleanore's Mantle.'" *ESQ*, no. 58 (1970), pp. 97–101.
See also 2825, 2835, 2865, 2871, 2892, 2893, 2895, 2898, 2907, 2948, 2989, 2991, 5388.

"The Lily's Quest"

2647. LEVY, LEO B. "The Temple and the Tomb: Hawthorne's 'The Lily's Quest.'" *Studies in Short Fiction*, 3 (1966), 334–42.
See also 2928.

"Little Annie's Ramble"

See 2842.

"Main-Street"

See 26, 38, 2839, 2841, 2842, 2860, 2892.

"The Man of Adamant"

2648. BLAND, R. LAMAR. "William Austin's 'The Man with the Cloaks: A Vermont Legend': An American Influence on Hawthorne's 'The Man of Adamant.'" *The Nathaniel Hawthorne Journal 1977*, pp. 139–45.
2649. GALLAGHER, EDWARD J. "Sir Kenelm Digby in Hawthorn's 'The Man of Adamant.'" *Notes and Queries*, NS 17 (1970), 15–16.
2650. GAUTREAU, HENRY W., JR. "A Note on Hawthorne's 'The Man of Adamant.'" *Philological Quarterly*, 52 (1973), 315–17.
2651. JONES, BUFORD. "'The Man of Adamant' and the Moral Picturesque." *American Transcendental Quarterly*, no. 14 (1972), pp. 33–41.
2652. SCHROEDER, JOHN W. "Hawthorne's 'The Man of Adamant': A Spenserian Source-Study." *Philological Quarterly*, 41 (1962), 744–56.
See also 2835, 2842, 2860, 2871, 2876, 2893, 2937, 2952, 2984, 3006, 5149.

"The May-Pole of Merry Mount"

2653. **DEMING, ROBERT H.** "The Use of the Past: Herrick and Hawthorne." *Journal of Popular Culture*, 2 (1968), 278–91.

2654. **FEENEY, JOSEPH J., S.J.** "The Structure of Ambiguity in Hawthorne's 'The Maypole of Merry Mount.' " *Studies in American Fiction*, 3 (1975), 211–16.

2655. **LIEBMAN, SHELDON W.** "Hawthorne's *Comus:* A Miltonic Source for 'The Maypole of Merry Mount.' " *Nineteenth-Century Fiction*, 27 (1972), 345–51.

2656. ———. "Moral Choice in 'The Maypole of Merry Mount.'" *Studies in Short Fiction*, 11 (1974), 173–80.

2657. **McWILLIAMS, JOHN P., JR.** "Fictions of Merry Mount." *American Quarterly*, 29 (1977), 3–30.

2658. **STERN, RICHARD CLARK.** "Puritans at Merry Mount: Variations on a Theme." *American Quarterly*, 22 (1970), 846–58.

See also 38, 47, 103, 363, 574, 2824, 2831, 2842, 2860, 2871, 2879, 2889, 2893, 2897, 2914, 2961, 2986, 2995, 3637, 6535.

"The Minister's Black Veil"

2659. **ALLEN, JOHN D.** "Behind 'The Minister's Black Veil.'" In *Essays in Memory of Christine Burleson in Language and Literature by Former Colleagues and Students.* Ed. Thomas G. Burton. Johnson City: Research Advisory Council, East Tennessee State Univ., 1969. pp. 3–12.

2660. **ALLEN, M. L.** "The Black Veil: Three Versions of a Symbol." *English Studies*, 47 (1966), 286–89.

2661. **ALTSCHULER, GLENN C.** "The Puritan Dilemma in 'The Minister's Black Veil.'" *American Transcendental Quarterly*, no. 24, Supplement One (1974), pp. 25–27.

2662. **BENOIT, RAYMOND.** "Hawthorne's Psychology of Death: 'The Minister's Black Veil.'" *Studies in Short Fiction*, 8 (1971), 553–60.

2663. **CANADAY, NICHOLAS, JR.** "Hawthorne's Minister and the Veiling Deceptions of Self." *Studies in Short Fiction*, 4 (1967), 135–42.

2664. **CARNOCHAN, W. B.** "'The Minister's Black Veil': Symbol, Meaning, and the Context of Hawthorne's Art." *Nineteenth-Century Fiction*, 24 (1969), 182–92.

2665. **CRIE, ROBERT D.** "'The Minister's Black Veil': Mr. Hopper's Symbolic Fig Leaf." *Literature and Psychology*, 17 (1967), 211–18.

2666. **MONTEIRO, GEORGE.** "The Full Particulars of the Minister's Behavior—According to Hale." *The Nathaniel Hawthorne Journal 1972*, pp. 173–82.

2667. _____. "Hawthorne's 'The Minister's Black Veil.'" *The Explicator*, 22 (1963), item 9.

2668. MORSBERGER, ROBERT E. "'The Minister's Black Veil': 'Shrouded in a Blackness, Ten Times Black.'" *The New England Quarterly*, 46 (1973), 454–63.

2669. QUINN, JAMES, AND ROSS BALDESSARINI. "Literary Technique and Psychological Effect in Hawthorne's 'The Minister's Black Veil.'" *Literature and Psychology*, 24 (1974), 115–23.

2670. REECE, JAMES B. "Mr. Hooper's Vow." *ESQ*, 21 (1975), 93–102.

2671. STIBITZ, E. EARLE. "Ironic Unity in Hawthorne's 'The Minister's Black Veil.'" *American Literature*, 34 (1962), 182–90.

2672. STRANDBERG, VICTOR. "The Artist's Black Veil." *The New England Quarterly*, 41 (1968), 567–74.

2673. TURNER, FREDERICK W., III. "Hawthorne's Black Veil." *Studies in Short Fiction*, 5 (1968), 186–87.

2674. WYCHERLEY, H. ALAN. "Hawthorne's 'The Minister's Black Veil.'" *The Explicator*, 23 (1964), item 11.

See also 377, 384, 454, 486, 2824, 2830, 2835, 2842, 2857, 2860, 2863, 2871, 2879, 2889, 2893, 2937, 2940, 2961, 2991, 2992, 2997.

"The Minotaur"

See 2956, 4529.

"The Miraculous Pitcher"

See 2956.

"Mr. Higginbotham's Catastrophe"

2675. BRUBAKER, B. R. "Hawthorne's Experiment in Popular Form: 'Mr. Higginbotham's Catastrophe.'" *Southern Humanities Review*, 7 (1973), 155–66.

2676. DUBAN, JAMES. "The Sceptical Context of Hawthorne's 'Mr. Higginbotham's Catastrophe.'" *American Literature*, 48 (1976), 292–301.

2677. MEHTA, R. N. "'Mr. Higginbotham's Catastrophe': An Unusual Hawthorne Story." In *Indian Essays in American Literature: Papers in Honour of Robert E. Spiller.* Ed. Sujit Mukherjee and D. V. K. Raghavacharyulu. Bombay: Popular Prakashan, 1969. pp. 113–19.

2678. PAULY, THOMAS H. "'Mr. Higginbotham's Catastrophe'— The Story Teller's Disaster." *American Transcendental Quarterly*, no. 14 (1972), pp. 171–74.

See also 47, 2892, 2991, 5549.

"Mrs. Bullfrog"

2679. **SOLENSTEN, JOHN M.** "Hawthorne's Ribald Classic: 'Mrs. Bullfrog' and the Folktale." *Journal of Popular Culture*, 7 (1973), 582-88.
See also 54, 2892.

"Monsieur du Miroir"

See 2898.

"My Kinsman, Major Molineux"

2680. **ABERNETHY, P. L.** "The Identity of Hawthorne's Major Molineux." *American Transcendental Quarterly*, no. 31 (1976), pp. 5-8.

2681. **ALLISON, ALEXANDER W.** "The Literary Contexts of 'My Kinsman, Major Molineux.'" *Nineteenth-Century Fiction*, 23 (1968), 304-11.

2682. **BENOIT, RAYMOND.** "Hawthorne's Ape Man: 'My Kinsman, Major Molineux.'" *American Transcendental Quarterly*, no. 14 (1972), pp 8-9.

2683. **BROES, ARTHUR T.** "Journey into Moral Darkness: 'My Kinsman, Major Molineux' as Allegory." *Nineteenth-Century Fiction*, 19 (1964), 171-84.

2684. **BROWN, DENNIS.** "Literature and Existential Psychoanalysis: 'My Kinsman, Major Molineux' and 'Young Goodman Brown.'" *The Canadian Review of American Studies*, 4 (1973), 65-73.

2685. **D'AVANZO, MARIO L.** "The Literary Sources of 'My Kinsman, Major Molineux': Shakespeare, Coleridge, and Milton." *Studies in Short Fiction*, 10 (1973), 121-36.

2686. **DAVIDSON, RICHARD ALLAN.** "Redburn, Pierre and Robin: Melville's Debt to Hawthorne?" *The Emerson Society Quarterly*, no. 47 (1967), pp. 32-34.

2687. **DENNIS, CARL.** "How to Live in Hell: The Bleak Vision of Hawthorne's 'My Kinsman, Major Molineux.'" *The University Review* (Kansas City), 37 (1971), 250-58.

2688. **DOLAN, PAUL J.** "Hawthorne: The Politics of Puberty." In *Of War and War's Alarms: Fiction and Politics in the Modern World*. New York: Free Press, 1976. pp. 16-35.

2689. **ENGLAND, A. B.** "Robin Molineux and the Young Ben Franklin: A Reconsideration." *Journal of American Studies*, 6 (1972), 181-88.

2690. **FASS, BARBARA.** "Rejection of Paternalism: Hawthorne's 'My Kinsman, Major Molineux' and Ellison's *Invisible Man*." *CLA Journal*, 14 (1971), 317-23.

2691. **Hoffman, Daniel G.** "Yankee Bumpkin and Scapegoat King." *The Sewanee Review*, 69 (1961), 48–60.
2692. **Jones, Bartlett C.** "The Ambiguity of Shrewdness in 'My Kinsman, Major Molineux.' " *Midcontinent American Studies Journal*, 3, no. 2 (1962), 42–47.
2693. **Kehler, Dorothea.** "Hawthorne and Shakespeare." *American Transcendental Quarterly*, no. 22 (1974), pp. 104–05.
2694. **Kim, Yong-Chol.** "Note on Hawthorne's 'My Kinsman, Major Molineux.'" *The English Language and Literature*, no. 19 (1966), pp. 85–88.
2695. **Kimmey, John L.** "Pierre and Robin: Melville's Debt to Hawthorne." *The Emerson Society Quarterly*, no. 38 (1965), pp. 90–92.
2696. **Kozikowski, Stanley J.** "'My Kinsman, Major Molineux' as Mock-Heroic." *American Transcendental Quarterly*, no. 31 (1976), pp. 20–21.
2697. **Liebman, Sheldon W.** "Robin's Conversion: The Design of 'My Kinsman, Major Molineux.'" *Studies in Short Fiction*, 8 (1971), 443–57.
2698. **Nilsen, Helge Normann.** "Hawthorne's 'My Kinsman, Major Molineux': Society and the Individual." In *Americana-Norvegica: Norwegian Contributions to American Studies Dedicated to Sigmund Skard*, Vol. 4. Ed. Brita Seyersted. Oslo: Universitetsforlaget, 1973. pp. 123–36.
2699. **Paul, Louis.** "A Psychoanalytic Reading of Hawthorne's 'Major Molineux': The Father Manqué and the Protégé Manqué." *American Imago*, 18 (1961), 279–88.
2700. **Pearce, Roy Harvey.** "Robin Molineux on the Analyst's Couch: A Note on the Limits of Psychoanalytic Criticism." *Criticism*, 1 (1959), 83–90.
2701. **Pinsker, Sanford.** "Hawthorne's 'Double-Faced Fellow': A Note on 'My Kinsman, Major Molineux.' " *The Nathaniel Hawthorne Journal 1972*, pp. 255–56.
2702. **Rose, Marilyn Gaddis.** "Theseus Motif in 'My Kinsman, Major Molineux.'" *The Emerson Society Quarterly*, no. 47 (1967), pp. 21–23.
2703. **Russell, John.** "Allegory and 'My Kinsman, Major Molineux.'" *The New England Quarterly*, 40 (1967), 432–40.
2704. **Sappenfield, James A.** "My Kinsman, Major Molineux." In *Instructor's Manual for* "The Art of Fiction," Second Edition. Ed. R. F. Dietrich and Roger H. Sundell. New York: Holt, Rinehart and Winston, 1974. pp. 23–29.
2705. **Sharma, T. R. S.** "Diabolic World and the Naive Hero in

'My Kinsman, Major Molineux.'" *Indian Journal of American Studies*, 1, no. 1 (1969), 35–43.

2706. SHAW, PETER. "Fathers, Sons, and the Ambiguities of Revolution in 'My Kinsman, Major Molineux.' " *The New England Quarterly*, 49 (1976), 559–76.

2707. _____. "Their Kinsman, Thomas Hutchinson: Hawthorne, the Boston Patriots, and His Majesty's Royal Governor." *Early American Literature*, 11 (1976), 183–90.

2708. SIMPSON, LEWIS P. "John Adams and Hawthorne: The Fiction of the Real American Revolution." *Studies in the Literary Imagination*, 9, no. 2 (1976), 1–17.

2709. SMITH, JULIAN. "Coming of Age in America: Young Ben Franklin and Robin Molineux." *American Quarterly*, 17 (1965), 550–58.

2710. _____. "Historical Ambiguity in 'My Kinsman, Major Molineux.'" *English Language Notes*, 8 (1970), 115–20.

2711. VANDERBEETS, RICHARD, AND PAUL WITHERINGTON. "My Kinsman, Brockden Brown: Robin Molineux and Arthur Mervyn." *American Transcendental Quarterly*, no. 1 (1969), pp. 13–15.

2712. WALLINS, ROGER P. "Robin and the Narrator in 'My Kinsman, Major Molineux.'" *Studies in Short Fiction*, 12 (1975), 173–79.

See also 47, 93, 103, 454, 463, 511, 537, 548, 565, 595, 2785, 2824, 2826, 2835, 2842, 2860, 2863, 2871, 2875, 2889, 2891–2894, 2898, 2903, 2914, 2934, 2938, 2958, 2960, 2961, 2973, 2976, 2978, 2986, 2991, 2995, 2997, 3006, 3009, 3012, 3019.

"The New Adam and Eve"

See 54, 2821, 2842, 2898.

"Night Sketches"

See 2997, 3005, 3006, 3009.

"The Old Apple-Dealer"

2713. WELDON, ROBERTA F. "Hawthorne's Old Apple-Dealer and Wordworth's Leechgatherer." *The Nathaniel Hawthorne Journal 1977*, pp. 249–59.

See also 2873, 2892, 3006, 3009, 4489.

"Old Esther Dudley"

2714. WALSH, THOMAS F., JR. "Hawthorne's Satire in 'Old Esther Dudley.'" *The Emerson Society Quarterly*, no. 22 (1961), pp. 31–33.

See also 2825, 2841, 2871, 2893, 2895, 2958, 2989.

"The Old Manse"

2715. **COX, JAMES M.** *"The Scarlet Letter*: Through 'The Old Manse' and 'The Custom House.'" *The Virginia Quarterly Review*, 51 (1975), 432–47.

2716. **WILLOUGHBY, JOHN C.** "'The Old Manse' Revisited: Some Analogues for Art." *The New England Quarterly*, 46 (1973), 45–61.

See also 9, 10, 2841, 2842, 2863, 2953, 2983, 4753, 4823.

"Old News"

See 2842, 2898, 2947, 2958, 2978.

"The Old Tory" (See "Old News")

"P.'s Correspondence"

See 2842, 2886.

"The Paradise of Children"

See 2956.

"Peter Goldthwaite's Treasure"

2717. **BUSH, SARGENT, JR.** "'Peter Goldthwaite's Treasure' and *The House of Seven Gables.*" *ESQ*, no. 62 (1971), pp. 35–38.

See also 92, 2842, 2898, 2991.

"The Pomegranate Seeds"

See 2898, 2956.

"The Procession of Life"

See 2821, 2842.

"The Prophetic Pictures"

See 54, 493, 2835, 2842, 2843, 2871, 2892, 2893, 2910, 2923, 2987, 2991, 2994.

"The Pygmies"

See 2956.

"Rappaccini's Daughter"

2718. **ALSEN, EBERHARD.** "The Ambitious Experiment of Dr. Rappaccini." *American Literature*, 43 (1971), 430–31.

2719. **ANDERSON, NORMAN A.** "'Rappaccini's Daughter': A Keatsian Analogue?" *PMLA*, 83 (1968), 271–83.

2720. **BRENZO, RICHARD.** "Beatrice Rappaccini: A Victim of Male Love and Horror." *American Literature*, 48 (1976), 152–64.

2721. **BRODSKY, PATRICIA POLLOCK.** "Fertile Fields and Poisoned Gardens: Sologub's Debt to Hoffman, Pushkin, and Hawthorne." *Essays in Literature* (Western Illinois University), 1 (1974), 96–108.

2722. **COHEN, HUBERT I.** "Hoffman's 'The Sandman': A Possible Source For 'Rappaccini's Daughter.' " *ESQ*, 18 (1972), 148–53.

2723. **CREWS, FREDERICK C.** "Giovanni's Garden." *American Quarterly*, 16 (1964), 402–18.

2724. **DALY, ROBERT.** "Fideism and the Allusive Mode in 'Rappaccini's Daughter.' " *Nineteenth-Century Fiction*, 28 (1973), 25–37.

2725. **DAVIS, JOE.** "The Myth of the Garden: Nathaniel Hawthorne's 'Rappaccini's Daughter.' " *Studies in the Literary Imagination*, 2, no. 1 (1969), 3–12.

2726. **DOBBS, JEANNINE.** "Hawthorne's Dr. Rappaccini and Father George Rapp." *American Literature*, 43 (1971), 427–30.

2727. **EVANS, OLIVER.** "Allegory and Incest in 'Rappaccini's Daughter.' " *Nineteenth-Century Fiction*, 19 (1964), 185–95.

2728. ———. "The Cavern and the Fountain: Paradox and Double Paradox in 'Rappaccini's Daughter.' " *College English*, 24 (1963), 461–63.

2729. **GALE, ROBERT L.** "Rappaccini's Baglioni." *Studi Americani*, 9 (1963), 83–87.

2730. **GALLAGHER, KATHLEEN.** "The Art of Snake Handling: *Lamia, Elsie Venner*, and 'Rappaccini's Daughter.' " *Studies in American Fiction*, 3 (1975), 51–64.

2731. **HOVEY, RICHARD B.** "Love and Hate in 'Rappaccini's Daughter.' " *The University of Kansas City Review*, 29 (1962), 137–45.

2732. **INGE, M. THOMAS.** "Dr. Rappaccini's Noble Experiment." *The Nathaniel Hawthorne Journal 1973*, pp. 200–01.

2733. **KARRFALT, DAVID H.** "Anima in Hawthorne and Haggard." *American Notes & Queries*, 2 (1964), 152–53.

2734. **KLOECKNER, ALFRED J.** "The Flower and the Fountain: Hawthorne's Chief Symbols in 'Rappaccini's Daughter.' " *American Literature*, 38 (1966), 323–36.

2735. **LA REGINA, GABRIELLA.** " 'Rappaccini's Daughter': The Gothic as a Catalyst for Hawthorne's Imagination." *Studi Americani*, 17 (1971), 29–74.

2736. **LEIBOWITZ, HERBERT A.** "Hawthorne and Spenser: Two Sources." *American Literature*, 30 (1959), 459–66.

2737. **LIEBMAN, SHELDON W.** "Hawthorne and Milton: The Second Fall in 'Rappaccini's Daughter.' " *The New England Quarterly*, 41 (1968), 521–35.

2738. **LONG, ROBERT EMMET.** "James's *Washington Square*: The Hawthorne Relation." *The New England Quarterly*, 46 (1973), 573–90.

2739. **LYTTLE, DAVID.** "Giovanni! My Poor Giovanni!" *Studies in Short Fiction*, 9 (1972), 147–56.

2740. **MOSS, SIDNEY P.** "A Reading of 'Rappaccini's Daughter.' " *Studies in Short Fiction*, 2 (1965), 145–56.

2741. **MURPHY, JOHN J.** "Willa Cather and Hawthorne: Significant Resemblances." *Renascence*, 27 (1975), 161–75.

2742. **POLLIN, BURTON R.** " 'Rappaccini's Daughter'—Sources and Names." *Names*, 14 (1966), 30–35.

2743. **ROSENBERRY, EDWARD H.** "Hawthorne's Allegory of Science: 'Rappaccini's Daughter.' " *American Literature*, 32 (1960), 39–46.

2744. **ROSS, MORTON L.** "What Happens in 'Rappaccini's Daughter.' " *American Literature*, 43 (1971), 336–45.

2745. **SCHERTING, JACK.** "The Upas Tree in Dr. Rappaccini's Garden: New Light on Hawthorne's Tale." *Studies in American Fiction*, 1 (1973), 203–07.

2746. **SMITH, JULIAN.** "Keats and Hawthorne: A Romantic Bloom in Rappaccini's Garden." *The Emerson Society Quarterly*, no. 42 (1966), pp. 8–12.

2747. **STERNE, RICHARD C.** "Hawthorne Transformed: Octavio Paz's *La hija de Rappaccini*." *Comparative Literature Studies*, 13 (1976), 230–39.

2748. _____. "A Mexican Flower in Rappaccini's Garden: Madame Calderon de la Barca's *Life in Mexico* Revisited." *The Nathaniel Hawthorne Journal 1974*, pp. 277–79.

2749. **THARPE, JAC.** "Hawthorne and Hindu Literature." *The Southern Quarterly*, 10 (1972), 107–15.

2750. **UROFF, M. D.** "The Doctors in 'Rappaccini's Daughter.' " *Nineteenth-Century Fiction*, 27 (1972), 61–70.

2751. **WALSH, THOMAS F., JR.** "Rappaccini's Literary Gardens." *The Emerson Society Quarterly*, no. 19 (1960), pp. 9–13.

2752. **WHITE, ROBERT L.** " 'Rappaccini's Daughter,' *The Cenci* and Cenci Legend." *Studi Americani*, 14 (1968), 63–86.

See also 35, 37, 50, 54, 604, 2820, 2821, 2824, 2835, 2836, 2841–2843, 2860, 2865, 2879, 2880, 2882, 2889, 2892, 2893, 2896, 2898, 2940, 2948, 2961, 2970, 2987, 2991, 2992, 2995, 2997, 3002, 3006, 3013, 3017, 3019, 3897.

"Roger Malvin's Burial"

2753. **BIRDSALL, VIRGINIA O.** "Hawthorne's Oak Tree Image." *Nineteenth-Century Fiction*, 15 (1960), 181–85.

2754. **BYERS, JOHN R., JR.** "The Geography and Framework of Hawthorne's 'Roger Malvin's Burial.'" *Tennessee Studies In Literature*, 21 (1976), 11–20.

2755. **CREWS, FREDERICK C.** "The Logic of Compulsion in 'Roger Malvin's Burial.'" *PMLA*, 79 (1964), 457–65.

2756. **DONOHUE, AGNES MCNEILL.** "'From Whose Bourn No Traveller Returns': A Reading of 'Roger Malvin's Burial.'" *Nineteenth-Century Fiction*, 18 (1963), 1–19.

2757. **ERLICH, GLORIA CHASSON.** "Guilt and Expiation in 'Roger Malvin's Burial.'" *Nineteenth-Century Fiction*, 26 (1972), 377–89.

2758. **FISHMAN, BURTON J.** "Imagined Redemption in 'Roger Malvin's Burial.'" *Studies in American Fiction*, 5 (1977), 257–62.

2759. **HERTENSTEIN, ROD.** "A Mythic Reading of 'Roger Malvin's Burial.'" In *Itinerary 3: Criticism.* Ed. Frank Baldanza. Bowling Green, OH: Bowling Green Univ. Press, 1977. pp. 39–48.

2760. **KLIGERMAN, JACK.** "A Stylistic Approach to Hawthorne's 'Roger Malvin's Burial.'" *Language and Style*, 4 (1971), 188–94.

2761. **LIEBMAN, SHELDON W.** "'Roger Malvin's Burial': Hawthorne's Allegory of the Heart." *Studies in Short Fiction*, 12 (1975), 253–60.

2762. **NAPLES, DIANE C.** "'Roger Malvin's Burial'—A Parable for Historians?" *American Transcendental Quarterly*, no. 13 (1972), pp. 45–48.

2763. **ROBILLARD, DOUGLAS.** "Hawthorne's 'Roger Malvin's Burial.'" *The Explicator*, 26 (1968), item 56.

2764. **ROBINSON, E. ARTHUR.** "'Roger Malvin's Burial': Hawthorne and the American Environment." *The Nathaniel Hawthorne Journal 1977*, pp. 147–66.

2765. **SCHECHTER, HAROLD.** "Death and Resurrection of the King: Elements of Primitive Mythology and Ritual in 'Roger Malvin's Burial.'" *English Language Notes*, 8 (1971), 201–05.

2766. **SCHULZ, DIETER.** "Imagination and Self-Imprisonment: The Ending of 'Roger Malvin's Burial.'" *Studies in Short Fiction*, 10 (1973), 183–86.

2767. **STOCK, ELY.** "History and the Bible in Hawthorne's 'Roger Malvin's Burial.'" *Essex Institute Historical Collections*, 100 (1964), 279–96.

2768. **THOMPSON, W. R.** "The Biblical Sources of Hawthorne's 'Roger Malvin's Burial.'" *PMLA*, 77 (1962), 92–96.

See also 5, 38, 90, 92, 548, 601, 2621, 2749, 2835, 2836, 2842, 2850, 2860, 2871, 2879, 2893, 2898, 2927, 2931, 2938, 2965, 2976, 2991, 3002, 3006.

"A Select Party"

2769. **NIVA, WELDON N.** " 'No-Names' in Literature." *Names*,
12 (1964), 89–97.
See also 2842, 2890, 2892, 2960, 2961.

"The Seven Vagabonds"

2770. **JANSSEN, JAMES G.** "Hawthorne's Seventh Vagabond: 'The
Outsetting Bard.' " *ESQ*, no. 62 (1971), pp. 22–28.
See also 38, 2853, 2893, 2968.

"The Shaker Bridal"

See 2871.

"Sights from a Steeple"

See 2873, 3003.

"Sketches from Memory"

See 38, 2873, 3003.

"The Snow-Image"

2771. **ABEL, DARREL.** " 'A Vast Deal of Human Sympathy': Idea
and Device in Hawthorne's 'The Snow-Image.' " *Criticism*, 12
(1970), 316–32.
See also 2833, 2842, 2843, 2850, 2934.

"Sunday at Home"

See 3006.

"The Three Golden Apples"

See 2892, 2956.

"The Threefold Destiny"

See 109, 2847, 2892, 2926.

"The Toll-Gatherer's Day"

See 2863.

"The Village Uncle"

2772. **ASQUINO, MARK L.** "Hawthorne's Village Uncle and Melville's Moby Dick." *Studies in Short Fiction*, 10 (1973), 413–14.
2773. **GUPTA, R. K.** "The Technique of Counterstatement:
Theme and Meaning in Hawthorne's 'The Village Uncle.' "
The Nathaniel Hawthorne Journal 1973, pp. 154–61.
2774. **HAWTHORNE, ELIZABETH.** "The Susan 'Affair.' " *The Nathaniel Hawthorne Journal 1971*, pp. 12–17.

2775. **LEVY, LEO B.** "The Mermaid and the Mirror: Hawthorne's 'The Village Uncle.' " *Nineteenth-Century Fiction*, 19 (1964), 205–11.
See also 47, 2843, 3003.

"A Virtuoso's Collection"
See 2849, 2871, 2882.

"Wakefield"

2776. **GATTA, JOHN, JR.** " 'Busy and Selfish London': The Urban Figure in Hawthorne's 'Wakefield.' " *ESQ*, 23 (1977), 164–72.
2777. **MORSBERGER, ROBERT E.** "Wakefield in the Twilight Zone." *American Transcendental Quarterly*, no. 14 (1972), pp. 6–8.
2778. **WALSH, THOMAS F., JR.** " 'Wakefield' and Hawthorne's Illustrated Ideas: A Study in Form." *The Emerson Society Quarterly*, no. 25 (1961), pp. 29–35.
2779. **WELDON, ROBERTA F.** "Wakefield's Second Journey." *Studies in Short Fiction*, 14 (1977), 69–74.
See also 54, 478, 483, 564, 2824, 2835, 2863, 2865, 2871, 3010.

"The Wedding-Knell"

2780. **HOMAN, JOHN, JR.** "Hawthorne's 'The Wedding Knell' and Cotton Mather." *The Emerson Society Quarterly*, no. 43 (1966), pp. 66–67.
See also 2830, 2863, 2922, 5383.

"The White Old Maid"
See 1885, 2965.

"The Wives of the Dead"

2781. **STEPHENSON, EDWARD R.** "Hawthorne's 'The Wives of the Dead.' " *The Explicator*, 25 (1967), item 63.
See also 2871, 2940.

"Young Goodman Brown"

2782. **ABCARIAN, RICHARD.** "The Ending of 'Young Goodman Brown.' " *Studies in Short Fiction*, 3 (1966), 343–45.
2783. **ABEL, DARREL.** "Black Glove and Pink Ribbon: Hawthorne's Metonymic Symbols." *The New England Quarterly*, 42 (1969), 163–80.
2784. **CAMPBELL, HARRY M.** "Freudianism, American Romanticism, and 'Young Goodman Brown.' " *The CEA Critic*, 33, no. 3 (1971), 3–6.

2785. **CARPENTER, RICHARD C.** "Hawthorne's Polar Explorations: 'Young Goodman Brown' and 'My Kinsman, Major Molineux.' " *Nineteenth-Century Fiction*, 24 (1969), 45–56.

2786. **COCHRAN, ROBERT W.** "Reply." *College English*, 24 (1962), 153–54.

2787. **CONNOLLY, THOMAS E.** "How Young Goodman Brown Became Old Badman Brown." *College English*, 24 (1962), 153.

2788. ———. "Introduction." In *Nathaniel Hawthorne: Young Goodman Brown*. Columbus, OH: Merrill, 1968. pp. 1–9.

2789. **COOK, REGINALD.** "The Forest of Goodman Brown's Night: A Reading of Hawthorne's 'Young Goodman Brown.' " *The New England Quarterly*, 43 (1970), 473–81.

2790. **DAVIDSON, FRANK.** " 'Young Goodman Brown'—Hawthorne's Intent." *The Emerson Society Quarterly*, no. 31 (1963), pp. 68–71.

2791. **DAVIS, WILLIAM V.** "Hawthorne's 'Young Goodman Brown.' " *The Nathaniel Hawthorne Journal 1973*, pp. 198–99.

2792. **DICKSON, WAYNE.** "Hawthorne's 'Young Goodman Brown.' " *The Explicator*, 29 (1971), item 44.

2793. **ENSOR, ALLISON.** " 'Whispers of the Bad Angel': A *Scarlet Letter* Passage as a Commentary on Hawthorne's 'Young Goodman Brown.' " *Studies in Short Fiction*, 7 (1970), 467–69.

2794. **ERISMAN, FRED.** " 'Young Goodman Brown'—Warning to Idealists." *American Transcendental Quarterly*, no. 14 (1972), pp. 156–58.

2795. **FERGUSON, J. M., JR.** "Hawthorne's 'Young Goodman Brown.' " *The Explicator*, 28 (1969), item 32.

2796. **GALLAGHER, EDWARD J.** "The Concluding Paragraph of 'Young Goodman Brown.' " *Studies in Short Fiction*, 12 (1975), 29–30.

2797. **HUMMA, JOHN B.** " 'Young Goodman Brown' and the Failure of Hawthorne's Ambiguity." *Colby Library Quarterly*, 9 (1971), 425–31.

2798. **HURLEY, PAUL J.** "Young Goodman Brown's 'Heart of Darkness.' " *American Literature*, 37 (1966), 410–19.

2799. **JOHNSON, CLAUDIA G.** " 'Young Goodman Brown' and Puritan Justification." *Studies in Short Fiction*, 11 (1974), 200–03.

2800. **KIM, CHONG-UN.** "Hawthorne's 'Young Goodman Brown.' " *The English Language and Literature*, no. 9 (1960), pp. 140–55.

2801. **LEVIN, DAVID.** "Shadows of Doubt: Specter Evidence in Hawthorne's 'Young Goodman Brown.' " *American Literature*, 34 (1962), 344–52.

2802. LEVY, LEO B. "The Problem of Faith in 'Young Goodman Brown.' " *Journal of English and Germanic Philology*, 74 (1975), 375–87.

2803. LIEBMAN, SHELDON W. "The Reader in 'Young Goodman Brown.' " *The Nathaniel Hawthorne Journal 1975*, pp. 156–69.

2804. MATHEWS, JAMES W. "Antinomianism in 'Young Goodman Brown.' " *Studies in Short Fiction*, 3 (1965), 73–75.

2805. MILLER, PAUL W. "Hawthorne's 'Young Goodman Brown': Cynicism or Meliorism?" *Nineteenth-Century Fiction*, 14 (1959), 255–64.

2806. MINOCK, DANIEL W. "Hawthorne and the Rumor about the Governor's Lady." *American Notes & Queries*, 13 (1975), 87–88.

2807. MORSBERGER, ROBERT E. "The Woe That Is Madness: Goodman Brown and the Face of the Fire." *The Nathaniel Hawthorne Journal 1973*, pp. 177–82.

2808. PAULITS, WALTER J. "Ambivalence in 'Young Goodman Brown.' " *American Literature*, 41 (1970), 577–84.

2809. REYNOLDS, LARRY J. "Melville's Use of 'Young Goodman Brown.' " *American Transcendental Quarterly*, no. 31 (1976), pp. 12–14.

2810. ROBINSON, E. ARTHUR. "The Vision of Goodman Brown: A Source and Interpretation." *American Literature*, 35 (1963), 218–25.

2811. ST. ARMAND, BARTON LEVI. " 'Young Goodman Brown' as Historical Allegory." *The Nathaniel Hawthorne Journal 1973*, pp. 183–97.

2812. SHRIVER, M. M. "Young Goody Brown." *Études Anglaises*, 30 (1977), 407–19.

2813. STOEHR, TAYLOR. " 'Young Goodman Brown' and Hawthorne's Theory of Mimesis." *Nineteenth-Century Fiction*, 23 (1969), 393–412.

2814. WALSH, THOMAS F., JR. "The Bedeviling of Young Goodman Brown." *Modern Language Quarterly*, 19 (1958), 331–36.

2815. WHELAN, ROBERT EMMET, JR. "Hawthorne Interprets 'Young Goodman Brown.' " *ESQ*, no. 62 (1971), pp. 2–4.

See also 38, 47, 85, 363, 399, 454, 544, 548, 597, 599, 601, 1240, 2684, 2736, 2824, 2826, 2842, 2857, 2860, 2863, 2871, 2879, 2884, 2889, 2891–2893, 2897, 2898, 2903, 2904, 2907, 2924, 2937, 2940, 2944, 2961, 2969, 2973, 2991, 2992, 2995, 2997, 3002, 3039.

General Studies

2816. ABEL, DARREL. "Giving Lustre to Gray Shadows: Hawthorne's Potent Art." *American Literature*, 41 (1969), 373–88.

2817. ———. "Hawthorne, Ghostland, and the Jurisdiction of Veracity." *American Transcendental Quarterly*, no. 24 (1974), pp. 30–38.

2818. ———. " 'A More Imaginative Pleasure': Hawthorne on the Play of Imagination." *ESQ*, no. 55 (1969), pp. 63–71.

2819. ———. " 'This Troublesome Mortality': Hawthorne's Marbles and Bubbles." *Studies in Romanticism*, 8 (1969), 193–97.

2820. ADAMS, JOHN F. "Hawthorne's Symbolic Gardens." *Texas Studies in Literature and Language*, 5 (1963), 242–54.

2821. ADAMS, RICHARD P. "Hawthorne: The Old Manse Period." *Tulane Studies in English*, 8 (1958), 115–51.

2822. ADAMS, TIMOTHY DOW. "To Prepare a Preface to Meet the Faces that You Meet: Autobiographical Rhetoric in Hawthorne's Prefaces." *ESQ*, 23 (1977), 89–98.

2823. ADKINS, NELSON F. "Hawthorne's Democratic New England Puritans." *The Emerson Society Quarterly*, no. 44 (1966), pp. 66–72.

2824. ALLEN, M. L. "Hawthorne's Art in his Short Stories." *Studi Americani*, 7 (1961), 9–41.

2825. ALLEN, MARGARET V. "Imagination and History in Hawthorne's 'Legends of the Province Hall.' " *American Literature*, 43 (1971), 432–37.

2826. ALLEN, MARY. "Smiles and Laughter in Hawthorne." *Philological Quarterly*, 52 (1973), 119–28.

2827. ALSEN, EBERHARD. "Poe's Theory of Hawthorne's Indebtedness to Tieck." *Anglia*, 91 (1973), 342–56.

2828. ANDERSON, QUENTIN. "Introduction." In *Twice-Told Tales and Other Short Stories*, by Nathaniel Hawthorne. New York: Washington Square Press, 1960. pp. v–xii.

2829. ARVIN, NEWTON. "The Relevance of Hawthorne." In *American Pantheon*. Ed. Daniel Aaron and Sylvan Schendler. New York: Delacorte Press, 1966. pp. 60–69.

2830. ASALS, FREDERICK. "Jeremy Taylor and Hawthorne's Early Tales." *American Transcendental Quarterly*, no. 14 (1972), pp. 15–23.

2831. ASKEW, MELVIN W. "Hawthorne, the Fall, and the Psychology of Maturity." *American Literature*, 34 (1962), 335–43.

2832. ATKINS, LOIS. "Psychological Symbolism of Guilt and Isolation in Hawthorne." *American Imago*, 11 (1954), 417–25.

2833. AUTREY, MAX L. "Hawthorne and the Beautiful Impulse." *American Transcendental Quarterly*, no. 14 (1972), pp. 48–54.

2834. ———. "Hawthorne's Study in Clay." *Xavier University Studies*, 11, no. 2 (1972), 1–5.

2835. **AXELSSON, ARNE.** *The Links in the Chain: Isolation and Interdependence in Nathaniel Hawthorne's Fictional Characters.* Stockholm: Almqvist & Wiksell, 1974.

2836. **BALES, KENT.** "Hawthorne's Prefaces and Romantic Perspectivism." *ESQ*, 23 (1977), 69–88.

2837. **BARTLETT, IRVING H.** "Nathaniel Hawthorne: The Democrat as Puritan." In *The American Mind in the Mid-Nineteenth Century.* New York: Crowell, 1967. pp. 105–09.

2838. **BAYM, NINA.** "Hawthorne's Myths for Children: The Author Versus His Audience." *Studies in Short Fiction*, 10 (1973), 35–46.

2839. _____. "Hawthorne's Women: The Tyranny of Social Myths." *The Centennial Review*, 15 (1971), 250–72.

2840. _____. "The Head, the Heart, and the Unpardonable Sin." *The New England Quarterly*, 40 (1967), 31–47.

2841. _____. *The Shape of Hawthorne's Career.* Ithaca, NY: Cornell Univ. Press, 1976.

2842. **BECKER, ISIDORE H.** *The Ironic Dimension in Hawthorne's Short Fiction.* New York: Carlton Press, 1971.

2843. **BELL, MILLICENT.** *Hawthorne's View of the Artist.* New York: State Univ. of New York, 1962.

2844. **BELLMAN, SAMUEL I.** " 'The Joke's on *You!*': Sudden Revelation in Hawthorne." *The Nathaniel Hawthorne Journal 1975*, pp. 192–99.

2845. _____. "Outward Bound from Hawthorne." *The CEA Critic*, 37, no. 2 (1975), 3–7.

2846. _____. " 'Outward Bound from Hawthorne' Once More." *The CEA Critic*, 38, no. 2 (1976), 27–28.

2847. **BLACKMUR, R. P.** "Afterword." In *The Celestial Railroad and Other Stories*, by Nathaniel Hawthorne. New York: New American Library, 1963. pp. 289–97.

2848. **BUNGE, NANCY.** "Dreams in Hawthorne's Tales." *The Nathaniel Hawthorne Journal 1977*, pp. 279–87.

2849. _____. "Unreliable Artist-Narrators in Hawthorne's Short Stories." *Studies in Short Fiction*, 14 (1977), 145–50.

2850. **BURNS, SHANNON.** "Hawthorne's Literary Theory in the Tales." *The Nathaniel Hawthorne Journal 1977*, pp. 261–77.

2851. **CARLSON, PATRICIA ANN.** "National Typology and Hawthorne's Historical Allegory." *The CEA Critic*, 37, no. 1 (1974), 11–13.

2852. **CECIL, L. MOFFITT.** "Hawthorne's Optical Device." *American Quarterly*, 15 (1963), 76–84.

2853. CLARK, C. E. FRAZER, JR. "New Light on the Editing of the 1842 Edition of *Twice-Told Tales.*" *The Nathaniel Hawthorne Journal 1972*, pp. 91–139.

2854. CLARK, HARRY HAYDEN. "Hawthorne: Tradition *versus* Innovation." In *Patterns of Commitment in American Literature.* Ed. Marston LaFrance. Toronto: Univ. of Toronto Press, 1967. pp. 19–37.

2855. CLARK, MARDEN J. "The Wages of Sin in Hawthorne." *Brigham Young University Studies*, 1, no. 1 (1959), 21–36.

2856. CLOUGH, WILSON O. "The Cost of Solitude." In *The Necessary Earth: Nature and Solitude in American Literature.* Austin: Univ. of Texas Press, 1964. pp. 116–31.

2857. COCHRAN, ROBERT W. "Hawthorne's Choice: The Veil or the Jaundiced Eye." *College English*, 23 (1962), 342–46.

2858. COHEN, B. BERNARD. "Hawthorne Debunkers Examined." *The Nathaniel Hawthorne Journal 1977*, pp. 99–107.

2859. COX, JAMES M. "Emerson and Hawthorne: Trust and Doubt." *The Virginia Quarterly Review*, 45 (1969), 88–107.

2860. CREWS, FREDERICK C. *The Sins of the Fathers: Hawthorne's Psychological Themes.* New York: Oxford Univ. Press, 1966.

2861. CROWLEY, J. DONALD. "The Artist as Mediator: The Rationale of Hawthorne's Large-Scale Revisions in His Collected Tales and Sketches." In *Melville & Hawthorne in the Berkshires: A Symposium.* Ed. Howard P. Vincent. Kent, OH: Kent State Univ. Press, 1968. pp. 79–88.

2862. _____. "A False Edition of Hawthorne's 'Twice-Told Tales.'" *The Papers of the Bibliographical Society of America*, 59 (1965), 182–88.

2863. _____. *Nathaniel Hawthorne.* London: Routledge & Kegan Paul, 1971.

2864. _____. "The Unity of Hawthorne's *Twice-Told Tales.*" *Studies in American Fiction*, 1 (1973), 35–61.

2865. DAUBER, KENNETH. *Rediscovering Hawthorne.* Princeton, NJ: Princeton Univ. Press, 1977.

2866. DAVIDSON, EDWARD H. "Nathaniel Hawthorne." In *Major Writers of America.* Ed. Perry Miller. 2 vols. New York: Harcourt, Brace & World, 1962. I, 683–94.

2867. DeHAYES, R. "Charting Hawthorne's Invisible World." *The CEA Critic*, 27, no. 8 (1965), 5–6.

2868. DeVILLIER, MARY ANNE. "'Outward Bound from Hawthorne': A Reply." *The CEA Critic*, 38, no. 2 (1976), 25–26.

2869. DOUBLEDAY, NEAL F. "Classroom Consideration of Hawthorne's Tales." *The Emerson Society Quarterly*, no. 25 (1961), pp. 4–6.

2870. ———. "Doctrine for Fiction in the *North American Review*, 1815–1826." In *Literature and Ideas in America: Essays in Memory of Harry Hayden Clark*. Ed. Robert Falk. Athens: Ohio Univ. Press, 1975. pp. 20–39.

2871. ———. *Hawthorne's Early Tales: A Critical Study*. Durham, NC: Duke Univ. Press, 1972.

2872. ———. "Hawthorne's Estimate of His Early Work." *American Literature*, 37 (1966), 403–09.

2873. DRYDEN, EDGAR A. *Nathaniel Hawthorne: The Poetics of Enchantment*. Ithaca, NY: Cornell Univ. Press, 1977.

2874. DURHAM, FRANK. "Hawthorne and Goldsmith: A Note." *Journal of American Studies*, 4 (1970), 103–05.

2875. DUSENBERY, ROBERT. "Hawthorne's Merry Company: The Anatomy of Laughter in the Tales and Short Stories." *PMLA*, 82 (1967), 285–88.

2876. DWIGHT, SHEILA. "Hawthorne and the Unpardonable Sin." *Studies in the Novel*, 2 (1970), 449–58.

2877. EBERWEIN, JANE DONAHUE. "Temporal Perspective in 'The Legends of the Province House.' " *American Transcendental Quarterly*, no. 14 (1972), pp. 41–45.

2878. EHRENPREIS, ANNE HENRY. "Elizabeth Gaskell and Nathaniel Hawthorne." *The Nathaniel Hawthorne Journal 1973*, pp. 89–119.

2879. ELDER, MARJORIE J. *Nathaniel Hawthorne: Transcendental Symbolist*. Athens: Ohio Univ. Press, 1969.

2880. ERLICH, GLORIA CHASSON. "Deadly Innocence: Hawthorne's Dark Women." *The New England Quarterly*, 41 (1968), 163–79.

2881. EVANS, WALTER. "Poe's Revisions in His Reviews of Hawthorne's *Twice-Told Tales*." *The Papers of the Bibliographical Society of America*, 66 (1972), 407–19.

2882. FAIRBANKS, HENRY G. *The Lasting Loneliness of Nathaniel Hawthorne: A Study of the Sources of Alienation in Modern Man*. Albany, NY: Magi Books, 1965.

2883. FAIRCHILD, B. H., JR. "A Technique of Discovery: The Dream-Vision in Hawthorne's Fiction." *Essays in Literature* (Univ. of Denver), 1, no. 2 (1973), 17–28.

2884. FERRELL, M. J. "Imbalance in Hawthorne's Characters." *South Dakota Review*, 10, no. 1 (1972), 45–59.

2885. FLINT, ALLEN. "The Saving Grace of Marriage in Hawthorne's Fiction." *ESQ*, 19 (1973), 112–16.

2886. FOGLE, RICHARD HARTER. "Byron and Nathaniel Hawthorne." In *Romantic and Victorian: Studies in Memory of William H. Marshall*. Ed. W. Paul Elledge and Richard L. Hoffman.

Rutherford, NJ: Fairleigh Dickinson Univ. Press, 1971. pp. 181–97.

2887. _____. "Hawthorne and Coleridge on Credibility." *Criticism*, 13 (1971), 234–41.

2888. _____. "Hawthorne, History, and the Human Heart." *Clio*, 5 (1976), 175–80.

2889. _____. *Hawthorne's Fiction: The Light & the Dark*. Rev. ed. Norman: Univ. of Oklahoma Press, 1964.

2890. _____. "Hawthorne's Variegated Lighting." *Bucknell Review*, 21, no. 2–3 (1973), 83–88.

2891. _____. "Weird Mockery: An Element of Hawthorne's Style." *Style*, 2 (1968), 191–200.

2892. FOLSOM, JAMES K. *Man's Accidents and God's Purposes: Multiplicity in Hawthorne's Fiction*. New Haven, CT: College & University Press, 1963.

2893. FOSSUM, ROBERT H. *Hawthorne's Inviolable Circle: The Problem of Time*. Deland, FL: Everett/Edwards, 1972.

2894. _____. "The Shadow of the Past: Hawthorne's Historical Tales." *Claremont Quarterly*, 11, no. 1 (1963), 45–56.

2895. _____. "Time and the Artist in 'Legends of the Province House.' " *Nineteenth-Century Fiction*, 21 (1967), 337–48.

2896. FRANKLIN, H. BRUCE. "Hawthorne and Science Fiction." *The Centennial Review*, 10 (1966), 112–30.

2897. FUSSELL, EDWIN. "Neutral Territory: Hawthorne and the Figurative Frontier." In *Hawthorne Centenary Essays*. Ed. Roy Harvey Pearce. Columbus: Ohio State Univ. Press, 1964. pp. 297–314, 467–68.

2898. GALE, ROBERT L. *Plots and Characters in the Fiction and Sketches of Nathaniel Hawthorne*. Hamden, CT: Archon Books, 1968.

2899. GARLITZ, BARBARA. "Teaching All of Hawthorne." *The Emerson Society Quarterly*, no. 25 (1961), pp. 6–8.

2900. GILKES, LILLIAN B. "Hawthorne, Park Benjamin, and S. G. Goodrich: A Three-Cornered Imbroglio." *The Nathaniel Hawthorne Journal 1971*, pp. 83–112.

2901. GREEN, MARTIN. "The Hawthorne Myth: A Protest." In *Re-Appraisals: Some Commonsense Readings in American Literature*. London: Hugh Evelyn, 1963. pp. 61–85.

2902. GROSS, SEYMOUR L. "Hawthorne and the London *Athenaeum*, 1834–1864." *The Nathaniel Hawthorne Journal 1973*, pp. 35–72.

2903. _____. "Hawthorne Versus Melville." *Bucknell Review*, 14, no. 3 (1966), 89–109.

2904. _____. "Hawthorne's Moral Realism." *The Emerson Society Quarterly*, no. 25 (1961), pp. 11–13.

2905. _____, AND ALFRED J. LEVY. "Some Remarks on the Extant Manuscripts of Hawthorne's Short Stories." *Studies in Bibliography*, 14 (1961), 254–57.

2906. GROSS, THEODORE L. "Nathaniel Hawthorne: The Absurdity of Heroism." *The Yale Review*, 57 (1967), 182–95.

2907. GRUNES, DENNIS. "Allegory versus Allegory in Hawthorne." *American Transcendental Quarterly*, no. 32 (1976), pp. 14–19.

2908. GUPTA, R. K. "Hawthorne's Ideal Reader." *Indian Journal of American Studies*, 1, no. 1 (1969), 97–99.

2909. _____. "Hawthorne's Theory of Art." *American Literature*, 40 (1968), 309–24.

2910. _____. "Hawthorne's Treatment of the Artist." *The New England Quarterly*, 45 (1972), 65–80.

2911. _____. "The Idea and the Image: Some Aspects of Imagery in the Minor Short Stories of Nathaniel Hawthorne." In *Studies in American Literature: Essays in Honour of William Mulder*. Ed. Jagdish Chander and Narindar S. Pradhan. Delhi: Oxford Univ. Press, 1976. pp. 62–76.

2912. HARRIS, JANET. "Reflections of the Byronic Hero in Hawthorne's Fiction." *The Nathaniel Hawthorne Journal 1977*, pp. 305–17.

2913. HATHAWAY, RICHARD D. "Hawthorne and the Paradise of Children." *Western Humanities Review*, 15 (1961), 161–72.

2914. HERNDON, JERRY A. "Hawthorne's Dream Imagery." *American Literature*, 46 (1975), 538–45.

2915. HOELTJE, HUBERT H. "Hawthorne, Melville, and 'Blackness.'" *American Literature*, 37 (1965), 41–51.

2916. _____. *Inward Sky: The Mind and Art of Nathaniel Hawthorne*. Durham, NC: Duke Univ. Press, 1962.

2917. HOFFMAN, DANIEL. "Myth, Romance, and the Childhood of Man." In *Hawthorne Centenary Essays*. Ed. Roy Harvey Pearce. Columbus: Ohio State Univ. Press, 1964. pp. 197–219, 465–66.

2918. HOLMES, EDWARD M. "Hawthorne and Romanticism." *The New England Quarterly*, 33 (1960), 476–88.

2919. HOWELL, ROGER. "A Note on Hawthorne's Ambivalence Towards Puritanism: His View of Sir Henry Vane The Younger." *The Nathaniel Hawthorne Journal 1972*, pp. 143–46.

2920. HULL, RAYMONA E. "Hawthorne and the Magic Elixir of Life: The Failure of a Gothic Theme." *ESQ*, 18 (1972), 97–107.

2921. JACOBSON, RICHARD J. *Hawthorne's Conception of the Creative Process.* Cambridge, MA: Harvard Univ. Press, 1965.

2922. JANSSEN, JAMES G. "The 'Dismal Merry-Making' in Hawthorne's Comic Vision." *Studies in American Humor*, 1 (1974), 107–17.

2923. _____. "Impaled Butterflies and the Misleading Moral in Hawthorne's Short Works." *The Nathaniel Hawthorne Journal 1976*, pp. 269–75.

2924. JOHNSTON, MARK EVAN. "The Receding Narrator: The *Spectator*, the *Rambler* and Hawthorne's Shorter Fiction." *Essays in Arts and Sciences*, 6, no. 2 (1977), 20–46.

2925. JONES, BUFORD. "After Long Apprenticeship: Hawthorne's Mature Romances." *ESQ*, 19 (1973), 1–7.

2926. _____. "*The Faery Land* of Hawthorne's Romances." *The Emerson Society Quarterly*, no. 48 (1967), pp. 106–24.

2927. JONES, WAYNE ALLEN. "The Hawthorne-Goodrich Relationship and a New Estimate of Hawthorne's Income from *The Token.*" *The Nathaniel Hawthorne Journal 1975*, pp. 91–140.

2928. _____. "New Light on Hawthorne and the *Southern Rose.*" *The Nathaniel Hawthorne Journal 1974*, pp. 31–46.

2929. _____. "Sometimes Things Just Don't Work Out: Hawthorne's Income from *Twice-Told Tales* (1837), and Another 'Good Thing' for Hawthorne." *The Nathaniel Hawthorne Journal 1975*, pp. 11–26.

2930. JOSIPOVICI, G[ABRIEL] D. "Hawthorne's Modernity." *The Critical Quarterly*, 8 (1966), 351–60.

2931. _____. *The World and the Book: A Study of Modern Fiction.* Stanford, CA: Stanford Univ. Press, 1971.

2932. KAUL, A. N. "Introduction." In *Hawthorne: A Collection of Critical Essays.* Englewood Cliffs, NJ: Prentice-Hall, 1966. pp. 1–10.

2933. KAY, CAROL MCGINNIS. "Hawthorne's Use of Clothing in His Short Stories." *The Nathaniel Hawthorne Journal 1972*, pp. 245–49.

2934. KAY, DONALD. "Hawthorne's Use of Laughter in Selected Short Stories." *Xavier University Studies*, 10, no. 2 (1971), 27–32.

2935. KAZIN, ALFRED. "Hawthorne: The Artist of New England." *The Atlantic Monthly*, 218, no. 6 (1966), 109–13.

2936. KERN, ALEXANDER C. "A Note on Hawthorne's Juveniles." *Philological Quarterly*, 39 (1960), 242–46.

2937. KESTERSON, DAVID B. "Nature and Hawthorne's Religious Isolationists." *The Nathaniel Hawthorne Journal 1974*, pp. 196–208.

2938. KJØRVEN, JOHANNES. "Hawthorne, and the Significance of History." In *Americana Norvegica: Norwegian Contributions to American Studies*, Vol. 1. Ed. Sigmund Skard and Henry H. Wasser. Oslo: Gyldendal Norsk, 1966. pp. 110–60.

2939. KOSKELINNA, HAZEL M. "Setting, Image, and Symbol in Scott and Hawthorne." *ESQ*, 19 (1973), 50–59.

2940. LANG, H. J. "How Ambiguous is Hawthorne?" In *Geist einer freien Gesellschaft: Festschrift zu Ehren von Senator James William Fulbright aus Anlass des zehnjährigen Bestehens des deutschen Fulbright-Programms*. Ed. Lewis Hammond, Dieter Sattler, and Emil Lehnartz. Heidelberg: Quelle & Meyer, 1962. pp. 195–200.

2941. LAUBER, JOHN. "Hawthorne's Shaker Tales." *Nineteenth-Century Fiction*, 18 (1963), 82–86.

2942. LAVERTY, CARROLL D. "Some Touchstones of Hawthorne's Style." *ESQ*, no. 60 (1970), pp. 30–36.

2943. LEASE, BENJAMIN. "Hawthorne and the Archaeology of the Cinema." *The Nathaniel Hawthorne Journal 1976*, pp. 133–71.

2944. LEVIN, DAVID. "Hawthorne's Romances: The Value of Puritan History." In *In Defense of Historical Literature: Essays on American History, Autobiography, Drama, and Fiction*. New York: Hill and Wang, 1967. pp. 98–117.

2945. LEVY, LEO B. "Hawthorne and the Sublime." *American Literature*, 37 (1966), 391–402.

2946. _____. " 'Lifelikeness' in Hawthorne's Fiction." *The Nathaniel Hawthorne Journal 1975*, pp. 141–45.

2947. _____. " 'Time's Portraiture': Hawthorne's Theory of History." *The Nathaniel Hawthorne Journal 1971*, pp. 192–200.

2948. LIEBMAN, SHELDON W. "The Forsaken Maiden in Hawthorne's Stories." *American Transcendental Quarterly*, no. 19 (1973), pp. 13–19.

2949. LOVING, JEROME M. "Melville's Pardonable Sin." *The New England Quarterly*, 47 (1974), 262–78.

2950. LUECKE, SISTER JANE MARIE, O.S.B. "Villains and Non-Villains in Hawthorne's Fiction." *PMLA*, 78 (1963), 551–58.

2951. MCCALL, DAN. "Hawthorne's 'Familiar Kind of Preface.' " *ELH*, 35 (1968), 422–39.

2952. MCCULLEN, JOSEPH T., AND JOHN C. GUILDS. "The Unpardonable Sin in Hawthorne: A Re-examination." *Nineteenth-Century Fiction*, 15 (1960), 221–37.

2953. MCDONALD, JOHN J. " 'The Old Manse' and Its Mosses: The Inception and Development of *Mosses from an Old Manse*." *Texas Studies in Literature and Language*, 16 (1974), 77–108.

2954. _____. "The Old Manse Period Canon." *The Nathaniel Hawthorne Journal 1972*, pp. 13-39.

2955. McELDERRY, B. R., JR. "The Transcendental Hawthorne." *The Midwest Quarterly*, 2 (1961), 307-23.

2956. McPHERSON, HUGO. *Hawthorne as Myth-Maker: A Study in Imagination*. Toronto: Univ. of Toronto Press, 1969.

2957. _____. "Hawthorne's Mythology: A Mirror for Puritans." *University of Toronto Quarterly*, 28 (1959), 267-78.

2958. McWILLIAMS, JOHN P., JR. " 'Thorough-going Democrat' and 'Modern Tory': Hawthorne and the Puritan Revolution of 1776." *Studies in Romanticism*, 15 (1976), 549-71.

2959. MALE, ROY R. "Hawthorne's Allegory of Guilt and Redemption." *The Emerson Society Quarterly*, no. 25 (1961), pp. 16-18.

2960. MARTIN, TERENCE. "The Method of Hawthorne's Tales." In *Hawthorne Centenary Essays*. Ed. Roy Harvey Pearce. Columbus: Ohio State Univ. Press, 1964. pp. 7-30.

2961. _____. *Nathaniel Hawthorne*. New York: Twayne, 1965.

2962. MATHEWS, JAMES W. "Hawthorne and the Periodical Tale: From Popular Lore to Art." *The Papers of the Bibliographical Society of America*, 68 (1974), 149-62.

2963. MORSBERGER, ROBERT E. "Hawthorne: The Civil War as the Unpardonable Sin." *The Nathaniel Hawthorne Journal 1977*, pp. 111-22.

2964. MOUNTS, CHARLES EUGENE. "Hawthorne's Echoes of Spenser and Milton." *The Nathaniel Hawthorne Journal 1973*, pp. 162-71.

2965. NEWLIN, PAUL A. " 'Vague Shapes of the Borderland': The Place of the Uncanny in Hawthorne's Gothic Fiction." *ESQ*, 18 (1972), 83-96.

2966. NORMAND, JEAN. *Nathaniel Hawthorne: An Approach to an Analysis of Artistic Creation*. Trans. Derek Coltman. Cleveland, OH: Press of Case Western Reserve Univ., 1970.

2967. PATTISON, JOSEPH C. "Point of View in Hawthorne." *PMLA*, 82 (1967), 363-69.

2968. PAULY, THOMAS H. "Hawthorne's Houses of Fiction." *American Literature*, 48 (1976), 271-91.

2969. PEARCE, ROY HARVEY. "Romance and the Study of History." In *Hawthorne Centenary Essays*. Ed. Roy Harvey Pearce. Columbus: Ohio State Univ. Press, 1964. pp. 221-44, 466.

2970. PETERICH, WERNER. "Hawthorne and the *Gesta Romanorum*: The Genesis of 'Rappaccini's Daughter' and 'Ethan Brand.' " In *Kleine Beiträge zur amerikanischen Literaturgeschichte: Arbeitsproben aus deutschen Seminaren und Instituten*. Ed. Hans Galinsky and Hans-Joachim Lang. Heidelberg: Carl Winter, 1961. pp. 11-18.

2971. REED, P. L. "The Telling Frame of Hawthorne's 'Legends of the Province House.' " *Studies in American Fiction*, 4 (1976), 105-11.

2972. REES, JOHN O., JR. "Hawthorne's Concept of Allegory: A Reconsideration." *Philological Quarterly*, 54 (1975), 494-510.

2973. RINGE, DONALD A. "Hawthorne's Night Journeys." *American Transcendental Quarterly*, no. 10 (1971), pp. 27-32.

2974. _____. "Teaching Hawthorne to Engineering Students." *The Emerson Society Quarterly*, no. 25 (1961), pp. 24-26.

2975. ROCKS, JAMES E. "Hawthorne and France: In Search of American Literary Nationalism." *Tulane Studies in English*, 17 (1969), 145-57.

2976. ROHRBERGER, MARY. "Hawthorne's Literary Theory and the Nature of his Short Stories." *Studies in Short Fiction*, 3 (1965), 23-30.

2977. ROULSTON, ROBERT. "Hawthorne's Attitude toward Jews." *American Transcendental Quarterly*, no. 29 (1976), pp. 3-8.

2978. ROUSE, BLAIR. "Hawthorne and the American Revolution: An Exploration." *The Nathaniel Hawthorne Journal 1976*, pp. 17-61.

2979. RUBIN, JOSEPH JAY. "Hawthorne's Theology: The Wide Plank." *The Emerson Society Quarterly*, no. 25 (1961), pp. 20-24.

2980. SAKAMOTO, MASAYUKI. "Hawthorne on Romance." In *American Literature in the 1940's*. Annual Report, 1975. Tokyo: Tokyo Chapter, American Literature Society of Japan, 1976. pp. 25-32.

2981. SALOMON, LOUIS B. "Hawthorne and His Father: A Conjecture." *Literature and Psychology*, 13 (1963), 12-17.

2982. SCHNEIDERMAN, LEO. "Hawthorne and the Refuge of the Heart." *The Connecticut Review*, 3, no. 2 (1970), 83-101.

2983. SCHWARTZ, JOSEPH. "Nathaniel Hawthorne and the Natural Desire for God." *The Nathaniel Hawthorne Journal 1972*, pp. 159-71.

2984. _____. "Three Aspects of Hawthorne's Puritanism." *The New England Quarterly*, 36 (1963), 192-208.

2985. SCOVILLE, SAMUEL. "Hawthorne's Houses and Hidden Treasures." *ESQ*, 19 (1973), 61-73.

2986. SHAW, PETER. "Hawthorne's Ritual Typology of the American Revolution." *Prospects*, no. 3 (1977), pp. 483-98.

2987. SHULMAN, ROBERT. "Hawthorne's Quiet Conflict." *Philological Quarterly*, 47 (1968), 216-36.

2988. SMITH, JULIAN. "A Hawthorne Source for *The House of the Seven Gables*." *American Transcendental Quarterly*, no. 1 (1969), pp. 18-19.

2989. _____. "Hawthorne's *Legends of the Province House.*" *Nineteenth-Century Fiction*, 24 (1969), 31–44.

2990. SMITH, LAURA. "Charactonyms in the Fiction of Nathaniel Hawthorne." In *Of Edsels and Marauders*. Ed. Fred Tarpley and Ann Moseley. Commerce, TX: Names Institute Press, 1971. pp. 75–81.

2991. STAAL, ARIE. *Hawthorne's Narrative Art.* New York: Revisionist Press, 1977.

2992. STAVROU, C. N. "Hawthorne's Quarrel with Man." *The Personalist*, 42 (1961), 352–60.

2993. STOEHR, TAYLOR. "Hawthorne and Mesmerism." *The Huntington Library Quarterly*, 33 (1969), 33–60.

2994. _____. "Physiognomy and Phrenology in Hawthorne." *The Huntington Library Quarterly*, 37 (1974), 355–400.

2995. STUBBS, JOHN CALDWELL. *The Pursuit of Form: A Study of Hawthorne and the Romance.* Urbana: Univ. of Illinois Press, 1970.

2996. SUH, IN-JAE. "Hawthorne's Attitude Toward New England Religious Doctrine." *The English Language and Literature*, no. 14 (1963), pp. 78–105.

2997. THARPE, JAC. *Nathaniel Hawthorne: Identity and Knowledge.* Carbondale and Edwardsville: Southern Illinois Univ. Press, 1967.

2998. THORSLEV, PETER L., JR. "Hawthorne's Determinism: An Analysis." *Nineteenth-Century Fiction*, 19 (1964), 141–57.

2999. TRILLING, LIONEL. "Our Hawthorne." *Partisan Review*, 31 (1964), 329–51.

3000. TURNER, ARLIN. "Consistency in the Mind and Work of Hawthorne." In *The Chief Glory of Every People: Essays on Classic American Writers*. Ed. Matthew J. Bruccoli. Carbondale and Edwardsville: Southern Illinois Univ. Press, 1973. pp. 97–116.

3001. _____. "Elizabeth Peabody Reviews *Twice-Told Tales.*" *The Nathaniel Hawthorne Journal 1974*, pp. 75–84.

3002. _____. *Nathaniel Hawthorne: An Introduction and Interpretation.* New York: Barnes & Noble, 1961.

3003. VANCE, WILLIAM L. "The Comic Element in Hawthorne's Sketches." *Studies in Romanticism*, 3 (1964), 144–60.

3004. WAGENKNECHT, EDWARD. *Nathaniel Hawthorne: Man and Writer.* New York: Oxford Univ. Press, 1961.

3005. WAGGONER, HYATT H. "Art and Belief." In *Hawthorne Centenary Essays*. Ed. Roy Harvey Pearce. Columbus: Ohio State Univ. Press, 1964. pp. 167–95, 464–65.

3006. _____. *Hawthorne: A Critical Study.* Rev. ed. Cambridge, MA: Harvard Univ. Press, 1963.

3007. _____. "Hawthorne's Presence in *Moby-Dick* and in Melville's Tales and Sketches." *The Nathaniel Hawthorne Journal 1977*, pp. 73–79.

3008. _____. "Introduction to Third Edition." In *Selected Tales and Sketches*, by Nathaniel Hawthorne. New York: Holt, Rinehart and Winston, 1970. pp. iii–xiii.

3009. _____. *Nathaniel Hawthorne*. Minneapolis: Univ. of Minnesota Press, 1962.

3010. WAGNER, VERN. "Hawthorne's Smile." *The Texas Quarterly*, 16, no. 4 (1973), 6–31.

3011. WALTER, JAMES F. "The Metaphysical Vision of History in Hawthorne's Fiction." *The Nathaniel Hawthorne Journal 1976*, pp. 276–85.

3012. WARREN, ROBERT PENN. "Hawthorne Revisited: Some Remarks on Hellfiredness." *The Sewanee Review*, 81 (1973), 75–111.

3013. WEBB, JANE CARTER. "The Implications of Control for the Human Personality: Hawthorne's Point of View." *Tulane Studies in English*, 21 (1974), 57–66.

3014. WEST, HARRY C. "Hawthorne's Editorial Pose." *American Literature*, 44 (1972), 208–21.

3015. _____. "Hawthorne's Magic Circle: The Artist as Magician." *Criticism*, 16 (1974), 311–25.

3016. WHEELER, OTIS B. "Hawthorne and the Fiction of Sensibility." *Nineteenth-Century Fiction*, 19 (1964), 159–70.

3017. _____. "Love among the Ruins: Hawthorne's Surrogate Religion." *The Southern Review*, NS 10 (1974), 535–65.

3018. WINSLOW, JOAN D. "New Light on Hawthorne's Miles Coverdale." *The Journal of Narrative Technique*, 7 (1977), 189–99.

3019. WRIGHT, JOHN. "Borges and Hawthorne." *TriQuarterly*, no. 25 (1972), pp. 334–55.

3020. YODER, R. A. "Hawthorne and His Artist." *Studies in Romanticism*, 7 (1968), 193–206.

3021. ZIFF, LARNER. "The Artist and Puritanism." In *Hawthorne Centenary Essays*. Ed. Roy Harvey Pearce. Columbus: Ohio State Univ. Press, 1964. pp. 245–69, 466.

Bibliography

3022. ADKINS, NELSON F. "Notes on the Hawthorne Canon." *The Papers of the Bibliographical Society of America*, 60 (1966), 364–67.

3023. ATKINSON, JENNIFER E. "Recent Hawthorne Scholarship— 1967–1970: A Checklist." *The Nathaniel Hawthorne Journal 1971*, pp. 295–305.

3024. BEEBE, MAURICE, AND JACK HARDIE. "Criticism of Nathaniel Hawthorne: A Selected Checklist." *Studies in the Novel*, 2 (1970), 519–87.

3025. BLAIR, WALTER. "Nathaniel Hawthorne." In *Eight American Authors: A Review of Research and Criticism*. Rev. ed. Ed. James Woodress. New York: Norton, 1971. pp. 85–128.

3026. BRUCCOLI, MATTHEW J. "Hawthorne as a Collector's Item, 1885–1924." In *Hawthorne Centenary Essays*. Ed. Roy Harvey Pearce. Columbus: Ohio State Univ. Press, 1964. pp. 387–400, 477–79.

3027. _____. "Nathaniel Hawthorne Stalks Columbus: An Ohio Ghost?" *The Serif*, 1, no. 1 (1964), 26–27.

3028. CADY, EDWIN H. "The Wizard Hand." In *Hawthorne Centenary Essays*. Ed. Roy Harvey Pearce. Columbus: Ohio State Univ. Press, 1964. pp. 317–34, 468–70.

3029. CAMERON, KENNETH WALTER. *Hawthorne Index to Themes, Motifs, Topics, Archetypes, Sources and Key Words Dealt with in Recent Criticism*. Hartford, CT: Transcendental Books, 1968.

3030. CLARK, C. E. FRAZER, JR. *The Merrill Checklist of Nathaniel Hawthorne*. Columbus, OH: Merrill, 1970.

3031. FRANCIS, GLORIA A. "Recent Hawthorne Scholarship, 1970–1972." *The Nathaniel Hawthorne Journal 1972*, pp. 273–78; *1973*, pp. 269–77.

3032. GROSS, SEYMOUR L., AND RANDALL STEWART. "The Hawthorne Revival." In *Hawthorne Centenary Essays*. Ed. Roy Harvey Pearce. Columbus: Ohio State Univ. Press, 1964. pp. 335–66.

3033. GROSS, THEODORE L., AND STANLEY WERTHEIM. *Hawthorne, Melville, Stephen Crane: A Critical Bibliography*. New York: Free Press, 1971.

3034. HULL, RAYMONA E. "British Periodical Printings of Hawthorne's Works, 1835–1900: A Partial Bibliography." *The Nathaniel Hawthorne Journal 1973*, pp. 73–88.

3035. JONES, BUFORD. "A Checklist of Hawthorne Criticism, 1951–1966." *The Emerson Society Quarterly*, no. 52, Supplement (1968), pp. 1–91.

3036. _____. "Current Hawthorne Bibliography." *The Nathaniel Hawthorne Society Newsletter*, 1, no. 2 (1975), 4–6; 2, no. 2 (1976), 4–10; 3, no. 2 (1977), 6–10.

3037. JONES, WAYNE ALLEN. "A Checklist of Recent Hawthorne Scholarship." *The Nathaniel Hawthorne Journal 1976*, pp. 313–20; *1977*, pp. 373–89.

3038. _____. "Recent Hawthorne Scholarship, 1973–1974, with Supplementary Entries from Other Years Added." *The Nathaniel Hawthorne Journal 1975*, pp. 281–316.

3039. **STANTON, ROBERT J.** "Secondary Studies on Hawthorne's 'Young Goodman Brown,' 1845–1975: A Bibliography." *Bulletin of Bibliography and Magazine Notes*, 33 (1976), 32–44, 52.

3040. **TANSELLE, G. THOMAS.** "*BAL* Addenda: Some Hawthorne Printings, 1884–1921." *The Papers of the Bibliographical Society of America*, 67 (1973), 65–66.

HAY, JOHN

"The Minstrel"

3041. **MONTEIRO, GEORGE.** " 'The Minstrel.' An Unpublished Story by John Hay." *Books at Brown*, 25 (1977), 27–42.

General Studies

*3042. **MONTEIRO, GEORGE.** "John Hay's Short Fiction." *Studies in Short Fiction*, 8 (1971), 543–52.

Bibliography

3043. **SLOANE, DAVID E. E.** "John Hay (1838–1905)." *American Literary Realism, 1870–1910*, 3 (1970), 178–88.

HAYCOX, ERNEST

General Studies

3044. **ETULAIN, RICHARD.** "Ernest Haycox: The Historical Western, 1937–43." *South Dakota Review*, 5, no. 1 (1967), 35–54.

HEARN, LAFCADIO

"Karma"

See 3051.

"Of a Promise Kept"

See 3045, 3046.

"A Passional Karma"

See 3045, 3046.

"The Story of Itō Norisuké"

See 3051.

"The Story of Kōgi the Priest"

See 3045, 3046.

General Studies

*3045. **KUNST, ARTHUR E.** *Lafcadio Hearn*. New York: Twayne, 1969.

3046. ———. "Lafcadio Hearn's Use of Japanese Sources." *Literature East & West*, 10 (1966), 245–63.

3047. **LEARY, LEWIS.** "Lafcadio Hearn, 'One of Our Southern Writers': A Footnote to Southern Literary History." In *Essays on American Literature in Honor of Jay B. Hubbell.* Ed. Clarence Gohdes. Durham, NC: Duke Univ. Press, 1967. pp. 202–14.

3048. **MANDEL, SIEGFRIED.** "Lafcadio Hearn and the Jikininkis." *Iowa English Yearbook*, no. 8 (1963), pp. 67–72.

3049. **MORDELL, ALBERT.** *Discoveries: Essays on Lafcadio Hearn.* Tokyo: Orient/West, 1964.

3050. **STEVENSON, ELIZABETH.** *Lafcadio Hearn.* New York: Macmillan, 1961.

3051. **YU, BEONGCHEON.** *An Ape of Gods: The Art and Thought of Lafcadio Hearn.* Detroit, MI: Wayne State Univ. Press, 1964.

3052. ———. "Lafcadio Hearn's Twice-Told Legends Reconsidered." *American Literature*, 34 (1962), 56–71.

Bibliography

3053. **YU, BEONGCHEON.** "Lafcadio Hearn (or Koizumi Yakumo)(1850–1904)." *American Literary Realism, 1870–1910*, 1, no. 1 (1967), 52–55.

HEGGEN, [ORLO] THOMAS

General Studies

*3054. **LEGGETT, JOHN.** *Ross and Tom: Two American Tragedies.* New York: Simon and Schuster, 1974.

HEINLEIN, ROBERT A.

" '*All You Zombies—*' "

See 3057.

"*By His Bootstraps*"

See 140, 365, 3059.

"*Common Sense*"

See 3059.

"*Coventry*"

See 140, 3057, 3059.

"Gulf"

See 293, 3057.

" '—If This Goes On' "

See 226, 3057, 3059.

"Life-Line"

See 3057, 3059.

"Magic, Inc."

See 3059.

"Requiem"

See 3059.

"Solution Unsatisfactory"

See 462.

"They"

3055. SCHUMAN, SAMUEL. "Vladimir Nabokov's *Invitation to a Beheading* and Robert Heinlein's 'They.' " *Twentieth Century Literature*, 19 (1973), 99–106.
See also 3059.

"Universe"

See 3059.

"The Unpleasant Profession of Jonathan Hoag"

See 3057.

"Waldo"

See 462, 3057, 3059.

General Studies

3056. LEHMAN-WILZIG, SAM N. "Science Fiction as Futurist Prediction: Alternative Visions of Heinlein and Clarke." *The Literary Review*, 20 (1977), 133–51.
3057. PANSHIN, ALEXEI. *Heinlein in Dimension.* Chicago: Advent, 1968.
3058. SAMUELSON, DAVID N. "The Frontier Worlds of Robert A. Heinlein." In *Voices for the Future: Essays on Major Science Fiction Writers.* Ed. Thomas D. Clareson. Bowling Green, OH: Bowling Green Univ. Popular Press, 1976. pp. 104–52.
3059. SLUSSER, GEORGE EDGAR. *The Classic Years of Robert A. Heinlein.* San Bernardino, CA: Borgo Press, 1977.

HEMINGWAY, ERNEST

"After the Storm"

3060. **ATKINS, ANSELM.** "Ironic Action in 'After the Storm.'" *Studies in Short Fiction*, 5 (1968), 189–92.

3061. **BUSCH, FREDERICK.** "Icebergs, Islands, Ships Beneath the Sea." In *A John Hawkes Symposium: Design and Debris.* Ed. Anthony C. Santore and Michael Pocalyko. New York: New Directions, 1977. pp. 50–63.

3062. **GARDNER, JOHN, AND LENNIS DUNLAP.** "Analysis." In *The Forms of Fiction.* New York: Random House, 1962. pp. 48–50.

3063. **WALKER, ROBERT G.** "Irony and Allusion in Hemingway's 'After the Storm.'" *Studies in Short Fiction*, 13 (1976), 374–76.
See also 3327, 3360.

"An Alpine Idyll"

3064. **ARMISTEAD, MYRA.** "Hemingway's 'An Alpine Idyll.'" *Studies in Short Fiction*, 14 (1977), 255–58.

3065. **HATTAM, EDWARD.** "Hemingway's 'An Alpine Idyll.'" *Modern Fiction Studies*, 12 (1966), 261–65.
See also 356, 3302, 3303, 3306.

"Banal Story"

3066. **KVAM, WAYNE.** "Hemingway's 'Banal Story.'" *Fitzgerald/Hemingway Annual 1974*, pp. 181–91.

3067. **YANNELLA, PHILLIP R.** "Notes on the Manuscript, Date, and Sources of Hemingway's 'Banal Story.'" *Fitzgerald/Hemingway Annual 1974*, pp. 175–79.
See also 3402.

"The Battler"

See 194, 3306, 3327, 3334, 3343, 3347, 3363, 3374, 3392, 3438, 3460, 5934.

"Big Two-Hearted River"

3068. **ADAIR, WILLIAM.** "Landscapes of the Mind: 'Big Two-Hearted River.'" *College Literature*, 4 (1977), 144–51.

3069. **ANDERSON, PAUL VICTOR.** "Nick's Story in Hemingway's 'Big Two-Hearted River.'" *Studies in Short Fiction*, 7 (1970), 564–72.

3070. **DOXEY, WILLIAM S.** "The Significance of Seney, Michigan, in Hemingway's 'Big Two-Hearted River.'" *Hemingway Notes*, 1, no. 2 (1971), 5–6.

3071. EVANS, ROBERT. "Hemingway and the Pale Cast of Thought." *American Literature*, 38 (1966), 161-76.

3072. GREEN, JAMES L. "Symbolic Sentences in 'Big Two-Hearted River.'" *Modern Fiction Studies*, 14 (1968), 307-12.

3073. GUTWINSKI, WALDEMAR. "Cohesion in Hemingway." In *Cohesion in Literary Texts: A Study of Some Grammatical and Lexical Features of English Discourse*. The Hague: Mouton, 1976. pp. 127-41, 164-66.

3074. KORN, BARBARA. "Form and Idea in Hemingway's 'Big Two-Hearted River.'" *English Journal*, 56 (1967), 979-81, 1014.

3075. STEIN, WILLIAM BYSSHE. "Ritual in Hemingway's 'Big Two-Hearted River.'" *Texas Studies in Literature and Language*, 1 (1960), 555-61.

3076. TWITCHELL, JAMES. "The Swamp in Hemingway's 'Big Two-Hearted River.'" *Studies in Short Fiction*, 9 (1972), 275-76.

3077. WEEKS, LEWIS E., JR. "Two Types of Tension: Art vs. Campcraft in Hemingway's 'Big Two-Hearted River.'" *Studies in Short Fiction*, 11 (1974), 433-34.

3078. WELLS, ELIZABETH. "A Comparative Statistical Analysis Of The Prose Styles Of F. Scott Fitzgerald And Ernest Hemingway." *Fitzgerald/Hemingway Annual 1969*, pp. 47-67.

3079. ———. "A Statistical Analysis of the Prose Style of Ernest Hemingway: 'Big Two-Hearted River.'" In *The Short Stories of Ernest Hemingway: Critical Essays*. Ed. Jackson J. Benson. Durham, NC: Duke Univ. Press, 1975. pp. 129-35.

See also 175, 209, 356, 455, 569, 574, 589, 599, 3212, 3301-3303, 3306, 3311, 3327, 3334, 3343, 3347, 3349, 3359, 3381, 3392, 3395, 3397, 3402, 3403, 3414, 3417, 3422, 3429, 3433, 3438, 3439, 3443, 3444, 3460.

"The Butterfly and the Tank"

See 3380, 3427.

"A Canary for One"

3080. ROUCH, JOHN S. "Jake Barnes as Narrator." *Modern Fiction Studies*, 11 (1965), 361-70.

3081. SMITH, JULIAN. "'A Canary for One': Hemingway in the Wasteland." *Studies in Short Fiction*, 5 (1968), 355-61.

See also 454, 3327.

"The Capital of the World"

3082. GREBSTEIN, SHELDON NORMAN. "Hemingway's Dark and Bloody Capital." In *The Thirties: Fiction, Poetry, Drama*. Ed. Warren French. Deland, FL: Everett/Edwards, 1967. pp. 21-30.

3083. **REID, STEPHEN A.** "The Oedipal Pattern in Hemingway's 'The Capital of the World.' " *Literature and Psychology*, 13 (1963), 37–43.
See also 3306, 3327, 3347, 3359, 3402, 3403.

"Cat in the Rain"

3084. **KRUSE, HORST.** "Hemingway's 'Cat in the Rain' and Joyce's *Ulysses.*" *Literatur in Wissenschaft und Unterricht*, 3 (1970), 28–30.
3085. **MAGEE, JOHN D.** "Hemingway's 'Cat in the Rain.' " *The Explicator*, 26 (1967), item 8.
3086. **SRIVASTAVA, RAMESH.** "Hemingway's 'Cat in the Rain': An Interpretation." *The Literary Criterion*, 9, no. 2 (1970), 79–84.
See also 454, 3327, 3330, 3372.

"Chapter III," In Our Time

See 269, 3389.

"Chapter V," In Our Time

3087. **SPIEGEL, ALAN.** "The Mud on Napoleon's Boots: The Adventitious Detail in Film and Fiction." *The Virginia Quarterly Review*, 52 (1976), 249–64.

"Chapter VI," In Our Time

See 3411, 3460.

"Chapter IX," In Our Time

See 3343, 3411.

"Chapter XV," In Our Time

See 3429.

"Che Ti Dice La Patria?"

See 3343, 3344.

"A Clean, Well-Lighted Place"

3088. **BENERT, ANNETTE.** "Survival through Irony: Hemingway's 'A Clean, Well-Lighted Place.' " *Studies in Short Fiction*, 11 (1974), 181–87.
3089. **BENNETT, WARREN.** "Character, Irony, and Resolution in 'A Clean, Well-Lighted Place.' " *American Literature*, 42 (1970), 70–79.
3090. ———. "The New Text of 'A Clean, Well-Lighted Place.' " *The Literary Half-Yearly*, 14, no. 1 (1973), 115–25.

3091. BROER, LAWRENCE. " 'A Clean, Well-Lighted Place' (Hemingway)." In *Instructor's Manual to Accompany* "The Realities of Literature." Ed. R. F. Dietrich. Waltham, MA: Xerox Publishing, 1971. pp. 82–89.

3092. _____. "The Iceberg in 'A Clean, Well-Lighted Place.' " *Lost Generation Journal*, 4, no. 2 (1976), 14–15, 21.

3093. CAMPBELL, HARRY M. "Comments on Mr. Stock's *'Nada* in Hemingway's "A Clean, Well-Lighted Place." ' " *Midcontinent American Studies Journal*, 3, no. 1 (1962), 57–59.

3094. COLBURN, WILLIAM E. "Confusion in 'A Clean, Well-Lighted Place.' " *College English*, 20 (1959), 241–42.

3095. EWELL, NATHANIEL M., III. "Dialogue in Hemingway's 'A Clean, Well-Lighted Place.' " *Fitzgerald/Hemingway Annual 1971*, pp. 305–06.

3096. GABRIEL, JOSEPH F. "The Logic of Confusion in Hemingway's 'A Clean, Well-Lighted Place.' " *College English*, 22 (1961), 539–46.

3097. HAGOPIAN, JOHN V. "Tidying Up Hemingway's Clean, Well-Lighted Place." *Studies in Short Fiction*, 1 (1964), 140–46.

3098. HURLEY, C. HAROLD. "The Attribution of the Waiters' Second Speech in Hemingway's 'A Clean, Well-Lighted Place.' " *Studies in Short Fiction*, 13 (1976), 81–85.

3099. KANN, HANS-JOACHIM. "Perpetual Confusion in 'A Clean, Well-Lighted Place': The Manuscript Evidence." *Fitzgerald/Hemingway Annual 1977*, pp. 115–18.

3100. KROEGER, F. P. "The Dialogue in 'A Clean, Well-Lighted Place.' " *College English*, 20 (1959), 240–41.

3101. LODGE, DAVID. "Hemingway's Clean, Well-Lighted, Puzzling Place." *Essays in Criticism*, 21 (1971), 33–56.

3102. MACDONALD, SCOTT. "The Confusing Dialogue in Hemingway's 'A Clean, Well-Lighted Place': A Final Word?" *Studies in American Fiction*, 1 (1973), 93–101.

3103. MAY, CHARLES E. "Is Hemingway's 'Well-Lighted Place' Really Clean Now?" *Studies in Short Fiction*, 8 (1971), 326–30.

3104. MONTEIRO, GEORGE. "Hemingway on Dialogue in 'A Clean, Well-Lighted Place.' " *Fitzgerald/Hemingway Annual 1974*, p. 243.

3105. _____. "Not Hemingway But Spain." *Fitzgerald/Hemingway Annual 1971*, pp. 309–11.

3106. REINERT, OTTO. "Hemingway's Waiters Once Again." *College English*, 20 (1959), 417–18.

3107. SCHORER, MARK. "Comment." In *The Story: A Critical Anthology*. 2nd ed. Englewood Cliffs, NJ: Prentice-Hall, 1967. pp. 323–25.

3108. **STOCK, ELY.** "*Nada* in Hemingway's 'A Clean, Well-Lighted Place.' " *Midcontinent American Studies Journal*, 3, no. 1 (1962), 54-57.

3109. **STONE, EDWARD.** "Hemingway's Waiters Yet Once More." *American Speech*, 37 (1962), 239-40.

See also 133, 454, 564, 3302, 3303, 3306, 3311, 3330, 3347, 3353, 3359, 3362, 3370, 3390, 3402, 3403, 3414, 3419, 3422, 3444.

"Cross-Country Snow"

See 455, 3327, 3334, 3374, 3438.

"A Day's Wait"

3110. **MAHONEY, PATRICK J.** "Hemingway's 'A Day's Wait.' " *The Explicator*, 27 (1968), item 18.

3111. **MONTEIRO, GEORGE.** "Hemingway, O. Henry, and the Surprise Ending." *Prairie Schooner*, 47 (1974), 296-302.

See also 454, 3327, 3344.

"The Denunciation"

See 3343, 3380, 3396, 3427.

"The Doctor and the Doctor's Wife"

3112. **ARNOLD, AEROL.** "Hemingway's 'The Doctor and the Doctor's Wife.' " *The Explicator*, 18 (1960), item 36.

3113. **DAVIS, ROBERT MURRAY.** "Hemingway's 'The Doctor and the Doctor's Wife.' " *The Explicator*, 25 (1966), item 1.

3114. **FOX, STEPHEN D.** "Hemingway's 'The Doctor and the Doctor's Wife.' " *The Arizona Quarterly*, 29 (1973), 19-25.

See also 356, 3306, 3311, 3327, 3334, 3336, 3343, 3344, 3359, 3392, 3397.

"The End of Something"

3115. **KRUSE, HORST H.** "Ernest Hemingway's 'The End of Something': Its Independence as a Short Story and its Place in the 'Education of Nick Adams.' " *Studies in Short Fiction*, 4 (1967), 152-66.

See also 356, 3306, 3327, 3347, 3392, 3416, 3438, 3460.

"The Faithful Bull"

3116. **JOHNSTON, KENNETH G.** "The Bull and the Lion: Hemingway's Fables for Critics." *Fitzgerald/Hemingway Annual 1977*, pp. 149-56.

"Fathers and Sons"

3117. **FLEMING, ROBERT E.** "Hemingway's Treatment of Sui-

cide: 'Fathers and Sons' and *For Whom the Bell Tolls.*" *The Arizona Quarterly,* 33 (1977), 121-32.
See also 3306, 3311, 3327, 3330, 3334, 3341, 3343, 3359, 3392, 3402, 3403, 3438, 3443, 3460.

"Fifty Grand"

3118. DAVIES, PHILLIPS G. AND ROSEMARY R. "Hemingway's 'Fifty Grand' and the Jack Britton-Mickey Walter Prize Fight." *American Literature,* 37 (1965), 251-58.
3119. MARTINE, JAMES J. "Hemingway's 'Fifty Grand': The Other Fight(s)." *Journal of Modern Literature,* 2 (1971), 123-27.
See also 133, 269, 574, 3306, 3327, 3343, 3347, 3389, 3460.

"The Gambler, the Nun, and the Radio"

3120. MONTGOMERY, MARION. "Hemingway's 'The Gambler, the Nun, and the Radio.' " *Forum* (University of Houston), 3, no. 9 (1962), 36-40.
3121. RODGERS, PAUL C., JR. "Levels of Irony in Hemingway's 'The Gambler, the Nun, and the Radio.' " *Studies in Short Fiction,* 7 (1970), 439-49.
3122. STONE, EDWARD. "Hemingway's Mr. Frazer: From Revolution to Radio." *Journal of Modern Literature,* 1 (1971), 375-88.
3123. WHITTLE, AMBERYS R. "A Reading of Hemingway's 'The Gambler, the Nun, and the Radio.' " *The Arizona Quarterly,* 33 (1977), 173-80.
See also 267, 269, 3306, 3327, 3340, 3343, 3359, 3362, 3372, 3402, 3460.

"Get A Seeing-Eyed Dog"

3124. WYLDER, DELBERT E. "Internal Treachery in the Last Published Short Stories of Ernest Hemingway." In *Hemingway in Our Time.* Ed. Richard Astro and Jackson J. Benson. Corvallis: Oregon State Univ. Press, 1974. pp. 53-65.
See also 3157.

"God Rest You Merry, Gentlemen"

3125. HAYS, PETER L. "Hemingway and the Fisher King." *The University Review* (Kansas City), 32 (1966), 225-28.
3126. MONTEIRO, GEORGE. "Hemingway's Christmas Carol." *Fitzgerald/Hemingway Annual 1972,* pp. 207-13.
See also 3359, 3428.

"The Good Lion"

See 3116.

"Hills Like White Elephants"

3127. **ELLIOTT, GARY D.** "Hemingway's 'Hills Like White Elephants.'" *The Explicator*, 35, no. 4 (1977), 22–23.

3128. **JAIN, S. P.** "'Hills Like White Elephants': A Study." *Indian Journal of American Studies*, 1, no. 3 (1970), 33–38.

3129. **MAYNARD, REID.** "Leitmotif and Irony in Hemingway's 'Hills Like White Elephants.'" *The University Review* (Kansas City), 37 (1971), 273–75.

3130. **MONTEIRO, GEORGE.** "The Wages of Love: 'Hills Like White Elephants.'" *Fitzgerald/Hemingway Annual 1976*, pp. 224–29.

3131. **RODRIGUES, EUSEBIO L.** "'Hills Like White Elephants': An Analysis:" *The Literary Criterion*, 5, no. 3 (1962), 105–09.

See also 274, 356, 399, 595, 3327, 3343, 3347, 3370, 3379.

"Homage to Switzerland"

See 3327, 3359, 3360.

"In Another Country"

3132. **IRWIN, RICHARD.** "'Of War, Wounds, and Silly Machines': An Examination of Hemingway's 'In Another Country.'" *The Serif*, 5, no. 2 (1968), 21–29.

3133. **STEPHENS, ROSEMARY.** "'In Another Country': *Three* as Symbol." *The University of Mississippi Studies in English*, 7 (1966), 77–83.

See also 133, 356, 548, 566, 3306, 3311, 3327, 3343, 3347, 3393, 3402, 3414, 3428, 3438, 3443.

"Indian Camp"

3134. **BERNARD, KENNETH.** "Hemingway's 'Indian Camp.'" *Studies in Short Fiction*, 2 (1965), 291.

3135. **GRIMES, LARRY.** "Night Terror and Morning Calm: A Reading of Hemingway's 'Indian Camp' as Sequel to 'Three Shots.'" *Studies in Short Fiction*, 12 (1975), 413–15.

3136. **MONTEIRO, GEORGE.** "The Limits of Professionalism: A Sociological Approach to Faulkner, Fitzgerald and Hemingway." *Criticism*, 15 (1973), 145–55.

3137. **PENNER, DICK.** "The First Nick Adams Story." *Fitzgerald/Hemingway Annual 1977*, pp. 195–202.

3138. **TANSELLE, G. THOMAS.** "Hemingway's 'Indian Camp.'" *The Explicator*, 20 (1962), item 53.

See also 356, 447, 3306, 3327, 3343, 3392, 3397, 3422, 3438, 3439, 3456, 3460.

"Judgment of Manitou"

See 3392.

"The Killers"

3139. B[RUCCOLI], M[ATTHEW] J. "Ole Anderson, Ole Andreson, and Carl Andreson." *Fitzgerald/Hemingway Annual 1971*, pp. 341–42.

3140. DAVIES, PHILLIP G. AND ROSEMARY R. "'A Killer Who Would Shoot You for the Fun of It': A Possible Source for Hemingway's 'The Killers.'" *Iowa English Yearbook*, no. 15 (1970), pp. 36–38.

3141. MOORE, L. HUGH, JR. "Mrs. Hirsch and Mrs. Bell in Hemingway's 'The Killers.'" *Modern Fiction Studies*, 11 (1965), 427–28.

3142. MORRIS, WILLIAM E. "Hemingway's 'The Killers.'" *The Explicator*, 18 (1959), item 1.

3143. NAGARJAN, M. S. "The Structure of 'The Killers.'" *The Literary Half-Yearly*, 15, no. 1 (1974), 114–19.

3144. OWEN, CHARLES A., JR. "Time and the Contagion of Flight in 'The Killers.'" *Forum* (University of Houston), 3, no. 5 (1960), 45–46.

3145. SCHLEPPER, WOLFGANG. "Hemingway's 'The Killers': An Absurd Happening." *Literatur in Wissenschaft und Unterricht*, 10 (1977), 104–14.

3146. STONE, EDWARD. "Some Questions about Hemingway's 'The Killers.'" *Studies in Short Fiction*, 5 (1967), 12–17.

3147. STUCKEY, W. J. "'The Killers' As Experience." *The Journal of Narrative Technique*, 5 (1975), 128–35.

3148. WALZ, LAWRENCE A. "Hemingway's 'The Killers.'" *The Explicator*, 25 (1967), item 38.

See also 356, 384, 394, 419, 454, 599, 1389, 3306, 3311, 3327, 3334, 3343, 3347, 3370, 3372, 3397, 3402, 3439, 3451, 3460.

"The Last Good Country"

See 3438, 3457.

"The Light of the World"

3149. BARBOUR, JAMES. " 'The Light of the World': Hemingway's Comedy of Errors." *Notes on Contemporary Literature*, 7, no. 5 (1977), 5–8.

3150. ———. " 'The Light of the World': The Real Ketchel and the Real Light." *Studies in Short Fiction*, 13 (1976), 17–23.

3151. BRUCCOLI, MATTHEW J. " 'The Light of the World': Stan Ketchel as 'My Sweet Christ.' " *Fitzgerald/Hemingway Annual 1969*, pp. 125–30.

3152. ———. "Stan Ketchel and Steve Ketchel: A Further Note on 'The Light of the World.' " *Fitzgerald/Hemingway Annual 1975*, pp. 325-26.

3153. CANADAY, NICHOLAS, JR. "Is There Any Light in Hemingway's 'The Light of the World'?" *Studies in Short Fiction*, 3 (1965), 75-76.

3154. LAYMAN, RICHARD. " 'C. and M.' in 'The Light of the World.' " *Fitzgerald/Hemingway Annual 1976*, pp. 243-44.

3155. MARTINE, JAMES J. "A Little Light on Hemingway's 'The Light of the World.' " *Studies in Short Fiction*, 7 (1970), 465-67.

See also 3306, 3311, 3327, 3359, 3392, 3432, 3438, 3443.

"A Man of the World"

3156. FERGUSON, J. M., JR. "Hemingway's Man of the World." *The Arizona Quarterly*, 33 (1977), 116-20.

3157. SMITH, JULIAN. "Eyeless in Wyoming, Blind in Venice— Hemingway's Last Stories." *The Connecticut Review*, 4, no. 2 (1971), 9-15.

See also 3124.

"Mr. and Mrs. Elliot"

3158. BROUSSARD, LOUIS. "Hemingway as a Literary Critic." *The Arizona Quarterly*, 20 (1964), 197-204.

3159. SHEPHERD, ALLEN. "Taking Apart 'Mr. and Mrs. Elliot.' " *The Markham Review*, 2, no. 1 (1969), 15-16.

See also 3327, 3403.

"The Mother of a Queen"

See 3343, 3359.

"My Old Man"

3160. KRAUSE, SYDNEY J. "Hemingway's 'My Old Man.' " *The Explicator*, 20 (1962), item 39.

See also 356, 3327, 3359, 3381, 3431.

"A Natural History of the Dead"

3161. JOHNSTON, KENNETH G. "Journeys into the Interior: Hemingway, Thoreau and Mungo Park." *Forum* (University of Houston), 10, no. 2 (1972), 27-31.

3162. PORTZ, JOHN. "Allusion and Structure in Hemingway's 'A Natural History of the Dead.' " *Tennessee Studies In Literature*, 10 (1965), 27-41.

3163. WEEKS, LEWIS E., JR. "Mark Twain and Hemingway: 'A Catastrophe' and 'A Natural History of the Dead.' " *The Mark Twain Journal*, 14, no. 2 (1968), 15-17.

3164.   YUNCK, JOHN A. "The Natural History of a Dead Quarrel: Hemingway and the Humanists." *The South Atlantic Quarterly*, 62 (1963), 29–42.
See also 3338, 3359, 3363, 3417, 3430.

"Night Before Battle"

See 3380, 3427.

"Night Before Landing"

See 3438.

"Nobody Ever Dies"

3165.   JOHNSTON, KENNETH G. " 'Nobody Ever Dies': Hemingway's Neglected Story of Freedom Fighters." *Kansas Quarterly*, 9, no. 2 (1977), 53–58.
See also 3440.

"Now I Lay Me"

3166.   GELLEY, ALEXANDER. "Setting and a Sense of World in the Novel." *The Yale Review*, 62 (1972), 186–201.
3167.   HOVEY, RICHARD B. "Hemingway's 'Now I Lay Me': A Psychological Interpretation." *Literature and Psychology*, 15 (1965), 70–78.
3168.   JOHNSTON, KENNETH G. "The Great Awakening: Nick Adams and the Silkworms in 'Now I Lay Me.' " *Hemingway Notes*, 1, no. 2 (1971), 7–10.
3169.   KUPPUSWAMY, B. "Hemingway on Insomnia." *The Literary Half-Yearly*, 1, no. 2 (1960), 58–60.
3170.   MACDONALD, SCOTT. "Implications of Narrative Perspective in Hemingway's 'Now I Lay Me.' " *Studies in American Fiction*, 1 (1973), 213–20.
See also 3306, 3310, 3327, 3334, 3356, 3359, 3402, 3428, 3432, 3438, 3440, 3443.

"The Old Man and the Sea"

3171.   BARBOUR, JAMES, AND ROBERT SATTELMEYER. "Baseball and Baseball Talk in *The Old Man and the Sea*." *Fitzgerald/Hemingway Annual 1975*, pp. 281–87.
3172.   BASKETT, SAM S. "The Great Santiago: Opium, Vocation, and Dream in *The Old Man and the Sea*." *Fitzgerald/Hemingway Annual 1976*, pp. 230–42.
3173.   _____. "Toward a 'Fifth Dimension' in *The Old Man and the Sea*." *The Centennial Review*, 19 (1975), 269–86.
3174.   BLUEFARB, SAM. "The Sea—Mirror and Maker of Character in Fiction and Drama." *The English Journal*, 48 (1959), 501–10.

3175. BRADFORD, M. E. "On the Importance of Discovering God: Faulkner and Hemingway's *The Old Man and the Sea*." *The Mississippi Quarterly*, 20 (1967), 158–62.

3176. BROADUS, ROBERT N. "The New Record Set by Hemingway's Old Man." *Notes and Queries*, NS 10 (1963), 152–53.

3177. BRUCCOLI, MATTHEW J. "Mary Welsh Hemingway." In *Conversations with Writers*, Vol. 1. Detroit, MI: Gale, 1977. pp. 181–94.

3178. BURHANS, CLINTON S., JR. "*The Old Man and the Sea*: Hemingway's Tragic Vision of Man." *American Literature*, 31 (1960), 446–55.

3179. CARLIN, STANLEY A. "Anselmo and Santiago: Two Old Men of the Sea." *The American Book Collector*, 19, no. 6 (1969), 12–14.

3180. COOPERMAN, STANLEY. "Hemingway and Old Age: Santiago as Priest of Time." *College English*, 27 (1965), 215–20.

3181. COTTER, JANET M. "*The Old Man and the Sea*: An 'Open' Literary Experience." *English Journal*, 51 (1962), 459–63.

3182. DAVIDSON, RICHARD ALLAN. "Carelessness and the Cincinnati Reds in *The Old Man and the Sea*." *Notes on Contemporary Literature*, 1, no. 1 (1971), 11–13.

3183. DEFALCO, JOSEPH M. "Hemingway's Islands and Streams: Minor Tactics for Heavy Pressure." In *Hemingway in Our Time*. Ed. Richard Astro and Jackson J. Benson. Corvallis: Oregon State Univ. Press, 1974. pp. 39–51.

3184. FLORA, JOSEPH M. "Biblical Allusion in 'The Old Man and the Sea.'" *Studies in Short Fiction*, 10 (1973), 143–47.

3185. GAHLOT, JAI S. "*The Old Man and the Sea*: A Reading." In *Variations on American Literature*. Ed. Darshan Singh Maini. New Delhi: U. S. Educational Foundation in India, 1968. pp. 89–92.

3186. GREBSTEIN, SHELDON NORMAN. "Hemingway's Craft in *The Old Man and the Sea*." In *The Fifties: Fiction, Poetry, Drama*. Ed. Warren French. Deland, FL: Everett/Edwards, 1970. pp. 41–50.

3187. HALVERSON, JOHN. "Christian Resonance in *The Old Man and the Sea*." *English Language Notes*, 2 (1964), 50–54.

3188. HAMILTON, JOHN BOWEN. "Hemingway and the Christian Paradox." *Renascence*, 24 (1972), 141–54.

3189. HANDY, WILLIAM J. "Hemingway's *The Old Man and the Sea*." In *Modern Fiction: A Formalist Approach*. Carbondale and Edwardsville: Southern Illinois Univ. Press, 1971. pp. 94–118.

3190. ———. "A New Dimension for a Hero: Santiago of *The Old Man and the Sea*." In *Six Contemporary Novels: Six Introducto-*

ry Essays in Modern Fiction. Ed. William O. S. Sutherland, Jr. Austin: Dept. of English, Univ. of Texas, 1962. pp. 58–75.

3191. **HEATON, C. P.** "Style in *The Old Man and the Sea.*" *Style*, 4 (1970), 11–27.

3192. **HOFLING, CHARLES K.** "Hemingway's *The Old Man and the Sea* and the Male Reader." *American Imago*, 20 (1963), 161–73.

3193. **JARRAWAY, DAVID R.** "*The Old Man and the Sea*: A Critical Reconsideration." *The English Quarterly*, 8, nos. 1-2 (1975), 21–30.

3194. **JOBES, KATHARINE T.** "Introduction." In *Twentieth Century Interpretations of* The Old Man and the Sea: *A Collection of Critical Essays.* Englewood Cliffs, NJ: Prentice-Hall, 1968. pp. 1–17.

3195. **JOHNSTON, KENNETH G.** "The Star in Hemingway's *The Old Man and the Sea.*" *American Literature*, 42 (1970), 388–91.

3196. **LONGMIRE, SAMUEL E.** "Hemingway's Praise of Dick Sisler in *The Old Man and the Sea.*" *American Literature*, 42 (1970), 96–98.

3197. **MANSELL, DARREL.** "When Did Hemingway Write *The Old Man and the Sea?*" *Fitzgerald/Hemingway Annual 1975*, pp. 311–24.

3198. **MEADOR, JOHN M., JR.** "Addendum to Hanneman: Hemingway's *The Old Man and the Sea.*" *The Papers of the Bibliographical Society of America*, 67 (1973), 454–57.

3199. **MONTEIRO, GEORGE.** "The Reds, the White Sox, and *The Old Man and the Sea.*" *Notes on Contemporary Literature*, 4, no. 3 (1974), 7–9.

3200. ———. "Santiago, DiMaggio, and Hemingway: The Ageing Professionals of *The Old Man and the Sea.*" *Fitzgerald/Hemingway Annual 1975*, pp. 273–80.

3201. **MOSELEY, EDWIN M.** "Christ as the Old Champion: Hemingway's *The Old Man and the Sea.*" In *Pseudonyms of Christ in the Modern Novel: Motifs and Methods.* Pittsburgh, PA: Univ. of Pittsburgh Press, 1962. pp. 205–13.

3202. **NAGLE, JOHN M.** "A View of Literature Too Often Neglected." *English Journal*, 58 (1969), 399–407.

3203. **OHASHI, KENZABURO.** "So Many Ishmaels: Some Notes on the Modern American Novel." *Studies in English Literature* (Tokyo), English no. 1960, pp. 71–83.

3204. **PARKER, STEPHEN JAN.** "Hemingway's Revival in the Soviet Union: 1955–1962." *American Literature*, 35 (1964), 485–501.

3205. **PRIZEL, YURI.** "Hemingway in Soviet Literary Criticism." *American Literature*, 44 (1972), 445–56.

3206. **SCHROETER, JAMES.** "Hemingway via Joyce." *The Southern Review*, NS 10 (1974), 95–114.

3207. SCOVILLE, SAMUEL. "The *Weltanschauung* of Steinbeck and Hemingway: An Analysis of Themes." *English Journal*, 56 (1967), 60–63, 66.

3208. SINHA, KRISHNA NANDAN. "*The Old Man and the Sea*: An Approach to Meaning." In *Indian Studies in American Fiction*. Ed. M. K. Naik, S. K. Desai, and S. Mokashi-Punekar. Dharwar: Karnatak Univ., 1974. pp. 219–28.

3209. STUCKEY, W. J. *The Pulitzer Prize Novels: A Critical Backward Look*. Norman: Univ. of Oklahoma Press, 1966.

3210. SYLVESTER, BICKFORD. "Hemingway's Extended Vision: *The Old Man and the Sea*." *PMLA*, 81 (1966), 130–38.

3211. ———. " 'They Went Through This Fiction Every Day': Informed Illusion in *The Old Man and the Sea*." *Modern Fiction Studies*, 12 (1966), 473–77.

3212. UENO, NAOZO. "An Oriental View of *The Old Man and the Sea*." *The East-West Review*, 2 (1965), 67–76.

3213. WAGNER, LINDA W. "The Poem of Santiago and Manolin." *Modern Fiction Studies*, 19 (1973), 517–29.

3214. WARNER, STEPHEN D. "Hemingway's 'The Old Man and the Sea.' " *The Explicator*, 33 (1974), item 9.

3215. WEEKS, ROBERT P. "Fakery in *The Old Man and the Sea*." *College English*, 24 (1962), 188–92.

3216. WELLS, ARVIN R. "A Ritual of Transfiguration: *The Old Man and the Sea*." *The University Review* (Kansas City), 30 (1963), 95–101.

3217. WILSON, G. R., JR. "Incarnation and Redemption in *The Old Man and the Sea*." *Studies in Short Fiction*, 14 (1977), 369–73.

See also 341, 347, 395, 454, 574, 597, 1739, 1787, 3298, 3301–3303, 3306, 3315, 3316, 3324, 3330, 3333, 3341, 3343, 3344, 3347, 3352, 3358a, 3359, 3362, 3365, 3366, 3372, 3377, 3393, 3397, 3402–3404, 3406, 3414, 3417, 3419, 3422, 3433, 3434, 3436, 3440, 3443, 3444, 3452, 3453, 3458–3460.

"Old Man at the Bridge"

See 3327, 3379, 3396.

"On the Quai at Smyrna"

3218. LEITER, LOUIS H. "Neural Projections in Hemingway's 'On the Quai at Smyrna.' " *Studies in Short Fiction*, 5 (1968), 384–86.

See also 3327, 3338, 3340.

"On Writing"

See 3438.

"One Reader Writes"

3219. EDELSON, MARK. "A Note on 'One Reader Writes.'" *Fitz-gerald/Hemingway Annual 1972*, pp. 329-31.
See also 3306.

"Out of Season"

3220. JOHNSTON, KENNETH G. "Hemingway's 'Out of Season' And The Psychology of Errors." *Literature and Psychology*, 21 (1971), 41-46.
See also 3327, 3417.

"A Pursuit Race"

See 3343.

"The Revolutionist"

3221. GROSECLOSE, BARBARA S. "Hemingway's 'The Revolu-tionist': An Aid to Interpretation." *Modern Fiction Studies*, 17 (1971), 565-70.
3222. HUNT, ANTHONY. "Another Turn for Hemingway's 'The Revolutionist': Sources and Meanings." *Fitzgerald/Hemingway Annual 1977*, pp. 119-35.
3223. JOHNSTON, KENNETH G. "Hemingway and Mantegna: The Bitter Nail Holes." *The Journal of Narrative Technique*, 1 (1971), 86-94.
See also 3327.

"The Sea Change"

3224. KOBLER, J. F. "Hemingway's 'The Sea Change': A Sympa-thetic View of Homosexuality." *The Arizona Quarterly*, 26 (1970), 318-24.
3225. WYCHERLEY, H. ALAN. "Hemingway's 'The Sea Change.'" *American Notes & Queries*, 7 (1969), 67-68.
See also 3327, 3370, 3403.

"Sepi Jingan"

See 3392.

"The Short Happy Life of Francis Macomber"

3226. BACHE, WILLIAM B. "*The Red Badge of Courage* and 'The Short Happy Life of Francis Macomber.'" *Western Humanities Review*, 15 (1961), 83-84.
3227. BECK, WARREN. "Mr. Spilka's Problem: A Reply." *Modern Fiction Studies*, 22 (1976), 256-69.

3228. **BELL, H. H., JR.** "Hemingway's 'The Short Happy Life of Francis Macomber.' " *The Explicator*, 32 (1974), item 78.

3229. **BOCAZ, SERGIO H.** "Senecan Stoicism in Hemingway's 'The Short Happy Life of Francis Macomber.' " In *Studies in Language and Literature*. Proceedings of the 23rd Mountain Interstate Foreign Language Conference. Ed. Charles Nelson. Richmond: Dept. of Foreign Languages, Eastern Kentucky Univ., 1976. pp. 81–86.

3230. **B[RUCCOLI], M[ATTHEW] J.** "Francis Macomber and Francis Fitzgerald." *Fitzgerald/Hemingway Annual 1970*, p. 223.

3231. **DAVIDSON, ARNOLD E.** "The Ambivalent End of Francis Macomber's Short, Happy Life." *Hemingway Notes*, 2, no. 1 (1972), 14–16.

3232. **GAILLARD, THEODORE L., JR.** "The Critical Menagerie in 'The Short Happy Life of Francis Macomber.' " *English Journal*, 60 (1971), 31–35.

3233. **GRECO, ANNE.** "Margot Macomber: 'Bitch Goddess,' Exonerated." *Fitzgerald/Hemingway Annual 1972*, pp. 273-80.

3234. **HERNDON, JERRY A.** "No 'Maggie's Drawers' for Margot Macomber." *Fitzgerald/Hemingway Annual 1975*, pp. 289–91.

3235. **HILL, JOHN S.** "Robert Wilson: Hemingway's Judge in 'Macomber.' " *The University Review* (Kansas City), 35 (1968), 129–32.

3236. **HOLLAND, ROBERT B.** "Macomber and the Critics." *Studies in Short Fiction*, 5 (1968), 171–78.

3237. **HOWELL, JOHN M.** "The Macomber Case." *Studies in Short Fiction*, 4 (1967), 171–72.

3238. ———, **AND CHARLES A. LAWLER.** "From Abercrombie & Fitch to *The First Forty-Nine Stories*: The Text of Ernest Hemingway's 'Francis Macomber.' " *Proof*, 2 (1972), 213–81.

3239. **HUTTON, VIRGIL.** "The Short Happy Life of Macomber." *The University Review* (Kansas City), 30 (1964), 253–63.

3240. **JACKSON, THOMAS J.** "The 'Macomber' Typescript." *Fitzgerald/Hemingway Annual 1970*, pp. 219–22.

3241. **KOBLER, J. F.** "Francis Macomber as Four-Letter Man." *Fitzgerald/Hemingway Annual 1972*, pp. 295–96.

3242. **LEWIS, CLIFFORD.** "The Short Happy Life of Francis Scott Macomber." *Études Anglaises*, 23 (1970), 256–61.

3243. **MORRIS, WILLIAM E.** "Hemingway's 'The Short Happy Life of Francis Macomber.' " *The Explicator*, 24 (1965), item 31.

3244. **SHEPHERD, ALLEN.** "The Lion in the Grass (Alas?): A Note on 'The Short Happy Life of Francis Macomber.' " *Fitzgerald/Hemingway Annual 1972*, pp. 297-99.

3245. SPILKA, MARK. "Warren Beck Revisited." *Modern Fiction Studies*, 22 (1976), 245-55.

3246. STEIN, WILLIAM BYSSHE. "Hemingway's 'The Short Happy Life of Francis Macomber.' " *The Explicator*, 19 (1961), item 47.

3247. STEPHENS, ROBERT O. "Macomber and That Somali Proverb: The Matrix of Knowledge." *Fitzgerald/Hemingway Annual 1977*, pp. 137-47.

3248. VAIDYANATHAN, T. G. "Did Margot Kill Francis Macomber?" *Indian Journal of American Studies*, 1, no. 3 (1970), 1-13.

3249. WATERMAN, ARTHUR E. "Hemingway's 'The Short Happy Life of Francis Macomber.' " *The Explicator*, 20 (1961), item 2.

3250. WATSON, JAMES GRAY. " 'A Sound Basis of Union': Structural and Thematic Balance in 'The Short Happy Life of Francis Macomber.' " *Fitzgerald/Hemingway Annual 1974*, pp. 215-28.

See also 133, 269, 455, 565, 574, 597, 1462, 2185, 3302, 3303, 3306, 3311, 3318, 3327, 3330, 3343, 3347, 3349, 3359, 3360, 3367, 3377, 3394, 3397, 3402, 3403, 3414, 3417, 3419, 3422, 3433, 3443, 3460.

"The Snows of Kilimanjaro"

3251. BAKER, CARLOS. "The Slopes of Kilimanjaro: A Biographical Perspective." *Novel*, 1 (1967), 19-23.

3252. BEVIS, R. W., M. A. J. SMITH, JR., AND G. BROSE. "Leopard Tracks in 'The Snows . . . .' " *American Notes & Queries*, 6 (1968), 115.

3253. CHILDS, BARNEY. "Hemingway and the Leopard of Kilimanjaro." *American Notes & Queries*, 2 (1963), 3.

3254. CRANE, JOHN KENNY. "Crossing the Bar Twice: Post-Mortem Consciousness in Bierce, Hemingway, and Golding." *Studies in Short Fiction*, 6 (1969), 361-76.

3255. CUNNINGHAM, DONALD H. "Hemingway's 'The Snows of Kilimanjaro.' " *The Explicator*, 22 (1964), item 41.

3256. DUSSINGER, GLORIA R. "Hemingway's 'The Snows of Kilimanjaro.' " *The Explicator*, 26 (1968), item 67.

3257. ———. " 'The Snows of Kilimanjaro': Harry's Second Chance." *Studies in Short Fiction*, 5 (1967), 54-59.

3258. EVANS, OLIVER. " 'The Snows of Kilimanjaro': A Revaluation." *PMLA*, 76 (1961), 601-07.

3259. FISHER, MARVIN. "More Snow on Kilimanjaro." In *Americana-Norvegica: Norwegian Contributions to American Studies*, Vol. 2. Ed. Sigmund Skard. Philadelphia: Univ. of Pennsylvania Press, 1968. pp. 343-53.

3260. **GEORGOUDAKI, EKATERINI.** "Some Comments on 'The Snows of Kilimanjaro.' " *Essays in Literature* (Univ. of Denver), 2, no. 1 (1974), 49–58.

3261. **HOWELL, JOHN M.** "Hemingway's Riddle and Kilimanjaro's Reusch." *Studies in Short Fiction*, 8 (1971), 469–70.

3262. _____. "What the Leopard Was Seeking." *American Notes & Queries*, 7 (1969), 68.

3263. **KOLB, ALFRED.** "Symbolic Structure in Hemingway's 'The Snows of Kilimanjaro.' " *Notes on Modern American Literature*, 1 (1976), item 4.

3264. **LEWIS, ROBERT W., JR., AND MAX WESTBROOK.** " 'The Snows of Kilimanjaro' Collated and Annotated." *The Texas Quarterly*, 13, no. 2 (1970), 67–143; 14, no. 3 (1971), 103.

3265. _____, AND _____. "The Texas Manuscript of 'The Snows of Kilimanjaro.' " *The Texas Quarterly*, 9, no. 4 (1966), 66–101.

3266. **LONGYEAR, CHRISTOPHER R.** *Linguistically Determined Categories of Meanings: A Comparative Analysis of Meaning in "The Snows of Kilimanjaro."* The Hague: Mouton, 1971.

3267. **MACDONALD, SCOTT.** "Hemingway's 'The Snows of Kilimanjaro': Three Critical Problems." *Studies in Short Fiction*, 11 (1974), 67–74.

3268. **MONTGOMERY, MARION.** "The Leopard and the Hyena: Symbol and Meaning in 'The Snows of Kilimanjaro.' " *The University of Kansas City Review*, 27 (1961), 277–82.

3269. **RAO, P. G. RAMA.** "A Note on the Structure of 'The Snows of Kilimanjaro.' " *Indian Journal of American Studies*, 1, no. 2 (1970), 13–20.

3270. **SANTANGELO, GENNARO.** "The Dark Snows of Kilimanjaro." In *The Short Stories of Ernest Hemingway: Critical Essays.* Ed. Jackson J. Benson. Durham, NC: Duke Univ. Press, 1975. pp. 251–61.

3271. **STALLMAN, R. W.** "A New Reading of 'The Snows of Kilimanjaro.' " In *The House That James Built and Other Literary Studies.* East Lansing: Michigan State Univ. Press, 1961. pp. 193–99.

3272. **STEPHENS, ROBERT O.** "Hemingway's Riddle of Kilimanjaro: Idea and Image." *American Literature*, 32 (1960), 84–87.

3273. **TARBOX, RAYMOND.** "Blank Hallucinations in the Fiction of Poe and Hemingway." *American Imago*, 24 (1967), 312–43.

3274. **TAYLOR, J. GOLDEN.** "Hemingway on the Flesh and the Spirit." *Western Humanities Review*, 15 (1961), 273–75.

3275. **THOMANECK, JURGEN K. A.** "Hemingway's Riddle of Kilimanjaro Once More." *Studies in Short Fiction*, 7 (1970), 326–27.

3276. **WALZ, LAWRENCE A.** " 'The Snows of Kilimanjaro': A New Reading." *Fitzgerald/Hemingway Annual 1971*, pp. 239-45.
See also 597, 2185, 2200, 3301–3303, 3306, 3311, 3327, 3330, 3343, 3347, 3359, 3360, 3377, 3397, 3399, 3403, 3414, 3417, 3422, 3433, 3440, 3443, 3444, 3460.

"Soldier's Home"

3277. **BROER, LAWRENCE.** "Soldier's Home." In *Instructor's Manual for* "The Art of Fiction," Second Edition. Ed. R. F. Dietrich and Roger H. Sundell. New York: Holt, Rinehart and Winston, 1974. pp. 18–23.
3278. _____. "Soldier's Home." *Lost Generation Journal*, 3, no. 2 (1975), 11, 32.
3279. **HAYS, PETER L.** " 'Soldier's Home' and Ford Madox Ford." *Hemingway Notes*, 1, no. 2 (1971), 21–22.
3280. **PETRARCA, ANTHONY J.** "Irony of Situation in Ernest Hemingway's 'Soldier's Home.' " *English Journal*, 58 (1969), 664–67.
3281. **ROBERTS, JOHN J.** "In Defense of Krebs." *Studies in Short Fiction*, 13 (1976), 515–18.
3282. **ROVIT, EARL.** "On Ernest Hemingway and 'Soldier's Home.' " In *The American Short Story*. Ed. Calvin Skaggs. New York: Dell, 1977. pp. 251–55.
See also 249, 3306, 3327, 3347, 3359, 3369, 3403.

"Summer People"

See 3438, 3457.

"Ten Indians"

3283. **AIKEN, WILLIAM.** "Hemingway's 'Ten Indians.' " *The Explicator*, 28 (1969), item 31.
See also 3311, 3327, 3343, 3392.

"The Three-Day Blow"

3284. **MONTEIRO, GEORGE.** "Dating the Events of 'The Three-Day Blow.' " *Fitzgerald/Hemingway Annual 1977*, pp. 207–10.
3285. **O'BRIEN, MATTHEW.** "Baseball in 'The Three-Day Blow.' " *American Notes & Queries*, 16 (1977), 24–26.
See also 3306, 3327, 3334, 3343, 3377, 3392, 3413, 3414, 3416, 3460.

"Three Shots"

See 3438.

"Today Is Friday"

See 3327, 3443.

"The Undefeated"

3286. JAIN, S. P. " 'The Undefeated': Triumph of the Ideal." *The Indian Journal of English Studies*, 12 (1971), 86–95.

3287. MacDONALD, SCOTT. "Implications of Narrative Perspective in Hemingway's 'The Undefeated.' " *The Journal of Narrative Technique*, 2 (1972), 1–15.

See also 493, 3306, 3327, 3343, 3347, 3432, 3433, 3444.

"Under the Ridge"

See 175, 3380, 3427, 3440.

"Up in Michigan"

3288. FLORA, JOSEPH M. "Hemingway's 'Up in Michigan.' " *Studies in Short Fiction*, 6 (1969), 465–66.

See also 3343, 3377, 3392.

"A Very Short Story"

3289. MYERS, MARSHALL. "A Tagmemic Analysis of Hemingway's 'A Very Short Story': An Exercise in the Applicability of Linguistic Methodology to Literature." In *From Soundstream to Discourse: Papers from the 1971 Mid-America Linguistics Conference.* Ed. Daniel G. Hays and Donald M. Lance. Columbia: Linguistics Area Program, Univ. of Missouri, 1972. pp. 158–66.

See also 3327.

"A Way You'll Never Be"

3290. MILLER, PATRICK. "Hemingway's 'A Way You'll Never Be.' " *The Explicator*, 23 (1964), item 18.

3291. WITHERINGTON, PAUL. "To Be and Not to Be: Paradox and Pun in Hemingway's 'A Way You'll Never Be.' " *Style*, 7 (1973), 56–63.

3292. YOKELSON, JOSEPH B. "A Dante-Parallel in Hemingway's 'A Way You'll Never Be.' " *American Literature*, 41 (1969), 279–80.

See also 3306, 3310, 3327, 3343, 3344, 3359, 3363, 3438, 3443, 3460.

"Wine of Wyoming"

3293. JOHNSTON, KENNETH G. "Hemingway's 'Wine of Wyoming': Disappointment in America." *Western American Literature*, 9 (1974), 159–67.

See also 3343.

General Studies

3294. ÅHNEBRINK, LARS. "Hemingway in Sweden." In *The Lit-*

erary Reputation of Hemingway in Europe. Ed. Roger Asselineau. New York: New York Univ. Press, 1965. pp. 151–75.

3295. **ALGREN, NELSON.** *Notes from a Sea Diary: Hemingway All the Way.* New York: Putnam's, 1965.

3296. **ANDERSON, DAVID D.** "Ernest Hemingway, the Voice of an Era." *The Personalist,* 47 (1966), 234–47.

3297. **ARNOLD, LLOYD R.** *High on the Wild with Hemingway.* Caldwell, ID: Caxton, 1968.

3298. **ARONOWITZ, ALFRED G., AND PETER HAMILL.** *Ernest Hemingway: The Life and Death of a Man.* New York: Lancer Books, 1961.

3299. **ASSELINEAU, ROGER.** "Ernest Hemingway: A Rebel Rediscovers Tradition or The Destruction and Rehabilitation of Traditional Values in E. Hemingway's Fiction." In *Studien zur englischen und amerikanischen Sprache und Literatur: Festschrift für Helmut Papajewski.* Ed. Paul G. Buchloh, Inge Leimberg, and Herbert Rauter. Neumünster: Karl Wachholtz, 1974. pp. 387–404.

3300. _____. "French Reactions to Hemingway's Works between the Two World Wars." In *The Literary Reputation of Hemingway in Europe.* Ed. Roger Asselineau. New York: New York Univ. Press, 1965. pp. 39–72.

3301. **BAKER, CARLOS.** *Ernest Hemingway: A Life Story.* New York: Scribner's, 1969.

3302. _____. *Hemingway: The Writer as Artist.* 3rd ed. Princeton, NJ: Princeton Univ. Press, 1963.

3303. _____. *Hemingway: The Writer as Artist.* 4th ed. Princeton, NJ: Princeton Univ. Press, 1972.

3304. _____. "Hemingway's Empirical Imagination." In *Individual and Community: Variations on a Theme in American Fiction.* Ed. Kenneth H. Baldwin and David K. Kirby. Durham, NC: Duke Univ. Press, 1975. pp. 94–111.

3305. _____. "Introduction: Citizen of the World." In *Hemingway and His Critics: An International Anthology.* Ed. Carlos Baker. New York: Hill and Wang, 1961. pp. 1–18.

3306. **BAKKER, J.** *Ernest Hemingway: The Artist as Man of Action.* Assen: Van Gorcum, 1972.

3307. **BARGER, JAMES.** *Ernest Hemingway: American Literary Giant.* Charlottesville, NY: SamHar, 1975.

3308. **BARNES, ROBERT J.** "Two Modes of Fiction: Hemingway and Greene." *Renascence,* 14 (1962), 193–98.

3309. **BELL, NEIL.** "Of the Company." *The Mark Twain Journal,* 11, no. 4 (1962), 18.

3310. BENSON, JACKSON J. "Ernest Hemingway as Short Story Writer." In *The Short Stories of Ernest Hemingway: Critical Essays*. Ed. Jackson J. Benson. Durham, NC: Duke Univ. Press, 1975. pp. 272–310.

3311. ———. *Hemingway: The Writer's Art of Self-Defense*. Minneapolis: Univ. of Minnesota Press, 1969.

3312. ———. "Introduction." In *The Short Stories of Ernest Hemingway: Critical Essays*. Ed. Jackson J. Benson. Durham, NC: Duke Univ. Press, 1975. pp. xi–xv.

3313. BIGSBY, C. W. E. "Hemingway: The Recoil from History." In *The Twenties: Fiction, Poetry, Drama*. Ed. Warren French. Deland, FL: Everett/Edwards, 1975. pp. 203–13.

3314. BODNÁR, GYÖRGY. "Hemingway and the New Realism." In *Littérature et réalité*. Ed. Béla Köpeczi and Péter Juhász. Budapest: Akadémiai Kiadó, 1966. pp. 246–63.

3315. BROER, LAWRENCE R. *Hemingway's Spanish Tragedy*. University: Univ. of Alabama Press, 1973.

3316. BRØGGER, FREDRIK CHR. "Love and Fellowship in Ernest Hemingway's Fiction." In *Americana-Norvegica: Norwegian Contributions to American Studies Dedicated to Sigmund Skard*, Vol. 4. Ed. Brita Seyersted. Oslo: Universitetsforlaget, 1973. pp. 269–89.

3317. BRUCCOLI, MATTHEW J., ED. *Ernest Hemingway's Apprenticeship: Oak Park, 1916-1917*. Washington, DC: NCR Microcard Editions, 1971.

3318. BRYAN, JAMES E. "Hemingway as Vivisector." *The University Review* (Kansas City), 30 (1963), 3–12.

3319. BURHANS, CLINTON S., JR. "The Complex Unity of *In Our Time*." *Modern Fiction Studies*, 14 (1968), 313–28.

3320. ———. "Hemingway and Vonnegut: Diminishing Vision in a Dying Age." *Modern Fiction Studies*, 21 (1975), 173–91.

3321. BURNS, STUART L. "Unscrambling the Unscrambleable: *The Nick Adams Stories*." *The Arizona Quarterly*, 33 (1977), 133–40.

3322. CLENDENNING, JOHN. "Hemingway's Gods, Dead and Alive." *Texas Studies in Literature and Language*, 3 (1962), 489–502.

3323. CROZIER, ROBERT D., S.J. "Home James: Hemingway's Jacob." *Papers on Language & Literature*, 11 (1975), 293–301.

3324. D'AGOSTINO, NEMI. "The Later Hemingway (1956)." *The Sewanee Review*, 68 (1960), 482–93.

3325. DASGUPTA, H. "Parent-Son Relationship in Ernest Hemingway." *The Indian Journal of English Studies*, 17 (1977), 110–18.

3326. DEFALCO, JOSEPH. "Hemingway, Sport, and the Larger Metaphor." *Lost Generation Journal*, 3, no. 2 (1975), 18–20.

3327. _____. *The Hero in Hemingway's Short Stories*. Pittsburgh, PA: Univ. of Pittsburgh Press, 1963.

3328. **DERLETH, AUGUST.** "A Superb Short Story Writer." *The Mark Twain Journal*, 11, no. 4 (1962), 16.

3329. **DIECKMANN, EDWARD A., JR.** "The Hemingway Hypnosis." *The Mark Twain Journal*, 11, no. 4 (1962), 3–4, 16.

3330. **DONALDSON, SCOTT.** *By Force of Will: The Life and Art of Ernest Hemingway.* New York: Viking, 1977.

3331. **DRINNON, RICHARD.** "In the American Heartland: Hemingway and Death." *The Psychoanalytic Review*, 52 (1965), 149–75.

3332. **FALBO, ERNEST S.** "Carlo Linati: Hemingway's First Italian Critic and Translator." *Fitzgerald/Hemingway Annual 1975*, pp. 293–306.

3333. **FARRINGTON, S. KIP, JR.** *Fishing with Hemingway and Glassell.* New York: McKay, 1971.

3334. **FICKEN, CARL.** "Point of View in the Nick Adams Stories." *Fitzgerald/Hemingway Annual 1971*, pp. 212–35.

3335. **FITZ, REGINALD.** "The Meaning of Impotence in Hemingway and Eliot." *The Connecticut Review*, 4, no. 2 (1971), 16–22.

3336. **FLORA, JOSEPH M.** "A Closer Look at the Young Nick Adams and His Father." *Studies in Short Fiction*, 14 (1977), 75–78.

3337. **FRIEDBERG, MICHAEL.** "Hemingway and the Modern Metaphysical Tradition." In *Hemingway in Our Time*. Ed. Richard Astro and Jackson J. Benson. Corvallis: Oregon State Univ. Press, 1974. pp. 175–89.

3338. **FUCHS, DANIEL.** "Ernest Hemingway, Literary Critic." *American Literature*, 36 (1965), 431–51.

3339. **GEISMAR, MAXWELL.** "Was 'Papa' a Truly Great Writer?" *The New York Times Book Review*, 1 July 1962, pp. 1, 16.

3340. **GIFFORD, WILLIAM.** "Ernest Hemingway: The Monsters and the Critics." *Modern Fiction Studies*, 14 (1968), 255–70.

3341. **GORDON, DAVID.** "The Son and the Father: Patterns of Response to Conflict in Hemingway's Fiction." *Literature and Psychology*, 16 (1966), 122–38.

3342. **GRANT, DOUGLAS.** "Ernest Hemingway—II: Men without Women." In *Purpose and Place: Essays on American Writers*. London: Macmillan, 1965. pp. 175–82.

3343. **GREBSTEIN, SHELDON NORMAN.** *Hemingway's Craft.* Carbondale and Edwardsville: Southern Illinois Univ. Press, 1973.

3344. _____. "The Structure of Hemingway's Short Stories." *Fitzgerald/Hemingway Annual 1972*, pp. 173–93.

3345. **GREINER, DONALD J.** "Emerson, Thoreau, and Hemingway: Some Suggestions About Literary Heritage." *Fitzgerald/Hemingway Annual 1971*, pp. 247–61.

3346. **GRIFFITH, JOHN.** "Rectitude in Hemingway's Fiction: How Rite Makes Right." In *Hemingway in Our Time*. Ed. Richard Astro and Jackson J. Benson. Corvallis: Oregon State Univ. Press, 1974. pp. 159–73.

3347. **GURKO, LEO.** *Ernest Hemingway and the Pursuit of Heroism.* New York: Crowell, 1968.

3348. **HAGOPIAN, JOHN V.** "Hemingway: Ultimate Exile." *Mosaic*, 8, no. 3 (1975), 77–87.

3349. **HALE, NANCY.** "Hemingway and the Courage to Be." *The Virginia Quarterly Review*, 38 (1962), 620–39.

3350. **HAMALIAN, LEO.** "Hemingway as Hunger Artist." *The Literary Review*, 16 (1972), 5–13.

3351. **HARRISON, JAMES M.** "Hemingway's *In Our Time*." *The Explicator*, 18 (1960), item 51.

3352. **HASSAN, IHAB.** "Hemingway: Valor Against the Void." In *The Dismemberment of Orpheus: Toward a Postmodern Literature*. New York: Oxford Univ. Press, 1971. pp. 80–109.

3353. ———. "The Silence of Ernest Hemingway." In *The Shaken Realist: Essays in Modern Literature in Honor of Frederick J. Hoffman*. Ed. Melvin J. Friedman and John B. Vickery. Baton Rouge: Louisiana State Univ. Press, 1970. pp. 5–20.

3354. **HAYES, CURTIS W.** "A Study in Prose Styles: Edward Gibbon and Ernest Hemingway." *Texas Studies in Literature and Language*, 7 (1966), 371–86.

3355. **HERTZEL, LEO J.** "The Look of Religion: Hemingway and Catholicism." *Renascence*, 17 (1965), 77–81.

3356. **HOLDER, ALAN.** "The Other Hemingway." *Twentieth Century Literature*, 9 (1963), 153–57.

3357. **HOLMAN, C. HUGH.** "Ernest Hemingway." *Shenandoah*, 10, no. 2 (1959), 4–11.

3358. ———. "Ernest Hemingway: A Tribute." *Books Abroad*, 36 (1962), 5–8.

3358a. **HOTCHNER, A. E.** *Papa Hemingway.* New York: Random House, 1966.

3359. **HOVEY, RICHARD B.** *Hemingway: The Inward Terrain.* Seattle: Univ. of Washington Press, 1968.

3360. **HOWELL, JOHN M.** "Hemingway's 'Metaphysics' in Four Stories of the Thirties: A Look at the Manuscripts." *ICarbS*, 1 (1973), 41–51.

3361. **HUGHES, LANGSTON.** "A Reader's Writer." *The Mark Twain Journal*, 11, no. 4 (1962), 19.

3362. **ISABELLE, JULANNE.** *Hemingway's Religious Experience.* New York: Vantage Press, 1964.

3363. JAIN, S. P. "Some Hemingway Stories: Perspectives and Responses." *The Literary Half-Yearly*, 12, no. 1 (1971), 53–64.

3364. KAPLAN, HAROLD. "Hemingway and the Passive Hero." In *The Passive Voice: An Approach to Modern Fiction*. Athens: Ohio Univ. Press, 1966. pp. 93–110.

3365. KAUSHAL, JOGENDRA. *Ernest Hemingway: A Critical Study*. Patiala: Chandi, 1974.

3366. KILLINGER, JOHN. "Hemingway and Our 'Essential Worldliness.'" In *Forms of Extremity in the Modern Novel*. Ed. Nathan A. Scott, Jr. Richmond, VA: John Knox Press, 1965. pp. 35–54.

3367. _____. *Hemingway and the Dead Gods: A Study in Existentialism*. Lexington: Univ. of Kentucky Press, 1960.

3368. KINNAMON, KENETH. "Hemingway, the *Corrida*, and Spain." *Texas Studies in Literature and Language*, 1 (1959), 44–61.

3369. KNIEGER, BERNARD. "The Concept of Maturity in Hemingway's Short Stories." *CLA Journal*, 8 (1964), 149–56.

3370. KOBLER, J. F. "Hemingway's Four Dramatic Short Stories." *Fitzgerald/Hemingway Annual 1975*, pp. 247–57.

3371. KRIEGEL, LEONARD. "Hemingway's Rites of Manhood." *Partisan Review*, 44 (1977), 415–30.

3372. KVAM, WAYNE E. *Hemingway in Germany: The Fiction, the Legend, and the Critics*. Athens: Ohio Univ. Press, 1973.

3373. LABOR, EARLE. "Crane and Hemingway: Anatomy of Trauma." *Renascence*, 11 (1959), 189–96.

3374. LEBOWITZ, ALAN. "Hemingway in Our Time." *The Yale Review*, 58 (1969), 321–41.

3375. LEHAN, RICHARD. "Hemingway among the Moderns." In *Hemingway in Our Time*. Ed. Richard Astro and Jackson J. Benson. Corvallis: Oregon State Univ. Press, 1974. pp. 191–212.

3376. LEIGH, DAVID J., S.J. "*In Our Time:* The Interchapters as Structural Guides to a Psychological Pattern." *Studies in Short Fiction*, 12 (1975), 1–8.

3377. LEWIS, ROBERT W., JR. *Hemingway on Love*. Austin: Univ. of Texas Press, 1965.

3378. _____. "Hemingway's Sense of Place." In *Hemingway in Our Time*. Ed. Richard Astro and Jackson J. Benson. Corvallis: Oregon State Univ. Press, 1974. pp. 113–43.

3379. LID, RICHARD W. "Hemingway and the Need for Speech." *Modern Fiction Studies*, 8 (1962), 401–07.

3380. LIGHT, MARTIN. "Of Wasteful Deaths: Hemingway's Stories about the Spanish War." *Western Humanities Review*, 23 (1969), 29–42.

3381. **LOWRY, E. D.** "Chaos and Cosmos in *In Our Time.*" *Literature and Psychology*, 26 (1976), 108–17.
3382. **MCCARTHY, PAUL.** "Opposites Meet: Melville, Hemingway, and Heroes." *Kansas Quarterly*, 7, no. 4 (1975), 40–54.
3383. **MCLENDON, JAMES.** *Papa: Hemingway in Key West.* Miami, FL: E. A. Seeman, 1972.
3384. **MACHLIN, MILT.** *The Private Hell of Ernest Hemingway.* New York: Paperback Library, 1962.
3385. **MAI, ROBERT P.** "Ernest Hemingway and Men Without Women." *Fitzgerald/Hemingway Annual 1970*, pp. 173–86.
3386. **MARGOLIES, ALAN.** "A Note on Fitzgerald's Lost and Unpublished Stories." *Fitzgerald/Hemingway Annual 1972*, pp. 335–36.
3387. **MERIWETHER, JAMES B.** "The Text of Ernest Hemingway." *The Papers of the Bibliographical Society of America*, 57 (1963), 403–21.
3388. **MILLS, GORDON.** "The Influence of Darwinism on the Style of Certain American Writers." In *The Impact of Darwinian Thought on American Life and Culture: Papers Read at the Fourth Annual Meeting of The American Studies Association of Texas at Houston, Texas, December 5, 1959.* Austin: Univ. of Texas, 1959. pp. 11–26.
3389. **MIZENER, ARTHUR.** "The Two Hemingways." In *The Great Experiment in American Literature: Six Lectures.* Ed. Carl Bode. London: Heinemann, 1961. pp. 135–51.
3390. **MONTEIRO, GEORGE.** "The Education of Ernest Hemingway." *Journal of American Studies*, 8 (1974), 91–99.
3391. ———. "Hemingway's Pléiade Ballplayers." *Fitzgerald/Hemingway Annual 1973*, pp. 299–301.
3392. **MONTGOMERY, CONSTANCE CAPPEL.** *Hemingway in Michigan.* New York: Fleet, 1966.
3393. **MORITZ, KEN.** "Ernest Hemingway." In *American Winners of the Nobel Literary Prize.* Ed. Warren G. French and Walter E. Kidd. Norman: Univ. of Oklahoma Press, 1968. pp. 158–92.
3394. **MOTOLA, GABRIEL.** "Hemingway's Code: Literature and Life." *Modern Fiction Studies*, 10 (1964), 319–29.
3395. **MULLER, GILBERT H.** "*In Our Time*: Hemingway and the Discontents of Civilization." *Renascence*, 29 (1977), 185–92.
3396. **MUSTE, JOHN M.** *Say That We Saw Spain Die: Literary Consequences of the Spanish Civil War.* Seattle: Univ. of Washington Press, 1966.
3397. **NAHAL, CHAMAN.** *The Narrative Pattern in Ernest Hemingway's Fiction.* Rutherford, NJ: Fairleigh Dickinson Univ. Press, 1971.

3398. **NOBLE, DAVID W.** *The Eternal Adam and the New World Garden: The Central Myth in the American Novel since 1830.* New York: Braziller, 1968.

3399. **OLDSEY, BERN.** "The Snows of Ernest Hemingway." *Wisconsin Studies in Contemporary Literature,* 4 (1963), 172–98.

3400. **PAPAJEWSKI, HELMUT.** "The Critical Reception of Hemingway's Works in Germany since 1920." In *The Literary Reputation of Hemingway in Europe.* Ed. Roger Asselineau. New York: New York Univ. Press, 1965. pp. 73–92.

3401. **PARKER, STEPHEN JAN.** "Hemingway's Revival in the Soviet Union, 1955–1962." In *The Literary Reputation of Hemingway in Europe.* Ed. Roger Asselineau. New York: New York Univ. Press, 1965. pp. 177–95.

3402. **PEARSALL, ROBERT BRAINARD.** *The Life and Writings of Ernest Hemingway.* Amsterdam: Rodopi, 1973.

3403. **PETERSON, RICHARD K.** *Hemingway: Direct and Oblique.* The Hague: Mouton, 1969.

3404. **PHILLIPS, STEVEN R.** "Hemingway and the Bullfight: The Archetypes of Tragedy." *The Arizona Quarterly,* 29 (1973), 37–56.

3405. **PICI, J. R.** "Hemingway: Openings of the Master Strategist." *Lost Generation Journal,* 5, no. 1 (1977), 9, 23.

3406. **PRATT, JOHN CLARK.** "A Sometimes Great Notion: Ernest Hemingway's Roman Catholicism." In *Hemingway in Our Time.* Ed. Richard Astro and Jackson J. Benson. Corvallis: Oregon State Univ. Press, 1974. pp. 145–57.

3407. **PRAZ, MARIO.** "Hemingway in Italy." In *The Literary Reputation of Hemingway in Europe.* Ed. Roger Asselineau. New York: New York Univ. Press, 1965. pp. 93–125.

3408. **PRESLEY, JOHN W.** "'Hawks Never Share': Women and Tragedy in Hemingway." *Hemingway Notes,* 3, no. 1 (1973), 3–10.

3409. **RAO, E. NAGESWARA.** "Note on Catharsis in Hemingway." *The Indian Journal of English Studies,* 16 (1976), 189–91.

3410. **RAO, K. S. NARAYANA.** "Women, Violence and Darkness in the World of Hemingway's Short Stories." *The Literary Criterion,* 4, no. 3 (1960), 32–38.

3411. **REYNOLDS, MICHAEL S.** "Two Hemingway Sources for *In Our Time.*" *Studies in Short Fiction,* 9 (1972), 81–86.

3412. **ROBERTS, JOHN J.** "Patrick Shaw's Hemingway: A Response." *The CEA Crit:* 39, no. 1 (1976), 20–21.

3413. **RODGERS, BERNARD F., JR.** *"The Nick Adams Stories:* Fiction or Fact?" *Fitzgerald/Hemingway Annual 1974,* pp. 155–62.

3414. **ROVIT, EARL.** *Ernest Hemingway.* New York: Twayne, 1963.

3415. **ST. JOHN, DONALD.** "Hemingway and Prudence." *The Connecticut Review,* 5, no. 2 (1972), 78–84.

3416. _____. "Interview with Hemingway's 'Bill Gorton.'" *The Connecticut Review*, 1, no. 2 (1968), 5–12; 3, no. 1 (1969), 5–23.

3417. SANDERSON, STEWART. *Ernest Hemingway*. Edinburgh: Oliver & Boyd, 1961.

3418. SCHNEIDERMAN, LEO. "Hemingway: A Psychological Study." *The Connecticut Review*, 6, no. 2 (1973), 34–49.

3419. SCOTT, NATHAN A., JR. *Ernest Hemingway: A Critical Essay*. Grand Rapids, MI: Eerdmans, 1966.

3420. SHARMA, D. R. "Vision and Design in Hemingway." *The Literary Criterion*, 8, no. 3 (1968), 42–51.

3421. SHAW, PATRICK W. "How Earnest Is the Image: Hemingway's Little Animals." *The CEA Critic*, 37, no. 3 (1975), 5–8.

3422. SHAW, SAMUEL. *Ernest Hemingway*. New York: Ungar, 1973.

3423. SHELTON, FRANK W. "The Family in Hemingway's Nick Adams Stories." *Studies in Short Fiction*, 11 (1974), 303–05.

3423a. SINGER, KURT. *Hemingway: Life and Death of a Giant*. Los Angeles, CA: Holloway House, 1961.

3424. SKARD, SIGMUND. "Hemingway in Norway." In *The Literary Reputation of Hemingway in Europe*. Ed. Roger Asselineau. New York: New York Univ. Press, 1965. pp. 127–49.

3425. SLABEY, ROBERT M. "The Structure of *In Our Time*." *South Dakota Review*, 3, no. 1 (1965), 38–52.

3426. SLAVUTYCH, YAR. "Ernest Hemingway in Ukranian Literature." In *Modern American Fiction: Insights and Foreign Lights*. Proceedings of the Comparative Literature Symposium, Vol. 5. Ed. Wolodymyr T. Zyla and Wendell M. Aycock. Lubbock: Interdepartmental Committee on Comparative Literature, Texas Tech Univ., 1972. pp. 67–76.

3427. SMITH, JULIAN. "Christ Times Four: Hemingway's Unknown Spanish Civil War Stories." *The Arizona Quarterly*, 25 (1969), 5–17.

3428. _____. "Hemingway and The Thing Left Out." *Journal of Modern Literature*, 1 (1970), 169–82.

3429. SOJKA, GREGORY S. "Who Is Sam Cardinella, and Why Is He Hanging?" *Fitzgerald/Hemingway Annual 1976*, pp. 217–23.

3430. SOMERS, PAUL P., JR. "Anderson's Twisted Apples and Hemingway's Crips." *Midamerica*, 1 (1974), 82–97.

3431. _____. "The Mark of Sherwood Anderson on Hemingway: A Look at the Texts." *The South Atlantic Quarterly*, 73 (1974), 487–503.

3432. STEIN, WILLIAM BYSSHE. "Love and Lust in Hemingway's Short Stories." *Texas Studies in Literature and Language*, 3 (1961), 234–42.

3433. STEPHENS, ROBERT O. *Hemingway's Nonfiction: The Public Voice*. Chapel Hill: Univ. of North Carolina Press, 1968.

3434. ———. "Hemingway's Old Man and the Iceberg." *Modern Fiction Studies*, 7 (1961), 295–304.

3435. ———. "Introduction." In *Ernest Hemingway: The Critical Reception*. New York: Burt Franklin, 1977. pp. ix–xxxv.

3436. SYLVESTER, BICKFORD. "Hemingway's Unpublished Remarks on War and Warriors." In *War and Society in North America*. Ed. J. L. Granastein and R. D. Cuff. Toronto: T. Nelson, 1971. pp. 135–52.

3437. TUTTLETON, JAMES W. "'Combat in the Erogenous Zone': Women in the American Novel between the Two World Wars." In *What Manner of Woman: Essays on English and American Life and Literature*. Ed. Marlene Springer. New York: New York Univ. Press, 1977. pp. 271–96.

3438. UNFRIED, SARAH P. *Man's Place in the Natural Order: A Study of Hemingway's Major Works*. New York: Gordon Press, 1976.

3439. VAIDYANATHAN, T. G. "The Nick Adams Stories and the Myth of Initiation." In *Indian Studies in American Fiction*. Ed. M. K. Naik, S. K. Desai, and S. Mokashi-Punekar. Dharwar: Karnatak Univ., 1974. pp. 203–18.

3440. WAGNER, LINDA WELSHIMER. *Hemingway and Faulkner: Inventors/Masters*. Metuchen, NJ: Scarecrow, 1975.

3441. ———. "Juxtaposition in Hemingway's *In Our Time*." *Studies in Short Fiction*, 12 (1975), 243–52.

3442. ———. "The Poetry in American Fiction." *Prospects*, 2 (1976), 513–26.

3443. WALDHORN, ARTHUR. *A Reader's Guide to Ernest Hemingway*. New York: Farrar, Straus and Giroux, 1972.

3444. WATTS, EMILY STIPES. *Ernest Hemingway and the Arts*. Urbana: Univ. of Illinois Press, 1971.

3445. WEBER, BROM. "Ernest Hemingway's Genteel Bullfight." In *The American Novel and the Nineteen Twenties*. Ed. Malcolm Bradbury and David Palmer. London: Edward Arnold, 1971. pp. 151–63.

3446. WEBSTER, HARVEY CURTIS. "Ernest Hemingway: The Pursuit of Death." *The Texas Quarterly*, 7, no. 2 (1964), 149–59.

3447. WEEKS, ROBERT P. "Cleaning Up Hemingway." *Fitzgerald/Hemingway Annual 1972*, pp. 311–13.

3448. ———. "Introduction." In *Hemingway: A Collection of Critical Essays*. Englewood Cliffs, NJ: Prentice-Hall, 1962. pp. 1–16.

3449. WEGELIN, CHRISTOF. "Hemingway and the Decline of International Fiction." *The Sewanee Review*, 73 (1965), 285–98.

3450. WELLAND, D. S. R. "Hemingway's English Reputation." In *The Literary Reputation of Hemingway in Europe*. Ed. Roger Asselineau. New York: New York Univ. Press, 1965. pp. 9–38.

3451. WELLS, DAVID J. "Hemingway in French." *Fitzgerald/Hemingway Annual 1974*, pp. 235–38.

3452. WHITE, WILLIAM. *The Merrill Guide to Ernest Hemingway*. Columbus, OH: Merrill, 1969.

3453. WHITLOW, ROGER. "The Destruction/Prevention of the Family Relationship in Hemingway's Fiction." *The Literary Review*, 20 (1976), 5–16.

3454. WILSON, DOUGLAS. "Ernest Hemingway, *The Nick Adams Stories*." *Western Humanities Review*, 27 (1973), 295–99.

3455. WYATT, BRYANT N. "Huckleberry Finn and the Art of Ernest Hemingway." *The Mark Twain Journal*, 13, no. 4 (1967), 1–8.

3456. WYATT, DAVID M. "Hemingway's Uncanny Beginnings." *The Georgia Review*, 31 (1977), 476–501.

3457. YOUNG, PHILIP. "'Big World Out There': The Nick Adams Stories." *Novel*, 6 (1972), 5–19.

3458. _____. *Ernest Hemingway*. Minneapolis: Univ. of Minnesota Press, 1959.

3459. _____. *Ernest Hemingway*. Rev. ed. Minneapolis: Univ. of Minnesota Press, 1965.

3460. _____. *Ernest Hemingway: A Reconsideration*. Rev. ed. University Park: Pennsylvania State Univ. Press, 1966.

3461. _____. "Hemingway's Manuscripts: The Vault Reconsidered." *Studies in American Fiction*, 2 (1974), 3–11.

3462. _____. "Posthumous Hemingway, and Nicholas Adams." In *Hemingway in Our Time*. Ed. Richard Astro and Jackson J. Benson. Corvallis: Oregon State Univ. Press, 1974. pp. 13–23.

3463. _____. "Preface." In *The Nick Adams Stories*, by Ernest Hemingway. New York: Scribner's, 1972. pp. 5–7.

3464. _____. "Scott Fitzgerald on his Thirtieth Birthday Sends a Small Gift to Ernest Hemingway." *Modern Fiction Studies*, 14 (1968), 229–30.

3465. _____. "Speaking of Books: In the Vault with Hemingway." *The New York Times Book Review*, 29 Sept. 1968, pp. 2, 28.

Interviews

3466. RODMAN, SELDEN. "Ernest Hemingway." In *Tongues of Fallen Angels*. New York: New Directions, 1974. pp. 51–61.

Bibliography

3467. A[LDERMAN], T[AYLOR], K[ENNETH] R[OSEN], AND W[IL-LIAM] W[HITE]. "Current Bibliography." *Hemingway Notes*, 1, no. 2 (1971), 10–13; 2, no. 1 (1972), 9–13; 2, no. 2 (1972), 7–12.

3468. _____, _____, AND _____. "Hemingway: A Current Bibliography." *Hemingway Notes*, 3, no. 1 (1973), 11–13; 3, no. 2 (1973), 12–16.

3469. ANON. "Hemingway Checklist." *Fitzgerald/Hemingway Annual 1972*, pp. 347–67.

3470. BAKER, CARLOS. "A Checklist of Hemingway Criticism." In *Hemingway and His Critics: An International Anthology*. Ed. Carlos Baker. New York: Hill and Wang, 1961. pp. 279–98.

3471. BEEBE, MAURICE, AND JOHN FEASTER. "Criticism of Ernest Hemingway: A Selected Checklist." *Modern Fiction Studies*, 14 (1968), 337–69.

3472. BENSON, JACKSON J. "A Comprehensive Checklist of Hemingway Short Fiction Criticism, Explication, and Commentary." In *The Short Stories of Ernest Hemingway: Critical Essays*. Ed. Jackson J. Benson. Durham, NC: Duke Univ. Press, 1975. pp. 312–75.

3473. DUGGAN, MARGARET M. "Hemingway Checklist." *Fitzgerald/Hemingway Annual 1973*, pp. 357–62; *1974*, pp. 323–29.

3474. HANNEMAN, AUDRE. *Ernest Hemingway: A Comprehensive Bibliography*. Princeton, NJ: Princeton Univ. Press, 1967.

3475. _____. "Hanneman Addenda." *Fitzgerald/Hemingway Annual 1970*, pp. 195–218; *1971*, pp. 343–46.

3476. _____. *Supplement to* Ernest Hemingway: A Comprehensive Bibliography. Princeton, NJ: Princeton Univ. Press, 1975.

3477. HOFFMAN, FREDERICK J. "Ernest Hemingway." In *Fifteen Modern American Authors: A Survey of Research and Criticism*. Ed Jackson R. Bryer. Durham, NC: Duke Univ. Press, 1969. pp. 275–300.

3478. _____, AND MELVIN J. FRIEDMAN. "Ernest Hemingway." In *Sixteen Modern American Authors: A Survey of Research and Criticism*. Ed. Jackson R. Bryer. Durham, NC: Duke Univ. Press, 1974. pp. 367–416.

3479. MONTEIRO, GEORGE. "Addenda to Hanneman's *Hemingway: Books on Trial.*" *The Papers of the Bibliographical Society of America*, 71 (1977), 514–15.

3480. ROGERS, JEAN MUIR, AND GORDON STEIN. "Bibliographical Notes on Hemingway's *Men Without Women.*" *The Papers of the Bibliographical Society of America*, 64 (1970), 210–13.

3481. WAGNER, LINDA WELSHIMER. *Ernest Hemingway: A Reference Guide*. Boston, MA: G. K. Hall, 1977.

3482. **WHITE, WILLIAM.** "Hemingway: A Current Bibliography." *Hemingway Notes*, 4, no. 1 (1974), 20–24.

3483. _____. "Hemingway Checklist." *Fitzgerald/Hemingway Annual 1975*, pp. 351–68; *1976*, pp. 260–72; *1977*, pp. 255–66.

3484. _____. "Hemingway-iana Annotated." *The Mark Twain Journal*, 11, no. 4 (1962), 11–13.

3485. _____. *The Merrill Checklist of Ernest Hemingway*. Columbus, OH: Merrill, 1970.

3486. _____. "Supplement to Hanneman: Articles, 1966–1970." *Hemingway Notes*, 1, no. 1 (1971), 3–12.

3487. _____. "Two More Hanneman Addenda." *Hemingway Notes*, 3, no. 1 (1973), 14–15.

3488. **YOUNG, PHILIP, AND CHARLES W. MANN.** *The Hemingway Manuscripts: An Inventory*. University Park: Pennsylvania State Univ. Press, 1969.

HERGESHEIMER, JOSEPH

General Studies

3489. **MARTIN, RONALD E.** *The Fiction of Joseph Hergesheimer*. Philadelphia: Univ. of Pennsylvania Press, 1965.

Bibliography

3490. **NAPIER, JAMES J.** "Joseph Hergesheimer: A Selected Bibliography, 1913–1945." *Bulletin of Bibliography and Magazine Notes*, 24 (1963–64), 46–48, 52, 69–70.

3491. **STAPPENBECK, HERB.** *A Catalogue of the Joseph Hergesheimer Collection at the University of Texas*. Austin: Humanities Research Center, Univ. of Texas, 1974.

HERRICK, ROBERT

"The Master of the Inn"

See 3492.

General Studies

3492. **BUDD, LOUIS J.** *Robert Herrick*. New York: Twayne, 1971.

3493. **FRANKLIN, PHYLLIS.** "The Influence of William James on Robert Herrick's Early Fiction." *American Literary Realism, 1870–1910*, 7 (1974), 395–402.

3494. **NEVIUS, BLAKE.** *Robert Herrick: The Development of a Novelist*. Berkeley: Univ. of California Press, 1962.

Bibliography

3495. **Carlson, Douglas O.** "Robert Herrick: An Addendum." *American Literary Realism, 1870–1910*, 1, no. 3 (1968), 67–68.

3496. **Franklin, Phyllis.** "A Handlist of the Robert Herrick Papers at the University of Chicago." *American Literary Realism, 1870–1910*, 8 (1975), 109–54.

3497. **Genthe, Charles V.** "Robert Herrick (1868–1938)." *American Literary Realism, 1870–1910*, 1, no. 1 (1967), 56–60.

HERSEY, JOHN

"A Fable South of Cancer"

3498. **Sanders, David.** *John Hersey.* New York: Twayne, 1967.

HEYERT, MURRAY

"The New Kid"

See 374.

HEYWARD, DuBOSE

"The Brute"

See 3500.

"The Half Pint Flask"

3499. **Durham, Frank M.** *DuBose Heyward's Use of Folklore in His Negro Fiction.* Charleston, SC: The Citadel, 1961.

"The Winning Loser"

See 3500.

General Studies

3500. **Durham, Frank.** "Dubose Heyward's 'Lost' Short Stories." *Studies in Short Fiction*, 2 (1965), 157–63.

HIGGINSON, THOMAS WENTWORTH

"The Monarch of Dreams"

See 35.

HIMES, CHESTER

"A Nigger"

3501. **LISTON, MAUREEN.** "Chester Himes, 'A Nigger' (1937)."
In *The Black American Short Story in the 20th Century: A Collection
of Critical Essays*. Ed. Peter Bruck. Amsterdam: B. R. Grüner,
1977. pp. 85–97.
See also 3505.

"Prediction"

See 3504, 3505.

General Studies

3502. **HIMES, CHESTER.** *My Life of Absurdity*. Vol. II of *The Autobiography of Chester Himes*. Garden City, NY: Doubleday, 1976.
3503. ———. *The Quality of Hurt*. Vol. I of *The Autobiography of
Chester Himes*. Garden City, NY: Doubleday, 1972.
3504. **LUNDQUIST, JAMES.** *Chester Himes*. New York: Ungar,
1976.
*3505. **MILLIKEN, STEPHEN F.** *Chester Himes: A Critical Appraisal*. Columbia: Univ. of Missouri Press, 1976.

Interviews

3506. **FULLER, HOYT W.** "Traveler on the Long, Rough, Lonely
Old Road: An Interview With Chester Himes." *Black World*, 21,
no. 5 (1972), 4–22, 87–98.
3507. **WILLIAMS, JOHN A.** "My Man Himes: An Interview with
Chester Himes." *Amistad*, no. 1 (1970), pp. 25–93.

Bibliography

3508. **FABRE, MICHEL.** "Chester Himes' Published Works: A
Tentative Check List." *Black World*, 21, no. 5 (1972), 76–78.
3509. **HILL, JAMES LEE.** "Bibliography of the Works of Chester
Himes, Ann Petry and Frank Yerby." *Black Books Bulletin*, 3,
no. 3 (1975), 60–72.

HINOJOSA, ROLANDO R.

"Fira the Blond"

See 3510.

"Por Esas Cosas Que Pasan"

See 205.

General Studies

3510. **SALINAS, JUDY.** "The Chicana Image." In *Proceedings of the
Fifth National Convention of the Popular Culture Association*, St.

Louis, Missouri, March 20–22, 1975. Ed. Michael T. Marsden. Bowling Green, OH: Bowling Green Univ. Popular Press, 1975. pp. 146–60.

HOCH, EDWARD D.

Bibliography

3511. **CLARK, WILLIAM J., EDWARD D. HOCH, AND FRANCIS M. NEVINS, JR.** "Edward D. Hoch: A Checklist." *The Armchair Detective*, 9 (1976), 102–11.

3512. **HOCH, EDWARD D.** "A Simon Ark Bibliography." *The Armchair Detective*, 3 (1970), 248–49.

HOOPER, JOHNSON JONES

"The Captain Attends a Camp-Meeting"

See 3514.

The 'Tallapoosy Vollantares' Meet the Enemy"

See 549.

General Studies

3513. **RACHAL, JOHN.** "Scotty Briggs and the Minister: An Idea from Hooper's Simon Suggs?" *Mark Twain Journal*, 17, no. 2 (1974), 10–11.

3514. **SMITH, WINSTON.** *"Simon Suggs* and the Satiric Tradition." In *Essays in Honor of Richebourg Gaillard McWilliams*. Ed. Howard Creed. Birmingham, AL: Birmingham-Southern College, 1970. pp. 49–56.

3515. **WELLMAN, MANLY WADE.** "Introduction." In *Adventures of Simon Suggs, Late of the Tallapoosa Volunteers*, by Johnson Jones Hooper. Chapel Hill: Univ. of North Carolina Press, 1969. pp. ix–xxviii.

HOPLEY-WOOLRICH, CORNELL GEORGE (*See* WOOLRICH, CORNELL)

HORGAN, PAUL

General Studies

3516. **DAY, JAMES M.** *Paul Horgan*. Austin, TX: Steck-Vaughn, 1967.

Bibliography

3517. McCONNELL, RICHARD M. M., AND SUSAN A. FREY. "Paul Horgan: A Bibliography." *Western American Literature*, 6 (1971), 137–50.
3518. _____, AND _____. *Paul Horgan's Humble Powers: A Bibliography*. Washington, DC: Information Resources Press, 1971.

HOWARD, [JOHN] HAYDEN

"Beyond Words"

See 293.

HOWE, E[DGAR] W[ATSON]

General Studies

3519. PICKETT, CALDER M. *Ed Howe: Country Town Philosopher*. Lawrence: Univ. Press of Kansas, 1968.

Bibliography

3520. BUCCO, MARTIN. "The Place." In *E. W. Howe*. Boise, ID: Boise State Univ., 1977. pp. 36–46.
3521. EICHELBERGER, CLAYTON L. "Edgar Watson Howe and Joseph Kirkland: More Critical Comment." *American Literary Realism, 1870–1910*, 4 (1971), 279–90.
3522. _____. "Edgar Watson Howe (1853–1937): A Critical Bibliography of Secondary Comment." *American Literary Realism, 1870–1910*, 2 (1969), 1–49.

HOWELLS, WILLIAM DEAN

"The Angel of the Lord"

See 3537.

"A Case of Metaphantasmia"

3523. CROW, CHARLES L. "Howells and William James: 'A Case of Metaphantasmia' Solved." *American Quarterly*, 27 (1975), 169–77.

"A Circle in the Water"

See 3536.

"The Critical Bookstore"

3524. SIMPSON, LEWIS P. "The Treason of William Dean Howells." In *The Man of Letters in New England and the South:*

Essays on the History of the Literary Vocation in America. Baton Rouge: Louisiana State Univ. Press, 1973. pp. 85-128.

"A Day's Pleasure"

See 3535, 3536.

"A Difficult Case"

3525. CROWLEY, JOHN W. "Howells' Minister in a Maze: 'A Difficult Case.'" *Colby Library Quarterly*, 13 (1977), 278-83.

"A Dream"

3526. MARLER, ROBERT F., JR. "'A Dream': Howells' Early Contribution to the American Short Story." *The Journal of Narrative Technique*, 4 (1974), 75-85.

"Editha"

3527. CROWLEY, JOHN W. "Howells's Obscure Hurt." *Journal of American Studies*, 9 (1975), 199-211.
3528. ENGELHART, CARL W. "Howells' 'Editha': Toward Realism." In *Americana-Austriaca: Beiträge zur Amerikakunde*, Vol. 3. Ed. Klaus Lanzinger. Vienna: Braumüller, 1974. pp. 3-9.
3529. FREE, WILLIAM J. "Howells' 'Editha' and Pragmatic Belief." *Studies in Short Fiction*, 3 (1966), 285-92.
3530. KEHLER, HAROLD. "Howells' 'Editha.'" *The Explicator*, 19 (1961), item 41.
See also 3536, 6445.

"Fennel and Rue"

3531. CROWLEY, JOHN W. "The Oedipal Theme in Howells's *Fennel and Rue.*" *Studies in the Novel*, 5 (1973), 104-09.

"Flitting"

See 3543.

"His Apparition"

See 3536.

"The Independent Candidate"

See 3536.

"Letters of an Alturian Traveller"

See 3536.

"The Magic of a Voice"

See 3536.

"A Pair of Patient Lovers"

See 3536.

"A Pedestrian Tour"

See 3543.

"A Romance of Real Life"

3532. SIMON, MYRON. "Howells on Romantic Fiction." *Studies in Short Fiction*, 2 (1965), 241–46.
See also 3535.

"Scene"

3533. AARON, DANIEL. "Howells' 'Maggie.'" *The New England Quarterly*, 38 (1965), 85–90.
See also 3535.

"A Sleep and a Forgetting"

3534. CROWLEY, JOHN W., AND CHARLES L. CROW. "Psychic and Psychological Themes in Howells' 'A Sleep and a Forgetting.'" *ESQ*, 23 (1977), 41–51.

"Though One Rose from the Dead"

See 3537.

General Studies

3535. CARRINGTON, GEORGE C., JR. *The Immense Complex Drama: The World and Art of the Howells Novel*. Columbus: Ohio State Univ. Press, 1966.
3536. ———, AND ILDIKÓ DE PAPP CARRINGTON. *Plots and Characters in the Fiction of William Dean Howells*. Hamden, CT: Archon Books, 1976.
3537. CROWLEY, JOHN W. "Howells' *Questionable Shapes*: From Psychologism to Psychic Romance." *ESQ*, 21 (1975), 169–78.
3538. GIBSON, WILLIAM M. *William D. Howells*. Minneapolis: Univ. of Minnesota Press, 1967.
3539. GILLESPIE, ROBERT. "The Fictions of Basil March." *Colby Library Quarterly*, 12 (1976), 14–28.
3540. KIRK, CLARA MARBURG. *W. D. Howells and Art in His Time*. New Brunswick, NJ: Rutgers Univ. Press, 1965.
3541. ———, AND RUDOLPH KIRK. *William Dean Howells*. New York: Twayne, 1962.
3542. KLINKOWITZ, JEROME. "Ethic and Aesthetic: The Basil and Isabel March Stories of William Dean Howells." *Modern Fiction Studies*, 16 (1970), 303–22.

3543. LYNN, KENNETH S. *William Dean Howells: An American Life*. New York: Harcourt Brace Jovanovich, 1971.

3544. VANDERBILT, KERMIT. *The Achievement of William Dean Howells: A Reinterpretation*. Princeton, NJ: Princeton Univ. Press, 1968.

3545. WAGENKNECHT, EDWARD. *William Dean Howells: The Friendly Eye*. New York: Oxford Univ. Press, 1969.

Interviews

3546. ROWLETTE, ROBERT. "More Addenda to Halfmann: Nine New Howells Interviews." *American Literary Realism, 1870–1910*, 9 (1976), 33–42.

Bibliography

3547. BEEBE, MAURICE. "Criticism of William Dean Howells: A Selected Checklist." *Modern Fiction Studies*, 16 (1970), 395–419.

3548. BRENNI, VITO J. *William Dean Howells: A Bibliography*. Metuchen, NJ: Scarecrow, 1973.

3549. EICHELBERGER, CLAYTON L. *Published Comment on William Dean Howells through 1920: A Research Bibliography*. Boston, MA: G. K. Hall, 1976.

3550. FORTENBERRY, GEORGE. "William Dean Howells." In *Fifteen American Authors before 1900: Bibliographic Essays on Research and Criticism*. Ed. Robert A. Rees and Earl N. Harbert. Madison: Univ. of Wisconsin Press, 1971. pp. 229–44.

3551. HALFMANN, ULRICH, AND DON R. SMITH. "William Dean Howells: A Revised and Annotated Bibliography of Secondary Comment in Periodicals and Newspapers, 1868–1919." *American Literary Realism, 1870–1910*, 5 (1972), 91–121.

3552. REEVES, JOHN K. "The Literary Manuscripts of W. D. Howells: A Supplement to the Descriptive Finding List." *Bulletin of The New York Public Library*, 65 (1961), 465–76.

3553. ROWLETTE, ROBERT. "Addenda to Halfmann and Smith: More New Howells Items." *American Literary Realism, 1870–1910*, 9 (1976), 43–55.

3554. VANDERBILT, KERMIT. "Howells Studies: Past, or Passing, or to Come." *American Literary Realism, 1870–1910*, 7 (1974), 143–53.

3555. WOODRESS, JAMES. "The Dean's Comeback: Four Decades of Howells Scholarship." *Texas Studies in Literature and Language*, 2 (1960), 115–23.

3556. _____, AND STANLEY P. ANDERSON. "A Bibliography of Writings about William Dean Howells." *American Literary Realism, 1870–1910*, Special no. (1969), 1–139.

HUBBARD, ELBERT
"How I Found My Brother"
See 3557.

General Studies
3557. **CHAMPNEY, FREEMAN.** *Art & Glory: The Story of Elbert Hubbard.* New York: Crown, 1968.

HUBBARD, L[AFAYETTE] RON[ALD]
"Fear"
See 226.

HUGHES, [JAMES] LANGSTON
"Big Meeting"
See 386, 3561.

"Blessed Assurance"
See 3562.

"The Blues I'm Playing"
3558. **BRUCK, PETER.** "Langston Hughes, 'The Blues I'm Playing' (1934)." In *The Black American Short Story in the 20th Century: A Collection of Critical Essays.* Ed. Peter Bruck. Amsterdam: B. R. Grüner, 1977. pp. 71–83.
See also 386, 3561.

"Christmas Song"
See 333.

"Cora Unashamed"
See 386, 3561.

"Father and Son"
See 3561.

"A Good Job Gone"
See 3561.

"Home"
See 3561.

"Little Dog"

See 3561.

"Mary Winowsky"

3559. **EMANUEL, JAMES A.** "Langston Hughes' First Short Story: 'Mary Winowsky.' " *Phylon*, 22 (1961), 267-72.

"Mother and Child"

See 3561.

"On the Road"

See 335, 386, 3561.

"On the Way Home"

See 386, 3561.

"One Christmas Eve"

See 3561.

"Poor Little Fellow"

See 3561.

"Powder-White Faces"

See 3561.

"Professor"

See 3561.

"Red-Headed Baby"

See 386, 3562.

"Rejuvenation through Joy"

See 3561.

"Sailor Ashore"

See 3561.

"Slave on the Block"

See 337, 3561.

"Spanish Blood"

See 3561.

General Studies

3560. **DANDRIDGE, RITA B.** "The Black Woman as a Freedom Fighter in Langston Hughes' *Simple's Uncle Sam.*" *CLA Journal*, 18 (1974), 273–83.

3561. **EMANUEL, JAMES A.** *Langston Hughes.* New York: Twayne, 1967.

3562. ———. "The Literary Experiments of Langston Hughes." *CLA Journal*, 11 (1968), 335–44.

3563. **FULLER, HOYT W.** "Langston Hughes and the Example of 'Simple.' " *Black World*, 19, no. 8 (1970), 35–38.

3564. **HASKINS, JAMES S.** *Always Movin' On: The Life of Langston Hughes.* New York: Franklin Watts, 1976.

3565. **JACKSON, BLYDEN.** "A Word About Simple." *CLA Journal*, 11 (1968), 310–18.

3566. **KLOTMAN, PHYLLIS R.** "Jesse B. Semple and the Narrative Art of Langston Hughes." *The Journal of Narrative Technique*, 3 (1973), 66–75.

3567. **MINTZ, LAWRENCE E.** "Langston Hughes's Jesse B. Semple: The Urban Negro as Wise Fool." *Satire Newsletter*, 7 (1969), 11–21.

3568. **O'DANIEL, THERMAN B.** "Langston Hughes." In *Langston Hughes, Black Genius: A Critical Evaluation.* Ed. Therman B. O'Daniel. New York: Morrow, 1971. pp. 1–17.

3569. **PRESLEY, JAMES.** "The American Dream of Langston Hughes." *Southwest Review*, 48 (1963), 380–86.

3570. ———. "The Birth of Jesse B. Semple." *Southwest Review*, 58 (1973), 219–25.

3571. **ROSENBLATT, ROGER.** "The 'Negro Everyman' and His Humor." In *Veins of Humor.* Ed. Harry Levin. Cambridge, MA: Harvard Univ. Press, 1972. pp. 225–41.

3572. **WATKINS, CHARLES A.** "Simple: The Alter Ego of Langston Hughes." *The Black Scholar*, 2, no. 10 (1971), 18–26.

3573. **WILLIAMS, MELVIN, G.** "The Gospel According to Simple." *Black American Literature Forum*, 11 (1977), 46–48.

3574. ———. "Langston Hughes's Jesse B. Semple: A Black Walter Mitty." *Negro American Literature Forum*, 10 (1976), 66–69.

Bibliography

3575. **DICKINSON, DONALD C.** *A Bio-Bibliography of Langston Hughes, 1902–1967.* Hamden, CT: Archon Books, 1967.

3576. ———. *A Bio-Bibliography of Langston Hughes, 1902–1967.* 2nd ed. Hamden, CT: Archon Books, 1972.

3577. **O'DANIEL, THERMAN B.** "Langston Hughes: A Selected Classified Bibliography." *CLA Journal*, 11 (1968), 349–66.

HUMPHREY, WILLIAM

General Studies

*3578. **LEE, JAMES W.** *William Humphrey.* Austin, TX: Steck-Vaughn, 1967.

HUNEKER, JAMES GIBBONS

General Studies

3579. **ROTTENBERG, ANNETTE T.** "Aesthete in America: The Short Stories of James Gibbons Huneker." *Studies in Short Fiction*, 2 (1965), 358–66.

HUNTER, EVAN

General Studies

3580. **PROZINI, BILL.** "The 'Mystery' Career of Evan Hunter." *The Armchair Detective*, 5 (1972), 129–32.

HURSTON, ZORA NEALE

"Black Death"

See 3582.

"Drenched in Light"

See 386.

"The Gilded Six-Bits"

See 386, 3584.

"John Redding Goes to Sea"

See 3582, 3584.

"Spunk"

See 3584.

"Sweat"

See 3582–3584.

General Studies

3581. **BABCOCK, C. MERTON.** "A Word-List from Zora Neale Hurston." *Publication of the American Dialect Society*, no. 40 (1963), pp. 1–11.

3582. HEMENWAY, ROBERT E. *Zora Neale Hurston: A Literary Biography*. Urbana: Univ. of Illinois Press, 1977.
3583. ———. "Zora Neale Hurston and the Eatonville Anthology." In *The Harlem Renaissance Remembered: Essays*. Ed. Arna Bontemps. New York: Dodd, Mead, 1972. pp. 190–214, 294–95.
3584. HOWARD, LILLIE P. "Marriage: Zora Neale Hurston's System of Values." *CLA Journal*, 21 (1977), 256–68.
3585. LOVE, THERESA R. "Zora Neale Hurston's America." *Papers on Language & Literature*, 12 (1976), 422–37.

IRVING, WASHINGTON

"The Adventure of My Uncle"

See 26.

"The Adventure of the German Student"

3586. GRIFFITH, KELLEY, JR. "Ambiguity and Gloom in Irving's 'Adventure of the German Student.' " *The CEA Critic*, 38, no. 1 (1975), 10–13.
See also 3607, 3613, 3635.

"Buckthorne, or The Young Man of Great Expectations"

See 3613.

"The Devil and Tom Walker"

See 3613.

"Dolph Heyliger"

See 26, 3613, 3626.

"The Grand Prior of Minorca"

3587. McLENDON, WILL L. "A Problem in Plagiarism: Washington Irving and Cousen de Courchamps." *Comparative Literature*, 20 (1968), 157–69.

"John Bull"

3588. GARTNER, DENNIS D. "The Influence of James Kirke Paulding's *Diverting History* on Washington Irving's Sketch 'John Bull.' " *The Papers of the Bibliographical Society of America*, 67 (1973), 310–14.

"The Legend of Sleepy Hollow"

3589. BONE, RICHARD A. "Irving's Headless Hessian: Prosperity and the Inner Life." *American Quarterly*, 15 (1963), 167–75.

3590. **BRUNER, MARJORIE W.** *"The Legend of Sleepy Hollow*: A Mythological Parody." *College English*, 25 (1964), 274, 279-83.
3591. **CONLEY, PATRICK T.** "The Real Ichabod Crane." *American Literature*, 40 (1968), 70-71.
3592. **EBY, CECIL B., JR.** "Ichabod Crane in Yoknapatawpha." *The Georgia Review*, 16 (1962), 465-69.
3593. **McCLARY, BEN HARRIS.** "Ichabod Crane's Scottish Origin." *Notes and Queries*, NS 15 (1968), 29.
3594. **MALIN, IRVING.** "Sleepy Oppositions." In *Approaches to the Short Story*. Ed. Neil D. Isaacs and Louis H. Leiter. San Francisco, CA: Chandler, 1963. pp. 56-62.
See also 47, 452, 597, 3601, 3605, 3607, 3611, 3613, 3619, 3620, 3625, 3636, 3637, 3640, 3642, 3643.

"May-Day"

See 3613.

"Rip Van Winkle"

3595. **CAMERON, KENNETH WALTER.** "The Long-Sleep-and-Changed-World Motif in 'Rip Van Winkle.' " *The Emerson Society Quarterly*, no. 19 (1960), pp. 35-36.
3596. **HEIMAN, MARCEL.** "Rip Van Winkle: A Psychoanalytic Note on the Story and Its Author." *American Imago*, 16 (1959), 3-47.
3597. **LARSON, CHARLES R.** "Dame Van Winkle's Burden." *The Colorado Quarterly*, 17 (1969), 407-10.
3598. **LEE, HELEN.** "Clue Patterns in 'Rip Van Winkle.' " *English Journal*, 55 (1966), 192-94.
3599. **MENGELING, MARVIN E.** "Characterization in 'Rip Van Winkle.' " *The English Journal*, 53 (1964), 643-46.
3600. **ROTH, MARTIN.** "The Final Chapter of Knickerbocker's New York." *Modern Philology*, 66 (1969), 248-55.
3601. **SHEAR, WALTER.** "Time in 'Rip Van Winkle' and 'The Legend of Sleepy Hollow.' " *The Midwest Quarterly*, 17 (1976), 158-72.
3602. **YOUNG, PHILIP.** "Fallen from Time: The Mythic Rip Van Winkle." *The Kenyon Review*, 22 (1960), 547-73.
See also 63, 433-435, 454, 461, 597, 3607, 3613, 3620, 3622, 3625, 3636, 3637, 3640, 3642, 3643.

"The Rookery"

See 3613.

"The Seven Sons of Lara"

3603. SCHEICK, WILLIAM J., ED. " 'The Seven Sons of Lara': A
Washington Irving Manuscript." *Resources for American Literary Study*, 2 (1972), 208–17.

"The Spectre Bridegroom"

See 3607, 3610.

"The Story of the Young Italian"

3604. WRIGHT, NATHALIA. "Irving's Use of His Italian Experiences in *Tales of a Traveller*: The Beginning of an American
Tradition." *American Literature*, 31 (1959), 191–96.
See also 3613.

"The Story of the Young Robber"

See 3613, 3634.

"The Stout Gentleman"

See 3613.

"Wolfert Webber"

3605. COUSER, G. THOMAS. "The Ruined Garden of Wolfert
Webber." *Studies in Short Fiction*, 12 (1975), 23–28.
See 102, 3613.

General Studies

3606. CARROLL, MARTIN C., JR. "Watersheds of American Literature." *The Literary Criterion*, 5, no. 3 (1962), 6–21.

3607. CLENDENNING, JOHN. "Irving and the Gothic Tradition."
Bucknell Review, 12, no. 2 (1964), 90–98.

3608. CURRENT-GARCIA, E. "Irving Sets the Pattern: Notes on
Professionalism and the Art of the Short Story." *Studies in Short
Fiction*, 10 (1973), 327–41.

3609. FOX, AUSTIN McC. "Introduction." In *The Legend of Sleepy
Hollow and Other Selections*, by Washington Irving. New York:
Washington Square Press, 1962. pp. vii–xxi.

3610. GATES, W. B. "Shakespearean Elements in Irving's *Sketch
Book*." *American Literature*, 30 (1959), 450–58.

3611. GUTTMANN, ALLEN. "Washington Irving and the Conservative Imagination." *American Literature*, 36 (1964), 165–73.

3612. HEDGES, WILLIAM L. "Washington Irving." In *Major Writers of America*. Ed. Perry Miller. 2 vols. New York: Harcourt,
Brace & World, 1962. I, 179–93.

3613. _____. *Washington Irving: An American Study, 1802–1832*.
Baltimore, MD: Johns Hopkins Press, 1965.

3614. ———. "Washington Irving: Nonsense, the Fat of the Land and the Dream of Indolence." In *The Chief Glory of Every People: Essays on Classic American Writers*. Ed. Matthew J. Bruccoli. Carbondale and Edwardsville: Southern Illinois Univ. Press, 1973. pp. 141–60.

3615. ———. "Washington Irving: *The Sketch Book of Geoffrey Crayon, Gent.*" In *Landmarks of American Writing*. Ed. Hennig Cohen. New York: Basic Books, 1969. pp. 56–65.

3616. KASSON, JOY S. " 'The Citadel Within': Washington Irving and the Search for Literary Vocation." *Prospects*, no. 3 (1977), pp. 371–417.

3617. KEMP, JOHN C. "Historians Manqués: Irving's Apologetic Personae." *American Transcendental Quarterly*, no. 24, Supplement Two (1974), pp. 15–19.

3618. KIME, WAYNE R. *Pierre M. Irving and Washington Irving: A Collaboration in Life and Letters*. Waterloo, Ontario: Wilfrid Laurier Univ. Press, 1977.

3619. LEARY, LEWIS. "The Two Voices of Washington Irving." In *From Irving to Steinbeck: Studies in American Literature in Honor of Harry R. Warfel*. Ed. Motley Deakin and Peter Lisca. Gainesville: Univ. of Florida Press, 1972. pp. 13–26.

3620. ———. *Washington Irving*. Minneapolis: Univ. of Minnesota Press, 1963.

3621. ———. "Washington Irving." In *The Comic Imagination in American Literature*. Ed. Louis D. Rubin, Jr. New Brunswick, NJ: Rutgers Univ. Press, 1973. pp. 63–76.

3622. ———. "Washington Irving: An End and a New Beginning." In *Soundings: Some Early American Writers*. Athens: Univ. of Georgia Press, 1975. pp. 292–329.

3623. LEASE, BENJAMIN. "*John Bull* Versus Washington Irving: More on the Shakespeare Committee Controversy." *English Language Notes*, 9 (1972), 272–77.

3624. McCLARY, BEN HARRIS, ED. *Washington Irving and the House of Murray: Geoffrey Crayon Charms the British, 1817–1856*. Knoxville: Univ. of Tennessee Press, 1969.

3625. MARTIN, TERENCE. "Rip, Ichabod, and the American Imagination." *American Literature*, 31 (1959), 137–49.

3626. MENGELING, MARVIN E. "The Crass Humor of Irving's Diedrich Knickerbocker." *Studies in American Humor*, 1 (1974), 66–72.

3627. MILLER, PERRY. "Afterword." In *The Sketch Book*, by Washington Irving. New York: New American Library, 1961. pp. 371–78.

3628. **MYERS, ANDREW B.** "Introduction." In *A Century of Commentary on the Works of Washington Irving, 1860–1974*. Tarrytown, NY: Sleepy Hollow Restorations, 1976. pp. xix–xxxviii.

3629. ———. "Introduction." In *Washington Irving: A Tribute*. Ed. Andrew B. Myers. Tarrytown, NY: Sleepy Hollow Restorations, 1972. pp. 1–19.

3630. **POCHMANN, HENRY A.** "Washington Irving: Amateur or Professional?" In *Essays on American Literature in Honor of Jay B. Hubbell*. Ed. Clarence Gohdes. Durham, NC: Duke Univ. Press, 1967. pp. 63–76.

3631. **PROFFER, CARL R.** "Washington Irving In Russia: Pushkin, Gogol, Marlinsky." *Comparative Literature*, 20 (1968), 329–42.

3632. **REED, KENNETH T.** " 'Oh These Women! These Women!': Irving's Shrews and Coquettes." *American Notes & Queries*, 8 (1970), 147–50.

3633. ———. "Washington Irving and the Negro." *Negro American Literature Forum*, 4 (1970), 43–44.

3634. **REICHERT, WALTER A.** "Some Sources of Irving's 'Italian Banditti' Stories." In *Festschrift für Walther Fischer*. Heidelberg: Carl Winter, 1959. pp. 181–86.

3635. **RINGE, DONALD A.** "Irving's Use of the Gothic Mode." *Studies in the Literary Imagination*, 7, no. 1 (1974), 51–65.

3636. ———. "New York and New England: Irving's Criticism of American Society." *American Literature*, 38 (1967), 455–67.

3637. **ROTH, MARTIN.** *Comedy and America: The Lost World of Washington Irving*. Port Washington, NY: Kennikat, 1976.

3638. ———. "Introduction." In *Washington Irving's Contributions to* The Corrector. Minneapolis: Univ. of Minnesota Press, 1968. pp. 3–40.

3639. **RUST, RICHARD D.** "Irving Rediscovers the Frontier." *American Transcendental Quarterly*, no. 18 (1973), pp. 40–44.

3640. **SANDERLIN, GEORGE.** *Washington Irving: As Others Saw Him*. New York: Coward, McCann & Geoghegan, 1975.

3641. **SMITH, HERBERT F.** "Introduction." In *Bracebridge Hall, or The Humourists: A Medley, by Geoffrey Crayon, Gent.*, by Washington Irving. Boston, MA: Twayne, 1977. pp. xiii–xxxiii.

3642. ———. "The Spell of Nature in Irving's Famous Stories." *American Transcendental Quarterly*, no. 5, Part One (1970), pp. 18–21.

3643. **SPRINGER, HASKELL S.** "Creative Contradictions in Irving." *American Transcendental Quarterly*, no. 5, Part One (1970), pp. 14–18.

3644. ———. "*The Sketch Book.*" In *Washington Irving: A Trib-*

ute. Ed. Andrew B. Myers. Tarrytown, NY: Sleepy Hollow Restorations, 1972. pp. 21-27.

3645. **TILLETT, A. S.** "Washington Irving in the *Revue Encyclopédique.*" *Revue de Littérature Comparée,* 34 (1960), 442-47.

3646. **WAGENKNECHT, EDWARD.** *Washington Irving: Moderation Displayed.* New York: Oxford Univ. Press, 1962.

3647. **WOODRING, CARL H.** "The English Literary Scene in the 1820s." In *Washington Irving: A Tribute.* Ed. Andrew B. Myers. Tarrytown, NY: Sleepy Hollow Restorations, 1972. pp. 37-41.

Bibliography

3648. **KLEINFIELD, H. L.** "A Census of Washington Irving Manuscripts." *Bulletin of The New York Public Library,* 68 (1964), 13-32.

3649. **LANGFELD, WILLIAM R., PHILIP C. BLACKBURN, AND H. L. KLEINFIELD.** *Washington Irving: A Bibliography, and A Census of Washington Irving Manuscripts.* Port Washington, NY: Kennikat, 1968.

3650. **POCHMANN, HENRY A.** "Washington Irving." In *Fifteen American Authors before 1900: Bibliographic Essays on Research and Criticism.* Ed. Robert A. Rees and Earl N. Harbert. Madison: Univ. of Wisconsin Press, 1971. pp. 245-61.

3651. **SPRINGER, HASKELL.** "Practical Editions: Washington Irving's *The Sketch Book.*" *Proof,* 4 (1975), 167-74.

3652. ———. *Washington Irving: A Reference Guide.* Boston, MA: G. K. Hall, 1976.

JACKSON, CHARLES [REGINALD]

Bibliography

3653. **LEONARD, SHIRLEY.** "Charles Reginald Jackson: A Checklist." *Bulletin of Bibliography and Magazine Notes,* 28 (1971), 137-41.

3654. ———. "Charles Reginald Jackson: A Critical Checklist." *The Serif,* 10, no. 3 (1973), 32-40.

JACKSON, HELEN HUNT

General Studies

3655. **BANNING, EVELYN I.** *Helen Hunt Jackson.* New York: Vanguard Press, 1973.

Bibliography

3656. **BYERS, JOHN R., JR.** "Helen Hunt Jackson (1830-1885)." *American Literary Realism, 1870-1910,* 2 (1969), 143-48.

3657. _____, AND ELIZABETH S. BYERS. "Helen Hunt Jackson
(1830–1885): A Critical Bibliography of Secondary Comment."
American Literary Realism, 1870–1910, 6 (1973), 197–241.

JACKSON, SHIRLEY

"Elizabeth"

See 3661.

"Flower Garden"

See 478.

"The Lottery"

3658. NEBEKER, HELEN E. " 'The Lottery': Symbolic Tour de
Force." *American Literature*, 46 (1974), 100–07.
See also 277, 384, 394, 454, 535, 565, 3660.

"Seven Types of Ambiguity"

See 564.

"The Witch"

3659. KELLY, ROBERT L. "Jackson's 'The Witch': A Satanic
Gem." *English Journal*, 60 (1971), 1204–08.

General Studies

*3660. FRIEDMAN, LENEMAJA. *Shirley Jackson*. Boston, MA:
Twayne, 1975.
3661. HOFFMAN, STEVEN K. "Individuation and Character Development in the Fiction of Shirley Jackson." *Hartford Studies in
Literature*, 8 (1976), 190–208.

Bibliography

3662. PHILLIPS, ROBERT S. "Shirley Jackson: A Chronology and
a Supplementary Checklist." *The Papers of the Bibliographical Society of America*, 60 (1966), 203–11.

JAMES, HENRY

"The Abasement of the Northmores"

3663. GALE, ROBERT L. "The Abasement of Mrs. Warren
Hope." *PMLA*, 78 (1963), 98–102.

"Adina"

3664. MACKENZIE, MANFRED. "Communities of Knowledge: Secret Society in Henry James." *ELH*, 39 (1972), 147–68.
See also 3946, 3996, 4004.

"The Altar of the Dead"

3665. FRAME, J. DOUGLAS. "The Practice of Creativity: Henry James' Approach." *The English Quarterly*, 6 (1973), 249–62.
3666. HARTSOCK, MILDRED E. "Dizzying Summit: James's 'The Altar of the Dead.' " *Studies in Short Fiction*, 11 (1974), 371–78.
See also 3948, 3961, 3982, 3988, 4015, 4023, 4032, 4054, 4058, 4067, 4073.

"The Aspern Papers"

3667. BLACKMUR, R. P. "Introduction." In *The Aspern Papers*; *The Spoils of Poynton*, by Henry James. New York: Dell, 1959. pp. 5–18.
3668. BRYLOWSKI, ANNA SALNE. "In Defense of the First Person Narrator in 'The Aspern Papers.' " *The Centennial Review*, 13 (1969), 215–40.
3669. CROWLEY, JOHN W. "The Wiles of a 'Witless' Woman: Tina in *The Aspern Papers*." *ESQ*, 22 (1976), 159–68.
3670. FORDE, SISTER VICTORIA M. " 'The Aspern Papers': What Price—Defeat." *Notre Dame English Journal*, NS 6 (1971), 17–24.
3671. FRANKLIN, ROSEMARY F. "Military Metaphors and the Organic Structure of Henry James's 'The Aspern Papers.' " *The Arizona Quarterly*, 32 (1976), 327–40.
3672. GARGANO, JAMES W. " 'The Aspern Papers': The Untold Story." *Studies in Short Fiction*, 10 (1973), 1–10.
3673. HARTSOCK, MILDRED. "Unweeded Garden: A View of *The Aspern Papers*." *Studies in Short Fiction*, 5 (1967), 60–68.
3674. HOLLAND, LAURENCE BEDWELL. *The Expense of Vision: Essays on the Craft of Henry James*. Princeton, NJ: Princeton Univ. Press, 1966.
3675. HUNTING, CONSTANCE. "The Identity of Miss Tina in *The Aspern Papers*." *Studies in the Humanities*, 5, no. 2 (1976), 28–31.
3676. HUX, SAMUEL. "Irony in *The Aspern Papers*: The Unreliable Symbolist." *Ball State University Forum*, 10, no. 1 (1969), 60–65.
3677. KADIR, DJELAL. "Another Sense of the Past: Henry James' *The Aspern Papers* and Carlos Fuentes' *Aura*." *Revue de Littérature Comparée*, 50 (1976), 448–54.
3678. KENNEDY, J. GERALD. "Jeffrey Aspern and Edgar Allan Poe: A Speculation." *Poe Studies*, 6 (1973), 17–18.

3679.   KORG, JACOB. "Reply." *College English*, 24 (1962), 155.

3680.   ———. "What Aspern Papers? A Hypothesis." *College English*, 23 (1962), 378–81.

3681.   LAITINEN, TUOMO. "Style in *The Aspern Papers*." In *Aspects of Henry James's Style*. Helsinki: Suomalainen Tiedeakatemia, 1975. pp. 60–75.

3682.   McLEAN, ROBERT C. " 'Poetic Justice' in James's *Aspern Papers*." *Papers on Language & Literature*, 3 (1967), 260–66.

3683.   MELLARD, JAMES M. "Modal Counterpoint in James's *The Aspern Papers*." *Papers on Language & Literature*, 4 (1968), 299–307.

3684.   PHILLIPS, ROBERT S. "A Note on 'What Aspern Papers? A Hypothesis.' " *College English*, 24 (1962), 154–55.

3685.   REED, KENNETH T. "Henry James, Andrew Marvell, and 'The Aspern Papers.' " *Notre Dame English Journal*, NS 6 (1971), 25–28.

3686.   RODGERS, PAUL C., JR. "Motive, Agency, and Act in James's *The Aspern Papers*." *The South Atlantic Quarterly*, 73 (1974), 377–87.

3687.   SAMUELS, CHARLES THOMAS. "At the Bottom of the *Fount*." *Novel*, 2 (1968), 46–54.

3688.   SCHNEIDER, DANIEL J. "The Unreliable Narrator: James's 'The Aspern Papers' and the Reading of Fiction." *Studies in Short Fiction*, 13 (1976), 43–49.

3689.   STEIN, WILLIAM BYSSHE. "*The Aspern Papers*: A Comedy of Masks." *Nineteenth-Century Fiction*, 14 (1959), 172–78.

See also 53, 389, 597, 3919, 3936, 3943, 3948, 3950, 3961, 3963, 3982, 3988, 3995, 3996, 4004, 4023, 4027, 4028, 4031, 4032, 4042, 4055, 4073.

"At Isella"

See 4004.

"The Author of Beltraffio*"*

3690.   PICKERING, SAMUEL F. "The Sources of 'The Author of Beltraffio.' " *The Arizona Quarterly*, 29 (1973), 177–90.

3691.   REIMAN, DONALD H. "The Inevitable Imitation: The Narrator in 'The Author of *Beltraffio*.' " *Texas Studies in Literature and Language*, 3 (1962), 503–09.

3692.   SCOGGINS, JAMES. " 'The Author of *Beltraffio*': A Reapportionment of Guilt." *Texas Studies in Literature and Language*, 5 (1963), 265–70.

3693.   WINNER, VIOLA HOPKINS. "The Artist and the Man in 'The Author of Beltraffio.' " *PMLA*, 83 (1968), 102–08.

See also 377, 583, 3924, 3948, 3961, 3964, 3974, 3982, 3998, 4023, 4031, 4035, 4042.

"The Beast in the Jungle"

3694. **BECK, RONALD.** "James' *The Beast in the Jungle*: Theme and Metaphor." *The Markham Review*, 2, no. 2 (1970), 37–40.

3695. **BIRJE-PATIL, J.** "*The Beast in the Jungle* and *Portrait of a Lady*." *The Literary Criterion*, 11, no. 4 (1975), 45–52.

3696. **CONN, PETER J.** "Seeing and Blindness in 'The Beast in the Jungle.' " *Studies in Short Fiction*, 7 (1970), 472–75.

3697. **CROWLEY, FRANCIS E.** "Henry James' *The Beast in the Jungle* and *The Ambassadors*." *The Psychoanalytic Review*, 61 (1975), 154–63.

3698. **DAWSON, ANTHONY B.** "The Reader and the Measurement of Time in 'The Beast in the Jungle.' " *English Studies in Canada*, 3 (1977), 458–65.

3699. **GEISMAR, MAXWELL.** "Henry James: 'The Beast in the Jungle.' " *Nineteenth-Century Fiction*, 18 (1963), 35–42.

3700. **JOHNSON, COURTNEY.** "John Marcher and the Paradox of the 'Unfortunate' Fall." *Studies in Short Fiction*, 6 (1969), 121–35.

3701. **KAU, JOSEPH.** "Henry James and the Garden: A Symbolic Setting for 'The Beast in the Jungle.' " *Studies in Short Fiction*, 10 (1973), 187–98.

3702. **KEHLER, JOEL R.** "Salvation and Resurrection in James's 'The Beast in the Jungle.' " *Essays in Literature* (Univ. of Denver), 1, no. 1 (1973), 13–29.

3703. **KRAFT, JAMES L.** "A Perspective on 'The Beast in the Jungle.' " *Literatur in Wissenschaft und Unterricht*, 2 (1969), 20–26.

3704. **NANCE, WILLIAM.** " 'The Beast in the Jungle': Two Versions of Oedipus." *Studies in Short Fiction*, 13 (1976), 433–40.

3705. **REID, STEPHEN.** "*The Beast in the Jungle* and *A Painful Case*: Two Different Sufferings." *American Imago*, 20 (1963), 221–39.

3706. **ROWE, JOHN CARLOS.** *Henry Adams and Henry James: The Emergence of a Modern Consciousness*. Ithaca, NY: Cornell Univ. Press, 1976.

3707. **SALZBERG, JOEL.** "The Gothic Hero in Transcendental Quest: Poe's 'Ligeia' and James' 'The Beast in the Jungle.' " *ESQ*, 18 (1972), 108–14.

3708. **TOMPKINS, JANE P.** " 'The Beast in the Jungle': An Analysis of James's Late Style." *Modern Fiction Studies*, 16 (1970), 185–91.

3709. **WALDRON, RANDALL H.** "Prefiguration in 'The Beast in the Jungle.' " *Studies in American Fiction*, 1 (1973), 101–04.

3710. **ZLOTNICK, JOAN.** "Influence or Coincidence: A Comparative Study of 'The Beast in the Jungle' and 'A Painful Case.' " *Colby Library Quarterly*, 11 (1975), 132–135.

See also 1, 11, 53, 315, 389, 565, 599, 3784, 3921, 3930, 3931, 3935,

3936, 3943, 3947, 3953, 3961, 3972, 3980, 3982, 3986, 4001,
4007, 4022, 4028, 4031, 4032, 4043, 4048, 4054, 4055, 4058,
4073, 4074.

"The Beldonald Holbein"

3711. MacNAUGHTON, W. R., AND W. R. MARTIN. " 'The Beldonald Holbein': Another Jamesian Trap for the Unwary." *English Essays in Canada*, 2 (1976), 299-305.
3712. THORBERG, RAYMOND. "Henry James and the Real Thing:
'The Beldonald Holbein.' " *Southern Humanities Review*, 3
(1968), 78-85.
See also 3982, 4002, 4073.

"The Bench of Desolation"

3713. SEGAL, ORA. "The Weak Wings of Pride: An Interpreta-
tion of James's 'The Bench of Desolation.' " *Nineteenth-Century
Fiction*, 20 (1965), 145-54.
See also 492, 3929, 3935, 3961, 3982, 3986, 3995, 4052, 4058, 4065.

"Benvolio"

3714. TINTNER, ADELINE R. "The Countess and Scholastica:
Henry James's 'L'Allegro' and 'Il Penseroso.' " *Studies in Short
Fiction*, 11 (1974), 267-76.
See also 3946, 3984, 3993, 4023, 4058.

"The Birthplace"

3715. ARMS, GEORGE. "James's 'The Birthplace': Over a Pulpit-
Edge." *Tennessee Studies In Literature*, 8 (1963), 61-69.
3716. HARTSOCK, MILDRED E. "The Conceivable Child: James
and the Poet." *Studies in Short Fiction*, 8 (1971), 569-74.
3717. HOLLERAN, JAMES V. "An Analysis of 'The Birthplace.' "
Papers on Language & Literature, 2 (1966), 76-80.
3718. McMURRAY, WILLIAM. "Reality in Henry James's 'The
Birthplace.' " *The Explicator*, 35, no. 1 (1976), 10-11.
3719. ROSE, MORTON L. "James's *The Birthplace*: A Double Turn
of the Narrative Screw." *Studies in Short Fiction*, 3 (1966), 321-28.
See also 25, 597, 3947, 3974, 3982, 4043, 4054, 4058.

"Broken Wings"

See 3930, 3974, 3982.

"Brooksmith"

3720. DOW, EDDY. "James' 'Brooksmith.' " *The Explicator*, 27
(1969), item 35.
See also 3961, 3974, 4015, 4058.

"A Bundle of Letters"

See 3984.

"The Chaperon"

See 3937, 4023.

"Collaboration"

See 3917.

"Covering End"

See 3952, 3982.

"The Coxon Fund"

See 3924, 3961, 3981, 4023, 4043.

"Crapy Cornelia"

3721. PURDY, STROTHER B. "Language as Art: The Ways of Knowing in Henry James's 'Crapy Cornelia.'" *Style*, 1 (1967), 139–49.
3722. TINTNER, ADELINE R. "Henry James at the Movies: Cinematograph and Photograph in 'Crapy Cornelia.'" *The Markham Review*, 6 (Fall 1976), 1–8.
See also 3933, 3961, 3982, 3986, 4008, 4023, 4032, 4051, 4052.

"Daisy Miller: A Study"

3723. CANADAY, NICHOLAS, JR. "Portrait of Daisy: Studies by James and Fitzgerald." *Forum* (University of Houston), 4, no. 10 (1966), 17–20.
3724. DAVIDSON, CATHY N. "'Circumsexualocution' in Henry James's *Daisy Miller*." *The Arizona Quarterly*, 32 (1976), 353–66.
3725. DEAKIN, MOTLEY F. "Daisy Miller, Tradition, and the European Heroine." *Comparative Literature Studies*, 6 (1969), 45–59.
3726. DRAPER, R. P. "Death of a Hero? Winterbourne and Daisy Miller." *Studies in Short Fiction*, 6 (1969), 601–08.
3727. GARGANO, JAMES W. "*Daisy Miller*: An Abortive Quest for Innocence." *The South Atlantic Quarterly*, 59 (1960), 114–20.
3728. GRANT, WILLIAM E. "'Daisy Miller': A Study of a Study." *Studies in Short Fiction*, 11 (1974), 17–25.
3729. HIRSCH, DAVID H. "William Dean Howells and Daisy Miller." *English Language Notes*, 1 (1963), 123–28.
3730. HOUGHTON, DONALD E. "Attitude and Illness in James' 'Daisy Miller.'" *Literature and Psychology*, 19 (1969), 51–60.
3731. KENNEDY, IAN. "Frederick Winterbourne: The Good Bad Boy in *Daisy Miller*." *The Arizona Quarterly*, 29 (1973), 139–50.

3732. **McCarthy, Harold T.** "Henry James and the American Aristocracy." *American Literary Realism, 1870–1910*, 4 (1971), 61–71.

3733. **Monteiro, George.** "'Girlhood on the American Plan'— A Contemporary Defense of *Daisy Miller*." *Books at Brown*, 19 (1963), 89–93.

3734. ———. "Henry James and Scott Fitzgerald: A Source." *Notes on Contemporary Literature*, 6, no. 2 (1976), 4–6.

3735. **Murray, D. M.** "Candy Christian as a Pop-Art Daisy Miller." *Journal of Popular Culture*, 5 (1971), 340–48.

3736. **Ohmann, Carol.** "*Daisy Miller*: A Study of Changing Intentions." *American Literature*, 36 (1964), 1–11.

3737. **Petty, George R., Jr., and William M. Gibson.** *Project OCCULT: The Ordered Computer Collation of Unprepared Literary Text*. New York: New York Univ. Press, 1970.

3738. **Randall, John H., III.** "The Genteel Reader and *Daisy Miller*." *American Quarterly*, 17 (1965), 568–81.

3739. **Shriber, Michael.** "Cognitive Apparatus in *Daisy Miller*, *The Ambassadors*, and Two Works by Howells: A Comparative Study of the Epistemology of Henry James." *Language and Style*, 2 (1969), 207–25.

3740. **Tanner, Tony.** "The Literary Children of James and Clemens." *Nineteenth-Century Fiction*, 16 (1961), 205–18.

3741. **Vann, Barbara.** "A Psychological Interpretation of *Daisy Miller*." In *A Festschrift for Professor Marguerite Roberts, on the Occasion of Her Retirement from Westhampton College, University of Richmond, Virginia*. Ed. Frieda Elaine Penninger. Richmond, VA: Univ. of Richmond, 1976. pp. 205–08.

3742. **Walker, Cheryl.** "The Energy of Fear in Henry James." In *Modern Occasions 2*. Ed. Philip Rahv. Port Washington, NY: Kennikat, 1974. pp. 153–76.

3743. **Wood, Ann.** "Reconsideration: *Daisy Miller*." *The New Republic*, 167, nos. 24–25 (1972), 31–33.

3744. **Wood, Carl.** "Frederick Winterbourne, James's Prisoner of Chillon." *Studies in the Novel*, 9 (1977), 33–45.

See also 28, 37, 53, 315, 389, 422, 454, 597, 604, 3919, 3932, 3943, 3944, 3946, 3950, 3961, 3963, 3970, 3980–3982, 3984, 3991, 3994, 3995, 4004, 4009, 4016, 4027, 4032, 4035, 4043.

"A Day of Days"

See 3982, 3984.

"The Death of the Lion"

3745. **Hoag, Gerald.** "The Death of the Paper Lion." *Studies in Short Fiction*, 12 (1975), 163–72.

3746. **KIRBY, DAVID. K.** "Possible Source for James's 'The Death of the Lion.'" *Colby Library Quarterly*, 10 (1973), 39–40.

3747. **MACK, STANLEY THOMAS.** "The Narrator in James's 'The Death of the Lion': A Religious Conversion of Sorts." *Thoth*, 16, no. 1 (1976), 19–25.

3748. **NICHOLAS, CHARLES A.** "A Second Glance at Henry James's 'The Death of the Lion.'" *Studies in Short Fiction*, 9 (1972), 143–46.

See also 315, 3924, 3961, 3974, 3975, 4023, 4032, 4058, 4061.

"De Grey: A Romance"

3749. **TYTELL, JOHN.** "Henry James and the Romance." *The Markham Review*, 1, no. 5 (1969), 1–2.

See also 3933.

"The Diary of a Man of Fifty"

See 3965, 3984, 4004, 4016.

"Eugene Pickering"

See 3982, 3984, 4016, 4023.

" 'Europe' "

3750. **HUDSPETH, ROBERT N.** "A Hard, Shining Sonnet: The Art of Short Fiction in James's 'Europe.' " *Studies in Short Fiction*, 12 (1975), 387–95.

See also 377, 456, 3933, 3981, 4058.

"The Figure in the Carpet"

3751. **BOLAND, DOROTHY M.** "Henry James's 'The Figure in the Carpet': A Fabric of the East." *Papers on Language & Literature*, 13 (1977), 424–29.

3752. **FINCH, G. A.** "A Retreading of James' Carpet." *Twentieth Century Literature*, 14 (1968), 98–101.

3753. **GOSSMAN, ANN.** "Operative Irony in 'The Figure in the Carpet.' " *Descant*, 6, no. 3 (1962), 20–25.

3754. **KANZER, MARK.** "The Figure in the Carpet." *American Imago*, 17 (1960), 339–48.

3755. **LAINOFF, SEYMOUR.** "Henry James' 'The Figure in the Carpet': What is Critical Responsiveness?" *Boston University Studies in English*, 5 (1961), 122–28.

3756. **LEVY, LEO B.** "A Reading of 'The Figure in the Carpet.' " *American Literature*, 33 (1962), 457–65.

3757. **POWERS, LYALL H.** "A Reperusal of James's 'The Figure in the Carpet.' " *American Literature*, 33 (1961), 224–28.

3758. **RECCHIA, EDWARD.** "James's 'The Figure in the Carpet':
The Quality of Fictional Experience." *Studies in Short Fiction*, 10
(1973), 357–65.
3759. **RIMMON, SHLOMITH.** "Barthes' 'Hermeneutic Code' and
Henry James's Literary Detective: Plot-Composition in 'The
Figure in the Carpet.' " *The Hebrew University Studies in Literature*, 1 (1973), 183–207.
See also 3927, 3949, 3961, 3974, 3982, 3987, 4001, 4017, 4023, 4025,
4043, 4054, 4058, 4061.

"Flickerbridge"

See 3982, 4032, 4037, 4056.

"Fordham Castle"

See 3981, 4023, 4058.

"Four Meetings"

3760. **AZIZ, MAQBOOL.** " 'Four Meetings': A Caveat for James
Critics." *Essays in Criticism*, 18 (1968), 258–74. Also see "Corri-
genda," *Essays in Criticism*, 19 (1969), 105.
3761. **GRIFFIN, ROBERT J.** "Notes toward an Exegesis: 'Four
Meetings.' " *The University of Kansas City Review*, 29 (1962),
45–49.
3762. **GURKO, LEO.** "The Missing Word in Henry James's 'Four
Meetings.' " *Studies in Short Fiction*, 7 (1970), 298–307.
3763. **JONES, LEONIDAS M.** "James' 'Four Meetings.' " *The Explicator*, 20 (1962), item 55.
3764. **TARTELLA, VINCENT.** "James's 'Four Meetings': Two
Texts Compared." *Nineteenth-Century Fiction*, 15 (1960), 17–28.
3765. **VANDERBILT, KERMIT.** "Notes Largely Musical on Henry
James's 'Four Meetings.' " *The Sewanee Review*, 81 (1973), 739–52.
See also 60, 3933, 3937, 3984, 4016, 4017, 4058.

"The Friends of the Friends"

See 3886, 4054.

"Gabrielle de Bergerac"

See 3914, 3941, 3984.

"Georgina's Reasons"

3766. **JONES, GRANVILLE H.** "Henry James's 'Georgina's Rea-
sons': The Underside of Washington Square." *Studies in Short
Fiction*, 11 (1974), 189–94.
See also 3982, 4023.

"The Ghostly Rental"

3767. ANDREACH, ROBERT J. "Literary Allusion as a Clue to Meaning: James's 'The Ghostly Rental' and Pascal's *Pensées*." *Comparative Literature Studies*, 4 (1967), 299–306.
See also 3921, 3933, 3984.

"Glasses"

3768. TINTNER, ADELINE R. "Poe's 'The Spectacles' and James' 'Glasses.' " *Poe Studies*, 9 (1976), 53–54.
3769. ———. "Why James Quoted Gibbon in 'Glasses.' " *Studies in Short Fiction*, 14 (1977), 287–88.
See also 3982.

"The Great Good Place"

3770. HERX, MARY ELLEN. "The Monomyth in 'The Great Good Place.' " *College English*, 24 (1963), 439–43.
3771. McMURRAY, WILLIAM. "Reality in James's 'The Great Good Place.' " *Studies in Short Fiction*, 14 (1977), 82–83.
3772. TINTNER, ADELINE R. "The Influence of Balzac's *L'Envers de L'Histoire Contemporaine* on James's 'The Great Good Place.' " *Studies in Short Fiction*, 9 (1972), 343–51.
See also 3949, 3961, 3974, 3982, 4023, 4038, 4058, 4073.

"Greville Fane"

See 3917, 3974, 3982, 3991, 4023, 4035, 4058.

"Guest's Confession"

See 3933, 3946, 4012.

"The Impressions of a Cousin"

3773. TINTNER, ADELINE R. " 'The Impressions of a Cousin': Henry James' Transformation of *The Marble Faun*." *The Nathaniel Hawthorne Journal 1976*, pp. 205–14.
See also 58, 3933, 3982.

"In the Cage"

3774. ASWELL, E. DUNCAN. "James's *In the Cage*: The Telegraphist as Artist." *Texas Studies in Literature and Language*, 8 (1966), 375–84.
3775. BLACKALL, JEAN FRANTZ. "James's *In the Cage*: An Approach through Figurative Language." *University of Toronto Quarterly*, 31 (1962), 164–79.
3776. FRANTZ, JEAN H. "Henry James and Saintine." *Notes and Queries*, NS 7 (1960), 266–68.

3777. **NORRMAN, RALF.** "The Intercepted Telegram Plot in Henry James's 'In the Cage.' " *Notes & Queries*, NS 24 (1977), 425–27.

3778. **STONE, WILLIAM B.** "On the Background of James's *In the Cage.*" *American Literary Realism, 1870–1910*, 6 (1973), 243–47.

3779. **WIESENFARTH, JOSEPH.** "The Dramatic Novel: Its Qualities and Elements." In *Henry James and the Dramatic Analogy: A Study of the Major Novels of the Middle Period.* New York: Fordham Univ. Press, 1963. pp. 1–43.

See also 589, 3801, 3886, 3941, 3949, 3950, 3982, 4014, 4027, 4035, 4036, 4054, 4065, 4073.

"An International Episode"

See 28, 3933, 3981, 3982, 3984, 3991, 4017, 4023.

"The Jolly Corner"

3780. **FREEDMAN, WILLIAM A.** "Universality in 'The Jolly Corner.' " *Texas Studies in Literature and Language*, 4 (1962), 12–15.

3781. **GRENANDER, M. E.** "Benjamin Franklin's Glass Armonica and Henry James's 'Jolly Corner.' " *Papers on Language & Literature*, 11 (1975), 415–17.

3782. **HENKLE, ROGER B.** "Narration and Point of View: Distrust the Teller and, Sometimes, the Tale." In *Reading the Novel: An Introduction to the Techniques of Interpreting Fiction.* New York: Harper & Row, 1977. pp. 65–85.

3783. **JOHNSON, COURTNEY.** "Henry James' 'The Jolly Corner': A Study in Integration." *American Imago*, 24 (1967), 344–59.

3784. **ROGERS, ROBERT.** "The Beast in Henry James." *American Imago*, 13 (1956), 427–54.

3785. **ROSENBLATT, JASON P.** "Bridegroom and Bride in 'The Jolly Corner.' " *Studies in Short Fiction*, 14 (1977), 282–84.

3786. **ROVIT, EARL.** "The Ghosts in James's 'The Jolly Corner.' " *Tennessee Studies In Literature*, 10 (1965), 65–72.

3787. **SMITH, HENRY NASH.** "On Henry James and 'The Jolly Corner.' " In *The American Short Story.* Ed. Calvin Skaggs. New York: Dell, 1977. pp. 122–27.

3788. **STEIN, ALLEN F.** "The Beast in 'The Jolly Corner': Spencer Brydon's Ironic Rebirth." *Studies in Short Fiction*, 11 (1974), 61–66.

3789. **THOMSON, FRED C.** "James' 'The Jolly Corner.' " *The Explicator*, 22 (1963), item 28.

3790. **TRAVIS, MILDRED K.** "Hawthorne's 'Egotism' and 'The Jolly Corner.' " *ESQ*, no. 63 (1971), pp. 13–18.

3791. **Tuveson, Ernest.** " 'The Jolly Corner': A Fable of Redemption." *Studies in Short Fiction*, 12 (1975), 271–80.
See also 267, 377, 610, 2016, 3919, 3921, 3933, 3935, 3937, 3947, 3961, 3972, 3982, 3986, 3996, 3997, 4007, 4022, 4023, 4028, 4032, 4034, 4037, 4048, 4051, 4055, 4056, 4058, 4073.

"Julia Bride"

3792. **Menikoff, Barry.** "The Subjective Pronoun in the Late Style of Henry James." *English Studies*, 52 (1971), 436–41.
See also 3932, 3933, 3982, 4008, 4023, 4051, 4069.

"Lady Barberina"

See 3961, 3975, 4023, 4031.

"A Landscape Painter"

See 3933, 4012.

"The Last of the Valerii"

See 3933, 3946, 4004, 4023, 4056.

"The Lesson of the Master"

3793. **Monteiro, George.** "Henry James and the Lessons of Sordello." *Western Humanities Review*, 31 (1977), 69–78.
3794. **Smith, Charles R.** " 'The Lesson of the Master': An Interpretative Note." *Studies in Short Fiction*, 6 (1969), 654–58.
3795. **Tintner, Adeline R.** "Iconic Analogy in 'The Lesson of the Master': Henry James's Legend of Saint George and the Dragon." *The Journal of Narrative Technique*, 5 (1975), 116–27.
See also 267, 356, 3961, 3964, 3974, 3982, 3996, 4001, 4025, 4031, 4059, 4073.

"The Liar"

3796. **Powers, Lyall H.** "Henry James and the Ethics of the Artist: 'The Real Thing' and 'The Liar.' " *Texas Studies in Literature and Language*, 3 (1961), 360–68.
See also 389, 597, 3996, 4002, 4023, 4031, 4043, 4073.

"A Light Man"

3797. **Fish, Charles K.** "Description in Henry James' 'A Light Man.' " *English Language Notes*, 2 (1965), 211–15.
See also 3982, 3984, 3993, 4012.

"A London Life"

See 3937, 3962, 3964, 4027, 4032, 4035, 4042.

"Lord Beaupre"

See 3982.

"Louisa Pallant"

3798. NICOLOFF, PHILLIP L. "At the Bottom of All Things in Henry James's 'Louisa Pallant.' " *Studies in Short Fiction,* 7 (1970), 409–20.
See also 3965, 4073.

"Mme. de Mauves"

3799. BOURAOUI, H. A. "Henry James and the French Mind: The International Theme in 'Madame de Mauves.' " *Novel,* 4 (1970), 69–76.
3800. HOCHMAN, BARUCH. "The Jamesian Spectacle: World as Spectacle." *The University of Denver Quarterly,* 11, no. 1 (1976), 48–66.
3801. INGLIS, TONY. "Reading Late James." In *The Modern English Novel: The Reader, the Writer, and the Work.* Ed. Gabriel Josipovici. London: Open Books, 1976. pp. 77–94.
3802. KAPLAN, CHARLES. "James' 'Madame de Mauves.' " *The Explicator,* 19 (1961), item 32.
3803. KIRKHAM, E. BRUCE. "A Study of Henry James' 'Mdme. de Mauves.' " *Ball State University Forum,* 12, no. 2 (1971), 63–69.
3804. KRAFT, JAMES. " 'Madame de Mauves' and *Roderick Hudson*: The Development of James's International Style." *The Texas Quarterly,* 11, no. 3 (1968), 143–60.
3805. MCLEAN, ROBERT C. "The Completed Vision: A Study of *Madame de Mauves* and *The Ambassadors.*" *Modern Language Quarterly,* 28 (1967), 446–61.
3806. PATTERSON, REBECCA. "Two Portraits of a Lady." *The Midwest Quarterly,* 1 (1960), 343–61.
3807. ROUNTREE, BENJAMIN C. "James's Madame de Mauves and Madame de la Fayette's Princess de Clèves." *Studies in Short Fiction,* 1 (1964), 264–71.
3808. SIMON, JOHN KENNETH. "A Study of Classical Gesture: Henry James and Madame de Lafayette." *Comparative Literature Studies,* 3 (1966), 273–83.
3809. WARD, J. A. "Structural Irony in *Madame de Mauves.*" *Studies in Short Fiction,* 2 (1965), 170–82.
See also 377, 3941, 3946, 3963, 3966, 3980–3982, 3984, 3993, 3995, 4023, 4027, 4031, 4042, 4058, 4067.

"The Madonna of the Future"

See 3946, 3964, 3974, 3980, 3993, 4004, 4017, 4018, 4058, 4072.

"The Marriages"

3810. **KRAMER, DALE AND CHERIS.** "James's 'The Marriages': Designs of Structure." *The University Review* (Kansas City), 33 (1966), 75–80.
See also 3982, 4023, 4033.

"Master Eustace"

See 4035.

"Maud-Evelyn"

3811. **D'AVANZO, MARIO L.** "James's 'Maud-Evelyn': Source, Allusion, and Meaning." *Iowa English Yearbook*, 13 (1968), 24–33.
3812. **SANTANGELO, GENNARO A.** "Henry James's 'Maud-Evelyn' and the Web of Consciousness." *Amerikastudien/American Studies*, 20 (1975), 45–54.
See also 4054, 4073.

"The Middle Years"

3813. **BABIN, JAMES L.** "Henry James's 'Middle Years' in Fiction and Autobiography." *The Southern Review*, NS 13 (1977), 505–17.
3814. **GALE, ROBERT L.** "James' 'The Middle Years,' II." *The Explicator*, 22 (1963), item 22.
See also 356, 3843, 3961, 3974, 3996, 4023, 4043, 4058.

"Miss Gunton of Poughkeepsie"

See 4004.

"The Modern Warning"

See 108, 3982.

"Mora Montravers"

See 3982, 3986, 4052, 4073.

"A Most Extraordinary Case"

See 3984, 4040, 4073.

"A New England Winter"

See 3933, 3964, 3982.

"The Next Time"

3815. **GALE, ROBERT L.** "James' 'The Next Time.' " *The Explicator*, 21 (1962), item 35.
See also 25, 389, 3924, 3974, 4023, 4037, 4058, 4059, 4061.

"Nona Vincent"

See 4032.

"Osborne's Revenge"

See 4035.

"Owen Wingrave"

See 3949.

"Pandora"

3816. GALE, ROBERT L. " 'Pandora' and Her President." *Studies in Short Fiction*, 1 (1964), 222–24.
3817. VANDERSEE, CHARLES. "James's 'Pandora': The Mixed Consequences of Revision." *Studies in Bibliography*, 21 (1968), 93–108.
See also 3933, 3996, 4023, 4035.

"The Papers"

See 3982, 4023.

"A Passionate Pilgrim"

See 3915, 3933, 3946, 3961, 3962, 3980, 3982, 3984, 3993, 3996, 3998, 4031, 4058, 4073.

"Paste"

3818. KNIEGER, BERNARD. "James's 'Paste.' " *Studies in Short Fiction*, 8 (1971), 468–69.
3819. SEGNITZ, T. M. "The Actual Genesis of Henry James's 'Paste.' " *American Literature*, 36 (1964), 216–19.
See also 356.

"The Patagonia"

3820. LABRIE, ROSS. "Henry James' Idea of Consciousness." *American Literature*, 39 (1968), 517–29.
See also 4023.

"The Pension Beaurepas"

See 3981, 3984, 3991, 4023.

"The Point of View"

3821. MONTEIRO, GEORGE. "The New York *Tribune* on Henry James, 1881–1882." *Bulletin of The New York Public Library*, 67 (1973), 71–81.
3822. WATSON, CHARLES N., JR. "The Comedy of Provincialism: James's 'The Point of View.' " *Southern Humanities Review*, 9 (1975), 173–83.
See also 3933, 3961, 3981, 3988, 4023, 4035, 4042.

"Poor Richard"

See 3933, 3984, 4012.

"The Private Life"

3823. **BARGAINNIER, EARL F.** "Browning, James, and 'The Private Life.' " *Studies in Short Fiction*, 14 (1977), 151–58.
See also 3917, 3980, 4054.

"Professor Fargo"

See 3921, 3933, 3982, 3993.

"The Pupil"

3824. **CANAVAN, THOMAS L.** "The Economics of Disease in James's 'The Pupil.' " *Criticism*, 15 (1973), 253–64.

3825. **CUMMINS, ELIZABETH.** " 'The Playroom of Superstition': An Analysis of Henry James's *The Pupil.*" *The Markham Review*, 2, no. 3 (1970), 53–56.

3826. **GRIFFITH, JOHN.** "James's 'The Pupil' as Whodunit: The Question of Moral Responsibility." *Studies in Short Fiction*, 9 (1972), 257–68.

3827. **HAGOPIAN, JOHN V.** "Seeing Through 'The Pupil' Again." *Modern Fiction Studies*, 5 (1959), 169–71.

3828. **HOWE, IRVING.** "The Pupil." In *Shoptalk—An Instructor's Manual for* "Classics of Modern Fiction: Eight Short Novels." New York: Harcourt, Brace & World, 1968. pp. 9–11.

3829. **KENNEY, WILLIAM.** "The Death of Morgan in James's 'The Pupil.' " *Studies in Short Fiction*, 8 (1971), 317–22.

3830. **LAINOFF, SEYMOUR.** "A Note on Henry James's 'The Pupil.' " *Nineteenth-Century Fiction*, 14 (1959), 75–77.

3831. **MARTIN, TERENCE.** "James's 'The Pupil': The Art of Seeing Through." *Modern Fiction Studies*, 4 (1958), 335–45.

3832. **RUCKER, MARY E.** "James's 'The Pupil': The Question of Moral Ambiguity." *The Arizona Quarterly*, 32 (1976), 301–15.

3833. **SNOW, LOTUS.** "Some Stray Fragrance of an Ideal: Henry James's Imagery for Youth's Discovery of Evil." *Harvard Library Bulletin*, 14 (1960), 107–25.

3834. **STEIN, WILLIAM BYSSHE.** " 'The Pupil': The Education of a Prude." *The Arizona Quarterly*, 15 (1959), 13–22.

See also 25, 37, 315, 595, 3949, 3950, 3961, 3976, 3981, 3982, 3996, 4013, 4017, 4027, 4035, 4043, 4058, 4073.

"The Real Thing"

3835. **BERKELMAN, ROBERT.** "Henry James and 'The Real Thing.' " *The University of Kansas City Review*, 26 (1959), 93–95.

3836. **BERNARD, KENNETH.** "The Real Thing in James's 'The Real Thing.' " *Brigham Young University Studies*, 5 (1962), 31–32.

3837. **FARNSWORTH, ROBERT M.** "The Real and the Exquisite in James's 'The Real Thing.' " *The Literary Criterion*, 7, no. 4 (1967), 29–31.

3838. **GALE, ROBERT L.** "H. J.'s J. H. in 'The Real Thing.' " *Studies in Short Fiction*, 14 (1977), 396–98.

3839. _____. "A Note on Henry James's 'The Real Thing.' " *Studies in Short Fiction*, 1 (1963), 65–66.

3840. **HORNE, HELEN.** "Henry James: *The Real Thing* (1890)—An Attempt at Interpretation." *Die Neueren Sprachen*, 58 (1959), 214–19.

3841. **KEHLER, HAROLD.** "James' 'The Real Thing.' " *The Explicator*, 25 (1967), item 79.

3842. **LABOR, EARLE.** "James's 'The Real Thing': Three Levels of Meaning." *College English*, 23 (1962), 376–78.

3843. **LYCETTE, RONALD L.** "Perceptual Touchstones for the Jamesian Artist-Hero." *Studies in Short Fiction*, 14 (1977), 55–62.

3844. **LYON, RICHARD C.** "Santayana and the Real Thing." *Shenandoah*, 17, no. 3 (1966), 41–60.

3845. **MUELLER, LAVONNE.** "Henry James: The Phenomenal Self as the 'Real Thing.' " *Forum* (University of Houston), 6, no. 2 (1968), 46–50.

3846. **SUNDELL, ROGER H.** "The Real Thing." In *Instructor's Manual for* "The Art of Fiction," Second Edition. Ed. R. F. Dietrich and Roger H. Sundell. New York: Holt, Rinehart and Winston, 1974. pp. 6–12.

3847. **TOOR, DAVID.** "Narrative Irony in Henry James' 'The Real Thing.' " *The University Review* (Kansas City), 34 (1967), 95–99.

3848. **UROFF, M. D.** "Perception in James's 'The Real Thing.' " *Studies in Short Fiction*, 9 (1972), 41–46.

See also 53, 157, 384, 481, 492, 493, 511, 565, 597, 599, 3796, 3917, 3941, 3972, 3974, 3980, 4017, 4023, 4054, 4072.

"A Romance of Certain Old Clothes"

See 3933, 3996.

"Rose-Agathe"

See 3941, 3982.

"A Round of Visits"

3849. **CHAPMAN, SARA S.** "The 'Obsession of Egotism' in Henry James's 'A Round of Visits.' " *The Arizona Quarterly*, 29 (1973), 130–38.

3850. **PURDY, STROTHER B.** "Conversation and Awareness in Henry James's 'A Round of Visits.' " *Studies in Short Fiction*, 6 (1969), 421–32.
See also 377, 3933, 3986, 4007, 4051, 4052, 4065.

"The Siege of London"

3851. **HABEGGER, ALFRED.** " 'The Seige of London': Henry James and the *Pièce Bien Faite.*" *Modern Fiction Studies*, 15 (1969), 219–30.
See also 3941, 4023, 4027, 4042.

"Sir Dominick Ferrand"

See 3917, 4054.

"Sir Edmund Orme"

See 3921, 4054.

"The Solution"

See 3982, 4004.

"The Special Type"

See 3998.

"The Story In It"

3852. **GARGANO, JAMES W.** "James's Stories in 'The Story In It.' " *Notes on Modern American Literature*, 1 (1976), item 2.
See also 3974, 3982.

"The Story of a Masterpiece"

3853. **FISH, CHARLES K.** "Indirection, Irony, and the Two Endings of James's 'The Story of a Masterpiece.' " *Modern Philology*, 62 (1965), 241–43.
See also 3933, 3984, 4002.

"The Story of a Year"

See 3933, 3984, 3993.

"The Third Person"

See 4043.

"The Tone of Time"

See 267, 3974, 3998.

"A Tragedy of Error"

See 3941, 4035, 4058.

"Travelling Companions"

See 107, 3993, 4004.

"The Tree of Knowledge"

3854. **BELLMAN, SAMUEL IRVING.** "Henry James's 'The Tree of Knowledge': A Biblical Parallel." *Studies in Short Fiction*, 1 (1964), 226–28.

3855. **TRUSS, TOM J., JR.** "Anti-Christian Myth in James's *The Tree of Knowledge.*" *The University of Mississippi Studies in English*, 6 (1965), 1–4.

See also 399, 3974.

"The Turn of the Screw"

3856. **ALDRICH, C. KNIGHT, M.D.** "Another Twist to *The Turn of the Screw.*" *Modern Fiction Studies*, 13 (1967), 167–78.

3857. **ALLEN, JEANNE THOMAS.** "*Turn of the Screw* and *The Innocents*: Two Types of Ambiguity." In *The Classic American Novel and the Movies.* Ed. Gerald Peary and Roger Shatzkin. New York: Ungar, 1977. pp. 132–42.

3858. **ALLOTT, MIRIAM.** "Mrs. Gaskell's 'The Old Nurse's Story': A Link between 'Wuthering Heights' and 'The Turn of the Screw.'" *Notes and Queries*, NS 8 (1961), 101–02.

3859. **ANON.** "The Lesson of the Master." *The Times* (London) *Literary Supplement*, 19 Jan. 1962, p. 44.

3860. **ARMSTRONG, NANCY.** "Character, Closure, and Impressionist Fiction." *Criticism*, 19 (1977), 317–37.

3861. **ASWELL, E. DUNCAN.** "Reflections of a Governess: Image and Distortion in *The Turn of the Screw.*" *Nineteenth-Century Fiction*, 23 (1968), 49–63.

3862. **BEIT-HALLAHMI, BENJAMIN.** "*The Turn of the Screw* and *The Exorcist*: Demoniacal Possession and Childhood Purity." *American Imago*, 33 (1976), 296–303.

3863. **BYERS, JOHN R., JR.** "*The Turn of the Screw*: A Hellish Point of View." *The Markham Review*, 2 (1971), 101–04.

3864. **CARGILL, OSCAR.** "*The Turn of the Screw* and Alice James." *PMLA*, 78 (1963), 238–49.

3865. **CRANFILL, THOMAS MABRY, AND ROBERT LANIER CLARK, JR.** *An Anatomy of* The Turn of the Screw. Austin: Univ. of Texas Press, 1965.

3866. ———, AND ———. "Caste in James's *The Turn of the Screw.*" *Texas Studies in Literature and Language*, 5 (1963), 189–98.

3867. ———, AND ———. "James's Revisions of *The Turn of the Screw.*" *Nineteenth-Century Fiction*, 19 (1965), 394–98.

3868. ———, AND ———. "The Provocativeness of *The Turn of the Screw*." *Texas Studies in Literature and Language*, 12 (1970), 93–100.

3869. CROWL, SUSAN. "Aesthetic Allegory in 'The Turn of the Screw.' " *Novel*, 4 (1971), 107–22.

3870. DE BELLIS, JACK. "Andrew Lytle's *A Name for Evil*: A Transformation of *The Turn of the Screw*." *Critique*, 8, no. 3 (1966), 26–40.

3871. DOMANIECKI, HILDEGARD. "Complementary Terms in *The Turn of the Screw*: The Straight Turning." *Jahrbuch für Amerikastudien*, 10 (1965), 206–14.

3872. FEINSTEIN, HERBERT. "Two Pairs of Gloves: Mark Twain and Henry James." *American Imago*, 17 (1960), 349–87.

3873. FEUERLICHT, IGNACE. " 'Erlkönig' and *The Turn of the Screw*." *Journal of English and Germanic Philology*, 58 (1959), 68–74.

3874. FRASER, JOHN. "*The Turn of the Screw* Again." *The Midwest Quarterly*, 7 (1966), 327–36.

3875. GARGANO, JAMES W. "*The Turn of the Screw*." *Western Humanities Review*, 15 (1961), 173–79.

3876. GARRETT, PETER K. "Henry James: The Creations of Consciousness." In *Scene and Symbol from George Eliot to James Joyce: Studies in Changing Fictional Mode*. New Haven, CT: Yale Univ. Press, 1969. pp. 76–159.

3877. HALLAB, MARY Y. "*The Turn of the Screw* Squared." *The Southern Review*, NS 13 (1977), 492–504.

3878. HEILMAN, ROBERT B. "The Lure of the Demonic: James and Dürrenmatt." *Comparative Literature*, 13 (1961), 346–57.

3879. HOUSTON, NEAL B. "A Footnote on the Death of Miles." *RE: Artes Liberales*, 3, no. 2 (1977), 25–27.

3880. HUNTLEY, H. ROBERT. "James' *The Turn of the Screw*: Its 'Fine Machinery.' " *American Imago*, 34 (1977), 224–37.

3881. IVES, C. B. "James's Ghosts in *The Turn of the Screw*." *Nineteenth-Century Fiction*, 18 (1963), 183–89.

3882. JONES, ALEXANDER E. "Point of View in *The Turn of the Screw*." *PMLA*, 74 (1959), 112–22.

3883. KIRBY, DAVID K. "Two Modern Versions of the Quest." *Southern Humanities Review*, 5 (1971), 387–95.

3884. KROOK, DOROTHEA. "Intentions and Intentions: The Problem of Intention and Henry James's 'The Turn of the Screw.' " In *The Theory of the Novel: New Essays*. Ed. John Halperin. New York: Oxford Univ. Press, 1974. pp. 353–72.

3885. LANG, HANS-JOACHIM. "The Turns in *The Turn of the Screw*." *Jahrbuch für Amerikastudien*, 9 (1964), 110–28.

3886.　LIND, SIDNEY E. " 'The Turn of the Screw': The Torment of Critics." *The Centennial Review*, 14 (1970), 225–40.

3887.　LYDENBERG, JOHN. "Comment on Mr. Spilka's Paper." *Literature and Psychology*, 14 (1964), 6–8.

3888.　McMASTER, JULIET. " 'The Full Image of a Repetition' in *The Turn of the Screw.*" *Studies in Short Fiction*, 6 (1969), 377–82.

3889.　MACKENZIE, MANFRED. "*The Turn of the Screw*: Jamesian Gothic." *Essays in Criticism*, 12 (1962), 34–38.

3890.　MacNAUGHTON, W. R. "Turning the Screw of Ordinary Human Virtue: The Governess and the First-Person Narrators." *The Canadian Review of American Studies*, 5 (1974), 18–25.

3891.　MOGAN, DAVID. "Agonies of Innocence: The Governess and Maggie Verver." *American Literary Realism, 1870–1910*, 9 (1976), 231–42.

3892.　NORTON, RICTOR. "*The Turn of the Screw*: Coincidentia Oppositorum." *American Imago*, 28 (1971), 373–90.

3893.　PURTON, VALERIE. "James' 'The Turn of the Screw,' Chapter 9." *The Explicator*, 34 (1975), item 24.

3894.　RADHA, K. "*The Turn of the Screw*: A Critical Examination of Its Meaning." In *Literary Studies: Homage to Dr. A. Sivaramasubramonia Aiyer*. Ed. K. P. K. Menon, M. Manuel, and K. Ayyappa Paniker. Trivandrum: Dr. A. Sivaramasubramonia Aiyer Memorial Committee, 1973. pp. 103–11.

3895.　RUBIN, LOUIS D., JR. "One More Turn of the Screw." *Modern Fiction Studies*, 9 (1963), 314–28.

3896.　_____. *The Teller in the Tale*. Seattle: Univ. of Washington Press, 1967.

3897.　SAMUELS, CHARLES THOMAS. "Giovanni and the Governess." *The American Scholar*, 37 (1968), 655–56, 658, 660, 662, 664, 666, 668–70, 672, 674, 678.

3898.　SHEPPARD, E. A. *Henry James and* The Turn of the Screw. Auckland, New Zealand: Auckland Univ. Press, 1974.

3899.　SIEGEL, ELI. *James and the Children: A Consideration of Henry James's* The Turn of the Screw. New York: Definition Press, 1968.

3900.　SIEGEL, PAUL N. " 'Miss Jessel': Mirror Image of the Governess." *Literature and Psychology*, 18 (1968), 30–38.

3901.　SLABEY, ROBERT M. " 'The Holy Innocents' and *The Turn of the Screw.*" *Die Neueren Sprachen*, 62 (1963), 170–73.

3902.　_____. " 'The Turn of the Screw': Grammar and Optics." *CLA Journal*, 9 (1965), 68–72.

3903.　SOLOMON, ERIC. "The Return of the Screw." *The University Review* (Kansas City), 30 (1964), 205–11.

3904. S[PILKA], M[ARK]. "Mr. Spilka's Reply." *Literature and Psychology*, 14 (1964), 8, 34.

3905. _____. "Turning the Freudian Screw: How Not To Do It." *Literature and Psychology*, 13 (1963), 105–11.

3906. TRACHTENBERG, STANLEY. "The Return of the Screw." *Modern Fiction Studies*, 11 (1965), 180–82.

3907. VOEGELIN, ERIC. "*The Turn of the Screw.*" With a note by Donald E. Stanford and a foreword by Robert B. Heilman. *The Southern Review*, NS 7 (1971), 3–48.

3908. WEST, MURIEL. "The Death of Miles in *The Turn of the Screw.*" *PMLA*, 79 (1964), 283–88.

3909. _____. *A Stormy Night with* The Turn of the Screw. Phoenix, AZ: Frye & Smith, 1964.

3910. WILLEN, GERALD. "Preface to the Second Edition." In *A Casebook on Henry James's* The Turn of the Screw. 2nd ed. New York: Crowell, 1969. pp. v–ix.

3911. YU, FREDERICK YEH-WEI. "Andrew Lytle's *A Name for Evil* as a Redaction of 'The Turn of the Screw.'" *The Michigan Quarterly Review*, 11 (1972), 186–90.

3912. ZIMMERMAN, EVERETT. "Literary Tradition and 'The Turn of the Screw.'" *Studies in Short Fiction*, 7 (1970), 634–37.

See also 81, 376, 389, 597, 3667, 3784, 3919, 3921, 3931, 3937, 3943, 3944, 3949–3952, 3961, 3969, 3972, 3982, 3983, 3985, 3986, 3995, 3996, 4001, 4010, 4013–4015, 4017, 4022, 4023, 4025, 4027, 4032, 4035, 4036, 4044, 4054, 4058, 4065, 4066, 4073, 4084, 5323.

"The Velvet Glove"

3913. STEIN, ALLEN F. "The Hack's Progress: A Reading of James's 'The Velvet Glove.'" *Essays in Literature* (Western Illinois University), 1 (1974), 219–26.

See also 3941, 3947, 3982, 3986, 4008, 4023, 4050, 4052, 4054.

"The Way It Came"

See 4073.

"The Wheel of Time"

See 3948.

General Studies

3914. ADAMS, PERCY G. "Young Henry James and the Lesson of His Master Balzac." *Revue de Littérature Comparée*, 35 (1961), 458–67.

3915. **ALTENBERND, LYNN.** "A Dispassionate Pilgrim: Henry James's Early Travel in Sketch and Story." *Exploration*, 5, no. 1 (1977), 1–14.

3916. **ANDERSON, CHARLES R.** "A Henry James Centenary." *The Georgia Review*, 30 (1976), 34–52.

3917. **ASWELL, E. DUNCAN.** "James's Treatment of Artistic Collaboration." *Criticism*, 8 (1966), 180–95.

3918. **AUCHINCLOSS, LOUIS.** "Henry James's Literary Use of His American Tour (1904)." *The South Atlantic Quarterly*, 74 (1975), 45–52.

3919. ———. *Reading Henry James.* Minneapolis: Univ. of Minnesota Press, 1975.

3920. ———. "A Strategy for James Readers." *The Nation*, 190 (1960), 364–67.

3921. **BANTA, MARTHA.** *Henry James and the Occult: The Great Extension.* Bloomington: Indiana Univ. Press, 1972.

3922. ———. "Henry James and the Others." *The New England Quarterly*, 37 (1964), 171–84.

3923. **BASS, EBEN.** "Henry James and the English Country House." *The Markham Review*, 2, no. 2 (1970), 24–30.

3924. ———. "Lemon-Colored Volumes and Henry James." *Studies in Short Fiction*, 1 (1964), 113–22.

3925. **BEACHCROFT, T. O.** "James, Conrad, and the Place of Narrative." In *The English Short Story.* 2 vols. London: Longmans, Green, 1964. II, 14–18.

3926. **BEATTIE, MUNRO.** "Henry James, Novelist." *Dalhousie Review*, 39 (1960), 455–63.

3927. ———. "The Many Marriages of Henry James." In *Patterns of Commitment in American Literature.* Ed. Marston LaFrance. Toronto: Univ. of Toronto Press, 1967. pp. 93–112.

3928. **BELL, MILLICENT.** *Edith Wharton & Henry James: The Story of Their Friendship.* New York: Braziller, 1965.

3929. **BENDER, BERT.** "Henry James's Late Lyric Meditations upon the Mysteries of Fate and Self-Sacrifice." *Genre*, 9 (1976), 247–62.

3930. **BLACKALL, JEAN FRANTZ.** *Jamesian Ambiguity and* The Sacred Fount. Ithaca, NY: Cornell Univ. Press, 1965.

3931. **BROOKS, PETER.** *The Melodramatic Imagination: Balzac, Henry James, Melodrama, and the Mode of Excess.* New Haven, CT: Yale Univ. Press, 1976.

3932. **BUITENHUIS, PETER.** "From *Daisy Miller* to *Julia Bride*: 'A Whole Passage of Intellectual History.' " *American Quarterly*, 11 (1959), 136–46.

3933. _____. *The Grasping Imagination: The American Writings of Henry James*. Toronto: Univ. of Toronto Press, 1970.

3934. BURGESS, C. F. "The Seeds of Art: Henry James's *donnée*." *Literature and Psychology*, 13 (1963), 67–73.

3935. CHAPMAN, SARA S. "Stalking the Beast: Egomania and Redemptive Suffering in James's 'Major Phase.'" *Colby Library Quarterly*, 11 (1975), 50–66.

3936. CHATMAN, SEYMOUR. *The Later Style of Henry James*. Oxford: Basil Blackwell, 1972.

3937. CLAIR, JOHN A. *The Ironic Dimension in the Fiction of Henry James*. Pittsburgh, PA: Duquesne Univ. Press, 1965.

3938. CORNWELL, ETHEL F. "The Jamesian Moment of Experience." In *The "Still Point": Theme and Variations in the Writings of T. S. Eliot, Coleridge, Yeats, Henry James, Virginia Woolf, and D. H. Lawrence*. New Brunswick, NJ: Rutgers Univ. Press, 1962. pp. 126–58.

3939. COY, JAVIER. "A Thematic and Character Approach to Henry James." *Studi Americani*, 21–22 (1976), 109–27.

3940. DEAKIN, MOTLEY F. "The Real and Fictive Quest of Henry James." *Bucknell Review*, 14, no. 2 (1966), 82–97.

3941. DELBAERE-GARANT, JEANNE. *Henry James: The Vision of France*. Paris: Belles Lettres, 1970.

3942. DOYLE, SISTER MARY BENEDICT, S.C.N. "The Unknown and Indefinite in the Novels of Henry James." *Notre Dame English Journal*, 4, no. 1 (1965), 23–37.

3943. DUPEE, FREDERICK W. *Henry James*. Rev. ed. New York: Delta Books, 1965.

3944. EDEL, LEON. *Henry James*. Minneapolis: Univ. of Minnesota Press, 1960.

3945. _____. "Henry James: The Americano-European Legend." *University of Toronto Quarterly*, 36 (1967), 321–34.

3946. _____. *Henry James: The Conquest of London, 1870–1881*. Philadelphia, PA: Lippincott, 1962.

3947. _____. *Henry James: The Master, 1901–1916*. Philadelphia, PA: Lippincott, 1972.

3948. _____. *Henry James: The Middle Years, 1882–1895*. Philadelphia, PA: Lippincott, 1962.

3949. _____. *Henry James: The Treacherous Years, 1895–1901*. Philadelphia, PA: Lippincott, 1969.

3950. _____. "Introduction[s]." In *The Complete Tales of Henry James*. 12 vols. London: Rupert Hart-Davis, 1962–64. I, 7–22; II, 7–11; III, 7–10; IV, 7–11; V, 7–11; VI, 7–12; VII, 7–13; VIII, 7–12; IX, 7–12; X, 7–13; XI, 7–11; XII, 7–11.

3951. _____. "The Point of View." In *The Modern Psychological Novel*. Rev. ed. New York: Grosset & Dunlap, 1964. pp. 35–52.

3952. EGAN, MICHAEL. *Henry James: The Ibsen Years*. London: Vision Press, 1972.

3953. FUSSELL, EDWIN. "Hawthorne, James, and 'The Common Doom.' " *American Quarterly*, 10 (1958), 438–53.

3954. GALE, ROBERT L. *The Caught Image: Figurative Language in the Fiction of Henry James*. Chapel Hill: Univ. of North Carolina Press, 1964.

3955. _____. "Freudian Imagery in James's Fiction." *American Imago*, 11 (1954), 181–90.

3956. _____. "Henry James and Italy." *Nineteenth-Century Fiction*, 14 (1959), 157–70.

3957. _____. "Henry James's Dream Children." *The Arizona Quarterly*, 15 (1959), 56–63.

3958. _____. "Names in James." *Names*, 14 (1966), 83–108.

3959. _____. *Plots and Characters in the Fiction of Henry James*. Hamden, CT: Archon Books, 1965.

3960. GARD, ROGER. "Introduction." In *Henry James: The Critical Heritage*. London: Routledge & Kegan Paul, 1968. pp. 1–18.

3961. GEISMAR, MAXWELL. *Henry James and the Jacobites*. Boston, MA: Houghton Mifflin, 1963.

3962. GILL, RICHARD. "The Great Good Place: Henry James and the Country House." In *Happy Rural Seat: The English Country House and the Literary Imagination*. New Haven, CT: Yale Univ. Press, 1972. pp. 19–93.

3963. GRAHAM, [GEORGE] KENNETH. *Henry James—The Drama of Fulfilment: An Approach to the Novels*. Oxford: Clarendon Press, 1975.

3964. GROVER, PHILIP. *Henry James and the French Novel: A Study in Inspiration*. London: Paul Elek, 1973.

3965. _____. "Henry James and the Theme of the Adventuress." *Revue de Littérature Comparée*, 47 (1973), 586–96.

3966. _____. "Mérimée's Influence on Henry James." *The Modern Language Review*, 63 (1968), 810–17.

3967. HAGEMANN, E. R. " 'Unexpected light in shady places': Henry James and *Life*, 1883–1916." *Western Humanities Review*, 24 (1970), 241–50.

3968. HARTSOCK, MILDRED E. "Henry James and the Cities of the Plain." *Modern Language Quarterly*, 29 (1968), 297–311.

3969. _____. "The Most Valuable Thing: James on Death." *Modern Fiction Studies*, 22 (1977), 507–24.

3970. HINZ, EVELYN J. "Henry James's Names: Tradition, Theory, and Method." *Colby Library Quarterly*, 9 (1972), 557–78.

3971. _____. "The Imagistic Evolution of James's Business-men." *The Canadian Review of American Studies*, 3 (1972), 81–95.

3972. HOCKS, RICHARD A. *Henry James and Pragmatic Thought: A Study in the Relationship between the Philosophy of William James and the Literary Art of Henry James*. Chapel Hill: Univ. of North Carolina Press, 1974.

3973. HOLDER, ALAN. *Three Voyagers in Search of Europe: A Study of Henry James, Ezra Pound, and T. S. Eliot*. Philadelphia: Univ. of Pennsylvania Press, 1966.

3974. HORNE, HELEN. *Basic Ideas of James' Aesthetics as Expressed in the Short Stories concerning Artists and Writers*. Marburg: Erich Mauersberger, 1960.

3975. HORRELL, JOYCE TAYLOE. "A 'Shade of a Special Sense': Henry James and the Art of Naming." *American Literature*, 42 (1970), 203–20.

3976. HORWITZ, B. D. "The Sense of Desolation in Henry James." *Psychocultural Review*, 1 (1977), 466–92.

3977. HYDE, H. MONTGOMERY. *Henry James at Home*. New York: Farrar, Straus & Giroux, 1969.

3978. HYNES, JOSEPH. "The Transparent Shroud: Henry James and William Story." *American Literature*, 46 (1975), 506–27.

3979. ISLE, WALTER. *Experiments in Form: Henry James's Novels, 1896–1901*. Cambridge, MA: Harvard Univ. Press, 1968.

3980. JEFFERSON, D. W. *Henry James*. Edinburgh: Oliver & Boyd, 1960.

3981. _____. *Henry James and the Modern Reader*. Edinburgh: Oliver & Boyd, 1964.

3982. JONES, GRANVILLE H. *Henry James's Psychology of Experience: Innocence, Responsibility, and Renunciation in the Fiction of Henry James*. The Hague: Mouton, 1975.

3983. KORENMAN, JOAN S. "Henry James and the Murderous Mind." *Essays in Literature* (Western Illinois University), 4 (1977), 198–211.

3984. KRAFT, JAMES. *The Early Tales of Henry James*. Carbondale and Edwardsville: Southern Illinois Univ. Press, 1969.

3985. KROOK, DORTHEA. "The Madness of Art: Further Reflections on the Ambiguity of Henry James." *The Hebrew University Studies in Literature*, 1 (1973), 25–38.

3986. _____. *The Ordeal of Consciousness in Henry James*. Cambridge: Cambridge Univ. Press, 1962.

3987. KRUPNICK, MARK L. "Henry James' Curiosity." *Modern Occasions*, 2 (1972), 168–80.

3988. _____. "Playing with the Silence: Henry James's Poetics of Loss." *Forum* (University of Houston), 13, no. 3 (1976), 37–42.

3989. **Lebowitz, Naomi.** *The Imagination of Loving: Henry James's Legacy to the Novel.* Detroit, MI: Wayne State Univ. Press, 1965.

3990. **Leeming, Glenda.** *Who's Who in Henry James.* New York: Taplinger, 1976.

3991. **Leyburn, Ellen Douglass.** *Strange Alloy: The Relation of Comedy to Tragedy in the Fiction of Henry James.* Chapel Hill: Univ. of North Carolina Press, 1968.

3992. **Long, E. Hudson.** "Introduction." In *Short Novels of Henry James.* New York: Dodd, Mead, 1961. pp. v–x.

3993. **Long, Robert Emmet.** "Henry James's Apprenticeship—the Hawthorne Aspect." *American Literature,* 48 (1976), 194–216.

3994. **Lucas, John.** "Manliest of Cities: The Image of Rome in Henry James." *Studi Americani,* 11 (1965), 117–36.

3995. **McElderry, Bruce R., Jr.** *Henry James.* New York: Twayne, 1965.

3996. **Mackenzie, Manfred.** *Communities of Honor and Love in Henry James.* Cambridge, MA: Harvard Univ. Press, 1976.

3997. ———. "A Theory of Henry James's Psychology." *The Yale Review,* 63 (1974), 347–71.

3998. **Macnaughton, W. R.** "The First-Person Narrators of Henry James." *Studies in American Fiction,* 2 (1974), 145–64.

3999. **Maini, Darshan Singh.** *Henry James—The Indirect Vision: Studies in Themes and Techniques.* Bombay: Tata McGraw-Hill, 1973.

4000. **Mariani, Umberto.** "The Italian Experience of Henry James." *Nineteenth-Century Fiction,* 19 (1964), 237–54.

4001. **Markow-Totevy, Georges.** *Henry James.* Trans. John Griffiths. London: Merlin Press, 1969.

4002. **Martineau, Barbara.** "Portraits Are Murdered in the Short Fiction of Henry James." *The Journal of Narrative Technique,* 2 (1972), 16–25.

4003. **Matheson, Gwen.** "Portraits of the Artist and the Lady in the Shorter Fiction of Henry James." *Dalhousie Review,* 48 (1968), 222–30.

4004. **Maves, Carl.** *Sensuous Pessimism: Italy in the Work of Henry James.* Bloomington: Indiana Univ. Press, 1973.

4005. **Maynard, Reid N.** "Autotelism in Henry James's Aesthetic." *Tennessee Studies In Literature,* 21 (1976), 35–42.

4006. **Mays, Milton A.** "Down-Town with Henry James." *Texas Studies in Literature and Language,* 14 (1972), 107–22.

4007. ———. "Henry James, or, The Beast in the Palace of Art." *American Literature,* 39 (1968), 467–87.

4008. MENIKOFF, BARRY. "Punctuation and Point of View in the Late Style of Henry James." *Style*, 4 (1970), 29–47.

4009. MONTEIRO, GEORGE. *Henry James and John Hay: The Record of a Friendship*. Providence, RI: Brown Univ. Press, 1965.

4010. MOORE, HARRY T. *Henry James and His World*. London: Thames and Hudson, 1974.

4011. MORGAN, ALICE. "Henry James: Money and Morality." *Texas Studies in Literature and Language*, 12 (1970), 76–92.

4012. MULL, DONALD L. *Henry James's "Sublime Economy": Money as Symbolic Center in the Fiction*. Middletown, CT: Wesleyan Univ. Press, 1973.

4013. NETTELS, ELSA. *James & Conrad*. Athens: Univ. of Georgia Press, 1977.

4014. NORRMAN, RALF. *Techniques of Ambiguity in the Fiction of Henry James, with Special Reference to* In the Cage *and* The Turn of the Screw. Acta Academiae Aboensis—Humaniora, Vol. 54, no. 2. Åbo: Åbo Akademi, 1977.

4015. PEARCE, HOWARD. "Henry James's Pastoral Fallacy." *PMLA*, 90 (1975), 834–47.

4016. PETERSON, DALE E. *The Clement Vision: Poetic Realism in Turgenev and James*. Port Washington, NY: Kennikat, 1975.

4017. POWERS, LYALL H. *Henry James: An Introduction and Interpretation*. New York: Barnes & Noble, 1970.

4018. ———. "Henry James's Antinomies." *University of Toronto Quarterly*, 31 (1962), 125–35.

4019. ———. *The Merrill Guide to Henry James*. Columbus, OH: Merrill, 1969.

4020. PURDY, STROTHER B. "Henry James and the Sacred Thrill." *Philological Quarterly*, 48 (1969), 247–60.

4021. ———. "Henry James's Abysses: A Semantic Note." *English Studies*, 51 (1970), 424–33.

4022. ———. *The Hole in the Fabric: Science, Contemporary Literature, and Henry James*. Pittsburgh, PA: Univ. of Pittsburgh Press, 1977.

4023. PUTT, S. GORLEY. *Henry James: A Reader's Guide*. With an intro. by Arthur Mizener. Ithaca, NY: Cornell Univ. Press, 1966.

4024. ———. "Introduction." In *The Aspern Papers, and Other Stories*, by Henry James. Harmondsworth, Middlesex: Penguin Books, 1976. pp. 7–10.

4025. RIMMON, SHLOMITH. *The Concept of Ambiguity: The Example of Henry James*. Chicago: Univ. of Chicago Press, 1977.

4026. ROVIT, EARL. "James and Emerson: The Lesson of the Master." *The American Scholar*, 33 (1964), 434–46.

4027. SAMUELS, CHARLES THOMAS. *The Ambiguity of Henry James.* Urbana: Univ. of Illinois Press, 1971.

4028. SANFORD, CHARLES L. "Henry James and the American Rush of Experience." In *The Quest for Paradise: Europe and the American Moral Imagination.* Urbana: Univ. of Illinois Press, 1961. pp. 203-27.

4029. SCHNEIDER, DANIEL J. "The Divided Self in the Fiction of Henry James." *PMLA*, 90 (1975), 447-60.

4030. SEARS, SALLIE. *The Negative Imagination: Form and Perspective in the Novels of Henry James.* Ithaca, NY: Cornell Univ. Press, 1968.

4031. SEGAL, ORA. *The Lucid Reflector: The Observer in Henry James' Fiction.* New Haven, CT: Yale Univ. Press, 1969.

4032. SHARP, SISTER M. CORONA, O.S.U. *The Confidante in Henry James: Evolution and Moral Value of a Fictive Character.* Notre Dame, IN: Univ. of Notre Dame Press, 1963.

4033. ———. "Fatherhood in Henry James." *University of Toronto Quarterly*, 35 (1966), 279-92.

4034. SHELDEN, PAMELA JACOBS. "Jamesian Gothicism: The Haunted Castle of the Mind." *Studies in the Literary Imagination*, 7, no. 1 (1974), 121-34.

4035. SHINE, MURIEL G. *The Fictional Children of Henry James.* Chapel Hill: Univ. of North Carolina Press, 1969.

4036. SHINN, THELMA J. "A Question of Survival: An Analysis of 'The Treacherous Years' of Henry James." *Literature and Psychology*, 23 (1973), 135-48.

4037. SHULMAN, ROBERT. "Henry James and the Modern Comedy of Knowledge." *Criticism*, 10 (1968), 41-53.

4038. SILVERSTEIN, HENRY. "The Utopia of Henry James." *The New England Quarterly*, 35 (1962), 458-68.

4039. SMITH, WILLIAM F., JR. "Sentence Structure in the Tales of Henry James." *Style*, 7 (1973), 157-72.

4040. STAFFORD, WILLIAM T. "William James As Critic of His Brother Henry." *The Personalist*, 40 (1959), 341-53.

4041. STEWART, J. I. M. "James." In *Eight Modern Writers*. Vol. XII of *The Oxford History of English Literature*. Oxford: Clarendon Press, 1963. pp. 71-121.

4042. STONE, DONALD DAVID. *Novelists in a Changing World: Meredith, James, and the Transformation of English Fiction in the 1880's.* Cambridge, MA: Harvard Univ. Press, 1972.

4043. STONE, EDWARD. *The Battle and the Books: Some Aspects of Henry James.* Athens: Ohio Univ. Press, 1964.

4044. ———. "Edition Architecture and 'The Turn of the Screw.'" *Studies in Short Fiction*, 13 (1976), 9-16.

4045. **STRUBLE, GEORGE G.** "Henry James and the Rise of the Cosmopolitan Spirit in American Literature." In *Actes du IVe Congrès de l'Association Internationale de Littérature Comparée.* Ed. François Jost. 2 vols. The Hague: Mouton, 1966. I, 80–85.

4046. **SWEETAPPLE, R.** "Accepting the Unacceptable." In *Australasian Universities Language and Literature Association: Proceedings and Papers of the Twelfth Congress Held at the University of Western Australia, 5–11 February 1969.* Sydney: AULLA, 1970. pp. 224–30.

4047. **TANNER, TONY.** "Introduction." In *Henry James: Modern Judgements.* London: Macmillan, 1969. pp. 11–41.

4048. **THORBERG, RAYMOND.** "Terror Made Relevant: James's Ghost Stories." *Dalhousie Review,* 47 (1967), 185–91.

4049. **THORP, WILLARD.** "Foreword." In *The Madonna of the Future and Other Early Stories,* by Henry James. New York: New American Library, 1962. pp. vii–xvi.

4050. **TINTNER, ADELINE R.** "James's Mock Epic: 'The Velvet Glove,' Edith Wharton, and Other Late Tales." *Modern Fiction Studies,* 17 (1971), 483–99.

4051. _____. "Landmarks of 'The Terrible Town': The New York Scene in Henry James' Last Stories." *Prospects,* 2 (1976), 399–435.

4052. _____. "The Metamorphoses of Edith Wharton in Henry James's *The Finer Grain.*" *Twentieth Century Literature,* 21 (1975), 355–79.

4053. _____. "Octave Feuillet, *La Petite Comtesse* and Henry James." *Revue de Littérature Comparée,* 48 (1974), 218–32.

4054. **TODOROV, TZVETAN.** "The Structural Analysis of Literature: The Tales of Henry James." In *Structuralism: An Introduction.* Ed. David Robey. Oxford: Clarendon Press, 1973. pp. 73–103.

4055. **TREMPER, ELLEN.** "Henry James's Altering Ego: An Examination of His Psychological Double in Three Tales." *The Texas Quarterly,* 19, no. 3 (1976), 59–75.

4056. **UNRUE, DARLENE.** "Henry James and the Grotesque." *The Arizona Quarterly,* 32 (1976), 293–300.

4057. _____. "Henry James's Extraordinary Use of Portraits." *RE: Artes Liberales,* 1, no. 2 (1975), 47–53.

4058. **VAID, KRISHNA BALDEV.** *Technique in the Tales of Henry James.* Cambridge, MA: Harvard Univ. Press, 1964.

4059. **VAN CROMPHOUT, G.** "Artist and Society in Henry James." *English Studies,* 49 (1968), 132–40.

4060. **VEEDER, WILLIAM.** *Henry James—the Lessons of the Master: Popular Fiction and Personal Style in the Nineteenth Century.* Chicago: Univ. of Chicago Press, 1975.

4061. **WALLACE, RONALD.** *Henry James and the Comic Form.* Ann Arbor: Univ. of Michigan Press, 1975.

4062. **WARD, J. A.** "The Ambiguities of Henry James." *The Sewanee Review,* 83 (1975), 39–60.

4063. ———. "Henry James and the Nature of Evil." *Twentieth Century Literature,* 6 (1960), 65–69.

4064. ———. "Henry James's America: Versions of Oppression." *The Mississippi Quarterly,* 13 (1960), 30–44.

4065. ———. *The Imagination of Disaster: Evil in the Fiction of Henry James.* Lincoln: Univ. of Nebraska Press, 1961.

4066. ———. "The Ineffectual Heroes of James's Middle Period." *Texas Studies in Literature and Language,* 2 (1960), 315–27.

4067. ———. *The Search for Form: Studies in the Structure of James's Fiction.* Chapel Hill: Univ. of North Carolina Press, 1967.

4068. ———. "Social Criticism in James's London Fiction." *The Arizona Quarterly,* 15 (1959), 36–48.

4069. **WEGELIN, CHRISTOF.** "Henry James and the Treasure of Consciousness." *Die Neueren Sprachen,* 72 (1973), 484–91.

4070. **WEINSTEIN, PHILIP M.** *Henry James and the Requirements of the Imagination.* Cambridge, MA: Harvard Univ. Press, 1971.

4071. **WILSON, RICHARD.** "Henry James and 'The Note Absolute.'" *English Studies,* 47 (1966), 31–35.

4072. **WINNER, VIOLA HOPKINS.** *Henry James and the Visual Arts.* Charlottesville: Univ. Press of Virginia, 1970.

4073. **WRIGHT, WALTER F.** *The Madness of Art: A Study of Henry James.* Lincoln: Univ. of Nebraska Press, 1962.

4074. **YEAZELL, RUTH BERNARD.** *Language and Knowledge in the Late Novels of Henry James.* Chicago: Univ. of Chicago Press, 1976.

4075. **ZABEL, MORTON DAUWEN.** "Introduction." In *Fifteen Short Stories,* by Henry James. New York: Bantam Books, 1961. pp. vii–xxx.

Bibliography

4076. **BEEBE, MAURICE, AND WILLIAM T. STAFFORD.** "Criticism of Henry James: A Selected Checklist." *Modern Fiction Studies,* 12 (1966), 117–77.

4077. **EDEL, LEON, AND DAN H. LAURENCE.** *A Bibliography of Henry James.* 2nd ed. London: Rupert Hart-Davis, 1961.

4078. **GALE, ROBERT L.** "Henry James." In *Eight American Authors: A Review of Research and Criticism.* Rev. ed. Ed. James Woodress. New York: Norton, 1971. pp. 321–75.

4079. **HAGEMANN, E. R.** *"Life* Buffets (and Comforts) Henry James, 1883-1916: An Introduction and An Annotated Checklist." *The Papers of the Bibliographical Society of America*, 62 (1968), 207-25.

4080. **MONTEIRO, GEORGE.** "Henry James and His Reviewers: Some Identifications." *The Papers of the Bibliographical Society of America*, 63 (1969), 300-04.

4081. **PUTT, S. GORLEY.** "James." In *The English Novel: Select Bibliographical Guides.* Ed. A. E. Dyson. London: Oxford Univ. Press, 1974. pp. 280-99.

4082. **RICKS, BEATRICE.** *Henry James: A Bibliography of Secondary Works.* Metuchen, NJ: Scarecrow, 1975.

4083. **TINTNER, ADELINE R.** "Henry James Criticism: A Current Perspective." *American Literary Realism, 1870-1910*, 7 (1974), 155-68.

4084. **WILLEN, GERALD.** "Bibliography." In *A Casebook on Henry James's "The Turn of the Screw".* 2nd ed. New York: Crowell, 1969. pp. 385-91.

JEWETT, SARAH ORNE

"An Autumn Holiday"

See 4112.

"The Country of the Pointed Firs"

4085. **BERTHOFF, WARNER.** "The Art of Jewett's *Pointed Firs.*" *The New England Quarterly*, 32 (1959), 31-53.

4086. **CHASE, MARY ELLEN.** "Sarah Orne Jewett as a Social Historian." *Prairie Schooner*, 36 (1962), 231-37.

4087. **FIKE, FRANCIS.** "An Interpretation of *Pointed Firs.*" *The New England Quarterly*, 34 (1961), 478-91.

4088. **GREEN, DAVID BONNELL.** "The World of Dunnet Landing." *The New England Quarterly*, 34 (1961), 514-17.

4089. **MAGOWAN, ROBIN.** "The Outer Island Sequence in *Pointed Firs.*" *Colby Library Quarterly*, 6 (1964), 418-24.

4090. ———. "Pastoral and the Art of Landscape in *The Country of the Pointed Firs.*" *The New England Quarterly*, 36 (1963), 229-40.

4091. **NOYES, SYLVIA GRAY.** "Mrs. Almira Todd, Herbalist-Conjurer." *Colby Library Quarterly*, 9 (1972), 643-49.

4092. **ST. ARMAND, BARTON L.** "Jewett and Marin: The Inner Vision." *Colby Library Quarterly*, 9 (1972), 632-43.

4093. **STEVENSON, CATHERINE BARNES.** "The Double Consciousness of the Narrator in Sarah Orne Jewett's Fiction." *Colby Library Quarterly*, 11 (1975), 1-12.

4094. **STOUCK, DAVID**. *"The Country of the Pointed Firs:* A Pastoral of Innocence." *Colby Library Quarterly*, 9 (1970), 213-20.

4095. **VELLA, MICHAEL W.** "Sarah Orne Jewett: A Reading of *The Country of the Pointed Firs. "ESQ*, 19 (1973), 275-82.

4096. **VOELKER, PAUL D.** *"The Country of the Pointed Firs*: A Novel by Sarah Orne Jewett." *Colby Library Quarterly*, 9 (1970), 201-13.

4097. **WAGGONER, HYATT H.** "The Unity of *The Country of the Pointed Firs."* *Twentieth Century Literature*, 5 (1959), 67-73.
See also 83, 366, 376, 507, 4104, 4107, 4112, 4114, 4115, 4118, 4120, 4121.

"The Courting of Sister Wisby"

4098. **HUMMA, JOHN B.** "The Art and Meaning of Sarah Orne Jewett's 'The Courting of Sister Wisby.' " *Studies in Short Fiction*, 10 (1973), 85-91.
See also 4112.

"Dan's Wife"

4099. **EPPARD, PHILIP B.** " 'Dan's Wife': A Newly Discovered Sarah Orne Jewett Story." *Colby Library Quarterly*, 12 (1976), 101-02.

"A Day's Night"

4100. **GREEN, DAVID BONNELL.** "Sarah Orne Jewett's 'A Dark Night.' " *The Papers of the Bibliographical Society of America*, 53 (1959), 331-34.

"Deephaven"

4101. **HORN, ROBERT L.** "The Power of Jewett's *Deephaven."* *Colby Library Quarterly*, 9 (1972), 617-31.
See also 83, 4106, 4108, 4112, 4115, 4120, 4121.

"The Dulham Ladies"

See 4112.

"A Dunnet Shepherdess"

See 4120.

"The Foreigner"

See 376, 4088, 4104.

"The Guests of Mrs. Timms"

See 4112.

"The King of Folly Island"

See 4112.

"Lady Ferry"

See 4112.

"The Landscape Chamber"

See 4112.

"Miss Tempy's Watchers"

See 1199.

"The Only Rose"

See 4120.

"River Driftwood"

See 4105.

"A White Heron"

4102. JOBES, KATHERINE T. "From Stowe's Eagle Island to Jewett's 'A White Heron.'" *Colby Library Quarterly*, 10 (1974), 515–21.

4103. PRATT, ANNIS. "Women and Nature in Modern Fiction." *Contemporary Literature*, 13 (1972), 476–90.
See also 4112, 4115, 4120.

"William's Wedding"

See 4115.

General Studies

4104. BENDER, BERT. "To Calm and Uplift 'Against the Dark': Sarah Orne Jewett's Lyric Narratives." *Colby Library Quarterly*, 11 (1975), 219–29.

4105. BISHOP, FERMAN. "The Sense of the Past in Sarah Orne Jewett." *University of Wichita Bulletin*, no. 41 (1959), pp. 3–10.

4106. BLANC, MARIE THÉRÈSE. "Le roman de la femme-médecin." Trans. by Archille H. Biron. *Colby Library Quarterly*, 7 (1967), 488–503.

4107. BOGGIO-SOLA, JEAN. "The Poetic Realism of Sarah Orne Jewett." *Colby Library Quarterly*, 7 (1965), 74–81.

4108. CARY, RICHARD. "Introduction." In *Deephaven and Other Stories*, by Sarah Orne Jewett. New Haven, CT: College & University Press, 1966. pp. 7–23.

4109. _____. "Introduction." In *The Uncollected Short Stories of Sarah Orne Jewett*. Waterville, ME: Colby College Press, 1971. pp. iii–xviii.

4110. _____. "Jewett on Writing Short Stories." *Colby Library Quarterly*, 6 (1964), 425–40.

4111. ———. "The Rise, Decline, and Rise of Sarah Orne Jewett." *Colby Library Quarterly*, 9 (1972), 650–63.
4112. ———. *Sarah Orne Jewett*. New York: Twayne, 1962.
4113. ———. "The Uncollected Short Stories of Sarah Orne Jewett." *Colby Library Quarterly*, 9 (1971), 385–408.
4114. CHASE, MARY ELLEN. "Sarah Orne Jewett and Her Coast of Maine: An Introduction." In *The Country of the Pointed Firs and Other Stories*, by Sarah Orne Jewett. New York: Norton, 1968. pp. vii–xiv.
4115. EAKIN, PAUL JOHN. "Sarah Orne Jewett and the Meaning of Country Life." *American Literature*, 38 (1967), 508–31.
4116. GREEN, DAVID BONNELL. "The Sarah Orne Jewett Collection: Additions and a Correction." *The Papers of the Bibliographical Society of America*, 55 (1961), 141–42.
4117. NYE, GEORGE P. "Jewett and the Juvenile Critics." *Colby Library Quarterly*, 5 (1959), 45–48.
4118. POOL, EUGENE HILLHOUSE. "The Child in Sarah Orne Jewett." *Colby Library Quarterly*, 7 (1967), 503–09.
4119. RHODE, ROBERT D. "Sarah Orne Jewett and 'The Palpable Present Intimate.' " *Colby Library Quarterly*, 8 (1968), 146–55.
4120. THORP, MARGARET FARRAND. *Sarah Orne Jewett*. Minneapolis: Univ. of Minnesota Press, 1966.
4121. TOTH, SUSAN ALLEN. "The Value of Age in the Fiction of Sarah Orne Jewett." *Studies in Short Fiction*, 8 (1971), 433–41.

Bibliography

4122. CARY, RICHARD. "Sarah Orne Jewett (1849–1909)." *American Literary Realism, 1870–1910*, 1, no. 1 (1967), 61–66.
4123. ———. "Some Bibliographic Ghosts of Sarah Orne Jewett." *Colby Library Quarterly*, 8 (1968), 139–45.
4124. EICHELBERGER, CLAYTON L. "Sarah Orne Jewett (1849–1909): A Critical Bibliography of Secondary Comment." *American Literary Realism, 1870–1910*, 2 (1969), 189–262.
4125. FROST, JOHN ELDRIDGE. "Sarah Orne Jewett Bibliography: 1949–1963." *Colby Library Quarterly*, 6 (1964), 405–17.

JOHNSTON, RICHARD MALCOLM

"Old Friends and New"

See 571.

General Studies

4126. VOYLES, JIMMY PONDER. "Richard Malcolm Johnston's Literary Career: An Estimate." *The Markham Review*, 4 (1974), 29–34.

JONES, GAYL

Interviews

4127. HARPER, MICHAEL S. "Gayl Jones: An Interview." *The Massachusetts Review*, 18 (1977), 692–715.

JONES, JAMES

"The Ice-Cream Headache"

4128. JONES, JAMES. Introduction to "The Ice-Cream Headache." In *Writer's Choice*. Ed. Rust Hills. New York: McKay, 1974. pp. 223–25.

Interviews

4129. NEWQUIST, ROY. "James Jones." In *Counterpoint*. Chicago: Rand McNally, 1964. pp. 376–84.

Bibliography

4130. HOPKINS, JOHN R. *James Jones: A Checklist*. Detroit, MI: Gale, 1974.

JONES, LeROI (See BARAKA, AMIRI)

JONES, LUCILLE

Interviews

4131. JONES, GAYL. "An Interview with Lucille Jones." *Obsidian*, 3, no. 3 (1977), 26–35.

KARCHMER, SYLVAN

"A Fistful of Alamo Heroes"

See 311.

KEELER, HARRY S.

General Studies

4132. NEVINS, FRANCIS M., JR. "The Wild and Woolly World of Harry Stephen Keeler: I." *Journal of Popular Culture*, 3 (1970), 635–43.

KELLEY, WILLIAM MELVIN

"The Life You Save"

See 225.

"The Poker Party"

4133. **GALLOWAY, DAVID.** "William Melvin Kelley, 'The Poker Party' (1961)." In *The Black American Short Story in the 20th Century: A Collection of Critical Essays.* Ed. Peter Bruck. Amsterdam: B. R. Grüner, 1977. pp. 129–40.

"Saint Paul and the Monkeys"

See 225.

General Studies

4134. **WEYANT, JILL.** "The Kelley Saga: Violence in America." *CLA Journal,* 19 (1975), 210–20.

Interviews

4135. **NEWQUIST, ROY.** "William Melvin Kelley." In *Conversations.* New York: Rand McNally, 1967. pp. 206–14.

KEROUAC, JACK

General Studies

4136. **BEAULIEU, VICTOR-LÉVY.** *Jack Kerouac: A Chicken-Essay.* Trans. Sheila Fischman. Toronto: Coach House Press, 1975.

4137. **CHARTERS, ANN.** *Kerouac: A Biography.* San Francisco, CA: Straight Arrow Books, 1973.

4138. **HIPKISS, ROBERT A.** *Jack Kerouac, Prophet of the New Romanticism: A Critical Study of the Published Works of Kerouac and a Comparison of Them to Those of J. D. Salinger, James Purdy, John Knowles, and Ken Kesey.* Lawrence: Regents Press of Kansas, 1976.

Bibliography

4139. **CHARTERS, ANN.** *A Bibliography of Works by Jack Kerouac.* New York: Phoenix Bookshop, 1967.

4140. ———. *A Bibliography of Works by Jack Kerouac.* Rev. ed. New York: Phoenix Bookshop, 1975.

KING, GRACE

"In the French Quarter, 1870"

See 571.

"Monsieur Motte"

See 4141, 4142.

General Studies

4141. **Bush, Robert.** "Grace King: The Emergence of a Southern Intellectual Woman." *The Southern Review*, NS 13 (1977), 272–88.

4142. _____. "Introduction." In *Grace King of New Orleans: A Selection of Her Writings*. Baton Rouge: Louisiana State Univ. Press, 1973. pp. 3–31.

Bibliography

4143. **Bush, Robert.** "Grace King (1852–1932)." *American Literary Realism, 1870–1910*, 8 (1975), 43–51.

KIRKLAND, CAROLINE M.

General Studies

4144. **Osborne, William S.** *Caroline M. Kirkland*. New York: Twayne, 1972.

KIRKLAND, JOSEPH

General Studies

4145. **Henson, Clyde E.** *Joseph Kirkland*. New York: Twayne, 1962.

Bibliography

4146. **Eichelberger, Clayton L.** "Edgar Watson Howe and Joseph Kirkland: More Critical Comment." *American Literary Realism, 1870–1910*, 4 (1971), 279–90.

4147. _____. "Joseph Kirkland (1830–1893): A Critical Bibliography of Secondary Comment." *American Literary Realism, 1870–1910*, 2 (1969), 51–69.

4148. **Henson, Clyde E.** "Joseph Kirkland (1830–1894)." *American Literary Realism, 1870–1910*, 1, no. 1 (1967), 67–70.

KLINE, OTIS ADELBERT

General Studies

4149. **McSherry, Frank D., Jr.** "Footsteps on the Golden Road: An Addendum to 'The Golden Road to Samarkand.' " *The Armchair Detective*, 7 (1974), 264, 282.

KUTTNER, HENRY

"The Fairy Chessmen"

See 226.

"Piggy Bank"

See 4150.

General Studies

4150. **GUNN, JAMES.** "Henry Kuttner, C. L. Moore, Lewis Padgett *et al.*" In *Voices for the Future: Essays on Major Science Fiction Writers*. Ed. Thomas D. Clareson. Bowling Green, OH: Bowling Green Univ. Popular Press, 1976. pp. 185-215.

LA FARGE, OLIVER

"All the Young Men"

See 4151.

"La Spécialté de M. Duclos"

See 4153.

"North Is Black"

See 4153.

General Studies

4151. **GILLIS, EVERETT A.** *Oliver La Farge*. Austin, TX: Steck-Vaughn, 1967.
4152. **McNICKLE, D'ARCY.** *Indian Man: A Life of Oliver La Farge*. Bloomington: Indiana Univ. Press, 1971.
4153. **PEARCE, T. M.** *Oliver La Farge*. New York: Twayne, 1972.

LARDNER, RING[GOLD]

"Alibi Ike"

See 4170.

"The Busher's Letters Home"

See 4167.

"A Caddy's Diary"

See 2185.

"Champion"

See 4157, 4163, 4170.

"A Chip of the Old Block"

See 4163.

"Cured!"

See 4170.

"Ex Parte"

See 4163.

"The First Game"

See 4167.

"The Golden Honeymoon"

See 4157, 4163, 4170.

"Gullible's Travels"

See 358, 4170.

"Haircut"

4154. G[OLDSTEIN], M[ELVIN]. "A Note on a Perfect Crime." *Literature and Psychology*, 11 (1961), 65–67.
4155. MAY, CHARLES E. "Lardner's 'Haircut.'" *The Explicator*, 31 (1973), item 69.
See also 394, 454, 511, 535, 4170.

"I Can't Breathe"

See 4170.

"Insomnia"

See 4170.

"The Love Nest"

See 4163, 4170.

"My Roomy"

See 574, 4157, 4163, 4164, 4169.

"The Pennant Pursuit"

See 4167.

Some Like Them Cold"

See 4157, 4170.

"The Young Immigrunts"

See 4170.

"Zone of Quiet"

See 4170.

General Studies

4156. COX, JAMES M. "Toward Vernacular Humor." *The Virginia Quarterly Review*, 46 (1970), 311–30.

4157. FRIEDRICH, OTTO. *Ring Lardner*. Minneapolis: Univ. of Minnesota Press, 1965.

4158. GEISMAR, MAXWELL. "Introduction." In *The Ring Lardner Reader*. New York: Scribner's, 1963. pp. xv–xxxiv.

4159. HASLEY, LOUIS. "Ring Lardner: The Ashes of Idealism." *The Arizona Quarterly*, 26 (1970), 219–32.

4160. HERBST, JOSEPHINE. "A Language Absolutely Unliterary: A New Introduction." In *Gullible's Travels, Etc.*, by Ring Lardner. Chicago: Univ. of Chicago Press, 1965. pp. v–xiv.

4161. INGRAM, FORREST L. "Fun at the Incinerating Plant: Lardner's Wry Waste Land." In *The Twenties: Fiction, Poetry, Drama*. Ed. Warren French. Deland, FL: Everett/Edwards, 1975. pp. 111–22.

4162. MESSENGER, CHRISTIAN. "Southwestern Humorists and Ring Lardner—Sport in American Literature." *Illinois Quarterly*, 39, no. 1 (1976), 5–21.

4163. PATRICK, WALTON R. *Ring Lardner*. New York: Twayne, 1963.

4164. SMITH, LEVERETT T., JR. " 'The Diameter of Frank Chance's Diamond': Ring Lardner and Professional Sports." *Journal of Popular Culture*, 6 (1972), 133–56.

4165. SPATZ, JONAS. "Ring Lardner: Not an Escape, but a Reflection." In *The Twenties: Fiction, Poetry, Drama*. Ed. Warren French. Deland, FL: Everett/Edwards, 1975. pp. 101–10.

4166. STEIN, ALLEN F. "This Unsporting Life: The Baseball Fiction of Ring Lardner." *The Markham Review*, 3 (1972), 27–33.

4167. WEBB, HOWARD W., JR. "The Development of a Style: The Lardner Idiom." *American Quarterly*, 12 (1960), 482–92.

4168. ———. "Mark Twain and Ring Lardner." *The Mark Twain Journal*, 11, no. 2 (1960), 13–15.

4169. ———. "The Meaning of Ring Lardner's Fiction: A Reevaluation." *American Literature*, 31 (1960), 434–45.

4170. YARDLEY, JONATHAN. *Ring: A Biography of Ring Lardner*. New York: Random House, 1977.

Bibliography

4171. BRUCCOLI, MATTHEW J., AND RICHARD LAYMAN. *Ring W. Lardner: A Descriptive Bibliography*. Pittsburgh, PA: Univ. of Pittsburgh Press, 1976.

LATHAM, PHILIP

"The Xi Effect"
See 114.

LEA, TOM

"Quite a Beach"
4172. **WEST, JOHN O.** *Tom Lea: Artist in Two Mediums*. Austin, TX: Steck-Vaughn, 1967.

LEGGETT, WILLIAM

"The Rifle"
4173. **SEELYE, JOHN.** "Buckskin and Ballistics: William Leggett and the American Detective Story." *Journal of Popular Culture*, 1 (1967), 52–57.

LE GUIN, URSULA

"The New Atlantis"
4174. **SUVIN, DARKO.** "Parables of De-Alienation: Le Guin's Widdershins Dance." *Science-Fiction Studies*, 2 (1975), 265–74.
See also 399.

"Nine Lives"
See 4179.

"Vaster Than Empires and More Slow"
See 4177, 4179.

"The Word for World is Forest"
4175. **BARBOUR, DOUGLAS.** "Wholeness and Balance in the Hainish Novels of Ursula K. Le Guin." *Science-Fiction Studies*, 1 (1974), 164–73.
4176. **COGELL, ELIZABETH CUMMINS.** "Setting as Analogue to Characterization in Ursula Le Guin." *Extrapolation*, 18 (1977), 131–41.
4177. **WATSON, IAN.** "The Forest as Metaphor for Mind: 'The Word for World is Forest' and 'Vaster Than Empires and More Slow.'" *Science-Fiction Studies*, 2 (1975), 231–37.
See also 4179.

General Studies
4178. **PORTER, DAVID L.** "The Politics of Le Guin's Opus." *Science-Fiction Studies*, 2 (1975), 243–48.

4179. **REMINGTON, THOMAS J.** "A Touch of Difference, A Touch of Love: Theme in Three Stories by Ursula K. Le Guin." *Extrapolation*, 18 (1976), 28–41.

4180. **SLUSSER, GEORGE EDGAR.** *The Farthest Shores of Ursula K. LeGuin.* San Bernardino, CA: Borgo Press, 1976.

Bibliography

4181. **LEVIN, JEFF.** "Ursula K. Le Guin: A Select Bibliography." *Science-Fiction Studies*, 2 (1975), 204–08.

LEWIS, ALFRED HENRY

General Studies

4182. **HUMPHRIES, ROLFE.** "Tall-Tale Americana." *The Nation*, 205 (1967), 153–57.

LEWIS, [HARRY] SINCLAIR

"Nature, Incorporated"

See 4184.

"The Scarlet Sign"

4183. **LIGHT, MARTIN.** "Lewis's 'Scarlet Sign': Accommodating to the Popular Market." *Journal of Popular Culture*, 1 (1967), 106–13.

"A Woman by Candlelight"

See 4184.

General Studies

4184. **DOOLEY, D. J.** *The Art of Sinclair Lewis.* Lincoln: Univ. of Nebraska Press, 1967.

4185. **GREBSTEIN, SHELDON NORMAN.** *Sinclair Lewis.* New York: Twayne, 1962.

4186. **LIGHT, MARTIN.** "Lewis' Finicky Girls and Faithful Workers." *The University Review* (Kansas City), 30 (1963), 151–59.

4187. ———. *The Quixotic Vision of Sinclair Lewis.* West Lafayette, IN: Purdue Univ. Press, 1975.

4188. **MOODIE, CLARA LEE.** "The Short Stories and Sinclair Lewis' Literary Development." *Studies in Short Fiction*, 12 (1975), 99–104.

4189. **SCHORER, MARK.** "Introduction." In *I'm a Stranger Here Myself and Other Stories,* by Sinclair Lewis. New York: Dell, 1962. pp. 7–16.

4190. _____. *Sinclair Lewis: An American Life*. New York: McGraw-Hill, 1961.

4191. YOSHIDA, HIROSHIGE. *A Sinclair Lewis Lexicon with a Critical Study of His Style and Method*. Tokyo: Hoyu Press, 1976.

Interviews

4192. DERLETH, AUGUST. "Sinclair Lewis." In *Three Literary Men: A Memoir of Sinclair Lewis, Sherwood Anderson, Edgar Lee Masters*. New York: Candlelight Press, 1963. pp. 9–27.

Bibliography

4193. LUNDQUIST, JAMES. *The Merrill Checklist of Sinclair Lewis*. Columbus, OH: Merrill, 1970.

4194. MOODIE, CLARA LEE. "Finding List of Sinclair Lewis's Short Stories." *Studies in Short Fiction*, 12 (1975), 104–07.

LEWIS, HENRY CLAY

"The Curious Widow"

See 460, 549.

"My Early Life"

See 4196.

"Stealing a Baby"

See 549.

"A Struggle for Life"

See 549, 4197.

"Valerian and the Panther"

See 4197.

General Studies

4195. ANDERSON, JOHN Q. "The Life of Henry Clay Lewis." In *Louisiana Swamp Doctor: The Life and Writings of Henry Clay Lewis, alias "Madison Tensas, M. D."* Baton Rouge: Louisiana State Univ. Press, 1962. pp. 3–70.

4196. ISRAEL, CHARLES. "Henry Clay Lewis's *Odd Leaves*: Studies in the Surreal and Grotesque." *The Mississippi Quarterly*, 28 (1975), 61–69.

4197. ROSE, ALAN H. "The Image of the Negro in the Writings of Henry Clay Lewis." *American Literature*, 41 (1969), 255–63.

LIBEN, MEYER

General Studies

4198. DENNISON, GEORGE. "A Good Man." *The New York Times Book Review*, 1 Aug. 1976, p. 23.

LINEBARGER, PAUL (See SMITH, CORDWAINER)

LOCKE, DAVID ROSS (See NASBY, PETROLEUM V.)

LONDON, JACK

"All Gold Canyon"

4199. LABOR, EARLE. "From 'All Gold Canyon' to *The Acorn-Planter*: Jack London's Agrarian Vision." *Western American Literature*, 11 (1976), 83–101.

"The Apostate"

See 4227, 4229.

"Bâtard"

4200. DODSON, MARY KAY. "Naturalism in the Works of Jack London." *Jack London Newsletter*, 4 (1971), 130–39.
See also 4241, 4250, 4251.

"The Bones of Kahelili"

See 4240, 4241.

"The Chinago"

See 4226, 4233.

"A Curious Fragment"

See 4227.

"A Day's Lodging"

4201. [WOODBRIDGE, HENSLEY C.] "A Further Note on *Gold* and 'A Day's Lodging.'" *Jack London Newsletter*, 9 (1976), 112–13.

"Diable—A Dog" (See "Bâtard")

"A Goboto Night"

See 4253.

"The God of His Fathers"

4202. ERBENTRAUT, EDWIN B. "The Balanced Vision: Mission-

aries and the Test of Spirit in Two Jack London Stories." *The American Book Collector*, 24, no. 4 (1974), 31–32.
See also 4241.

"Goliah"

See 4252.

"The Great Interrogation"

See 4255.

"In a Far Country"

See 4235, 4241.

"The Kanaka Surf"

4203. LACHTMAN, HOWARD. "Man and Superwoman in Jack London's 'The Kanaka Surf.' " *Western American Literature*, 7 (1972), 101–10.
See also 4241.

"Keesh, The Son of Keesh"

See 4241.

"Koolau"

See 4235.

"The Law of Life"

4204. ERBENTRAUT, EDWIN B. "Jack London, William Shakespeare, and 'The Law of Life.' " *Jack London Newsletter*, 10 (1977), 138–41.
See also 4233, 4241.

"The League of Old Men"

See 4241.

"Like Argus of the Ancient Times"

See 4240, 4241, 4254.

"Love of Life"

4205. BURTON, LOU. " 'Some Monstrous Worm.' " *Jack London Newsletter*, 7 (1974), 117–21.
See also 4233, 4241, 4254.

"The Master of Mystery"

See 4253.

"Mauki"

See 4235.

"The Men of Forty-Mile"

See 4241.

"The Mexican"

See 449, 4241.

"The Mistake of Creation"

4206. HENSLEY, DENNIS E. "Sherlock Holmes and Smoke Bel-
lew." *Jack London Newsletter*, 8 (1975), 129–32.

"A Night's Swim in Yeddo Bay"

4207. WATSON, CHARLES N., JR. "Jack London's Yokohama
Swim and His First Tall Tale." *Studies in American Humor*, 3
(1976), 84–95.

"An Odyssey of the North"

See 4241.

"The One Thousand Dozen"

See 4254.

"A Piece of Steak"

4208. HATCHEL, LINDA. "Animal Imagery in London's 'A Piece
of Steak.' " *Jack London Newsletter*, 8 (1975), 119–21.

"The Priestly Prerogative"

See 4241, 4255.

"The Red One"

4209. COLLINS, BILLY G. "Jack London's 'The Red One': Journey to a Lost Heart." *Jack London Newsletter*, 10 (1977), 1–6.
4210. JØRGENSON, JENS PETER. "Jack London's 'The Red One':
A Freudian Approach." *Jack London Newsletter*, 8 (1975), 101–03.
4211. RIBER, JØRGEN. "Archetypal Patterns in 'The Red
One.' " *Jack London Newsletter*, 8 (1975), 104–06.
See also 4252.

"The Scarlet Plague"

See 4237.

"The Seed of McCoy"

See 4241.

"Shin Bones"

See 4240, 4241.

"The Sickness of Lone Chief"

See 4241.

"The Son of the Wolf"

See 4232, 4249.

"The Sun-Dog Trail"

See 4241.

"The Tears of Ah Kim"

See 4240, 4241.

"The Terrible Solomons"

See 4241.

"A Thousand Deaths"

4212. ERBENTRAUT, EDWIN B. " 'A Thousand Deaths': Hyperbolic Anger." *Jack London Newsletter*, 4 (1971), 125–29.

"To Build a Fire"

4213. BOWEN, JAMES K. "Jack London's 'To Build a Fire': Epistemology and the White Wilderness." *Western American Literature*, 5 (1971), 287–89.

4214. FINDLEY, SUE. "Naturalism in 'To Build a Fire.' " *Jack London Newsletter*, 2 (1969), 45–48.

4215. LABOR, EARLE, AND KING HENDRICKS. "Jack London's Twice-Told Tale." *Studies in Short Fiction*, 4 (1967), 334–47.

4216. PETERSON, CLELL T. "The Theme of Jack London's 'To Build a Fire.' " *The American Book Collector*, 17, no. 3 (1966), 15–18.

See also 447, 483, 4233, 4235, 4241, 4242, 4254.

"To the Man on Trail"

4217. LABOR, EARL. " 'To the Man on Trail': Jack London's Christmas Carol." *Jack London Newsletter*, 3 (1970), 90–94.

See also 4235, 4241.

"The Unexpected"

See 4223, 4254.

"War"

4218. HENSLEY, DENNIS E. " 'War': Jack London's the Red and the Black." *Jack London Newsletter*, 9 (1976), 73–77.

4219. **WOODWARD, ROBERT H.** "Another Reading of Jack London's 'War.' " *Jack London Newsletter*, 10 (1977), 151–56.
See also 4252.

"The Water Baby"

See 4240, 4241.

"The Whale Tooth"

See 4202.

"When God Laughs"

See 4226.

"The White Silence"

See 4241.

"The Wife of a King"

4220. **TAVERNIER-COURBIN, JACQUELINE.** " 'The Wife of a King': A Defense." *Jack London Newsletter*, 10 (1977), 34–38.
See also 4241.

"The Wisdom of the Trail"

See 4241.

"The Wit of Porportuk"

4221. **MEHL, R. F., JR.** "Jack London, Alfred Henry Lewis, and Primitive Woman." *Jack London Newsletter*, 6 (1973), 66–70.

General Studies

4222. **BARLTROP, ROBERT.** *Jack London: The Man, the Writer, the Rebel.* London: Pluto Press, 1976.

4223. **CALDER-MARSHALL, ARTHUR.** "Introduction[s]." In *The Bodley Head Jack London.* 4 vols. London: Bodley Head, 1963–66. I, 7–16; II, 7–27; IV, 7–18.

4224. **COURBIN, JACQUELINE M.** "Jack London's Portrayal of the Natives in His First Four Collections of Arctic Tales." *Jack London Newsletter*, 10 (1977), 127–37.

4225. **DAY, A. GROVE.** "Introduction." In *Stories of Hawaii*, by Jack London. New York: Appleton-Century, 1965. pp. 3–20.

4226. **DHONDT, STEVEN T.** "Jack London's *When God Laughs*: Overman, Underdog and Satire." *Jack London Newsletter*, 2 (1969), 51–57.

4227. _____. " 'There is a good time coming': Jack London's Spirit of Proletarian Revolt." *Jack London Newsletter*, 3 (1970), 25–34.

4228. DUC DUC, DO. "Jack London's Dream at the Turn of the Century." Trans. N. T. Ngoc-Phuong. *Jack London Newsletter*, 6 (1973), 133–45.

4229. FEIED, FREDERICK. *No Pie in the Sky: The Hobo as Cultural Hero in the Works of Jack London, John Dos Passos, and Jack Kerouac.* New York: Citadel Press, 1964.

4230. FRANCHERE, RUTH. *Jack London: The Pursuit of a Dream.* New York: Crowell, 1962.

4231. GEISMAR, MAXWELL. "Introduction: Jack London—The White Logic." In *Short Stories*, by Jack London. New York: Hill and Wang, 1960. pp. ix–xx.

4232. GILES, JAMES R. "Beneficial Atavism in Frank Norris and Jack London." *Western American Literature*, 4 (1969), 15–27.

4233. HENDRICKS, KING. *Jack London: Master Craftsman of the Short Story.* Logan: Faculty Association, Utah State. Univ., 1966.

4234. HENSLEY, DENNIS E. "Jack London Speaks about Writing" (An Imagined Interview). *Jack London Newsletter*, 10 (1977), 43–47.

4235. LABOR, EARLE. *Jack London.* New York: Twayne, 1974.

4236. ———. "Jack London's Symbolic Wilderness: Four Versions." *Nineteenth-Century Fiction*, 17 (1962), 149–61.

4237. LACASSIN, FRANCIS. "Jack London between the Challenge of the Supernatural and the Last Judgment." Trans. Jack Hockett. *Jack London Newsletter*, 8 (1975), 59–65.

4238. LITTELL, KATHERINE M. "The 'Nietzschean' and the Individualist in Jack London's Socialist Writings." *Amerikastudien/American Studies*, 22 (1977), 309–23.

4239. McCLINTOCK, JAMES I. "Jack London: Finding the Proper Trend of Literary Art." *The CEA Critic*, 34, no. 4 (1972), 25–28.

4240. ———. "Jack London's Use of Carl Jung's *Psychology of the Unconscious.*" *American Literature*, 42 (1970), 336–47.

4241. ———. *White Logic: Jack London's Short Stories.* Grand Rapids, MI: Wolf House Books, 1975.

4242. NICHOL, JOHN. "The Role of 'Local Color' in Jack London's Alaskan Wilderness Tales." *Western Review* (Western New Mexico University), 6, no. 2 (1969), 51–56.

4243. O'CONNOR, RICHARD. *Jack London: A Biography.* Boston, MA: Little, Brown, 1964.

4244. PETERSON, CLELL T. "Jack London's Alaskan Stories." *The American Book Collector*, 9, no. 8 (1959), 15–22.

4245. SCHRIBER, MARY SUE. "London in France, 1905–1939." *American Literary Realism, 1870–1910*, 9 (1976), 171–77.

4246. SHIVERS, ALFRED S. "Jack London's Mate-Women." *The American Book Collector*, 15, no. 2 (1964), 17–21.

4247. SHIVERS, SAMUEL A. "The Demoniacs in Jack London." *The American Book Collector*, 12, no. 1 (1961), 11–14.

4248. SINCLAIR, ANDREW. *Jack: A Biography of Jack London*. New York: Harper & Row, 1977.

4249. VANDERBEETS, RICHARD. "Nietzsche of the North: Heredity and Race in London's *The Son of the Wolf*." *Western American Literature*, 2 (1967), 229–33.

4250. WALCUTT, CHARLES CHILD. *Jack London*. Minneapolis: Univ. of Minnesota Press, 1966.

4251. _____. "Jack London." In *Seven Novelists in the American Naturalist Tradition: An Introduction*. Ed. Charles Child Walcutt. Minneapolis: Univ. of Minnesota Press, 1974. pp. 131–67.

4252. WALKER, DALE L. *The Alien Worlds of Jack London*. Grand Rapids, MI: Wolf House Books, 1973.

4253. _____. *Jack London, Sherlock Holmes, & Sir Arthur Conan Doyle*. Amsterdam, NY: Alvin S. Fick, 1974.

4254. WALKER, FRANKLIN. *Jack London and the Klondike: The Genesis of an American Writer*. San Marino, CA: Huntington Library, 1966.

4255. WILCOX, EARL. " 'The Kipling of the Klondike': Naturalism in London's Early Fiction." *Jack London Newsletter*, 6 (1973), 1–12.

Bibliography

4256. HAYDOCK, JAMES. "Jack London: A Bibliography of Criticism." *Bulletin of Bibliography and Magazine Notes*, 23 (1960), 42–46.

4257. LABOR, EARLE. "Jack London: An Addendum." *American Literary Realism, 1870–1910*, 1, no. 2 (1968), 91–93.

4258. LACHTMAN, HOWARD. "Criticism of Jack London: A Selected Checklist." *Modern Fiction Studies*, 22 (1976), 107–25.

4259. LEITZ, ROBERT C. "Additions to the London Bibliography." *Jack London Newsletter*, 9 (1976), 15.

4260. _____. "London in *Life*: An Annotated Checklist." *Jack London Newsletter*, 9 (1976), 10–14.

4261. MONTEIRO, GEORGE. "Jack London: Additions to the Bibliography." *Jack London Newsletter*, 8 (1975), 78–79.

4262. NICHOL, JOHN W. "*Jack London: A Bibliography*, Addenda I." *Jack London Newsletter*, 2 (1969), 84–87.

4263. SHERMAN, JOAN R. *Jack London: A Reference Guide*. Boston, MA: G. K. Hall, 1977.

4264. **SUVIN, DARKO, AND DAVID DOUGLAS.** "Jack London and His Science Fiction: An Annotated Chronological Select Bibliography." *Science-Fiction Studies*, 3 (1976), 181–87.

4265. **TWENEY, GEORGE H.** "Jack London: Bibliographically and Biographically Speaking." *Jack London Newsletter*, 7 (1974), 9–22.

4266. **WALKER, DALE L.** "Jack London (1876–1916)." *American Literary Realism, 1870–1910*, 1, no. 1 (1967), 71–78.

4267. _____, AND JAMES E. SISSON, III. *The Fiction of Jack London: A Chronological Bibliography*. El Paso: Texas Western Press, 1972.

4268. _____, ET AL. "*Jack London: A Bibliography*—A Supplement." *Jack London Newsletter*, 2 (1969), 5–25.

4269. **WOODBRIDGE, HENSLEY C.** "Jack London: A Bibliography—A Supplement." *The American Book Collector*, 17, no. 3 (1966), 32–35.

4270. _____. "More References Concerning Jack London." *Jack London Newsletter*, 1 (1968), 34–40.

4271. _____. "WLT²: Supplement." *Jack London Newsletter*, 6 (1973), 31–56, 123–30; 7 (1974), 48–54, 85–89, 127–31; 8 (1975), 28–31, 80–82, 133–37; 9 (1976), 46–51, 104–06, 156–59; 10 (1977), 52–53.

4272a. _____, JOHN LONDON, AND GEORGE H. TWENEY. *Jack London: A Bibliography*. Georgetown, CA: Talisman Press, 1966.

4272b. _____, _____, AND _____. *Jack London: A Bibliography*. Enlarged ed. Millwood, NY: Kraus Reprint, 1973.

4273. **WOODWARD, ROBERT H.** "*Jack London: A Bibliography*, Addenda II." *Jack London Newsletter*, 2 (1969), 88–90.

LONGSTREET, AUGUSTUS BALDWIN

"A Dance"

See 571.

"The Fight"

See 64, 571.

"The Gander Pulling"

4274. **SILVERMAN, KENNETH.** "Longstreet's 'The Gander Pulling.' " *American Quarterly*, 18 (1966), 548–49.

"Georgia Theatrics"

See 20, 64.

"The Mother and Her Child"

See 549.

General Studies

4275. **Downs, Robert B.** "Yarns of Frontier Life: Augustus Baldwin Longstreet's *Georgia Scenes.*" In *Books That Changed the South*. Chapel Hill: Univ. of North Carolina Press, 1977. pp. 74–81.

LOOMIS, EDWARD

"Wounds"

4276. **Gallagher, Edward J.** "Edward Loomis's 'Wounds.' " *Studies in Short Fiction*, 9 (1972), 247–56.

LOVECRAFT, H[OWARD] P[HILLIPS]

"At the Mountains of Madness"

See 4279.

"The Call of Cthulhu"

See 4278, 4279, 4284.

"The Dreams in the Witch-House"

See 4284.

"The Dunwich Horror"

See 4278, 4279, 4283, 4284.

"The Festival"

See 4284.

"The Haunter of the Dark"

See 4278, 4284.

"The Horror at Red Hook"

See 4279.

"The Hound"

See 4278, 4284.

"The Lair of the Star-Spawn"

See 4278.

"The Nameless City"

See 4278.

"The Outsider"

See 4283.

"Polaris"

See 4279.

"The Rats in the Walls"

See 4283.

"The Shadow Out of Time"

See 4278, 4279.

"The Shadow Over Innsmouth"

See 4278, 4279, 4284.

"The Shunned House"

See 4279, 4284.

"The Statement of Randolph Carter"

See 4279.

"The Terrible Old Man"

See 4284.

"The Thing on the Doorstep"

See 4279, 4284.

"Through the Gates of the Silver Key"

See 4279.

"The Whisperer in Darkness"

See 4278, 4284.

General Studies

4277. BUHLE, PAUL. "Dystopia as Utopia: Howard Phillips Lovecraft and the Unknown Content of American Horror Literature." *The Minnesota Review*, NS no. 6 (1976), pp. 118–31.

4278. CARTER, LIN. *Lovecraft: A Look Behind the "Cthulhu Mythos."* New York: Ballantine Books, 1972.

4279. DE CAMP, L. SPRAGUE. *Lovecraft: A Biography.* Garden City, NY: Doubleday, 1975.

4280. DERLETH, AUGUST. "H. P. Lovecraft: The Making of a Literary Reputation, 1937–1971." *Books at Brown*, 25 (1977), 13–25.

4281. _____. *Some Notes on H. P. Lovecraft.* Sauk City, WI: Arkham House, 1959.

4282. **LONG, FRANK BELKNAP.** *Howard Phillips Lovecraft: Dreamer on the Nightside.* Sauk City, WI: Arkham House, 1975.

4283. **ST. ARMAND, BARTON LEVI.** *The Roots of Horror in the Fiction of H. P. Lovecraft.* Elizabethtown, NY: Dragon Press, 1977.

4284. **SHREFFLER, PHILIP A.** *The H. P. Lovecraft Companion.* Westport, CT: Greenwood Press, 1977.

4285. **TALMAN, WILFRED B.** *The Normal Lovecraft.* Saddle River, NJ: Gerry de la Ree, 1973.

Bibliography

4286. **OWINGS, MARK, AND JACK CHALKER.** *The Revised H. P. Lovecraft Bibliography.* Baltimore, MD: Mirage Press, 1973.

4287. **WEINBERG, R. E., AND E. P. BERGLUND.** *A Reader's Guide to the Cthulhu Mythos.* Albuquerque, NM: Silver Scarab Press, 1973.

LYON, HARRIS MERTON

"The Man with the Broken Fingers"

See 4289.

"The Riding Beggar"

4288. **LYON, ZOË.** "A Brief Analysis of 'The Riding Beggar.' " *Studies in Short Fiction,* 10 (1973), 25–26.

"Scarlet and White"

See 4289.

General Studies

4289. **LYON, ZOË.** "Harris Merton Lyon: Early American Realist." *Studies in Short Fiction,* 5 (1968), 368–77.

Bibliography

4290. **EICHELBERGER, CLAYTON L., AND ZOË LYON.** "A Partial Listing of the Published Work of Harris Merton Lyon." *American Literary Realism, 1870–1910,* 3 (1970), 41–52.

4291. **LYON, ZOË.** "Harris Merton Lyon (1883–1916)." *American Literary Realism, 1870–1910,* 3 (1970), 36–40.

LYON, KATE

"Lorraine's Last Voyage"

4292. **GARNER, STANTON B.** "Kate Lyon—Author." *The Frederic Herald,* 1, no. 2 (1967), 2.

LYTLE, ANDREW

"Alchemy"

4293. BRADFORD, M. E. "Toward a Dark Shape: Lytle's 'Alchemy' and the Conquest of the New World." *The Mississippi Quarterly*, 23 (1970), 407–14.

"The Hind Tit"

See 185.

"Jerico, Jerico, Jerico"

4294. HURT, JAMES R. "Lytle's 'Jerico, Jerico, Jerico.'" *The Explicator*, 20 (1962), item 52.
4295. LANDMAN, SIDNEY J. "The Walls of Mortality." *The Mississippi Quarterly*, 23 (1970), 415–23.

"The Mahogany Frame"

4296. KRICKEL, EDWARD. "The Whole and the Parts: Initiation in 'The Mahogany Frame.'" *The Mississippi Quarterly*, 23 (1970), 391–405.

"Mister McGregor"

4297. JONES, MADISON. "A Look at 'Mister McGregor.'" *The Mississippi Quarterly*, 23 (1970), 363–70.
See also 267, 4298.

General Studies

4298. JOYNER, NANCY. "The Myth of Matriarch in Andrew Lytle's Fiction." *The Southern Literary Journal*, 7, no. 1 (1974), 67–77.

Bibliography

4299. POLK, NOEL. "Andrew Nelson Lytle: A Bibliography of His Writings." *The Mississippi Quarterly*, 23 (1970), 435–91.

McALMON, ROBERT

"Distinguished Air"

See 116, 4300.

"The Lodging House"

See 4300.

"Miss Knight"

See 4300.

General Studies

4300. **Smoller, Sanford J.** *Adrift Among Geniuses: Robert Mc-Almon, Writer and Publisher of the Twenties.* University Park: Pennsylvania State Univ. Press, 1975.

McCARTHY, MARY

"Artists in Uniform"
See 267.

"The Cicerone"
4301. **McKenzie, Barbara.** "The Arid Plain of 'The Cicerone.'" In *The Process of Fiction: Contemporary Stories and Criticism.* Ed. Barbara McKenzie. New York: Harcourt, Brace & World, 1969. pp. 76–83.
See also 4305.

"The Company Is Not Responsible"
See 4305.

"Cruel and Barbarous Treatment"
See 384, 4306.

"Ghostly Father, I Confess"
See 4305, 4306.

"The Hounds of Summer"
See 4305.

"The Man in the Brooks Brothers Suit"
See 4305, 4306.

"The Old Men"
See 4306.

"Portrait of an Intellectual as a Yale Man"
See 4305, 4306.

"The Unspoiled Reaction"
4302. **Gillen, Francis.** "The Failure of Ritual in 'The Unspoiled Reaction.'" *Renascence,* 24 (1972), 155–58.
4303. **Kreutz, Irving.** "Mary McCarthy's 'The Unspoiled Reaction': Pejorative as Satire." *Descant,* 13, no. 1 (1968), 32–48.
See also 565, 4305.

"The Weeds"

See 4305, 4306.

General Studies

4304. **CHAMBERLAIN, JOHN.** "The Novels of Mary McCarthy." In *The Creative Present: Notes on Contemporary American Fiction.* Ed. Nona Balakian and Charles Simmons. Garden City, NY: Doubleday, 1963. pp. 241-55.

4305. **GRUMBACH, DORIS.** *The Company She Kept.* New York: Coward-McCann, 1967.

4306. **McKENZIE, BARBARA.** *Mary McCarthy.* New York: Twayne, 1966.

4307. **SCHLUETER, PAUL.** "The Dissections of Mary McCarthy." In *Contemporary American Novelists.* Ed. Harry T. Moore. Carbondale: Southern Illinois Univ. Press, 1964. pp. 54-64.

4308. **WIDMER, ELEANOR.** "Finally a Lady: Mary McCarthy." In *The Fifties: Fiction, Poetry, Drama.* Ed. Warren French. Deland, FL: Everett/Edwards, 1970. pp. 93-102.

Interviews

4309. **McCARTHY, MARY.** "The Art of Fiction XXVII." With Elisabeth Niebuhr. *The Paris Review,* no. 27 (1962), pp. 59-94.

4310. **[RAHV, PHILIP].** "The Editor Interviews Mary McCarthy." *Modern Occasions,* 1 (1970), 14-25.

4311. **REVEL, JEAN-FRANCOIS.** "Miss McCarthy Explains." *The New York Times Book Review,* 16 May 1971, pp. 2, 24, 26, 28, 30.

Bibliography

4312. **GOLDMAN, SHERLI EVANS.** *Mary McCarthy: A Bibliography.* New York: Harcourt, Brace & World, 1968.

McCULLERS, CARSON

"The Ballad of the Sad Cafe"

4313. **BROUGHTON, PANTHEA REID.** "Rejection of the Feminine in Carson McCullers' *The Ballad of the Sad Cafe." Twentieth Century Literature,* 20 (1974), 34-43.

4314. **DODD, WAYNE D.** "The Development of Theme through Symbol in the Novels of Carson McCullers." *The Georgia Review,* 17 (1963), 206-13.

4315. **EVANS, OLIVER.** "The Case of Carson McCullers." *The Georgia Review,* 18 (1964), 40-45.

4316. **GAILLARD, DAWSON F.** "The Presence of the Narrator in Carson McCullers' *The Ballad of the Sad Cafe." The Mississippi Quarterly,* 25 (1972), 419-27.

4317. GRIFFITH, ALBERT J. "Carson McCullers' Myth of the Sad Café." *The Georgia Review*, 21 (1967), 46–56.

4318. HAMILTON, ALICE. "Loneliness and Alienation: The Life and Work of Carson McCullers." *Dalhousie Review*, 50 (1970), 215–29.

4319. HASSAN, IHAB H. "Carson McCullers: The Alchemy of Love and Aesthetics of Pain." *Modern Fiction Studies*, 5 (1959), 311–26.

4320. LUBBERS, KLAUS. "The Necessary Order: A Study of Theme and Structure in Carson McCullers' Fiction." *Jahrbuch für Amerikastudien*, 8 (1963), 187–204.

4321. MILLICHAP, JOSEPH R. "Carson McCullers' Literary Ballad." *The Georgia Review*, 27 (1973), 329–39.

4322. MOORE, JANICE TOWNLEY. "McCullers' 'The Ballad of the Sad Café.' " *The Explicator*, 29 (1970), item 27.

4323. OHKOSO, YOSHIKO. "Solitary Love: Carson McCullers's Novels." In *American Literature in the 1940's*. Annual Report, 1975. Tokyo: Tokyo Chapter, American Literary Society of Japan, 1976. pp. 40–57.

4324. PHILLIPS, ROBERT S. "Dinesen's 'Monkey' and McCullers' 'Ballad': A Study in Literary Affinity." *Studies in Short Fiction*, 1 (1964), 184–90.

4325. _____. "Painful Love: Carson McCullers' Parable." *Southwest Review*, 51 (1966), 80–86.

4326. RECHNITZ, ROBERT M. "The Failure of Love: The Grotesque in Two Novels by Carson McCullers." *The Georgia Review*, 22 (1968), 454–63.

4327. VICKERY, JOHN B. "Carson McCullers: A Map of Love." *Wisconsin Studies in Contemporary Literature*, 1, no. 1 (1960), 13–24.
See also 162, 166, 185, 200, 206, 257, 277, 4334–4336, 4338–4341.

"Correspondence"

4328. EDMUNDS, DALE. " 'Correspondence': A 'Forgotten' Carson McCullers Short Story." *Studies in Short Fiction*, 9 (1972), 89–92.

"A Domestic Dilemma"

4329. GRINNELL, JAMES W. "Delving 'A Domestic Dilemma.' " *Studies in Short Fiction*, 9 (1972), 270–71.

4330. PERRINE, LAURENCE. "Restoring 'A Domestic Dilemma.' " *Studies in Short Fiction*, 11 (1974), 101–04.

"The Sojourner"

See 194, 384, 564, 4336, 4339.

"A Tree. A Rock. A Cloud"

4331. MISSEY, JAMES. "A McCullers Influence on Albee's *The Zoo Story.*" *American Notes & Queries*, 13 (1975), 121–23.
See also 565, 4338.

"Wunderkind"

See 4338.

General Studies

4332. BUCHEN, IRVING H. "Carson McCullers, A Case of Convergence." *Bucknell Review*, 21, no. 1 (1973), 15–28.
4333. ———. "Divine Collusion: The Art of Carson McCullers." *Dalhousie Review*, 54 (1974), 529–41.
4334. CARR, VIRGINIA SPENCER. *The Lonely Hunter: A Biography of Carson McCullers.* Garden City, NY: Doubleday, 1975.
4335. COOK, RICHARD M. *Carson McCullers.* New York: Ungar, 1975.
4336. EDMONDS, DALE. *Carson McCullers.* Austin, TX: Steck-Vaughn, 1969.
4337. EVANS, OLIVER. "The Achievement of Carson McCullers." *English Journal*, 51 (1962), 301–08.
4338. ———. *Carson McCullers: Her Life and Work.* London: Peter Owen, 1965.
4339. FOLK, BARBARA NAUER. "The Sad Sweet Music of Carson McCullers." *The Georgia Review*, 16 (1962), 202–09.
4340. GRAVER, LAWRENCE. *Carson McCullers.* Minneapolis: Univ. of Minnesota Press, 1969.
4341. ROBINSON, W. R. "The Life of Carson McCullers' Imagination." *Southern Humanities Review*, 2 (1968), 291–302.

Bibliography

4342. KIERNAN, ROBERT F. *Katherine Anne Porter and Carson McCullers: A Reference Guide.* Boston, MA: G. K. Hall, 1976.
4343. PHILLIPS, ROBERT S. "Carson McCullers, 1956–1964: A Selected Checklist." *Bulletin of Bibliography and Magazine Notes*, 24 (1964), 113–16.
4344. STANLEY, WILLIAM T. "Carson McCullers, 1965–1969: A Selected Checklist." *Bulletin of Bibliography and Magazine Notes*, 27 (1970), 91–93.
4345. STEWART, STANLEY. "Carson McCullers, 1940–1956: A Selected Checklist." *Bulletin of Bibliography and Magazine Notes*, 22 (1959), 182–85.

MacDOWELL, CATHERINE SHERWOOD
(See BONNER, SHERWOOD)

MacLEAN, KATHERINE
"Pictures Don't Lie"
See 114.

"Unhuman Sacrifice"
See 114.

McKAY, CLAUDE
"The Agricultural Show"
See 386.

"High Ball"
See 283, 4347.

"The Strange Burial of Sue"
See 386, 4347.

"Truant"
See 337, 386.

General Studies
4346. CONROY, SISTER MARY. "The Vagabond Motif in the Writings of Claude McKay." *Negro American Literature Forum*, 5 (1971), 15–23.
*4347. GILES, JAMES R. *Claude McKay.* Boston, MA: Twayne, 1976.

Bibliography
4348. LOPEZ, MANUEL D. "Claude McKay." *Bulletin of Bibliography and Magazine Notes*, 29 (1972), 128–34.

McMURTRY, LARRY
Bibliography
4349. PEAVY, CHARLES D. "A Larry McMurtry Bibliography." *Western American Literature*, 3 (1968), 235–48.

McPHERSON, JAMES ALAN
"Gold Coast"
See 268, 483.

"Hue and Cry"

See 333.

"A Solo Song: For Doc"

4350. **LAUGHLIN, ROSEMARY M.** "Attention, American Folklore: Doc Craft Comes Marching In." *Studies in American Fiction*, 1 (1973), 220–27.
See also 399.

MADDEN, DAVID

Interviews

4351. **LANEY, RUTH.** "An Interview with David Madden." *The Southern Review*, NS 11 (1975), 167–80.
4352. **PINSKER, SANFORD.** "A Conversation with David Madden." *Critique*, 15, no. 2 (1973), 5–14.

MAILER, NORMAN

"The Man Who Studied Yoga"

4353. **ADAMS, LAURA.** *Existential Battles: The Growth of Norman Mailer*. Athens: Ohio Univ. Press, 1976.
4354. **BUSCH, FREDERICK.** "The Whale as Shaggy Dog: Melville and 'The Man Who Studied Yoga.'" *Modern Fiction Studies*, 19 (1973), 193–206.
4355. **TRILLING, DIANA.** "The Radical Moralism of Norman Mailer." In *The Creative Present: Notes on Contemporary American Fiction*. Ed. Nona Balakian and Charles Simmons. Garden City, NY: Doubleday, 1963. pp. 145–71.
See also 4358, 4361, 4362.

"The Paper House"

See 4357, 4358.

"The Time of Her Time"

4356. **RAINES, HELON HOWELL.** "Norman Mailer's Sergius O'Shaughnessy, Villain and Victim." *Frontiers*, 2, no. 1 (1977), 71–75.
See also 4355, 4361.

"Way Out"

See 4361.

General Studies

4357. **FOSTER, RICHARD.** *Norman Mailer*. Minneapolis: Univ. of Minnesota Press, 1968.

4358. **IWAMOTO, IWAO.** "Norman Mailer's Short Fiction in the Fifties." In *American Literature in the 1950's.* Annual Report, 1976. Tokyo: Tokyo Chapter, American Literary Society of Japan, 1977. pp. 22–31.

4359. **KAUFMANN, DONALD L.** *Norman Mailer: The Countdown (The First Twenty Years).* Carbondale and Edwardsville: Southern Illinois Univ. Press, 1969.

4360. **POIRIER, RICHARD.** *Norman Mailer.* New York: Viking, 1972.

4361. **RADFORD, JEAN.** *Norman Mailer: A Critical Study.* London: Macmillan, 1975.

4362. **SOLOTAROFF, ROBERT.** *Down Mailer's Way.* Urbana: Univ. of Illinois Press, 1974.

4363. **WEATHERBY, W. J.** *Squaring Off: Mailer vs. Baldwin.* New York: Mason/Charter, 1977.

Interviews

4364. **ADAMS, LAURA.** "Existential Aesthetics: An Interview with Norman Mailer." *Partisan Review,* 42 (1975), 197–214.

4365. **MAILER, NORMAN.** "The Art of Fiction XXXII." With Steve Marcus. *The Paris Review,* no. 31 (1964), pp. 29–58.

4366. ———. "Mailer on Mailer: An Interview." With Matthew Grace and Steve Roday. *The New Orleans Review,* 3 (1973), 229–34.

4367. ———. "Mr. Mailer Interviews Himself." *The New York Times Book Review,* 17 Sept. 1967, pp. 4–5, 40.

4368. **RODMAN, SELDEN.** "Norman Mailer." In *Tongues of Fallen Angels.* New York: New Directions, 1974. pp. 163–81.

4369. **STERN, RICHARD G.** "Hip, Hell, and the Navigator: An Interview with Norman Mailer." *The Western Review* (State University of Iowa), 23 (1959), 101–09.

Bibliography

4370. **ADAMS, LAURA.** "Criticism of Norman Mailer: A Selected Checklist." *Modern Fiction Studies,* 17 (1971), 455–63.

4371. ———. *Norman Mailer: A Comprehensive Bibliography.* Metuchen, NJ: Scarecrow, 1974.

4372. **LUCID, ROBERT F.** "A Checklist of Mailer's Published Work." In *Norman Mailer: The Man and His Work.* Ed. Robert F. Lucid. Boston, MA: Little, Brown, 1971. pp. 299–310.

4373. **SHEPARD, DOUGLAS H.** "Norman Mailer: A Preliminary Bibliography of Secondary Comment, 1948–1968." *Bulletin of Bibliography and Magazine Notes,* 29 (1972), 37–45.

4374. **SOKOLOFF, B. A.** *A Bibliography of Norman Mailer.* Folcroft, PA: Folcroft Press, 1970.

MAINWARING, DANIEL

"Fruit Tramp"

4375. ASTRO, RICHARD. "Steinbeck and Mainwaring: Two Californians of the Earth." *Steinbeck Quarterly*, 3 (1970), 3–11.

MAJOR, CLARENCE

Interviews

4376. O'BRIEN, JOHN. "Clarence Major." In *Interviews with Black Writers*. Ed. John O'Brien. New York: Liveright, 1973. pp. 125–39.

MALAMUD, BERNARD

"Angel Levine"

See 4393, 4400, 4409, 4413.

"Behold the Key"

4377. SWEET, CHARLES A., JR. "Unlocking the Door: Malamud's 'Behold the Key.' " *Notes on Contemporary Literature*, 5, no. 5 (1975), 11–12.
See also 4395.

"Benefit Performance"

See 222.

"The Bill"

See 4409.

"Black Is My Favorite Color"

4378. SKAGGS, MERRILL MAGUIRE. "A Complex Black-and-White Matter." In *The Process of Fiction: Contemporary Stories and Criticism*. Ed. Barbara McKenzie. New York: Harcourt, Brace & World, 1969. pp. 384–91.
See also 4409.

"A Choice of Profession"

See 4409.

"The First Seven Years"

See 4409.

"The German Refugee"

See 256, 4409.

"The Girl of My Dreams"

See 4393, 4409.

"The Glass Blower of Venice"

See 4395.

"Idiots First"

See 4409, 4413.

"The Jewbird"

4379. RUDIN, NEIL. "Malamud's Jewbird and Kafka's Gracchus: Birds of a Feather." *Studies in American Jewish Literature*, 1, no. 1 (1975), 10–15.
See also 113, 456, 4409, 4413.

"The Lady of the Lake"

4380. HILL, JOHN S. "Malamud's 'The Lady of the Lake'—A Lesson in Rejection." *The University Review* (Kansas City), 36 (1969), 149–50.
See also 453, 4400, 4409.

"The Last Mohican"

4381. MESHER, DAVID R. "The Remembrance of Things Unknown: Malamud's 'The Last Mohican.' " *Studies in Short Fiction*, 12 (1975), 397–404.
4382. WINN, H. HARBOUR, III. "Malamud's Uncas: 'Last Mohican.' " *Notes on Contemporary Literature*, 5, no. 2 (1975), 13–14.
See also 256, 4392, 4395, 4396, 4400, 4409, 4412.

"Life Is Better Than Death"

See 4409.

"The Loan"

4383. MAY, CHARLES E. "The Bread of Tears: Malamud's 'The Loan.' " *Studies in Short Fiction*, 7 (1970), 652–54.
See also 4409.

"The Magic Barrel"

4384. MILLER, THEODORE C. "The Minister and the Whore: An Examination of Bernard Malamud's 'The Magic Barrel.' " *Studies in the Humanities*, 3, no. 1 (1972), 43–44.
4385. PINSKER, SANFORD. "The Achievement of Bernard Malamud." *The Midwest Quarterly*, 10 (1969), 379–89.
4386. REYNOLDS, RICHARD. " 'The Magic Barrel': Pinye Salzman's Kadish." *Studies in Short Fiction*, 10 (1973), 100–02.

See also 222, 286, 564, 595, 4393, 4400, 4402, 4409, 4413, 5868.

"The Maid's Shoes"
See 4409.

"The Mourners"
See 4393.

"Naked Nude"
See 4395, 4409.

"Pictures of the Artist"
See 4396, 4411.

"A Pimp's Revenge"
See 4395.

"The Prison"
4387. **WECHSLER, DIANE.** "An Analysis of 'The Prison' by Bernard Malamud." *English Journal*, 59 (1970), 782–84.
See also 564.

"The Silver Crown"
See 483, 535.

"Still Life"
See 4395, 4409.

"A Summer's Reading"
4388. **MAY, CHARLES E.** "Bernard Malamud's 'A Summer's Reading.' " *Notes on Contemporary Literature*, 2, no. 4 (1972), 11–13.

"Take Pity"
4389. **PERRINE, LAURENCE.** "Malamud's 'Take Pity.' " *Studies in Short Fiction*, 2 (1964), 84–86.
4390. **PINSKER, SANFORD.** "A Note on Bernard Malamud's 'Take Pity.' " *Studies in Short Fiction*, 6 (1969), 212–13.
See also 267, 564, 4413.

General Studies
4391. **BELLMAN, SAMUEL IRVING.** "Women, Children, and Idiots First: The Transformational Psychology of Bernard Malamud." *Critique*, 7, no. 2 (1965), 123–38.

4392. **BENSON, JACKSON J.** "An Introduction: Bernard Malamud and the Haunting of America." In *The Fiction of Bernard Malamud*. Ed. Richard Astro and Jackson J. Benson. Corvallis: Oregon State Univ. Press, 1977. pp. 13–42.

4393. **BLUEFARB, SAM.** "Bernard Malamud: The Scope of Caricature." *The English Journal*, 53 (1964), 319–26, 335.

4394. ———. "The Syncretism of Bernard Malamud." In *Bernard Malamud: A Collection of Critical Essays*. Ed. Leslie A. Field and Joyce W. Field. Englewood Cliffs, NJ: Prentice-Hall, 1975. pp. 72–79.

4395. **COHEN, SANDY.** *Bernard Malamud and the Trial by Love*. Amsterdam: Rodopi, 1974.

4396. **DUCHARME, ROBERT.** "Structure and Content in Malamud's *Pictures of Fidelman*." *The Connecticut Review*, 5, no. 1 (1971), 26–36.

4397. **FIELD, LESLIE.** "Bernard Malamud and the Marginal Jew." In *The Fiction of Bernard Malamud*. Ed. Richard Astro and Jackson J. Benson. Corvallis: Oregon State Univ. Press, 1977. pp. 97–116.

4398. ———. "Portrait of the Artist as *Schlemiel (Pictures of Fidelman)*." In *Bernard Malamud: A Collection of Critical Essays*. Ed. Leslie A. Field and Joyce W. Field. Englewood Cliffs, NJ: Prentice-Hall, 1975. pp. 117–29.

4399. **FIELD, LESLIE AND JOYCE.** "Introduction: Malamud, Mercy, and Menschlechkeit." In *Bernard Malamud: A Collection of Critical Essays*. Ed. Leslie A. Field and Joyce W. Field. Englewood Cliffs, NJ: Prentice-Hall, 1975. pp. 1–7.

4400. **GOLDMAN, MARK.** "Bernard Malamud's Comic Vision and the Theme of Identity." *Critique*, 7, no. 2 (1965), 92–109.

4401. **GREBSTEIN, SHELDON NORMAN.** "Bernard Malamud and the Jewish Movement." In *Contemporary American-Jewish Literature*. Ed. Irving Malin. Bloomington: Indiana Univ. Press, 1973. pp. 175–212.

4402. **GUNN, GILES B.** "Bernard Malamud and the High Cost of Living." In *Adversity and Grace: Studies in Recent American Literature*. Ed. Nathan A. Scott, Jr. Chicago: Univ. of Chicago Press, 1968. pp. 59–85.

4403. **HASSAN, IHAB.** "Bernard Malamud, 1976: Fictions within Our Fictions." In *The Fiction of Bernard Malamud*. Ed. Richard Astro and Jackson J. Benson. Corvallis: Oregon State Univ. Press, 1977. pp. 43–64.

4404. **HAYS, PETER L.** "Malamud's Yiddish-Accented Medieval Stories." In *The Fiction of Bernard Malamud*. Ed. Richard Astro and Jackson J. Benson. Corvallis: Oregon State Univ. Press, 1977. pp. 87–96.

4405. **Hoyt, Charles Alva.** "Bernard Malamud and the New Romanticism." In *Contemporary American Novelists.* Ed. Harry T. Moore. Carbondale: Southern Illinois Univ. Press, 1964. pp. 65–79.

4406. **Lamdin, Lois S.** "Malamud's Schlemiels." In *A Modern Miscellany.* Ed. David P. Demarest, Jr., Lois S. Lamdin, and Joseph Baim. Pittsburgh, PA: Carnegie-Mellon Univ., 1970. pp. 31–42.

4407. **Malamud, Bernard.** "Speaking of Books: Theme, Content and the 'New Novel.'" *The New York Times Book Review,* 26 Mar. 1967, pp. 2, 29.

4408. **Ratner, Marc L.** "Style and Humanity in Malamud's Fiction." *The Massachusetts Review,* 5 (1964), 663–83.

4409. **Richman, Sidney.** *Bernard Malamud.* New York: Twayne, 1966.

4410. **Rovit, Earl H.** "Bernard Malamud and the Jewish Literary Tradition." *Critique,* 3, no. 2 (1960), 3–10.

4411. **Schwartz, Helen J.** "Malamud's Turning Point: The End of Redemption in *Pictures of Fidelman.*" *Studies in American Jewish Literature,* 2, no. 2 (1976), 26–37.

4412. **Siegel, Ben.** "Through a Glass Darkly: Bernard Malamud's Painful Views of the Self." In *The Fiction of Bernard Malamud.* Ed. Richard Astro and Jackson J. Benson. Corvallis: Oregon State Univ. Press, 1977. pp. 117–47.

4413. **Warburton, Robert W.** "Fantasy and the Fiction of Bernard Malamud." In *Imagination and the Spirit: Essays in Literature and the Christian Faith Presented to Clyde S. Kilby.* Ed. Charles A. Huttar. Grand Rapids, MI: Eerdmans, 1971. pp. 387–416.

Interviews

4414. **Anon.** Interview with Bernard Malamud. *The New York Times Book Review,* 13 Oct. 1963, p. 5.

4415. **Anon.** "A Talk with B. Malamud." *The New York Times Book Review,* 8 Oct. 1961, p. 28.

4416. **Field, Leslie and Joyce.** "An Interview with Bernard Malamud." In *Bernard Malamud: A Collection of Critical Essays.* Ed. Leslie A. Field and Joyce W. Field. Englewood Cliffs, NJ: Prentice-Hall, 1975. pp. 8–17.

4417. **Hicks, Granville.** "His Hopes on the Human Heart." *Saturday Review,* 46 (12 Oct. 1963), 31–32.

4418. **Malamud, Bernard.** "The Art of Fiction LII." With Daniel Stern. *The Paris Review,* no. 61 (1975), pp. 41–64.

4419. **Shenker, Israel.** "For Malamud It's Story." *The New York Times Book Review*, 3 Oct. 1971, pp. 20, 22.

Bibliography

4420. **[Field, Leslie and Joyce.]** "Selected Bibliography." In *Bernard Malamud: A Collection of Critical Essays*. Ed. Leslie A. Field and Joyce W. Field. Englewood Cliffs, NJ: Prentice-Hall, 1975. pp. 172–79.

4421. _____. "Works of Bernard Malamud." In *Bernard Malamud: A Collection of Critical Essays*. Ed. Leslie A. Field and Joyce W. Field. Englewood Cliffs, NJ: Prentice-Hall, 1975. pp. 170–71.

4422. **Kosofsky, Rita Nathalie.** *Bernard Malamud: An Annotated Checklist*. Kent, OH: Kent State Univ. Press, 1969.

4423. **Risty, Donald.** "A Comprehensive Checklist of Malamud Criticism." In *The Fiction of Bernard Malamud*. Ed. Richard Astro and Jackson J. Benson. Corvallis: Oregon State Univ. Press, 1977. pp. 163–90.

MALTZ, ALBERT

General Studies

4424. **Eisinger, Chester E.** "Character and Self in Fiction on the Left." In *Proletarian Writers of the Thirties*. Ed. David Madden. Carbondale and Edwardsville: Southern Illinois Univ. Press, 1968. pp. 158–83.

MANFRED, FREDERICK

Interviews

4425. **Milton, John R.** *Conversations with Frederick Manfred*. Salt Lake City: Univ. of Utah Press, 1974.

4426. _____. "Interview with Frederick Manfred." *South Dakota Review*, 7, no. 4 (1970), 110–30.

Bibliography

4427. **Kellogg, George.** "Frederick Manfred: A Bibliography." *Twentieth Century Literature*, 11 (1965), 30–35.

MARCH, WILLIAM

"Aesop's Last Fable"

See 478.

"The Dappled Fawn"

See 4434.

"The Little Wife"

4428. GOING, WILLIAM T. "March's 'The Little Wife.' " *The Explicator*, 20 (1962), item 66.

"A Memorial to the Slain"

See 4431.

"Nine Prisoners"

See 4430, 4434.

"Personal Letter"

See 4435.

"The Unploughed Patch"

See 4430.

General Studies

4429. GOING, WILLIAM T. "Introduction." In *99 Fables*, by William March. University: Univ. of Alabama Press, 1960. pp. xiii–xxii.

4430. _____. "Some in Addition: The Uncollected Stories of William March." In *Essays on Alabama Literature*. University: Univ. of Alabama Press, 1975. pp. 80–96.

4431. _____. "William March's Alabama." In *Essays on Alabama Literature*. University: Univ. of Alabama Press, 1975. pp. 97–113.

4432. MEDLICOTT, ALEXANDER, JR. " 'Soldiers Are Citizens of Death's Gray Land': William March's *Company K*." *The Arizona Quarterly*, 28 (1972), 209–24.

4433. SIMMONDS, ROY S. "An Unending Circle of Pain: William March's *Company K*." *Ball State University Forum*, 16, no. 2 (1975), 33–46.

4434. _____. "William March's *Company K*: A Short Textual Study." *Studies in American Fiction*, 2 (1974), 105–13.

4435. _____. "William March's 'Personal Letter': Fact into Fiction." *The Mississippi Quarterly*, 30 (1977), 625–37.

Bibliography

4436. SIMMONDS, ROY S. "A William March Checklist." *The Mississippi Quarterly*, 28 (1975), 461–88.

MARQUAND, J[OHN] P[HILLIPS]
"The End Game"

See 4437.

"Good Morning, Major"

See 4437.

General Studies

4437. **BIRMINGHAM, STEPHEN.** *The Late John Marquand: A Biography.* Philadelphia, PA: Lippincott, 1972.
4438. **HOLMAN, C. HUGH.** *John P. Marquand.* Minneapolis: Univ. of Minnesota Press, 1965.

Bibliography

4439. **WHITE, WILLIAM.** "More Marquandiana, 1956–1968." *The Serif,* 6, no. 2 (1969), 33–36.

MARQUIS, DON[ALD]
General Studies

4440. **ANTHONY, EDWARD.** *O Rare Don Marquis: A Biography.* Garden City, NY: Doubleday, 1962.
4441. **HASLEY, LOUIS.** "Don Marquis: Ambivalent Humorist." *Prairie Schooner,* 45 (1971), 59–73.
4442. **HILL, HAMLIN L.** "Archy and Uncle Remus: Don Marquis's Debt to Joel Chandler Harris." *The Georgia Review,* 15 (1961), 78–87.

MARSHALL, PAULE
"Reena"

See 340.

General Studies

4443. **BROWN, LLOYD W.** "The Rhythms of Power in Paule Marshall's Fiction." *Novel,* 7 (1974), 159–67.
4444. **KAPAI, LEELA.** "Dominant Themes and Technique in Paule Marshall's Fiction." *CLA Journal,* 16 (1972), 49–59.
4445. **KEIZS, MARCIA.** "Themes and Style in the Works of Paule Marshall." *Negro American Literature Forum,* 9 (1975), 67, 71–76.
4446. **MARSHALL, PAULE.** "Shaping the World of My Art." *New Letters,* 40, no. 1 (1973), 97–112.

MATHEUS, JOHN
"Fog"
See 283.

MATHEWS, CORNELIUS
General Studies
*4447. STEIN, ALLEN F. *Cornelius Mathews*. New York: Twayne, 1974.

MAYER, TOM
General Studies
*4448. DAVIS, KENNETH W. "The Themes of Initiation in the Works of Larry McMurtry and Tom Mayer." *The Arlington Quarterly*, 2, no. 3 (1970), 29–43.

MELVILLE, HERMAN
"The Apple-Tree Table"
4449. BREINIG, HELMBRECHT. "Symbol, Satire, and the Will to Communicate in Melville's 'The Apple-Tree Table.' " *Amerikastudien/American Studies*, 22 (1977), 269–85.
4450. FISHER, MARVIN. "Bug and Humbug in Melville's 'Apple-Tree Table.' " *Studies in Short Fiction*, 8 (1971), 459–66.
4451. KARCHER, CAROLYN L. "The 'Spiritual Lesson' of Melville's 'The Apple-Tree Table.' " *American Quarterly*, 23 (1971), 101–09.
4452. MAGAW, MALCOLM O. "Apocalyptic Imagery in Melville's 'The Apple-Tree Table.' " *The Midwest Quarterly*, 8 (1967), 357–69.
See also 56, 4770, 4776, 4784, 4788, 4789, 4793, 4813, 4831.

"Bartleby the Scrivener"
4453. ABCARIAN, RICHARD. "The World of Love and the Spheres of Fright: Melville's 'Bartleby the Scrivener.' " *Studies in Short Fiction*, 1 (1964), 207–15.
4454. ASCHAFFENBURG, WALTER. "*Bartleby*: Genesis of an Opera 1." In *Melville Annual 1965, A Symposium:* Bartleby the Scrivener. Ed. Howard P. Vincent. Kent, OH: Kent State Univ. Press, 1966. pp. 25–41.
4455. AYO, NICHOLAS. "Bartleby's Lawyer on Trial." *The Arizona Quarterly*, 28 (1972), 27–38.

4456. **BALL, ROLAND C.** "American Reinterpretations of European Romantic Themes: The Rebel-Hero in Cooper and Melville." In *Actes du IVe Congrès de l'Association Internationale de Littérature Comparée.* Ed. François Jost. 2 vols. The Hague: Mouton, 1966. II, 1113–21.

4457. **BARBER, PATRICIA.** "What If Bartleby Were a Woman?" In *The Authority of Experience: Essays in Feminist Criticism.* Ed. Arlyn Diamond and Lee R. Edwards. Amherst: Univ. of Massachusetts Press, 1977. pp. 212–23, 298–300.

4458. **BARNETT, LOUISE K.** "Bartleby as Alienated Worker." *Studies in Short Fiction,* 11 (1974), 379–85.

4459. **BERGMANN, JOHANNES DIETRICH.** " 'Bartleby' and *The Lawyer's Story."* *American Literature,* 47 (1975), 432–36.

4460. **BIGELOW, GORDON E.** "The Problem of Symbolist Form in Melville's 'Bartleby the Scrivener.' " *Modern Language Quarterly,* 31 (1970), 345–58..

4461. **BILLY, TED.** "Eros and Thanatos in 'Bartleby.' " *The Arizona Quarterly,* 31 (1975), 21–32.

4462. **BLUESTONE, GEORGE.** *"Bartleby:* The Tale, the Film." In *Melville Annual 1965, A Symposium:* Bartleby the Scrivener. Ed. Howard P. Vincent. Kent, OH: Kent State Univ. Press, 1966. pp. 45–54.

4463. **BOLLAS, CHRISTOPHER.** "Melville's Lost Self: *Bartleby."* *American Imago,* 31 (1974), 401–11.

4464. **BOWEN, JAMES K.** "Alienation and Withdrawal Are Not the Absurd: Renunciation and Preference in 'Bartleby the Scrivener.' " *Studies in Short Fiction,* 8 (1971), 633–35.

4465. **BROWNE, RAY B.** "The Affirmation of 'Bartleby.' " In *Folklore International: Essays in Traditional Literature, Belief, and Custom in Honor of Wayland Debs Hand.* Ed. D. K. Wilgus and Carol Sommer. Hatsboro, PA: Folklore Associates, 1967. pp. 11–21.

4466. **BUSCH, FREDERICK.** "Thoreau and Melville as Cellmates." *Modern Fiction Studies,* 23 (1977), 239–42.

4467. **CERVO, NATHAN A.** "Melville's Bartleby—*Imago Dei."* *American Transcendental Quarterly,* no. 14 (1972), pp. 152–56.

4468. **COLWELL, JAMES L., AND GARY SPITZER.** " 'Bartleby' and 'The Raven': Parallels of the Irrational." *The Georgia Review,* 23 (1969), 37–43.

4469. **CONARROE, JOEL O.** "Melville's Bartleby and Charles Lamb." *Studies in Short Fiction,* 5 (1968), 113–18.

4470. **D'AVANZO, MARIO L.** "Melville's 'Bartleby' and Carlyle." In *Melville Annual 1965, A Symposium:* Bartleby the Scrivener. Ed. Howard P. Vincent. Kent, OH: Kent State Univ. Press, 1966. pp. 113–39.

4471. _____. "Melville's 'Bartleby' and John Jacob Astor." *The New England Quarterly*, 41 (1968), 259–64.

4472. DAVIDSON, FRANK. " 'Bartleby': A Few Observations." *The Emerson Society Quarterly*, no. 27 (1962), pp. 25–32.

4473. DEW, MARJORIE. "The Attorney and the Scrivener: Quoth the Raven, 'Nevermore.' " In *Melville Annual 1965, A Symposium:* Bartleby the Scrivener. Ed. Howard P. Vincent. Kent, OH: Kent State Univ. Press, 1966. pp. 94–103.

4474. EMERY, ALLAN MOORE. "The Alternatives of Melville's 'Bartleby.' " *Nineteenth-Century Fiction*, 31 (1976), 170–87.

4475. FELHEIM, MARVIN. "Meaning and Structure in 'Bartleby.' " *College English*, 23 (1962), 369–70, 375–76.

4476. FIENE, DONALD M. "Bartleby the Christ." *American Transcendental Quarterly*, no. 7 (1970), pp. 18–23.

4477. FIRCHOW, PETER E. "*Bartleby*: Man and Metaphor." *Studies in Short Fiction*, 5 (1968), 342–48.

4478. FISHER, MARVIN. " 'Bartleby,' Melville's Circumscribed Scrivener." *The Southern Review*, NS 10 (1974), 59–79.

4479. FRIEDMAN, MAURICE. "Bartleby and the Modern Exile." In *Melville Annual 1965, A Symposium:* Bartleby the Scrivener. Ed. Howard P. Vincent. Kent, OH: Kent State Univ. Press, 1966. pp. 64–81.

4480. GARDNER, JOHN. "*Bartleby*: Art and Social Commitment." *Philological Quarterly*, 43 (1964), 87–98.

4481. GIBSON, WILLIAM M. "Herman Melville's 'Bartleby the Scrivener' and 'Benito Cereno.' " In *The American Renaissance—The History of an Era: Essays and Interpretations*. Ed. George Hendrick. Frankfurt am Main: Moritz Diesterweg, 1961. pp. 107–16.

4482. GIDDINGS, T. H. "Melville, The Colt-Adams Murder, and 'Bartleby.' " *Studies in American Fiction*, 2 (1974), 123–32.

4483. GUPTA, R. K. " 'Bartleby': Melville's Critique of Reason." *Indian Journal of American Studies*, 4, nos. 1–2 (1974), 66–71.

4484. HAAG, JOHN. "Bartleby-ing for the Camera." In *Melville Annual 1965, A Symposium:* Bartleby the Scrivener. Ed. Howard P. Vincent. Kent, OH: Kent State Univ. Press, 1966. pp. 55–63.

4485. HOWARD, FRANCES K. "The Catalyst of Language: Melville's Symbol." *English Journal*, 57 (1968), 825–31.

4486. KISSANE, LEEDICE. "Dangling Constructions in Melville's 'Bartleby.' " *American Speech*, 36 (1961), 195–200.

4487. KNIGHT, KARL F. "Melville's Variations of the Theme of Failure: 'Bartleby' and *Billy Budd*." *The Arlington Quarterly*, 2, no. 2 (1969), 44–58.

4488. KORNFIELD, MILTON. "Bartleby and the Presentation of Self in Everyday Life." *The Arizona Quarterly*, 31 (1975), 51–56.

4489.   LEVY, LEO B. "Hawthorne and the Idea of 'Bartleby.' "
The Emerson Society Quarterly, no. 47 (1967), pp. 66–69.

4490.   LEYDA, JAY. *"Bartleby*: Genesis of an Opera 2." In *Melville Annual 1965, A Symposium:* Bartleby the Scrivener. Ed. Howard P. Vincent. Kent, OH: Kent State Univ. Press, 1966. pp. 42–44.

4491.   MARCUS, MORDECAI. "Melville's Bartleby as a Psychological Double." *College English*, 23 (1962), 365–68.

4492.   MILLS, NICOLAUS C. "Prison and Society in Nineteenth-Century American Fiction." *Western Humanities Review*, 24 (1970), 325–31.

4493.   MONTEIRO, GEORGE. " 'Bartleby the Scrivener' and Melville's Contemporary Reputation." *Studies in Bibliography*, 24 (1971), 195–96.

4494.   ———. "Melville, 'Timothy Quicksand,' and the Dead-Letter Office." *Studies in Short Fiction*, 9 (1972), 198–201.

4495.   MOORE, JACK B. "Ahab and Bartleby: Energy and Indolence." *Studies in Short Fiction*, 1 (1964), 291–94.

4496.   MURRAY, HENRY A. "Bartleby and I." In *Melville Annual 1965, A Symposium:* Bartleby the Scrivener. Ed. Howard P. Vincent. Kent, OH: Kent State Univ. Press, 1966. pp. 3–24.

4497.   NORMAN, LIANE. "Bartleby and the Reader." *The New England Quarterly*, 44 (1971), 23–39.

4498.   PARKER, HERSHEL. "Dead Letters and Melville's Bartleby." *Resources for American Literary Study*, 4 (1974), 90–99.

4499.   PATRICK, WALTON R. "Melville's 'Bartleby' and the Doctrine of Necessity." *American Literature*, 41 (1969), 39–54.

4500.   PINSKER, SANFORD. " 'Bartleby the Scrivener': Language as Wall." *College Literature*, 2 (1975), 17–27.

4501.   PLUMSTEAD, A. W. *"Bartleby*: Melville's Venture in a New Genre." In *Melville Annual 1965, A Symposium:* Bartleby the Scrivener. Ed. Howard P. Vincent. Kent, OH: Kent State Univ. Press, 1966. pp. 82–93.

4502.   RANDALL, JOHN H., III. "Bartleby *vs.* Wall Street: New York in the 1850s." *Bulletin of The New York Public Library*, 78 (1975), 138–44.

4503.   REINERT, OTTO. "Bartleby the Inscrutable: Notes on a Melville Motif." In *Americana Norvegica: Norwegian Contributions to American Studies*, Vol. 1. Ed. Sigmund Skard and Henry H. Wasser. Oslo: Gyldendal Norsk, 1966. pp. 180–205.

4504.   ST. ARMAND, BARTON LEVI. "Curtis's 'Bartleby': An Unrecorded Melville Reference." *The Papers of the Bibliographical Society of America*, 71 (1977), 219–20.

4505.   SEELYE, JOHN. "The Contemporary 'Bartleby.' " *American Transcendental Quarterly*, no. 7 (1970), pp. 12–18.

4506. SHUSTERMAN, DAVID. "The 'Reader Fallacy' and 'Bartleby the Scrivener.' " *The New England Quarterly*, 45 (1972), 118-24.

4507. SINGLETON, MARVIN. "Melville's 'Bartleby': Over the Republic, a Ciceronian Shadow." *The Canadian Review of American Studies*, 6 (1975), 165-73.

4508. SMITH, HERBERT F. "Melville's Master in Chancery and His Recalcitrant Clerk." *American Quarterly*, 17 (1965), 734-41.

4509. SOLOMONT, SUSAN, AND RITCHIE DARLING. *Bartleby: An Essay*. Amherst, MA: Green Knight Press, 1969.

4510. SPECTOR, ROBERT DONALD. "Melville's 'Bartleby' and the Absurd." *Nineteenth-Century Fiction*, 16 (1961), 175-77.

4511. SPRINGER, NORMAN. "Bartleby and the Terror of Limitation." *PMLA*, 80 (1965), 410-18.

4512. STEIN, ALLEN F. "The Motif of Voracity in 'Bartleby.' " *ESQ*, 21 (1975), 29-34.

4513. STEIN, WILLIAM BYSSHE. "Bartleby: The Christian Conscience." In *Melville Annual 1965, A Symposium:* Bartleby the Scrivener. Ed. Howard P. Vincent. Kent, OH: Kent State Univ. Press, 1966. pp. 104-12.

4514. STEMPEL, DANIEL, AND BRUCE M. STILLIANS. *"Bartleby the Scrivener:* A Parable of Pessimism." *Nineteenth-Century Fiction*, 27 (1972), 268-82.

4515. STEN, CHRISTOPHER W. "Bartleby the Transcendentalist: Melville's Dead Letter to Emerson." *Modern Language Quarterly*, 35 (1974), 30-44.

4516. STONE, EDWARD. "Bartleby and Miss Norman." *Studies in Short Fiction*, 9 (1972), 271-74.

4517. STOUT, JANIS P. "The Encroaching Sodom: Melville's Urban Fiction." *Texas Studies in Literature and Language*, 17 (1975), 157-73.

4518. TUERK, RICHARD. "Melville's 'Bartleby' and Isaac D'Israeli's *Curiosities of Literature*, Second Series." *Studies in Short Fiction*, 7 (1970), 647-49.

4519. WELLS, DANIEL A. " 'Bartleby the Scrivener,' Poe, and the Duyckinck Circle." *ESQ*, 21 (1975), 35-39.

4520. WIDMER, KINGSLEY. "Melville's Radical Resistance: The Method and Meaning of *Bartleby*." *Studies in the Novel*, 1 (1969), 444-58.

4521. _____. "The Negative Affirmation: Melville's 'Bartleby.' " *Modern Fiction Studies*, 8 (1962), 276-86.

4522. WRIGHT, NATHALIA. "Melville and 'Old Burton,' with 'Bartleby' as an Anatomy of Melancholy." *Tennessee Studies In Literature*, 15 (1970), 1-13.

4523. ZINK, DAVID D. "Bartleby and the Contemporary Search for Meaning." *Forum* (University of Houston), 8, no. 2 (1970), 46–50.

See also 53, 93, 360, 399, 446, 454, 461, 466, 484, 486, 492, 505, 565, 569, 583, 595, 597, 598, 3737, 4724, 4765, 4766, 4768, 4770, 4772, 4776, 4784, 4788–4795, 4798, 4799, 4802, 4803, 4815, 4817, 4820, 4822, 4824, 4828, 4829, 4835, 4836, 4840, 4845.

"The Bell-Tower"

4524. COSTELLO, JACQUELINE A., AND ROBERT J. KLOSS. "The Psychological Depths of Melville's 'The Bell-Tower.' " *ESQ*, 19 (1971), 254–61.

4525. FISHER, MARVIN. "Melville's 'Bell-Tower': A Double Thrust." *American Quarterly*, 18 (1966), 200–07.

4526. KIME, WAYNE R. " 'The Bell-Tower': Melville's Reply to a Review." *ESQ*, 22 (1976), 28–38.

4527. MORSBERGER, ROBERT E. "Melville's 'The Bell-Tower' and Benvenuto Cellini." *American Literature*, 44 (1972), 459–62.

4528. SALZBERG, JOEL. "The Artist Manqué: Tower Symbolism in Melville and Crane." *American Transcendental Quarterly*, no. 29 (1976), pp. 55–61.

4529. SWEENEY, GERARD M. "Melville's Hawthornian Bell-Tower: A Fairy-Tale Source." *American Literature*, 45 (1973), 279–85.

4530. TRAVIS, MILDRED K. "A Note on 'The Bell-Tower': Melville's 'Blackwood Article.' " *Poe Studies*, 6 (1973), 28–29.

4531. VERNON, JOHN. "Melville's 'The Bell-Tower.' " *Studies in Short Fiction*, 7 (1970), 264–76.

See also 35, 503, 4770, 4776, 4784, 4788, 4789, 4793, 4820, 4834.

"Benito Cereno"

4532. ALTSCHULER, GLENN C. "Whose Foot on Whose Throat? A Re-Examination of Melville's *Benito Cereno*." *CLA Journal*, 18 (1975), 383–92.

4533. BERNSTEIN, JOHN. "*Benito Cereno* and the Spanish Inquisition." *Nineteenth-Century Fiction*, 16 (1962), 345–50.

4534. BROPHY, ROBERT J. "Benito Cereno, Oakum, and Hatchets." *American Transcendental Quarterly*, no. 1 (1969), pp. 89–90.

4535. CANADAY, NICHOLAS, JR. "A New Reading of Melville's 'Benito Cereno.' " In *Studies in American Literature*. Ed. Waldo McNeir and Leo B. Levy. Baton Rouge: Louisiana State Univ. Press, 1960. pp. 49–57.

4536. CARDWELL, GUY A. "Melville's Gray Story: Symbols and Meaning in 'Benito Cereno.' " *Bucknell Review*, 8 (1959), 154–67.

4537. _____. "A Surprising World: Amaso Delano in Kentucky." *The Mark Twain Journal*, 16, no. 4 (1973), 12-13.

4538. CARLISLE, E. F. "Captain Amasa Delano: Melville's American Fool." *Criticism*, 7 (1965), 349-62.

4539. COCHRAN, ROBERT. "Babo's Name in 'Benito Cereno': An Unnecessary Controversy?" *American Literature*, 48 (1976), 217-19.

4540. ENSSLEN, KLAUS. "Melville's 'Benito Cereno.' " In *Kleine Beiträge zur amerikanische Literaturgeschichte: Arbeitsproben aus deutschen Seminaren und Instituten*. Ed. Hans Galinsky and Hans-Joachim Lang. Heidelberg: Carl Winter, 1961. pp. 27-33.

4541. FARNSWORTH, ROBERT M. "Slavery and Innocence in 'Benito Cereno.' " *The Emerson Society Quarterly*, no. 44 (1966), pp. 94-96.

4542. FISHER, MARVIN. " 'Benito Cereno': Old World Experience, New World Expectations and Third World Realities." *Forum* (University of Houston), 13, no. 3 (1976), 31-36.

4543. FRANKLIN, H. BRUCE. " 'Apparent Symbol of Despotic Command': Melville's *Benito Cereno*." *The New England Quarterly*, 34 (1961), 462-77.

4544. GAILLARD, THEODORE L., JR. "Melville's Riddle for Our Time: 'Benito Cereno.' " *English Journal*, 61 (1972), 479-87.

4545. GALLOWAY, DAVID D. "Herman Melville's *Benito Cereno*: An Anatomy." *Texas Studies in Literature and Language*, 9 (1967), 239-52.

4546. GREEN, JESSE D. "Diabolism, Pessimism, and Democracy: Notes on Melville and Conrad." *Modern Fiction Studies*, 8 (1962), 287-305.

4547. GREJDA, EDWARD S. "*Benito Cereno*." In *The Common Continent of Men: Racial Equality in the Writings of Herman Melville*. Port Washington, NY: Kennikat, 1974. pp. 135-47.

4548. GROSS, SEYMOUR L. "Mungo Park and Ledyard in Melville's *Benito Cereno*." *English Language Notes*, 3 (1965), 122-23.

4549. GUTTMANN, ALLEN. "The Enduring Innocence of Captain Amasa Delano." *Boston University Studies in English*, 5 (1961), 35-45.

4550. HAYS, PETER. "Slavery and *Benito Cereno*: An Aristotelian View." *Études Anglaises*, 23 (1970), 38-46.

4551. JACKSON, MARGARET Y. "Melville's Use of a Real Slave Mutiny in 'Benito Cereno.' " *CLA Journal*, 4 (1960), 79-93.

4552. KARCHER, CAROLYN L. "Melville and Racial Prejudice: A Re-evaluation." *The Southern Review*, NS 12 (1976), 287-310.

4553. KEELER, CLINTON. "Melville's Delano: Our Cheerful Axiologist." *CLA Journal*, 10 (1966), 49-55.

4554. KIM, U-CHANG. "The Agony of Passivity: A Note on Melville's 'Benito Cereno.' " *The English Language and Literature*, nos. 51–52 (1974), pp. 248–57.

4555. KNOX, GEORGE. "Lost Command: *Benito Cereno* Reconsidered." *The Personalist*, 40 (1959), 280–91.

4556. LANNON, DIEDRE. "A Note on Melville's 'Benito Cereno.' " *Massachusetts Studies in English*, 2 (1970), 68–70.

4557. LOWANCE, MASON I., JR. "Veils and Illusion in *Benito Cereno*." *The Arizona Quarterly*, 26 (1970), 113–26.

4558. McELROY, JOHN HARMON. "Cannibalism in Melville's *Benito Cereno*." *Essays in Literature* (Western Illinois University), 1 (1974), 206–18.

4559. MAGOWAN, ROBIN. "Masque and Symbol in Melville's 'Benito Cereno.' " *College English*, 23 (1962), 346–51.

4560. MANDEL, RUTH B. "The Two Mystery Stories in *Benito Cereno*." *Texas Studies in Literature and Language*, 14 (1973), 631–42.

4561. MARGOLIES, EDWARD. "Melville and the Blacks." *CLA Journal*, 18 (1975), 364–73.

4562. METZGER, CHARLES R. "Melville's Saints: Allusion in *Benito Cereno*." *ESQ*, no. 58 (1970), pp. 88–90.

4563. NICHOLS, CHARLES H. "Color, Conscience and Crucifixion: A Study of Racial Attitudes in American Literature and Criticism." *Jahrbuch für Amerikastudien*, 6 (1961), 37–47.

4564. NICOL, CHARLES. "The Iconography of Evil and Ideal in 'Benito Cereno.' " *American Transcendental Quarterly*, no. 7 (1970), pp. 25–31.

4565. NNOLIM, E. CHARLES. *Melville's "Benito Cereno": A Study in Meaning of Name Symbolism.* New York: New Voices, 1974.

4566. PARKER, HERSHEL. " 'Benito Cereno' and *Cloister-Life*: A Re-Scrutiny of a 'Source.' " *Studies in Short Fiction*, 9 (1972), 221–32.

4567. PATTERSON, FRANK M. "The *San Dominick*'s Anchor." *American Notes & Queries*, 3 (1964), 19–20.

4568. PAVESE, CESARE. "Preface to 'Benito Cereno.' " In *American Literature: Essays and Opinions*. Trans. Edwin Fussell. Berkeley: Univ. of California Press, 1970. pp. 156–60.

4569. PHILLIPS, BARRY. " 'The Good Captain': A Reading of *Benito Cereno*." *Texas Studies in Literature and Language*, 4 (1962), 188–97.

4570. PILKINGTON, WILLIAM T. " 'Benito Cereno' and the 'Valor-Ruined Man' of *Moby-Dick*." *Texas Studies in Literature and Language*, 7 (1965), 201–07.

4571. ———. "Melville's *Benito Cereno*: Source and Technique." *Studies in Short Fiction*, 2 (1965), 247–55.

4572. PUTZEL, MAX. "The Source and the Symbols of Melville's 'Benito Cereno.' " *American Literature*, 34 (1962), 191–206.

4573. RAY, RICHARD E. " 'Benito Cereno': Babo as Leader." *American Transcendental Quarterly*, no. 7 (1970), pp. 31–37.

4574. RAY, TOMMY JOE. "Delano's Devils; or, A Case of Libel." *The University of Mississippi Studies in English*, 12 (1971), 59–64.

4575. RICE, JULIAN C. "The Ship as Cosmic Symbol in *Moby Dick* and *Benito Cereno.*" *The Centennial Review*, 16 (1972), 138–50.

4576. RIDGE, GEORGE ROSS, AND DAVY S. RIDGE. "A Bird and a Motto: Source for 'Benito Cereno.' " *The Mississippi Quarterly*, 13 (1960), 22–29.

4577. ROHRBERGER, MARY. "Point of View in 'Benito Cereno': Machinations and Deceptions." *College English*, 27 (1966), 541–46.

4578. ROSENTHAL, BERNARD. "Melville's Island." *Studies in Short Fiction*, 11 (1974), 1–9.

4579. SCOUTEN, ARTHUR H. "The Derelict Slave Ship in Melville's *Benito Cereno* and Defoe's *Captain Singleton.*" *Colby Library Quarterly*, 12 (1976), 122–25.

4580. SHETTY, NALINI V. "Melville's Use of the Gothic Tradition." In *Studies in American Literature: Essays in Honour of William Mulder.* Ed. Jagdish Chander and Narindar S. Pradhan. Delhi: Oxford Univ. Press, 1976. pp. 144–53.

4581. SIMBOLI, DAVID. " 'Benito Cereno' as Pedagogy." *CLA Journal*, 9 (1965), 159–64.

4582. SIMPSON, ELEANOR E. "Melville and the Negro: From *Typee* to 'Benito Cereno.' " *American Literature*, 41 (1969), 19–38.

4583. STONE, ALBERT E. "American Innocence Revisited: Robert Lowell's *Benito Cereno.*" In *Acta Universitatis Carolinae—Philologica 5.* Prague Studies in English, Vol. 14. Prague: Univ. Karlova, 1971. pp. 117–31.

4584. SWANSON, DONALD R. "The Exercise of Irony in 'Benito Cereno.' " *American Transcendental Quarterly*, no. 7 (1970), pp. 23–25.

4585. TAYLOR, J. CHESLEY. " 'Aranda' in *Benito Cereno.*" *American Notes & Queries*, 10 (1972), 118.

4586. VANDERBILT, KERMIT. " 'Benito Cereno': Melville's Fable of Black Complicity." *The Southern Review*, NS 12 (1976), 311–22.

4587. VANDERHAAR, MARGARET M. "A Re-Examination of 'Benito Cereno.' " *American Literature*, 40 (1968), 179–91.

4588. WELSH, HOWARD. "The Politics of Race in 'Benito Cereno.' " *American Literature*, 46 (1975), 556–66.

4589. WIDMER, KINGSLEY. "The Perplexity of Melville: *Benito Cereno.*" *Studies in Short Fiction*, 5 (1968), 225–38.

4590. YELLIN, JEAN FAGAN. "Black Masks: Melville's 'Benito Cereno.' " *American Quarterly*, 22 (1970), 678–89.

4591. _____. "Melville's 'Benito Cereno.' " In *The Intricate Knot: Black Figures in American Literature, 1776–1863*. New York: New York Univ. Press, 1972. pp. 215–27.

See also 40, 53, 85, 103, 389, 433, 434, 446, 454, 463, 544, 576, 597, 598, 2903, 4481, 4624, 4765, 4768–4770, 4772, 4776, 4782, 4784, 4786, 4788, 4789, 4791, 4793–4795, 4799, 4802, 4803, 4811, 4815, 4820, 4822, 4824, 4825, 4828, 4829, 4835, 4836, 4838, 4840.

"Billy Budd, Sailor"

4592. ADLER, JOYCE SPARER. "*Billy Budd* and Melville's Philosophy of War." *PMLA*, 91 (1976), 266–78.

4593. BARITZ, LOREN. "The Demonic: Herman Melville." In *City on a Hill: A History of Ideas and Myths in America*. New York: Wiley, 1964. pp. 271–332.

4594. BARNET, SYLVAN. "The Execution in *Billy Budd*." *American Literature*, 33 (1962), 517–19.

4595. BERCOVITCH, SACVAN. "Melville's Search for National Identity: Son and Father in *Redburn, Pierre*, and *Billy Budd*." *CLA Journal*, 10 (1967), 217–28.

4596. BERTHOFF, WARNER. " 'Certain Phenomenal Men': The Example of *Billy Budd*." *ELH*, 27 (1960), 334–51.

4597. BREDAHL, A. CARL, JR. "Conclusion—*Billy Budd, Sailor*." In *Melville's Angles of Vision*. Gainesville: Univ. of Florida Press, 1972. pp. 63–74.

4598. BRODTKORB, PAUL, JR. "The Definitive *Billy Budd*: 'But aren't it all sham?' " *PMLA*, 82 (1967), 602–12.

4599. BROWNE, RAY B. "*Billy Budd*: Gospel of Democracy." *Nineteenth-Century Fiction*, 17 (1963), 321–37.

4600. CALLAN, RICHARD J. "The Burden of Innocence In Melville and Twain." *Renascence*, 17 (1965), 191–94.

4601. CAMERON, KENNETH WALTER. "Another Newspaper Anticipation of *Billy Budd*." *American Transcendental Quarterly*, no. 14 (1972), pp. 167–68.

4602. CHANDLER, ALICE. "Captain Vere and the 'Tragedies of the Palace.' " *Modern Fiction Studies*, 13 (1967), 259–61.

4603. _____. "The Name Symbolism of Captain Vere." *Nineteenth-Century Fiction*, 22 (1967), 86–89.

4604. CIFELLI, EDWARD M. "*Billy Budd*: Boggy Ground to Build On." *Studies in Short Fiction*, 13 (1976), 463–69.

4605. _____. "Melville's *Billy Budd*." *The Explicator*, 31 (1973), item 60.

4606. DEW, MARJORIE. "The Prudent Captain Vere." *American Transcendental Quarterly*, no. 7 (1970), pp. 81-85.

4607. DILLISTONE, F. W. *The Novelist and the Passion Story*. London: Collins, 1960.

4608. DONOW, HERBERT S. "Herman Melville and the Craft of Fiction." *Modern Language Quarterly*, 25 (1964), 181-86.

4609. DOUBLEDAY, NEAL F. "Jack Easy and Billy Budd." *English Language Notes*, 2 (1964), 39-42.

4610. DUERKSEN, ROLAND A. "*Caleb Williams, Political Justice*, and *Billy Budd*." *American Literature*, 38 (1966), 372-76.

4611. _____. "The Deep Quandary in *Billy Budd*." *The New England Quarterly*, 41 (1968), 51-66.

4612. EBERWEIN, ROBERT T. "The Impure Fiction of *Billy Budd*." *Studies in the Novel*, 6 (1974), 318-26.

4613. ELLEN, SISTER MARY, I.H.M. "Parallels in Contrast: A Study of Melville's Imagery in *Moby Dick* and *Billy Budd*." *Studies in Short Fiction*, 2 (1965), 284-90.

4614. FITE, OLIVE L. "Billy Budd, Claggart, and Schopenhauer." *Nineteenth-Century Fiction*, 23 (1968), 336-43.

4615. FLOYD, NATHANIEL M. "*Billy Budd*: A Psychological Autopsy." *American Imago*, 34 (1977), 28-49.

4616. FOGLE, RICHARD HARTER. "*Billy Budd*—Acceptance or Irony." *Tulane Studies in English*, 8 (1958), 107-13.

4617. _____. "*Billy Budd*: The Order of the Fall." *Nineteenth-Century Fiction*, 15 (1960), 189-205.

4618. FOLEY, MARY. "The Digressions in *Billy Budd*." In *Melville's* Billy Budd *and the Critics*. Ed. William T. Stafford. Belmont, CA: Wadsworth, 1961. pp. 161-64.

4619. FRIEDMAN, IRENE. "Melville's Billy Budd: 'A Sort of Upright Barbarian.' " *The Canadian Review of American Studies*, 4 (1973), 87-95.

4620. FULWILER, TOBY. "The Death of the Handsome Sailor: A Study of *Billy Budd* and *The Red Badge of Courage*." *The Arizona Quarterly*, 26 (1970), 101-12.

4621. FUSSELL, MARY EVERETT BURTON. "*Billy Budd*: Melville's Happy Ending." *Studies in Romanticism*, 15 (1976), 43-57.

4622. GARNER, STANTON. "Melville and Thomas Campbell: The 'Deadly Space Between.' " *English Language Notes*, 14 (1976), 289-90.

4623. GASKINS, AVERY F. "The Symbolic Nature of Claggart's Name." *American Notes & Queries*, 6 (1967), 56.

4624. GEISMAR, MAXWELL. "Introduction." In *Billy Budd and Benito Cereno*, by Herman Melville. New York: Heritage Press, 1965. pp. v-xv.

4625. _____. "Introduction." In *Billy Budd and Typee*. New York: Washington Square Press, 1962. pp. xiii–xxvi.

4626. **HALL, JOAN JOFFE.** "The Historical Chapters in *Billy Budd*." *The University Review* (Kansas City), 30 (1963), 35–40.

4627. **HAYFORD, HARRISON, AND MERTON M. SEALTS, JR., ED.,** with an intro., variorum notes and commentary, and manuscript analysis. *Billy Budd, Sailor (An Inside Narrative), by Herman Melville*. Chicago: Univ. of Chicago Press, 1962.

4628. **HAYFORD, HARRISON, ED.** *The* Somers *Mutiny Affair*. Englewood Cliffs, NJ: Prentice-Hall, 1959.

4629. **HENDRICKSON, JOHN.** "*Billy Budd*: Affirmation of Absurdity." *RE: Arts & Letters*, 2, no. 1 (1969), 30–38.

4630. **HILLWAY, TYRUS.** "Melville and the Young Revolutionaries." In *Americana-Austriaca: Beiträge zur Amerikakunde*, Vol. 3. Ed. Klaus Lanzinger. Vienna: Braumüller, 1974. pp. 43–58.

4631. **HINER, JAMES.** "Only Catastrophe." *The Minnesota Review*, 10, nos. 3–4 (1970), 82–89.

4632. **HOUSE, KAY S.** "Francesco Caracciolo, Fenimore Cooper, and 'Billy Budd.'" *Studi Americani*, 19–20 (1973–74), 83–100.

4633. **HUMMA, JOHN B.** "Melville's *Billy Budd* and Lawrence's 'The Prussian Officer': Old Adams and New." *Essays in Literature* (Western Illinois University), 1 (1974), 83–88.

4634. **IVES, C. B.** "*Billy Budd* and the Articles of War." *American Literature*, 34 (1962), 31–39.

4635. **KEARNS, EDWARD A.** "Omniscient Ambiguity: The Narrators of *Moby-Dick* and *Billy Budd*." *ESQ*, no. 58 (1970), pp. 117–20.

4636. **KELLY, MICHAEL J.** "Claggart's 'Equivocal Words' and Lamb's 'Popular Fallacies.'" *Studies in Short Fiction*, 9 (1972), 183–86.

4637. **KENNEY, BLAIR G.** "Melville's *Billy Budd*." *American Notes & Queries*, 9 (1971), 151–52.

4638. **KETTERER, DAVID.** "Some Co-ordinates in *Billy Budd*." *Journal of American Studies*, 3 (1969), 221–37.

4639. **KILBOURNE, W. G., JR.** "Montaigne and Captain Vere." *American Literature*, 33 (1962), 514–17.

4640. **KINNAMON, JON M.** "*Billy Budd*: Political Philosophies in a Sea of Thought." *The Arizona Quarterly*, 26 (1970), 164–72.

4641. **LEDBETTER, KENNETH.** "The Ambiguity of *Billy Budd*." *Texas Studies in Literature and Language*, 4 (1962), 130–34.

4642. **LEMON, LEE T.** "Billy Budd: The Plot Against The Story." *Studies in Short Fiction*, 2 (1964), 32–43.

4643. **LONDON, PHILIP W.** "The Military Necessity: *Billy Budd* and Vigny." *Comparative Literature*, 14 (1962), 174–86.

4644. LONGENECKER, MARLENE. "Captain Vere and the Form of Truth." *Studies in Short Fiction*, 14 (1977), 337-43.

4645. MCENIRY, HUGH. "Some Contrapuntal Themes in Herman Melville." In *Essays in Modern American Literature*. Ed. Richard E. Langford, et al. Deland, FL: Stetson Univ. Press, 1963. pp. 14-25.

4646. MCNAMARA, ANNE. "Melville's 'Billy Budd.' " *The Explicator*, 21 (1962), item 11.

4647. MALBONE, RAYMOND G. "How Shall We Teach the New *Billy Budd, Sailor?*" *College English*, 27 (1966), 449-500.

4648. MANSFIELD, LUTHER STEARNS. "Some Patterns from Melville's 'Loom of Time.' " In *Essays on Determinism in American Literature*. Ed. Sydney J. Krause. Kent, OH: Kent State Univ. Press, 1964. pp. 19-35.

4649. MERRILL, ROBERT. "The Narrative Voice in *Billy Budd*." *Modern Language Quarterly*, 34 (1973), 283-91.

4650. MILLER, JAMES E. "Melville's Search for Form." *Bucknell Review*, 8 (1959), 260-76.

4651. MILLER, RUTH. "But Laugh or Die: A Comparison of *The Mysterious Stranger* and *Billy Budd*." *The Literary Half-Yearly*, 11, no. 1 (1970), 25-29.

4652. MILLGATE, MICHAEL. "Melville and Marvell: A Note on *Billy Budd*." *English Studies*, 49 (1968), 47-50.

4653. MONTALE, EUGENIO. "An Introduction to *Billy Budd* (1942)." *The Sewanee Review*, 68 (1960), 419-22.

4654. MONTEIRO, GEORGE. "Melville and Keats." *The Emerson Society Quarterly*, no. 31 (1963), p. 55.

4655. MYERS, MARGARET. "Mark Twain and Melville." *The Mark Twain Journal*, 14, no. 2 (1968), 5-8.

4656. NADEAU, ROBERT L. "Melville's Sailor in the Sixties." In *The Classic American Novel and the Movies*. Ed. Gerald Peary and Roger Shatzkin. New York: Ungar, 1977. pp. 124-31.

4657. NARVESON, ROBERT. "The Name 'Claggart' in 'Billy Budd.' " *American Speech*, 43 (1968), 229-32.

4658. NATHANSON, LEONARD. "Melville's *Billy Budd*, Chapter 1." *The Explicator*, 22 (1964), item 75.

4659. OATES, J. C. "Melville and the Manichean Illusion." *Texas Studies in Literature and Language*, 4 (1962), 117-29.

4660. ORTEGO, PHILIP D. "The Existential Roots of *Billy Budd*." *The Connecticut Review*, 4, no. 1 (1970), 80-87.

4661. O'SHAUGHNESSY, REVEREND RICHARD, S.M. "Father Mapple's Sermon and *Billy Budd*." *Notre Dame English Journal*, 2, no. 1 (1963), 13-15.

4662. PERRY, ROBERT L. *"Billy Budd*: Melville's *Paradise Lost."* *The Midwest Quarterly*, 10 (1969), 173–85.

4663. RACHAL, JOHN. "Melville on Vere: A Revealing Letter?" *American Notes & Queries*, 15 (1976), 36–38.

4664. RATHBUN, JOHN W. *"Billy Budd* and the Limits of Perception." *Nineteenth-Century Fiction*, 20 (1965), 19–34.

4665. REED, WALTER L. "The Measured Forms of Captain Vere." *Modern Fiction Studies*, 23 (1977), 227–35.

4666. REICH, CHARLES A. "The Tragedy of Justice in *Billy Budd."* *The Yale Review*, 56 (1967), 368–89.

4667. REID, B. L. "Old Melville's Fable." *The Massachusetts Review*, 9 (1968), 529–46.

4668. REINERT, OTTO. " 'Secret Mines and Dubious Side': The World of *Billy Budd."* In *Americana-Norvegica: Norwegian Contributions to American Studies Dedicated to Sigmund Skard*, Vol. 4. Ed. Brita Seyersted. Oslo: Universitetsforlaget, 1973. pp. 183–92.

4669. ROGERS, ROBERT. "The 'Ineludible Gripe' of Billy Budd." *Literature and Psychology*, 14 (1964), 9–22.

4670. ROSENBERRY, EDWARD H. "The Problem of *Billy Budd."* *PMLA*, 80 (1965), 489–98.

4671. ROSENTHAL, BERNARD. "Elegy for Jack Chase." *Studies in Romanticism*, 10 (1971), 213–29.

4672. SCHROTH, EVELYN. "Melville's Judgment on Captain Vere." *The Midwest Quarterly*, 10 (1969), 189–200.

4673. SHATTUCK, ROGER. "Two Inside Narratives: *Billy Budd* and *L'Etranger." Texas Studies in Literature and Language*, 4 (1962), 314–20.

4674. SHERWOOD, JOHN C. "Vere as Collingwood: A Key to *Billy Budd." American Literature*, 35 (1964), 476–84.

4675. SHULMAN, ROBERT. "Melville's 'Timoleon': From Plutarch to the Early Stages of *Billy Budd." Comparative Literature*, 19 (1967), 350–61.

4676. _____. "Montaigne and the Techniques and Tragedy of Melville's *Billy Budd." Comparative Literature*, 16 (1964), 322–30.

4677. SKERRY, PHILIP J. *"Billy Budd*: From Novella to Libretto." *RE: Artes Liberales*, 3, no. 1 (1976), 19–27.

4678. SMITH, HERBERT F. "Melville's Sea-Lawyers." *English Essays in Canada*, 2 (1976), 423–38.

4679. SPOFFORD, WILLIAM K. "Melville's Ambiguities: A Reevaluation of 'The *Town-Ho's* Story.' " *American Literature*, 41 (1969), 264–70.

4680. SPRINGER, HASKELL. "Preface." In *The Merrill Studies in Billy Budd*. Columbus, OH: Merrill, 1970. pp. v–x.

4681. STEIN, WILLIAM BYSSHE. " 'Billy Budd': The Nightmare of History." *Criticism*, 3 (1961), 237–50.

4682. ———. "The Motif of the Wise Old Man in *Billy Budd.*" *Western Humanities Review*, 14 (1960), 99–101.

4683. STEINMANN, THEO. "The Perverted Pattern of *Billy Budd* in *The Nigger of the 'Narcissus.'*" *English Studies*, 55 (1974), 239–46.

4684. STEN, CHRISTOPHER W. "Vere's Use of the 'Forms': Means and Ends in *Billy Budd.*" *American Literature*, 47 (1975), 37–51.

4685. STITT, PETER A. "Herman Melville's *Billy Budd*: Sympathy and Rebellion." *The Arizona Quarterly*, 28 (1972), 39–54.

4686. STOKES, GARY. "The Dansker, Melville's Manifesto on Survival." *English Journal*, 57 (1968), 980–81.

4687. STRANDBERG, VICTOR H. "God and the Critics of Melville." *Texas Studies in Literature and Language*, 6 (1964), 322–33.

4688. SUITS, BERNARD. "*Billy Budd* and Historical Evidence: A Rejoinder." *Nineteenth-Century Fiction*, 18 (1963), 288–91.

4689. SUTTON, WALTER. "Melville and the Great God Budd." *Prairie Schooner*, 34 (1960), 128–33.

4690. TURNAGE, MAXINE. "Melville's Concern with the Arts in *Billy Budd.*" *The Arizona Quarterly*, 28 (1972), 74–82.

4691. VINCENT, HOWARD P. "Introduction." In *Twentieth Century Interpretations of* Billy Budd. Englewood Cliffs, NJ: Prentice-Hall, 1971. pp. 1–10.

4692. WALLACE, ROBERT K. "*Billy Budd* and the Haymarket Hangings." *American Literature*, 47 (1975), 108–13.

4693. WEALES, GERALD. "Getting Billy off the Page." *The Michigan Quarterly Review*, 13 (1974), 382–400.

4694. WIDMER, KINGSLEY. "The Perplexed Myths of Melville: *Billy Budd.*" *Novel*, 2 (1968), 25–35.

4695. WILLETT, RALPH W. "Nelson and Vere: Hero and Victim in *Billy Budd, Sailor.*" *PMLA*, 82 (1967), 370–76.

4696. WILSON, G. R., JR. "*Billy Budd* and Melville's Use of Dramatic Technique." *Studies in Short Fiction*, 4 (1967), 105–11.

4697. WITHIM, PHIL. "*Billy Budd*: Testament of Resistance." *Modern Language Quarterly*, 20 (1959), 115–27.

See also 13, 40, 53, 54, 85, 92, 381, 433, 434, 452, 454, 460, 463, 470, 499, 509, 597, 598, 2903, 4487, 4765, 4766, 4768, 4769, 4772, 4774, 4776, 4779, 4781, 4782, 4786, 4790–4795, 4799, 4802, 4804, 4805, 4809, 4815–4817, 4819–4822, 4825, 4828, 4829, 4833, 4836, 4840, 4850, 4851.

"Cock-A-Doodle-Doo!"

4698. GREEN, MARTIN. "Melville and the American Romance." In *Re-Appraisals: Some Commonsense Readings in American Literature*. London: Hugh Evelyn, 1963. pp. 87–112.

4699. MOSS, SIDNEY P. " 'Cock-A-Doodle-Doo!' and Some Legends in Melville Scholarship." *American Literature*, 40 (1968), 192–210.

4700. STEIN, WILLIAM BYSSHE. "Melville's Cock and the Bell of Saint Paul." *The Emerson Society Quarterly*, no. 27 (1962), pp. 5–10.

See also 4708, 4770, 4773, 4776, 4784, 4788, 4789, 4793, 4805, 4820, 4831.

"Daniel Orme"

See 4828.

"The Encantadas, or Enchanted Isles"

4701. ALBRECHT, ROBERT C. "The Thematic Unity of Melville's 'The Encantadas.' " *Texas Studies in Literature and Language*, 14 (1972), 463–77.

4702. CANADAY, NICHOLAS, JR. "Melville's 'The Encantadas': The Deceptive Enchantment of the Absolute." *Papers on Language & Literature*, 10 (1974), 58–69.

4703. COXE, LOUIS. "Reconsideration: Melville's *The Encantadas*." *The New Republic*, 168, no. 19 (1973), 32–35.

4704. EDDY, D. MATHIS. "Melville's Response to Beaumont and Fletcher: A New Source for *The Encantadas*." *American Literature*, 40 (1968), 374–80.

4705. FRANKLIN, H. BRUCE. "The Island Worlds of Darwin and Melville." *The Centennial Review*, 11 (1967), 353–70.

4706. FRANZOSA, JOHN. "Darwin and Melville: Why a Tortoise?" *American Imago*, 33 (1976), 361–79.

4707. FURROW, SHARON. "The Terrible Made Visible: Melville, Salvator Rosa, and Piranesi." *ESQ*, 19 (1973), 237–53.

4708. HABER, RICHARD. "Patience and Charity in *The Encantadas*' 'Chola Widow' Sketch and in 'Cock-A-Doodle-Doo!' " *Massachusetts Studies in English*, 3 (1972), 100–07.

4709. HOWINGTON, DON S. "Melville's 'The Encantadas': Imagery and Meaning." *Studies in the Literary Imagination*, 2, no. 1 (1969), 69–75.

4710. JACKSON, ARLENE M. "Technique and Discovery in Melville's *Encantadas*." *Studies in American Fiction*, 1 (1973), 133–40.

4711. JONES, BUFORD. "Melville's Buccaneers and Crébillon's Sofa." *English Language Notes*, 2 (1964), 122–26.

4712. ―――. "Spenser and Shakespeare in *The Encantadas*, Sketch VI." *The Emerson Society Quarterly*, no. 35 (1964), pp. 68–73.

4713. MENGELING, MARVIN E. "Through 'The Encantadas': An Experienced Guide and You." *American Transcendental Quarterly*, no. 7 (1970), pp. 37–43.

4714. NEWBERY, I. " 'The Encantadas': Melville's *Inferno.*" *American Literature*, 38 (1966), 49-68.

4715. PEARCE, HOWARD D. "The Narrator of 'Norfolk Isle and the Chola Widow.' " *Studies in Short Fiction*, 3 (1965), 56-62.

4716. RESINK, G. J. "Samburan Encantada." *English Studies*, 47 (1966), 35-44.

4717. ROBERTS, DAVID A. "Structure and Meaning in Melville's 'The Encantadas.' " *ESQ*, 22 (1976), 234-44.

4718. WATSON, CHARLES N., JR. "Melville's Agatha and Hunilla: A Literary Reincarnation." *English Language Notes*, 6 (1968), 114-18.

4719. YARINA, MARGARET. "The Dualistic Vision of Herman Melville's 'The Encantadas.' " *The Journal of Narrative Technique*, 3 (1973), 141-48.

See also 16, 4765, 4768-4770, 4776, 4784, 4788, 4789, 4793, 4803, 4807, 4811, 4820, 4824, 4828, 4839.

"The Fiddler"

4720. BIER, JESSE. "Melville's 'The Fiddler' Reconsidered." *American Transcendental Quarterly*, no. 14 (1972), pp. 2-4.

4721. EASTWOOD, DAVID R. "O'Brien's Fiddler—or Melville's?" *American Transcendental Quarterly*, no. 29 (1976), pp. 39-46.

4722. FISHER, MARVIN. "Melville's 'The Fiddler': Succumbing to the Drummer." *Studies in Short Fiction*, 11 (1974), 153-60.

4723. GUPTA, R. K. "Hautboy and Plinlimmon: A Reinterpretation of Melville's 'The Fiddler.' " *American Literature*, 43 (1971), 437-42.

4724. THOMPSON, W. R. "Melville's 'The Fiddler': A Study in Dissolution." *Texas Studies in Literature and Language*, 2 (1961), 492-500.

See also 493, 4770, 4776, 4778, 4784, 4788, 4789.

"Fragments from a Writing Desk"

See 4770, 4787, 4817.

"The 'Gees"

See 4770, 4771.

"The Happy Failure"

4725. LYNDE, RICHARD D. "Melville's Success in 'The Happy Failure: A Story of the River Hudson.' " *CLA Journal*, 13 (1969), 119-30.

See also 4770, 4776, 4784, 4788.

"I and My Chimney"

4726. CHATFIELD, E. HALE. "Levels of Meaning in Melville's 'I and My Chimney.' " *American Imago*, 19 (1962), 163–69.

4727. CROWLEY, WILLIAM G. "Melville's Chimney." *The Emerson Society Quarterly*, no. 14 (1959), pp. 2–6.

4728. MCCULLAGH, JAMES C. "More Smoke from Melville's Chimney." *American Transcendental Quarterly*, no. 17 (1973), pp. 17–22.

4729. SOWDER, WILLIAM J. "Melville's 'I and My Chimney': A Southern Exposure." *The Mississippi Quarterly*, 16 (1963), 128–45.

4730. STEIN, WILLIAM BYSSHE. "Melville's Chimney Chivy." *The Emerson Society Quarterly*, no. 35 (1964), pp. 63–65.

4731. TURNER, DARWIN T. "Smoke from Melville's Chimney." *CLA Journal*, 7 (1963), 107–13.

4732. WOODRUFF, STUART C. "Melville and His Chimney." *PMLA*, 75 (1960), 283–92.

See also 4770, 4773, 4776, 4784, 4787–4789, 4793, 4803, 4812, 4831.

"Jimmy Rose"

4733. FISHER, MARVIN. "Melville's 'Jimmy Rose': Truly Risen?" *Studies in Short Fiction*, 4 (1966), 1–11.

4734. GARGANO, JAMES W. "Melville's 'Jimmy Rose.' " *Western Humanities Review*, 16 (1962), 276–80.

4735. JEFFREY, DAVID K. "Unreliable Narration in Melville's 'Jimmy Rose.' " *The Arizona Quarterly*, 31 (1975), 69–72.

4736. TUTT, RALPH M. " 'Jimmy Rose'—Melville's Displaced Noble." *The Emerson Society Quarterly*, no. 33 (1963), pp. 28–32.

See also 4770, 4773, 4776, 4784, 4788, 4789, 4793, 4831, 4839.

"The Lightning-Rod Man"

4737. FISHER, MARVIN. " 'The Lightning-Rod Man': Melville's Testament of Rejection." *Studies in Short Fiction*, 7 (1970), 433–38.

4738. MASTRIANO, MARY. "Melville's 'The Lightning-Rod Man.' " *Studies in Short Fiction*, 14 (1977), 29–33.

4739. PARKER, HERSHEL. "Melville's Salesman Story." *Studies in Short Fiction*, 1 (1964), 154–58.

4740. SHUSTERMAN, ALAN. "Melville's 'The Lightning-Rod Man': A Reading." *Studies in Short Fiction*, 9 (1972), 165–74.

4741. WILSON, HARRY B. "The Double View: Melville's 'The Lightning-Rod Man.' " In *Approaches to the Short Story*. Ed. Neil D. Isaacs and Louis H. Leiter. San Francisco, CA: Chandler, 1963. pp. 16–23.

See also 40, 4770, 4776, 4784, 4788, 4789, 4831.

"The Paradise of Bachelors and the Tartarus of Maids"

4742. BROWNE, RAY B. "Two Views of Commitment: 'The Paradise of Bachelors' and 'The Tartarus of Maids.' " *American Transcendental Quarterly*, no. 7 (1970), pp. 43–47.

4743. FISHER, MARVIN. "Melville's 'Tartarus': The Deflowering of New England." *American Quarterly*, 23 (1971), 79–100.

4744. ROWLAND, BERYL. "Melville's Bachelors and Maids: Interpretation Through Symbol and Metaphor." *American Literature*, 41 (1969), 389–405.

4745. SANDBERG, A. "Erotic Patterns in 'The Paradise of Bachelors and the Tartarus of Maids.' " *Literature and Psychology*, 18 (1968), 2–8.

4746. STEIN, WILLIAM BYSSHE. "Melville's Eros." *Texas Studies in Literature and Language*, 3 (1961), 297–308.

See also 4767, 4770, 4771, 4776, 4784, 4788–4790, 4793.

"The Piazza"

4747. AVALLONE, C. SHERMAN. "Melville's 'Piazza.' " *ESQ*, 22 (1976), 221–33.

4748. FISHER, MARVIN. "Prospect and Perspective in Melville's 'Piazza.' " *Criticism*, 16 (1974), 203–16.

4749. MOSES, CAROLE. "Melville's Use of Spenser in 'The Piazza.' " *CLA Journal*, 20 (1976), 222–31.

4750. POENICKE, KLAUS. "A View from the Piazza: Herman Melville and the Legacy of the European Sublime." *Comparative Literature Studies*, 4 (1967), 267–81.

4751. ROUNDY, NANCY. "Fancies, Reflections and Things: The Imagination as Perception in 'The Piazza.' " *CLA Journal*, 20 (1977), 539–46.

4752. TURNER, DARWIN T. "A View of Melville's 'Piazza.' " *CLA Journal*, 7 (1963), 56–62.

4753. WAGGONER, HYATT H. "Hawthorne and Melville Acquaint the Reader with Their Abodes." *Studies in the Novel*, 2 (1970), 420–24.

See also 9, 81, 4472, 4770, 4773, 4784, 4788, 4789, 4793, 4831, 4832.

"Poor Man's Pudding and Rich Man's Crumbs"

4754. FISHER, MARVIN. " 'Poor Man's Pudding': Melville's Meditation on Grace." *American Transcendental Quarterly*, no. 13 (1972), pp. 32–36.

4755. ROWLAND, BERYL. "Melville's Waterloo in 'Rich Man's Crumbs.' " *Nineteenth-Century Fiction*, 25 (1970), 216–21.

4756. _____. "Sitting Up with a Corpse: Malthaus according to Melville in "Poor Man's Pudding and Rich Man's Crumbs.' " *Journal of American Studies*, 6 (1972), 69–83.
See also 4770, 4771, 4776, 4784, 4788, 4789, 4793.

"Rip Van Winkle's Lilac"
See 4828.

"The Two Temples"

4757. ASALS, FREDERICK. "Satire and Skepticism in 'The Two Temples.' " *Books at Brown*, 24 (1971), 7–18.

4758. FISHER, MARVIN. "Focus on Herman Melville's 'The Two Temples': The Denigration of the American Dream." In *American Dreams, American Nightmares*. Ed. David Madden. Carbondale and Edwardsville: Southern Illinois Univ. Press, 1970. pp. 76–86.

4759. ROWLAND, BERYL. "Grace Church and Melville's Story of 'The Two Temples.' " *Nineteenth-Century Fiction*, 28 (1973), 339–46.

4760. _____. "Melville Answers the Theologians: The Ladder of Charity in 'The Two Temples.' " *Mosaic*, 7, no. 4 (1974), 1–13.
See also 4770, 4776, 4784, 4788, 4789, 4793.

"Under the Rose"
See 4787, 4828.

General Studies

4761. ADLER, JOYCE. "The Imagination and Melville's Endless Probe for Relation." *American Transcendental Quarterly*, no. 19 (1973), pp. 37–42.

4762. ALLEN, GAY WILSON. *Melville and His World*. New York: Viking, 1971.

4763. BABCOCK, C. MERTON. "Some Expressions from Herman Melville." *Publication of the American Dialect Society*, no. 31 (1959), pp. 3–13.

4764. BACH, BERT C. "Melville's Theatrical Mask: The Role of Narrative Perspective in his Short Fiction." *Studies in the Literary Imagination*, 2, no. 1 (1969), 43–55.

4765. BEAVER, HAROLD. "Introduction." In *Billy Budd, Sailor, and Other Stories*, by Herman Melville. Harmondsworth, Middlesex: Penguin Books, 1967. pp. 9–50.

4766. BENDER, BERT. "Melville's Shock of Genius and His Three Tales of the Shock Unrecognized." *Forum* (University of Houston), 13, no. 3 (1976), 24–30.

4767. BERINGAUSE, A. F. "Melville and Chretien de Troyes." *American Notes & Queries*, 2 (1963), 20–21.

4768. BERNSTEIN, JOHN. *Pacifism and Rebellion in the Writings of Herman Melville*. The Hague: Mouton, 1964.

4769. BERTHOFF, WARNER. *The Example of Melville*. Princeton, NJ: Princeton Univ. Press, 1962.

4770. BICKLEY, R. BRUCE, JR. *The Method of Melville's Short Fiction*. Durham, NC: Duke Univ. Press, 1975.

4771. _____. "The Triple Thrust of Satire in Melville's Short Stories: Society, the Narrator, and the Reader." *Studies in American Humor*, 1 (1975), 172–79.

4772. BOWEN, MERLIN. *The Long Encounter: Self and Experience in the Writings of Herman Melville*. Chicago: Univ. of Chicago Press, 1960.

4773. BRACK, VIDA K. AND O. M., JR. "Weathering Cape Horn: Survivors in Melville's Minor Short Fiction." *The Arizona Quarterly*, 28 (1972), 61–73.

4774. BRANCH, WATSON G. "Introduction." In *Melville: The Critical Heritage*. London: Routledge & Kegan Paul, 1974. pp. 1–49.

4775. BRIDGMAN, RICHARD. "Melville's Roses." *Texas Studies in Literature and Language*, 8 (1966), 235–44.

4776. BROWNE, RAY B. *Melville's Drive To Humanism*. Lafayette, IN: Purdue Univ. Studies, 1971.

4777. CAMPBELL, MARIE A. "A Quiet Crusade: Melville's Tales of the Fifties." *American Transcendental Quarterly*, no. 7 (1970), pp. 8–12.

4778. CHARVAT, WILLIAM. "Melville and the Common Reader." *Studies in Bibliography*, 12 (1959), 41–57.

4779. CHASE, RICHARD. "Herman Melville." In *Major Writers of America*. Ed. Perry Miller. 2 vols. New York: Harcourt, Brace & World, 1962. I, 877–91.

4780. _____. "Introduction." In *Melville: A Collection of Critical Essays*. Englewood Cliffs, NJ: Prentice-Hall, 1962. pp. 1–10.

4781. COHEN, HENNIG. "Wordplay on Personal Names in the Writings of Herman Melville." *Tennessee Studies In Literature*, 8 (1963), 85–97.

4782. CREEGER, GEORGE R. "The Symbolism of Whiteness in Melville's Prose Fiction." *Jahrbuch für Amerikastudien*, 5 (1960), 147–63.

4783. DEANE, PAUL. "Herman Melville: The Quality of Balance." *The Serif*, 7, no. 2 (1970), 12–17.

4784. DILLINGHAM, WILLIAM B. *Melville's Short Fiction, 1853–1856*. Athens: Univ. of Georgia Press, 1977.

4785. DONALDSON, SCOTT. "The Dark Truth of *The Piazza Tales.*" *PMLA*, 85 (1970), 1082–86.

4786. DRYDEN, EDGAR A. *Melville's Thematics of Form: The Great Art of Telling the Truth.* Baltimore, MD: Johns Hopkins Press, 1968.

4787. FINKELSTEIN, DOROTHEE METLITSKY. *Melville's Orienda.* New Haven, CT: Yale Univ. Press, 1961.

4788. FISHER, MARVIN. *Going Under: Melville's Short Fiction and the American 1850s.* Baton Rouge: Louisiana State Univ. Press, 1977.

4789. FOGLE, RICHARD HARTER. *Melville's Shorter Tales.* Norman: Univ. of Oklahoma Press, 1960.

4790. FRANKLIN, H. BRUCE. "Herman Melville: Artist of the Worker's World." In *Weapons of Criticism: Marxism in America and the Literary Tradition.* Ed. Norman Rudich. Palo Alto, CA: Ramparts Press, 1976. pp. 287–309.

4791. ———. *The Wake of the Gods: Melville's Mythology.* Stanford, CA: Stanford Univ. Press, 1963.

4792. FRIEDMAN, MAURICE. *Problematic Rebel: Melville, Dostoievsky, Kafka, Camus.* Rev. ed. Chicago: Univ. of Chicago Press, 1970.

4793. GALE, ROBERT L. *Plots and Characters in the Fiction and Narrative Poetry of Herman Melville.* Hamden, CT: Archon Books, 1969.

4794. GROSS, THEODORE. "Herman Melville: The Nature of Authority." *The Colorado Quarterly*, 16 (1968), 397–412.

4795. HAGOPIAN, JOHN V. "Melville's *L'Homme Révolté.*" *English Studies*, 46 (1965), 390–402.

4796. HAYMAN, ALLEN. "The Real and the Original: Herman Melville's Theory of Prose Fiction." *Modern Fiction Studies*, 8 (1962), 211–32.

4797. HENNELLY, MARK. "Ishmael's Nightmare and The American Eve." *American Imago*, 30 (1973), 274–93.

4798. HETHERINGTON, HUGH W. *Melville's Reviewers, British and American, 1846–1891.* Chapel Hill: Univ. of North Carolina Press, 1961.

4799. HILLWAY, TYRUS. *Herman Melville.* New York: Twayne, 1963.

4800. ———. "Herman Melville's Major Themes." In *Americana-Austriaca: Festschrift des Amerika-Instituts der Universität Innsbruck anlässlich seines zehnjährigen Bestehens.* Ed. Klaus Lanzinger. Vienna: Braumüller, 1966. pp. 170–80.

4801. ———. "Melville's Education in Science." *Texas Studies in Literature and Language*, 16 (1974), 411–25.

4802. HOWARD, LEON. *Herman Melville*. Minneapolis: Univ. of Minnesota Press, 1961.

4803. ———. "The Mystery of Melville's Short Stories." In *Americana-Austriaca: Festschrift des Amerika-Instituts der Universität Innsbruck anlässlich seines zehnjährigen Bestehens*. Ed. Klaus Lanzinger. Vienna: Braumüller, 1966. pp. 204-16.

4804. HOWARD, VINCENT P. *The Merrill Guide to Herman Melville*. Columbus, OH: Merrill, 1969.

4805. HUMPHREYS, A. R. *Herman Melville*. Edinburgh: Oliver and Boyd, 1962.

4806. KEHLER, JOEL R. "The House Divided: A Version of American Romantic 'Double Consciousness.' " *Papers on Language & Literature*, 13 (1977), 148-67.

4807. KELLNER, ROBERT. "Herman Melville: The Sketch as Genre." *Massachusetts Studies in English*, 3 (1971), 22-26.

4808. KENNY, VINCENT. "Melville's Problem of Detachment and Engagement." *American Transcendental Quarterly*, no. 19 (1973), pp. 30-37.

4809. LANE, LAURIAT, JR. "Dickens and Melville: Our Mutual Friends." *Dalhousie Review*, 51 (1971), 315-31.

4810. LEBOWITZ, ALAN. *Progress into Silence: A Study of Melville's Heroes*. Bloomington: Indiana Univ. Press, 1970.

4811. LEWIS, R. W. B. "Introduction." In *Herman Melville*. New York: Dell, 1962. pp. 7-35.

4812. LITMAN, VICKI HALPER. "The Cottage and the Temple: Melville's Symbolic Use of Architecture." *American Quarterly*, 21 (1969), 630-38.

4813. McCARTHY, PAUL. "Melville's Families: Facts, Figures, and Fates." *South Dakota Review*, 15, no. 1 (1977), 73-93.

4814. MAENO, SHIGERU. *A Melville Dictionary*. Tokyo: Kaibunsha, 1976.

4815. MAXWELL, D. E. S. *Herman Melville*. London: Routledge & Kegan Paul, 1968.

4816. MAYOUX, JEAN-JACQUES. *Melville*. Trans. John Ashbery. New York: Grove Press, 1960.

4817. MILLER, EDWIN HAVILAND. *Melville*. New York: Braziller, 1975.

4818. MILLER, JAMES E., JR. "The Achievement of Melville." *The University of Kansas City Review*, 26 (1959), 59-67.

4819. ———. "The Complex Figure in Melville's Carpet." *The Arizona Quarterly*, 15 (1959), 197-210.

4820. ———. *A Reader's Guide to Herman Melville*. New York: Farrar, Straus and Cudahy, 1962.

4821.　**MITCHELL, CHARLES.** "Melville and the Spurious Truth of Legalism." *The Centennial Review*, 12 (1968), 110–26.

4822.　**MUMFORD, LEWIS.** *Herman Melville: A Study of His Life and Vision.* Rev. ed. New York: Harcourt, Brace & World, 1962.

4823.　**ROSENBERRY, EDWARD H.** "Melville and His *Mosses*." *American Transcendental Quarterly*, no. 7 (1970), pp. 47–51.

4824.　**SCHIFFMAN, JOSEPH.** "On *Three Shorter Novels of Herman Melville*." In *Three Shorter Novels of Herman Melville.* New York: Harper, 1962. pp. 229–40.

4825.　**SCHROEDER, FRED E. H.** "*Enter Ahab, Then All*: Theatrical Elements in Melville's Fiction." *Dalhousie Review*, 46 (1966), 223–32.

4826.　**SEALTS, MERTON M., JR.** "Melville's 'Geniality.'" In *Essays in American and English Literature Presented to Bruce Robert McElderry, Jr.* Ed. Max F. Schulz, et al. Athens: Ohio Univ. Press, 1967. pp. 3–26.

4827.　———, ED. WITH AN INTRO. *The Early Lives of Melville: Nineteenth-Century Biographical Sketches and Their Authors.* Madison: Univ. of Wisconsin Press, 1974.

4828.　**SEELYE, JOHN.** *Melville: The Ironic Diagram.* Evanston, IL: Northwestern Univ. Press, 1970.

4829.　**SELTZER, LEON F.** *The Vision of Melville and Conrad.* Athens: Ohio Univ. Press, 1970.

4830.　**SHNEIDMAN, EDWIN S.** "The Deaths of Herman Melville." In *Melville & Hawthorne in the Berkshires: A Symposium.* Ed. Howard P. Vincent. Kent, OH: Kent State Univ. Press, 1968. pp. 118–43.

4831.　**SLATER, JUDITH.** "The Domestic Adventurer in Melville's Tales." *American Literature*, 37 (1965), 267–79.

4832.　**STEIN, WILLIAM BYSSHE.** "Melville's Comedy of Faith." *ELH*, 27 (1960), 315–33.

4833.　**STOUT, JANIS.** "Melville's Use of the Book of Job." *Nineteenth-Century Fiction*, 25 (1970), 69–83.

4834.　**SWEENEY, GERARD M.** *Melville's Use of Classical Mythology.* Amsterdam: Rodopi, 1975.

4835.　**THAKUR, D.** "The Tales of Melville." *The Literary Criterion*, 8, no. 4 (1969), 39–53.

4836.　**THORP, WILLARD.** "Afterword." In *Billy Budd and Other Tales*, by Herman Melville. New York: New American Library, 1961. pp. 325–34.

4837.　**TURNER, FREDERICK W., III.** "Melville's Post-Meridian Fiction." *Midcontinent American Studies Journal*, 10, no. 2 (1969), 60–67.

4838. **WAITE, ROBERT.** "Melville's *Momento Mori.*" *Studies in American Fiction*, 5 (1977), 187–97.

4839. **WATSON, CHARLES N., JR.** "Melville and the Theme of Timonism: From *Pierre* to *The Confidence-Man.*" *American Literature*, 44 (1972), 398–413.

4840. **WIDMER, KINGSLEY.** *The Ways of Nihilism: A Study of Herman Melville's Short Novels.* Los Angeles: The California State Colleges, 1970.

4841. **WILLETT, MAURITA.** "The Silences of Herman Melville." *American Transcendental Quarterly*, no. 7 (1970), pp. 85–92.

Bibliography

4842. **ANDERSON, DAVID D.** "Melville Criticism . . . Past and Present." *The Midwest Quarterly*, 2 (1961), 169–84.

4843. **BEEBE, MAURICE, HARRISON HAYFORD, AND GORDON ROPER.** "Criticism of Herman Melville: A Selected Checklist." *Modern Fiction Studies*, 8 (1962), 312–46.

4844. **BOWEN, JAMES K., AND RICHARD VANDERBEETS.** *A Critical Guide to Herman Melville: Abstracts of Forty Years of Criticism.* Glenview, IL: Scott, Foresman, 1971.

4845. **FIENE, DONALD M.** "A Bibliography of Criticism of 'Bartleby the Scrivener.' " In *Melville Annual 1965, A Symposium: Bartleby the Scrivener.* Ed. Howard P. Vincent. Kent, OH: Kent State Univ. Press, 1966. pp. 140–90.

4846. **GROSS, THEODORE L., AND STANLEY WERTHEIM.** *Hawthorne, Melville, Stephen Crane: A Critical Bibliography.* New York: Free Press, 1971.

4847. **MAILLOUX, STEVE, AND HERSHEL PARKER.** *Checklist of Melville Reviews.* np: Melville Society, 1975.

4848. **RICKS, BEATRICE, AND JOSEPH D. ADAMS.** *Herman Melville: A Reference Bibliography, 1900–1972, with Selected Nineteenth Century Materials.* Boston, MA: G. K. Hall, 1973.

4849. **SHERMAN, STUART C., JOHN H. BIRSS, AND GORDON ROPER.** *Melville Bibliography, 1952–1957.* Providence, RI: Providence Public Library, 1959.

4850. **STAFFORD, WILLIAM T.** "An Annotated Checklist of Studies of *Billy Budd.*" In *Melville's* Billy Budd *and the Critics.* Ed. William T. Stafford. Belmont, CA: Wadsworth, 1961. pp. 174–80.

4851. ———. "An Annotated Checklist of Studies of *Billy Budd.*" In *Melville's* Billy Budd *and the Critics.* 2nd ed. Ed. William T. Stafford. Belmont, CA: Wadsworth, 1968. pp. 263–72.

4852. **VANN, J. DON.** "A Selected Checklist of Melville Criticism, 1958-1968." *Studies in the Novel*, 1 (1969), 507-35.
4853. **VINCENT, HOWARD PATON.** *The Merrill Checklist of Herman Melville.* Columbus, OH: Merrill, 1969.
4854. **WRIGHT, NATHALIA.** "Herman Melville." In *Eight American Authors: A Review of Research and Criticism*. Rev. ed. Ed. James Woodress. New York: Norton, 1971. pp. 173-224.
4855. **ZIMMERMAN, MICHAEL.** "Herman Melville in the 1920's: An Annotated Bibliography." *Bulletin of Bibliography and Magazine Notes*, 24 (1964-65), 117-20, 139-44.

MENCKEN, SARA HAARDT

General Studies

4856. **GOING, WILLIAM T.** "Zelda Sayre Fitzgerald and Sara Haardt Mencken." In *Essays on Alabama Literature*. University: Univ. of Alabama Press, 1975. pp. 114-41.

MICHENER, JAMES A.

"Until They Sail"

See 4857.

General Studies

4857. **DAY, A. GROVE.** *James A. Michener.* New York: Twayne, 1964.

MILLAY, EDNA ST. VINCENT

"The White Peacock"

See 4858.

General Studies

4858. **BRITTIN, NORMAN A.** "Edna St. Vincent Millay's 'Nancy Boyd' Stories." *Ball State University Forum*, 10, no. 2 (1969), 31-36.

Bibliography

4859. **BRITTIN, NORMAN A.** "Millay Bibliography: Additions and Corrections." *American Notes & Queries*, 8 (1969), 52.

MILLER, ARTHUR

"Fame"

See 4864.

"Fitter's Night"

See 4864.

"I Don't Need You Any More"

4860. JACOBSON, IRVING. "The Child as Guilty Witness." *Literature and Psychology*, 24 (1974), 12–23.
See also 4862, 4864.

"The Misfits"

4861. WELLAND, DENNIS. *Arthur Miller*. Edinburgh: Oliver & Boyd, 1961.
See also 4864.

"Monte Sant' Angelo"

4862. JACOBSON, IRVING. "The Vestigial Jews on Monte Sant' Angelo." *Studies in Short Fiction*, 13 (1976), 507–12.
See also 4864.

"Please Don't Kill Anything"

See 4864.

General Studies

4863. MOSS, LEONARD. *Arthur Miller*. New York: Twayne, 1967.
4864. SHEPHERD, ALLEN. " 'What Comes Easier—': The Short Stories of Arthur Miller." *Illinois Quarterly*, 34, no. 3 (1972), 37–49.

Bibliography

4865. HAYASHI, TETSUMARO. *Arthur Miller Criticism (1930–1967)*. Metuchen, NJ: Scarecrow, 1969.
4866. _____. "Arthur Miller—The Dimension of His Art: A Checklist of His Published Writings." *The Serif*, 4, no. 2 (1967), 26–32.
4867. _____. *An Index to Arthur Miller Criticism*. 2nd ed. Metuchen, NJ: Scarecrow, 1976.
4868. UNGAR, HARRIET. "The Writings of and about Arthur Miller: A Check List 1936–1967." *Bulletin of The New York Public Library*, 74 (1970), 107–34.

MILLER, HENRY

"The Smile at the Foot of the Ladder"

4869. ARMITAGE, MERLE. "The Man Behind the Smile: Doing Business with Henry Miller." *The Texas Quarterly*, 4, no. 4 (1961), 154–61.

General Studies

4870. **BAXTER, ANNETTE KAR.** *Henry Miller: Expatriate.* Pittsburgh, PA: Univ. of Pittsburgh Press, 1961.

4871. **DICK, KENNETH C.** *Henry Miller: Collossus of One.* Sittard: Alberts, 1967.

4872. **GORDON, WILLIAM A.** *The Mind and Art of Henry Miller.* Baton Rouge: Louisiana State Univ. Press, 1967.

4873. **MILLER, HENRY.** "On His Sins of Omission." *The New York Times Book Review,* 2 Jan. 1972, pp. 10–11.

4874. **NELSON, JANE A.** *Form and Image in the Fiction of Henry Miller.* Detroit, MI: Wayne State Univ. Press, 1970.

4875. **OMARR, SYDNEY.** *Henry Miller: His World of Urania.* With a foreword by Henry Miller. London: Villiers, 1960.

4876. **WIDMER, KINGSLEY.** *Henry Miller.* New York: Twayne, 1963.

Interviews

4877. **JONES, ROGER.** "Henry Miller at Eighty-Four: An Interview." *Queen's Quarterly,* 84 (1977), 351–65.

4878. **MILLER, HENRY.** "The Art of Fiction XXVIII." With George Wickes. *The Paris Review,* no. 28 (1962), pp. 129–59.

4879. **SNYDER, ROBERT.** *This Is Henry, Henry Miller from Brooklyn: Conversations with the Author from* The Henry Miller Odyssey. Los Angeles, CA: Nash Publishing, 1974.

4880. **WICKES, GEORGE.** "Henry Miller at Seventy." *Claremont Quarterly,* 9, no. 2 (1962), 5–20.

Bibliography

4881. **[MITCHELL, EDWARD.]** "Selected Checklist." In *Henry Miller: Three Decades of Criticism.* Ed. Edward Mitchell. New York: New York Univ. Press, 1971. pp. 185–216.

4882. **MOORE, THOMAS HAMILTON.** *Bibliography: Henry Miller.* Minneapolis, MN: Henry Miller Literary Society, 1961.

4883. **RENKEN, MAXINE.** "Bibliography of Henry Miller: 1945–1961." *Twentieth Century Literature,* 7 (1962), 180–90.

4884. ———. *A Bibliography of Henry Miller, 1945–1961.* Denver, CO: Swallow, 1962.

4885. **RILEY, ESTA LOU.** *Henry Miller: An Informal Bibliography, 1924–1960.* Hays: Fort Hays Kansas State College, 1961.

MILLER, WALTER M., JR.

"Crucifixus Etiam"

See 4886.

"The Darfsteller"

See 4886.

General Studies

4886. SAMUELSON, DAVID N. "The Lost Canticles of Walter M. Miller, Jr." *Science-Fiction Studies*, 3 (1976), 3–26.

MINOT, STEPHEN

"Sausage and Beer"

See 518.

MITCHELL, S[ILAS] WEIR

"The Autobiography of a Quack"

See 4888.

"Was He Dead?"

See 4888.

General Studies

4887. LOVERING, JOSEPH P. *S. Weir Mitchell*. New York: Twayne, 1971.

4888. WALTER, RICHARD D. *S. Weir Mitchell, M.D.—Neurologist: A Medical Biography*. Springfield, IL: Charles C. Thomas, 1970.

Bibliography

4889. HAYNE, BARRIE. "S. Weir Mitchell (1829–1914)." *American Literary Realism, 1870–1910*, 2 (1969), 149–55.

MOFFETT, CLEVELAND

General Studies

4890. LAUTERBACH, EDWARD S. *"The Mysterious Card* Unsealed." *The Armchair Detective*, 4 (1970), 41–43.

MONTGOMERY, MARION

"Ye Olde Bluebird"

4891. LANDESS, THOMAS H. "The Present Course of Southern Fiction: *Everynegro* and Other Alternatives." *The Arlington Quarterly*, 1, no. 2 (1968), 61–85.

Interviews

4892. COLVERT, JAMES B. "An Interview With Marion Montgomery." *The Southern Review*, NS 6 (1970), 1041–53.

MOORE, C[ATHERINE] L[UCILLE]

"The Fairy Chessmen"

See 226.

"There Shall Be Darkness"

See 140.

"Vintage Season"

See 4893.

General Studies

4893. GUNN, JAMES. "Henry Kuttner, C. L. Moore, Lewis Padgett *et al.*" In *Voices for the Future: Essays on Major Science Fiction
Writers*. Ed. Thomas D. Clareson. Bowling Green, OH: Bowling Green Univ. Popular Press, 1976. pp. 185–215.

MORRIS, WRIGHT

Bibliography

4894. BOYCE, ROBERT L. "A Wright Morris Bibliography." In
Conversations with Wright Morris: Critical Views and Responses.
Ed. Robert E. Knoll. Lincoln: Univ. of Nebraska Press, 1977.
pp. 169–206.

MOTLEY, WILLARD

General Studies

4895. GILES, JAMES R., AND N. JILL WEYANT. "The Short Fiction
of Willard Motley." *Negro American Literature Forum*, 9 (1975),
3–10.

Bibliography

4896. ABBOTT, CRAIG, AND KAY VAN MOL. "The Willard Motley Papers at Northern Illinois University." *Resources for American Literary Study*, 7 (1977), 3–26.

4897. KLINKOWITZ, JEROME, JAMES GILES, AND JOHN T. O'BRIEN.
"The Willard Motley Papers at The University of Wisconsin."
Resources for American Literary Study, 2 (1972), 218–73.

MULLICAN, ARTHENIA BATES

Interviews

4898. **WARD, JERRY W.** "Legitimate Resources of the Soul: An Interview with Arthenia Bates Mullican." *Obsidian*, 3, no. 1 (1977), 14–34.

MURFREE, MARY NOAILLES
(See *CRADDOCK, CHARLES EGBERT*)

MURO, AMADO

General Studies

4899. **HASLAM, GERALD.** "The Enigma of Amado Jesus Muro." *Western American Literature*, 10 (1975), 3–9.

NABOKOV, VLADIMIR

"The Assistant Producer"

See 4902.

"A Christmas Story"

See 4904.

"Cloud, Castle, Lake"

See 4907.

"Conversation Piece, 1945"

See 4909, 4910.

"First Love"

See 4914.

"A Forgotten Poet"

See 4909.

"Lance"

See 4915.

"Lips to Lips"

See 4904.

"The Potato Elf"

See 483, 4912.

"Scenes from the Life of a Double Monster"

See 4909.

"Signs and Symbols"

4900. **CARROLL, WILLIAM.** "Nabokov's Signs and Symbols." In *A Book of Things about Vladimir Nabokov.* Ed. Carl R. Proffer. Ann Arbor, MI: Ardis, 1974. pp. 203–17.
See also 399, 4915.

"Spring in Fialta"

4901. **MONTER, BARBARA HELDT.** " 'Spring in Fialta': The Choice That Mimics Chance." *TriQuarterly,* no. 17 (1970), pp. 128–35.
See also 4907, 4909, 4910, 4914.

" 'That in Aleppo Once . . .' "

See 566, 4909.

"Time and Ebb"

See 4902, 4903.

"Triangle within Circle"

See 4907.

General Studies

4902. **APPEL, ALFRED, JR.** *Nabokov's Dark Cinema.* New York: Oxford Univ. Press, 1974.

4903. ———. "The Road to *Lolita,* or the Americanization of an Emigré." *Journal of Modern Literature,* 4 (1974), 3–31.

4904. **FIELD, ANDREW.** "The Artist as Failure in Nabokov's Early Prose." *Wisconsin Studies in Contemporary Literature,* 8 (1967), 165–73.

4905. ———. *Nabokov: His Life in Art.* Boston, MA: Little, Brown, 1967.

4906. ———. *Nabokov: His Life in Part.* New York: Viking, 1977.

4907. **FOWLER, DOUGLAS.** *Reading Nabokov.* Ithaca, NY: Cornell Univ. Press, 1974.

4908. **GRAYSON, JANE.** *Nabokov Translated: A Comparison of Nabokov's Russian and English Prose.* Oxford: Oxford Univ. Press, 1977.

4909. **LEE, L. L.** "Duplexity in V. Nabokov's Short Stories." *Studies in Short Fiction,* 2 (1965), 307–15.

4910. ———. *Vladimir Nabokov.* Boston, MA: Twayne, 1976.

4911. **NABOKOV, VLADIMIR.** "Inspiration." *Saturday Review of the Arts*, 1 (6 Jan. 1973), 30, 32.

4912. **ROWE, WILLIAM WOODIN.** *Nabokov's Deceptive World*. New York: New York Univ. Press, 1971.

4913. **STEGNER, PAGE.** "Editor's Introduction." In *Nabokov's Congeries*, by Vladimir Nabokov. New York: Viking, 1968. pp. ix–xxxii.

4914. ———. *Escape into Aesthetics: The Art of Vladimir Nabokov*. New York: Dial, 1966.

4915. **WILLIAMS, CAROL T.** "Nabokov's Dozen Short Stories: His World in Microcosm." *Studies in Short Fiction*, 12 (1975), 213–22.

Interviews

4916. **ANON.** "Nabokov on Nabokov and Things." *The New York Times Book Review*, 12 May 1968, pp. 4, 50–51.

4917. **APPEL, ALFRED, JR.** "Conversations With Nabokov." *Novel*, 4 (1971), 209–22.

4918. ———. "An Interview with Vladimir Nabokov." *Wisconsin Studies in Contemporary Literature*, 8 (1967), 127–52.

4919. **FEIFER, GEORGE.** "An Interview with Vladimir Nabokov." *Saturday Review*, 4 (27 Nov. 1976), 20–24, 26.

4920. **HAYMAN, JOHN G.** "A Conversation with Vladimir Nabokov—with Digressions." *The Twentieth Century*, 166 (1959), 444–50.

4921. **NABOKOV, VLADIMIR.** "The Art of Fiction XL." With Herbert Gold. *The Paris Review*, no. 41 (1967), pp. 92–111.

4922. **SHENKER, ISRAEL.** "The Old Magician at Home." *The New York Times Book Review*, 9 Jan. 1972, p. 2.

Bibliography

4923. **BRYER, JACKSON R., AND THOMAS J. BERGIN, JR.** "Vladimir Nabokov's Critical Reputation in English: A Note and a Checklist." *Wisconsin Studies in Contemporary Literature*, 8 (1967), 312–64.

4924. **FIELD, ANDREW.** *Nabokov: A Bibliography*. New York: McGraw-Hill, 1973.

NASBY, PETROLEUM V.

"A Fictitious Fact"

See 4925.

General Studies

4925. **AUSTIN, JAMES C.** *Petroleum V. Nasby (David Ross Locke)*. New York: Twayne, 1965.

4926. **HARRISON, JOHN M.** *The Man Who Made Nasby, David Ross Locke.* Chapel Hill: Univ. of North Carolina Press, 1969.
4927. **JONES, JOSEPH.** "Introduction: Abe Lincoln's Copperhead." In *The Struggles of Petroleum V. Nasby*, by David Ross Locke. Boston, MA: Beacon Press, 1963. pp. xiii–xxvi.

NEAL, JOHN

"David Whicher"

4928. **LEASE, BENJAMIN.** "The Authorship of 'David Whicher': The Case for John Neal." *Jahrbuch für Amerikastudien*, 12 (1967), 124–36.
4929. **RICHARDS, IRVING T.** "A Note on the Authorship of 'David Whicher.' " *Jahrbuch für Amerikastudien*, 7 (1962), 293–96.
See also 4930, 4931.

General Studies

4930. **LANG, HANS-JOACHIM, ED. WITH AN INTRO.** "Critical Essays and Stories by John Neal." *Jahrbuch für Amerikastudien*, 7 (1962), 204–93.
*4931. **LEASE, BENJAMIN.** *That Wild Fellow John Neal and the American Literary Revolution.* Chicago: Univ. of Chicago Press, 1972.

Bibliography

4932. **RICHARDS, IRVING T.** "John Neal: A Bibliography." *Jahrbuch für Amerikastudien*, 7 (1962), 296–319.

NEIDIG, WILLIAM J.

General Studies

4933. **DENT, GENE H.** "The Multi-Faceted World of William J. Neidig." In *Proceedings of the Sixth National Convention of the Popular Culture Association, Chicago, Illinois, April 22–24, 1976.* Ed. Michael T. Marsden. Bowling Green, OH: Bowling Green Univ. Popular Press, 1976. pp. 218–32.

NEMEROV, HOWARD

Bibliography

4934. **DUNCAN, BOWIE, ED.** *The Critical Reception of Howard Nemerov: A Selection of Essays and a Bibliography.* Intro. by Reed Whitmore. Metuchen, NJ: Scarecrow, 1971.

NIN, ANAÏS
"The All Seeing"
See 4939.

"Birth"
See 4939.

"The Child Born Out of the Fog"
See 4939.

"Djuna"
See 4939.

"Hejda"
See 4939, 4942.

"Houseboat"
See 4939.

"Je suis le plus malade des surréalistes"
See 4939.

"The Mouse"
See 4939.

"Ragtime"
4935. WATSON, FRED. "Allegories in 'Ragtime': Balance, Growth, Disintegration." *Under the Sign of Pisces: Anaïs Nin and Her Circle,* 7, no. 2 (1976), 1–5.
See also 4939, 4942.

"Stella"
See 4939, 4942.

"Under a Glass Bell"
4936. TYTELL, JOHN. "Anaïs Nin and 'The Fall of the House of Usher.'" *Under the Sign of Pisces,* 2, no. 1 (1971), 5–11.
See also 4939.

"The Voice"
See 4939, 4942.

"Winter of Artifice"
See 4942.

General Studies

4937. **BALAKIAN, ANNA.** "The Poetic Reality of Anaïs Nin." In *A Casebook on Anaïs Nin.* Ed. Robert Zaller. New York: New American Library, 1974. pp. 113-31.

4938. **EKBERG, KENT.** "The Importance of *Under a Glass Bell.*" *Under the Sign of Pisces: Anaïs Nin and Her Circle,* 8, no. 2 (1977), 4-18.

4939. **EVANS, OLIVER.** *Anaïs Nin.* Carbondale and Edwardsville: Southern Illinois Univ. Press, 1968.

4940. **KUNTZ, PAUL GRIMLEY.** "Art as Public Dream: The Practice and Theory of Anaïs Nin." In *A Casebook on Anaïs Nin.* Ed. Robert Zaller. New York: New American Library, 1974. pp. 77-99.

4941. **NIN, ANAÏS.** *The Novel of the Future.* New York: Macmillan, 1968.

4942. **SPENCER, SHARON.** *Collage of Dreams: The Writings of Anaïs Nin.* Chicago: Swallow, 1977.

Interviews

4943. **ALDEN, DAISY.** "A[naïs] N[in] Interviewed by Daisy Alden." *Under the Sign of Pisces,* 1, no. 2 (1970), 7-9.

4944. **BAILEY, JEFFREY.** "Link in the Chain of Feeling: An Interview with Anaïs Nin." *The New Orleans Review,* 5 (1976), 113-18.

4945. **ENGLISH, PRISCILLA.** "An Interview with Anaïs Nin." In *A Casebook on Anaïs Nin.* Ed. Robert Zaller. New York: New American Library, 1974. pp. 185-97.

4946. **FREEMAN, BARBARA.** "A Dialogue with Anaïs Nin." *Chicago Review,* 24, no. 2 (1972), 29-35.

4947. **McBRIEN, WILLIAM.** "Anaïs Nin: An Interview." *Twentieth Century Literature,* 20 (1974), 277-90.

4948. **SCHNEIDER, DUANE.** *An Interview with Anaïs Nin.* Athens, OH: Duane Schneider Press, 1970.

Bibliography

4949. **FRANKLIN, BENJAMIN, [V].** "Anaïs Nin: A Bibliographical Essay." In *A Casebook on Anaïs Nin.* Ed. Robert Zaller. New York: New American Library, 1974. pp. 25-33.

4950. _____. *Anaïs Nin: A Bibliography.* Kent, OH: Kent State Univ. Press, 1973.

4951. _____. "A[naïs] N[in]: A Selected Current Checklist." *Under the Sign of Pisces,* 1, no. 2 (1970), 15-16; 1, no. 3 (1970), 15-16.

4952. **MARCINCZYK, REESA.** "A Checklist of the Writings of Anaïs Nin, 1973-1976." *Under the Sign of Pisces: Anaïs Nin and Her Circle,* 8, no. 1 (1977), 2-14.

4953. ZEE, NANCY SCHOLAR. "A Checklist of Nin Materials at Northwestern University Library." *Under the Sign of Pisces*, 3, no. 2 (1972), 3–11.

NISSENSON, HUGH
"The Well"

See 564.

NIVEN, LARRY
"Flash Crowd"

See 233.

NORDHOFF, CHARLES
General Studies

4954. BRIAND, PAUL L., JR. *In Search of Paradise: The Nordhoff-Hall Story*. New York: Duell, Sloan & Pearce, 1966.

NORRIS, [BENJAMIN] FRANK[LIN]
"A Deal in Wheat"

See 456.

"Dying Fires"

See 79.

"The Great Corner in Hannibal and St Jo."

4955. SWENSSON, JOHN K. " 'The Great Corner in Hannibal and St Jo.': A Previously Unpublished Short Story by Frank Norris." *American Literary Realism, 1870–1910*, 4 (1971), 205–26.
4956. WESTBROOK, WAYNE W. " 'The Great Corner in Hannibal & St Jo.'—Another Look." *American Literary Realism, 1870–1910*, 10 (1977), 213–14.

"Lauth"

See 559, 4957, 4962.

General Studies

4957. DILLINGHAM, WILLIAM B. *Frank Norris: Instinct and Art*. Lincoln: Univ. of Nebraska Press, 1969.
4958. FRENCH, WARREN. *Frank Norris*. New York: Twayne, 1962.

4959. HILL, JOHN S. "The Influence of Cesare Lombroso on Frank Norris's Early Fiction." *American Literature*, 42 (1970), 89–91.

4960. _____. "Poe's 'Fall of the House of Usher' and Frank Norris' Early Short Stories." *The Huntington Library Quarterly*, 26 (1962), 111–12.

4961. JOHNSON, LEE ANN. "Western Literary Realism: The California Tales of Norris and Austin." *American Literary Realism, 1870–1910*, 7 (1974), 278–80.

4962. PIZER, DONALD. *The Novels of Frank Norris*. Bloomington: Indiana Univ. Press, 1966.

Bibliography

4963. CRISLER, JESSE S., AND JOSEPH R. MCELRATH, JR. *Frank Norris: A Reference Guide*. Boston, MA: G. K. Hall, 1974.

4964. DILLINGHAM, WILLIAM B. "Frank Norris." In *Fifteen American Authors before 1900: Bibliographic Essays on Research and Criticism*. Ed. Robert A. Rees and Earl N. Harbert. Madison: Univ. of Wisconsin Press, 1971. pp. 307–32.

4965. FRENCH, WARREN. "Frank Norris (1870–1902)." *American Literary Realism, 1870–1910*, 1, no. 1 (1967), 84–89.

4966. HILL, JOHN S. *The Merrill Checklist of Frank Norris*. Columbus, OH: Merrill, 1970.

4967. KATZ, JOSEPH. "The Shorter Publications of Frank Norris: A Checklist." *Proof*, 3 (1973), 155–220.

4968. LOHF, KENNETH A., AND EUGENE P. SHEEHY. *Frank Norris: A Bibliography*. Los Gatos, CA: Talisman Press, 1959.

4969. WHITE, WILLIAM. "Frank Norris: Bibliographical Addenda." *Bulletin of Bibliography and Magazine Notes*, 22 (1959), 227–28.

NYE, BILL

General Studies

4970. KESTERSON, DAVID B. *Bill Nye: The Western Writings*. Boise, ID: Boise State Univ., 1976.

O. HENRY

"An Afternoon Miracle"

See 4977.

"The Atavism of John Tom Little Bear"

See 4977.

"The Badge of Policeman O'Roon"

See 4976.

"The Caballero's Way"

See 4977.

"A Call Loan"

See 4977.

"The Chair of Philanthromathematics"

See 4977.

"A Chaparrel Christmas Gift"

See 4977.

"Elsie in New York"

4971. **MARKS, PATRICIA.** "O. Henry and Dickens: Elsie in the Bleak House of Moral Decay." *English Language Notes*, 12 (1974), 35–37.

"The Ethics of Pig"

See 4977.

"The Furnished Room"

See 394.

"The Gift of the Magi"

4972. **REA, JOHN A.** "The Idea for O. Henry's 'Gift of the Magi.' " *Southern Humanities Review*, 7 (1973), 311–14.

"The Handbook of Hymen"

See 4977.

"The Hiding of Black Bill"

See 4977.

"Hostages to Momus"

See 4977.

"Hygeia at the Solito"

See 4977.

"The Last Leaf"

See 3111.

"The Last of the Troubadours"
See 4977.

"The Lonesome Road"
See 4977.

"The Marquis and Miss Sally"
See 4977.

"The Moment of Victory"
See 4977.

"A Municipal Report"
See 535, 576.

"A Night in New Arabia"
See 4976.

"The Passing of Black Eagle"
See 4977.

"The Plutonian Fire"
See 4976.

"Princess and the Puma"
See 4977.

"Proof of the Pudding"
See 4976.

"The Ransom of Mack"
See 4974, 4977.

"The Ransom of Red Chief"
See 616.

"Roads to Destiny"
See 4976.

"Telemachus, Friend"
See 4977.

"Tommy's Burglar"
See 4976.

"Two Renegades"

See 457.

"The Venturers"

See 4974.

"Vereton Villa"

See 4974.

General Studies

4973. **ARNETT, ETHEL STEPHENS.** *O. Henry from Polecat Creek.* Greensboro, NC: Piedmont Press, 1962.

4974. **CURRENT-GARCIA, EUGENE.** *O. Henry (William Sydney Porter).* New York: Twayne, 1965.

4975. _____. "O. Henry's Southern Heritage." *Studies in Short Fiction,* 2 (1964), 1–12.

4976. **ÈJXENBAUM, BORIS M.** "O. Henry and the Theory of the Short Story." In *Readings in Russian Poetics: Formalist and Structuralist Views.* Ed. Ladislav Matejka and Krystyna Pomorska. Cambridge, MA: M. I. T. Press, 1971. pp. 227–70.

4977. **GALLEGLY, JOSEPH.** *From Alamo Plaza to Jack Harris's Saloon: O. Henry and the Southwest He Knew.* The Hague: Mouton, 1970.

4978. **HANSEN, HARRY.** "Foreword." In *The Complete Works of O. Henry.* 2 vols. Garden City, NY: Doubleday, 1960. I, v–x.

4979. **LONG, E. HUDSON.** *O. Henry: American Regionalist.* Austin, TX: Steck-Vaughn, 1969.

4980. _____. "O. Henry as a Regional Artist." In *Essays on American Literature in Honor of Jay B. Hubbell.* Ed. Clarence Gohdes. Durham, NC: Duke Univ. Press, 1967. pp. 229–40.

4981. _____. "Social Customs in O. Henry's Texas Stories." In *A Good Tale and a Bonny Tune.* Ed. Mody C. Boatright, Wilson M. Hudson, and Allen Maxwell. Dallas, TX: Southern Methodist Univ. Press, 1964. pp. 148–67.

4982. **McLEAN, MALCOLM D.** "O. Henry in Honduras." *American Literary Realism, 1870–1910,* 1, no. 3 (1968), 39–46.

4983. **PAVESE, CESARE.** "O. Henry; or, The Literary Trick." In *American Literature: Essays and Opinions.* Trans. Edwin Fussell. Berkeley: Univ. of California Press, 1970. pp. 79–90.

4984. **SAROYAN, WILLIAM.** "O What a Man Was O. Henry." *The Kenyon Review,* 29 (1967), 671–75.

Bibliography

4985. **LONG, E. HUDSON.** "O. Henry (William Sydney Porter) (1862-1910)." *American Literary Realism, 1870–1910,* 1, no. 1 (1967), 93–99.

OATES, JOYCE CAROL

"Accomplished Desires"

4986. **EVANS, ELIZABETH.** "Joyce Carol Oates' 'Patient Grisel-da.' " *Notes on Contemporary Literature*, 6, no. 4 (1976), 2–5.

"The Dead"

See 111.

"Dreams"

See 4992.

"The Heavy Sorrow of the Body"

See 4992.

"How I Contemplated the World from the Detroit House of Correction and Began My Life over Again"

4987. **PARK, SUE SIMPSON.** "A Study in Counterpoint: Joyce Carol Oates's 'How I Contemplated the World from the Detroit House of Correction and Began My Life over Again.' " *Modern Fiction Studies*, 22 (1976), 213–24.
See also 399.

"The Loves of Franklin Ambrose"

See 333.

"The Metamorphosis"

See 483.

"Normal Love"

See 111.

"Plot"

4988. **WALKER, CAROLYN.** "Fear, Love, and Art in Oates' 'Plot.' " *Critique*, 15, no. 1 (1973), 59–69.

"Where Are You Going, Where Have You Been?"

4989. **WEGS, JOYCE M.** " 'Don't You Know Who I Am?': The Grotesque in Oates's 'Where Are You Going, Where Have You Been?' " *The Journal of Narrative Technique*, 5 (1975), 66–72.
See also 111.

General Studies

4990. **DENNE, CONSTANCE AYERS.** "Joyce Carol Oates's Women." *The Nation*, 219 (1974), 597–99.

4991. GOODMAN, CHARLOTTE. "Women and Madness in the Fiction of Joyce Carol Oates." *Women & Literature*, 5, no. 2 (1977), 17–28.

4992. PETITE, JOSEPH. " 'Out of the Machine': Joyce Carol Oates and the Liberation of Women." *Kansas Quarterly*, 9, no. 2 (1977), 75–79.

4993. PICKERING, SAMUEL F., JR. "The Short Stories of Joyce Carol Oates." *The Georgia Review*, 28 (1974), 218–26.

4994. SULLIVAN, WALTER. "The Artificial Demon: Joyce Carol Oates and the Dimensions of the Real." *The Hollins Critic*, 9, no. 4 (1972), 1–6, 8–12.

Interviews

4995. ANON. "Transformations of Self: An Interview With Joyce Carol Oates." *The Ohio Review*, 15, no. 1 (1973), 51–61.

4996. BELLAMY, JOE DAVID. "The Dark Lady of American Letters: An Interview With Joyce Carol Oates." *The Atlantic Monthly*, 229, no. 2 (1972), 63–67.

4997. BOWER, WARREN. An Interview with Joyce Carol Oates. *Saturday Review*, 51 (26 Oct. 1968), 34–35.

4998. CLEMONS, WALTER. "Joyce Carol Oates at Home." *The New York Times Book Review*, 28 Sept. 1969, pp. 4–5, 48.

Bibliography

4999. CATRON, DOUGLAS M. "A Contribution to a Bibliography of Works by and about Joyce Carol Oates." *American Literature*, 49 (1977), 399–414.

5000. McCORMICK, LUCIENNE P. "A Bibliography of Works by and about Joyce Carol Oates." *American Literature*, 43 (1971), 124–32.

O'BRIEN, FITZ-JAMES

"The Diamond Lens"
See 35, 56.

"How I Overcame My Gravity"
See 35.

"The Pot of Tulips"
See 56.

"What Was It?"
See 56.

O'CONNOR, EDWIN

General Studies

5001.　**RANK, HUGH.** *Edwin O'Connor.* New York: Twayne, 1974.

O'CONNOR, FLANNERY

"The Artificial Nigger"

5002.　**BYRD, TURNER F.** "Ironic Dimension in Flannery O'Connor's 'The Artificial Nigger.' " *The Mississippi Quarterly*, 21 (1968), 243–51.

5003.　**DESMOND, JOHN F.** "Mr. Head's Epiphany in Flannery O'Connor's 'The Artificial Nigger.' " *Notes on Modern American Literature*, 1 (1977), item 20.

5004.　**HAYS, PETER L.** "Dante, Tobit, and 'The Artificial Nigger.' " *Studies in Short Fiction*, 5 (1968), 263–68.

5005.　**MULLER, GILBERT H.** "The City of Woe: Flannery O'Connor's Dantean Vision." *The Georgia Review*, 23 (1969), 206–13.

5006.　**RUBIN, LOUIS D., JR.** "Flannery O'Connor's Company of Southerners: or, 'The Artificial Nigger' Read as Fiction Rather Than Theology." *The Flannery O'Connor Bulletin*, 6 (1977), 47–71.

See also 219, 257, 267, 478, 549, 564, 597, 5064, 5087, 5089, 5091, 5121, 5124, 5129, 5131, 5141, 5142, 5149, 5162, 5168.

"The Barber"

See 5072, 5123, 5129.

"The Capture"

See 5063, 5072, 5087, 5149, 5162.

"A Circle in the Fire"

5007.　**RYAN, THOMAS P.** " 'A Circle in the Fire' by Flannery O'Connor." *Notre Dame English Journal*, 4, no. 1 (1965), 13–14.

See also 5064, 5068, 5075, 5089, 5091, 5124, 5129, 5144, 5162, 5168.

"The Comforts of Home"

5008.　**MILLICHAP, JOSEPH R.** "The Pauline 'Old Man' in Flannery O'Connor's 'The Comforts of Home.' " *Studies in Short Fiction*, 11 (1974), 96–99.

See also 5076, 5087, 5089, 5091, 5104, 5119, 5124, 5128, 5129, 5141, 5142, 5151, 5168.

"The Crop"

See 5072, 5129.

"The Displaced Person"

5009. BALDESHWILER, EILEEN. "Thematic Centers in 'The Displaced Person.' " In *The Process of Fiction: Contemporary Stories and Criticism*. Ed. Barbara McKenzie. New York: Harcourt, Brace & World, 1969. pp. 529–37.

5010. COX, JAMES M. "On Flannery O'Connor and 'The Displaced Person.' " In *The American Short Story*. Ed. Calvin Skaggs. New York: Dell, 1977. pp. 337–44.

5011. FITZGERALD, ROBERT. "The Countryside and the True Country." *The Sewanee Review*, 70 (1962), 380–94.

5012. JOSELYN, SISTER M., O.S.B. "Thematic Centers in 'The Displaced Person.' " *Studies in Short Fiction*, 1 (1964), 85–92.

5013. MALE, ROY R. "The Two Versions of 'The Displaced Person.' " *Studies in Short Fiction*, 7 (1970), 450–57.

See also 257, 298, 571, 5064, 5073, 5083, 5087, 5089, 5091, 5109, 5114, 5119, 5121, 5124, 5129, 5141, 5142, 5144, 5149, 5163, 5166, 5168.

"The Enduring Chill"

5014. AIKEN, DAVID. "Flannery O'Connor's Portrait of the Artist as a Young Failure." *The Arizona Quarterly*, 32 (1976), 245–59.

See also 257, 5074, 5076, 5083, 5087, 5089, 5091, 5104, 5119, 5124, 5128, 5129, 5149, 5168.

"Enoch and the Gorilla"

See 483, 5071, 5129.

"Everything That Rises Must Converge"

5015. BROER, CARMEN AVILA. " 'Everything That Rises Must Converge' (O'Connor)." In *Instructor's Manual to Accompany* "The Realities of Literature." Ed. R. F. Dietrich. Waltham, MA: Xerox Publishing, 1971. pp. 72–76.

5016. DENHAM, ROBERT D. "The World of Guilt and Sorrow: Flannery O'Connor's 'Everything That Rises Must Converge.' " *The Flannery O'Connor Bulletin*, 4 (1975), 42–51.

5017. DESMOND, JOHN F. "The Lessons of History: Flannery O'Connor's 'Everything That Rises Must Converge.' " *The Flannery O'Connor Bulletin*, 1 (1972), 39–45.

5018. ESCH, ROBERT M. "O'Connor's 'Everything That Rises Must Converge.' " *The Explicator*, 27 (1969), item 58.

5019. FOWLER, DOREEN FERLAINO. "Mrs. Chestny's Saving Graces." *The Flannery O'Connor Bulletin*, 6 (1977), 99–106.

5020. McDERMOTT, JOHN V. "Julian's Journey into Hell: Flannery O'Connor's Allegory of Pride." *The Mississippi Quarterly*, 28 (1975), 171–79.

5021.　MAIDA, PATRICIA DINNEEN. " 'Convergence' in Flannery O'Connor's 'Everything That Rises Must Converge.' " *Studies in Short Fiction*, 7 (1970), 549–55.

5022.　MONTGOMERY, MARION. "On Flannery O'Connor's 'Everything That Rises Must Converge.' " *Critique*, 13, no. 2 (1971), 15–29.

See also 298, 399, 566, 5070, 5076, 5087, 5091, 5102, 5104, 5119, 5124, 5128, 5129, 5142, 5145, 5149, 5168.

"The Geranium"

See 5063, 5072, 5091, 5096, 5129, 5142, 5149, 5162.

"Good Country People"

5023.　JONES, BARTLETT C. "Depth Psychology and Literary Study." *Midcontinent American Studies Journal*, 5, no. 2 (1964), 50–56.

5024.　PIERCE, CONSTANCE. "The Mechanical World of 'Good Country People.' " *The Flannery O'Connor Bulletin*, 5 (1976), 30–38.

5025.　THOMAS, ALFRED. "O'Connor's 'Good Country People.' " *The Explicator*, 33 (1974), item 30.

See also 257, 416, 478, 484, 565, 5064, 5068, 5089, 5091, 5104, 5119, 5124, 5128, 5129, 5132, 5149, 5154, 5166, 5168, 5170.

"A Good Man Is Hard to Find"

5026.　BRITTAIN, JOAN TUCKER. "O'Connor's 'A Good Man Is Hard to Find.' " *The Explicator*, 26 (1967), item 1.

5027.　DOXEY, WILLIAM S. "A Dissenting Opinion of Flannery O'Connor's 'A Good Man Is Hard to Find.' " *Studies in Short Fiction*, 10 (1973), 199–204.

5028.　HAMBLEN, ABIGAIL ANN. "Flannery O'Connor's Study of Innocence and Evil." *The University Review* (Kansas City), 34 (1968), 295–97.

5029.　KROPF, C. R. "Theme and Setting in 'A Good Man Is Hard to Find.' " *Renascence*, 24 (1972), 177–80, 206.

5030.　LORENTZEN, MELVIN E. "A Good Writer Is Hard to Find." In *Imagination and the Spirit: Essays in Literature and the Christian Faith Presented to Clyde S. Kilby*. Ed. Charles A. Huttar. Grand Rapids, MI: Eerdmans, 1971. pp. 417–35.

5031.　MARKS, W. S., III. "Advertisements for Grace: Flannery O'Connor's 'A Good Man Is Hard to Find.' " *Studies in Short Fiction*, 4 (1966), 19–27.

5032.　MARTIN, CARTER. "Comedy and Humor in Flannery O'Connor's Fiction." *The Flannery O'Connor Bulletin*, 4 (1975), 1–12.

5033. **MARTIN, SISTER M., O.P.** "O'Connor's 'A Good Man Is Hard to Find.' " *The Explicator*, 24 (1965), item 19.

5034. **MONTGOMERY, MARION.** "Miss Flannery's 'Good Man.' " *The University of Denver Quarterly*, 3, no. 3 (1968), 1–19.

5035. **SPIVEY, TED R.** "Religion and the Reintegration of Man in Flannery O'Connor and Walker Percy." In *The Poetry of Community: Essays on the Southern Sensibility of History and Literature.* Ed. Lewis P. Simpson. Spectrum: Monograph Series in the Arts and Sciences, Vol. 2. Atlanta: School of Arts and Sciences, Georgia State Univ., 1972. pp. 67–79.

5036. **SULLIVAN, WALTER.** "Southerners in the City: Flannery O'Connor and Walker Percy." In *The Comic Imagination in American Literature.* Ed. Louis D. Rubin, Jr. New Brunswick, NJ: Rutgers Univ. Press, 1973. pp. 339–48.

5037. **WOODWARD, ROBERT H.** "A Good Route Is Hard to Find: Place Names and Setting in O'Connor's 'A Good Man Is Hard to Find.' " *Notes on Contemporary Literature*, 3, no. 5 (1973), 2–6.

See also 181, 257, 324, 333, 399, 564, 5039, 5068, 5073, 5076, 5087, 5089, 5091, 5097, 5098, 5102, 5104, 5119, 5121, 5124, 5129, 5136, 5142, 5149–5152, 5154, 5162, 5168, 5170.

"Greenleaf"

5038. **ASALS, FREDERICK.** "The Mythic Dimensions of Flannery O'Connor's 'Greenleaf.' " *Studies in Short Fiction*, 5 (1968), 317–30.

5039. **EVANS, ELIZABETH.** "Three Notes on Flannery O'Connor." *Notes on Contemporary Literature*, 3, no. 3 (1973), 11–15.

See also 298, 478, 535, 5064, 5074–5076, 5087, 5089, 5091, 5093, 5104, 5119, 5124, 5129, 5142, 5149, 5162, 5167, 5168.

"The Heart of the Park"

See 5071, 5129.

"Judgement Day"

5040. **HOWELL, ELMO.** "Flannery O'Connor and the Home Country." *Renascence*, 24 (1972), 171–76.

See also 5064, 5086, 5087, 5091, 5093, 5119, 5124, 5129, 5149, 5162, 5168.

"The Lame Shall Enter First"

5041. **ASALS, FREDERICK.** "Flannery O'Connor's 'The Lame Shall Enter First.' " *The Mississippi Quarterly*, 23 (1970), 103–20.

5042. ———. "Hawthorne, Mary Ann, and 'The Lame Shall Enter First.' " *The Flannery O'Connor Bulletin*, 2 (1973), 3–18.

5043. **GRIMSHAW, JAMES A., JR.** "The Mistaken Identity of Rufus [Florida] Johnson." *Notes on Modern American Literature*, 1 (1977), item 31.

5044. **LORCH, THOMAS M.** "Flannery O'Connor: Christian Allegorist." *Critique*, 10, no. 2 (1968), 69–80.

5045. **SPIVEY, TED.** "Flannery O'Connor's View of God and Man." *Studies in Short Fiction*, 1 (1964), 200–06.

See also 298, 324, 5067, 5073, 5076, 5083, 5087, 5091, 5093, 5095, 5096, 5113, 5119, 5124, 5129, 5131, 5141, 5145, 5148, 5149, 5156, 5166, 5168.

"A Late Encounter with the Enemy"

See 5091, 5114, 5119, 5124, 5129, 5149, 5168.

"The Life You Save May Be Your Own"

5046. **DESMOND, JOHN F.** "The Shifting of Mr. Shiftlet: Flannery O'Connor's 'The Life You Save May Be Your Own.' " *The Mississippi Quarterly*, 28 (1975), 55–59.

5047. **DETTELBACH, CYNTHIA GOLOMB.** *In the Driver's Seat: The Automobile in American Literature and Popular Culture*. Westport, CT: Greenwood, 1976.

5048. **GRIFFITH, ALBERT J.** "Flannery O'Connor's Salvation Road." *Studies in Short Fiction*, 3 (1966), 329–33.

5049. **HEGARTY, CHARLES M., S.J.** "A Man Though Not Yet a Whole One: Mr. Shiftlet's Genesis." *The Flannery O'Connor Bulletin*, 1 (1972), 24–38.

5050. **MONTGOMERY, MARION.** "In Defense of Flannery O'Connor's Dragon." *The Georgia Review*, 25 (1971), 302–16.

See also 257, 5075, 5088, 5091, 5104, 5119, 5124, 5129, 5132, 5135, 5142, 5149, 5166, 5168.

"Mary Ann: The Story of a Little Girl"

See 5087.

"Parker's Back"

5051. **BROWNING, PRESTON, JR.** " 'Parker's Back': Flannery O'Connor's Iconography of Salvation by Profanity." *Studies in Short Fiction*, 6 (1969), 525–35.

5052. **FAHEY, WILLIAM A.** "Flannery O'Connor's 'Parker's Back.' " *Renascence*, 20 (1968), 162–64, 166.

5053. **GORDON, CAROLINE.** "Heresy in Dixie." *The Sewanee Review*, 76 (1968), 263–97.

See also 399, 5073, 5074, 5076, 5086, 5087, 5089, 5091, 5093, 5099, 5104, 5105, 5119, 5124, 5129, 5141, 5142, 5148, 5149, 5152, 5162, 5168.

"The Partridge Festival"

See 5064, 5086, 5087, 5091, 5124, 5128, 5129, 5154.

"The Peeler"

See 5071, 5129.

"Revelation"

See 324, 481, 571, 5035, 5075, 5076, 5081, 5089, 5104, 5108, 5111, 5119, 5120, 5124, 5128, 5129, 5131, 5142, 5145, 5152, 5168, 5170.

"The River"

See 257, 5064, 5069, 5087, 5089, 5091, 5124, 5129, 5141, 5142, 5168.

"A Stroke of Good Fortune"

5054. **MONTGOMERY, MARION.** "Flannery O'Connor's 'Leaden Tract Against Complacency and Contraception.' " *The Arizona Quarterly*, 24 (1968), 133–46.

5055. **ZOLLER, PETER T.** "The Irony of Preserving the Self: Flannery O'Connor's 'A Stroke of Good Fortune.' " *Kansas Quarterly*, 9, no. 2 (1977), 61–66.

See also 5063, 5072, 5129, 5168.

"A Temple of the Holy Ghost"

5056. **BASSAN, MAURICE.** "Flannery O'Connor's Way: Shock, With Moral Intent." *Renascence*, 15 (1963), 195–99, 211.

5057. **MAYER, DAVID R.** "Apologia for the Imagination: Flannery O'Connor's 'A Temple of the Holy Ghost.' " *Studies in Short Fiction*, 11 (1974), 147–52.

5058. **ROBINSON, GABRIELE SCOTT.** "Irish Joyce and Southern O'Connor." *The Flannery O'Connor Bulletin*, 5 (1976), 82–97.

5059. **WALDEN, DANIEL, AND JANE SALVIA.** "Flannery O'Connor's Dragon: Vision in 'A Temple of the Holy Ghost.' " *Studies in American Fiction*, 4 (1976), 230–35.

See also 5073, 5089, 5091, 5104, 5119, 5124, 5129, 5135, 5149, 5162, 5168.

"The Train"

5060. **HARRISON, MARGARET.** "Hazel Motes in Transit: A Comparison of Two Versions of Flannery O'Connor's 'The Train' With Chapter 1 of 'Wise Blood.' " *Studies in Short Fiction*, 8 (1971), 287–93.

See also 5063, 5071, 5087, 5129, 5149, 5162.

"The Turkey"

See 5129.

"A View of the Woods"

5061. **RISO, DON, S.J.** "Blood and Land in 'A View of the Woods.' " *The New Orleans Review*, 1 (1969), 255–57.
See also 298, 5064, 5076, 5087, 5089, 5091, 5104, 5119, 5124, 5129, 5149, 5168, 5170.

"Why Do the Heathen Rage?"

See 5129.

"Wildcat"

See 5072, 5129.

"You Can't Be Any Poorer Than Dead"

See 5129.

General Studies

5062. **ALICE, SISTER ROSE, S.S.J.** "Flannery O'Connor: Poet to the Outcast." *Renascence*, 16 (1964), 126–32.

5063. **ASALS, FREDERICK.** "The Road to *Wise Blood*." *Renascence*, 21 (1969), 181–94.

5064. **BASS, EBEN.** "Flannery O'Connor and Henry James: The Vision of Grace." *Studies in the Twentieth Century*, no. 14 (1974), pp. 43–67.

5065. **BRITTAIN, JOAN.** "The Fictional Family of Flannery O'Connor." *Renascence*, 19 (1966), 48–52.

5066. _____, **AND LEON V. DRISKELL.** "O'Connor and the Eternal Crossroads." *Renascence*, 22 (1969), 49–55.

5067. **BROWNING, PRESTON M., JR.** "Flannery O'Connor and the Demonic." *Modern Fiction Studies*, 19 (1973), 29–41.

5068. _____. "Flannery O'Connor and the Grotesque Recovery of the Holy." In *Adversity and Grace: Studies in Recent American Literature*. Ed. Nathan A. Scott, Jr. Chicago: Univ. of Chicago Press, 1968. pp. 133–61.

5069. _____. "Flannery O'Connor's Devil Revisited." *Southern Humanities Review*, 10 (1976), 325–33.

5070. **BURKE, JOHN J., JR., S.J.** "Convergence of Flannery O'Connor and Chardin." *Renascence*, 19 (1966), 41–47, 52.

5071. **BURNS, STUART L.** "The Evolution of *Wise Blood*." *Modern Fiction Studies*, 16 (1970), 147–62.

5072. _____. "Flannery O'Connor's Literary Apprenticeship." *Renascence*, 22 (1969), 3–16.

5073. _____. "Freaks in a Circus Tent: Flannery O'Connor's Christ-Haunted Characters." *The Flannery O'Connor Bulletin*, 1 (1972), 3-23.

5074. _____. "How Wide Did 'The Heathen' Range?" *The Flannery O'Connor Bulletin*, 4 (1975), 25-41.

5075. _____. " 'torn by the Lord's eye': Flannery O'Connor's Use of Sun Imagery." *Twentieth Century Literature*, 13 (1967), 154-66.

5076. CARLSON, THOMAS M. "Flannery O'Connor: The Manichaean Dilemma." *The Sewanee Review*, 77 (1969), 254-76.

5077. CASPER, LEONARD. "The Unspeakable Peacock: Apocalypse in Flannery O'Connor." In *The Shaken Realist: Essays in Modern Literature in Honor of Frederick J. Hoffman*. Ed. Melvin J. Friedman and John B. Vickery. Baton Rouge: Louisiana State Univ. Press, 1970. pp. 287-99.

5078. COFFEY, WARREN. "Flannery O'Connor." *Commentary*, 40, no. 5 (1965), 93-99.

5079. DESMOND, JOHN F. "Flannery O'Connor's Sense of Place." *Southern Humanities Review*, 10 (1976), 251-59.

5080. DETWEILER, ROBERT. "The Curse of Christ in Flannery O'Connor's Fiction." *Comparative Literature Studies*, 3 (1966), 235-45.

5081. DOWELL, BOB. "The Moment of Grace in the Fiction of Flannery O'Connor." *College English*, 27 (1965), 235-39.

5082. DRAKE, ROBERT. " 'The Bleeding Stinking Mad Shadow of Jesus' in the Fiction of Flannery O'Connor." *Comparative Literature Studies*, 3 (1966), 183-96.

5083. _____. *Flannery O'Connor: A Critical Essay*. Grand Rapids, MI: Eerdmans, 1966.

5084. _____. "Flannery O'Connor and American Literature." *The Flannery O'Connor Bulletin*, 3 (1974), 1-22.

5085. _____. "The Paradigm of Flannery O'Connor's True Country." *Studies in Short Fiction*, 6 (1969), 433-42.

5086. DRISKELL, LEON. " 'Parker's Back' vs. 'The Partridge Festival': Flannery O'Connor's Critical Choice." *The Georgia Review*, 21 (1967), 476-90.

5087. _____, AND JOAN T. BRITTAIN. *The Eternal Crossroads: The Art of Flannery O'Connor*. Lexington: Univ. Press of Kentucky, 1971.

5088. EDELSTEIN, MARK G. "Flannery O'Connor and the Problem of Modern Satire." *Studies in Short Fiction*, 12 (1975), 139-44.

5089. EGGENSCHWILER, DAVID. *The Christian Humanism of Flannery O'Connor*. Detroit, MI: Wayne State Univ. Press, 1972.

5090. FARNHAM, JAMES F. "Disintegration of Myth in the Writings of Flannery O'Connor." *The Connecticut Review*, 8, no. 1 (1974), 11–19.

√5091. FEELEY, SISTER KATHLEEN, S.S.N.D. *Flannery O'Connor: Voice of the Peacock*. New Brunswick, NJ: Rutgers Univ. Press, 1972.

5092. _____. "Thematic Imagery in the Fiction of Flannery O'Connor." *Southern Humanities Review*, 3 (1968), 14–32.

5093. FITZGERALD, ROBERT H., S.J. "Flannery O'Connor's *Everything That Rises Must Converge*." *Notre Dame English Journal*, NS 2, no. 2 (1967), 36–50.

5094. FRIEDMAN, MELVIN J. "Flannery O'Connor: Another Legend in Southern Fiction." *English Journal*, 51 (1962), 233–43.

5095. _____. "Flannery O'Connor's Sacred Objects." In *The Added Dimension: The Art and Mind of Flannery O'Connor*. Ed. Melvin J. Friedman and Lewis A. Lawson. New York: Fordham Univ. Press, 1966. pp. 196–206.

5096. _____. "Introduction." In *The Added Dimension: The Art and Mind of Flannery O'Connor*. Ed. Melvin J. Friedman and Lewis A. Lawson. New York: Fordham Univ. Press, 1966. pp. 1–31.

5097. FRIELING, KENNETH. "Flannery O'Connor's Vision: The Violence of Revelation." In *The Fifties: Fiction, Poetry, Drama*. Ed. Warren French. Deland, FL: Everett/Edwards, 1970. pp. 111–20.

5098. GARDINER, HAROLD C., S.J. "Flannery O'Connor's Clarity of Vision." In *The Added Dimension: The Art and Mind of Flannery O'Connor*. Ed. Melvin J. Friedman and Lewis A. Lawson. New York: Fordham Univ. Press, 1966. pp. 184–95.

5099. GORDON, CAROLINE. "An American Girl." In *The Added Dimension: The Art and Mind of Flannery O'Connor*. Ed. Melvin J. Friedman and Lewis A. Lawson. New York: Fordham Univ. Press, 1966. pp. 123–37.

5100. _____. "Rebels and Revolutionaries: The New American Scene." *The Flannery O'Connor Bulletin*, 3 (1974), 40–56.

5101. _____, ET AL. "Panel Discussion." *The Flannery O'Connor Bulletin*, 3 (1974), 57–78.

5102. GOSSETT, THOMAS F. "Flannery O'Connor on Her Fiction." *Southwest Review*, 59 (1974), 34–42.

5103. HAWKES, JOHN. "Flannery O'Connor's Devil." *The Sewanee Review*, 70 (1962), 395–407.

5104. HENDIN, JOSEPHINE. *The World of Flannery O'Connor*. Bloomington: Indiana Univ. Press, 1970.

5105. HINES, MELISSA. "Grotesque Conversations and Critical Piety." *The Flannery O'Connor Bulletin*, 6 (1977), 17–35.

5106. HOFFMAN, FREDERICK J. "The Search for Redemption: Flannery O'Connor's Fiction." In *The Added Dimension: The Art and Mind of Flannery O'Connor*. Ed. Melvin J. Friedman and Lewis A. Lawson. New York: Fordham Univ. Press, 1966. pp. 32–48.

5107. HOLMAN, C. HUGH. "Her Rue with a Difference: Flannery O'Connor and the Southern Literary Tradition." In *The Added Dimension: The Art and Mind of Flannery O'Connor*. Ed. Melvin J. Friedman and Lewis A. Lawson. New York: Fordham Univ. Press, 1966. pp. 73–87.

5108. HOWELL, ELMO. "The Developing Art of Flannery O'Connor." *The Arizona Quarterly*, 29 (1973), 266–76.

5109. HYMAN, STANLEY EDGAR. *Flannery O'Connor*. Minneapolis: Univ. of Minnesota Press, 1966.

5110. INGRAM, FORREST L. "American Short Story Cycles: Foreign Influences and Parallels." In *Modern American Fiction: Insights and Foreign Lights*. Proceedings of the Comparative Literature Symposium, Vol. 5. Ed. Wolodymyr T. Zyla and Wendell M. Aycock. Lubbock: Interdepartmental Committee on Comparative Literature, Texas Tech Univ., 1972. pp. 19–37.

5111. _____. "O'Connor's Seven-Story Cycle." *The Flannery O'Connor Bulletin*, 2 (1973), 19–28.

5112. KATZ, CLAIRE. "Flannery O'Connor's Range of Vision." *American Literature*, 46 (1974), 54–67.

5113. KELLER, JANE CARTER. "The Figures of the Empiricist and the Rationalist in the Fiction of Flannery O'Connor." *The Arizona Quarterly*, 28 (1972), 263–73.

5114. KLEVAR, HARVEY. "Image and Imagination: Flannery O'Connor's Front Page Fiction." *Journal of Modern Literature*, 4 (1974), 121–32.

5115. LAWSON, LEWIS A. "A Collection of Statements." In *The Added Dimension: The Art and Mind of Flannery O'Connor*. Ed. Melvin J. Friedman and Lewis A. Lawson. New York: Fordham Univ. Press, 1966. pp. 226–63.

5116. LENSING, GEORGE. "De Chardin's Ideas In Flannery O'Connor." *Renascence*, 18 (1966), 171–75.

5117. LEVINE, PAUL. "Flannery O'Connor: The Soul of the Grotesque." In *Minor American Novelists*. Ed. Charles Alva Hoyt. Carbondale and Edwardsville: Southern Illinois Univ. Press, 1970. pp. 95–117.

5118. MCCARTHY, JOHN F. "Human Intelligence Versus Divine Truth: The Intellectual in Flannery O'Connor's Works." *English Journal*, 55 (1966), 1143–48.

5119. MCFARLAND, DOROTHY TUCK. *Flannery O'Connor*. New York: Ungar, 1976.

5120. **MAIDA, PATRICIA D.** "Light and Enlightenment in Flannery O'Connor's Fiction." *Studies in Short Fiction*, 13 (1976), 31–36.

5121. **MALIN, IRVING.** "Flannery O'Connor and the Grotesque." In *The Added Dimension: The Art and Mind of Flannery O'Connor.* Ed. Melvin J. Friedman and Lewis A. Lawson. New York: Fordham Univ. Press, 1966. pp. 108–22.

5122. **MARTIN, CARTER W.** "Flannery O'Connor and Fundamental Poverty." *English Journal,* 60 (1971), 458–61.

5123. _____. "Flannery O'Connor's Early Fiction." *Southern Humanities Review*, 7 (1973), 210–14.

√5124. _____. *The True Country: Themes in the Fiction of Flannery O'Connor.* Nashville, TN: Vanderbilt Univ. Press, 1969.

5125. **MAY, JOHN R., S.J.** "Flannery O'Connor: Critical Consensus and the 'Objective' Interpretation." *Renascence*, 27 (1975), 179–92.

5126. _____. "Flannery O'Connor and the New Hermeneutic." *The Flannery O'Connor Bulletin*, 2 (1973), 29–42.

5127. _____. "Of Huckleberry Bushes and the New Hermeneutic." *Renascence*, 24 (1972), 85–95.

5128. _____. "The Pruning Word: Flannery O'Connor's Judgment of Intellectuals." *Southern Humanities Review*, 4 (1970), 325–38.

√5129. _____. *The Pruning Word: The Parables of Flannery O'Connor.* Notre Dame, IN: Univ. of Notre Dame Press, 1976.

5130. **MELLARD, JAMES M.** "Violence and Belief in Mauriac and O'Connor." *Renascence*, 26 (1974), 158–68.

5131. **MILDER, ROBERT.** "The Protestantism of Flannery O'Connor." *The Southern Review*, NS 11 (1975), 802–19.

5132. **MONTGOMERY, MARION.** "Flannery O'Connor and the Natural Man." *The Mississippi Quarterly*, 21 (1968), 235–42.

5133. _____. "Flannery O'Connor's Imitation of Significant Action." *Studies in the Twentieth Century*, no. 3 (1969), pp. 55–64.

5134. _____. "Flannery O'Connor's Territorial Center." *Critique*, 11, no. 3 (1969), 5–10.

5135. _____. "Flannery O'Connor's Transformation of the Sentimental." *The Mississippi Quarterly*, 25 (1972), 1–18.

5136. _____. "Miss O'Connor and the Christ-Haunted." *The Southern Review*, NS 4 (1968), 665–72.

5137. _____. "A Note on Flannery O'Connor's Terrible and Violent Prophecy of Mercy." *Forum* (University of Houston), 7, no. 3 (1969), 4–7.

5138. _____. "O'Connor and Teilhard de Chardin: The Problem of Evil." *Renascence*, 22 (1969), 34–42.

5139. ———. "Some Reflections on Miss O'Connor and the Dixie Limited." *The Flannery O'Connor Bulletin*, 5 (1976), 70–81.

5140. ———, ET AL. "Panel Discussion." *The Flannery O'Connor Bulletin*, 6 (1977), 72–81.

5141. MOONEY, HARRY J., JR. "Moments of Eternity: A Study in the Short Stories of Flannery O'Connor." In *The Shapeless God: Essays on Modern Fiction*. Ed. Harry J. Mooney, Jr., and Thomas F. Staley. Pittsburgh, PA: Univ. of Pittsburgh Press, 1968. pp. 117–38.

5142. MULLER, GILBERT H. *Nightmares and Visions: Flannery O'Connor and the Catholic Grotesque*. Athens: Univ. of Georgia Press, 1972.

5143. NANCE, WILLIAM L. "Flannery O'Connor: The Trouble with Being a Prophet." *The University Review* (Kansas City), 36 (1969), 101–08.

5144. NELIGAN, PATRICK, JR., AND VICTOR NUNEZ. "Flannery and the Film Makers." *The Flannery O'Connor Bulletin*, 5 (1976), 98–104.

5145. OATES, JOYCE CAROL. "The Visionary Art of Flannery O'Connor." *Southern Humanities Review*, 7 (1973), 235–46.

5146. O'CONNOR, FLANNERY. "Fiction Is a Subject with a History—It Should Be Taught That Way." In *The Added Dimension: The Art and Mind of Flannery O'Connor*. Ed. Melvin J. Friedman and Lewis A. Lawson. New York: Fordham Univ. Press, 1966. pp. 264–68.

5147. ———. "Some Aspects of the Grotesque in Southern Literature." In *The Added Dimension: The Art and Mind of Flannery O'Connor*. Ed. Melvin J. Friedman and Lewis A. Lawson. New York: Fordham Univ. Press, 1966. pp. 269–79.

5148. OPPEGAARD, SUSAN HILL. "Flannery O'Connor and the Backwoods Prophet." In *Americana-Norvegica: Norwegian Contributions to American Studies Dedicated to Sigmund Skard*, Vol. 4. Ed. Brita Seyersted. Oslo: Universitetsforlaget, 1973. pp. 305–25.

5149. ORVELL, MILES. *Invisible Parade: The Fiction of Flannery O'Connor*. Philadelphia, PA: Temple Univ. Press, 1972.

5150. PEARCE, HOWARD D. "Flannery O'Connor's Ineffable 'Recognitions.' " *Genre*, 6 (1973), 298–312.

5151. PEARCE, RICHARD. "The World Upside Down I: Flannery O'Connor." In *Stages of the Clown: Perspectives on Modern Fiction from Dostoyevsky to Beckett*. Carbondale and Edwardsville: Southern Illinois Univ. Press, 1970. pp. 67–83.

5152. QUINN, SISTER M. BERNETTA, O.S.F. "Flannery O'Connor, a Realist of Distances." In *The Added Dimension: The Art and Mind of Flannery O'Connor*. Ed. Melvin J. Friedman and Lewis A. Lawson. New York: Fordham Univ. Press, 1966. pp. 157–83.

5153. RUBIN, LOUIS D., JR. "Flannery O'Connor and the Bible Belt." In *The Added Dimension: The Art and Mind of Flannery O'Connor*. Ed. Melvin J. Friedman and Lewis A. Lawson. New York: Fordham Univ. Press, 1966. pp. 49–72.

5154. SCOUTEN, KENNETH. "The Mythological Dimensions of Five of Flannery O'Connor's Works." *The Flannery O'Connor Bulletin*, 2 (1973), 59–72.

5155. SHEAR, WALTER. "Flannery O'Connor: Character and Characterization." *Renascence*, 20 (1968), 140–46. '

5156. SHINN, THELMA J. "Flannery O'Connor and the Violence of Grace." *Contemporary Literature*, 9 (1968), 58–73.

5157. SNOW, OLLYE TINE. "The Functional Gothic of Flannery O'Connor." *Southwest Review*, 50 (1965), 286–99.

5158. SONNENFELD, ALBERT. "Flannery O'Connor: The Catholic Writer as Baptist." *Contemporary Literature*, 13 (1972), 445–57.

5159. SPIVEY, TED R. "Flannery's South: Don Quixote Rides Again." *The Flannery O'Connor Bulletin*, 1 (1972), 46–53.

5160. STELZMANN, RAINULF. "Shock and Orthodoxy: An Interpretation of Flannery O'Connor's Novels and Short Stories." *Xavier University Studies*, 2 (1963), 4–21.

5161. STEPHENS, MARTHA. "Flannery O'Connor and the Sanctified-Sinner Tradition." *The Arizona Quarterly*, 24 (1968), 223–39.

5162. _____. *The Question of Flannery O'Connor*. Baton Rouge: Louisiana State Univ. Press, 1973.

5163. SULLIVAN, WALTER. "The Achievement of Flannery O'Connor." *Southern Humanities Review*, 2 (1968), 303–09.

5164. _____. "Flannery O'Connor, Sin, and Grace: *Everything That Rises Must Converge*." *The Hollins Critic*, 2, no. 4 (1965), 1–8, 10.

5165. TATE, J. O. "The Uses of Banality." *The Flannery O'Connor Bulletin*, 4 (1975), 13–24.

5166. TAYLOR, HENRY. "The Halt Shall Be Gathered Together: Physical Deformity in the Fiction of Flannery O'Connor." *Western Humanities Review*, 22 (1968), 325–38.

5167. VANDE KIEFT, RUTH M. "Judgment in the Fiction of Flannery O'Connor." *The Sewanee Review*, 76 (1968), 337–56.

√ 5168. WALTERS, DOROTHY. *Flannery O'Connor*. New York: Twayne, 1973.

5169. WILLIAMS, MELVIN G. "Black and White: A Study in Flannery O'Connor's Characters." *Black American Literature Forum*, 10 (1976), 130–32.

5170. WYNNE, JUDITH F. "The Sacramental Irony of Flannery O'Connor." *The Southern Literary Journal*, 7, no. 2 (1975), 33–49.

Interviews

5171. **HICKS, GRANVILLE.** "A Writer at Home with Her Heritage." *Saturday Review*, 45 (12 May 1962), 22-23.

5172. **SESSIONS, WILLIAM.** "A Correspondence." In *The Added Dimension: The Art and Mind of Flannery O'Connor*. Ed. Melvin J. Friedman and Lewis A. Lawson. New York: Fordham Univ. Press, 1966. pp. 209-25.

Bibliography

5173. **BECHAM, GERALD.** "Flannery O'Connor Collection." *The Flannery O'Connor Bulletin*, 1 (1972), 66-71.

5174. **BRITTAIN, JOAN T.** "Flannery O'Connor: A Bibliography." *Bulletin of Bibliography and Magazine Notes*, 25 (1967-68), 98-100, 123-24, 142.

5175. **DUNN, ROBERT J.** "The Manuscripts of Flannery O'Connor at Georgia College." *The Flannery O'Connor Bulletin*, 5 (1976), 61-69.

5176. **FRIEDMAN, MELVIN J.** " 'The Perplex Business': Flannery O'Connor and Her Critics Enter the 1970s." In *The Added Dimension: The Art and Mind of Flannery O'Connor*. 2nd ed. Ed. Melvin J. Friedman and Lewis A. Lawson. New York: Fordham Univ. Press, 1977. pp. 207-34.

5177. **GOLDEN, ROBERT E., AND MARY C. SULLIVAN.** *Flannery O'Connor and Caroline Gordon: A Reference Guide*. Boston, MA: G. K. Hall, 1977.

5178. **LACKEY, ALLEN D.** "Flannery O'Connor: A Supplemental Bibliography of Secondary Sources." *Bulletin of Bibliography and Magazine Notes*, 30 (1973), 170-75.

5179. **LAWSON, LEWIS A.** "Bibliography." In *The Added Dimension: The Art and Mind of Flannery O'Connor*. Ed. Melvin J. Friedman and Lewis A. Lawson. New York: Fordham Univ. Press, 1966. pp. 281-302.

O'HARA, JOHN

"The Chink in the Armor"

See 5183.

"Decision"

See 5183.

"The Doctor's Son"

See 5183, 5184.

"The Gangster"

5180. SHAWEN, EDGAR. "Social Interaction in John O'Hara's 'The Gangster.' " *Studies in Short Fiction*, 11 (1974), 367–70.

"Horizon"

See 5185.

"Leonard"

See 5184.

"Over the River and Through the Woods"

See 5183.

"Pal Joey"

See 5181.

"Radio"

See 5185.

"Summer's Day"

See 595.

"Transaction"

See 5183.

"Zero"

See 5181.

General Studies

5181. BRUCCOLI, MATTHEW J. *The O'Hara Concern*. New York: Random House, 1975.

5182. ———, ED. *"An Artist Is His Own Fault": John O'Hara on Writers and Writing*. Carbondale and Edwardsville: Southern Illinois Univ. Press, 1977.

5183. CARSON, EDWARD RUSSELL. *The Fiction of John O'Hara*. Pittsburgh, PA: Univ. of Pittsburgh Press, 1961.

5184. FARR, FINIS. *O'Hara: A Biography*. Boston, MA: Little, Brown, 1973.

5185. GREBSTEIN, SHELDON NORMAN. *John O'Hara*. New York: Twayne, 1966.

Bibliography

5186. BRUCCOLI, MATTHEW J. *John O'Hara: A Checklist*. New York: Random House, 1972.

5187. _____. "John O'Hara's Works/About John O'Hara." In *The O'Hara Concern*. New York: Random House, 1975. pp. 358–99.

5188. EPPARD, PHILIP B. "Addenda to Bruccoli: O'Hara." *The Papers of the Bibliographical Society of America*, 68 (1974), 444–45.

OLIVER, DIANE
"Neighbors"

See 268.

OLSEN, TILLIE
"I Stand Here Ironing"

See 5190.

"The Iron Throat"

See 5189.

"Oh Yes"

See 5190.

"Tell Me a Riddle"

See 399, 5189–5191.

General Studies

5189. BURKOM, SELMA, AND MARGARET WILLIAMS. "De-Riddling Tillie Olsen's Writings." *San José Studies*, 2, no. 1 (1976), 65–83.

5190. McELHINEY, ANNETTE BENNINGTON. "Alternative Responses to Life in Tillie Olsen's Work." *Frontiers*, 2, no. 1 (1977), 76–91.

5191. O'CONNOR, WILLIAM VAN. "The Short Stories of Tillie Olsen." *Studies in Short Fiction*, 1 (1963), 21–25.

5192. ROSE, ELLEN CRONAN. "Limning: or Why Tillie Writes." *The Hollins Critic*, 13, no. 2 (1976), 1–9, 11, 13.

ORTEGA, PHILIP D.
"The Coming of Zamora"

See 311.

OSKISON, JOHN MILTON

General Studies

5193. **STRICKLAND, ARNEY L.** "John Milton Oskison: A Writer of the Transitional Period of the Oklahoma Indian Territory." *Southwestern American Literature*, 2 (1972), 125–34.

OWENS, WILLIAM A.

"Hangerman John"

See 5194.

General Studies

5194. **PILKINGTON, WILLIAM T.** *William A. Owens.* Austin, TX: Steck-Vaughn, 1968.

OZICK, CYNTHIA

General Studies

*5195. **KNOPP, JOSEPHINE Z.** "The Jewish Stories of Cynthia Ozick." *Studies in American Jewish Literature*, 1, no. 1 (1975), 31–38.

5196. **OZICK, CYNTHIA.** "A Response to Josephine Knopp's 'The Jewish Stories of Cynthia Ozick.' " *Studies in American Jewish Literature*, 1, no. 2 (1975), 49–50.

5197. **WISSE, RUTH R.** "American Jewish Writing, Act II." *Commentary*, 61, no. 6 (1976), 40–45.

PAGE, THOMAS NELSON

"The Burial of the Guns"

See 5200.

"Elsket"

See 5200.

"The Gray Jacket of No. 4"

See 5200.

"Little Darby"

See 83, 5200.

"Marse Chan"

See 446, 5199–5201, 5203.

"Meh Lady: A Story of the War"

See 5199, 5200, 5203.

" 'No Haid Pawn' "

5198. **RUBIN, LOUIS D., JR.** "The Other Side of Slavery: Thomas Nelson Page's ' "No Haid Pawn." ' " *Studies in the Literary Imagination*, 7, no. 1 (1974), 95–99.
See also 553, 5203.

"The Old Gentleman of the Black Stock"

See 5200.

"Old Jabe's Marital Experiment"

See 5200.

"Ole 'Stracted"

See 5200, 5201.

"Polly: A Christmas Recollection"

See 5200, 5205.

"A Soldier of the Empire"

See 5200.

"Unc' Edinburg's Drowndin' "

See 5200, 5203.

General Studies

5199. **DOWNS, ROBERT B.** "Moonlight and Magnolia: Thomas Nelson Page's *In Ole Virginia*." In *Books That Changed the South*. Chapel Hill: Univ. of North Carolina Press, 1977. pp. 176–85.
5200. **GROSS, THEODORE L.** *Thomas Nelson Page*. New York: Twayne, 1967.
5201. ———. "Thomas Nelson Page: Creator of a Virginia Classic." *The Georgia Review*, 20 (1966), 338–51.
5202. **HOLMAN, HARRIET R.** "Magazine Editors and the Stories of Thomas Nelson Page's Late Flowering." In *Essays Mostly on Periodical Publishing in America: A Collection in Honor of Clarence Gohdes*. Ed. James Woodress, et al. Durham, NC: Duke Univ. Press, 1973. pp. 148–61.
5203. **KING, KIMBALL.** "Introduction." In *In Ole Virginia; or Marse Chan and Other Stories*, by Thomas Nelson Page. Chapel Hill: Univ. of North Carolina Press, 1969. pp. ix–xxxvi.

5204. SIMMS, L. MOODY, JR. "Corra Harris on the Declining Influence of Thomas Nelson Page." *The Mississippi Quarterly*, 28 (1975), 505–09.

5205. SOWDER, WILLIAM J. "Gerald W. Johnson, Thomas Nelson Page, and the South." *The Mississippi Quarterly*, 14 (1961), 197–203.

Bibliography

5206. GROSS, THEODORE L. "Thomas Nelson Page (1853–1922)." *American Literary Realism, 1870–1910*, 1, no. 1 (1967), 90–92.

PARKER, DOROTHY

"Big Blonde"

See 5207.

"The Sexes"

See 548.

"Soldiers of the Republic"

See 5207.

"Such a Pretty Little Picture"

See 5207.

"The Waltz"

See 374.

"You Were Perfectly Fine"

See 454.

General Studies

5207. KEATS, JOHN. *You Might As Well Live: The Life and Times of Dorothy Parker*. New York: Simon and Schuster, 1970.

5208. LABRIE, ROSS. "Dorothy Parker Revisited." *The Canadian Review of American Studies*, 7 (1976), 48–56.

5209. TOTH, EMILY. "Dorothy Parker, Erica Jong, and New Feminist Humor." *Regionalism and the Female Imagination*, 3, nos. 2–3 (1977), 70–85.

PAULDING, JAMES KIRKE

"The Dumb Girl"

5210. OWENS, LOUIS. "Paulding's 'The Dumb Girl': A Source

for *The Scarlet Letter.*" *The Nathaniel Hawthorne Journal 1974*, pp. 240–49.

General Studies

5211. **ADERMAN, RALPH M.** "James Kirke Paulding as Social Critic." *Papers on English Language & Literature*, 1 (1965), 217–29.
5212. ———. "James Kirke Paulding's Literary Income." *Bulletin of The New York Public Library*, 64 (1960), 117–29.

Bibliography

5213. **ADERMAN, RALPH M.** "James Kirke Paulding's Contributions to American Magazines." *Studies in Bibliography*, 17 (1964), 142–51.

PERRY, GEORGE SESSIONS

General Studies

5214. **ALEXANDER, STANLEY G.** *George Sessions Perry.* Austin, TX: Steck-Vaughn, 1967.

PETERKIN, JULIA

General Studies

5215. **LANDESS, THOMAS H.** "The Achievement of Julia Peterkin." *The Mississippi Quarterly*, 29 (1976), 221–32.
*5216. ———. *Julia Peterkin.* Boston, MA: Twayne, 1976.
5217. **SHEALY, ANN.** "Julia Peterkin: A Souvenir." In *The Passionate Mind: Four Studies including "Julia Peterkin: A Souvenir."* Philadelphia, PA: Dorrance, 1976. pp. 31–54.

PETRAKIS, HARRY MARK

General Studies

5218. **CHAPIN, HELEN GERACIMOS.** " 'Chicagopolis'—The Double World of Harry Mark Petrakis." *The Old Northwest*, 2 (1976), 401–13.

Interviews

5219. **NEWQUIST, ROY.** "Harry Mark Petrakis." In *Conversations.* New York: Rand McNally, 1967. pp. 288–99.
5220. **RODGERS, BERNARD F., JR.** "The Song of the Thrush: An Interview with Harry Mark Petrakis." *Chicago Review*, 28, no. 3 (1977), 97–119.

PETRY, ANN

"In Darkness and Confusion"

5221. ADAMS, GEORGE R. "Riot as Ritual: Ann Petry's 'In Darkness and Confusion.' " *Negro American Literature Forum*, 6 (1972), 54–57, 60.
See also 484.

"The Witness"

5222. MADDEN, DAVID. "Ann Petry: 'The Witness.' " *Studies in Black Literature*, 6, no. 3 (1975), 24–26.

Interviews

5223. O'BRIEN, JOHN. "Ann Petry." In *Interviews with Black Writers*. Ed. John O'Brien. New York: Liveright, 1973. pp. 153–63.

Bibliography

5224. HILL, JAMES LEE. "Bibliography of the Works of Chester Himes, Ann Petry and Frank Yerby." *Black Books Bulletin*, 3, no. 3 (1975), 60–72.

PHELPS, ELIZABETH STUART

"The Angel Over the Right Shoulder"

5225. CULLEY, MARGARET M. "Vain Dreams: The Dream Convention in Some Nineteenth-Century American Women's Fiction." *Frontiers*, 1, no. 3 (1976), 94–102.

General Studies

5226. KESSLER, CAROL F. "The Feminist Mock-Heroics of Elizabeth Stuart Phelps (1844–1911)." *Regionalism and the Female Imagination*, 3, nos. 2–3 (1977), 20–28.

PHILLIPS, DAVID GRAHAM

General Studies

5227. RAVITZ, ABE C. *David Graham Phillips*. New York: Twayne, 1966.

PHILLIPS, THOMAS HAL

Interviews

5228. KELLY, GEORGE M. "An Interview with Thomas Hal Phillips." *Notes on Mississippi Writers*, 6 (1973), 3–13.

PIERSON, HELEN W.

"Chip"

See 18.

PIKE, ALBERT

General Studies

5229. WEBER, DAVID J. "Introduction." In *Prose Sketches and Poems Written in the Western Country (With Additional Stories)*, by Albert Pike. Albuquerque, NM: Calvin Horn, 1968. pp. ix–xxv.

POE, EDGAR ALLAN

"The Angel of the Odd"

5230. BANDY, W. T. "More on 'The Angel of the Odd.' " *Poe Newsletter*, 3 (1970), 22.
5231. GERBER, GERALD E. "Poe's Odd Angel." *Nineteenth-Century Fiction*, 23 (1968), 88–93.
5232. RICHARD, CLAUDE. "Arrant Bubbles: Poe's 'The Angel of the Odd.' " *Poe Newsletter*, 2 (1969), 46–48.

"The Assignation"

5233. BENTON, RICHARD P. "Is Poe's 'The Assignation' a Hoax?" *Nineteenth-Century Fiction*, 18 (1963), 193–97.
5234. FISHER, BENJAMIN FRANKLIN, IV. "To 'The Assignation' from 'The Visionary' and Poe's Decade of Revising." *The Library Chronicle*, 39 (1973), 89–105; 40 (1976), 221–51.
See also 93, 556, 5600, 5630.

"The Balloon-Hoax"

5235. FALK, DORIS V. "Thomas Low Nichols, Poe, and the 'Balloon Hoax.' " *Poe Studies*, 5 (1972), 48–49.
5236. WILKINSON, RONALD STERNE. "Poe's 'Balloon-Hoax' Once More." *American Literature*, 32 (1960), 313–17.
See also 5511, 5549, 5592, 5643.

"Berenice"

5237. SLOANE, DAVID E. E. "Gothic Romanticism and Rational Empiricism in Poe's 'Berenice.' " *American Transcendental Quarterly*, no. 19 (1973), pp. 19–26.
5238. _____, AND BENJAMIN FRANKLIN FISHER, IV. "Poe's Revisions in 'Berenice': Beyond the Gothic." *American Transcendental Quarterly*, no. 24, Supplement Two (1974), pp. 19–23.
See also 81, 5464, 5492, 5506, 5521, 5522, 5524, 5600, 5617, 5643.

"The Black Cat"

5239. **ANDERSON, GAYLE DENINGTON.** "Demonology in 'The Black Cat.' " *Poe Studies*, 10 (1977), 43–44.

5240. **FRUSHELL, RICHARD C.** " 'An Incarnate Night-Mare': Moral Grotesquerie in 'The Black Cat.' " *Poe Studies*, 5 (1972), 43–44.

5241. **GARGANO, JAMES W.** " 'The Black Cat': Perverseness Reconsidered." *Texas Studies in Literature and Language*, 2 (1960), 172–78.

5242. **McELROY, JOHN HARMON.** "The Kindred Artist; or, the Case of the Black Cat." *Studies in American Humor*, 3 (1976), 103–17.

5243. **REEDER, ROBERTA.** " 'The Black Cat' as a Study in Repression." *Poe Studies*, 7 (1974), 20–22.

See also 456, 503, 548, 5263, 5507, 5511, 5522, 5524, 5600, 5602, 5614, 5615, 5617.

"Bon-Bon"

5244. **CHRISTIE, JAMES W.** "Poe's 'Diabolical' Humor: Revisions of 'Bon-Bon.' " *The Library Chronicle*, 41 (1976), 44–55.

"The Cask of Amontillado"

5245. **BALES, KENT.** "Poetic Justice in 'The Cask of Amontillado.' " *Poe Studies*, 5 (1972), 51.

5246. **BURNS, SHANNON.** " 'The Cask of Amontillado': Montresor's Revenge." *Poe Studies*, 7 (1974), 24.

5247. **CAROLAN, KATHERINE.** " 'The Cask of Amontillado': Some Further Ironies." *Studies in Short Fiction*, 11 (1974), 195–99.

5248. **CLARK, GEORGE P.** "A Further Word on Poe and *Lolita*." *Poe Newsletter*, 3 (1970), 39.

5249. **CLENDENNING, JOHN.** "Anything Goes: Comic Aspects in 'The Cask of Amontillado.' " In *American Humor: Essays Presented to John C. Gerber*. Ed. O. M. Brack, Jr. Scottsdale, AZ: Arete, 1977. pp. 13–26.

5250. **DAMERON, J. LASLEY.** "The Poe Theme in Junior High Literature." *Interpretations*, 2 (1969), 11–18.

5251. **DOXEY, WILLIAM S.** "Concerning Fortunato's 'Courtesy.' " *Studies in Short Fiction*, 4 (1967), 266.

5252. **FOOTE, DOROTHY NORRIS.** "Poe's 'The Cask of Amontillado.' " *The Explicator*, 20 (1961), item 27.

5253. **FREEHAFER, JOHN.** "Poe's 'Cask of Amontillado': A Tale of Effect." *Jahrbuch für Amerikastudien*, 13 (1968), 134–42.

5254. **GARGANO, JAMES W.** " 'The Cask of Amontillado': A Masquerade of Motive and Identity." *Studies in Short Fiction*, 4 (1967), 119–26.

5255. **GOLDHURST, WILLIAM, ALFRED APPEL, JR., AND GEORGE P. CLARK.** "Three Observations on 'Amontillado' and *Lolita.*" *Poe Studies*, 5 (1972), 51.

5256. **HARKEY, JOSEPH H.** "A Note on Fortunato's Coughing." *Poe Newsletter*, 3 (1970), 22.

5257. **HARRIS, KATHRYN MONTGOMERY.** "Ironic Revenge in Poe's 'The Cask of Amontillado.' " *Studies in Short Fiction*, 6 (1969), 333-35.

5258. **JACOBS, EDWARD CRANEY.** "A Possible Debt to Cooper." *Poe Studies*, 9 (1976), 23.

5259. **MABBOTT, THOMAS OLLIVE.** "Poe's 'The Cask of Amontillado.' " *The Explicator*, 25 (1966), item 30.

5260. **NEVI, CHARLES N.** "Irony and 'The Cask of Amontillado.' " *English Journal*, 56 (1967), 461-63.

5261. **PITTMAN, PHILIP McM.** "Method and Motive in 'The Cask of Amontillado.' " *The Malahat Review*, no. 34 (1975), pp. 87-100.

5262. **REA, J.** "In Defense of Fortunato's Courtesy." *Studies in Short Fiction*, 4 (1967), 267-68.

5263. ———. "Poe's 'The Cask of Amontillado.' " *Studies in Short Fiction*, 4 (1966), 57-69.

5264. **ROCKS, JAMES E.** "Conflict and Motive in 'The Cask of Amontillado.' " *Poe Studies*, 5 (1972), 50-51.

5265. **SHURR, WILLIAM H.** "Montresor's Audience in 'The Cask of Amontillado.' " *Poe Studies*, 10 (1977), 28-29.

5266. **STEELE, CHARLES W.** "Poe's 'The Cask of Amontillado.' " *The Explicator*, 18 (1960), item 43.

5267. **STEPP, WALTER.** "The Ironic Double in Poe's 'The Cask of Amontillado.' " *Studies in Short Fiction*, 13 (1976), 447-53.

5268. **SWEET, CHARLES A., JR.** "Retapping Poe's 'Cask of Amontillado.' " *Poe Studies*, 8 (1975), 10-12.

5269. **WATERMAN, ARTHUR E.** "Point of View in Poe." *The CEA Critic*, 27, no. 4 (1965), 5.

See also 2, 454, 597, 5476, 5492, 5503, 5513, 5549, 5583, 5600, 5618, 6430.

"The Colloquy of Monos and Una"

5270. **SUTHER, JUDITH D.** "Rousseau, Poe, and the Idea of Progress." *Papers on Language & Literature*, 12 (1976), 469-75.

See also 13, 5507, 5511, 5524, 5537, 5549, 5609, 5627, 5630.

"The Conversation of Eiros and Charmion"

See 5497, 5507, 5524, 5549, 5616.

"A Descent into the Maelström"

5271. **FINHOLT, RICHARD D.** "The Vision at the Brink of the Abyss: 'A Descent into the Maelstrom' in the Light of Poe's Cosmology." *The Georgia Review,* 27 (1973), 356-66.
5272. **FRANK, FREDERICK S.** "The Aqua-Gothic Voyage of 'A Descent into the Maelström.' " *American Transcendental Quarterly,* no. 29 (1976), pp. 85-93.
5273. **HENNELLY, MARK M., JR.** "Oedipus and Orpheus in the Maelström: The Traumatic Rebirth of the Artist." *Poe Studies,* 9 (1976), 6-11.
5274. **MURPHY, CHRISTINA J.** "The Philosophical Pattern of 'A Descent into the Maelström.' " *Poe Studies,* 6 (1973), 25-26.
5275. **SWEENEY, GERALD M.** "Beauty and Truth: Poe's 'A Descent into the Maelström.' " *Poe Studies,* 6 (1973), 22-25.
See also 38, 63, 5474, 5477, 5497, 5510, 5511, 5549, 5556, 5615.

"The Devil in the Belfry"

5276. **POLLIN, BURTON R.** "*Nicholas Nickleby* and 'The Devil in the Belfry.' " *Poe Studies,* 8 (1975), 23.

"Diddling Considered as One of the Exact Sciences"

5277. **POLLIN, BURTON R.** "Poe's 'Diddling': More on the Dating and the Aim." *Poe Studies,* 9 (1976), 11-13.
5278. ———. "Poe's 'Diddling': The Source of Title and Tale." *The Southern Literary Journal,* 2, no. 1 (1969), 106-11.
5279. **RICHARD, CLAUDE.** "Poe and the Yankee Hero: An Interpretation of 'Diddling Considered as One of the Exact Sciences.' " *The Mississippi Quarterly,* 21 (1968), 93-109.
See also 5527.

"The Domain of Arnheim"

5280. **HESS, JEFFREY A.** "Sources and Aesthetics of Poe's Landscape Fiction." *American Quarterly,* 22 (1970), 177-89.
5281. **JEFFREY, DAVID K.** "The Johnsonian Influence: *Rasselas* and Poe's 'The Domain of Arnheim.' " *Poe Newsletter,* 3 (1970), 26-29.
5282. **MIZE, GEORGE E.** "The Matter of Taste in Poe's 'Domain of Arnheim' and 'Landor's Cottage.' " *The Connecticut Review,* 6, no. 1 (1972), 93-99.
See also 34, 5511, 5524, 5539, 5542, 5549, 5630, 5642.

"The Duc De L'Omelette"

5283. **CARSON, DAVID L.** "Ortolans and Geese: The Origin of Poe's *Duc De L'Omelette.*" *CLA Journal,* 8 (1965), 277-83.

5284. HIRSCH, DAVID H. "Another Source for Poe's 'The Duc De L'Omelette.' " *American Literature*, 38 (1967), 532–36.

5285. _____. " 'The Duc De L'Omelette' as Anti-Visionary Tale." *Poe Studies*, 10 (1977), 36–39.

See also 5630.

"Eleonora"

5286. BENTON, RICHARD P. "Platonic Allegory in Poe's 'Eleonora.' " *Nineteenth-Century Fiction*, 22 (1967), 293–97.

5287. LJUNGQUIST, KENT. "The Influence of 'Adonais' on 'Eleonora.' " *Poe Studies*, 10 (1977), 27–28.

5288. POLLIN, B[URTON] R. "Poe's Use of the Name Ermengarde in 'Eleonora.' " *Notes and Queries*, NS 17 (1970), 332–33.

5289. ROBINSON, E. ARTHUR. "Comic Vision in Poe's 'Eleonora.' " *Poe Studies*, 9 (1976), 44–46.

See also 5474, 5511, 5524, 5583, 5590, 5630, 5642.

"The Facts in the Case of M. Valdemar"

5290. BARTHES, ROLAND. "Textual Analysis of a Tale By Edgar Poe." Trans. Donald G. Marshall. *Poe Studies*, 10 (1977), 1–12.

See also 35, 5497, 5501, 5511, 5549, 5630.

"The Fall of the House of Usher"

5291. AMUR, G. S. " 'The Heart of Darkness' and 'The Fall of the House of Usher': The Tale as Discovery." *The Literary Criterion*, 9, no. 4 (1971), 59–70.

5292. BAILEY, J. O. "What Happens in 'The Fall of the House of Usher'?" *American Literature*, 35 (1964), 445–66.

5293. BOUDREAU, GORDON V. "Of Pale Ushers and Gothic Piles: Melville's Architectural Symbology." *ESQ*, 18 (1972), 67–82.

5294. CARLSON, ERIC W. "Introduction." In *Edgar Allan Poe: "The Fall of the House of Usher."* Columbus, OH: Merrill, 1971. pp. 1–7.

5295. COHEN, HENNIG. "Roderick Usher's Tragic Struggle." *Nineteenth-Century Fiction*, 14 (1959), 270–72.

5296. DAMERON, J. LASLEY. "Arthur Symons on Poe's 'The Fall of the House of Usher.' " *Poe Studies*, 9 (1976), 46–49.

5297. EVANS, WALTER. " 'The Fall of the House of Usher' and Poe's Theory of the Tale." *Studies in Short Fiction*, 14 (1977), 137–44.

5298. GARMON, GERALD M. "Roderick Usher: Portrait of the Madman as an Artist." *Poe Studies*, 5 (1972), 11–14.

5299. GOLD, JOSEPH. "Reconstructing the 'House of Usher.' " *The Emerson Society Quarterly*, no. 37 (1964), pp. 74–76.

5300. **GOODWIN, K. L.** "Roderick Usher's Overrated Knowledge." *Nineteenth-Century Fiction*, 16 (1961), 173–75.

5301. **HAFLEY, JAMES.** "A Tour of the House of Usher." *The Emerson Society Quarterly*, no. 31 (1963), pp. 18–20.

5302. **HARTLEY, LODWICK.** "From Crazy Castle to the House of Usher: A Note toward a Source." *Studies in Short Fiction*, 2 (1965), 256–61.

5303. **HILL, JOHN S.** "The Dual Hallucination in 'The Fall of the House of Usher.' " *Southwest Review*, 48 (1963), 396–402.

5304. **HOFFMAN, MICHAEL J.** "The House of Usher and Negative Romanticism." *Studies in Romanticism*, 4 (1965), 158–68.

5305. **KENDALL, LYLE H., JR.** "The Vampire Motif in 'The Fall of the House of Usher.' " *College English*, 24 (1963), 450–53.

5306. **LAVERTY, CARROLL D.** "Poe in His Place—in His Time." *The Emerson Society Quarterly*, no. 31 (1963), pp. 23–25.

5307. **MABBOTT, THOMAS OLLIVE.** "The Books in the House of Usher." *Books at Iowa*, no. 19 (1973), pp. 3–7.

5308. **McALEER, JOHN J.** "Poe and Gothic Elements in *Moby-Dick*." *The Emerson Society Quarterly*, no. 27 (1962), p. 34.

5309. **MARSH, JOHN L.** "The Psycho-Sexual Reading of 'The Fall of the House of Usher.' " *Poe Studies*, 5 (1972), 8–9.

5310. **MARTINDALE, COLIN.** "Archetype and Reality in 'The Fall of the House of Usher.' " *Poe Studies*, 5 (1972), 9–11.

5311. **OBUCHOWSKI, PETER.** "Unity of Effect in Poe's 'The Fall of the House of Usher.' " *Studies in Short Fiction*, 12 (1975), 407–12.

5312. **PHILLIPS, H. WELLS.** "Poe's Usher: Precursor of Abstract Art." *Poe Studies*, 5 (1972), 14–16.

5313. **POLLIN, BURTON R.** "Poe's Pen of Iron." *American Transcendental Quarterly*, no. 2 (1969), pp. 16–18.

5314. **ROBINSON, E. ARTHUR.** "Order and Sentience in 'The Fall of the House of Usher.' " *PMLA*, 76 (1961), 68–81.

5315. **ROUNTREE, THOMAS J.** "Poe's Universe: The House of Usher and the Narrator." *Tulane Studies in English*, 20 (1972), 123–34.

5316. **ST. ARMAND, BARTON LEVI.** "The 'Mysteries' of Edgar Poe: The Quest for a Monomyth in Gothic Literature." In *The Gothic Imagination: Essays in Dark Romanticism*. Ed. G. R. Thompson. Pullman: Washington State Univ. Press, 1974. pp. 65–93.

5317. _____. "Usher Unveiled: Poe and the Metaphysic of Gnosticism." *Poe Studies*, 5 (1972), 1–8.

5318. **SAMUELS, CHARLES THOMAS.** "Usher's Fall; Poe's Rise." *The Georgia Review*, 18 (1964), 208–16.

5319. **SIMPSON, LEWIS P.** *The Dispossessed Garden: Pastoral and*

History in Southern Literature. Athens: Univ. of Georgia Press, 1975.

5320. SMITH, HERBERT F. "Is Roderick Usher a Caricature?" *Poe Studies*, 6 (1973), 49–50.

5321. _____. "Usher's Madness and Poe's Organicism: A Source." *American Literature*, 39 (1967), 379–89.

5322. THOMPSON, G. R. "The Face in the Pool: Reflections on the Doppelgänger Motif in 'The Fall of the House of Usher.' " *Poe Studies*, 5 (1972), 16–21.

5323. VISWANATHAN, JACQUELINE. "The Innocent Bystander: The Narrator's Position in Poe's 'The Fall of the House of Usher,' James's 'The Turn of the Screw' and Butor's *L'Emploi du temps.*" *The Hebrew University Studies in Literature*, 4 (1976), 27–47.

5324. WALKER, I. M. "The 'Legitimate Sources' of Terror in 'The Fall of the House of Usher.' " *The Modern Language Review*, 61 (1966), 585–92.

5325. WASSERMAN, RENATA R. MAUTNER. "The Self, the Mirror, the Other: 'The Fall of the House of Usher.' " *Poe Studies*, 10 (1977), 33–35.

5326. WILCOX, EARL J. "Poe's Usher and Ussher's Chronology." *Poe Newsletter*, 1 (1968), 31.

5327. WRIGHT, NATHALIA. "Roderick Usher: Poe's Turn-of-the-Century Artist." In *Artful Thunder: Versions of the Romantic Tradition in American Literature in Honor of Howard P. Vincent.* Ed. Robert J. DeMott and Sanford E. Marovitz. Kent, OH: Kent State Univ. Press, 1975. pp. 55–67.

See also 53, 63, 81, 106, 363, 384, 389, 399, 481, 511, 583, 2597, 4936, 5477, 5479–5481, 5483, 5484, 5488, 5491, 5492, 5499, 5505, 5517, 5522, 5524, 5549, 5552, 5562, 5583, 5590, 5592, 5595, 5596, 5600, 5602, 5611, 5612, 5626, 5628, 5630, 5642, 5657.

"Four Beasts in One: The Homo-Cameleopard"

See 5466, 5550, 5566.

"The Gold-Bug"

5328. DELANEY, JOAN. "Poe's 'The Gold-Bug' in Russia: A Note on First Impressions." *American Literature*, 42 (1970), 375–79.

5329. RICARDOU, JEAN. "Gold in the Bug." Trans. Frank Towne. *Poe Studies*, 9 (1976), 33–39.

5330. ST. ARMAND, BARTON LEVI. "Poe's 'Sober Mystification': The Uses of Alchemy in 'The Gold-Bug.' " *Poe Studies*, 4 (1971), 1–7.

See also 102, 454, 597, 5464, 5470, 5503, 5511, 5518, 5522, 5531.

"Hans Pfaal"

5331. **GRAVELY, WILLIAM H., JR.** "A Few Words of Clarification on 'Hans Pfaal.' " *Poe Studies*, 5 (1972), 56.

5332. _____. "New Sources for Poe's 'Hans Pfaall.' " *Tennessee Studies In Literature*, 17 (1972), 139–49.

5333. _____. "A Note on the Composition of Poe's 'Hans Pfaal.' " *Poe Newsletter*, 3 (1970), 2–5.

5334. **GREER, H. ALLEN.** "Poe's 'Hans Pfaall' and the Political Scene." *ESQ*, no. 60, Supplement (1970), pp. 67–73.

5335. **WILKINSON, RICHARD STERNE.** "Poe's 'Hans Pfaall' Reconsidered." *Notes and Queries*, NS 13 (1966), 333–37.

See also 524, 5470, 5511, 5524, 5544, 5549.

"Hop-Frog"

5336. **MARTIN, BRUCE K.** "Poe's 'Hop-Frog' and the Retreat from Comedy." *Studies in Short Fiction*, 10 (1973), 288–90.

5337. **PAULY, THOMAS H.** " 'Hop-Frog'—Is the Last Laugh Best?" *Studies in Short Fiction*, 11 (1974), 307–09.

See also 16, 466, 548, 5466, 5503, 5513, 5549, 5566, 5615.

"How to Write a Blackwood Article"

5338. **McCLARY, BEN HARRIS.** "Poe's 'Turkish Fig-Pedler.' " *Poe Newsletter*, 2 (1969), 56.

5339. **POLLIN, BURTON R.** "Poe's Tale of Psyche Zenobia: A Reading for Humor and Ingenious Construction." In *Papers on Poe: Essays in Honor of John Ward Ostrom*. Ed. Richard P. Veler. Springfield, OH: Chantry Music Press, Wittenberg Univ., 1972. pp. 92–103.

5340. **SCHUSTER, RICHARD.** "More on the 'Fig-Pedler.' " *Poe Newsletter*, 3 (1970), 22.

See also 5463, 5516, 5560, 5630.

"The Imp of the Perverse"

5341. **KANJO, EUGENE R.** " 'The Imp of the Perverse': Poe's Dark Comedy of Art and Death." *Poe Newsletter*, 2 (1969), 41–44.

5342. **POLLIN, BURTON R.** "The Self-Destructive Fall: A Theme from Shakespeare Used in *Pym* and 'The Imp of the Perverse.' " *Études Anglaises*, 29 (1976), 199–202.

See also 5263, 5515, 5529, 5549, 5616.

"The Island of the Fay"

5343. **LJUNGQUIST, KENT.** "Poe's 'The Island of the Fay': The Passing of Fairyland." *Studies in Short Fiction*, 14 (1977), 265–71.

See also 34, 5464, 5524, 5583, 5590.

"The Journal of Julius Rodman"

5344. **JACKSON, DAVID K.** "A Poe Hoax Comes Before the U.S. Senate." *Poe Studies*, 7 (1974), 47–48.

5345. **KIME, WAYNE R.** "Poe's Use of Irving's *Astoria* in 'The Journal of Julius Rodman.' " *American Literature*, 40 (1968), 215–22.

5346. _____. "Poe's Use of Mackenzie's *Voyages* in 'The Journal of Julius Rodman.' " *Western American Literature*, 3 (1968), 61–67.

5347. **LEVINE, STUART.** "Poe's *Julius Rodman*: Judaism, Plagiarism, and the Wild West." *The Midwest Quarterly*, 1 (1960), 245–59.

5348. **SAXENA, M. C.** "Evident Rapture: Poe's *Journal of Julius Rodman* as a Western Narrative." *Indian Journal of American Studies*, 7, no. 1 (1977), 40–53.

See also 38, 435, 5511, 5549.

"King Pest"

5349. **GOLDHURST, WILLIAM.** "Poe's Multiple King Pest: A Source Study." *Tulane Studies in English*, 20 (1972), 107–21.

See also 93, 5513.

"Landor's Cottage"

5350. **ROSENFELD, ALVIN.** "Description in Poe's 'Landor's Cottage.' " *Studies in Short Fiction*, 4 (1967), 264–66.

See also 5282, 5524, 5542.

"The Landscape Garden"

See 5542, 5600, 5601.

"Ligeia"

5351. **BASLER, ROY P., AND JAMES SCHROETER.** "Poe's 'Ligeia.' " *PMLA*, 77 (1962), 675.

5352. **DAVIS, JUNE AND JACK L.** "An Error in Some Recent Printings of 'Ligeia.' " *Poe Newsletter*, 3 (1970), 21.

5353. **FISHER, BENJAMIN FRANKLIN, IV.** "Dickens and Poe: *Pickwick* and 'Ligeia.' " *Poe Studies*, 6 (1973), 14–16.

5354. **GARGANO, JAMES W.** "Poe's 'Ligeia': Dream and Destruction." *College English*, 23 (1962), 337–42.

5355. **GARRETT, WALTER.** "The 'Moral' of 'Ligeia' Reconsidered." *Poe Studies*, 4 (1971), 19–20.

5356. **GARRISON, JOSEPH M., JR.** "The Irony of 'Ligeia.' " *ESQ*, no. 60, Supplement (1970), pp. 13–17.

5357.　**HOFFMAN, DANIEL.** "I Have Been Faithful to You in My Fashion: The Remarriage of Ligeia's Husband." *The Southern Review*, NS 8 (1972), 89–105.

5358.　**HUMMA, JOHN B.** "Poe's 'Ligeia': Glanvill's Will or Blake's Will?" *The Mississippi Quarterly*, 26 (1973), 55–62.

5359.　**LAUBER, JOHN.** " 'Ligeia' and Its Critics: A Plea for Literalism." *Studies in Short Fiction*, 4 (1966), 28–32.

5360.　**MORRISON, CLAUDIA C.** "Poe's 'Ligeia': An Analysis." *Studies in Short Fiction*, 4 (1967), 234–44.

5361.　**RAMAKRISHNA, D.** "The Conclusion of Poe's 'Ligeia.' " *The Emerson Society Quarterly*, no. 47 (1967), pp. 69–70.

5362.　————. "Poe's 'Ligeia.' " *The Explicator*, 25 (1966), item 19.

5363.　**REA, J.** "Classicism and Romanticism in Poe's 'Ligeia.' " *Ball State University Forum*, 8, no. 1 (1967), 25–29.

5364.　**REED, KENNETH T.** " 'Ligeia': The Story as Sermon." *Poe Studies*, 4 (1971), 20.

5365.　**SCHROETER, JAMES.** "A Misreading of Poe's 'Ligeia.' " *PMLA*, 76 (1961), 397–406.

5366.　**SWEET, CHARLES A., JR.** " 'Ligeia' and the Warlock." *Studies in Short Fiction*, 13 (1976), 85–88.

5367.　**THOMPSON, G. R.** " 'Proper Evidences of Madness': American Gothic and the Interpretation of 'Ligeia.' " *ESQ*, 18 (1972), 30–49.

5368.　**TRITT, MICHAEL.** " 'Ligeia' and 'The Conqueror Worm.' " *Poe Studies*, 9 (1976), 21–22.

5369.　**WEST, MURIEL.** "Poe's 'Ligeia.' " *The Explicator*, 22 (1963), item 15.

5370.　————. "Poe's 'Ligeia' and Issac D'Israeli." *Comparative Literature*, 16 (1964), 19–28.

See also 13, 81, 360, 484, 3707, 5318, 5470, 5476, 5478, 5483, 5484, 5491, 5497, 5499, 5503, 5520, 5522, 5524, 5545, 5549, 5553, 5562, 5592, 5595, 5600, 5602, 5623, 5630, 5641.

"The Light-House"

See 5583, 5600.

"Lionizing"

5371.　**ARNOLD, JOHN.** "Poe's 'Lionizing': The Wound and the Bawdry." *Literature and Psychology*, 17 (1967), 52–54.

5372.　**BENTON, RICHARD P.** "Poe's 'Lionizing': A Quiz on Willis and Lady Blessington." *Studies in Short Fiction*, 5 (1968), 239–44.

5373.　————. "Reply to Professor Thompson." *Studies in Short Fiction*, 6 (1968), 97.

5374. **Hammond, Alexander.** "Poe's 'Lionizing' and the Design of *Tales of the Folio Club*." *ESQ*, 18 (1972), 154–65.

5375. **Thompson, G. R.** "On the Nose—Further Speculation on the Sources and Meaning of Poe's 'Lionizing.' " *Studies in Short Fiction*, 6 (1968), 94–96.

"The Literary Life of Thingum Bob, Esq.,
Late Editor of the 'Goosetherumfoodle' "

See 5511.

"Loss of Breath"

See 5466, 5511, 5600, 5630, 5631.

"The Man of the Crowd"

5376. **Shelden, Pamela J.** "Poe's Urban Nightmare: 'The Man of the Crowd' and the Gothic Tradition." *Studies in the Humanities*, 4, no. 2 (1975), 31–35.
See also 93, 610, 5543, 5549, 5592.

"The Man That Was Used Up."

5377. **Mabbott, Thomas O.** "Poe's 'The Man That Was Used Up.' " *The Explicator*, 25 (1967), item 70.

5378. **Pry, Elmer R.** "A Folklore Source for 'The Man That Was Used Up.' " *Poe Studies*, 8 (1975), 46.
See also 16, 5406, 5566, 5630.

"MS. Found in a Bottle"

5379. **Richard, Claude.** " 'MS. Found in a Bottle' and The Folio Club." *Poe Newsletter*, 2 (1969), 23.

5380. **Stauffer, Donald Barlow.** "The Two Styles of Poe's 'MS. Found in a Bottle.' " *Style*, 1 (1967), 107–20.
See also 524, 3273, 5477, 5486, 5498, 5524, 5556, 5600, 5636, 5643.

"The Masque of the Red Death"

5381. **Benton, Richard P.** " 'The Masque of the Red Death'— The Primary Source." *American Transcendental Quarterly*, no. 1 (1969), pp. 12–13.

5382. **Cary, Richard.** " 'The Masque of the Red Death' Again." *Nineteenth-Century Fiction*, 17 (1962), 76–78.

5383. **Evans, Walter.** "Poe's 'The Masque of the Red Death' and Hawthorne's 'The Wedding Knell.' " *Poe Studies*, 10 (1977), 42–43.

5384. **Gerber, Gerald E.** "Additional Sources for 'The Masque of the Red Death.' " *American Literature*, 37 (1965), 52–54.

5385. HEWITT, SANDRA. "The Satiric Echoes of Edgar Allan Poe's 'The Masque of the Red Death' in 'La máscara olvidada' by Leopoldo Lugones." In *Essays in Honor of Jorge Guillén on the Occasion of His 85th Year*. Cambridge, MA: Abedul Press, 1977. pp. 10–19.

5386. PITCHER, EDWARD WILLIAM. "Horological and Chronological Time in 'Masque of the Red Death.'" *American Transcendental Quarterly*, no. 29 (1976), pp. 71–75.

5387. POLLIN, BURTON R. "Poe's 'Shadow' as a Source for His 'The Masque of the Red Death.'" *Studies in Short Fiction*, 6 (1968), 104–06.

5388. REGAN, ROBERT. "Hawthorne's 'Plagiary'; Poe's Duplicity." *Nineteenth-Century Fiction*, 25 (1970), 281–98.

5389. ROPPOLO, JOSEPH PATRICK. "Meaning and 'The Masque of the Red Death.'" *Tulane Studies in English*, 13 (1963), 59–69.

5390. VANDERBILT, KERMIT. "Art and Nature in 'The Masque of the Red Death.'" *Nineteenth-Century Fiction*, 22 (1968), 379–89.

See also 38, 5513, 5524, 5549, 5559, 5583, 5591, 5600, 5615, 5618, 5630.

"Mellonta Tauta"

5391. POLLIN, BURTON R. "Politics and History in Poe's 'Mellonta Tauta': Two Allusions Explained." *Studies in Short Fiction*, 8 (1971), 627–31.

See also 5511.

"Mesmeric Revelation"

5392. STERN, MADELEINE B. "Poe: 'The Mental Temperament' for Phrenologists." *American Literature*, 40 (1968), 155–63.

See also 5501, 5507, 5524, 5630.

"Metzengerstein"

5393. FISHER, BENJAMIN F. "Poe's 'Metzengerstein': Not a Hoax." *American Literature*, 42 (1971), 487–94.

5394. LEVINE, SUSAN AND STUART. "Poe's Use of Jacob Bryant in 'Metzengerstein.'" *Poe Studies*, 9 (1976), 53.

See also 5511, 5552, 5600, 5601, 5630, 5631.

"Morella"

5395. BICKMAN, MARTIN. "Animatopoeia: Morella as Siren of the Self." *Poe Studies*, 8 (1975), 29–32.

5396. GARGANO, JAMES W. "Poe's 'Morella': A Note on Her Name." *American Literature*, 47 (1975), 259–64.

5397. HOLT, PALMER C. "Poe and H. N. Coleridge's *Greek Clas-*

sic Poets: 'Pinakidia,' 'Politian,' and 'Morella' Sources." *American Literature*, 34 (1962), 8–30.

5398. McCARTHY, KEVIN M. " 'Sameness' versus 'Saneness' in Poe's 'Morella.' " *American Notes & Queries*, 11 (1973), 149–50.

5399. RICHARD, LEE J. "Edgar Allan Poe's 'Morella': Vampire of Volition." *Studies in Short Fiction*, 9 (1972), 93–94.

See also 5522, 5524, 5609.

"The Murders in the Rue Morgue"

5400. ASARCH, JOEL KENNETH. "A Telling Tale: Poe's Revisions in 'The Murders in the Rue Morgue.' " *The Library Chronicle*, 41 (1976), 83–90.

5401. BANDY, W. T. "Who Was Monsieur Dupin?" *PMLA*, 79 (1964), 508–09.

5402. BRONZWAER, W. "Deixis as a Structuring Device in Narrative Discourse: An Analysis of Poe's 'The Murders in the Rue Morgue.' " *English Studies*, 56 (1975), 345–59.

5403. DISKIN, PATRICK. "Poe, Le Fanu and the Sealed Room Mystery." *Notes and Queries*, NS 13 (1966), 337–39.

5404. FISHER, BENJAMIN FRANKLIN, IV. "Poe, Blackwood's, and 'The Murders in the Rue Morgue.' " *American Notes & Queries*, 12 (1974), 109–11.

5405. GROSS, SEYMOUR. "*Native Son* and 'The Murders in the Rue Morgue': An Addendum." *Poe Studies*, 8 (1975), 23.

5406. HATVARY, GEORGE E. "Introduction." In *Prose Romances: The Murders in the Rue Morgue and The Man that was Used Up*, by Edgar Allan Poe. Jamaica, NY: St. John's Univ. Press, 1968. pp. i–vi.

5407. HAWKINS, JOHN. "Poe's 'The Murders in the Rue Morgue.' " *The Explicator*, 23 (1965), item 49.

5408. HOLMAN, HARRIET R. "Longfellow in 'The Rue Morgue.' " *ESQ*, no. 60, Supplement (1970), pp. 58–60.

5409. JONES, BUFORD, AND KENT LJUNGQUIST. "Monsieur Dupin: Further Details On the Reality Behind the Legend." *The Southern Literary Journal*, 9, no. 1 (1976), 70–77.

5410. KELLER, MARK. "Dupin in the 'Rue Morgue': Another Form of Madness?" *The Arizona Quarterly*, 33 (1977), 249–55.

5411. OUSBY, IAN V. K. " 'The Murders in the Rue Morgue' and 'Doctor D'Arsac': A Poe Source." *Poe Studies*, 5 (1972), 52.

5412. STAUFFER, DONALD BARLOW. "Poe as Phrenologist: The Example of Monsieur Dupin." In *Papers on Poe: Essays in Honor of John Ward Ostrom*. Ed. Richard P. Veler. Springfield, OH: Chantry Music Press, Wittenberg Univ., 1972. pp. 113–25.

See also 555, 583, 597, 5466, 5470, 5476, 5479, 5485, 5491, 5511, 5549, 5562, 5592, 5611, 5616, 5617, 5630, 5643.

"The Mystery of Marie Rogêt"

5413. BENTON, RICHARD P. " 'The Mystery of Marie Rogêt'—A Defense." *Studies in Short Fiction*, 6 (1969), 144–51.

5414. FUSCO, RICHARD. "Poe's Revisions of 'The Mystery of Marie Rogêt'—A Hoax?" *The Library Chronicle*, 41 (1976), 91–99.

5415. WALSH, JOHN. *Poe the Detective: The Curious Circumstances Behind* The Mystery of Marie Rogêt. New Brunswick, NJ: Rutgers Univ. Press, 1968.

See also 597, 5511, 5524, 5592.

"Mystification"

5416. POLLIN, BURTON R. "Poe's 'Mystification': Its Source in Fay's *Norman Leslie*." *The Mississippi Quarterly*, 25 (1972), 111–30.

See also 5549, 5630.

"Never Bet the Devil Your Head"

5417. GLASSHEIM, ELIOT. "A Dogged Interpretation of 'Never Bet the Devil Your Head.' " *Poe Newsletter*, 2 (1969), 44–45.

"The Oblong Box"

See 5543, 5549, 5600, 5601.

"The Oval Portrait"

5418. DOWELL, RICHARD W. "The Ironic History of Poe's 'Life in Death': A Literary Skeleton in the Closet." *American Literature*, 42 (1971), 478–86.

5419. THOMPSON, G. R. "Dramatic Irony in 'The Oval Portrait': A Reconsideration of Poe's Revisions." *English Language Notes*, 6 (1968), 107–14.

See also 43, 5477, 5559, 5600, 5601, 5630, 5635, 5636.

"The Philosophy of Furniture"

See 5524.

"The Pit and the Pendulum"

5420. HIRSCH, DAVID H. "Another Source for 'The Pit and the Pendulum.' " *The Mississippi Quarterly*, 23 (1970), 35–43.

5421. ———. "The Pit and the Apocalypse." *The Sewanee Review*, 76 (1968), 632–52.

5422. MURTUZA, ATHAR. "An Arabian Source for Poe's 'The Pit and the Pendulum.' " *Poe Studies*, 5 (1972), 52.

See also 4283, 5499, 5503, 5524, 5549, 5552, 5583, 5591, 5616, 5618, 5630.

"The Power of Words"

See 5524, 5549, 5627.

"A Predicament"

5423. **GERBER, GERALD E.** "Milton and Poe's 'Modern Woman.' " *Poe Newsletter*, 3 (1970), 25–26.

5424. **POLLIN, BURTON R.** "Poe's Dr. Ollapod." *American Literature*, 42 (1970), 80–82.

5425. **ROCHE, A. JOHN.** "Another Look at Poe's Dr. Ollapod." *Poe Studies*, 6 (1973), 28.

See also 5339, 5516, 5560.

"The Premature Burial"

See 5524, 5630, 5638.

"The Purloined Letter"

5426. **BELLEI, SERGIO L. P.** " 'The Purloined Letter': A Theory of Perception." *Poe Studies*, 9 (1976), 40–42.

5427. **HATVARY, GEORGE EGON.** "Poe's Borrowings from H. B. Wallace." *American Literature*, 38 (1966), 365–72.

5428. **HAYCRAFT, HOWARD.** "Poe's 'Purloined Letter.' " *The Papers of the Bibliographical Society of America*, 56 (1962), 486–87.

5429. **VARNADO, S. L.** "The Case of the Sublime Purloin; or Burke's *Inquiry* as the Source of an Anecdote in 'The Purloined Letter.' " *Poe Newsletter*, 1 (1968), 27.

See also 597, 5464, 5479, 5485, 5503, 5511, 5549, 5609, 5615.

"Shadow—A Parable"

5430. **DEFALCO, JOSEPH M.** "The Source of Terror in Poe's 'Shadow—A Parable.' " *Studies in Short Fiction*, 6 (1969), 643–48.

See also 5387, 5550, 5584, 5600, 5601.

"Silence—A Fable"

5431. **FISHER, BENJAMIN FRANKLIN, IV.** "The Power of Words in Poe's 'Silence.' " *The Library Chronicle*, 41 (1976), 56–72.

5432. **THOMPSON, G. R.** " 'Silence' and the Folio Club: Who Were the 'Psychological Autobiographists'?" *Poe Newsletter*, 2 (1969), 23.

See also 5550, 5600.

"Some Words with a Mummy"

5433. **POLLIN, BURTON R.** "Poe's 'Some Words with a Mummy' Reconsidered." *ESQ*, no. 60, Supplement (1970), pp. 60–67.

See also 5511, 5630.

"The Spectacles"

5434. **POLLIN, BURTON R.** " 'The Spectacles' of Poe—Sources and Significance." *American Literature*, 37 (1965), 185–90.

5435. **SALZBERG, JOEL.** "Preposition and Meaning in Poe's 'The Spectacles.' " *Poe Newsletter*, 3 (1970), 21.

See also 5511, 5566.

"The System of Dr. Tarr and Prof. Fether"

5436. **BENTON, RICHARD P.** "Poe's 'The System of Dr. Tarr and Prof. Fether': Dickens or Willis?" *Poe Newsletter*, 1 (1968), 7–9.

5437. **DRABECK, BERNARD A.** " 'Tarr and Fether'—Poe and Abolitionism." *American Transcendental Quarterly*, no. 14 (1972), pp. 177–84.

5438. **FISHER, BENJAMIN FRANKLIN, IV.** "Poe's 'Usher' Tarred & Fethered." *Poe Studies*, 6 (1973), 49.

See also 5466, 5511, 5566.

"A Tale of the Ragged Mountains"

5439. **ISANI, MUKHTAR ALI.** "Some Sources for Poe's 'Tale of the Ragged Mountains.' " *Poe Studies*, 5 (1972), 38–40.

5440. **THOMPSON, G. R.** "Is Poe's 'A Tale of the Ragged Mountains' a Hoax?" *Studies in Short Fiction*, 6 (1969), 454–60.

See also 38, 5501, 5511, 5549, 5583, 5630.

"The Tell-Tale Heart"

5441. **CANARIO, JOHN W.** "The Dream in 'The Tell-Tale Heart.' " *English Language Notes*, 7 (1970), 194–97.

5442. **GARGANO, JAMES W.** "The Theme of Time in 'The Tell-Tale Heart.' " *Studies in Short Fiction*, 5 (1968), 378–82.

5443. **McILVAINE, ROBERT.** "A Shakespearean Echo in 'The Tell-Tale Heart.' " *American Notes & Queries*, 15 (1976), 38–40.

5444. **POLLIN, BURTON R.** "Bulwer Lytton and 'The Tell-Tale Heart.' " *American Notes & Queries*, 4 (1965), 7–8.

5445. **REILLY, JOHN E.** "The Lesser Death-Watch and 'The Tell-Tale Heart.' " *American Transcendental Quarterly*, no. 2 (1969), pp. 3–9.

5446. **ROBINSON, E. ARTHUR.** "Poe's 'The Tell-Tale Heart.' " *Nineteenth-Century Fiction*, 19 (1965), 369–78.

5447. ———. "Thoreau and the Deathwatch in Poe's 'The Tell-Tale Heart.' " *Poe Studies*, 4 (1971), 14–16.

5448. **SENELICK, LAURENCE.** "Charles Dickens and 'The Tell-Tale Heart.' " *Poe Studies*, 6 (1973), 12–14.

5449. **STRICKLAND, EDWARD.** "Dickens' 'A Madman's Manuscript' and 'The Tell-Tale Heart.' " *Poe Studies*, 9 (1976), 22–23.

See also 454, 565, 585, 5263, 5464, 5492, 5503, 5522, 5524, 5600, 5614, 5618, 5624.

"Thou Art the Man"

5450. **MURPHY, GEORGE D.** "A Source for Ballistics in Poe." *American Notes & Queries*, 4 (1966), 99.
See also 5511, 5549.

"The Thousand-and-Second Tale of Scheherazade"

5451. **POLLIN, BURTON R.** "Poe and the Incubator." *American Notes & Queries*, 12 (1974), 146–49.
See also 5486, 5511.

"Three Sundays in a Week"

5452. **PRY, ELMER R., JR.** "Bawdy Punning in 'Three Sundays in a Week.' " *Poe Studies*, 9 (1976), 54.

"Von Kempelen and His Discovery"

5453. **HALL, THOMAS.** "Poe's Use of a Source: Davy's Chemical Researches and 'Von Kempelen and His Discovery.' " *Poe Newsletter*, 1 (1968), 28.
5454. **POLLIN, BURTON R.** "Poe's *Von Kempelen and His Discovery*: Sources and Significance." *Études Anglaises*, 20 (1967), 12–23.
See also 5583, 5638.

"William Wilson"

5455. **COSKREN, ROBERT.** " 'William Wilson' and the Disintegration of Self." *Studies in Short Fiction*, 12 (1975), 155–62.
5456. **GARGANO, JAMES W.** "Art and Irony in 'William Wilson.' " *ESQ*, no. 60, Supplement (1970), pp. 18–22.
5457. **MONTGOMERY, MARION.** "Vision and the Eye for Detail in Poe and O'Connor." *The Flannery O'Connor Bulletin*, 6 (1977), 36–46.
5458. **PORTE, JOEL.** "In the Hands of an Angry God: Religious Terror in Gothic Fiction." In *The Gothic Imagination: Essays in Dark Romanticism*. Ed. G. R. Thompson. Pullman: Washington State Univ. Press, 1974. pp. 42–64.
5459. **ROVNER, MARC LESLIE.** "What William Wilson Knew: Poe's Dramatization of an Errant Mind." *The Library Chronicle*, 41 (1976), 73–82.
5460. **SULLIVAN, RUTH.** "William Wilson's Double." *Studies in Romanticism*, 15 (1976), 253–63.
5461. **WALSH, THOMAS F.** "The Other William Wilson." *American Transcendental Quarterly*, no. 10 (1971), pp. 17–26.

See also 5388, 5464, 5491, 5499, 5503, 5511, 5513, 5522, 5524, 5549, 5558, 5559, 5601, 5616, 5623, 5625, 5636, 5643.

General Studies

5462. ALEXANDER, JEAN. "Introduction." In *Affidavits of Genius: Edgar Allan Poe and the French Critics, 1847–1924*. Port Washington, NY: Kennikat, 1971. pp. 3–76.

5463. ALLEN, MICHAEL. *Poe and the British Magazine Tradition*. New York: Oxford Univ. Press, 1969.

5464. ANDERSON, CARL L. *Poe in Northlight: The Scandinavian Response to His Life and Work*. Durham, NC: Duke Univ. Press, 1973.

5465. ARNOLD, ARMIN. *D. H. Lawrence and America*. London: Philosophical Library, 1959.

5466. AUTREY, MAX L. "Edgar Allan Poe's Satiric View of Evolution." *Extrapolation*, 18 (1977), 186–99.

5467. BANDY, WILLIAM T. *The Influence and Reputation of Edgar Allan Poe in Europe*. Baltimore, MD: Edgar Allan Poe Society, 1962.

5468. BAUDELAIRE, CHARLES. "Edgar Allan Poe, His Life and Works (1852)." In *Affadavits of Genius: Edgar Allan Poe and the French Critics, 1847–1924*. Ed. and trans. Jean Alexander. Port Washington, NY: Kennikat, 1971. pp. 99–121.

5469. BAYM, NINA. "The Function of Poe's Pictorialism." *The South Atlantic Quarterly*, 65 (1966), 46–54.

5470. BITTNER, WILLIAM. *Poe: A Biography*. Boston, MA: Little, Brown, 1962.

5471. ———. "Poe and the 'Invisible Demon.' " *The Georgia Review*, 17 (1963), 134–38.

5472. BLACKMUR, R. P. "Afterword." In *The Fall of the House of Usher and Other Tales*, by Edgar Allan Poe. New York: New American Library, 1960. pp. 375–83.

5473. BLISH, JAMES. "The Climate of Insult." *The Sewanee Review*, 80 (1972), 340–46.

5474. BLOCK, HASKELL M. "Poe, Baudelaire and His Rival Translators." In *Translation in the Humanities*. Ed. Marilyn Gaddis Rose. Binghamton: State Univ. of New York at Binghamton, 1977. pp. 59–66.

5475. BRADDY, HALDEEN. "Poe's Flight from Reality." *Texas Studies in Literature and Language*, 1 (1959), 394–400.

5476. BROUSSARD, LOUIS. *The Measure of Poe*. Norman: Univ. of Oklahoma Press, 1969.

5477. BUDICK, E. MILLER. "The Fall of the House: A Reappraisal of Poe's Attitudes toward Life and Death." *The Southern Literary Journal*, 9, no. 2 (1977), 30-50.

5478. ———. "Poe's Gothic Idea: The Cosmic Geniture of Horror." *Essays in Literature* (Western Illinois University), 3 (1976), 73-85.

5479. BURANELLI, VINCENT. *Edgar Allan Poe*. New York: Twayne, 1961.

5480. ———. *Edgar Allan Poe*. 2nd ed. Boston, MA: Twayne, 1977.

5481. BUTLER, DAVID W. "Usher's Hypochondriasis: Mental Alienation and Romantic Idealism in Poe's Gothic Tales." *American Literature*, 48 (1976), 1-12.

5482. CARLSON, ERIC W. "Introduction." In *Introduction to Poe: A Thematic Reader*. Glenview, IL: Scott, Foresman, 1967. pp. xv-xxxv.

5483. ———. *Poe on the Soul of Man*. Baltimore, MD: Edgar Allan Poe Society and Enoch Pratt Free Library, 1973.

5484. ———. "Poe's Vision of Man." In *Papers on Poe: Essays in Honor of John Ward Ostrom*. Ed. Richard P. Veler. Springfield, OH: Chantry Music Press, Wittenberg Univ., 1972. pp. 7-20.

5485. CAWELTI, JOHN G. *Adventure, Mystery, and Romance: Formula Stories as Art and Popular Culture*. Chicago: Univ. of Chicago Press, 1976.

5486. CECIL, L. MOFFITT. "Poe's 'Arabesque.'" *Comparative Literature*, 18 (1966), 55-70.

5487. ———. "Poe's Wine List." *Poe Studies*, 5 (1972), 41-42.

5488. CHANDLER, ALICE. "'The Visionary Race': Poe's Attitude toward His Dreamers." *ESQ*, no. 60, Supplement (1970), pp. 73-81.

5489. CHRISTOPHER, J. R. "Poe and the Detective Story." *The Armchair Detective*, 2 (1968), 49-51.

5490. COLEMAN, ALEXANDER. "Notes on Borges and American Literature." *TriQuarterly*, no. 25 (1972), pp. 356-77.

5491. COX, JAMES M. "Edgar Poe: Style as Pose." *The Virginia Quarterly Review*, 44 (1968), 67-89.

5492. CROSSLEY, ROBERT. "Poe's Closet Monologues." *Genre*, 10 (1977), 215-32.

5493. D'AUREVILLY, J. BARBEY. "The King of the Bohemians, or Edgar Poe." In *Affidavits of Genius: Edgar Allan Poe and the French Critics, 1847-1924*. Ed. and trans. Jean Alexander. Port Washington, NY: Kennikat, 1971. pp. 145-52.

5494. DE GOURMONT, REMY. "Marginalia on Edgar Poe and Baudelaire." In *Affidavits of Genius: Edgar Allan Poe and the*

French Critics, 1847–1924. Ed. and trans. Jean Alexander. Port Washington, NY: Kennikat, 1971. pp. 219–32.

5495. DE MOÜY, CHARLES. "Contemporary Studies—Edgar Poe." In *Affidavits of Genius: Edgar Allan Poe and the French Critics, 1847–1924.* Ed. and trans. Jean Alexander. Port Washington, NY: Kennikat, 1971. pp. 153–66.

5496. DE PONTMARTIN, ARMAND. "The Storytellers." In *Affidavits of Genius: Edgar Allan Poe and the French Critics, 1847–1924.* Ed. and trans. Jean Alexander. Port Washington, NY: Kennikat, 1971. pp. 126–30.

5497. EAKIN, PAUL JOHN. "Poe's Sense of an Ending." *American Literature,* 45 (1973), 1–22.

5498. ELKINS, WILLIAM R. "The Dream World and the Dream Vision: Meaning and Structure in Poe's Art." *The Emporia State Research Studies,* 17, no. 1 (1968), 5–17.

5499. ENGELBERG, EDWARD. "Consciousness and Will: Poe and Mann." In *The Unknown Distance: From Consciousness to Conscience—Goethe to Camus.* Cambridge, MA: Harvard Univ. Press, 1972. pp. 117–43.

5500. ETIENNE, LOUIS. "The American Storytellers—Edgar Allan Poe." In *Affidavits of Genius: Edgar Allan Poe and the French Critics, 1847–1924.* Ed. and trans. Jean Alexander. Port Washington, NY: Kennikat, 1971. pp. 132–44.

5501. FALK, DORIS V. "Poe and the Power of Animal Magnetism." *PMLA,* 84 (1969), 536–46.

5502. FISHER, BENJAMIN FRANKLIN, IV. "Poe and the Art of the Well Wrought Tale." *The Library Chronicle,* 41 (1976), 5–12.

5503. FLETCHER, RICHARD M. *The Stylistic Development of Edgar Allan Poe.* The Hague: Mouton, 1973.

5504. FLORY, WENDY STALLARD. "Rehearsals for Dying in Poe and Emily Dickinson." *American Transcendental Quarterly,* no. 18 (1973), pp. 13–18.

5505. ———. "Usher's Fear and the Flaw in Poe's Theories of the Metamorphosis of the Senses." *Poe Studies,* 7 (1974), 17–19.

5506. FORCLAZ, ROGER. "A Source for 'Berenice' And A Note on Poe's Reading." *Poe Newsletter,* 1 (1968), 25–27.

5507. FORGUES, E. D. "Studies in the English and American Novel: The Tales of Edgar A. Poe." In *Affidavits of Genius: Edgar Allan Poe and the French Critics, 1847–1924.* Ed. and trans. Jean Alexander. Port Washington, NY: Kennikat, 1971. pp. 79–96.

5508. FRAIBERG, LOUIS. "Joseph Wood Krutch: Poe's Art as an Abnormal Condition of the Nerves." In *Psychoanalysis & Ameri-*

can Literary Criticism. Detroit, MI: Wayne State Univ. Press, 1960. pp. 134–44.

5509. FRANKLIN, ROSEMARY F. "The Cabin by the Lake: Pastoral Landscapes of Poe, Cooper, Hawthorne, and Thoreau." *ESQ*, 22 (1976), 59–70.

5510. FURROW, SHARON. "Psyche and Setting: Poe's Picturesque Landscapes." *Criticism*, 15 (1973), 16–27.

5511. GALE, ROBERT L. *Plots and Characters in the Fiction and Poetry of Edgar Allan Poe*. Hamden, CT: Archon Books, 1970.

5512. GALLOWAY, DAVID. "Introduction." In *Selected Writings of Edgar Allan Poe: Poems, Tales, Essays and Reviews*. Harmondsworth, Middlesex: Penguin Books, 1967. pp. 9–46.

5513. GARGANO, JAMES W. *The Masquerade Vision in Poe's Short Stories*. Baltimore, MD: Enoch Pratt Free Library, Edgar Allan Poe Society, and Library of the Univ. of Baltimore, 1977.

5514. ———. "The Question of Poe's Narrators." *College English*, 25 (1963), 177–81.

5515. GARRISON, JOSEPH M., JR. "The Function of Terror in the Work of Edgar Allan Poe." *American Quarterly*, 18 (1966), 136–50.

5516. GERBER, GERALD E. "The Coleridgean Context of Poe's *Blackwood* Satires." *ESQ*, no. 60, Supplement (1970), pp. 87–91.

5517. GIRGUS, SAM B. "Poe and R. D. Laing: The Transcendent Self." *Studies in Short Fiction*, 13 (1976), 299–309.

5518. GOLDHURST, WILLIAM. "Edgar Allan Poe and the Conquest of Death." *The New Orleans Review*, 1 (1969), 316–19.

5519. ———. "Poe-esque Themes." In *Papers on Poe: Essays in Honor of John Ward Ostrom*. Ed. Richard P. Veler. Springfield, OH: Chantry Music Press, Wittenberg Univ., 1972. pp. 126–39.

5520. GRANT, VERNON W. *Great Abnormals: The Pathological Genius of Kafka, Van Gogh, Strindberg and Poe*. New York: Hawthorn Books, 1968.

5521. GRIFFITH, CLARK. "Poe and the Gothic." In *Papers on Poe: Essays in Honor of John Ward Ostrom*. Ed. Richard P. Veler. Springfield, OH: Chantry Music Press, Wittenberg Univ., 1972. pp. 21–27.

5522. GROSSMAN, JOAN DELANEY. *Edgar Allan Poe in Russia: A Study of Legend and Literary Influence*. Würzburg: Jal, 1973.

5523. HALIO, JAY L. "The Moral Mr. Poe." *Poe Newsletter*, 1 (1968), 23–24.

5524. HALLIBURTON, DAVID. *Edgar Allan Poe: A Phenomenological View*. Princeton, NJ: Princeton Univ. Press, 1973.

5525. HAMMOND, ALEXANDER. "Edgar Allan Poe's *Tales of the Folio Club*: The Evolution of a Lost Book." *The Library Chronicle*, 41 (1976), 13–43.

5526. _____. "Further Notes on Poe's Folio Club Tales." *Poe Studies*, 8 (1975), 38–42.

5527. _____. "A Reconstruction of Poe's 1833 *Tales of the Folio Club*: Preliminary Notes." *Poe Studies*, 5 (1972), 25–32.

5528. HARAP, LOUIS. "Edgar Allan Poe and Journalism." *Zeitschrift für Anglistik und Amerikanistik*, 19 (1971), 164–81.

5529. _____. "Poe and Dostoevsky: A Case of Affinity." In *Weapons of Criticism: Marxism in America and the Literary Tradition*. Ed. Norman Rudich. Palo Alto, CA: Ramparts Press, 1976. pp. 271–85.

5530. HODGSON, JOHN. "Poe's Criticism: The Circular Pursuit." *The Centennial Review*, 21 (1977), 140–49.

5531. HOFRICHTER, LAURA. "From Poe to Kafka." *University of Toronto Quarterly*, 29 (1960), 405–19.

5532. HOLQUIST, MICHAEL. "Whodunit and Other Questions: Metaphysical Detective Stories in Post-War Fiction." *New Literary History*, 3 (1971), 135–56.

5533. HOWARTH, WILLIAM L. "Introduction." In *Twentieth Century Interpretations of Poe's Tales*. Englewood Cliffs, NJ: Prentice-Hall, 1971. pp. 1–22.

5534. HUBBELL, JAY B. "Introduction." In *Tales and The Raven and Other Poems*, by Edgar Allan Poe. Columbus, OH: Merrill, 1969. pp. v–xxvi.

5535. _____. "The Literary Apprenticeship of Edgar Allan Poe." *The Southern Literary Journal*, 2, no. 1 (1969), 99–105.

5536. _____. "Poe and the Southern Literary Tradition." *Texas Studies in Literature and Language*, 2 (1960), 151–71.

5537. HUBERT, THOMAS. "The Southern Element in Poe's Fiction." *The Georgia Review*, 28 (1974), 200–11.

5538. HUSSEY, JOHN P. "Narrative Voice and Classical Rhetoric in *Eureka*." *American Transcendental Quarterly*, no. 26 (1975), pp. 37–42.

5539. JACOBS, ROBERT D. "Poe's Earthly Paradise." *American Quarterly*, 12 (1960), 404–13.

5540. JACOBS, WILLIAM JAY. *Edgar Allan Poe: Genius in Torment*. New York: McGraw-Hill, 1975.

5541. JOSEPH, GERHARD J. "Poe and Tennyson." *PMLA*, 88 (1973), 418–28.

5542. KEHLER, JOEL R. "New Light on the Genesis and Progress of Poe's Landscape Fiction." *American Literature*, 47 (1975), 173–83.

5543. KENNEDY, J. GERALD. "The Limits of Reason: Poe's Deluded Detectives." *American Literature*, 47 (1975), 184–96.

5544. KETTERER, DAVID. "Poe's Usage of the Hoax and the Unity of 'Hans Phaall.' " *Criticism*, 13 (1971), 377–85.

5545. KOSTER, DONALD N. "Poe, Romance and Reality." *American Transcendental Quarterly*, no. 19 (1973), pp. 8–13.

5546. KRONEGGER, M. E. "Joyce's Debt to Poe and the French Symbolists." *Revue de Littérature Comparée*, 39 (1965), 243–54.

5547. ———. "The Theory of Unity and Effect in the Works of E. A. Poe and James Joyce." *Revue de Littérature Comparée*, 40 (1966), 226–34.

5548. LAWSON, LEWIS A. "Poe's Conception of the Grotesque." *The Mississippi Quarterly*, 19 (1966), 200–05.

5549. LEVINE, STUART. *Edgar Poe: Seer and Craftsman*. Deland, FL: Everett/Edwards, 1972.

5550. LEVINE, STUART AND SUSAN. "History, Myth, Fable, and Satire: Poe's Use of Jacob Bryant." *ESQ*, 21 (1975), 197–214.

5551. ———, ED. *The Short Fiction of Edgar Allan Poe: An Annotated Edition*. Indianapolis, IN: Bobbs-Merrill, 1976.

5552. LÉVY, MAURICE. "Poe and the Gothic Tradition." Trans. Richard Henry Haswell. *ESQ*, 18 (1972), 19–29.

5553. LIEBMAN, SHELDON W. "Poe's Tales and His Theory of the Poetic Experience." *Studies in Short Fiction*, 7 (1970), 582–96.

5554. LIPPIT, NORIKO M. "Natsume Sōseki on Poe." *Comparative Literature Studies*, 14 (1977), 30–37.

5555. ———. "Tanizaki and Poe: The Grotesque and the Quest for Supernal Beauty." *Comparative Literature*, 29 (1977), 221–40.

5556. LJUNGQUIST, KENT. "Poe and the Sublime: His Two Short Sea Tales in the Context of an Aesthetic Tradition." *Criticism*, 17 (1975), 131–51.

5557. LOMBARD, CHARLES. "Poe and French Romanticism." *Poe Newsletter*, 3 (1970), 30–35.

5558. LYONS, NATHAN. "Kafka and Poe—and Hope." *The Minnesota Review*, 5 (1965), 158–68.

5559. McKEITHAN, D. M. "Poe and the Second Edition of Hawthorne's *Twice-Told Tales*." *The Nathaniel Hawthorne Journal 1974*, pp. 257–69.

5560. MARTIN, TERENCE. "The Imagination at Play: Edgar Allan Poe." *The Kenyon Review*, 28 (1966), 194–209.

5561. MAZOW, JULIA WOLF. "The Survival Theme in Selected Tales of Edgar Allan Poe." *Studies in American Fiction*, 3 (1975), 216–23.

5562. MENGELING, MARVIN AND FRANCES. "From Fancy to Failure: A Study of the Narrators in the Tales of Edgar Allan Poe." *The University Review* (Kansas City), 33 (1967), 293–98; 34 (1967), 31–37.

5563. **MILLER, JOHN CARL.** *Building Poe Biography*. Baton Rouge: Louisiana State Univ. Press, 1977.

5564. **MOKASHI-PUNEKAR, S.** "Indra—The Mind of Edgar Allan Poe." In *Indian Studies in American Fiction*. Ed. M. K. Naik, S. K. Desai, and S. Mokashi-Punekar. Dharwar: Karnatak Univ., 1974. pp. 16–30.

5565. **MOLDENHAUER, JOSEPH J.** "Murder as a Fine Art: Basic Connections between Poe's Aesthetics, Psychology, and Moral Vision." *PMLA*, 83 (1968), 284–97.

5566. **MOONEY, STEPHEN L.** "The Comic in Poe's Fiction." *American Literature*, 33 (1962), 433–41.

5567. ———. "Poe's Gothic Waste Land." *The Sewanee Review*, 70 (1962), 261–83.

5568. **MOSKOWITZ, SAM.** "Poe on 'Trial.' " *The Armchair Detective*, 4 (1970), 10–11.

5569. **MOSS, SIDNEY P.** "Duyckinck Defends Mr. Poe Against New York's Penny-A-Liners." *Papers on Language & Literature*, 5 (1969), 74–81.

5570. ———. "Poe as Probabilist in Forgues' Critique of the *Tales*." *ESQ*, no. 60, Supplement (1970), pp. 4–13.

5571. ———. "Poe's Apocalyptic Vision." In *Papers on Poe: Essays in Honor of John Ward Ostrom*. Ed. Richard P. Veler. Springfield, OH: Chantry Music Press, Wittenberg Univ., 1972. pp. 42–53.

5572. ———. *Poe's Literary Battles: The Critic in the Context of His Literary Milieu*. Durham, NC: Duke Univ. Press, 1963.

5573. **NEWLIN, PAUL A.** "Scott's Influence on Poe's Grotesque and Arabesque Tales." *American Transcendental Quarterly*, no. 2 (1969), pp. 9–12.

5574. **OLNEY, CLARKE.** "Edgar Allan Poe—Science-Fiction Pioneer." *The Georgia Review*, 12 (1958), 416–21.

5575. **OSOWSKI, JUDY.** "T. S. Eliot on 'Poe the Detective.' " *Poe Newsletter*, 3 (1970), 39.

5576. **PALEY, ALAN L.** *Edgar Allan Poe: American Poet and Mystery Writer*. Charlottesville, NY: SamHar, 1975.

5577. **PANEK, LEROY L.** "Play and Games: An Approach to Poe's Detective Tales." *Poe Studies*, 10 (1977), 39–41.

5578. **PETERSON, PAM.** "Mesmerism, Popular Science, and Poe." In *Proceedings of the Sixth National Convention of the Popular Culture Association, Chicago, Illinois, April 22–24, 1976*. Ed. Michael T. Marsden. Bowling Green, OH: Bowling Green Univ. Popular Press, 1976. pp. 251–62.

5579. **PITCHER, EDWARD W.** "A Note on Anagrams in Edgar Allan Poe's Stories." *American Notes & Queries*, 14 (1976), 22–23.

5580. **POLLIN, BURTON R.** "Byron, Poe, and Miss Matilda." *Names*, 16 (1968), 390–414.

5581. ———. "Dean Swift in the Works of Poe." *Notes and Queries*, NS 20 (1973), 244–46.

5582. ———. *Dictionary of Names and Titles in Poe's Collected Works*. New York: Da Capo Press, 1968.

5583. ———. *Discoveries in Poe*. Notre Dame, IN: Univ. of Notre Dame Press, 1970.

5584. ———. "Light on 'Shadow' and Other Pieces by Poe; Or, More of Thomas Moore." *ESQ*, 18 (1972), 166–73.

5585. ———. "Names Used for Humor in Poe's Fiction." In *Love and Wrestling, Butch and O. K.* Ed. Fred Tarpley. Commerce, TX: Names Institute Press, 1973. pp. 51–57.

5586. ———. "Place Names in Poe's Creative Writings." *Poe Studies*, 6 (1973), 43–48.

5587. ———. *Poe, Creator of Words*. Baltimore, MD: Enoch Pratt Free Library, Edgar Allan Poe Society, and Library of the Univ. of Baltimore, 1974.

5588. ———. "Poe in the *Boston Notion*." *The New England Quarterly*, 42 (1969), 585–89.

5589. ———. "Poe's Literary Use of 'Oppodeldoc' and Other Patent Medicines." *Poe Studies*, 4 (1971), 30–32.

5590. ———. "*Undine* in the Works of Poe." *Studies in Romanticism*, 14 (1975), 59–74.

5591. ———. "Victor Hugo and Poe." *Revue de Littérature Comparée*, 42 (1968), 494–519.

5592. **PORGES, IRWIN.** *Edgar Allan Poe*. Philadelphia, PA: Chilton Books, 1963.

5593. **PURDY, S. B.** "Poe and Dostoyevsky." *Studies in Short Fiction*, 4 (1967), 169–71.

5594. **QUINN, PATRICK F.** "Four Views of Edgar Poe." *Jahrbuch für Amerikastudien*, 5 (1960), 138–46.

5595. **RAMACHANDRAN, MEERA.** "Naturalism in the Grotesque: A New Look at Poe's *Eureka* and His Tales of the Grotesque." *Indian Journal of American Studies*, 6 (1976), 30–43.

5596. **RANS, GEOFFREY.** *Edgar Allan Poe*. Edinburgh: Oliver and Boyd, 1965.

5597. **REES, THOMAS R.** "Why Poe? Some Notes on the Artistic Qualities of the Prose Fiction of Edgar Allan Poe." *Forum* (University of Houston), 12, no. 1 (1974), 11–15.

5598. **REGAN, ROBERT.** "Introduction." In *Poe: A Collection of Critical Essays*. Englewood Cliffs, NJ: Prentice-Hall, 1967. pp. 1–13.

5599. REIN, DAVID M. "The Appeal of Poe Today." *ESQ*, no. 60, Supplement (1970), pp. 29–33.

5600. ———. *Edgar A. Poe: The Inner Pattern*. New York: Philosophical Library, 1960.

5601. ———. "Poe's Dreams." *The London Magazine*, NS 2, no. 1 (1962), 42–58.

5602. REISS, T. J. "The Universe and the Dialectic of Imagination in Edgar Allan Poe." *Études Anglaises*, 27 (1974), 16–25.

5603. RICHARD, CLAUDE. "Poe and 'Young America.' " *Studies in Bibliography*, 21 (1968), 25–58.

5604. ROBBINS, J. ALBERT. "The State of Poe Studies." *Poe Newsletter*, 1 (1968), 1–2.

5605. ROSE, MARILYN GADDIS. " 'Emmanuèle'—'Morella': Gide's Poe Affinities." *Texas Studies in Literature and Language*, 5 (1963), 127–37.

5606. RUBIN, LOUIS D., JR. "Edgar Allan Poe: A Study in Heroism." In *The Curious Death of the Novel: Essays in American Literature*. Baton Rouge: Louisiana State Univ. Press, 1967. pp. 47–66.

5607. RUSSELL, J. THOMAS. *Edgar Allan Poe: The Army Years*. West Point, NY: U.S. Military Academy, 1972.

5608. SAMUEL, DOROTHY J. "Poe and Baudelaire: Parallels in Form and Symbol." *CLA Journal*, 3 (1959), 88–105.

5609. SANDLER, S. GERALD. "Poe's Indebtedness to Locke's *An Essay Concerning Human Understanding*." *Boston University Studies in English*, 5 (1961), 107–21.

5610. SANFORD, CHARLES L. "Edgar Allan Poe: A Blight upon the Landscape." *American Quarterly*, 20 (1968), 54–66.

5611. SCHWABER, PAUL. "On Reading Poe." *Literature and Psychology*, 21 (1971), 81–99.

5612. SEELYE, JOHN. "Edgar Allan Poe: *Tales of the Grotesque and Arabesque*." In *Landmarks of American Writing*. Ed. Hennig Cohen. New York: Basic Books, 1969. pp. 101–10.

5613. SERIO, JOHN N. "From Edwards to Poe." *The Connecticut Review*, 6, no. 1 (1972), 88–92.

5614. SHELDEN, PAMELA J. " 'True Originality': Poe's Manipulation of the Gothic Tradition." *American Transcendental Quarterly*, no. 29 (1976), pp. 75–80.

5615. SHULMAN, ROBERT. "Poe and the Powers of the Mind." *ELH*, 37 (1970), 245–62.

5616. SIPPEL, ERICH W. "Bolting the Whole Shebang Together: Poe's Predicament." *Criticism*, 15 (1973), 289–308.

5617. SMITH, ALLAN. "The Psychological Context of Three Tales by Poe." *Journal of American Studies*, 7 (1973), 279–92.

5618. **SOLOMONT, SUSAN, AND RITCHIE DARLING.** *Four Stories by Poe: An Essay.* Norwich, CT: Green Knight Press, 1965.

5619. **SOULE, GEORGE H., JR.** "Another Source for Poe: Trelawny's *The Adventures of a Younger Son.*" *Poe Studies*, 8 (1975), 35–37.

5620. **SPILLER, ROBERT E.** "The American Literary Dilemma and Edgar Allan Poe." In *The Great Experiment in American Literature: Six Lectures.* Ed. Carl Bode. London: Heinemann, 1961. pp. 3–25.

5621. **SPROUT, MONIQUE.** "The Influence of Poe on Jules Verne." *Revue de Littérature Comparée*, 41 (1967), 37–53.

5622. **STAUFFER, DONALD BARLOW.** "Poe's Views on the Nature and Function of Style." *ESQ*, no. 60 (1970), pp. 23–30.

5623. ———. "Style and Meaning in 'Ligeia' and 'William Wilson.' " *Studies in Short Fiction*, 2 (1965), 316–30.

5624. **STONE, EDWARD.** "Poe in and out of His Time." *The Emerson Society Quarterly*, no. 31 (1963), pp. 14–17.

5625. **STRANDBERG, VICTOR.** "Poe's Hollow Men." *The University Review* (Kansas City), 35 (1969), 203–12.

5626. **SWIGG, RICHARD.** *Lawrence, Hardy, and American Literature.* London: Oxford Univ. Press, 1972.

5627. **TATE, ALLEN.** "The Angelic Imagination: Poe as God." In *Collected Essays.* Denver, CO: Swallow, 1959. pp. 432–54.

5628. ———. "Our Cousin, Mr. Poe." In *Collected Essays.* Denver, CO: Swallow, 1959. pp. 455–71.

5629. **THOMPSON, G. R.** "Poe and 'Romantic Irony.' " In *Papers on Poe: Essays in Honor of John Ward Ostrom.* Ed. Richard P. Veler. Springfield, OH: Chantry Music Press, Wittenberg Univ., 1972. pp. 28–41.

5630. ———. *Poe's Fiction: Romantic Irony in the Gothic Tales.* Madison: Univ. of Wisconsin Press, 1973.

5631. ———. "Poe's 'Flawed' Gothic: Absurdist Techniques in 'Metzengerstein' and the *Courier* Satires." *ESQ*, no. 60, Supplement (1970), pp. 38–58.

5632. ———. "Unity, Death, and Nothingness—Poe's 'Romantic Skepticism.' " *PMLA*, 85 (1970), 297–300.

5633. **TRIEBER, J. MARSHALL.** "The Scornful Grin: A Study of Poesque Humor." *Poe Studies*, 4 (1971), 32–34.

5634. **TUTTLETON, JAMES W.** "The Presence of Poe in *This Side of Paradise.*" *English Language Notes*, 3 (1966), 284–89.

5635. **TWITCHELL, JAMES.** "Poe's 'The Oval Portrait' and the Vampire Motif." *Studies in Short Fiction*, 14 (1977), 387–93.

5636. **UNRUE, DARLENE.** "Poe and the Subjective Reality." *Ariel*, 7, no. 3 (1976), 68–76.

5637. WAGENKNECHT, EDWARD. *Edgar Allan Poe: The Man Behind the Legend*. New York: Oxford Univ. Press, 1963.

5638. WEINER, BRUCE IRA. "Poe's Subversion of Verisimilitude." *American Transcendental Quarterly*, no. 24, Supplement Two (1974), pp. 2–8.

5639. WEISS, MIRIAM. "Poe's Catterina." *The Mississippi Quarterly*, 19 (1966), 29–33.

5640. WERTZ, S. K. AND LINDA L. "On Poe's Use of 'Mystery.' " *Poe Studies*, 4 (1971), 7–10.

5641. WILBUR, RICHARD. "Edgar Allan Poe." In *Major Writers of America*. Ed. Perry Miller. 2 vols. New York: Harcourt, Brace & World, 1962. I, 369–82.

5642. ———. "Introduction." In *Poe*. New York: Dell, 1959. pp. 7–39.

5643. WINWAR, FRANCES. *The Haunted Palace: A Life of Edgar Allan Poe*. New York: Harper & Row, 1959.

5644. ZIMMERMAN, MELVIN. "Baudelaire's Early Conception of Poe's Fate." *Revue de Littérature Comparée*, 44 (1970), 117–20.

Bibliography

5645. BENTON, RICHARD P. "Current Bibliography on Edgar Allan Poe." *The Emerson Society Quarterly*, no. 38 (1965), pp. 144–47; no. 47 (1967), pp. 84–87.

5646. ———. "Edgar Allan Poe: Current Bibliography." *Poe Newsletter*, 2 (1969), 4–12; 3 (1970), 11–16; *Poe Studies*, 4 (1971), 38–44.

5647. DAMERON, J. LASLEY. *Edgar Allan Poe: A Checklist of Criticism, 1942–1960*. Charlottesville: Bibliographical Society of the Univ. of Virginia, 1966.

5648. ———. "Poe at Mid-Century: Anglo-American Criticism, 1928–1960." *Ball State University Forum*, 8, no. 1 (1967), 36–44.

5649. ———. "The State of the Complete Bibliography of Poe Criticism, 1827–1967." *Poe Newsletter*, 2 (1969), 3.

5650. ———, AND IRBY B. CAUTHEN, JR. *Edgar Allan Poe: A Bibliography of Criticism, 1827–1967*. Charlottesville: Univ. Press of Virginia, 1974.

5651. ———, THOMAS C. CARLSON, AND JOHN E. REILLY. "Current Poe Bibliography." *Poe Studies*, 8 (1975), 15–21.

5652. ———, ———, ———, AND JUDY OSOWSKI. "Current Poe Bibliography." *Poe Studies*, 6 (1973), 36–42; 8 (1975), 43–46; 10 (1977), 21–27.

5653. HUBBELL, JAY B. "Edgar Allan Poe." In *Eight American Authors: A Review of Research and Criticism*. Rev. ed. Ed. James Woodress. New York: Norton, 1971. pp. 3–36.

5654. HYNEMAN, ESTHER F. *Edgar Allan Poe: An Annotated Bib-

liography of Books and Articles in English, 1827–1973. Boston, MA: G. K. Hall, 1974.

5655. **KETTERER, DAVID.** "The SF Element in the Work of Poe: A Chronological Survey." *Science-Fiction Studies,* 1 (1974), 197–213.

5656. **LAWSON, LEWIS A.** "Poe and the Grotesque: A Bibliography, 1695–1965." *Poe Newsletter,* 1 (1968), 9–10.

5657. **MARRS, ROBERT L.** " 'The Fall of the House of Usher': A Checklist of Criticism Since 1960." *Poe Studies,* 5 (1972), 23–24.

5658. _____. "Fugitive Poe References: A Bibliography." *Poe Newsletter,* 2 (1969), 12–18.

5659. **MILLER, JOHN CARL.** *John Henry Ingram's Poe Collection at the University of Virginia: A Calendar of Letters and Other Manuscripts* . . . . Charlottesville: Univ. Press of Virginia, 1960.

5660. **MOLDENHAUER, JOSEPH J.** "A Descriptive Catalog of Edgar Allan Poe Manuscripts in The Humanities Research Center Library, The University of Texas at Austin." *Texas Quarterly,* 16, no. 3, Supplement (1973), i–xxii, 1–88.

5661. **OSOWSKI, JUDY.** "Fugitive Poe References: A Bibliography." *Poe Newsletter,* 3 (1970), 16–19; *Poe Studies,* 4 (1971), 44–46; 8 (1975), 21–22; 9 (1976), 49–51.

5662. **PAVNASKAR, SADANAND R.** "Poe in India: A Bibliography, 1955–1969." *Poe Studies,* 5 (1972), 49–50.

5663. **REILLY, JOHN E.** "Recently Published." *Poe Studies,* 7 (1974), 27–28.

5664. **ROBBINS, J. ALBERT.** *The Merrill Checklist of Edgar Allan Poe.* Columbus, OH: Merrill, 1969.

5665. **STRONKS, JAMES.** "Addenda to the Bibliographies of Emily Dickinson and Edgar Allan Poe." *The Papers of the Bibliographical Society of America,* 71 (1977), 360–62.

5666. **TANSELLE, G. THOMAS.** "The State of Poe Bibliography." *Poe Newsletter,* 2 (1969), 1–3.

5667. _____. "Unrecorded Early Reprintings of Two Poe Tales." *The Papers of the Bibliographical Society of America,* 56 (1962), 252.

POHL, FREDERICK

"The Tunnel under the World"

See 114.

POOLE, ERNEST

"An Author's Predicament"

5668. **KEEFER, TRUMAN FREDERICK.** *Ernest Poole.* New York: Twayne, 1966.

PORTER, KATHERINE ANNE

"The Circus"
See 5714, 5715, 5724, 5729, 5731, 5736, 5743.

"The Cracked Looking Glass"
5669. JOHNSON, JAMES W. "The Cracked Looking Glass." *The Virginia Quarterly Review*, 36 (1960), 604–07.
See also 5722, 5724, 5731, 5734, 5736, 5740.

"A Day's Work"
See 5724, 5736, 5740.

"The Downward Path to Wisdom"
5670. HARTLEY, LODWICK. "Stephen's Lost World: The Background of Katherine Anne Porter's 'The Downward Path to Wisdom.'" *Studies in Short Fiction*, 6 (1969), 574–79.
See also 5709, 5724, 5729, 5731, 5734, 5736, 5740, 5751.

"The Fig Tree"
See 5714, 5722, 5724, 5731, 5736.

"Flowering Judas"
5671. BLUEFARB, SAM. "Loss of Innocence in 'Flowering Judas.'" *CLA Journal*, 7 (1964), 256–62.
5672. BRIDE, SISTER MARY, O.P. "Laura and the Unlit Lamp." *Studies in Short Fiction*, 1 (1963), 61–63.
5673. GOTTFRIED, LEON. "Death's Other Kingdom: Dantesque and Theological Symbolism in 'Flowering Judas.'" *PMLA*, 84 (1969), 112–24.
5674. GROSS, BEVERLY. "The Poetic Narrative: A Reading of 'Flowering Judas.'" *Style*, 2 (1968), 129–39.
5675. MADDEN, DAVID. "The Changed Image in Katherine Anne Porter's 'Flowering Judas.'" *Studies in Short Fiction*, 7 (1970), 277–89.
5676. REDDEN, DOROTHY S. "'Flowering Judas': Two Voices." *Studies in Short Fiction*, 6 (1969), 194–204.
5677. ROHRBERGER, MARY. "Betrayer or Betrayed: Another View of 'Flowering Judas.'" *Notes on Modern American Literature*, 2 (1977), item 10.
See also 356, 385, 449, 481, 500, 544, 565, 597, 5713, 5722, 5724, 5729, 5731, 5732, 5736, 5737, 5746, 5750.

"The Grave"
5678. BELL, VEREEN M. "'The Grave' Revisited." *Studies in Short Fiction*, 3 (1965), 39–45.

5679. **BROOKS, CLEANTH.** "On 'The Grave.' " *The Yale Review*, 55 (1965), 275-79.
5680. **CURLEY, DANIEL.** "Treasure in 'The Grave.' " *Modern Fiction Studies*, 9 (1963), 377-84.
5681. **JOSELYN, SISTER M., O.S.B.** " 'The Grave' as Lyrical Short Story." *Studies in Short Fiction*, 1 (1964), 216-21.
5682. **KRAMER, DALE.** "Notes on Lyricism and Symbolism in 'The Grave.' " *Studies in Short Fiction*, 2 (1965), 331-36.
5683. **PRATER, WILLIAM.** " 'The Grave': Form and Symbol." *Studies in Short Fiction*, 6 (1969), 336-38.
See also 267, 447, 5713-5715, 5722, 5724, 5725, 5730, 5731, 5736, 5743, 5750.

"Hacienda"

5684. **PERRY, ROBERT L.** "Porter's 'Hacienda' and the Theme of Change." *The Midwest Quarterly*, 6 (1965), 403-15.
See also 5709, 5722, 5724, 5731, 5734, 5736, 5737.

"He"

See 5714, 5722, 5724, 5732, 5736.

"Holiday"

See 454, 597, 5714, 5724, 5731, 5732.

"The Jilting of Granny Weatherall"

5685. **BARNES, DANIEL R. AND MADELINE T.** "The Secret Sin of Granny Weatherall." *Renascence*, 21 (1969), 162-65.
5686. **BECKER, LAURENCE A.** " 'The Jilting of Granny Weatherall': The Discovery of Pattern." *English Journal*, 55 (1966), 1164-69.
5687. **COWSER, ROBERT G.** "Porter's 'The Jilting of Granny Weatherall.' " *The Explicator*, 21 (1962), item 34.
5688. **WIESENFARTH, JOSEPH.** "Internal Opposition in Porter's 'Granny Weatherall.' " *Critique*, 11, no. 2 (1969), 47-55.
5689. **WOLFE, PETER.** "The Problems of Granny Weatherall." *CLA Journal*, 11 (1967), 142-48.
See also 360, 454, 484, 5722, 5724, 5736.

"The Journey"

See 454, 5714, 5715, 5724, 5731, 5734, 5736, 5750.

"The Last Leaf"

See 5714, 5715, 5724, 5731, 5736.

"The Leaning Tower"

5690. **GIVNER, JOAN.** " 'Her Great Art, Her Sober Craft': Kath-

erine Anne Porter's Creative Process." *Southwest Review*, 62 (1977), 217–30.
See also 366, 5708, 5713, 5719, 5724, 5729, 5731, 5734, 5736, 5750.

"Magic"

See 5722, 5724, 5736.

"María Concepción"

See 449, 546, 5709, 5713, 5724, 5731, 5736, 5737.

"The Martyr"

See 5724, 5737.

"Noon Wine"

5691. **GROFF, EDWARD.** " 'Noon Wine': A Texas Tragedy." *Descant*, 22, no. 1 (1977), 39–47.
5692. **PIERCE, MARVIN.** "Point of View: Katherine Anne Porter's *Noon Wine*." *The Ohio University Review*, 3 (1961), 95–113.
5693. **SMITH, J. OATES.** "Porter's *Noon Wine*: A Stifled Tragedy." *Renascence*, 17 (1965), 157–62.
5694. **THOMAS, M. WYNN.** "Strangers in a Strange Land: A Reading of 'Noon Wine.' " *American Literature*, 47 (1975), 230–46.
5695. **WALSH, THOMAS F.** "Deep Similarities in 'Noon Wine.' " *Mosaic*, 9, no. 1 (1975), 83–91.
5696. ———. "The 'Noon Wine' Devils." *The Georgia Review*, 22 (1968), 90–96.
See also 206, 366, 597, 5708, 5709, 5714, 5722, 5724, 5731, 5732, 5734, 5736, 5742, 5749–5751.

"Old Mortality"

5697. **SULLIVAN, WALTER.** "The Decline of Myth in Southern Fiction." *The Southern Review*, NS 12 (1976), 16–31.
See also 134, 185, 206, 315, 325, 399, 597, 5708, 5712–5714, 5716, 5721, 5722, 5724, 5725, 5727, 5730–5732, 5734, 5736, 5742–5744, 5747, 5750.

"The Old Order" [story] (See *"The Journey"*)

"Pale Horse, Pale Rider"

5698. **NANCE, WILLIAM L.** "Variations on a Dream: Katherine Anne Porter and Truman Capote." *Southern Humanities Review*, 3 (1969), 338–45.
5699. **YANNELLA, PHILIP R.** "The Problems of Dislocation in

'Pale Horse, Pale Rider.' " *Studies in Short Fiction*, 6 (1969), 637–42.

5700. YOUNGBLOOD, SARAH. "Structure and Imagery in Katherine Anne Porter's 'Pale Horse, Pale Rider.' " *Modern Fiction Studies*, 5 (1959), 344–52.

See also 389, 566, 597, 5707, 5708, 5712, 5722, 5724, 5725, 5729, 5731, 5734, 5736, 5742, 5743, 5745, 5749, 5750.

"Rope"

See 178, 493, 5724, 5736.

"The Source"

See 5714, 5724, 5731, 5736.

"That Tree"

See 449, 5724, 5736.

"Theft"

5701. GIVNER, JOAN. "Katherine Anne Porter, Eudora Welty and *Ethan Brand*." *The International Fiction Review*, 1 (1974), 32–37.

5702. _____. "A Re-Reading of Katherine Anne Porter's 'Theft.' " *Studies in Short Fiction*, 6 (1969), 463–65.

5703. MURAD, ORLENE, AND JOAN GIVNER. "On Joan Givner's Article 'Katherine Anne Porter, Eudora Welty and *Ethan Brand*.' " *The International Fiction Review*, 1 (1974), 162–64.

5704. SMITH, CHARLES W. "A Flaw in Katherine Anne Porter's 'Theft': The Teacher Taught." *The CEA Critic*, 38, no. 2 (1976), 19–21.

5705. _____. "Rebuttal." *The CEA Critic*, 39, no. 4 (1977), 9–11.

5706. STERN, CAROL SIMPSON. " 'A Flaw in Katherine Anne Porter's "Theft": The Teacher Taught'—A Reply." *The CEA Critic*, 39, no. 4 (1977), 4–8.

See also 564, 5719, 5722, 5724, 5736.

"Virgin Violeta"

See 5724, 5737, 5744.

"The Witness"

See 5724, 5731, 5736, 5738.

General Studies

5707. ALEXANDER, JEAN. "Katherine Anne Porter's Ship in the Jungle." *Twentieth Century Literature*, 11 (1966), 179–88.

5708. **ALLEN, CHARLES A.** "The Nouvelles of Katherine Anne Porter." *The University of Kansas City Review*, 29 (1962), 87–93.

5709. **BAKER, HOWARD.** "The Upward Path: Notes on the Work of Katherine Anne Porter." *The Southern Review*, NS 4 (1968), 1–19.

5710. **BALDESHWILER, EILEEN.** "Structural Patterns in Katherine Anne Porter's Fiction." *South Dakota Review*, 11, no. 2 (1973), 45–53.

5711. **BROWN, JOHN L.** "Mexican-American Literary and Artistic Relations: 1920–1940." In *Studies in Honor of Tatiana Fotitch*. Ed. Josep M. Sola-Solé, Alessandro S. Crisafulli, and Siegfried A. Schulz. Washington, DC: Catholic Univ. of America Press, 1973, pp. 317–31.

5712. **CARSON, BARBARA HARRELL.** "Winning: Katherine Anne Porter's Women." In *The Authority of Experience: Essays in Feminist Criticism*. Ed. Arlyn Diamond and Lee R. Edwards. Amherst: Univ. of Massachusetts Press, 1977. pp. 239–56, 301.

5713. **CURLEY, DANIEL.** "Katherine Anne Porter: The Larger Plan." *The Kenyon Review*, 25 (1963), 671–95.

5714. **EMMONS, WINIFRED S.** *Katherine Anne Porter: The Regional Stories*. Austin, TX: Steck-Vaughn, 1967.

5715. **FETTERLEY, JUDITH.** "The Struggle for Authenticity: Growing Up Female in *The Old Order*." *The Kate Chopin Newsletter*, 2, no. 2 (1976), 11–19.

5716. **FLANDERS, JANE.** "Katherine Anne Porter and the Ordeal of Southern Womanhood." *The Southern Literary Journal*, 9, no. 1 (1976), 47–60.

5717. **GASTON, EDWIN W., JR.** "The Mythic South of Katherine Anne Porter." *Southwestern American Literature*, 3 (1973), 81–85.

5718. **GESSEL, MICHAEL.** "Katherine Anne Porter: The Low Comedy of Sex." In *American Humor: Essays Presented to John C. Gerber*. Ed. O. M. Brack, Jr. Scottsdale, AZ: Arete, 1977. pp. 139–52.

5719. **GIVNER, JOAN.** "Katherine Anne Porter and the Art of Caricature." *Genre*, 5 (1972), 51–60.

5720. _____. "Porter's Subsidiary Art." *Southwest Review*, 59 (1974), 265–76.

5721. **GRAY, R. J.** "The Grace of Pure Awareness: Katherine Anne Porter." *Southwestern American Literature*, 4 (1974), 1–13.

5722. **HARDY, JOHN EDWARD.** *Katherine Anne Porter*. New York: Ungar, 1973.

5723. **HARTLEY, LODWICK, AND GEORGE CORE.** "Introduction." In *Katherine Anne Porter: A Critical Symposium*. Athens: Univ. of Georgia Press, 1969. pp. xi–xxii.

5724. HENDRICK, GEORGE. *Katherine Anne Porter.* New York: Twayne, 1965.

5725. HENNESSY, ROSEMARY. "Katherine Anne Porter's Model for Heroines." *The Colorado Quarterly,* 25 (1977), 301-15.

5726. HERNÁNDEZ, FRANCES. "Katherine Anne Porter and Julio Cortázar." In *Modern American Fiction: Insights and Foreign Lights.* Proceedings of the Comparative Literature Symposium, Vol. 5. Ed. Wolodymyr T. Zyla and Wendell M. Aycock. Lubbock: Interdepartmental Committee on Comparative Literature, Texas Tech Univ., 1972. pp. 55-66.

5727. HOWELL, ELMO. "Katherine Anne Porter as a Southern Writer." *The South Carolina Review,* 4, no. 1 (1971), 5-15.

5728. JOHNSON, JAMES WILLIAM. "Another Look at Katherine Anne Porter." *The Virginia Quarterly Review,* 36 (1960), 598-613.

5729. JOSELYN, SISTER M., O.S.B. "Animal Imagery in Katherine Anne Porter's Fiction." In *Myth and Symbol: Critical Approaches and Applications.* Ed. Bernice Slote. Lincoln: Univ. of Nebraska Press, 1963. pp. 101-15.

5730. KAPLAN, CHARLES. "True Witness: Katherine Anne Porter." *The Colorado Quarterly,* 7 (1959), 319-27.

5731. KRISHNAMURTHI, M. G. *Katherine Anne Porter: A Study.* Mysore: Rao and Raghavan, 1971.

5732. LIBERMAN, M. M. *Katherine Anne Porter's Fiction.* Detroit, MI: Wayne State Univ. Press, 1971.

5733. MARSDEN, MALCOLM M. "Love As Threat in Katherine Anne Porter's Fiction." *Twentieth Century Literature,* 13 (1967), 29-38.

5734. MOONEY, HARRY JOHN, JR. *The Fiction and Criticism of Katherine Anne Porter.* Rev. ed. Pittsburgh, PA: Univ. of Pittsburgh Press, 1962.

5735. NANCE, WILLIAM L. "Katherine Anne Porter and Mexico." *Southwest Review,* 55 (1970), 143-53.

5736. _____. *Katherine Anne Porter & the Art of Rejection.* Chapel Hill: Univ. of North Carolina Press, 1964.

5737. PARTRIDGE, COLIN. " 'My Familiar Country': An Image of Mexico in the Work of Katherine Anne Porter." *Studies in Short Fiction,* 7 (1970), 597-614.

5738. PINKERTON, JAN. "Katherine Anne Porter's Portrayal of Black Resentment." *The University Review* (Kansas City), 36 (1970), 315-17.

5739. ROBINSON, CECIL. "A Kaleidoscope of Images: Mexicans and Chicanos as Reflected in American Literature." In *Bilingualism in the Southwest.* Ed. Paul R. Turner. Tucson: Univ. of Arizona Press, 1973. pp. 107-29.

5740. **RYAN, MARJORIE.** *"Dubliners* and the Stories of Katherine Anne Porter." *American Literature,* 31 (1960), 464–73.

5741. _____. "Katherine Anne Porter: *Ship of Fools* and the Short Stories." *Bucknell Review,* 12, no. 1 (1964), 51–63.

5742. **SCHORER, MARK.** "Afterword." In *Pale Horse, Pale Rider,* by Katherine Anne Porter. New York: New American Library, 1962. pp. 167–75.

5743. **SCHWARTZ, EDWARD GREENFIELD.** "The Fictions of Memory." *Southwest Review,* 45 (1960), 204–15.

5744. **SHURBUTT, S.** "The Short Fiction of Katherine Anne Porter: *Momentos de Verdades." Southwestern American Literature,* 5 (1975), 40–46.

5745. **SUZUE, AKIKO.** "Katherine Anne Porter: The Abyss beneath the Smooth Surface." In *American Literature in the 1940's.* Annual Report, 1975. Tokyo: Tokyo Chapter, American Literary Society of Japan, 1976. pp. 92–100.

5746. **VAN ZYL, JOHN.** "Surface Elegance, Grotesque Content— A Note on the Short Stories of Katherine Anne Porter." *English Studies in Africa,* 9 (1966), 168–75.

5747. **WARREN, ROBERT PENN.** "Uncorrupted Consciousness: The Stories of Katherine Anne Porter." *The Yale Review,* 55 (1965), 280–90.

5748. **WELTY, EUDORA.** "The Eye of the Story." *The Yale Review,* 55 (1965), 265–74.

5749. **WESCOTT, GLENWAY.** "Katherine Anne Porter Personally." In *Images of Truth: Remembrances and Criticism.* New York: Harper & Row, 1962. pp. 25–58.

5750. **WEST, RAY B., JR.** *Katherine Anne Porter.* Minneapolis: Univ. of Minnesota Press, 1963.

5751. **WIESENFARTH, JOSEPH.** "Negatives of Hope: A Reading of Katherine Anne Porter." *Renascence,* 25 (1973), 85–94.

Interviews

5752. **FRANKEL, HASKEL.** Interview with Katherine Anne Porter. *Saturday Review,* 48 (25 Sept. 1965), 36.

5753. **JANEWAY, ELIZABETH.** "For Katherine Anne Porter, 'Ship of Fools' Was a Lively Twenty-Two Year Voyage." *The New York Times Book Review,* 1 Apr. 1962, pp. 4–5.

5754. **LOPEZ, HANK.** "A Country and Some People I Love: An Interview with Katherine Anne Porter." *Harper's Magazine,* 231 (Sept. 1965), 58–62, 65–68.

5755. **NEWQUIST, ROY.** "Katherine Anne Porter." In *Conversations.* New York: Rand McNally, 1967. pp. 302–23.

5756. **PORTER, KATHERINE ANNE.** "The Art of Fiction XXIX." With Barbara Thompson. *The Paris Review*, no. 29 (1963), pp. 87–114.

5757. **RUOFF, JAMES.** "Katherine Anne Porter Comes to Kansas." *The Midwest Quarterly*, 4 (1963), 305–14.

Bibliography

5758. **KIERNAN, ROBERT F.** *Katherine Anne Porter and Carson McCullers: A Reference Guide.* Boston, MA: G. K. Hall, 1976.

5759. **WALDRIP, LOUISE, AND SHIRLEY ANN BAUER.** *A Bibliography of the Works of Katherine Anne Porter and A Bibliography of the Criticism of the Works of Katherine Anne Porter.* Metuchen, NJ: Scarecrow, 1969.

PORTER, WILLIAM SYDNEY (See O. HENRY)

PORTILLO DE TRAMBLEY, ESTHER

"The Apple Trees"

5760. **CASTELLANO, OLIVIA.** "Of Clarity and the Moon: A Study of Two Women in Rebellion." *De Colores*, 3, no. 3 (1977), 25–30.

POST, MELVILLE DAVISSON

"The Corpus Delicti"

See 5761, 5762.

General Studies

*5761. **NORTON, CHARLES A.** *Melville Davisson Post: Man of Many Mysteries.* Bowling Green, OH: Bowling Green Univ. Popular Press, 1973.

5762. _____. "The Randolph Mason Stories." *The Armchair Detective*, 6 (1973), 86–96.

POSTEN, TED

"The Revolt of the Evil Fairies"

See 126.

POSTL, KARL ANTON (See SEALSFIELD, CHARLES)

POWERS, J[AMES] F[ARL]

"Blessing"
See 5769.

"Blue Island"
See 5769.

"Dawn"
See 5769.

"Death of a Favorite"
See 5769.

"Defection of a Favorite"
See 5769.

"The Devil Was a Joker"
See 5769, 5777.

"The Forks"
5763. **KELLY, RICHARD.** "Father Eudex, the Judge and the Judged: An Analysis of J. F. Powers' 'The Forks.' " *The University Review* (Kansas City), 35 (1969), 316–18.
See also 178, 219, 333, 454, 565, 5766, 5767, 5769, 5776, 5777.

"He Don't Plant Cotton"
See 5769.

"Jamesie"
See 5769.

"The Keystone"
See 5766, 5769, 5772.

"Lions, Harts, Leaping Does"
5764. **SCHLER, ARLENE.** "How to Recognize Heaven When You See It: The Theology of St. John in J. F. Powers' 'Lions, Harts, Leaping Does.' " *Studies in Short Fiction*, 14 (1977), 159–64.
See also 5766, 5768, 5769, 5776.

"Look How the Fish Live"
See 5769.

"The Lord's Day"
See 5769, 5772.

"A Losing Game"

See 267.

"The Old Bird, A Love Story"

See 5769.

"The Poor Thing"

See 5769.

"The Presence of Grace"

See 5769, 5771.

"The Prince of Darkness"

See 219, 5766, 5768, 5769.

"Renner"

See 5769.

"The Trouble"

See 5769.

"The Valiant Woman"

5765. BARNET, SYLVAN. "Powers' 'The Valiant Woman.' " *The Explicator*, 20 (1962), item 56.
See also 384, 5769.

"Zeal"

See 5769.

General Studies

5766. BOYLE, ROBERT, S.J. "To Look Outside: The Fiction of J. F. Powers." In *The Shapeless God: Essays on Modern Fiction*. Ed. Harry J. Mooney, Jr., and Thomas F. Staley. Pittsburgh, PA: Univ. of Pittsburgh Press, 1968. pp. 91–115.
5767. DEGNAN, JAMES P. "J. F. Powers: Comic Satirist." *The Colorado Quarterly*, 16 (1968), 325–33.
5768. HAGOPIAN, JOHN V. "The Fathers of J. F. Powers." *Studies in Short Fiction*, 5 (1968), 139–53.
5769. _____. *J. F. Powers*. New York: Twayne, 1968.
5770. HERTZEL, LEO J. "Brother Juniper, Father Urban, and The Unworldly Tradition." *Renascence*, 17 (1965), 207–10, 215.
5771. HYNES, JOSEPH. "A Couple of Thousand Years after Christmas: J. F. Powers' Traditionalism." *Forum* (University of Houston), 15, no. 1 (1977), 52–59.

5772. **KAUFMAN, MAYNARD.** "J. F. Powers and Secularity." In *Adversity and Grace: Studies in Recent American Literature.* Ed. Nathan A. Scott, Jr. Chicago: Univ. of Chicago Press, 1968. pp. 163–81.

5773. **LA GUARDIA, DAVID M.** "A Critical Dilemma: J. F. Powers and the Durability of Catholic Fiction." In *Challenges in American Culture.* Ed. Ray B. Browne, Larry N. Landrum, and William K. Bottorff. Bowling Green, OH: Bowling Green Univ. Popular Press, 1970. pp. 265–76.

5774. **PHELPS, DONALD.** "Reasonable, Holy and Living." *The Minnesota Review,* 9 (1969), 57–62.

5775. **POSS, STANLEY.** "J. F. Powers: The Gin of Irony." *Twentieth Century Literature,* 14 (1968), 65–74.

5776. **PRESTON, THOMAS R.** "Christian Folly in the Fiction of J. F. Powers." *Critique,* 16, no. 2 (1974), 91–107.

5777. **TWOMBLY, ROBERT G.** "Hubris, Health, and Holiness: The Despair of J. F. Powers." In *Seven Contemporary Authors: Essays on Cozzens, Miller, West, Golding, Heller, Albee, and Powers.* Ed. Thomas B. Whitbread. Austin: Univ. of Texas Press, 1966. pp. 141–62.

PRESCOTT, HARRIET E.

"Down the River"

See 18.

PRICE, REYNOLDS

"A Chain of Love"

See 5782.

"The Names and Faces of Heroes"

See 5782.

"A Sign of Blood"

See 5781.

"Uncle Grant"

See 267.

"Walking Lessons"

See 5781.

"The Warrior Princess Ozimba"

5778. **SHEPHERD, ALLEN.** " 'The Legitimate Heir' Making It

New, or Fairly So." *Studies in the Humanities*, 3, no. 1 (1972), 37–39.

General Studies

5779. **EICHELBERGER, CLAYTON L.** "Reynolds Price: 'A Banner in Defeat.' " *Journal of Popular Culture*, 1 (1968), 410–17.
5780. **PRICE, REYNOLDS.** "Speaking of Books: A Question of Influence." *The New York Times Book Review*, 29 May 1966, pp. 2, 12–13.
5781. **SHEPHERD, ALLEN.** "Notes on Nature in the Fiction of Reynolds Price." *Critique*, 15, no. 2 (1973), 83–94.
5782. **STEVENSON, JOHN W.** "The Faces of Reynolds Price's Short Fiction." *Studies in Short Fiction*, 3 (1966), 300–06.

Interviews

5783. **KAUFMAN, WALLACE.** "A Conversation with Reynolds Price." *Shenandoah*, 17, no. 4 (1966), 3–25.
5784. **MERAS, PHYLLIS.** "Talk with Reynolds Price." *The New York Times Book Review*, 27 Mar. 1966, p. 44.

PURDY, JAMES

"Color of Darkness"

See 257, 5791, 5793, 5795.

"Cutting Edge"

See 5791.

"Daddy Wolf"

5785. **BURRIS, SHIRLEY W.** "The Emergency in Purdy's 'Daddy Wolf.' " *Renascence*, 20 (1968), 94–98, 103.
5786. **GRINNELL, JAMES W.** "Who's Afraid of 'Daddy Wolf'?" *Journal of Popular Culture*, 3 (1970), 750–52.
See also 5791, 5795.

"Don't Call Me By My Right Name"

See 511.

"Encore"

See 5793.

"Eventide"

See 394, 5791, 5793.

"Everything Under the Sun"

See 5792.

"Goodnight, Sweetheart"

See 5795.

"Home by Dark"

See 5791, 5793.

"The Lesson"

See 5795.

"Mr. Evening"

5787. **BALDANZA, FRANK.** "The Paradoxes of Patronage in Purdy." *American Literature*, 46 (1974), 347–56.

"Mrs. Benson"

See 5795.

"Night and Day"

See 5793.

"Sermon"

See 5794.

"63: Dream Palace"

5788. **KENNARD, JEAN E.** *Number and Nightmare: Forms of Fantasy in Contemporary Fiction.* Hamden, CT: Archon Books, 1975.
5789. **SKERRETT, JOSEPH TAYLOR, JR.** "James Purdy and the Works: Love and Tragedy in Five Novels." *Twentieth Century Literature*, 15 (1969), 25–33.
See also 257, 275, 277, 278, 327, 5791, 5792, 5795, 5797, 5800.

"Why Can't They Tell You Why?"

5790. **SKAGGS, CALVIN.** "The Sexual Nightmare of 'Why Can't They Tell You Why?' " In *The Process of Fiction: Contemporary Stories and Criticism.* Ed. Barbara McKenzie. New York: Harcourt, Brace & World, 1969. pp. 305–10.
See also 5791, 5793.

General Studies

5791. **ADAMS, STEPHEN D.** *James Purdy.* New York: Barnes & Noble, 1976.
5792. **BALDANZA, FRANK.** "James Purdy and the Corruption of Innocents." *Contemporary Literature*, 15 (1974), 315–30.
5793. _____. "James Purdy's Half-Orphans." *The Centennial Review*, 18 (1974), 255–72.

5794. _____. "Northern Gothic." *The Southern Review*, NS 10 (1974), 566–82.

5795. **CHUPACK, HENRY.** *James Purdy*. Boston, MA: Twayne, 1975.

5796. **FRENCH, WARREN.** "The Quaking World of James Purdy." In *Essays in Modern American Literature*. Ed. Richard E. Langford, et al. Deland, FL: Stetson Univ. Press, 1963. pp. 112–22.

5797. **PEASE, DONALD.** "James Purdy: Shaman in Nowhere Land." In *The Fifties: Fiction, Poetry, Drama*. Ed. Warren French. Deland, FL: Everett/Edwards, 1970. pp. 145–54.

5798. **POMERANZ, REGINA.** "The Hell of Not Loving: Purdy's Modern Tragedy." *Renascence*, 16 (1964), 149–53.

5799. **SCHOTT, WEBSTER.** "James Purdy: American Dreams." *The Nation*, 198 (1964), 300–02.

5800. **SCHWARTZSCHILD, BETTINA.** *The Not-Right House: Essays on James Purdy*. Columbia: Univ. of Missouri Press, 1968.

5801. **WEALES, GERALD.** "No Face and No Exit: The Fiction of James Purdy and J. P. Donleavy." In *Contemporary American Novelists*. Ed. Harry T. Moore. Carbondale: Southern Illinois Univ. Press, 1964. pp. 143–54.

Bibliography

5802. **BUSH, GEORGE E.** "James Purdy." *Bulletin of Bibliography and Magazine Notes*, 28 (1971), 5–6.

PYNCHON, THOMAS

"Entropy"

5803. **MIZENER, ARTHUR.** "The New Romance." *The Southern Review*, NS 8 (1972), 106–17.

5804. **SIMONS, JOHN.** "Third Story Man: Biblical Irony in Thomas Pynchon's 'Entropy.'" *Studies in Short Fiction*, 14 (1977), 88–93.

See also 268, 327, 5805, 5807.

"Low-Lands"

See 5807.

"Mortality and Mercy in Vienna"

See 5807.

"The Secret Integration"

See 5807.

"Under the Rose"

5805. **COWART, DAVID.** "Love and Death: Variations on a Theme in Pynchon's Early Fiction." *The Journal of Narrative Technique*, 7 (1977), 157–69.

General Studies

5806. **POIRIER, RICHARD.** "The Importance of Thomas Pynchon." In *Mindful Pleasures: Essays on Thomas Pynchon.* Ed. George Levine and David Leverenz. Boston, MA: Little, Brown, 1976. pp. 15–29.

5807. **SLADE, JOSEPH W.** *Thomas Pynchon.* New York: Warner, 1974.

5808. **WINSTON, MATHEW.** "The Quest for Pynchon." In *Mindful Pleasures: Essays on Thomas Pynchon.* Ed. George Levine and David Leverenz. Boston, MA: Little, Brown, 1976. pp. 251–63.

Bibliography

5809. **HERZBERG, BRUCE.** "Selected Articles on Thomas Pynchon: An Annotated Bibliography." *Twentieth Century Literature*, 21 (1975), 221–25.

5810. **SCOTTO, ROBERT M.** *Three Contemporary Novelists: An Annotated Bibliography of Works by and about John Hawkes, Joseph Heller, and Thomas Pynchon.* New York: Garland, 1977.

5811. **WALSH, THOMAS P.** *John Barth, Jerzy Kosinski, and Thomas Pynchon: A Reference Guide.* Boston, MA: G. K. Hall, 1977.

5812. **WEIXLMANN, JOSEPH.** "Thomas Pynchon: A Bibliography." *Critique*, 14, no. 2 (1972), 34–43.

RANDOLPH, GEORGIANA ANN (See *RICE, CRAIG*)

RAWLINGS, MARJORIE KINNAN

"Alligators"

See 5815.

"Cocks Must Crow"

See 5813.

"Cracker Chidlings"

See 5813.

"Gal Young Un"

See 5813.

"Jacob's Ladder"

See 5813.

"A Mother in Mannville"

See 178, 5813.

General Studies

5813. **Bellman, Samuel I.** *Marjorie Kinnan Rawlings.* Boston, MA: Twayne, 1974.

5814. ———. "Marjorie Kinnan Rawlings: A Solitary Sojourner in the Florida Backwoods." *Kansas Quarterly*, 2, no. 2 (1970), 78–87.

5815. **Bigelow, Gordon E.** *Frontier Eden: The Literary Career of Marjorie Kinnan Rawlings.* Gainesville: Univ. of Florida Press, 1966.

RAWSON, CLAYTON

General Studies

5816. **Nevins, Francis M., Jr.** "The Diavolo Quartet." *The Armchair Detective*, 3 (1970), 243–44.

READ, OPIE

General Studies

5817. **Morris, Robert L.** *Opie Read: American Humorist (1852–1939).* New York: Helios Books, 1966.

REMINGTON, FREDERIC

General Studies

5818. **Erisman, Fred.** *Frederic Remington.* Boise, ID: Boise State Univ., 1975.

RHODES, EUGENE MANLOVE

"Beyond the Desert"

See 439.

"No Mean City"

5819. **Skillman, Richard, and Jerry C. Hoke.** "The Portrait of the New Mexican in the Fiction of Eugene Rhodes." *Western Review* (Western New Mexico University), 6, no. 1 (1969), 26–36. *See also* 439.

General Studies

5820.   **FIFE, JIM L.** "Two Views of The American West." *Western American Literature,* 1 (1966), 34–43.

5821.   **GASTON, EDWIN W., JR.** *Eugene Manlove Rhodes: Cowboy Chronicler.* Austin, TX: Steck-Vaughn, 1967.

RICE, CRAIG

Bibliography

5822.   **JASEN, DAVID A.** "The Mysterious Craig Rice." *The Armchair Detective,* 5 (1971), 25–27, 34.

RICHARDS, LAURA E.

Bibliography

5823.   **CALHOUN, PHILO, AND HOWELL J. HEANEY.** "A Checklist of the Separately Published Works of Laura E. Richards." *Colby Library Quarterly,* 5 (1961), 337–43.

5824.   **CARY, RICHARD.** "Some Richards Manuscripts and Correspondence." *Colby Library Quarterly,* 5 (1961), 344–56.

RICHARDSON, ROBERT SHIRLEY
(See *LATHAM, PHILIP*)

RICHTER, CONRAD

General Studies

5825.   **WILSON, DAWN.** "The Influence of the West on Conrad Richter's Fiction." *The Old Northwest,* 1 (1975), 375–89.

RITCHIE, JACK

Interviews

5826.   **PUECHNER, RAY.** "Jack Ritchie: An Interview." *The Armchair Detective,* 6 (1972), 12–14.

RIVERA, TOMÁS

" *. . . and the earth did not part* "

5827.   **DE LA GARZA, RUDOLPH O., AND ROWENA RIVERA.** "The Socio-Political World of the Chicano: A Comparative Analysis of Social Scientific and Literary Perspectives." In *Minority Language and Literature: Retrospective and Perspective.* Ed. Dexter Fisher. New York: Modern Language Association of America, 1977. pp. 42–64.

5828. **Pino, Frank, Jr.** "The Outsider and 'El Otro' in Tomás Rivera's '. . . *y no se lo tragó la tierra.*' " *Books Abroad*, 49 (1975), 453–58.

5829. **Rocard, Marcienne.** "The Cycle of Chicano Experience in '. . . *and the earth did not part*' by Tomás Rivera." *Caliban* (University of Toulouse), no. 11 (1974), pp. 141–51.

5830. **Valdés Fallis, Guadalupe.** "Metaphysical Anxiety and the Existence of God in Contemporary Chicano Fiction." *Revista Chicano-Riqueña*, 3, no. 1 (1975), 26–33.

See also 136.

" ' . . . *and the earth did not part*' "

See 5829.

"*His Hand in His Pocket*"

See 5828.

"*Trapped*"

See 5829.

ROBB, JOHN S.

General Studies

5831. **McDermott, John Francis.** "Introduction." In *Streaks of Squatter Life, and Far-West Scenes*, by John S. Robb. Gainesville, FL: Scholars' Facsimiles & Reprints, 1962. pp. v–xvi.

ROBERTS, ELIZABETH MADOX

General Studies

5832. **McDowell, Frederick P. W.** *Elizabeth Madox Roberts.* New York: Twayne, 1963.

ROBERTS, KENNETH

Bibliography

5833. **Ellis, Marjorie Mosser.** "Supplementary Bibliography of Kenneth Roberts." *Colby Library Quarterly*, 6 (1962), 99–105.

ROBINSON, E[DWIN] A[RLINGTON]

"Scattered Lives"

5834. **Anderson, Wallace L.** "E. A. Robinson's 'Scattered Lives.' " *American Literature*, 38 (1967), 498–507.

ROBINSON, ROWLAND E.

General Studies

*5835. **BAKER, RONALD L.** *Folklore in the Writings of Rowland E. Robinson.* Bowling Green, OH: Bowling Green Univ. Popular Press, 1973.

Bibliography

5836. **BAKER, RONALD L.** "Rowland E. Robinson (1833–1900)." *American Literary Realism, 1870–1910*, 2 (1969), 156–59.

ROMANO, OCTAVIO

"A Rosary for Doña Marina"

See 3510.

ROSCOE, THEODORE

"Corday and the Seven League Boots"

See 253.

"The Wonderful Lamp of Thibaut Corday"

See 253.

ROSENFELD, ISAAC

"The Brigadier"

See 456.

"Coney Island Revisited"

See 5837.

General Studies

5837. **LYONS, BONNIE.** "Isaac Rosenfeld's Fiction: A Reappraisal." *Studies in American Jewish Literature*, 1, no. 1 (1975), 3–9.

ROSTEN, LEO

Interviews

5838. **NEWQUIST, ROY.** "Leo Rosten." In *Counterpoint*. Chicago: Rand McNally, 1964. pp. 522–36.

ROTH, HENRY

"At Times in Flight"

See 5841, 5842.

"Broker"

5839. LYONS, BONNIE. " 'Broker': An Overlooked Story by Henry Roth." *Studies in Short Fiction*, 10 (1973), 97–98.
See also 5842.

"The Dun Dakotas"

See 5841, 5842.

"Final Dwarf"

See 5842.

"If We Had Bacon"

5840. LYONS, BONNIE. "After *Call It Sleep*." *American Literature*, 45 (1974), 610–12.
See also 5842.

"Petey and Yotsee and Mario"

See 5842.

"Somebody Always Grabs the Purple"

See 5842.

"The Surveyor"

See 5842.

General Studies

5841. KNOWLES, A. SIDNEY, JR. "The Fiction of Henry Roth." *Modern Fiction Studies*, 11 (1965), 393–404.
5842. LYONS, BONNIE. *Henry Roth: The Man and His Work.* New York: Cooper Square, 1976.

Interviews

5843. BRONSEN, DAVID. "A Conversation with Henry Roth." *Partisan Review*, 36 (1969), 265–80.
5844. FREEDMAN, WILLIAM. "A Conversation with Henry Roth." *The Literary Review*, 18 (1975), 149–57.
5845. LYONS, BONNIE. "An Interview with Henry Roth." *Shenandoah*, 25, no. 1 (1973), 48–71.
5846. RIBALOW, HAROLD U. "Interview with Henry Roth." *The New York Times Book Review*, 25 Oct. 1964, p. 60.
5847. ROTH, HENRY. "On Being Blocked & Other Literary Matters: An Interview." *Commentary*, 64, no. 2 (1977), 27–38.

ROTH, PHILIP

"The Contest for Aaron Gold"

See 5866.

"The Conversion of the Jews"

5848. PINSKER, SANFORD. "Joseph in Chederland: A Note on 'The Conversion of the Jews.' " *Studies in American Jewish Literature*, 1, no. 2 (1975), 36–37.
5849. SHAHEEN, NASEEB. "Binder Unbound, or, How Not to Convert the Jews." *Studies in Short Fiction*, 13 (1976), 376–78.
See also 335, 399, 453, 484, 5865, 5866, 5868.

"Courting Disaster"

See 5866.

"Defender of the Faith"

5850. DEER, IRVING. "Defender of the Faith." In *Instructor's Manual for* "The Art of Fiction," Second Edition. Ed. R. F. Dietrich and Roger H. Sundell. New York: Holt, Rinehart and Winston, 1974, pp. 104–08.
See also 267, 453, 535, 565, 5862, 5864, 5868, 5871.

"Eli, the Fanatic"

5851. HOLLIS, JAMES R. "Eli Agonistes: Philip Roth's Knight of Faith." In *The Process of Fiction: Contemporary Stories and Criticism*. Ed. Barbara McKenzie. New York: Harcourt, Brace & World, 1969. pp. 241–45.
5852. KNOPP, JOSEPHINE ZADOVSKY. *The Trial of Judaism in Contemporary Jewish Writing*. Urbana: Univ. of Illinois Press, 1975.
See also 453, 4400, 5857, 5862, 5864–5866, 5868, 5871.

"Epstein"

See 5866, 5868.

"Goodbye, Columbus"

5853. COHEN, SARAH BLACHER. "Philip Roth's Would-be Patriarchs and Their *Shikses* and Shrews." *Studies in American Jewish Literature*, 1, no. 1 (1975), 16–22.
5854. FONTANA, ERNEST. "Philip Roth's *Goodbye, Columbus*." *Notre Dame English Journal*, 4, no. 1 (1965), 38–44.
5855. GRAHAM, DON. "The Common Ground of *Goodbye, Columbus* and *The Great Gatsby*." *Forum* (University of Houston), 13, no. 3 (1976), 68–71.

5856. ISRAEL, CHARLES M. "The Fractured Hero of Roth's *Goodbye, Columbus.*" *Critique*, 16, no. 2 (1974), 5–11.

5857. ROCKLAND, MICHAEL AARON. "The Jewish Side of Philip Roth." *Studies in American Jewish Literature*, 1, no. 2 (1975), 29–36.

5858. TRACHTENBERG, STANLEY. "The Hero in Stasis." *Critique*, 7, no. 2 (1965), 5–17.

See also 244, 256, 453, 542, 5861–5866, 5868, 5872.

" 'I Always Wanted You to Admire My Fasting'; or, Looking at Kafka"

5859. MALIN, IRVING. "Looking at Roth's Kafka; or Some Hints about Comedy." *Studies in Short Fiction*, 14 (1977), 273–75.

See also 5866.

"Marriage à la Mode"

See 5866.

"Novotny's Pain"

See 5866.

"On the Air"

5860. MICHEL, PIERRE. " 'On the Air': Philip Roth's Arid World." *Études Anglaises*, 29 (1976), 556–60.

See also 5866.

"You Can't Tell a Man by the Song He Sings"

See 5868.

General Studies

5861. BENDER, EILEEN. "Philip Roth: The Clown in the Garden." *Studies in Contemporary Satire*, 3 (1976), 17–30.

5862. DEER, IRVING AND HARRIET. "Philip Roth and the Crisis in American Fiction." *The Minnesota Review*, 6 (1966), 353–60.

5863. HOWE, IRVING. "Philip Roth Reconsidered." *Commentary*, 54, no. 6 (1972), 69–77.

5864. ISAAC, DAN. "In Defense of Philip Roth." *Chicago Review*, 17, nos. 2–3 (1964), 84–96.

5865. LANDIS, JOSEPH C. "The Sadness of Philip Roth: An Interim Report." *The Massachusetts Review*, 3 (1962), 259–68.

5866. McDANIEL, JOHN N. *The Fiction of Philip Roth*. Haddonfield, NJ: Haddonfield House, 1974.

5867. MICHEL, PIERRE. "What Price Misanthropy? Philip Roth's Fiction." *English Studies*, 58 (1977), 232–39.

5868. PINSKER, SANFORD. *The Comedy That "Hoits": An Essay on the Fiction of Philip Roth*. Columbia: Univ. of Missouri Press, 1975.

5869. _____. "The Rise-and-Fall of the American-Jewish Novel." *The Connecticut Review*, 7, no. 1 (1973), 16–23.

5870. **SOLOTAROFF, THEODORE**. "The Journey of Philip Roth." *The Atlantic Monthly*, 223, no. 4 (1969), 64–72.

5871. _____. "Philip Roth and the Jewish Moralists." *Chicago Review*, 13, no. 4 (1959), 87–99.

5872. **WALDEN, DANIEL**. "Goodbye Columbus, Hello Portnoy— and Beyond: The Ordeal of Philip Roth." *Studies in American Jewish Literature*, 3, no. 2 (1977), 3–13.

Interviews

5873. **DAVIDSON, SARA**. "Talk with Philip Roth." *The New York Times Book Review*, 18 Sept. 1977, pp. 1, 51–53.

5874. **OATES, JOYCE CAROL**. "Philip Roth in Conversation." *The New Review*, 2, no. 14 (1975), 3–7.

5875. **PLIMPTON, GEORGE**. "Philip Roth's Exact Intact." *The New York Times Book Review*, 23 Feb. 1969, pp. 2, 23–25.

Bibliography

5876. **McDANIEL, JOHN N**. "Philip Roth: A Bibliography." In *The Fiction of Philip Roth*. Haddonfield, NJ: Haddonfield House, 1974. pp. 235–43.

5877. _____. "Philip Roth: A Checklist 1954–1973." *Bulletin of Bibliography and Magazine Notes*, 31 (1974), 51–53.

5878. **RODGERS, BERNARD F., JR**. *Philip Roth: A Bibliography*. Metuchen, NJ: Scarecrow, 1974.

RUFFNER, HENRY

"Judith Bensaddi"

See 46.

RUNYON, [ALFRED] DAMON

General Studies

*5879. **WAGNER, JEAN**. *Runyonese: The Mind and Craft of Damon Runyon*. Paris: Stechert-Hafner, 1965.

RUSS, JOANNA

Interviews

5880. **ANON**. "Reflections on Science Fiction: An Interview with Joanna Russ." *Quest*, 2, no. 1 (1975), 40–49.

5881. **HACKER, MARILYN**. "Science Fiction and Feminism: The Work of Joanna Russ." *Chrysalis*, no. 4 (1977), pp. 67–79.

RUSSELL, CHARLES M.

General Studies

5882. **BRUNVAND, JAN HAROLD.** "From Western Folklore to Fiction in the Stories of Charles M. Russell." *Western Review* (Western New Mexico University), 5, no. 1 (1968), 41–49.

SABERHAGEN, FRED

"The Face of the Deep"

See 5883.

"Starsong"

See 5883.

General Studies

5883. **STEWART, A. D.** "Fred Saberhagen: Cybernetic Psychologist—A Study of the Berserker Stories." *Extrapolation*, 18 (1976), 42–51.

SALINGER, J[EROME] D[AVID]

"Blue Melody"

See 5928, 5929.

"De Daumier-Smith's Blue Period"

5884. **RUSSELL, JOHN.** "Salinger, From Daumier to Smith." *Wisconsin Studies in Contemporary Literature*, 4 (1963), 70–87.
See also 195, 583, 5917, 5928, 5929, 5931, 5932, 5937, 5950, 5951, 5958.

"Down at the Dinghy"

See 194, 200, 454, 5928, 5929, 5951.

"Elaine"

See 5928, 5929.

"For Esmé—With Love and Squalor"

5885. **BROWNE, ROBERT M.** "In Defense of Esmé." *College English*, 22 (1961), 584–85.
5886. **BRYAN, JAMES.** "A Reading of Salinger's 'For Esmé—with Love and Squalor.'" *Criticism*, 9 (1967), 275–88.
5887. **BURKE, BROTHER FIDELIAN, F.S.C.** "Salinger's 'Esmé': Some Matters of Balance." *Modern Fiction Studies*, 12 (1966), 341–47.

5888. **DAVIS, TOM.** "J. D. Salinger: The Identity of Sergeant X." *Western Humanities Review*, 16 (1962), 181–83.

5889. **FREEMAN, FRED B., JR.** "Who Was Salinger's Sergeant X?" *American Notes & Queries*, 11 (1972), 6.

5890. **HERMANN, JOHN.** "J. D. Salinger: Hello Hello Hello." *College English*, 22 (1961), 262–64.

5891. **SLABEY, ROBERT M.** "Sergeant X and Seymour Glass." *Western Humanities Review*, 16 (1962), 376–77.

5892. **TOSTA, MICHAEL R.** " 'Will the Real Sergeant X Please Stand Up.' " *Western Humanities Review*, 16 (1962), 376.

See also 195, 200, 257, 5916, 5917, 5926, 5928, 5929, 5931, 5932, 5950, 5951, 5954, 5958.

"Franny"

5893. **SEITZMAN, DANIEL.** "Salinger's 'Franny': Homoerotic Imagery." *American Imago*, 22 (1965), 57–76.

See also 169, 195, 298, 308, 5914, 5928, 5929, 5931, 5932, 5938, 5943, 5945, 5947, 5954, 5958, 5963, 5968, 5974.

"A Girl I Knew"

See 5928.

"Go See Eddie"

5894. **FRENCH, WARREN.** "An Unnoticed Salinger Story." *College English*, 26 (1965), 394–95.

"Hapworth 16, 1924"

5895. **QUAGLIANO, ANTHONY.** "*Hapworth 16, 1924*: A Problem in Hagiography." *The University of Dayton Review*, 8, no. 2 (1971), 35–43.

See also 195, 298, 308, 446, 5896, 5907, 5935, 5958, 5968.

"I'm Crazy"

See 5928, 5929.

"The Inverted Forest"

See 5928, 5929.

"Just Before the War with the Eskimos"

See 5920, 5928, 5929, 5934, 5951.

"The Last Day of the Furlough"

See 5928, 5929.

"The Laughing Man"

See 257, 5928, 5929, 5937, 5951, 5975.

"The Long Debut of Lois Taggett"

See 5928, 5929.

"A Perfect Day for Bananafish"

5896. BELLMAN, SAMUEL IRVING. "New Light on Seymour's Suicide: Salinger's *Hapworth 16, 1924."* *Studies in Short Fiction*, 3 (1966), 348–51.
5897. LANE, GARY. "Seymour's Suicide Again: A New Reading of J. D. Salinger's 'A Perfect Day for Bananafish.' " *Studies in Short Fiction*, 10 (1973), 27–33.
5898. METCALF, FRANK. "The Suicide of Salinger's Seymour Glass." *Studies in Short Fiction*, 9 (1972), 243–46.
5899. OUGHTON, ROBYN. "Suicides in Salinger and Sôseki." In *Sôseki and Salinger: American Students on Japanese Fiction.* Ed. George Saitô and Philip Williams. Tokyo: Eihôsha, 1971. pp. 11–24.
5900. WASHIZU, HIROKO. "The Sound of One Hand Clapping: A Note on 'A Perfect Day for Bananafish.' " In *American Literature in the 1950's.* Annual Report, 1976. Tokyo: Tokyo Chapter, American Literary Society of Japan, 1977. pp. 83–89.
5901. WIEBE, DALLAS E. "Salinger's 'A Perfect Day for Bananafish.' " *The Explicator*, 23 (1964), item 3.
See also 195, 269, 298, 308, 5922, 5927–5929, 5931–5933, 5937, 5943, 5950, 5951, 5954, 5958.

"Pretty Mouth and Green My Eyes"

5902. HAGOPIAN, JOHN V. " 'Pretty Mouth and Green My Eyes': Salinger's Paolo and Francesca in New York." *Modern Fiction Studies*, 12 (1966), 349–54.
5903. HAMILTON, KENNETH. "Hell in New York: J. D. Salinger's 'Pretty Mouth and Green My Eyes.' " *Dalhousie Review*, 47 (1967), 394–99.
See also 5928, 5929, 5951.

"Raise High the Roof Beam, Carpenters"

See 195, 200, 218, 257, 298, 5918, 5924, 5928, 5929, 5936, 5946, 5958, 5966, 5968, 5974, 5975.

"Seymour: An Introduction"

5904. GLAZIER, LYLE. "The Glass Family Saga: Argument and Epiphany." *College English*, 27 (1965), 248–51.
5905. GOLDSTEIN, BERNICE AND SANFORD. " 'Seymour: An Introduction'—Writing as Discovery." *Studies in Short Fiction*, 7 (1970), 248–56.

5906.   LYONS, JOHN O. "The Romantic Style of Salinger's 'Seymour: An Introduction.' " *Wisconsin Studies in Contemporary Literature*, 4 (1963), 62–69.

5907.   SCHULZ, MAX F. "Epilogue to *Seymour: An Introduction:* Salinger and the Crisis of Consciousness." *Studies in Short Fiction*, 5 (1968), 128–38.

See also 195, 200, 269, 308, 345, 446, 589, 5884, 5918, 5919, 5928, 5929, 5936, 5938, 5941, 5945, 5946, 5952, 5956, 5958, 5966, 5968, 5969, 5973–5975.

"Slight Rebellion off Madison"

See 5928, 5929.

"Teddy"

5908.   BRYAN, JAMES. "A Reading of Salinger's 'Teddy.' " *American Literature*, 40 (1968), 352–69.

5909.   KRANIDAS, THOMAS. "Point of View in Salinger's 'Teddy.' " *Studies in Short Fiction*, 2 (1964), 89–91.

5910.   PERRINE, LAURENCE. "Teddy? Booper? or Blooper?" *Studies in Short Fiction*, 4 (1967), 217–24.

5911.   STEIN, WILLIAM BYSSHE. "Salinger's 'Teddy': *Tat Tvam Asi* or That Thou Art." *The Arizona Quarterly*, 29 (1973), 253–65.

5912.   SUBRAMANIAM, K. S. "A Study of J. D. Salinger's 'Teddy.' " *The Indian Journal of English Studies*, 13 (1972), 148–54.

See also 195, 5928, 5929, 5950, 5951, 5958.

"This Sandwich Has No Mayonnaise"

See 5928, 5929.

"Uncle Wiggily in Connecticut"

5913.   FRENCH, WARREN G. "The Phony World and the Nice World." *Wisconsin Studies in Contemporary Literature*, 4 (1963), 21–30.

See also 257, 5928, 5929, 5934, 5937, 5951, 5954, 5975.

"The Varioni Brothers"

See 5928, 5929.

"The Young Folks"

See 5928, 5929.

"A Young Girl in 1941 with No Waist at All"

See 5928, 5929.

"Zooey"

5914. **DETWEILER, ROBERT.** *Four Spiritual Crises in Mid-Century American Fiction.* Gainesville: Univ. of Florida Press, 1963.

5915. **SEITZMAN, DANIEL.** "Therapy and Antitherapy in Salinger's 'Zooey.' " *American Imago,* 25 (1968), 140–62.

See also 169, 195, 200, 269, 298, 589, 5916, 5918, 5920, 5924, 5926, 5928, 5929, 5931, 5932, 5938, 5940, 5943, 5945–5947, 5954, 5956, 5958, 5966, 5968, 5974.

General Studies

5916. **ANTICO, JOHN.** "The Parody of J. D. Salinger: Esme and the Fat Lady Exposed." *Modern Fiction Studies,* 12 (1966), 325–40.

5917. **BARR, DONALD.** "Ah, Buddy: Salinger." In *The Creative Present: Notes on Contemporary American Fiction.* Ed. Nona Balakian and Charles Simmons. Garden City, NY: Doubleday, 1963. pp. 27–62.

5918. **BASKETT, SAM S.** "The Splendid/Squalid World of J. D. Salinger." *Wisconsin Studies in Contemporary Literature,* 4 (1963), 48–61.

5919. **BLOTNER, JOSEPH L.** "Salinger Now: An Appraisal." *Wisconsin Studies in Contemporary Literature,* 4 (1963), 100–08.

5920. **BRYAN, JAMES E.** "J. D. Salinger: The Fat Lady and the Chicken Sandwich." *College English,* 23 (1961), 226–29.

5921. ———. "Reply." *College English,* 24 (1963), 563–64.

5922. ———. "Salinger's Seymour Suicide." *College English,* 24 (1962), 226–29.

5923. **CARTER, ALBERT HOWARD.** "The New Dickens." *Western Humanities Review,* 16 (1962), 239–41.

5924. **CHESTER, ALFRED.** "Salinger: How to Love without Love." *Commentary,* 35 (1963), 467–74.

5925. **COLES, ROBERT.** "Reconsideration: J. D. Salinger." *The New Republic,* 168, no. 17 (1973), 30–32.

5926. **DAVIS, TOM.** "J. D. Salinger: 'The Sound of One Hand Clapping.' " *Wisconsin Studies in Contemporary Literature,* 4 (1963), 41–47.

5927. **FRENCH, WARREN.** "The Age of Salinger." In *The Fifties: Fiction, Poetry, Drama.* Ed. Warren French. Deland, FL: Everett/Edwards, 1970. pp. 1–39.

5928. ———. *J. D. Salinger.* New York: Twayne, 1963.

5929. ———. *J. D. Salinger.* Rev. ed. Boston, MA: Twayne, 1976.

5930. ———. "Salinger's Seymour: Another Autopsy." *College English,* 24 (1963), 563.

5931. **GALLOWAY, DAVID D.** *The Absurd Hero in American Fiction: Updike, Styron, Bellow, Salinger.* Austin: Univ. of Texas Press, 1966.

5932. _____. *The Absurd Hero in American Fiction: Updike, Styron, Bellow, Salinger.* Rev. ed. Austin: Univ. of Texas Press, 1970.

5933. **GENTHE, CHARLES V.** "Six, Sex, Sick: Seymour, Some Comments." *Twentieth Century Literature,* 10 (1965), 170–71.

5934. **GOLDHURST, WILLIAM.** "The Hyphenated Ham Sandwich of Ernest Hemingway and J. D. Salinger: A Study in Literary Continuity." *Fitzgerald/Hemingway Annual 1970,* pp. 136–50.

5935. **GOLDSTEIN, BERNICE AND SANFORD.** "Ego and 'Hapworth 16, 1924.' " *Renascence,* 24 (1972), 159–67.

5936. _____. "Some Zen References in Salinger." *Literature East & West,* 15 (1971), 83–95.

5937. _____. "Zen and *Nine Stories.*" *Renascence,* 22 (1970), 171–82.

5938. _____. "Zen and Salinger." *Modern Fiction Studies,* 12 (1966), 313–24.

5939. **GREEN, MARTIN.** "American Rococo: Salinger and Nabokov." In *Re-Appraisals: Some Commonsense Readings in American Literature.* London: Hugh Evelyn, 1963. pp. 211–29.

5940. _____. "Franny and Zooey." In *Re-Appraisals: Some Commonsense Readings in American Literature.* London: Hugh Evelyn, 1963. pp. 197–210.

5941. **GROSS, THEODORE L.** "J. D. Salinger: Suicide and Survival in the Modern World." *The South Atlantic Quarterly,* 68 (1969), 454–62.

5942. **GRUNWALD, HENRY ANATOLE.** "Introduction." In *Salinger: A Critical and Personal Portrait.* New York: Harper, 1962. pp. ix–xxviii.

5943. **HAMILTON, KENNETH.** *J. D. Salinger: A Critical Essay.* Grand Rapids, MI: Eerdmans, 1967.

5944. _____. "J. D. Salinger's Happy Family." *Queen's Quarterly,* 71 (1964), 176–87.

5945. **HARADA, KEIICHI.** "After *Franny and Zooey.*" In *American Literature in the 1950's.* Annual Report, 1976. Tokyo: Tokyo Chapter, American Literary Society of Japan, 1977. pp. 90–95.

5946. **HASSAN, IHAB.** "Almost the Voice of Silence: The Later Novelettes of J. D. Salinger." *Wisconsin Studies in Contemporary Literature,* 4 (1963), 5–20.

5947. **HAYES, ANN L.** "J. D. Salinger: A Reputation and a Promise." In *Lectures on Modern Novelists.* Ed. A. Fred Sochatoff, Beekman W. Cottrell, and Ann L. Hayes. Pittsburgh, PA: Carnegie Institute of Technology, 1963. pp. 15–24.

5948. HICKS, GRANVILLE. "J. D. Salinger: Search for Wisdom."
Saturday Review, 42 (25 July 1959), 13, 30.

5949. KAZIN, ALFRED. "J. D. Salinger: 'Everybody's Favorite.' "
The Atlantic Monthly, 208, no. 2 (1961), 27–31.

5950. KINNEY, ARTHUR F. "J. D. Salinger and the Search for
Love." *Texas Studies in Literature and Language*, 5 (1963), 111–26.

5951. KIRSCHNER, PAUL. "Salinger and His Society: The Pattern
of *Nine Stories*." *The Literary Half-Yearly*, 12, no. 2 (1971), 51–60;
14, no. 2 (1973), 63–78.

5952. LARNER, JEREMY. "Salinger's Audience: An Explanation."
Partisan Review, 29 (1962), 594–98.

5953. LEITCH, DAVID. "The Salinger Myth." *The Twentieth Century*, 168 (1960), 428–35.

5954. LIVINGSTON, JAMES T. "J. D. Salinger: The Artist's Struggle to Stand on Holy Ground." In *Adversity and Grace: Studies in
Recent American Literature*. Ed. Nathan A. Scott, Jr. Chicago:
Univ. of Chicago Press, 1968. pp. 113–32.

5955. LODGE, DAVID. "Family Romances." *The Times* (London)
Literary Supplement, 13 June 1975, p. 642.

5956. LORCH, THOMAS M. "J. D. Salinger: The Artist, the Audience, and the Popular Arts." *South Dakota Review*, 5, no. 4
(1968), 3–13.

5957. McINTYRE, JOHN P., S.J. "The Modes of Disillusionment:
Irony in Modern Fiction." *Renascence*, 17 (1965), 70–76, 96.

5958. MILLER, JAMES E., JR. *J. D. Salinger*. Minneapolis: Univ. of
Minnesota Press, 1965.

5959. ———, AND ARTHUR HEISERMAN. "J. D. Salinger: Some
Crazy Cliff." In *Quests Surd and Absurd: Essays in American Literature*. Chicago: Univ. of Chicago Press, 1967. pp. 31–40.

5960. MIZENER, ARTHUR. "The Love Song of J. D. Salinger."
Harper's Magazine, 218 (Feb. 1959), 83–90.

5961. MURPHY, CAROL. "Some Last Puritans." *Approach*, no. 53
(1964), pp. 38–43.

5962. NOLAND, RICHARD W. "The Novel of Personal Formula:
J. D. Salinger." *The University Review* (Kansas City), 33 (1966),
19–24.

5963. REES, RICHARD. "The Salinger Situation." In *Contemporary
American Novelists*. Ed. Harry T. Moore. Carbondale: Southern
Illinois Univ. Press. 1964. pp. 95–105.

5964. ROSEN, GERALD. *Zen in the Art of J. D. Salinger*. Berkeley,
CA: Creative Arts, 1977.

5965. RUSSELL, JOHN. "Salinger's Feat." *Modern Fiction Studies*,
12 (1966), 299–311.

5966. SCHWARTZ, ARTHUR. "For Seymour—With Love and Judgment." *Wisconsin Studies in Contemporary Literature*, 4 (1963), 88–99.

5967. SIMMS, L. MOODY, JR. "Seymour Glass: The Salingerian Hero as Vulgarian." *Notes on Contemporary Literature*, 5, no. 5 (1975), 6–8.

5968. SLETHAUG, G[ORDON] E. "Form in Salinger's Shorter Fiction." *The Canadian Review of American Studies*, 3 (1972), 50–59.

5969. ———. "Seymour: A Clarification." *Renascence*, 23 (1971), 115–28.

5970. STEINER, GEORGE. "The Salinger Industry." *The Nation*, 189 (1959), 360–63.

5971. STONE, EDWARD. "Naming in Salinger." *Notes on Contemporary Literature*, 1, no. 2 (1971), 2–3.

5972. STRAUCH, CARL F. "Salinger: The Romantic Background." *Wisconsin Studies in Contemporary Literature*, 4 (1963), 31–40.

5973. WIEGAND, WILLIAM. "The Knighthood of J. D. Salinger." *The New Republic*, 141, no. 16 (1959), 19–21.

5974. ———. "Salinger and Kierkegaard." *The Minnesota Review*, 5 (1965), 137–56.

5975. YAMAYA, SABURO. "J. D. Salinger's Quest of 'The Valley of the Sick.' " *Studies in English Literature* (Tokyo), 40 (1964), 215–43.

Bibliography

5976. BEEBE, MAURICE, AND JENNIFER SPERRY. "Criticism of J. D. Salinger: A Selected Checklist." *Modern Fiction Studies*, 12 (1966), 377–90.

5977. BRUCCOLI, MATTHEW J. "States of Salinger Book." *American Notes & Queries*, 2 (1963), 21–22.

5978. DAVIS, TOM. "J. D. Salinger: A Checklist." *The Papers of the Bibliographical Society of America*, 53 (1959), 69–71.

5979. FIENE, DONALD M. "J. D. Salinger: A Bibliography." *Wisconsin Studies in Contemporary Literature*, 4 (1963), 109–49.

5980. GALLOWAY, DAVID D. "A J. D. Salinger Checklist." In *The Absurd Hero in American Fiction: Updike, Styron, Bellow, Salinger*. Austin: Univ. of Texas Press, 1966. pp. 226–51.

5981. ———. "A J. D. Salinger Checklist." In *The Absurd Hero in American Fiction: Updike, Styron, Bellow, Salinger*. Rev. ed. Austin: Univ. of Texas Press, 1970. pp. 239–67.

5982. STAROSCIAK, KENNETH. *J. D. Salinger: A Thirty-Year Bibliography, 1938-1968*. St. Paul, MN: Croixside Press, 1971.

SALTUS, EDGAR

General Studies

5983. **SPRAGUE, CLAIRE.** *Edgar Saltus.* New York: Twayne, 1968.

SANTEE, ROSS

General Studies

5984. **HOUSTON, NEAL B.** *Ross Santee.* Austin, TX: Steck-Vaughn, 1968.

SAROYAN, WILLIAM

"The Daring Young Man on the Flying Trapeze"
See 5987.

"The Living and the Dead"
See 5987.

"Seventy Thousand Assyrians"
See 5987.

"With a Hey Nonny, Nonny"
See 311.

General Studies

5985. **ANGOFF, CHARLES.** "William Saroyan: Some Footnotes." In *The Tone of the Twenties and Other Essays.* New York: Barnes, 1966. pp. 203–08.

5986. **BALAKIAN, NONA.** *The Armenian-American Writer: A New Accent in American Fiction.* New York: Armenian General Benevolent Union of America, 1958.

5987. **FLOAN, HOWARD R.** *William Saroyan.* New York: Twayne, 1966.

Bibliography

5988. **KHERDIAN, DAVID.** *A Bibliography of William Saroyan, 1934–1964.* San Francisco, CA: Roger Beacham, 1965.

SAWYER, RUTH

General Studies

5989. **HAVILAND, VIRGINIA.** *Ruth Sawyer.* London: Bodley Head, 1965.

SCHACHNER, NAT[HAN]

"Sterile Planet"

See 140.

SCHAEFER, JACK

General Studies

5990. HASLAM, GERALD. *Jack Schaefer*. Boise, ID: Boise State Univ., 1975.

Interviews

5991. NUWER, HENRY JOSEPH. "An Interview with Jack Schaefer." *South Dakota Review*, 11, no. 1 (1973), 48–58.

SCHOOLCRAFT, HENRY ROWE

General Studies

5992. MCALEER, JOHN J. "Schoolcraft's Vulnerable Red Men." *American Transcendental Quarterly*, no. 30, Part One (1976), pp. 13–18.

SCHORER, MARK

"The Face within the Face"

See 564.

"What We Don't Know Hurts Us"

5993. BLUEFARB, SAM. "What We Don't Know *Can* Hurt Us." *Studies in Short Fiction*, 5 (1968), 163–70.
See also 565.

SCHWARTZ, DELMORE

"America! America!"

See 5998.

"The Child Is the Meaning of This Life"

See 5998.

"In Dreams Begin Responsibilities"

5994. NOVAK, MICHAEL PAUL. "The Dream as Film: Delmore Schwartz's 'In Dreams Begin Responsibilities.'" *Kansas Quarterly*, 9, no. 2 (1977), 87–91.

See also 566, 5995, 5998.

"New Year's Eve"
See 5998.

"Successful Love"
See 256.

"The World Is a Wedding"
See 5997, 5998.

General Studies

5995. **ATLAS, JAMES.** *Delmore Schwartz: The Life of an American Poet.* New York: Farrar, Straus & Giroux, 1977.
5996. **FLINT, ROBERT W.** "The Stories of Delmore Schwartz." *Commentary*, 33 (1962), 336–39.
5997. **LYONS, BONNIE.** "Delmore Schwartz and the Whole Truth." *Studies in Short Fiction*, 14 (1977), 259–64.
5998. **McDOUGALL, RICHARD.** *Delmore Schwartz.* New York: Twayne, 1974.

SEAGER, ALLAN

"The Bang on the Head"
See 6000.

"The Old Man of the Mountain"
See 5999.

"Pommery 1921"
See 6000.

General Studies

5999. **HANNA, ALLAN.** "The Muse of History: Allan Seager and the Criticism of Culture." *Critique*, 5, no. 3 (1963), 37–61.
6000. **KENNER, HUGH.** "The Insider." *Critique*, 2, no. 3 (1959), 3–15.
6001. **QUIGLEY, GENEVIEVE L.** "Allan Seager of Tecumseh." *The Michigan Quarterly Review*, 9 (1970), 247–51.

Bibliography

6002. **HANNA, ALLAN.** "An Allan Seager Bibliography." *Critique*, 5, no. 3 (1963), 75–90.

SEALSFIELD, CHARLES
General Studies

6003. **CARRINGTON, ULRICH S.** "Charles Sealsfield: His Life and Times." In *The Making of an American: An Adaptation of Memorable Tales by Charles Sealsfield.* Dallas, TX: Southern Methodist Univ. Press, 1974. pp. 3–20.

SELBY, HUBERT
"Another Day Another Dollar"
See 6007.

"The Queen Is Back"
See 6006.

"Strike"
See 6006, 6007.

"Tralala"
See 6006.

General Studies

6004. **LANE, JAMES B.** "Violence and Sex in the Post-War Popular Urban Novel: With a Consideration of Harold Robbins's *A Stone for Danny Fisher* and Hubert Selby, Jr.'s *Last Exit to Brooklyn.*" *Journal of Popular Culture*, 8 (1974), 295–308.

6005. **PEAVY, CHARLES D.** "Hubert Selby and the Tradition of Moral Satire." *Satire Newsletter*, 6, no. 2 (1969), 35–39.

6006. ———. "The Sin of Pride and Selby's *Last Exit to Brooklyn.*" *Critique*, 11, no. 3 (1969), 35–42.

6007. **WERTIME, RICHARD A.** "Psychic Vengeance in *Last Exit to Brooklyn.*" *Literature and Psychology*, 24 (1974), 153–66.

Interviews

6008. **FRANKEL, HASKEL.** " 'Call Me Cubby.' " *Saturday Review*, 48 (23 Jan. 1965), 40–41.

SELTZER, CHESTER (See *MURO, AMADO*)

SHAW, HENRY WHEELER (See *BILLINGS, JOSH*)

SHAW, IRWIN

"The Girls in Their Summer Dresses"
See 394, 478, 565.

"Strawberry Ice Cream Soda"
See 374.

Interviews

6009. HARSENT, DAVID. "Irwin Shaw in Conversation." *The New Review*, 2, no. 22 (1976), 52–56.
6010. MITGANG, HERBERT. "Behind the Best Sellers: Irwin Shaw." *The New York Times Book Review*, 13 Nov. 1977, p. 88.
6011. NEWQUIST, ROY. "Irwin Shaw." In *Counterpoint*. Chicago: Rand McNally, 1964. pp. 544–51.

SHECKLEY, ROBERT

"The Academy"
See 114.

"A Ticket to Tranai"
See 114.

SHEPHERD, JEAN

"Hairy Gertz and the Forty-Seven Crappies"
See 6012.

General Studies

6012. TRIMMER, JOSEPH F. "Memoryscape: Jean Shepherd's Midwest." *The Old Northwest*, 2 (1976), 357–69.

SHILLABER, BENJAMIN PENHALLOW

General Studies

6013. REED, JOHN Q. *Benjamin Penhallow Shillaber*. New York: Twayne, 1972.

SILKO, LESLIE MARMON

Interviews

6014. EVERS, LARRY, AND DENNY CARR. "A Conversation with Leslie Marmon Silko." *Sun Tracks*, 3, no. 1 (1976), 28–33.

SILVERBERG, ROBERT

"After the Myths Went Home"

See 174.

SIMAK, CLIFFORD D.

"The World of the Red Sun"

See 6015.

General Studies

6015.   **CLARESON, THOMAS D.** "Clifford D. Simak: The Inhabited Universe." In *Voices for the Future: Essays on Major Science Fiction Writers*. Ed. Thomas D. Clareson. Bowling Green, OH: Bowling Green Univ. Popular Press, 1976. pp. 64–87.

SIMMS, WILLIAM GILMORE

"Confessions of a Murderer"

6016.   **GUILDS, JOHN C.** "The 'Lost' Number of the *Southern Literary Gazette*." *Studies in Bibliography*, 22 (1969), 266–73.

"How Sharp Snaffles Got His Capital and Wife"

6017.   **KIBLER, JAMES E., JR.** "Simms' Indebtedness to Folk Tradition in 'Sharp Snaffles.' " *The Southern Literary Journal*, 4, no. 2 (1972), 55–68.

"Major Rocket"

See 6026.

"Oaktibbe"

6018.   **DAVIS, JACK L.** "W. Gilmore Simms' 'Oaktibbe' and the Failure of the Westering Imagination." In *The Westering Experience in American Literature: Bicentennial Essays*. Ed. Merrill Lewis and L. L. Lee. Bellingham: Bureau for Faculty Research, Western Washington Univ., 1977. pp. 112–21.

"The Plank"

See 6026.

"Ponce de Leon"

See 6026.

"Sweet William"

See 6026.

"The Two Camps"
See 549.

General Studies

6019. CURRENT-GARCIA, EUGENE. "Simm's Short Stories: Art or Commercialism?" *The Mississippi Quarterly*, 15 (1962), 56–67.
6020. GUILDS, JOHN C. "The Achievement of William Gilmore Simms: His Short Fiction." In *The Poetry of Community: Essays on the Southern Sensibility of History and Literature.* Ed. Lewis P. Simpson. Spectrum: Monograph Series in the Arts and Sciences, Vol. 2. Atlanta: School of Arts and Sciences, Georgia State Univ., 1972. pp. 25–35.
6021. ———. "Introduction." In *The Writings of William Gilmore Simms. Volume V: Stories and Tales.* Columbia: Univ. of South Carolina Press, 1974. pp. xi–xxiv.
6022. ———. "William Gilmore Simms and the *Southern Literary Gazette.*" *Studies in Bibliography*, 21 (1968), 59–92.
6023. RIDGELY, J. V. *William Gilmore Simms.* New York: Twayne, 1962.
6024. WAKELYN, JON L. *The Politics of a Literary Man: William Gilmore Simms.* Westport, CT: Greenwood Press, 1973.
6025. WIMSATT, MARY ANN. "Simms and Irving." *The Mississippi Quarterly*, 20 (1967), 25–37.
6026. ———. "Simms's Early Short Shories." *The Library Chronicle*, 41 (1977), 163–79.

Bibliography

6027. KIBLER, JAMES E., JR. *Pseudonymous Publications of William Gilmore Simms.* Athens: Univ. of Georgia Press, 1976.
6028. STRICKLAND, BETTY JO. "The Short Fiction of William Gilmore Simms: A Checklist." *The Mississippi Quarterly*, 29 (1976), 591–608.
6029. WATSON, CHARLES S. "William Gilmore Simms: An Essay in Bibliography." *Resources for American Literary Study*, 3 (1973), 3–26.

SINGER, I[SAAC] B[ASHEVIS]
"Alone"
See 6043, 6044, 6048.
"The Black Wedding"
See 300, 6045.

"Blood"

See 6045.

"The Cafeteria"

See 6045.

"The Captive"

6030. RICE, JULIAN C. "I. B. Singer's 'The Captive': A False Messiah in the Promised Land." *Studies in American Fiction*, 5 (1977), 269–75.

"Caricature"

See 6046.

"Cockadoodledoo"

See 6045.

"Fool's Paradise"

See 6047.

"The Gentleman from Cracow"

See 6043, 6045.

"Gimpel the Fool"

6031. SIEGEL, PAUL N. "Gimpel and the Archetype of the Wise Fool." In *The Achievement of Isaac Bashevis Singer*. Ed. Marcia Allentuck. Carbondale and Edwardsville: Southern Illinois Univ. Press, 1969. pp. 159–73.
See also 191, 286, 385, 511, 6033, 6045, 6049, 6052.

"The Last Demon"

See 113, 300, 6045.

"The Little Shoemakers"

See 6045

"The Man Who Came Back"

See 6045.

"The Mirror"

6032. SALAMON, GEORGE. "In a Glass Darkly: The Morality of the Mirror in E. T. A. Hoffmann and I. B. Singer." *Studies in Short Fiction*, 7 (1970), 625–33.
See also 6048.

"Powers"

See 483.

"The Séance"

See 6033, 6039, 6045.

"Shiddah and Kuziba"

See 6045.

"The Slaughterer"

See 6044, 6045.

"The Spinoza of Market Street"

See 535, 6038, 6045, 6046.

"The Third One"

See 283.

"Zlateh the Goat"

See 6047.

General Studies

6033. **BEZANKER, ABRAHAM.** "I. B. Singer's Crises of Identity." *Critique*, 14, no. 2 (1972), 70–88.

6034. **BUCHEN, IRVING H.** "Isaac Bashevis Singer and the Eternal Past." *Critique*, 8, no. 3 (1966), 5–18.

6035. **FIXLER, MICHAEL.** "The Redeemers: Themes in the Fiction of Isaac Bashevis Singer." *The Kenyon Review*, 26 (1964), 371–86.

6036. **GASS, WILLIAM H.** "The Shut-In." In *The Achievement of Isaac Bashevis Singer*. Ed. Marcia Allentuck. Carbondale and Edwardsville: Southern Illinois Univ. Press, 1969. pp. 1–13.

6037. **GITTLEMAN, EDWIN.** "Dybbukianism: The Meaning of Method in Singer's Short Stories." In *Contemporary American-Jewish Literature*. Ed. Irving Malin. Bloomington: Indiana Univ. Press, 1973. pp. 248–69.

6038. **GOLDEN, MORRIS.** "Dr. Fischelson's Miracle: Duality and Vision in Singer's Fiction." In *The Achievement of Isaac Bashevis Singer*. Ed. Marcia Allentuck. Carbondale and Edwardsville: Southern Illinois Univ. Press, 1969. pp. 26–43.

6039. **GOTTLIEB, ELAINE.** "Singer and Hawthorne: A Prevalence of Satan." *The Southern Review*, NS 8 (1972), 359–70.

6040. **HOWE, IRVING.** "I. B. Singer." *Encounter*, 26, no. 3 (1966), 60–68, 70.

6041. JACOBSON, DAN. "The Problem of Isaac Bashevis Singer."
Commentary, 39, no. 2 (1965), 48–52.

6042. KATZ, ELI. "Isaac Bashevis Singer and the Classical Yiddish Tradition." In *The Achievement of Isaac Bashevis Singer*. Ed.
Marcia Allentuck. Carbondale and Edwardsville: Southern Illinois Univ. Press, 1969. pp. 14–25.

6043. LEE, GRACE FARRELL. "The Hidden God of Isaac Bashevis
Singer." *The Hollins Critic*, 10, no. 6 (1973), 1–4, 6–15.

6044. MALIN, IRVING. "Introduction." In *Critical Views of Isaac
Bashevis Singer*. Ed. Irving Malin. New York: New York Univ.
Press, 1969. pp. xi–xix.

6045. _____. *Isaac Bashevis Singer*. New York: Ungar, 1972.

6046. MINTZ, SAMUEL I. "Spinoza and Spinozaism in Singer's
Shorter Fiction." In *Critical Views of Isaac Bashevis Singer*. Ed.
Irving Malin. New York: New York Univ. Press, 1969. pp.
207–17.

6047. MORSE, NAOMI S. "Values for Children in the Stories of
Isaac Bashevis Singer." In *Children's Literature: Selected Essays
and Bibliographies*. Ed. Anne S. MacLeod. College Park: College
of Library and Information Services, Univ. of Maryland, 1977.
pp. 16–35.

6048. NOVAK, MAXIMILLIAN E. "Moral Grotesque and Decora-
tive Grotesque in Singer's Fiction." In *The Achievement of Isaac
Bashevis Singer*. Ed. Marcia Allentuck. Carbondale and Edwardsville: Southern Illinois Univ. Press, 1969. pp. 44–63.

6049. PINSKER, SANFORD. "The Fictive Worlds of Isaac Bashevis
Singer." *Critique*, 11, no. 2 (1969), 26–39.

6050. SEED, DAVID. "The Fiction of Isaac Bashevis Singer." *The
Critical Quarterly*, 18, no. 1 (1976), 73–79.

6051. SIEGEL, BEN. *Isaac Bashevis Singer*. Minneapolis: Univ. of
Minnesota Press, 1969.

6052. _____. "Sacred and Profane: Isaac Bashevis Singer's Em-
battled Spirits." *Critique*, 6, no. 1 (1963), 24–47.

6053. SLOMAN, JUDITH. "Existentialism in Pär Lagerkvist and
Isaac Bashevis Singer." *The Minnesota Review*, 5 (1965), 206–12.

6054. ZATLIN, LINDA G. "The Themes of Isaac Bashevis Singer's
Short Fiction." *Critique*, 11, no. 2 (1969), 40–46.

Interviews

6055. ANDERSEN, DAVID M. "Isaac Bashevis Singer: Conversations in California." *Modern Fiction Studies*, 16 (1970), 423–39.

6056. BRAGG, MELVIN. "Profile 12: Isaac Bashevis Singer." *The
New Review*, 2, no. 15 (1975), 43–52.

6057. **FRANKEL, HASKEL.** "On the Fringe." *Saturday Review*, 51 (27 Apr. 1968), 35.

6058. **LEE, GRACE FARRELL.** "Seeing and Blindness: A Conversation With Isaac Bashevis Singer." *Novel*, 9 (1976), 151–64.

6059. **PINSKER, SANFORD.** "Isaac Bashevis Singer: An Interview." *Critique*, 11, no. 2 (1969), 16–25.

6060. **PONDROM, CYRENA N.** "Isaac Bashevis Singer: An Interview and a Biographical Sketch." *Contemporary Literature*, 10 (1969), 1–38.

6061. ———. "Isaac Bashevis Singer: An Interview, Part II." *Contemporary Literature*, 10 (1969), 332–51.

6062. **ROSENBLATT, PAUL, AND GENE KOPPEL.** *A Certain Bridge: Isaac Bashevis Singer on Literature and Life.* Tucson: Univ. of Arizona, 1971.

6063. **ROTH, PHILIP.** "Roth and Singer on Bruno Schulz." *The New York Times Book Review*, 13 Feb. 1977, pp. 5, 14, 16, 20.

6064. **SINGER, ISAAC BASHEVIS.** "The Art of Fiction XLII." With Harold Flender. *The Paris Review*, no. 44 (1968), pp. 53–73.

Bibliography

6065. **BRYER, JACKSON R., AND PAUL E. ROCKWELL.** "Isaac Bashevis Singer in English: A Bibliography." In *Critical Views of Isaac Bashevis Singer.* Ed. Irving Malin. New York: New York Univ. Press, 1969. pp. 220–65.

6066. **CHRISTENSEN, BONNIEJEAN McGUIRE.** "Isaac Bashevis Singer: A Bibliography." *Bulletin of Bibliography and Magazine Notes*, 26 (1969), 3–6.

SLESINGER, TESS

General Studies

6067. **BIAGI, SHIRLEY.** "Forgive Me for Dying." *The Antioch Review*, 35 (1977), 224–36.

SMITH, CHARLES HENRY (See ARP, BILL)

SMITH, CORDWAINER

"The Dead Lady of Clown Town"

See 293.

"The Game of Rat and Dragon"

6068. **WOLFE, GARY K.** "Mythic Structures in Cordwainer

Smith's 'The Game of Rat and Dragon.' " *Science-Fiction Studies*, 4 (1977), 144–50.

SMITH, JEAN

"Frankie Mae"

See 340.

SMITH, SEBA

General Studies

*6069. **RICKELS, MILTON AND PATRICIA.** *Seba Smith.* Boston, MA: Twayne, 1977.

SNELLING, WILLIAM JOSEPH

"The Bois Brulé"

See 6070.

General Studies

6070. **SCHEICK, WILLIAM J.** "The Half-Breed in Snelling's *Tales of the Northwest.*" *The Old Northwest*, 2 (1976), 141–51.

SONTAG, SUSAN

Interviews

6071. **BELLAMY, JOE DAVID.** "Susan Sontag." In *The New Fiction: Interviews with Innovative American Writers.* Ed. Joe David Bellamy. Urbana: Univ. of Illinois Press, 1974. pp. 113–29.

SOUTHERN, TERRY

General Studies

6072. **ALGEN, NELSON.** "The Donkeyman by Twilight." *The Nation*, 198 (1964), 509–12.

SPENCER, ELIZABETH

"First Dark"

See 576.

General Studies

6073. **SPENCER, ELIZABETH.** "On Writing Fiction." *Notes on Mississippi Writers*, 3 (1970), 71–72.

Interviews

6074. **BUNTING, CHARLES T.** " 'In That Time and at That Place': The Literary World of Elizabeth Spencer." *The Mississippi Quarterly*, 28 (1975), 435–60.

6075. **COLE, HUNTER MCKELVA.** "Elizabeth Spencer at Sycamore Fair." *Notes on Mississippi Writers*, 6 (1974), 81–86.

6076. **HALEY, JOSEPHINE.** "An Interview with Elizabeth Spencer." *Notes on Mississippi Writers*, 1 (1968), 42–53.

Bibliography

6077. **BARGE, LAURA.** "An Elizabeth Spencer Checklist, 1948 to 1976." *The Mississippi Quarterly*, 29 (1976), 569–90.

SPENCER, SHARON

Bibliography

6078. **ANON.** "A Checklist of the Publications of Sharon Spencer." *Under the Sign of Pisces*, 4, no. 4 (1973), 9–10.

STAFFORD, JEAN

"A Country Love Story"

See 278, 318.

"In the Zoo"

See 173, 399.

General Studies

6079. **JENSON, SID.** "The Noble Wicked West of Jean Stafford." *Western American Literature*, 7 (1973), 261–70.

6080. **VICKERY, OLGA W.** "Jean Stafford and the Ironic Vision." *The South Atlantic Quarterly*, 61 (1962), 484–91.

STEELE, WILBUR DANIEL

"How Beautiful with Shoes"

6081. **SUNDELL, JULIE PEARCE AND ROGER H.** "How Beautiful with Shoes." In *Instructor's Manual for* "The Art of Fiction," Second Edition. Ed. R. F. Dietrich and Roger H. Sundell. New York: Holt, Rinehart and Winston, 1974. pp. 95–104. *See also* 6082.

General Studies

*6082. **BUCCO, MARTIN.** *Wilbur Daniel Steele.* New York: Twayne, 1972.

STEGNER, WALLACE

"The Blue-Winged Teal"

6083. FERGUSON, J. M., JR. "Cellars of Consciousness: Stegner's
'The Blue-Winged Teal.' " *Studies in Short Fiction*, 14 (1977),
180–82.
See also 6088.

"Butcher Bird"

See 564.

"Carrion Spring"

See 6085.

"The Chink"

See 6088.

"Field Guide to the Western Birds"

See 6086, 6088.

"Genesis"

See 594.

"Goin' to Town"

See 399.

"Maiden in a Tower"

See 564.

"Saw Gang"

See 6088.

"The Traveler"

See 6088.

"Two Rivers"

See 6086.

"The View from the Balcony"

6084. FLORA, JOSEPH M. "Vardis Fisher and Wallace Stegner:
Teacher and Student." *Western American Literature*, 5 (1970),
121–28.

"The Women on the Wall"

See 6088.

General Studies

6085. AHEARN, KERRY. "Heroes vs. Women: Conflict and Duplicity in Stegner." *Western Humanities Review*, 31 (1977), 125–41.

6086. CANZONERI, ROBERT. "Wallace Stegner: Trial by Existence." *The Southern Review*, NS 9 (1973), 796–827.

6087. LEWIS, MERRILL AND LORENE. *Wallace Stegner*. Boise, ID: Boise State College, 1972.

6088. ROBINSON, FORREST G., AND MARGARET G. ROBINSON. *Wallace Stegner*. Boston, MA: Twayne, 1977.

6089. STEGNER, WALLACE. "One Way to Spell Man." *The Literary Criterion*, 3, no. 4 (1959), 23–35.

6090. ———. "Sensibility and Intelligence." *Saturday Review*, 41 (13 Dec. 1958), 24.

Interviews

6091. ANON. "Interview: Wallace Stegner." *The Great Lakes Review*, 2, no. 1 (1975), 1–25.

6092. DILLON, DAVID. "Time's Prisoners: An Interview with Wallace Stegner." *Southwest Review*, 61 (1976), 252–67.

6093. HOFHEINS, ROGER, AND DAN TOOKER. "Interview with Wallace Stegner." *The Southern Review*, NS 11 (1975), 794–801.

6094. MILTON, [JOHN R.]. "Conversation with Wallace Stegner." *South Dakota Review*, 9, no. 1 (1971), 45–57.

STEIN, GERTRUDE

"The Gentle Lena"

6095. WAGNER, LINDA W. "Modern American Literature: The Poetics of the Individual Voice." *The Centennial Review*, 21 (1977), 333–54.
See also 6103, 6104, 6108, 6115.

"The Good Anna"

6096. ROSE, MARILYN GADDIS. "Gertrude Stein and Cubist Narrative." *Modern Fiction Studies*, 22 (1977), 543–55.
See also 339, 1118, 6103, 6104, 6108, 6115.

"Melanctha"

6097. BRIDGMAN, RICHARD. "Melanctha." *American Literature*, 33 (1961), 350–59.

6098. FITZ, L. T. "Gertrude Stein and Picasso: The Language of Surfaces." *American Literature*, 45 (1973), 228–37.

6099. LOWENKRON, DAVID. "The Linguistic World of Melanctha." *Lost Generation Journal*, 2, no. 1 (1974), 8–11.

6100. **STIMPSON, CATHARINE R.** "The Mind, the Body, and Gertrude Stein." *Critical Inquiry*, 3 (1977), 489–506.

6101. **WEINSTEIN, NORMAN.** " 'Melanctha': Toward a Definition of Character." In *Gertrude Stein and the Literature of the Modern Consciousness.* New York: Ungar, 1970. pp. 11–26.

See also 207, 315, 381, 393, 576, 6102–6104, 6107–6111, 6115.

General Studies

6102. **BRINNIN, JOHN MALCOLM.** *The Third Rose: Gertrude Stein and Her World.* Boston, MA: Little, Brown, 1959.

6103. **COPELAND, CAROLYN FAUNCE.** *Language & Time & Gertrude Stein.* Iowa City: Univ. of Iowa Press, 1975.

6104. **FARBER, LAWREN.** "Fading: A Way. Gertrude Stein's Sources for *Three Lives.*" *Journal of Modern Literature*, 5 (1976), 463–80.

6105. **GREENFELD, HOWARD.** *Gertrude Stein: A Biography.* New York: Crown, 1973.

6106. **HOBHOUSE, JANET.** *Everybody Who Was Anybody: A Biography of Gertrude Stein.* London: Weidenfeld and Nicolson, 1975.

6107. **HOFFMAN, FREDERICK J.** *Gertrude Stein.* Minneapolis: Univ. of Minnesota Press, 1961.

6108. **HOFFMAN, MICHAEL J.** *The Development of Abstractionism in the Writings of Gertrude Stein.* Philadelphia: Univ. of Pennsylvania Press, 1965.

6109. _____. *Gertrude Stein.* Boston, MA: Twayne, 1976.

6110. **MAYNARD, REID.** "Abstractionism in Gertrude Stein's *Three Lives.*" *Ball State University Forum*, 13, no. 1 (1972), 68–71.

6111. **MELLOW, JAMES R.** *Charmed Circle: Gertrude Stein & Company.* New York: Praeger, 1974.

6112. **PAVESE, CESARE.** "Preface to *Three Lives.*" In *American Literature: Essays and Opinions.* Trans. Edwin Fussell. Berkeley: Univ. of California Press, 1970. pp. 161–64.

6113. **ROBINSON, ELEANOR.** "Gertrude Stein: Cubist Teacher." *Lost Generation Journal*, 2, no. 1 (1974), 12–15.

6114. **STEWART, ALLEGRA.** *Gertrude Stein and the Present.* Cambridge, MA: Harvard Univ. Press, 1967.

6115. **WOOD, CARL.** "Continuity of Romantic Irony: Stein's Homage to Laforgue in *Three Lives.*" *Comparative Literature Studies*, 12 (1975), 147–58.

Bibliography

6116. **WILSON, ROBERT A.** *Gertrude Stein: A Bibliography.* New York: Phoenix Bookshop, 1974.

STEINBECK, JOHN

"Breakfast"

6117. **BENTON, RICHARD M.** " 'Breakfast' I and II." In *A Study Guide to Steinbeck's* The Long Valley. Ed. Tetsumaro Hayashi. Ann Arbor, MI: Pierian Press, 1976. pp. 33–39.

6118. **HAMBY, JAMES A.** "Steinbeck's Biblical Vision: 'Breakfast' and the Nobel Acceptance Speech." *Western Review* (Western New Mexico University), 10, no. 1 (1973), 57–59.

"The Chrysanthemums"

6119. **DIETRICH, R. F.** "The Chrysanthemums." In *Instructor's Manual for* "The Art of Fiction," Second Edition. Ed. R. F. Dietrich and Roger H. Sundell. New York: Holt, Rinehart and Winston, 1974. pp. 69–74.

6120. **McMAHAN, ELIZABETH E.** " 'The Chrysanthemums': Study of a Woman's Sexuality." *Modern Fiction Studies*, 14 (1968), 453–58.

6121. **MARCUS, MORDECAI.** "The Lost Dream of Sex and Childbirth in 'The Chrysanthemums.' " *Modern Fiction Studies*, 11 (1965), 54–58.

6122. **MILLER, WILLIAM V.** "Sexual and Spiritual Ambiguity in 'The Chrysanthemums.' " *Steinbeck Quarterly*, 5 (1972), 68–75.

6123. **NOONAN, GERALD.** "A Note on 'The Chrysanthemums.' " *Modern Fiction Studies*, 15 (1969), 542.

6124. **OSBORNE, WILLIAM.** "The Education of Elisa Allen: Another Reading of John Steinbeck's 'The Chrysanthemums.' " *Interpretations*, 8 (1976), 10–15.

6125. ———. "The Texts of Steinbeck's 'The Chrysanthemums.' " *Modern Fiction Studies*, 12 (1966), 479–84.

6126. **SIMMONDS, ROY S.** "The Original Manuscript of Steinbeck's 'The Chrysanthemums.' " *Steinbeck Quarterly*, 7 (1974), 102–11.

6127. **SWEET, CHARLES A., JR.** "Ms. Elisa Allen and Steinbeck's 'The Chrysanthemums.' " *Modern Fiction Studies*, 20 (1974), 210–14.

See also 157, 188, 399, 566, 612, 6160, 6172, 6177, 6188, 6196.

"Flight"

6128. **ANDERSON, HILTON.** "Steinbeck's 'Flight.' " *The Explicator*, 28 (1969), item 12.

6129. **ANTICO, JOHN.** "A Reading of Steinbeck's 'Flight.' " *Modern Fiction Studies*, 11 (1965), 45–53.

6130. **CHAPIN, CHESTER F.** "Pepé Torres: A Steinbeck 'Natural.' " *College English*, 23 (1962), 676.

6131. **DITSKY, JOHN M.** "Steinbeck's 'Flight': The Ambiguity of Manhood." *Steinbeck Quarterly*, 5 (1972), 80–85.

6132. **GORDON, WALTER K.** "Steinbeck's 'Flight': Journey *to* or *from* Maturity?" *Studies in Short Fiction*, 3 (1966), 453–55.

6133. **GROENE, HORST.** "The Themes of Manliness and Human Dignity in Steinbeck's Initiation Story 'Flight.'" *Die Neueren Sprachen*, 72 (1973), 278–84.

6134. **JONES, WILLIAM M.** "Steinbeck's 'Flight.'" *The Explicator*, 18 (1959), item 11.

6135. **OWENS, LOUIS D.** "Steinbeck's 'Flight': Into the Jaws of Death." *Steinbeck Quarterly*, 10 (1977), 103–08.

6136. **VOGEL, DAN.** "Steinbeck's 'Flight': The Myth of Manhood." *College English*, 23 (1961), 225–26.

See also 6161, 6172, 6177, 6192.

"The Gift"

6137. **BENTON, ROBERT M.** "Realism, Growth, and Contrast in 'The Gift.'" *Steinbeck Quarterly*, 6 (1973), 3–9.

See also 6159, 6163, 6176, 6177.

"The Great Mountains"

6138. **PETERSON, RICHARD F.** "The Grail Legend and Steinbeck's 'The Great Mountains.'" *Steinbeck Quarterly*, 6 (1973), 9–15.

See also 6159.

"The Harness"

6139. **FONTENROSE, JOSEPH.** "'The Harness.'" *Steinbeck Quarterly*, 5 (1972), 94–98.

"How Edith McGillcuddy Met R. L. Stevenson"

6140. **SIMMONDS, ROY S.** "John Steinbeck, Robert Louis Stevenson, and Edith McGillcuddy." *San José Studies*, 1, no. 3 (1975), 29–39.

"How Mr. Hogan Robbed a Bank"

6141. **FRENCH, WARREN.** "Steinbeck's Winter Tale." *Modern Fiction Studies*, 11 (1965), 66–74.

"Johnny Bear"

6142. **FRENCH, WARREN.** "'Johnny Bear'—Steinbeck's 'Yellow Peril' Story." *Steinbeck Quarterly*, 5 (1972), 101–07.

See also 6176.

"The Leader of the People"

6143. Astro, Richard. "Something That Happened: A Non-Teleological Approach to 'The Leader of the People.' " *Steinbeck Quarterly*, 6 (1973), 19–23.

6144. Autrey, Max L. "Men, Mice, and Moths: Gradation in Steinbeck's 'The Leader of the People.' " *Western American Literature*, 10 (1975), 195–204.

6145. Grommon, Alfred H. "Who *Is* 'The Leader of the People'?: Helping Students Examine Fiction." *The English Journal*, 48 (1959), 449–56, 461, 476.

6146. Martin, Bruce K. " 'The Leader of the People' Reëxamined." *Studies in Short Fiction*, 8 (1971), 423–32.

6147. Morsberger, Robert E. "In Defense of 'Westering.' " *Western American Literature*, 5 (1970), 143–46.

6148. Simmonds, Roy S. "The First Publication of Steinbeck's 'The Leader of the People.' " *Steinbeck Quarterly*, 8 (1975), 13–18.

6149. West, Philip J. "Steinbeck's 'The Leader of the People': A Crisis in Style." *Western American Literature*, 5 (1970), 137–41.
See also 454, 565, 6158, 6162, 6171, 6176, 6177.

"The Murder"

6150. Davis, Robert Murray. "Steinbeck's 'The Murder.' " *Studies in Short Fiction*, 14 (1977), 63–68.

6151. Morsberger, Katharine M. and Robert E. " 'The Murder': Realism or Ritual?" In *A Study Guide to Steinbeck's* The Long Valley. Ed. Tetsumaro Hayashi. Ann Arbor, MI: Pierian Press, 1976. pp. 65–71.

6152. Simmonds, Roy S. "Steinbeck's 'The Murder': A Critical and Bibliographical Study." *Steinbeck Quarterly*, 9 (1976), 45–51.
See also 6171.

"Murder at Full Moon"

6153. Lewis, Clifford. "Jungian Psychology and the Artistic Design of John Steinbeck." *Steinbeck Quarterly*, 10 (1977), 89–97.

"The Promise"

6154. Woodward, Robert H. "The Promise of Steinbeck's 'The Promise.' " In *A Study Guide to Steinbeck's* The Long Valley. Ed. Tetsumaro Hayashi. Ann Arbor, MI: Pierian Press, 1976. pp. 97–102.

6155. ———. "Steinbeck's 'The Promise.' " *Steinbeck Quarterly*, 6 (1973), 15–19.
See also 6159.

"The Raid"

6156.   LISCA, PETER. " 'The Raid' and *In Dubious Battle.*" *Steinbeck Quarterly*, 5 (1972), 90–94.
See also 6192.

"The Red Pony" [story sequence]

6157.   GOLDSMITH, ARNOLD L. "Thematic Rhythm in *The Red Pony.*" *College English*, 26 (1965), 391–94.
6158.   HOUGHTON, DONALD E. " 'Westering' in 'Leader of the People.' " *Western American Literature*, 4 (1969), 117–24.
6159.   LEVANT, HOWARD. "John Steinbeck's *The Red Pony*: A Study in Narrative Technique." *The Journal of Narrative Technique*, 1 (1971), 77–85.
6160.   LIEDLOFF, HELMUT. *Steinbeck in German Translation: A Study of Translational Practices.* Carbondale and Edwardsville: Southern Illinois Univ. Press, 1965.
6161.   MORSBERGER, ROBERT E. "Steinbeck on Screen." In *A Study Guide to Steinbeck: A Handbook to His Major Works.* Ed. Tetsumaro Hayashi. Metuchen, NJ: Scarecrow, 1974. pp. 258–98.
6162.   PEARCE, HOWARD D. "Steinbeck's 'The Leader of the People': Dialectic and Symbol." *Papers on Language & Literature*, 8 (1972), 415–26.
6163.   SHUMAN, R. BAIRD. "Initiation Rites in Steinbeck's *The Red Pony.*" *English Journal*, 59 (1970), 1252–55.
See also 428, 597, 6171, 6172, 6175–6178, 6192, 6196.

"St. Katy, The Virgin"

6164.   KRAUSE, SYDNEY J. "Steinbeck and Mark Twain." *Steinbeck Quarterly*, 6 (1973), 104–11.
6165.   MAROVITZ, SANFORD E. "The Cryptic Raillery of 'Saint Katy the Virgin.' " *Steinbeck Quarterly*, 5 (1972), 107–12.
See also 6176.

"The Short Story of Mankind"

6166.   JONES, LAWRENCE WILLIAM. "An Uncited Post-War Steinbeck Story: 'The Short Story of Mankind.' " *Steinbeck Quarterly*, 3 (1970), 30–31.

"The Snake"

6167.   GARCIA, RELOY. "Steinbeck's 'The Snake': An Explication." *Steinbeck Quarterly*, 5 (1972), 85–90.
6168.   MAY, CHARLES E. "Myth and Mystery in Steinbeck's 'The Snake': A Jungian View." *Criticism*, 15 (1973), 322–35.

"The Time the Wolves Ate the Vice-Principal"
See also 6177.

"Vigilante"

6169. **Court, Franklin E.** "A Vigilante's Fantasy." *Steinbeck Quarterly*, 5 (1972), 98–101.
See also 6171.

"The White Quail"

6170. **Simpson, Arthur L., Jr.** " 'The White Quail': A Portrait of an Artist." *Steinbeck Quarterly*, 5 (1972), 76–80.
See also 6171, 6188.

General Studies

6171. **Barbour, Brian M.** "Steinbeck as a Short Story Writer." In *A Study Guide to Steinbeck's* The Long Valley. Ed. Tetsumaro Hayashi. Ann Arbor, MI: Pierian Press, 1976. pp. 113–28.

6172. **Benton, Robert M.** "Steinbeck's *The Long Valley* (1938)." In *A Study Guide to Steinbeck: A Handbook to His Major Works.* Ed. Tetsumaro Hayashi. Metuchen, NJ: Scarecrow, 1974. pp. 69–86.

6173. **Crouch, Steve.** *Steinbeck Country.* Palo Alto, CA: American West Publishing, 1973.

6174. **Davis, Robert Murray.** "Introduction." In *Steinbeck: A Collection of Critical Essays.* Englewood Cliffs, NJ: Prentice-Hall, 1972. pp. 1–17.

6175. **Fontenrose, Joseph.** *John Steinbeck: An Introduction and Interpretation.* New York: Barnes & Noble, 1963.

6176. **French, Warren.** *John Steinbeck.* New York: Twayne, 1961.

6177. ———. *John Steinbeck.* 2nd ed. Boston, MA: Twayne, 1975.

6178. ———. "John Steinbeck." In *American Winners of the Nobel Literary Prize.* Ed. Warren G. French and Walter E. Kidd. Norman: Univ. of Oklahoma Press, 1968. pp. 193–223.

6179. ———. "John Steinbeck: A Usable Concept of Naturalism." In *American Literary Naturalism: A Reassessment.* Ed. Yoshinobu Hakutani and Lewis Fried. Heidelberg: Carl Winter, 1975. pp. 122–35.

6180. **Garcia, Reloy.** *Steinbeck and D. H. Lawrence: Fictive Voices and the Ethical Imperative.* Steinbeck Monograph Series, no. 2. Muncie, IN: Steinbeck Society, 1972.

6181. **Gray, James.** *John Steinbeck.* Minneapolis: Univ. of Minnesota Press, 1971.

6182. ———. "John Steinbeck." In *Seven Novelists in the American Naturalist Tradition: An Introduction*. Ed. Charles Child Walcutt. Minneapolis: Univ. of Minnesota Press, 1974. pp. 205-44.

6183. HAYASHI, TETSUMARO. "Steinbeck's Reputation: What Values Does He Communicate to Us?" In *Steinbeck's Prophetic Vision of America: Proceedings of the Taylor University-Ball State University Bicentennial Steinbeck Seminar*. Ed. Tetsumaro Hayashi and Kenneth D. Swan. Upland, IN: Taylor Univ. (for The John Steinbeck Society of America), 1976. pp. 28-34.

6184. ———, ED. *John Steinbeck: A Dictionary of His Fictional Characters*. Metuchen, NJ: Scarcrow, 1976.

6185. JONES, LAWRENCE W. "A Note on Steinbeck's Earliest Stories." *Steinbeck Quarterly*, 2 (1969), 59-60.

6186. LEWIS, CLIFFORD L. "Four Dubious Steinbeck Stories." *Steinbeck Quarterly*, 5 (1972), 17-19.

6187. MARKS, LESTER JAY. *Thematic Design in the Novels of John Steinbeck*. The Hague: Mouton, 1969.

6188. MITCHELL, MARILYN L. "Steinbeck's Strong Women: Feminine Identity in the Short Stories." *Southwest Review*, 61 (1976), 304-15.

6189. O'CONNOR, RICHARD. *John Steinbeck*. New York: McGraw-Hill, 1970.

6190. PETERSON, RICHARD F. "The God in the Darkness: A Study of John Steinbeck and D. H. Lawrence." In *Steinbeck's Literary Dimension: A Guide to Comparative Studies*. Ed. Tetsumaro Hayashi. Metuchen, NJ: Scarecrow, 1973. pp. 67-82.

6191. PRATT, JOHN CLARK. *John Steinbeck*. Grand Rapids, MI: Eerdmans, 1970.

6192. SATYANARAYANA, M. R. " 'And Then the Child Becomes a Man': Three Initiation Stories of John Steinbeck." *Indian Journal of American Studies*, 1, no. 4 (1971), 87-93.

6193. SIMMONDS, ROY S. *Steinbeck's Literary Achievement*. Steinbeck Monograph Series, no. 6. Muncie, IN: John Steinbeck Society of America, 1976.

6194. STREET, WEBSTER. "John Steinbeck: A Reminiscence." In *Steinbeck: The Man and His Work*. Ed. Richard Astro and Tetsumaro Hayashi. Corvallis: Oregon State Univ. Press, 1971. pp. 35-41.

6195. VALJEAN, NELSON. *John Steinbeck, The Errant Knight: An Intimate Biography of His California Years*. San Francisco, CA: Chronicle Books, 1975.

6196. WATT, F. W. *Steinbeck*. Edinburgh: Oliver and Boyd, 1962.

Interviews

6197. STEINBECK, JOHN. "The Art of Fiction XLV." *The Paris Review*, no. 48 (1969), pp. 161-88; no. 63 (1975), pp. 180-94.

Bibliography

6198. BEEBE, MAURICE, AND JACKSON R. BRYER. "Criticism of John Steinbeck: A Selected Checklist." *Modern Fiction Studies*, 11 (1965), 90-103.

6199. FRENCH, WARREN. "John Steinbeck." In *Fifteen Modern American Authors: A Survey of Research and Criticism*. Ed. Jackson R. Bryer. Durham, NC: Duke Univ. Press, 1969. pp. 369-87.

6200. ———. "John Steinbeck." In *Sixteen Modern American Authors: A Survey of Research and Criticism*. Ed. Jackson R. Bryer. Durham, NC: Duke Univ. Press, 1974. pp. 499-527.

6201. HAYASHI, TETSUMARO. "A Checklist of Steinbeck Criticism after 1965: First Supplement to Tetsumaro Hayashi's *John Steinbeck: A Concise Bibliography (1930-1965)*." *Steinbeck Newsletter*, 1, no. 3 (1968), 1-9.

6202. ———. *John Steinbeck: A Concise Bibliography (1930-65)*. Metuchen, NJ: Scarecrow, 1967.

6203. ———. *A New Steinbeck Bibliography, 1929-1971*. Metuchen, NJ: Scarcrow, 1973.

6204. ———. "A Selected Bibliography." In *Steinbeck's Literary Dimension: A Guide to Comparative Studies*. Ed. Tetsumaro Hayashi. Metuchen, NJ: Scarecrow, 1973. pp. 174-79.

6205. ———. "Steinbeck Scholarship: Recent Trends in the United States." In *Steinbeck's Literary Dimension: A Guide to Comparative Studies*. Ed. Tetsumaro Hayashi. Metuchen, NJ: Scarecrow, 1973. pp. 168-73.

6206. ———, AND DONALD L. SIEFKER. *The Special Steinbeck Collection of the Ball State University Library: A Bibliographical Handbook*. Muncie, IN: Steinbeck Society of America, 1972.

6207. ———, AND ROY S. SIMMONDS. "John Steinbeck's British Publications." *Steinbeck Quarterly*, 8 (1975), 79-89.

6208. ———, ED. *Steinbeck Criticism: A Review of Book-Length Studies (1939-1973)*. Steinbeck Monograph Series, no. 4. Muncie, IN: Steinbeck Society, 1974.

6209. LISCA, PETER. "A Survey of Steinbeck Criticism to 1971." In *Steinbeck's Literary Dimension: A Guide to Comparative Studies*. Ed. Tetsumaro Hayashi. Metuchen, NJ: Scarecrow, 1973. pp. 148-67.

6210. SIMMONDS, ROY S. "John Steinbeck: Works Published in the British Magazine *Argosy*." *Steinbeck Quarterly*, 4 (1971), 101-05.

6211. **STEELE, JOAN.** "John Steinbeck: A Checklist of Biographical, Critical, and Bibliographical Material." *Bulletin of Bibliography and Magazine Notes*, 24 (1965), 149–52, 162–63.

STEPHENS, MICHAEL

General Studies

6212. **KLINKOWITZ, JEROME.** "Michael Stephens' Superfiction." *TriQuarterly*, no. 34 (1975), pp. 219–32.

STERN, RICHARD

Interviews

6213. **RAEDER, ROBERT L.** "An Interview with Richard G. Stern." *Chicago Review*, 18, nos. 3–4 (1966), 170–75.

6214. **RIMA, LARRY.** "An Interview with Richard Stern." *Chicago Review*, 28, no. 3 (1977), 145–48.

STODDARD, ELIZABETH DREW BARSTOW

Bibliography

6215. **KELLER, DEAN H.** "Mrs. Stoddard's 'Stories.'" *American Notes & Queries*, 7 (1969), 131–33.

STONE, ALMA

"I'm Waving Tomorrow"

See 348.

STONE, WILLIAM LEETE

"The Grave of the Indian King"

See 26.

"Lake St. Sacrament"

See 26.

"Mercy Disborough"

See 26.

"The Skeleton Hand"

See 26.

"The Spectre Fire-Ship"

See 26.

STOUT, REX

General Studies

6216. GERHARDT, MIA I. " 'Homicide West': Some Observations on the Nero Wolfe Stories of Rex Stout." *English Studies*, 49 (1968), 107–27.

Interviews

6217. FRANKEL, HASKEL. "Interview with Rex Stout." *Saturday Review*, 48 (9 Oct. 1965), 55.

STOWE, HARRIET BEECHER

"Love versus *Law"*

See 6218.

General Studies

6218. ADAMS, JOHN R. *Harriet Beecher Stowe*. New York: Twayne, 1963.

Bibliography

6219. ADAMS, JOHN R. "Harriet Beecher Stowe (1811–1896)." *American Literary Realism, 1870–1910*, 2 (1969), 160–64.

6220. ASHTON, JEAN W. *Harriet Beecher Stowe: A Reference Guide*. Boston, MA: G. K. Hall, 1977.

6221. HILDRETH, MARGARET HOLBROOK. *Harriet Beecher Stowe: A Bibliography*. Hamden, CT: Archon Books, 1976.

STREET, JAMES

Bibliography

6222. COOPER, RUTH. "James Street: A Biographical and Bibliographical Study." *Notes on Mississippi Writers*, 9 (1976), 10–23.

STUART, JESSE

"Angel in the Pasture"

See 6224.

"Another April"

6223. LEAVELL, FRANK H. "The Boy Narrator in Jesse Stuart's 'Another April.' " *Jack London Newsletter*, 8 (1975), 83–91.
See also 6224.

General Studies

6224. **BLAIR, EVERETTA LOVE.** *Jesse Stuart: His Life and Works.* Columbia: Univ. of South Carolina Press, 1967.

6225. **CLARKE, KENNETH.** "Jesse Stuart's Use of Folklore." In *Jesse Stuart: Essays on His Work.* Ed. J. R. LeMaster and Mary Washington Clarke. Lexington: Univ. Press of Kentucky, 1977. pp. 117–29.

6226. **CLARKE, MARY WASHINGTON.** *Jesse Stuart's Kentucky.* New York: McGraw-Hill, 1968.

6227. _____. "Jesse Stuart's Use of Local Legends." *Jack London Newsletter,* 10 (1977), 63–70.

6228. **FOSTER, RUEL E.** "Jesse Stuart, Short Story Writer." In *Reality of Myth: Essays in American Literature in Memory of Richmond Croom Beatty.* Ed. William E. Walker and Robert L. Welker. Nashville, TN: Vanderbilt Univ. Press, 1964. pp. 145–60.

6229. _____. "Jesse Stuart's Way With Short Fiction." *Kansas Quarterly,* 9, no. 2 (1977), 21–29.

6230. _____. "Jesse Stuart's W-Hollow—Microcosm of the Appalachians." *Kansas Quarterly,* 2, no. 2 (1970), 66–72.

6231. _____. "The Short Stories of Jesse Stuart." In *Jesse Stuart: Essays on His Work.* Ed. J. R. LeMaster and Mary Washington Clarke. Lexington: Univ. Press of Kentucky, 1977. pp. 40–53.

6232. **GIBBS, SYLVIA.** "Jesse Stuart: The Dark Hills and Beyond." *Jack London Newsletter,* 4 (1971), 56–69.

6233. **HALL, WADE.** "Humor in Jesse Stuart's Fiction." In *Jesse Stuart: Essays on His Work.* Ed. J. R. LeMaster and Mary Washington Clarke. Lexington: Univ. Press of Kentucky, 1977. pp. 89–102.

6234. **MILLER, JIM WAYNE.** "The Gift Outright: W-Hollow." In *Jesse Stuart: Essays on His Work.* Ed. J. R. LeMaster and Mary Washington Clarke. Lexington: Univ. Press of Kentucky, 1977. pp. 103–16.

6235. **RICHARDSON, H. EDWARD.** "Stuart Country: The Man-Artist and the Myth." In *Jesse Stuart: Essays on His Work.* Ed. J. R. LeMaster and Mary Washington Clarke. Lexington: Univ. Press of Kentucky, 1977. pp. 1–18.

6236. **STUART, JESSE.** *A Jesse Stuart Reader: Stories and Poems Selected and Introduced by Jesse Stuart.* With an intro. by Max Bogart. New York: McGraw-Hill, 1963.

Interviews

6237. **PERRY, DICK.** *Reflections of Jesse Stuart on a Land of Many Moods.* New York: McGraw-Hill, 1971.

Bibliography

6238. **WOODBRIDGE, HENSLEY C.** *"Jesse and Jane Stuart: A Bibliography,* Supplement." *Jack London Newsletter,* 2 (1969), 118–20; 3 (1970), 37–41, 65–69, 132–34, 101; 4 (1971), 70–73, 115–18, 161–63; 5 (1972), 45–47, 139–41, 184–85; 6 (1973), 55–56, 89–90, 163–64; 7 (1974), 55–57, 90–91, 132–33; 8 (1975), 32–33, 92–93, 138–41.

6239. _____. *Jesse Stuart: A Bibliography.* Harrogate, TN: Lincoln Memorial Univ. Press, 1960.

6240. _____. "Jesse Stuart: A Critical Bibliography." *The American Book Collector,* 16, no. 6 (1966), 11–13.

STUART, RUTH [McENERY]

"Uncle Mingo's 'Speculations' "

See 571.

STURGEON, THEODORE

"Bulkhead"

See 353.

"Slow Sculpture"

See 303.

"The World Well Lost"

See 6241.

General Studies

6241. **FRIEND, BEVERLY.** "The Sturgeon Connection." In *Voices for the Future: Essays on Major Science Fiction Writers.* Ed. Thomas D. Clareson. Bowling Green, OH: Bowling Green Univ. Popular Press, 1976. pp. 153–66.

6242. **STURGEON, THEODORE.** "Future Writers in a Future World." In *The Craft of Science Fiction.* Ed. Reginald Bretnor. New York: Harper & Row, 1976. pp. 89–101.

STYRON, WILLIAM

"The Enormous Window"

See 6244.

"The Long Dark Road"

See 6244.

"Sun on the River"

6243.   LEON, PHILIP W. *"The Lost Boy* and a Lost Girl." *The Southern Literary Journal*, 9, no. 1 (1976), 61–69.

General Studies

6244.   RATNER, MARC L. *William Styron*. New York: Twayne, 1972.

Interviews

6245.   MERAS, PHYLLIS. An Interview with William Styron. *Saturday Review*, 50 (7 Oct. 1967), 30.
6246.   MORRIS, ROBERT K. "An Interview with William Styron." In *The Achievement of William Styron*. Ed. Robert K. Morris and Irving Malin. Athens: Univ. of Georgia Press, 1975. pp. 24–50.
6247.   PLIMPTON, GEORGE. "William Styron: A Shared Ordeal." *The New York Times Book Review*, 8 Oct. 1967, pp. 2–3, 30, 32, 34.
6248.   [RAHV, PHILIP]. "The Editor Interviews William Styron." *Modern Occasions*, 1 (1971), 501–10.

Bibliography

6249.   BRYER, JACKSON R. "William Styron: A Bibliography." In *The Achievement of William Styron*. Ed. Robert K. Morris and Irving Malin. Athens: Univ. of Georgia Press, 1975. pp. 242–77.
6250.   GALLOWAY, DAVID D. "A William Styron Checklist." In *The Absurd Hero in American Fiction: Updike, Styron, Bellow, Salinger*. Austin: Univ. of Texas Press, 1966. pp. 200–10.
6251.   ———. "A William Styron Checklist." In *The Absurd Hero in American Fiction: Updike, Styron, Bellow, Salinger*. Rev. ed. Austin: Univ. of Texas Press, 1970. pp. 208–20.
6252.   SCHNEIDER, HAROLD W. "Two Bibliographies: Saul Bellow/William Styron." *Critique*, 3, no. 3 (1960), 71–91.
6253.   WEST, JAMES L. W., III. *William Styron: A Descriptive Bibliography*. Boston, MA: G. K. Hall, 1977.

SUCKOW, RUTH

"Auntie Bissel"

See 6256.

"Elegy for Alma's Aunt Amy"

See 6254.

"Eltha"

See 6254.

"Eminence"

See 6256.

"Four Generations"

See 6254, 6256.

"Golden Wedding"

See 6254, 6256.

"Good Pals"

See 6256.

"A Home-Coming"

See 6254.

"Mame"

See 6254, 6256.

"Mrs. Vogel and Ollie"

See 6254.

"A Rural Community"

See 6256.

"Spinster and Cat"

See 6254.

"A Start in Life"

See 6256.

"Uprooted"

See 6254, 6256.

"What Have I"

See 6254.

General Studies

6254. KISSANE, LEEDICE MCANELLY. *Ruth Suckow.* New York: Twayne, 1969.

6255. MUEHL, LOIS B. "Ruth Suckow's Art of Fiction." *Books at Iowa*, no. 13 (1970), pp. 3–12.

6256. OMRČANIN, MARGARET STEWART. *Ruth Suckow: A Critical Study of Her Fiction.* Philadelphia, PA: Dorrance, 1972.

SUKENICK, RONALD

"The Death of the Novel"

See 328, 6257.

"Momentum"

See 239.

General Studies

6257. **KLINKOWITZ, JEROME.** "Getting Real: Making It (Up) with Ronald Sukenick." *Chicago Review*, 23, no. 3 (1972), 73–82.

6258. **NOEL, DANIEL C.** "Tales of Fictive Power: Dreaming and Imagination in Ronald Sukenick's Postmodern Fiction." *boundary 2*, 5 (1976), 117–35.

Interviews

6259. **BELLAMY, JOE DAVID.** "Imagination as Perception: An Interview with Ronald Sukenick." *Chicago Review*, 23, no. 3 (1972), 59–72.

SWADOS, HARVEY

General Studies

6260. **SHAPIRO, CHARLES.** "Harvey Swados: Private Stories and Public Fiction." In *Contemporary American Novelists*. Ed. Harry T. Moore. Carbondale: Southern Illinois Univ. Press, 1964. pp. 182–92, 232.

SWEET, ALEXANDER E.

General Studies

6261. **SPECK, ERNEST B.** "Alex. Sweet, Texas Humorist." *Southwestern American Literature*, 3 (1973), 49–60.

TALIAFERRO, HARDEN E.

General Studies

6262. **COFFIN, TRISTRAM P.** "Harden E. Taliaferro and the Use of Folklore by American Literary Figures." *The South Atlantic Quarterly*, 64 (1965), 241–46.

6263. **WALSER, RICHARD.** "Skitt Taliaferro: Facts and Reappraisal." *American Humor*, 4, no. 1 (1977), 7–10.

TAYLOR, BAYARD

General Studies

6264. **WERMUTH, PAUL C.** *Bayard Taylor.* New York: Twayne, 1973.

TAYLOR, PETER

"Allegiance"

See 6273.

"At the Drugstore"

6265. **PINKERTON, JAN.** "A Critical Distortion of Peter Taylor's 'At the Drugstore.' " *Notes on Contemporary Literature,* 1, no. 4 (1971), 6–7.
See also 6273, 6279.

"Bad Dreams"

See 6273.

"The Captain's Son"

See 6272, 6275.

"The Dark Walk"

See 6273.

"Dean of Men"

See 399.

"The End of Play"

See 6273.

"The Fancy Woman"

6266. **OVERMYER, JANET.** "Sex and the Fancy Woman." *Notes on Contemporary Literature,* 4, no. 4 (1974), 8–10.
See also 6270, 6273.

"A Friend and Protector"

See 6273.

"Guests"

See 6273.

"Heads of Houses"

See 6273.

"In the Miro District"

See 6272.

"Je suis perdu"

See 6269, 6273.

"The Little Cousins"

See 6269, 6273.

"A Long Fourth"

See 6270, 6273.

"Miss Leonora When Last Seen"

6267.   **BROOKS, CLEANTH.** "The Southern Temper." *Archiv für das Studium der Neueren Sprachen und Literaturen*, 206 (May 1969), 1–15.
See also 6273, 6279.

"Nerves"

See 6273.

"1939"

See 6269, 6273.

"The Other Times"

See 6273.

"An Overwhelming Question"

See 6273.

"Promise of Rain"

See 6273.

"Rain in the Heart"

See 6273.

"Reservations: A Love Story"

See 564, 6273.

"The Scoutmaster"

See 6273.

"Sky Line"

See 6270, 6273, 6279.

"A Spinster's Tale"

6268. PINKERTON, JAN. "The Vagaries of Taste and Peter Taylor's 'A Spinster's Tale.' " *Kansas Quarterly*, 9, no. 2 (1977), 81–85.
See also 6270, 6273.

"A Strange Story"

See 6273.

"Their Losses"

See 278, 6273.

"There"

See 6273.

"The Throughway"

See 6273.

"Two Ladies in Retirement"

See 6269, 6273.

"Two Pilgrims"

See 6273.

"Venus, Cupid, Folly and Time"

See 6273.

"A Walled Garden"

See 6279.

"What You Hear From 'Em?"

See 267, 6273.

"A Wife of Nashville"

See 6273.

General Studies

6269. BLUM, MORGAN. "Peter Taylor: Self-Limitation in Fiction." *The Sewanee Review*, 70 (1962), 559–78.
6270. BROWN, ASHLEY. "The Early Fiction of Peter Taylor."
The Sewanee Review, 70 (1962), 588–602.
6271. ———. "Peter Taylor at Sixty." *Shenandoah*, 28, no. 2
(1977), 48–53.
6272. GOWER, HERSCHEL. "The Nashville Stories." *Shenandoah*,
28, no. 2 (1977), 37–47.

6273. **Griffith, Albert J.** *Peter Taylor.* New York: Twayne, 1970.

6274. **Howard, Richard.** " 'Urgent Need and Unbearable Fear.' " *Shenandoah*, 24, no. 2 (1973), 44–47.

6275. **Lytle, Andrew.** "On a Birthday." *Shenandoah*, 28, no. 2 (1977), 11–17.

6276. **Peden, William.** "A Hard and Admirable Toughness: The Stories of Peter Taylor." *The Hollins Critic*, 7, no. 1 (1970), 1–9.

6277. **Pinkerton, Jan.** "The Non-Regionalism of Peter Taylor." *The Georgia Review*, 24 (1970), 432–40.

6278. **Powers, J. F.** "Peter Taylor's New Book." *Shenandoah*, 28, no. 2 (1977), 84–85.

6279. **Schuler, Barbara.** "The House of Peter Taylor." *Critique*, 9, no. 3 (1967), 6–18.

Interviews

6280. **Goodwin, Stephen.** "An Interview with Peter Taylor." *Shenandoah*, 24, no. 2 (1973), 3–20.

6281. **Smith, James Penny.** "A Peter Taylor Checklist." *Critique*, 9, no. 3 (1967), 31–36.

THANET, OCTAVE

General Studies

*6282. **McMichael, George.** *Journey to Obscurity: The Life of Octave Thanet.* Lincoln: Univ. of Nebraska Press, 1965.

THOMASON, JOHN W., JR.

General Studies

*6283. **Norwood, W. D., Jr.** *John W. Thomason, Jr.* Austin, TX: Steck-Vaughn, 1969.

THOMPSON, MAURICE

General Studies

6284. **Wheeler, Otis B.** *The Literary Career of Maurice Thompson.* Baton Rouge: Louisiana State Univ. Press, 1965.

THORPE, T[HOMAS] B[ANGS]

"The Big Bear of Arkansas"

6285. **Lemay, J. A. Leo.** "The Text, Tradition, and Themes of

'The Big Bear of Arkansas.' " *American Literature*, 47 (1975), 321–42.

See also 19, 20, 64, 87, 90, 383, 460, 6286.

"The Devil's Summer Retreat in Arkansas"

See 6286.

"The Disgraced Scalp-Lock"

See 64, 6286.

"Tom Owen, The Bee Hunter"

See 6286.

General Studies

6286. **RICKELS, MILTON**. *Thomas Bangs Thorpe, Humorist of the Old Southwest*. Baton Rouge: Louisiana State Univ. Press, 1962.

THURBER, JAMES
"Am Not I Your Rosalind?"

See 6302, 6303.

"Aunt Ida"

See 6304.

"Back to the Grades"

See 6303.

"The Beast in the Dingle"

See 6301, 6314.

"A Box to Hide In"

See 6303.

"The Breaking Up of the Winships"

See 6314.

"The Cane in the Corridor"

See 6303.

"The Car We Had to Push"

See 6303, 6304.

"The Case for the Daydreamer"

See 6303.

"The Cat in the Lifeboat"

See 6314.

"The Catbird Seat"

6287. **DIAS, EARL J.** "The Upside-Down World of Thurber's 'The Catbird Seat.' " *The CEA Critic*, 30, no. 5 (1968), 6–7.
6288. **KANE, THOMAS S.** "A Note on the Chronology of 'The Catbird Seat.' " *The CEA Critic*, 30, no. 7 (1968), 8–9.
See also 178, 384, 478, 565, 566, 6303, 6314.

"Do You Want to Make Something Out of It?"

See 6307.

"Doc Marlowe"

See 6303, 6304, 6314.

"File and Forget"

See 6303.

"A Friend to Alexander"

See 6302, 6303.

"The Gentleman Is Cold"

See 6314.

"The Greatest Man in the World"

See 6303, 6309, 6314.

"Josephine Has Her Day"

See 6303.

"The Ladies' and Gentlemen's Guide to Modern English Usage"

See 6307, 6314.

"The Last Clock"

See 6308.

"The Lover and His Lass"

6289. **BERNSTEIN, JARED, AND KENNETH LEE PIKE.** "The Emic Structure of Individuals in Relation to Dialogue." In *Grammars and Descriptions: Studies in Text Theory and Text Analysis*. Ed. Teun A. van Dijk and János S. Petöfi. Berlin: Walter de Gruyter, 1977. pp. 1–10.
6290. **FOWLER, ROGER.** "Cohesive, Progressive, and Localizing Aspects of Text Structure." In *Grammars and Descriptions: Stud-*

ies in Text Theory and Text Analysis. Ed. Teun A. van Dijk and János S. Petöfi. Berlin: Walter de Gruyter, 1977. pp. 64–84.

6291. **HALLIDAY, M. A. K.** "Text as Semantic Choice in Social Contexts." In *Grammars and Descriptions: Studies in Text Theory and Text Analysis.* Ed. Teun A. van Dijk and János S. Petöfi. Berlin: Walter de Gruyter, 1977. pp. 176–225.

6292. **LONGACRE, R. E.** "A Taxonomic Deep and Surface Structure Analysis of 'The Lover and His Lass.' " In *Grammars and Descriptions: Studies in Text Theory and Text Analysis.* Ed. Teun A. van Dijk and János S. Petöfi. Berlin: Walter de Gruyter, 1977. pp. 314–41.

6293. **PALEK, BOHUMIL.** "Reference and Text." In *Grammars and Descriptions: Studies in Text Theory and Text Analysis.* Ed. Teun A. van Dijk and János S. Petöfi. Berlin: Walter de Gruyter, 1977. pp. 359–94.

6294. **VAN DIJK, TEUN A.** "Connectives in Text Grammar and Text Logic." In *Grammars and Descriptions: Studies in Text Theory and Text Analysis.* Ed. Teun A. van Dijk and János S. Petöfi. Berlin: Walter de Gruyter, 1977. pp. 11–63.

"The Luck of Jad Peters"

See 6303, 6304.

"The Macbeth Murder Mystery"

See 454.

"Menaces in May"

See 6307.

"Mr. and Mrs. Monroe"

See 6314.

"Mr. Preble Gets Rid of His Wife"

See 6303.

"More Alarms at Night"

See 6303.

"The Night the Ghost Got In"

See 6303.

"One Is a Wanderer"

See 6303, 6304.

"The Ordeal of Mr. Matthews"

See 6303.

"The Other Room"

See 6303.

"The Pet Department"

See 6314.

"The Remarkable Case of Mr. Bruhl"

See 6303.

"The Secret Life of Walter Mitty"

6295. **ELLIS, JAMES.** "The Allusions in 'The Secret Life of Walter Mitty.' " *English Journal*, 54 (1965), 310–13.
6296. **FITZ GERALD, GREGORY.** "An Example of Associationism as an Organizational Technique from Thurber's 'Walter Mitty.' " *The CEA Critic*, 31, no. 4 (1969), 11.
6297. **LINDNER, CARL M.** "Thurber's Walter Mitty—The Underground American Hero." *The Georgia Review*, 28 (1974), 283–89.
6298. **SATTERFIELD, LEON.** "Thurber's 'The Secret Life of Walter Mitty.' " *The Explicator*, 27 (1969), item 57.
6299. **SUNDELL, CARL.** "The Architecture of Walter Mitty's Secret Life." *English Journal*, 56 (1967), 1284–87.
See also 394, 454, 479, 548, 6301, 6303, 6307, 6309, 6310, 6314.

"Something to Say"

See 6303, 6314.

"Teacher's Pet"

See 6309, 6314.

"The Unicorn in the Garden"

See 466.

"The Waters of the Moon"

See 6308, 6314.

"The Whip-poor-will"

See 6302, 6303, 6307, 6314.

"The Wood Duck"

See 6314.

"*You Could Look It Up*"

See 399.

General Studies

6300. **BALDWIN, ALICE.** "James Thurber's Compounds." *Language and Style*, 3 (1970), 185–96.

6301. **BERNSTEIN, BURTON.** *Thurber: A Biography.* New York: Dodd, Mead, 1975.

6302. **BLACK, STEPHEN A.** "The Claw of the Sea-Puss: James Thurber's Sense of Experience." *Wisconsin Studies in Contemporary Literature*, 5 (1964), 222–36.

6303. ———. *James Thurber: His Masquerades.* The Hague: Mouton, 1970.

6304. ———. "Thurber's Education for Hard Times." *The University Review* (Kansas City), 32 (1966), 257–67.

6305. **BRANSCOMB, LEWIS.** "James Thurber and Oral History at Ohio State University." *Lost Generation Journal*, 3, no. 1 (1975), 16–19.

6306. **HASLEY, LOUIS.** "James Thurber: Artist in Humor." *The South Atlantic Quarterly*, 73 (1974), 504–15.

6307. **HOLMES, CHARLES S.** *The Clocks of Columbus: The Literary Career of James Thurber.* New York: Atheneum, 1972.

6308. ———. "James Thurber and the Art of Fantasy." *The Yale Review*, 55 (1965), 17–33.

6309. **MORSBERGER, ROBERT E.** *James Thurber.* New York: Twayne, 1964.

6310. **NENADÁL, RADOSLAV.** "E. Hemingway and J. Thurber: Their Part in the Process of 'The Patterning of a Modern Hero.' " In *Acta Universitatis Carolinae—Philologica 5.* Prague Studies in English, Vol. 14. Prague: Univ. Karlova, 1971. pp. 75–88.

6311. **SCHOLL, PETER A.** "Thurber's Walter Ego—The Little Man Hero." *Lost Generation Journal*, 3, no. 1 (1975), 8–9, 26.

6312. **THURBER, JAMES.** "The Future, If Any, of Comedy; or Where Do We Non-Go from Here?" *The Times* (London) *Literary Supplement*, 11 Aug. 1961, pp. 512–13.

6313. **TIBBETTS, ROBERT.** "The Thurber Collection at Ohio State University." *Lost Generation Journal*, 3, no. 1 (1975), 12–15, 38.

6314. **TOBIAS, RICHARD C.** *The Art of James Thurber.* Athens: Ohio Univ. Press, 1969.

6315. ———. "Thurber in Paris: 'Clocks' Kept Different Time." *Lost Generation Journal*, 3, no. 1 (1975), 2–6.

6316. **TRIESCH, MANFRED.** "Men and Animals: James Thurber and the Conversion of a Literary Genre." *Studies in Short Fiction*, 3 (1966), 307–13.

Bibliography

6317. BOWDEN, EDWIN T. *James Thurber: A Bibliography*. Columbus: Ohio State Univ. Press, 1968.

6318. ———. "*The Thurber Carnival*: Bibliography and Printing History." *Texas Studies in Literature and Language*, 9 (1968), 555–66.

TOOMER, JEAN

"*Avey*"

See 6321, 6329, 6344.

"*Becky*"

See 192, 6321, 6325, 6329, 6338.

"*Blood-Burning Moon*"

See 192, 263, 337, 511, 6322, 6324, 6325, 6329, 6338.

"*Bona and Paul*"

6319. CHRIST, JACK M. "Jean Toomer's 'Bona and Paul.'" *Negro American Literature Forum*, 9 (1975), 44–46.
See also 192, 386, 6321, 6325, 6329, 6360.

"*Box Seat*"

See 192, 296, 387, 6322, 6323, 6328, 6329, 6360, 6363.

Cane

6320. ACKLEY, DONALD G. "Theme and Vision in Jean Toomer's *Cane*." *Studies in Black Literature*, 1, no. 1 (1970), 45–65.

6321. BAKER, HOUSTON A., JR. "Journey toward Black Art: Jean Toomer's *Cane*." In *Singers of Daybreak: Studies in Black American Literature*. Washington, DC: Howard Univ. Press, 1974. pp. 53–80, 97–99.

6322. BELL, BERNARD W. "Portrait of the Artist as High Priest of Soul: Jean Toomer's *Cane*." *Black World*, 23, no. 11 (1974), 4–19, 92–97.

6323. BERGHAHN, MARION. *Images of Africa in Black American Literature*. London: Macmillan, 1977.

6324. BLACKWELL, LOUISE. "Jean Toomer's *Cane* and Biblical Myth." *CLA Journal*, 16 (1974), 535–42.

6325. BLAKE, SUSAN L. "The Spectatorial Artist and the Structure of *Cane*." *CLA Journal*, 16 (1974), 516–34.

6326. BONTEMPS, ARNA. "Introduction." In *Cane*, by Jean Toomer. New York: Harper & Row, 1969. pp. vii–xvi.

6327. ———. "The Negro Renaissance: Jean Toomer and the Harlem Writers of the 1920's." In *Anger, and Beyond: The Negro Writer in the United States.* Ed. Herbert Hill. New York: Harper & Row, 1966. pp. 20–36.

6328. CANCEL, RAFAEL A. "Male and Female Interrelationships in Toomer's *Cane.*" *Negro American Literature Forum*, 5 (1971), 25–31.

6329. CHASE, PATRICIA. "The Women in *Cane.*" *CLA Journal*, 14 (1971), 259–73.

6330. DAVIS, CHARLES T. "Jean Toomer and the South: Region and Race as Elements within a Literary Imagination." *Studies in the Literary Imagination*, 7, no. 2 (1974), 23–37.

6331. DICKERSON, MARY JANE. "Sherwood Anderson and Jean Toomer: A Literary Relationship." *Studies in American Fiction*, 1 (1973), 163–75.

6332. DUNCAN, BOWIE. "Jean Toomer's *Cane*: A Modern Black Oracle." *CLA Journal*, 15 (1972), 323–33.

6333. DURHAM, FRANK. "Jean Toomer's Vision of the Southern Negro." *Southern Humanities Review*, 6 (1972), 13–22.

6334. ———. "Preface." In *The Merrill Studies in* Cane. Ed. Frank Durham. Columbus, OH: Merrill, 1971. pp. iii–ix.

6335. EMERSON, O. B. "Cultural Nationalism in Afro-American Literature." In *The Cry of Home: Cultural Nationalism and the Modern Writer.* Ed. H. Ernest Lewald. Knoxville: Univ. of Tennessee Press, 1972. pp. 211–44.

6336. FARRISON, W. EDWARD. "Jean Toomer's *Cane* Again." *CLA Journal*, 15 (1972), 295–302.

6337. FAULKNER, HOWARD. "The Buried Life: Jean Toomer's *Cane.*" *Studies in Black Literature*, 7, no. 1 (1976), 1–5.

6338. FISCHER, WILLIAM C. "The Aggregate Man in Jean Toomer's *Cane.*" *Studies in the Novel*, 3 (1971), 190–215.

6339. FISHER, ALICE POINDEXTER. "The Influence of Ouspensky's *Tertium Organum* upon Jean Toomer's *Cane.*" *CLA Journal*, 17 (1974), 504–15.

6340. FOREMAN, RONALD C., JR. "The '20's and the Blues/Jazz of Black Fiction." In *Proceedings of the Fifth National Convention of the Popular Culture Association, St. Louis, Missouri, March 20–22, 1975.* Ed. Michael T. Marsden. Bowling Green, OH: Bowling Green Univ. Popular Press, 1975. pp. 1559–73.

6341. GRANT, SISTER MARY KATHRYN. "Images of Celebration in *Cane.*" *Negro American Literature Forum*, 5 (1971), 32–34, 36.

6342. HELBLING, MARK. "Sherwood Anderson and Jean Toomer." *Negro American Literature Forum*, 9 (1975), 35–39.

6343. HOWELL, ELMO. "Jean Toomer's Hamlet: A Note on *Cane.*" *Interpretations*, 9 (1977), 70–73.

6344. INNES, CATHERINE L. "The Unity of Jean Toomer's *Cane.*" *CLA Journal*, 15 (1972), 306–22.

6345. JACKSON, BLYDEN. "Jean Toomer's *Cane*: An Issue of Genre." With an intro. and afternote by Warren French. In *The Twenties: Fiction, Poetry, Drama.* Ed. Warren French. Deland, FL: Everett/Edwards, 1975. pp. 317–33.

6346. KERMAN, CYNTHIA E. "Jean Toomer?—Enigma." *Indian Journal of American Studies*, 7, no. 1 (1977), 67–78.

6347. KRAFT, JAMES. "Jean Toomer's *Cane.*" *The Markham Review*, 2 (1970), 61–63.

6348. KRAMER, VICTOR A. "The 'Mid-Kingdom' of Crane's 'Black Tambourine' and Toomer's *Cane.*" *CLA Journal*, 16 (1974), 486–97.

6349. KRASNY, MICHAEL. "The Aesthetic Structure of Jean Toomer's *Cane.*" *Negro American Literature Forum*, 9 (1975), 42–43.

6350. LARSON, CHARLES R. "Reconsideration: *Cane* by Jean Toomer." *The New Republic*, 174, no. 25 (1976), 30–32.

6351. LIEBER, TODD. "Design and Movement in *Cane.*" *CLA Journal*, 13 (1969), 35–50.

6352. McKEEVER, BENJAMIN F. "*Cane* as Blues." *Negro American Literature Forum*, 4 (1970), 61–63.

6353. MacKETHAN, LUCINDA H. "Jean Toomer's *Cane*: A Pastoral Problem." *The Mississippi Quarterly*, 28 (1975), 423–34.

6354. MARTIN, ODETTE C. "*Cane*: Method and Myth." *Obsidian*, 2, no. 1 (1976), 5–20.

6355. MATTHEWS, GEORGE C. "Toomer's *Cane*: The Artist and His World." *CLA Journal*, 16 (1974), 543–59.

6356. RANKIN, WILLIAM. "Ineffability in the Fiction of Jean Toomer and Katherine Mansfield." In *Renaissance and Modern: Essays in Honor of Edwin M. Moseley.* Ed. Murray J. Levith. Saratoga Springs, NY: Skidmore College, 1976, pp. 160–71.

6357. REILLY, JOHN M. "The Search for Black Redemption: Jean Toomer's *Cane.*" *Studies in the Novel*, 2 (1970), 312–24.

6358. RILEY, ROBERTA. "Search for Identity and Artistry." *CLA Journal*, 16 (1974), 480–85.

6359. SCRUGGS, CHARLES. "Jean Toomer: Fugitive." *American Literature*, 47 (1975), 84–96.

6360. _____. "The Mark of Cain and the Redemption of Art: A Study in Theme and Structure of Jean Toomer's *Cane.*" *American Literature*, 44 (1972), 276–91.

6361. SINGH, AMRITJIT. *The Novels of the Harlem Renaissance: Twelve Black Writers, 1923-1933.* University Park: Pennsylvania State Univ. Press, 1976.

6362. SPOFFORD, WILLIAM K. "The Unity of Part One of Jean Toomer's *Cane.*" *The Markham Review*, 3 (1972), 58-60.

6363. TAYLOR, CLYDE. "The Second Coming of Jean Toomer." *Obsidian*, 1, no. 3 (1975), 37-57.

6364. THOMPSON, LARRY E. "Jean Toomer: As Modern Man." In *The Harlem Renaissance Remembered: Essays.* Ed. Arna Bontemps. New York: Dodd, Mead, 1972. pp. 51-62, 279.

6365. TURNER, DARWIN T. "An Intersection of Paths: Correspondence Between Jean Toomer and Sherwood Anderson." *CLA Journal*, 16 (1974), 455-67.

6366. ———. "Introduction." In *Cane*, by Jean Toomer. New York: Liveright, 1975. pp. ix–xxv.

6367. ———. "Jean Toomer's *Cane.*" *Negro Digest*, 18, no. 3 (1969), 54-61.

6368. VAN MOL, KAY R. "Primitivism and Intellect in Toomer's *Cane* and McKay's *Banana Bottom*: The Need for an Integrated Black Consciousness." *Negro American Literature Forum*, 10 (1976), 48-52.

6369. WATKINS, PATRICIA. "Is There a Unifying Theme in *Cane?*" *CLA Journal*, 15 (1972), 303-05.

See also 119, 150, 163, 192, 210, 258, 283, 296, 350, 386, 387, 443, 446, 494, 611, 6378.

"Carma"

See 6321, 6324, 6329, 6338.

"Esther"

6370. WALDRON, EDWARD E. "The Search for Identity in Jean Toomer's 'Esther.' " *CLA Journal*, 14 (1971), 277-80.

See also 192, 283, 6321, 6322, 6338, 6344, 6354.

"Fern"

6371. JUNG, UDO O. H. "Jean Toomer, 'Fern' (1922)." In *The Black American Short Story in the 20th Century: A Collection of Critical Essays.* Ed. Peter Bruck. Amsterdam: B. R. Grüner, 1977. pp. 53-69.

6372. STEIN, MARIAN L. "The Poet-Observer and Fern in Jean Toomer's *Cane.*" *The Markham Review*, 2 (1970), 64-65.

6373. WESTERFIELD, HARGIS. "Jean Toomer's 'Fern': A Mythical Dimension." *CLA Journal*, 14 (1971), 274-76.

See also 210, 386, 6321, 6322, 6325, 6329, 6338.

"Kabnis"

6374.   COOKE, MICHAEL G. "The Descent into the Underworld and Modern Black Fiction." *Iowa Review*, 5, no. 4 (1974), 72–90.
6375.   SOLARD, ALAIN. "The Impossible Unity: Jean Toomer's 'Kabnis.' " In *Myth and Ideology in American Culture*. Ed. Régis Durand. Villeneuve-d'Ascq: Univ. de Lille III, 1976. pp. 175–94.
See also 150, 163, 192, 210, 283, 296, 387, 443, 6320–6323, 6325, 6328, 6329, 6332, 6333, 6335, 6338, 6344, 6348, 6351–6355, 6357, 6358, 6360, 6363, 6364, 6367, 6378.

"Karintha"

See 6321, 6325, 6332, 6344.

"Mr. Costyve Duditch"

See 386, 6378.

"Rhobert"

See 192.

"Theater"

6376.   KOPF, GEORGE. "The Tensions in Jean Toomer's 'Theater.' " *CLA Journal*, 16 (1974), 498–503.
See also 360, 386, 484, 6360.

General Studies

6377.   DILLARD, MABEL MAYLE. "Behind the Veil: Jean Toomer's Aesthetic." In *The Merrill Studies in* Cane. Ed. Philip Durham. Columbus, OH: Merrill, 1971. pp. 2–10.
6378.   TURNER, DARWIN T. "Jean Toomer: Exile." In *In a Minor Chord: Three Afro-American Writers and Their Search for Identity.* Carbondale and Edwardsville: Southern Illinois Univ. Press, 1971. pp. 1–59.

Bibliography

6379.   GRIFFIN, JOHN C. "Jean Toomer: A Bibliography." *The South Carolina Review*, 7, no. 2 (1975), 61–64.
6380.   REILLY, JOHN M. "Jean Toomer: An Annotated Checklist of Criticism." *Resources for American Literary Study*, 4 (1974), 27–56.

TOURGÉE, ALBION W.

General Studies

6381.   OLSEN, OTTO H. *Carpetbagger's Crusade: The Life of Albion Winegar Tourgée.* Baltimore, MD: Johns Hopkins Press, 1965.

Bibliography

6382. **EALY, MARGUERITE, AND SANFORD E. MAROVITZ.** "Albion Winegar Tourgée (1838-1905)." *American Literary Realism, 1870-1910,* 8 (1975), 53-80.
6383. **KELLER, DEAN H.** "A Checklist of the Writings of Albion W. Tourgée (1838-1905)." *Studies in Bibliography,* 18 (1965), 269-79.

TRAVEN, B.

"Macario"

See 6386.

"Midnight Call"

See 6386.

"The Night Visitor"

6384. **WARNER, JOHN M.** "Tragic Vision in B. Traven's 'The Night Visitor.' " *Studies in Short Fiction,* 7 (1970), 377-84.
See also 6386.

General Studies

6385. **BAUMANN, MICHAEL L.** *B. Traven: An Introduction.* Albuquerque: Univ. of New Mexico Press, 1976.
6386. **CHANKIN, DONALD O.** *Anonymity and Death: The Fiction of B. Traven.* University Park: Pennsylvania State Univ. Press, 1975.
6387. **MILLER, CHARLES.** "B. Traven, American Author." *The Texas Quarterly,* 6, no. 4 (1963), 162-68.
6388. _____. "B. Traven, Pure Proletarian Writer." In *Proletarian Writers of the Thirties.* Ed. David Madden. Carbondale and Edwardsville: Southern Illinois Univ. Press, 1968. pp. 114-33.
6389. **STONE, JUDY.** *The Mystery of B. Traven.* Los Altos, CA: William Kaufmann, 1977.

Bibliography

6390. **HAGEMANN, E. R.** "A Checklist of the Work of B. Traven and the Critical Estimates and Biographical Essays on Him; together with a Brief Biography." *The Papers of the Bibliographical Society of America,* 53 (1959), 37-67.

TRILLING, LIONEL

"Of This Time, Of That Place"

6391. **BOYERS, ROBERT.** *Lionel Trilling: Negative Capability and the Wisdom of Avoidance.* Columbia: Univ. of Missouri Press, 1977.

6392. **GEORGE, DIANA L.** "Thematic Structure in Lionel Trilling's 'Of This Time, Of That Place.' " *Studies in Short Fiction*, 13 (1976), 1–8.

6393. **KEECH, JAMES M.** "Trilling's 'Of This Time, Of That Place.' " *The Explicator*, 23 (1965), item 66.

6394. **KENDLE, BURTON S.** "Trilling's 'Of This Time, Of That Place.' " *The Explicator*, 22 (1964), item 61.

See also 152, 566, 595.

"The Other Margaret"

6395. **HAGOPIAN, JOHN V.** "The Technique and Meaning of Lionel Trilling's *The Other Margaret.*" *Études Anglaises*, 16 (1963), 225–29.

See also 454, 486, 6391.

TRUMBO, DALTON

General Studies

6396. **COOK, BRUCE.** *Dalton Trumbo.* New York: Scribner's, 1977.

TWAIN, MARK

"Autobiography of a Damned Fool"

See 6464.

"The Autobiography of Belshazzar"

See 6397.

"The Boy's Manuscript"

See 6447, 6489, 6496.

"The Californian's Tale"

See 83.

"A Cat Tale"

6397. **ANDERSON, FREDERICK.** "Introduction." In *Concerning Cats: Two Tales by Mark Twain.* San Francisco, CA: Book Club of California, 1959. pp. iii–xvi.

"The Celebrated Jumping Frog of Calaveras County"

6398. **BAENDER, PAUL.** "The 'Jumping Frog' as a Comedian's First Virtue." *Modern Philology*, 60 (1963), 192–200.

6399. **BRANCH, EDGAR M.** " 'My voice is still for Setchell': A Background Study of 'Jim Smiley and His Jumping Frog.' " *PMLA*, 82 (1967), 591–601.

6400. **KRAUSE, S. J.** "The Art and Satire of Twain's 'Jumping Frog' Story." *American Quarterly*, 16 (1964), 562–76.

6401. **RODGERS, Paul C., JR.** "Artemus Ward and Mark Twain's 'Jumping Frog.' " *Nineteenth-Century Fiction*, 28 (1973), 273–86.

6402. **SMITH, PAUL.** "The Infernal Reminiscence: Mythic Patterns in Mark Twain's 'The Celebrated Jumping Frog of Calaveras County.' " *Satire Newsletter*, 1 (1964), 41–44.

6403. **WILSON, MARK K.** "Mr. Clemens and Madame Blanc: Mark Twain's First French Critic." *American Literature*, 45 (1974), 537–56.

See also 64, 399, 454, 512, 597, 6457, 6458, 6466, 6468, 6469, 6475, 6495.

"A Cure for the Blues"

6404. **CARDWELL, GUY A.** "Mark Twain's Failures in Comedy and *The Enemy Conquered*." *The Georgia Review*, 13 (1959), 424–36.

"The Curious Republic of Gondour"

See 6456, 6468.

"The Dandy Frightening the Squatter"

6405. **WHITE, WILLIAM.** "Roger Butterfield and the Earliest Mark Twain." *The Mark Twain Journal*, 13, no. 4 (1967), 20.
See also 6457.

"The Death Disk"

See 6496.

"A Dog's Tale"

See 6464.

"A Double-Barreled Detective Story"

6406. **KRUAS, W. KEITH.** "Mark Twain's 'A Double-Barreled Detective Story': A Source for the Solitary Oesophagus." *The Mark Twain Journal*, 16, no. 2 (1972), 10–12.
See also 83, 6447, 6464, 6472.

"Down the Rhône"

See 6464.

"The Enchanted Sea-Wilderness"

See 6498.

"The Enemy Conquered, or Love Triumphant"

See 83, 6404.

"Eve's Diary"

See 6454, 6461, 6464.

"Extracts from Adam's Diary"

See 6454, 6461.

"Extracts from Captain Stormfield's Visit to Heaven"

See 6448, 6464, 6468, 6500.

"A Fable"

6407. PRINCE, GILBERT. "Mark Twain's 'A Fable': The Teacher as Jackass." *The Mark Twain Journal*, 17, no. 3 (1975), 7–8.

"The Facts Concerning the Recent Carnival of Crime in Connecticut"
See 64, 6468.

"The Golden Arm"

6408. BURRISON, JOHN A. *"The Golden Arm": The Folk Tale and Its Literary Use by Mark Twain and Joel C. Harris.* Atlanta: Georgia State College, 1968.

"Goldsmith's Friend Abroad Again"

See 6468.

"The Great Dark"

6409. DENNIS, LARRY R. "Mark Twain and the Dark Angel." *The Midwest Quarterly*, 8 (1967), 181–97.
6410. JONES, DARYL E. "The *Hornet* Disaster: Twain's Adaptation in 'The Great Dark.'" *American Literary Realism, 1870–1910*, 9 (1976), 243–47.
See also 35, 64, 460, 6457, 6464, 6484, 6491, 6498.

"The Great Revolution in Pitcairn"

See 6451.

"Hellfire Hotchkiss"

See 6464.

"A Horse's Tale"
See 6464.

"Indiantown"
See 6464, 6498.

"The International Lightning Trust"
See 6464.

"The Invalid's Story"
6411. **AUSTIN, JAMES C.** "Artemus Ward, Mark Twain and the Limburger Cheese." *Midcontinent American Studies Journal*, 4, no. 2 (1963), 70–73.

6412. **HOROWITZ, FLOYD R.** " 'The Invalid's Story': An Early Mark Twain Commentary on Institutional Christianity." *Midcontinent American Studies Journal*, 7, no. 1 (1966), 37–44.

"Jim Baker's Blue-Jay Yarn"
6413. **BLAIR, WALTER.** "Mark Twain's Other Masterpiece: 'Jim Baker's Blue-Jay Yarn.' " *Studies in American Humor*, 1 (1975), 132–47.

6414. **HANSON, R. GALEN.** "Bluejays and Man: Twain's Exercise in Understanding." *Mark Twain Journal*, 17, no. 1 (1974), 18–19.

6415. **SHRELL, DARWIN H.** "Twain's Owl and His Bluejays." In *Essays in Honor of Esmond Linworth Marilla*. Ed. Thomas Austin Kirby and William John Olive. Baton Rouge: Louisiana State Univ. Press, 1970. pp. 283–90.

See also 6468.

"Jim Wolf and the Tom-Cats"
See 6496.

"The Latest Sensation"
6416. **MILLER, WILLIAM C.** "Mark Twain's Source for 'The Latest Sensation' Hoax?" *American Literature*, 32 (1960), 75–78.

"Letters from the Earth"
See 6461.

"The Loves of Alonzo Fitz Clarence and Rosannah Ethelton"
6417. **HOROWITZ, FLOYD R.** "Mark Twain's Belle Lettre in 'The Loves of Alonzo Fitz Clarence and Rosannah Ethelton.' " *The Mark Twain Journal*, 13, no. 1 (1966), 16.

"The Man That Corrupted Hadleyburg"

6418. **BERTOLOTTI, D. S.** "Structural Unity in 'The Man That Corrupted Hadleyburg.' " *The Mark Twain Journal*, 14, no. 1 (1968), 19–21.

6419. **BURHANS, CLINTON S., JR.** "The Sober Affirmation of Mark Twain's Hadleyburg." *American Literature*, 34 (1962), 375–84.

6420.. **CHARD, LESLIE F., II.** "Mark Twain's 'Hadleyburg' and Fredonia, New York." *American Quarterly*, 16 (1964), 595–601.

6421. **CLARK, GEORGE PIERCE.** "The Devil That Corrupted Hadleyburg." *The Mark Twain Journal*, 10, no. 2 (1956), 1–4.

6422. **KRAUSE, SYDNEY J.** "*The Pearl* and 'Hadleyburg': From Desire to Renunciation." *Steinbeck Quarterly*, 7 (1974), 3–18.

6423. **LAING, NITA.** "The Later Satire of Mark Twain." *The Midwest Quarterly*, 2 (1960), 35–48.

6424. **McKEITHAN, D. M.** "The Morgan Manuscript of *The Man That Corrupted Hadleyburg*." *Texas Studies in Literature and Language*, 2 (1961), 476–80.

6425. **MALIN, IRVING.** "Mark Twain: The Boy as Artist." *Literature and Psychology*, 11 (1961), 78–84.

6426. **NEBEKER, HELEN E.** "The Great Corruption or Satan Rehabilitated." *Studies in Short Fiction*, 8 (1971), 635–37.

6427. **PARK, MARTHA M.** "Mark Twain's Hadleyburg: A House Built on Sand." *CLA Journal*, 16 (1973), 508–13.

6428. **RUCKER, MARY E.** "Moralism and Determinism in 'The Man That Corrupted Hadleyburg.' " *Studies in Short Fiction*, 14 (1977), 49–54.

6429. **RULE, HENRY B.** "The Role of Satan in 'The Man That Corrupted Hadleyburg.' " *Studies in Short Fiction*, 6 (1969), 619–29.

6430. **SCHERTING, JACK.** "Poe's 'The Cask of Amontillado': A Source for Twain's 'The Man That Corrupted Hadleyburg.' " *The Mark Twain Journal*, 16, no. 2 (1972), 18–19.

6431. **SMITH, HENRY NASH.** "Pudd'nhead Wilson and After." *The Massachusetts Review*, 3 (1962), 233–53.

6432. **SPANGLER, GEORGE M.** "Locating Hadleyburg." *The Mark Twain Journal*, 14, no. 4 (1969), 20.

6433. **WERGE, THOMAS.** "Mark Twain and the Fall of Adam." *The Mark Twain Journal*, 15, no. 2 (1970), 5–13.

6434. ———. "The Sin of Hypocrisy in *The Man That Corrupted Hadleyburg* and *Inferno* XXIII." *The Mark Twain Journal*, 18, no. 1 (1976), 17–18.

See also 203, 381, 384, 6447, 6448, 6452, 6455, 6457, 6464, 6468, 6494.

"A Medieval Romance"

See 6464.

"Methuselah's Diary"

See 6461.

"Mock Marriage"

See 6464.

"My Bloody Massacre"

See 6457.

"My Platonic Sweetheart"

6435. **BAETZHOLD, HOWARD G.** "Found: Mark Twain's 'Lost Sweetheart.' " *American Literature*, 44 (1972), 414–29.
6436. **MCNAMARA, EUGENE.** "A Note on 'My Platonic Sweetheart.' " *The Mark Twain Journal*, 12, no. 1 (1963), 18–19, 21.
6437. **STONE, ALBERT E., JR.** "Mark Twain's *Joan of Arc*: The Child as Goddess." *American Literature*, 31 (1959), 1–20.
See also 6496.

"The £1,000,000 Bank-Note"

See 6464, 6487.

"1002d Arabian Night"

See 6464.

"Papers of the Adam Family"

See 6464.

"The Private History of a Campaign That Failed"

6438. **ALTIERI, JOANNE.** "The Structure of 'The Private History of a Campaign That Failed.' " *The Mark Twain Journal*, 13, no. 3 (1967), 2–5.
6439. **KIMBALL, WILLIAM J.** "Samuel Clemens as a Confederate Soldier: Some Observations about 'The Private History of a Campaign That Failed.' " *Studies in Short Fiction*, 5 (1968), 382–84.
6440. **MATTSON, J. STANLEY.** "Mark Twain on War and Peace: The Missouri Rebel and 'The Campaign That Failed.' " *American Quarterly*, 20 (1968), 783–94.
6441. **RACKHAM, JEFF.** "The Mysterious Stranger in 'The Campaign That Failed.' " *Southern Humanities Review*, 5 (1971), 63–67.
See also 6458, 6464, 6466, 6476, 6484, 6495, 6499, 6500.

"The Professor's Yarn"
See 60.

"The Refuge of the Derelicts"
See 6455, 6464.

"Sabbath Reflections"
See 6494.

"Schoolhouse Hill"
See 6464.

"The Secret History of Eddypus, The World-Empire"
See 6464, 6490.

"Sold to Satan"
See 6455.

"Some Learned Fables for Good Old Boys and Girls"
6442. BAETZHOLD, HOWARD G. "Mark Twain on Scientific Investigation: Contemporary Allusions in 'Some Learned Fables for Good Old Boys and Girls.' " In *Literature and Ideas in America: Essays in Memory of Harry Hayden Clark.* Ed. Robert Falk. Athens: Ohio Univ. Press, 1975. pp. 128–54.
See also 6459, 6464.

"Some Rambling Notes of an Idle Excursion"
See 6464.

"The Stolen White Elephant"
6443. BAETZHOLD, HOWARD G. "Of Detectives and Their Derring-Do: The Genesis of Mark Twain's 'The Stolen White Elephant.' " *Studies in American Humor*, 2 (1976), 183–95.

"The Story of Mamie Grant, The Child-Missionary"
See 6489.

"That Day in Eden"
See 6454, 6461.

"The $30,000 Bequest"
See 6457, 6464.

"Those Extraordinary Twins"
See 6448, 6464.

"Tom Sawyer's Conspiracy"

See 6464, 6484, 6492, 6496.

"Traveling with a Reformer"

See 454, 6487.

"A True Story, Repeated Word for Word As I Heard It"

See 11, 6468, 6484.

"Wapping Alice"

See 6464.

"The War Prayer"

6444. ANDREWS, WILLIAM L. "The Source of Mark Twain's 'The War Prayer.' " *Mark Twain Journal*, 17, no. 4 (1975), 8–9.

6445. ENSOR, ALLISON. "Mark Twain's 'The War Prayer': Its Ties to Howells and to Hymnology." *Modern Fiction Studies*, 16 (1970), 535–39.

"What Stumped the Bluejays" (See *"Jim Baker's Blue-Jay Yarn"*)

"Which Was It?"

See 6484.

"Which Was the Dream?"

See 6464, 6498.

" 'You've Been a Dam Fool, Mary. You Always Was!' "

See 6464.

General Studies

6446. ANDERSON, FREDERICK. "Introduction." In *Mark Twain: The Critical Heritage*. London: Routledge & Kegan Paul, 1971. pp. 1–19.

6447. BAETZHOLD, HOWARD G. *Mark Twain and John Bull: The British Connection*. Bloomington: Indiana Univ. Press, 1970.

6448. BALDANZA, FRANK. *Mark Twain: An Introduction and Interpretation*. New York: Barnes & Noble, 1961.

6449. BATES, ALLAN. "Sam Clemens, Pilot-Humorist of a Tramp Steamboat." *American Literature*, 39 (1967), 102–09.

6450. BLAIR, WALTER. "Introduction." In *Selected Shorter Writings of Mark Twain*. Boston, MA: Houghton Mifflin, 1962. pp. vii–xxvi.

6451. _____. *Mark Twain & Huck Finn*. Berkeley: Univ. of California Press, 1960.

6452. **BLUES, THOMAS.** *Mark Twain & the Community.* Lexington: Univ. Press of Kentucky, 1970.

6453. **BRANCH, EDGAR M.** "Samuel Clemens: Learning to Venture a Miracle." *American Literary Realism, 1870–1910,* 8 (1975), 91–99.

6454. **BRODWIN, STANLEY.** "The Humor of the Absurd: Mark Twain's Adamic Diaries." *Criticism,* 14 (1972), 49–64.

6455. ———. "Mark Twain's Masks of Satan: The Final Phase." *American Literature,* 45 (1973), 206–27.

6456. **BUDD, LOUIS J.** *Mark Twain: Social Philosopher.* Bloomington: Indiana Univ. Press, 1962.

6457. **COVICI, PASCAL, JR.** *Mark Twain's Humor: The Image of a World.* Dallas, TX: Southern Methodist Univ. Press, 1962.

6458. **COX, JAMES M.** *Mark Twain: The Fate of Humor.* Princeton, NJ: Princeton Univ. Press, 1966.

6459. **CUMMINGS, SHERWOOD.** "Mark Twain's Acceptance of Science." *The Centennial Review,* 6 (1962), 245–61.

6460. **DAVIS, PHILIP E.** "Mark Twain as Moral Philosopher." *San José Studies,* 2, no. 2 (1976), 83–93.

6461. **ENSOR, ALLISON.** *Mark Twain & the Bible.* Lexington: Univ. of Kentucky Press, 1969.

6462. **FATOUT, PAUL.** *Mark Twain in Virginia City.* Bloomington: Indiana Univ. Press, 1964.

6463. ———. *Mark Twain on the Lecture Circuit.* Bloomington: Indiana Univ. Press, 1960.

6464. **GALE, ROBERT L.** *Plots and Characters in the Works of Mark Twain.* 2 vols. Hamden, CT: Archon Books, 1973.

6465. **GANZEL, DEWEY.** "Samuel Clemens and John Camden Hotten." *The Library,* 5th Series, 20 (1965), 230–42.

6466. **GEISMAR, MAXWELL.** *Mark Twain: An American Prophet.* Boston, MA: Houghton Mifflin, 1970.

6467. **GERBER, JOHN C.** "Mark Twain's Use of the Comic Pose." *PMLA,* 77 (1962), 297–304.

6468. **GIBSON, WILLIAM M.** *The Art of Mark Twain.* New York: Oxford Univ. Press, 1976.

6469. **GRANT, DOUGLAS.** *Mark Twain.* Edinburgh: Oliver and Boyd, 1962.

6470. **HARRELL, DON W.** "A Chaser of Phantoms: Mark Twain and Romanticism." *The Midwest Quarterly,* 13 (1972), 201–12.

6471. **HARRIS, HELEN L.** "Mark Twain's Response to the Native American." *American Literature,* 46 (1975), 495–505.

6472. **HILL, HAMLIN.** *Mark Twain: God's Fool.* New York: Harper & Row, 1973.

6473. _____. *Mark Twain and Elisha Bliss*. Columbia: Univ. of Missouri Press, 1964.

6474. **KAHN, SHOLOM J.** "Mark Twain as American Rabelais." *The Hebrew University Studies in Literature*, 1 (1973), 47–75.

6475. **KAPLAN, JUSTIN.** *Mark Twain and His World*. New York: Simon and Schuster, 1974.

6476. _____. *Mr. Clemens and Mark Twain: A Biography*. New York: Simon and Schuster, 1966.

6477. _____. "On Mark Twain: 'Never Quite Sane in the Night.' " *The Psychoanalytic Review*, 56 (1969), 113–27.

6478. **KRAUSE, SYDNEY J.** *Mark Twain as Critic*. Baltimore, MD: Johns Hopkins Press, 1967.

6479. **McCOLLOUGH, JOSEPH B.** "Mark Twain and the Hy Slocum-Carl Byng Controversy." *American Literature*, 43 (1971), 42–59.

6480. **McELDERRY, BRUCE R., JR.** "Introduction." In *Contributions to* The Galaxy, *1868–1871, by Mark Twain*. Gainesville, FL: Scholars' Facsimiles & Reprints, 1961. pp. ix–xx.

6481. **MALONE, DAVID H.** "Mark Twain and the Literature of the Frontier." In *The Frontier in American History and Literature: Essays and Interpretations*. Ed. Hans Galinsky. Frankfurt am Main: Moritz Diesterweg, 1960. pp. 65–79.

6482. **NEIDER, CHARLES.** "Introduction." In *The Comic Mark Twain Reader: The Most Humorous Selections from His Stories, Sketches, Novels, Travel Books, and Lectures*. Garden City, NY: Doubleday, 1977. pp. xv–xxx.

6483. _____. "Mark Twain and No Hogwash." In *The Complete Humorous Sketches and Tales of Mark Twain*. Garden City, NY: Doubleday, 1961. pp. 13–22.

6484. **PETTIT, ARTHUR G.** *Mark Twain & the South*. Lexington: Univ. Press of Kentucky, 1974.

6485. **RAMSAY, ROBERT, AND FRANCES G. EMBERSON.** *A Mark Twain Lexicon*. New York: Russell & Russell, 1963.

6486. **REED, JOHN Q.** "Mark Twain: West Coast Journalist." *The Midwest Quarterly*, 1 (1960), 141–61.

6487. **REGAN, ROBERT.** *Unpromising Heroes: Mark Twain and His Characters*. Berkeley: Univ. of California Press, 1966.

6488. **REISS, EDMUND.** "Foreword." In *The Mysterious Stranger and Other Stories*, by Mark Twain. New York: New American Library, 1962. pp. vii–xv.

6489. **ROGERS, FRANKLIN R.** *Mark Twain's Burlesque Patterns as Seen in the Novels and Narratives, 1855–1885*. Dallas, TX: Southern Methodist Univ. Press, 1960.

6490.   SALOMON, ROGER B. *Twain and the Image of History.* New Haven, CT: Yale Univ. Press, 1961.

6491.   SEARLE, WILLIAM. *The Saint & the Skeptics: Joan of Arc in the Work of Mark Twain, Anatole France, and Bernard Shaw.* Detroit, MI: Wayne State Univ. Press, 1976.

6492.   SIMPSON, CLAUDE M., JR. "Huck Finn after *Huck Finn.*" In *American Humor: Essays Presented to John C. Gerber.* Ed. O. M. Brack, Jr. Scottsdale, AZ: Arete, 1977. pp. 59–72.

6493.   SLOANE, DAVID E. E. "Mark Twain's Comedy: The 1870s." *Studies in American Humor*, 2 (1976), 146–56.

6494.   SMITH, HENRY NASH. *Mark Twain: The Development of a Writer.* Cambridge, MA: Harvard Univ. Press, 1962.

6495.   SPENGEMANN, WILLIAM C. *Mark Twain and the Backwoods Angel: The Matter of Innocence in the Works of Samuel L. Clemens.* Kent, OH: Kent State Univ. Press, 1966.

6496.   STONE, ALBERT E., JR. *The Innocent Eye: Childhood in Mark Twain's Imagination.* New Haven, CT: Yale Univ. Press, 1961.

6497.   TRENSKY, ANNE. "The Bad Boy in Nineteenth-Century American Fiction." *The Georgia Review*, 27 (1973), 503–17.

6498.   TUCKEY, JOHN S. "Introduction." In *Mark Twain's Which Was the Dream? and Other Symbolic Writings of the Later Years.* Berkeley: Univ. of California Press, 1967. pp. 1–29.

6499.   WAGENKNECHT, EDWARD. *Mark Twain: The Man and His Work.* Rev. ed. Norman: Univ. of Oklahoma Press, 1961.

6500.   ———. *Mark Twain: The Man and His Work.* 3rd ed. Norman: Univ. of Oklahoma Press, 1967.

6501.   WIGGINS, ROBERT A. *Mark Twain: Jackleg Novelist.* Seattle: Univ. of Washington Press, 1964.

6502.   YU, BEONGCHEON. "The Immortal Twins—An Aspect of Mark Twain." *The English Language and Literature*, no. 22 (1967), pp. 48–77.

Interviews

6503.   BUDD, LOUIS J., ED. "A Listing of and Selection from Newspaper and Magazine Interviews with Samuel L. Clemens, 1874–1910." *American Literary Realism, 1870–1910*, 10 (1977), ix–xii, 1–100. [Note: p. 85a follows p. 326.]

Bibliography

6504.   BEEBE, MAURICE, AND JOHN FEASTER. "Criticism of Mark Twain: A Selected Checklist." *Modern Fiction Studies*, 14 (1968), 93–139.

6505.   CLARK, HARRY HAYDEN. "Mark Twain." In *Eight Ameri-*

can *Authors: A Review of Research and Criticism.* Rev. ed. Ed.
James Woodress. New York: Norton, 1971. pp. 273–320.
6506. McCullough, Joseph B. "A Listing of Mark Twain's
Contributions to The Buffalo *Express*, 1869–1871." *American Literary Realism, 1870–1910,* 5 (1972), 61–70.
6507. Tenney, Thomas Asa. *Mark Twain: A Reference Guide.*
Boston, MA: G. K. Hall, 1977.
6508. _____. "Mark Twain: A Reference Guide—First Annual
Supplement." *American Literary Realism, 1870–1910,* 10 (1977),
327–412.
6509. Wagenknecht, Edward. "A Commentary on Mark
Twain Criticism and Scholarship since 1960." In *Mark Twain: The Man and His Work.* 3rd ed. Norman: Univ. of Oklahoma
Press, 1967. pp. 265–94.

UPDIKE, JOHN

"A & P"

6510. Overmyer, Janet. "Courtly Love in the A & P." *Notes on Contemporary Literature,* 2, no. 3 (1972), 4–5.
6511. Porter, M. Gilbert. "John Updike's 'A & P': The Establishment and an Emersonian Cashier." *English Journal,* 61 (1972),
1155–58.
See also 127, 399, 6523.

"Ace in the Hole"

See 6523.

"The Astronomer"

6512. Sykes, Robert H. "A Commentary on Updike's Astronomer." *Studies in Short Fiction,* 8 (1971), 575–79.
See also 6525.

"Bech Panics"

See 6523.

"Bech Swings?"

See 6523.

"The Blessed Man of Boston, My Grandmother's Thimble, and Fanning Island"

See 6536, 6538.

"The Bulgarian Poetess"

See 6534, 6535.

"The Christian Roommates"

See 6534.

"The Crow in the Woods"

See 6522, 6525.

"The Dark"

See 6525.

"Dentistry and Doubt"

See 6525.

"Eros Rampant"

See 6525.

"Flight"

See 6534.

"Friends from Philadelphia"

See 518, 6523, 6535.

"A Gift from the City"

6513.   **WARNER, JOHN M.** "Charity in 'A Gift from the City.' " In *The Process of Fiction: Contemporary Stories and Criticism.* Ed. Barbara McKenzie. New York: Harcourt, Brace & World, 1969. pp. 118–23.
See also 6523.

"Giving Blood"

See 6523, 6525.

"The Happiest I've Been"

See 6522, 6523.

"Harv Is Plowing Now"

See 6523, 6527.

"The Hermit"

See 6522, 6535.

"In Football Season"

See 6535.

"Lifeguard"

See 6523, 6525–6527.

"Marching through Boston"

See 6525.

"Mobile of Birds"

See 6522.

"Museums and Women"

6514. ROSA, ALFRED F. "The Psycholinguistics of Updike's 'Museums and Women.'" *Modern Fiction Studies*, 20 (1974), 107–11.
See also 6525.

"The Music School"

6515. MARKLE, JOYCE B. "On John Updike and 'The Music School.'" In *The American Short Story*. Ed. Calvin Skaggs. New York: Dell, 1977. pp. 389–93.
See also 6523, 6526, 6535, 6536.

"My Lover Has Dirty Fingernails"

See 6523.

"Packed Dirt, Churchgoing, A Dying Cat, A Traded Car"
See 269, 6522, 6525, 6529, 6536, 6538.

"The Persistence of Desire"

See 6523.

"The Peruvian in the Heart of Lake Winnipesaukee"
See 6528.

"Pigeon Feathers"

6516. SHURR, WILLIAM H. "The Lutheran Experience in John Updike's 'Pigeon Feathers.'" *Studies in Short Fiction*, 14 (1977), 329–35.
See also 6522, 6523, 6525, 6529, 6532, 6535.

"The Rescue"

See 6523.

"A Sense of Shelter"

6517. EDWARDS, A. S. G. "Updike's 'A Sense of Shelter.'" *Studies in Short Fiction*, 8 (1971), 467–68.
6518. REISING, R. W. "Updike's 'A Sense of Shelter.'" *Studies in Short Fiction*, 7 (1970), 651–52.
See also 267, 270, 6525.

"Should Wizard Hit Mommy?"

6519.   **GRIFFITH, ALBERT J.** "Updike's Artist's Dilemma: 'Should Wizard Hit Mommy?' " *Modern Fiction Studies*, 20 (1974), 111-15.

"Snowing in Greenwich Village"

See 6523, 6525.

"The Taste of Metal"

See 6525.

"Tomorrow and Tomorrow and So Forth"

6520.   **BANKS, R. JEFF.** "The Uses of Weather in 'Tomorrow and Tomorrow and So Forth.' " *Notes on Contemporary Literature*, 3, no. 5 (1973), 8-9.
6521.   **FRIEDMAN, RUBEN.** "An Interpretation of John Updike's 'Tomorrow and Tomorrow and So Forth.' " *English Journal*, 61 (1972), 1159-62.
See also 6523.

"Toward Evening"

See 6525, 6526.

"Twin Beds in Rome"

See 6523, 6525.

"The Wait"

See 6535.

"Who Made Yellow Roses Yellow?"

See 565.

"Wife-Wooing"

See 6527.

"You'll Never Know, Dear, How Much I Love You"
See 6523, 6525.

"Your Lover Just Called"

See 6525.

General Studies

6522.   **BURCHARD, RACHAEL C.** *John Updike: Yea Sayings.* Carbondale and Edwardsville: Southern Illinois Univ. Press, 1971.

6523. **DETWEILER, ROBERT.** *John Updike.* New York: Twayne, 1972.

6524. **GINGHER, ROBERT S.** "Has John Updike Anything to Say?" *Modern Fiction Studies,* 20 (1974), 97–105.

6525. **HAMILTON, ALICE AND KENNETH.** *The Elements of John Updike.* Grand Rapids, MI: Eerdmans, 1970.

6526. _____. *John Updike: A Critical Essay.* Grand Rapids, MI: Eerdmans, 1967.

6527. **LARSEN, R. B.** "John Updike: The Story as Lyrical Meditation." *Thoth,* 13, no. 1 (1972), 33–39.

6528. **McCOY, ROBERT.** "John Updike's Literary Apprenticeship on *The Harvard Lampoon.*" *Modern Fiction Studies,* 20 (1974), 3–12.

6529. **MARKLE, JOYCE B.** *Fighters and Lovers: Theme in the Novels of John Updike.* New York: New York Univ. Press, 1973.

6530. **MURADIAN, THADDEUS.** "The World of Updike." *The English Journal,* 54 (1965), 577–84.

6531. **OATES, JOYCE CAROL.** "Updike's American Comedies." *Modern Fiction Studies,* 21 (1975), 459–72.

6532. **REGAN, ROBERT ALTON.** "Updike's Symbol of the Center." *Modern Fiction Studies,* 20 (1974), 77–96.

6533. **RUPP, RICHARD H.** "John Updike: Style in Search of a Center." *The Sewanee Review,* 75 (1967), 693–709.

6534. **SAMUELS, CHARLES THOMAS.** *John Updike.* Minneapolis: Univ. of Minnesota Press, 1969.

6535. **TAYLOR, LARRY E.** *Pastoral and Anti-Pastoral Patterns in John Updike's Fiction.* Carbondale and Edwardsville: Southern Illinois Univ. Press, 1971.

6536. **VARGO, EDWARD P.** *Rainstorms and Fire: Ritual in the Novels of John Updike.* Port Washington, NY: Kennikat, 1973.

6537. **WARD, J. A.** "John Updike's Fiction." *Critique,* 5, no. 1 (1962), 27–40.

6538. **WAXMAN, ROBERT E.** "Invitations to Dread: John Updike's Metaphysical Quest." *Renascence,* 29 (1977), 201–10.

Interviews

6539. **GADO, FRANK.** "John Updike." In *First Person: Conversations on Writers & Writing.* Ed. Frank Gado, Schenectady, NY: Union College Press, 1973. pp. 80–109.

6540. **NICHOLS, LEWIS.** "Talk with John Updike." *The New York Times Book Review,* 7 Apr. 1968, pp. 34–35.

6541. **UPDIKE, JOHN.** "The Art of Fiction XLIII." With Charles Thomas Samuels. *The Paris Review,* no. 45 (1968), pp. 85–117.

Bibliography

6542. **GALLOWAY, DAVID D.** "A John Updike Checklist." In *The Absurd Hero in American Fiction: Updike, Styron, Bellow, Salinger.* Austin: Univ. of Texas Press, 1966. pp. 183–200.

6543. ———. "A John Updike Checklist." In *The Absurd Hero in American Fiction: Updike, Styron, Bellow, Salinger.* Rev. ed. Austin: Univ. of Texas Press, 1970. pp. 184–208.

6544. **MEYER, ARLIN G., AND MICHAEL A. OLIVAS.** "Criticism of John Updike: A Selected Checklist." *Modern Fiction Studies*, 20 (1974), 121–33.

6545. **OLIVAS, MICHAEL A.** *An Annotated Bibliography of John Updike Criticism, 1967–1973, and A Checklist of His Works.* New York: Garland, 1975.

6546. **SOKOLOFF, B. A., AND DAVID E. ARNASON.** *John Updike: A Comprehensive Bibliography.* Folcroft, PA: Folcroft Press, 1971.

6547. **TAYLOR, C. CLARKE.** *John Updike: A Bibliography.* Kent, OH: Kent State Univ. Press, 1968.

VAN VECHTEN, CARL

General Studies

6548. **KELLNER, BRUCE.** *Carl Van Vechten and the Irreverent Decades.* Norman: Univ. of Oklahoma Press, 1968.

VIDAL, GORE

General Studies

6549. **DICK, BERNARD F.** *The Apostate Angel: A Critical Study of Gore Vidal.* New York: Random House, 1974.

Interviews

6550. **BROCKRIS, VICTOR, AND ANDREW WYLIE.** "Opinions: An Interview with Gore Vidal." *Fiction*, no. 7 (1974), pp. 12–13, 70–71.

6551. **JOHNSON, DIANE.** "Gore Vidal, Scorekeeper." *The New York Times Book Review*, 17 Apr. 1977, p. 47.

6552. **VIDAL, GORE.** "The Art of Fiction L." With Gerald Clarke. *The Paris Review*, no. 59 (1974), pp. 131–65.

Bibliography

6553. **GILLIAM, LORETTA MURRELL.** "Gore Vidal: A Checklist, 1945–1969." *Bulletin of Bibliography and Magazine Notes*, 30 (1973), 1–9, 44.

VONNEGUT, KURT, JR.

"EPICAC"

See 6562.

"The Manned Missles"

See 399.

"Report on the Barnhouse Effect"

See 6562.

"Thanasphere"

See 6555.

"Tomorrow and Tomorrow and Tomorrow"

See 6562.

"Welcome to the Monkey House"

See 6562.

General Studies

6554. **BELLAMY, JOE DAVID.** "Kurt Vonnegut for President: The Making of an Academic Reputation." In *The Vonnegut Statement*. Ed. Jerome Klinkowitz and John Somer. New York: Delacorte, 1973. pp. 71–89.

6555. **KLINKOWITZ, JEROME.** "A Do-It-Yourself Story Collection by Kurt Vonnegut." In *Vonnegut in America: An Introduction to the Life and Work of Kurt Vonnegut*. Ed. Jerome Klinkowitz and Donald L. Lawler. New York: Delta, 1977. pp. 53–60.

6556. ———. "Kurt Vonnegut, Jr.: The Canary in a Cathouse." In *The Vonnegut Statement*. Ed. Jerome Klinkowitz and John Somer. New York: Delacorte, 1973. pp. 7–17.

6557. ———. "Vonnegut in America." In *Vonnegut in America: An Introduction to the Life and Work of Kurt Vonnegut*. Ed. Jerome Klinkowitz and Donald L. Lawler. New York: Delta, 1977. pp. 7–36.

6558. ———. "Why They Read Vonnegut." In *The Vonnegut Statement*. Ed. Jerome Klinkowitz and John Somer. New York: Delacorte, 1973. pp. 18–30.

6559. **LAWLER, DONALD L., ET AL.** "Vonnegut in Academe (II)." In *Vonnegut in America: An Introduction to the Life and Work of Kurt Vonnegut*. Ed. Jerome Klinkowitz and Donald L. Lawler. New York: Delta, 1977. pp. 187–214.

6560. **MAYO, CLARK.** *Kurt Vonnegut: The Gospel from Outer Space (or, Yes We Have No Nirvanas).* San Bernardino, CA: Borgo Press, 1977.

6561. **RITTER, JESS.** "Teaching Kurt Vonnegut on the Firing Line." In *The Vonnegut Statement.* Ed. Jerome Klinkowitz and John Somer. New York: Delacorte, 1973. pp. 31–42.

6562. **SCHATT, STANLEY.** *Kurt Vonnegut, Jr.* Boston, MA: Twayne, 1976.

6563. **SCHOLES, ROBERT.** "Chasing a Lone Eagle: Vonnegut's College Writing." In *The Vonnegut Statement.* Ed. Jerome Klinkowitz and John Somer. New York: Delacorte, 1973. pp. 45–54.

6564. **WAKEFIELD, DAN.** "In Vonnegut's Karass." In *The Vonnegut Statement.* Ed. Jerome Klinkowitz and John Somer. New York: Delacorte, 1973. pp. 55–70.

6565. **WOOD, KAREN AND CHARLES.** "The Vonnegut Effect: Science Fiction and Beyond." In *The Vonnegut Statement.* Ed. Jerome Klinkowitz and John Somer. New York: Delacorte, 1973. pp. 133–57.

Interviews

6566. **BYRAN, C. D. B.** "Kurt Vonnegut, Head Bokononist." *The New York Times Book Review*, 6 Apr. 1969, pp. 2, 25.

6567. **CASEY, JOHN, AND JOE DAVID BELLAMY.** "Kurt Vonnegut, Jr." In *The New Fiction: Interviews with Innovative American Writers.* Ed. Joe David Bellamy. Urbana: Univ. of Illinois Press, 1974. pp. 194–207.

6568. **KNIGHT, JOSEPH.** "Interview with Kurt Vonnegut." *Fiction*, no. 5 (1972), pp. 8–9, 75.

6569. **SCHOLES, ROBERT.** "A Talk with Kurt Vonnegut, Jr." In *The Vonnegut Statement.* Ed. Jerome Klinkowitz and John Somer. New York: Delacorte, 1973. pp. 90–118.

6570. **VONNEGUT, KURT.** "The Art of Fiction LXIV." With David Hayman, David Michaels, George Plimpton, and Richard L. Rhodes. *The Paris Review*, no. 69 (1977), pp. 57–103.

Bibliography

6571. **HASKELL, JOHN D., JR.** "Addendum to Pieratt and Klinkowitz: Kurt Vonnegut, Jr." *The Papers of the Bibliographical Society of America*, 70 (1976), 122.

6572. **HUDGENS, BETTY LENHARDT.** *Kurt Vonnegut, Jr.: A Checklist.* Detroit, MI: Gale, 1972.

6573. **KLINKOWITZ, JEROME.** "The Vonnegut Bibliography." In *Vonnegut in America: An Introduction to the Life and Work of Kurt*

Vonnegut. Ed. Jerome Klinkowitz and Donald L. Lawler. New York: Delta, 1977. pp. 217–52.

6574. _____, ASA B. PIERATT, JR., AND STANLEY SCHATT. "The Vonnegut Bibliography." In *The Vonnegut Statement.* Ed. Jerome Klinkowitz and John Somer. New York: Delacorte, 1973. pp. 255–77.

6575. LERCANGÉE, FRANCINE. *Kurt Vonnegut, Jr.: A Selected Bibliography.* Brussels: Center for American Studies, 1976.

6576. PIERATT, ASA B., JR., AND JEROME KLINKOWITZ. *Kurt Vonnegut, Jr.: A Descriptive Bibliography and Annotated Secondary Checklist.* Hamden, CT: Archon Books, 1974.

6577. SCHATT, STANLEY, AND JEROME KLINKOWITZ. "A Kurt Vonnegut Checklist." *Critique,* 12, no. 3 (1971), 70–76.

WADE, JOHN DONALD

"The Duggone Bust"

See 6578.

"The Life and Death of Cousin Lucius"

See 6578.

General Studies

6578. BENSON, ROBERT G. "The Excellence of John Donald Wade." *The Mississippi Quarterly,* 29 (1976), 233–39.

Bibliography

6579. SMITH, GERALD J. "John Donald Wade: A Bibliographical Note." *The Mississippi Quarterly,* 29 (1976), 241–44.

WADSWORTH, OLIVE

"A Woman"

See 18.

WAGONER, DAVID

"The Spinning Ladies"

6580. SCHAFER, WILLIAM J. "David Wagoner's Fiction: In the Mills of Satan." *Critique,* 9, no. 1 (1966), 71–89.

WALDO, EDWARD HAMILTON
(See STURGEON, THEODORE)

WALKER, ALICE

"Revenge"
See 6581.

"Strong Horse Tea"
See 6581.

General Studies
6581. **HARRIS, TRUDIER.** "Folklore in the Fiction of Alice Walker: A Perpetuation of Historical and Literary Traditions." *Black American Literature Forum*, 11 (1977), 3–8.

Interviews
6582. **O'BRIEN, JOHN.** "Alice Walker." In *Interviews with Black Writers.* Ed. John O'Brien. New York: Liveright, 1973. pp. 185–211.

WALLACE, HORACE BINNEY

General Studies
6583. **HATVARY, GEORGE EGON.** *Horace Binney Wallace.* Boston, MA: Twayne, 1977.

WALLANT, EDWARD LEWIS

Bibliography
6584. **AYO, NICHOLAS.** "Edward Lewis Wallant, 1926–1962." *Bulletin of Bibliography and Magazine Notes*, 28 (1971), 119.

WALROND, ERIC

"The Black Pin"
See 386.

"City Love"
See 386.

"Miss Kenny's Marriage"
See 386.

"Tropic Death"
See 386.

"The White Snake"
See 386.

"The Yellow One"
See 386.

WARD, ARTEMUS
General Studies

6585. **Austin, James C.** *Artemus Ward.* New York: Twayne, 1964.

6586. **Reed, John Q.** "Artemus Ward: The Minor Writer in American Studies." *The Midwest Quarterly*, 7 (1966), 241–51.

6587. **Weber, Brom.** "The Mispellers." In *The Comic Imagination in American Literature.* Ed. Louis D. Rubin, Jr. New Brunswick, NJ: Rutgers Univ. Press, 1973. pp. 127–37.

WARREN, ROBERT PENN
"Blackberry Winter"

6588. **Davidson, Richard Allan.** "Physical Imagery in Robert Penn Warren's 'Blackberry Winter.' " *The Georgia Review*, 22 (1968), 482–88.

6589. **Warren, Robert Penn.** "Writer at Work: How a Story Was Born and How, Bit by Bit, It Grew." *The New York Times Book Review*, 1 Mar. 1959, pp. 4–5, 36.

6590. **Weathers, Winston.** " 'Blackberry Winter' and the Use of Archetypes." *Studies in Short Fiction*, 1 (1963), 45–51.

See also 454, 502, 511, 6592, 6594.

"The Circus in the Attic"
See 6594.

"The Patented Gate and the Mean Hamburger"
See 565.

"Prime Leaf"

6591. **Shepherd, Allen.** "Robert Penn Warren's 'Prime Leaf' as Prototype of *Night Rider*." *Studies in Short Fiction*, 7 (1970), 469–71.

See also 6594.

"The Unvexed Isles"
See 6594.

"When the Light Gets Green"

See 267.

General Studies

6592. **BOHNER, CHARLES H.** *Robert Penn Warren.* New York: Twayne, 1964.

6593. **MOORE, L. HUGH, JR.** *Robert Penn Warren and History: "The Big Myth We Live."* The Hague: Mouton, 1970.

6594. **SCOTT, JAMES B.** "The Theme of Betrayal in Robert Penn Warren's Stories." *Thoth,* 5 (1964), 74–84.

6595. **WARREN, ROBERT PENN.** "On Writing." *The Texas Quarterly,* 3, no. 2, Supplement (1960), 59–63.

6596. **WEST, PAUL.** *Robert Penn Warren.* Minneapolis: Univ. of Minnesota Press, 1964.

Interviews

6597. **BAKER, JOHN.** "Robert Penn Warren." In *Conversations with Writers,* Vol. 1. Detroit, MI: Gale, 1977. pp. 279–302.

6598. **DE MOTT, BENJAMIN.** "Talk with Robert Penn Warren." *The New York Times Book Review,* 9 Jan. 1977, pp. 1, 22–25.

6599. **GADO, FRANK.** "Robert Penn Warren." In *First Person: Conversations on Writers & Writing.* Ed. Frank Gado. Schenectady, NY: Union College Press, 1973. pp. 63–79.

6600. **NEWQUIST, ROY.** "Robert Penn Warren." In *Conversations.* New York: Rand McNally, 1967. pp. 83–93.

6601. **STITT, PETER.** "An Interview with Robert Penn Warren." *The Sewanee Review,* 85 (1977), 467–77.

6602. **WALKER, MARSHALL.** "Robert Penn Warren: An Interview." *Journal of American Studies,* 8 (1974), 229–45.

6603. **WARREN, ROBERT PENN.** "An Interview in New Haven with Robert Penn Warren." *Studies in the Novel,* 2 (1970), 325–54.

Bibliography

6604. **BEEBE, MAURICE, AND ERIN MARCUS.** "Criticism of Robert Penn Warren: A Selected Checklist." *Modern Fiction Studies,* 6 (1960), 83–88.

6605. **HUFF, MARY NANCE.** *Robert Penn Warren: A Bibliography.* New York: David Lewis, 1968.

WASSON, GEORGE S.

General Studies

6606. **EBY, CECIL D., JR.** "Americanisms in the Down-East Fiction of George S. Wasson." *American Speech,* 37 (1962), 249–54.

WEATHERS, WINSTON

Interviews

6607. **KIDNEY-WELLS, JENNIFER.** "The Writer in His Region: An Interview with Winston Weathers." *Kansas Quarterly*, 9, no. 2 (1977), 11–18.

WEAVER, GORDON

Interviews

6608. **ROHRBERGER, MARY.** "An Interview with Gordon Weaver." *Cimarron Review*, no. 34 (1976), pp. 46–52.

WEBBER, CHARLES WILKINS

"Jack Long; or, The Shot in the Eye"

6609. **MAROVITZ, SANFORD E.** "Poe's Reception of C. W. Webber's Gothic Western, 'Jack Long; or, The Shot in the Eye.' " *Poe Studies*, 4 (1971), 11–13.

WEIDMAN, JEROME

Interviews

6610. **NEWQUIST, ROY.** "Jerome Weidman." In *Counterpoint*. Chicago: Rand McNally, 1964. pp. 626–34.

WEINSTEIN, NATHAN WALLENSTEIN
(See *WEST, NATHANAEL*)

WELLS, LINTON

"Fauntleroy Fights"

See 374.

WELTY, EUDORA

"Asphodel"

See 6679, 6684, 6715.

"At the Landing"

See 162, 6679, 6715.

"The Bride of Innisfallen"

6611. **HARRELL, DON.** "Death in Eudora Welty's 'The Bride of

Innisfallen.' " *Notes on Contemporary Literature*, 3, no. 4 (1973), 2–7.
See also 6679, 6680, 6698, 6715, 6716.

"The Burning"

6612.   HOWELL, ELMO. "Eudora Welty's Civil War Story." *Notes on Mississippi Writers*, 2 (1969), 3–12.
See also 6679, 6680, 6715.

"Circe"

6613.   GOUDIE, ANDREA. "Eudora Welty's Circe: A Goddess Who Strove with Men." *Studies in Short Fiction*, 13 (1976), 481–89.
See also 6679, 6716.

"Clytie"

6614.   GRIFFITH, ALBERT J. "The Numimous Vision: Eudora Welty's 'Clytie.' " *Studies in Short Fiction*, 4 (1966), 80–82.
See also 206, 6679, 6691, 6699, 6714, 6715.

"A Curtain of Green"

6615.   CARSON, GARY. "The Romantic Tradition of Eudora Welty's *A Curtain of Green*." *Notes on Mississippi Writers*, 9 (1976), 97–100.
See also 6679, 6715, 6716.

"Death of a Traveling Salesman"

6616.   GRIFFITH, ALBERT J. "Welty's 'Death of a Traveling Salesman.' " *The Explicator*, 20 (1962), item 38.
6617.   HEILMAN, ROBERT B. "Salesmen's Deaths: Documentary and Myth." *Shenandoah*, 20, no. 3 (1969), 20–28.
6618.   JONES, WILLIAM M. "Eudora Welty's Use of Myth in 'Death of a Traveling Salesman.' " *Journal of American Folklore*, 73 (1960), 18–23.
6619.   SCHORER, MARK. "Comment." In *The Story: A Critical Anthology*. 2nd ed. Englewood Cliffs, NJ: Prentice-Hall, 1967. pp. 285–87.
See also 206, 384, 564, 6679, 6700, 6703, 6714, 6715, 6721.

"The Demonstrators"

6620.   OATES, JOYCE CAROL. "The Art of Eudora Welty." *Shenandoah*, 20, no. 3 (1969), 54–57.
6621.   PRENSHAW, PEGGY. "Cultural Patterns in Eudora Welty's *Delta Wedding* and 'The Demonstrators.' " *Notes on Mississippi Writers*, 3 (1970), 51–70.

6622. **VANDE KIEFT, RUTH M.** "Demonstrators in a Stricken Land." In *The Process of Fiction: Contemporary Stories and Criticism*. Ed. Barbara McKenzie. New York: Harcourt, Brace & World, 1969. pp. 342–49.
See also 6693.

"First Love"

6623. **THOMPSON, VICTOR H.** "Aaron Burr in Eudora Welty's 'First Love.' " *Notes on Mississippi Writers*, 8 (1976), 75–83.
6624. **WARNER, JOHN M.** "Eudora Welty: The Artist in 'First Love.' " *Notes on Mississippi Writers*, 9 (1976), 77–87.
See also 6679, 6686, 6688, 6715.

"Flowers for Marjorie"
See 6679, 6693, 6715.

"Going to Naples"
See 6679, 6698.

"The Hitch-Hikers"
See 6679, 6693.

"June Recital"

6625. **KREYLING, MICHAEL.** "The Reginald Birch Illustration in *The Golden Apples*." *Eudora Welty Newsletter*, 1, no. 1 (1977), 3–5.
See also 325, 6679–6681, 6695, 6701, 6704, 6712, 6715, 6717.

"Keela, the Outcast Indian Maiden"

6626. **McDONALD, W. U., JR.** "Welty's 'Keela': Irony, Ambiguity, and the Ancient Mariner." *Studies in Short Fiction*, 1 (1963), 59–61.
6627. **MAY, CHARLES E.** "*Le Roi Mehaigné* in Welty's 'Keela, the Outcast Indian Maiden.' " *Modern Fiction Studies*, 18 (1972), 559–66.
See also 597, 6679, 6685, 6694, 6703, 6715.

"The Key"

6628. **HARRIS, WENDELL V.** "Welty's 'The Key.' " *The Explicator*, 17 (1959), item 61.
See also 6679, 6686, 6707, 6715.

"Kin"

See 571, 6679, 6697, 6712.

"Ladies in Spring"

6629. **BOLSTERLI, MARGARET.** "Mythic Elements in 'Ladies in Spring.'" *Notes on Mississippi Writers*, 6 (1974), 69–72.
See also 6679, 6680.

"Lily Daw and the Three Ladies"

6630. **DRAKE, ROBERT Y., JR.** "Comments on Two Eudora Welty Stories." *The Mississippi Quarterly*, 13 (1960), 123–31.
See also 291, 6679, 6718.

"Livvie"

6631. **HENLEY, ELTON F.** "Confinement-Escape Symbolism in Eudora Welty's 'Livvie.'" *Iowa English Yearbook*, 10 (1965), 60–63.
6632. **KLOSS, ROBERT J.** "The Symbolic Structure of Eudora Welty's 'Livvie.'" *Notes on Mississippi Writers*, 7 (1975), 70–82.
6633. **SMITH, JULIAN.** "'Livvie'—Eudora Welty's Song of Solomon." *Studies in Short Fiction*, 5 (1967), 73–74.
See also 564, 566, 6679, 6696, 6715.

"A Memory"

6634. **GRAY, R. J.** "Eudora Welty: A Dance to the Music of Order." *The Canadian Review of American Studies*, 7 (1976), 57–65.
6635. **LIEF, RUTH ANN.** "A Progression of Answers." *Studies in Short Fiction*, 2 (1965), 343–50.
See also 185, 6679, 6714–6716.

"Moon Lake"

See 325, 6679, 6704, 6715.

"Music from Spain"

See 6679, 6704, 6707, 6715.

"No Place for You, My Love"

See 6679, 6698.

"Old Mr. Marblehall"

6636. **COULTHARD, A. R.** "Point of View in Eudora Welty's 'Old Mr. Marblehall.'" *Notes on Mississippi Writers*, 8 (1975), 22–27.
6637. **DAVIS, CHARLES E.** "Welty's 'Old Mr. Marblehall.'" *The Explicator*, 30 (1972), item 40.
6638. **DETWEILER, ROBERT.** "Eudora Welty's Blazing Butterfly: The Dynamics of Response." *Language and Style*, 6 (1973), 58–71.
6639. **TRAVIS, MILDRED K.** "A Note on 'Wakefield' and 'Old Mr.

Marblehall.' " *Notes on Contemporary Literature*, 4, no. 3 (1974), 9–10.
See also 6679, 6715.

"Pageant of Birds"

6640. **McDonald, W. U., Jr.** "Eudora Welty's Revisions of 'Pageant of Birds.' " *Notes on Mississippi Writers*, 10 (1977), 1–10.
See also 6679.

"Petrified Man"

6641. **Arnold, St. George Tucker, Jr.** "Mythic Patterns and Satiric Effect in Eudora Welty's 'Petrified Man.' " *Studies in Contemporary Satire*, 4 (1977), 21–27.
6642. **Cochran, Robert W.** "Welty's 'Petrified Man.' " *The Explicator*, 27 (1968), item 25.
6643. **Helterman, Jeffrey.** "Gorgons in Mississippi: Eudora Welty's 'Petrified Man.' " *Notes on Mississippi Writers*, 7 (1974), 12–20.
6644. **Kraus, W. Keith.** "Welty's 'Petrified Man.' " *The Explicator*, 29 (1971), item 63.
6645. **Richmond, Lee J.** "Symbol and Theme in Eudora Welty's 'Petrified Man.' " *English Journal*, 60 (1971), 1201–03.
6646. **Ringe, Donald A.** " 'Pike': To Be Nosy, To Pry." *American Speech*, 34 (1959), 306–07.
6647. ———. "Welty's 'Petrified Man.' " *The Explicator*, 18 (1960), item 32.
See also 478, 481, 548, 565, 5701, 6679, 6702, 6715, 6718.

"A Piece of News"

6648. **Brooks, Cleanth.** *American Literature: Mirror, Lens, or Prism?* Leicester: Leicester Univ. Press, 1967.
6649. **Hollenbaugh, Carol.** "Ruby Fisher and Her Demon-Lover." *Notes on Mississippi Writers*, 7 (1974), 63–68.
6650. **McDonald, W. U., Jr.** "Eudora Welty's Revisions of 'A Piece of News.' " *Studies in Short Fiction*, 7 (1970), 232–47.
See also 166, 394, 6679.

"Powerhouse"

6651. **Adams, Timothy Dow.** "A Curtain of Black: White and Black Jazz Styles in 'Powerhouse.' " *Notes on Mississippi Writers*, 10 (1977), 57–61.
6652. **Appel, Alfred, Jr.** "Powerhouse's Blues." *Studies in Short Fiction*, 2 (1965), 221–34.
6653. **Griffith, Benjamin W.** " 'Powerhouse' as a Showcase of

Eudora Welty's Methods and Themes." *The Mississippi Quarterly*, 19 (1966), 79–84.

6654. **KIRKPATRICK, SMITH.** "The Anointed Powerhouse." *The Sewanee Review*, 77 (1969), 94–108.

6655. **STONE, WILLIAM B.** "Eudora Welty's Hydrodynamic 'Powerhouse.' " *Studies in Short Fiction*, 11 (1974), 93–96.
See also 298, 399, 6679, 6685, 6686, 6694, 6715.

"The Purple Hat"

See 6679, 6715.

"Shower of Gold"

See 6679, 6680, 6697, 6704, 6710, 6715.

"Sir Rabbit"

6656. **CARSON, FRANKLIN D.** "The Passage of Time in Eudora Welty's 'Sir Rabbit.' " *Studies in Short Fiction*, 12 (1975), 284–86.
See also 6679.

"A Southern Landscape"

See 6684.

"A Still Moment"

6657. **DEVLIN, ALBERT J.** "From Horse to Heron: A Source for Eudora Welty." *Notes on Mississippi Writers*, 10 (1977), 62–68.

6658. **THOMPSON, VICTOR H.** "The Natchez Trace in Eudora Welty's 'A Still Moment.' " *The Southern Literary Journal*, 6, no. 1 (1973), 59–69.
See also 162, 6679, 6686, 6688, 6696, 6715, 6717, 6721.

"A Visit of Charity"

6659. **BRADHAM, JO ALLEN.** " 'A Visit of Charity': Menippean Satire." *Studies in Short Fiction*, 1 (1964), 258–63.

6660. **MAY, CHARLES E.** "The Difficulty of Loving in 'A Visit of Charity.' " *Studies in Short Fiction*, 6 (1969), 338–41.

6661. **PALMER, MELVIN DELMAR.** "Welty's 'A Visit of Charity.' " *The Explicator*, 22 (1964), item 69.

6662. **TOOLE, WILLIAM B., III.** "The Texture of 'A Visit of Charity.' " *The Mississippi Quarterly*, 20 (1967), 43–46.
See also 6679, 6715.

"The Wanderers"

See 162, 325, 6678–6680, 6701, 6704, 6715, 6717.

"Where Is the Voice Coming From?"

See 6710.

"The Whistle"

6663. McDONALD, W. U., JR. "Welty's 'Social Consciousness': Revisions of 'The Whistle.' " *Modern Fiction Studies*, 16 (1970), 193-98.
See also 6679.

"The Whole World Knows"

See 6679, 6704, 6715.

"Why I Live at the P. O."

6664. GRAVES, NORA CALHOUN. "Shirley-T. in Eudora Welty's 'Why I Live at the P. O.' " *Notes on Contemporary Literature*, 7, no. 2 (1977), 6-7.

6665. HERRSCHER, WALTER. "Is Sister Really Insane? Another Look at 'Why I Live at the P. O.' " *Notes on Contemporary Literature*, 5, no. 1 (1975), 5-7.

6666. SEMEL, JAY M. "Eudora Welty's Freak Show: A Pattern in 'Why I Live at the P. O.' " *Notes on Contemporary Literature*, 3, no. 3 (1973), 2-3.
See also 6630, 6679, 6710, 6714, 6715, 6718.

"The Wide Net"

6667. BOLSTERLI, MARGARET. "A Fertility Rite in Mississippi." *Notes on Mississippi Writers*, 8 (1975), 69-71.
See also 298, 6679, 6686, 6715.

"The Winds"

See 6679.

"A Worn Path"

6668. ARDOLINO, FRANK R. "Life out of Death: Ancient Myth and Ritual in Welty's 'A Worn Path.' " *Notes on Mississippi Writers*, 9 (1976), 1-9.

6669. BARTEL, ROLAND. "Life and Death in Eudora Welty's 'A Worn Path.' " *Studies in Short Fiction*, 14 (1977), 288-90.

6670. DALY, SARALYN R. " 'A Worn Path' Retrod." *Studies in Short Fiction*, 1 (1964), 133-39.

6671. HOWELL, ELMO. "Eudora Welty's Negroes: A Note on 'A Worn Path.' " *Xavier University Studies*, 9, no. 1 (1970), 28-32.

6672. ISAACS, NEIL D. "Life for Phoenix." *The Sewanee Review*, 71 (1963), 75-81.

6673. MOSS, GRANT, JR. " 'A Worn Path' Retrod." *CLA Journal*, 15 (1971), 144-52.

6674. NOSTRANDT, JEANNE R. "Welty's 'A Worn Path.' " *The Explicator*, 34 (1976), item 33.

6675. SEIDL, FRANCES. "Eudora Welty's Phoenix." *Notes on Mississippi Writers*, 6 (1973), 53–55.

6676. TREFMAN, SARA. "Welty's 'A Worn Path.' " *The Explicator*, 24 (1966), item 56.

6677. WELTY, EUDORA. " 'Is Phoenix Jackson's Grandson Really Dead?' " *Critical Inquiry*, 1 (1974), 219–21.

See also 267, 493, 6679, 6685, 6694.

General Studies

6678. ALLEN, JOHN A. "Eudora Welty: The Three Moments." *The Virginia Quarterly Review*, 51 (1975), 605–27.

6679. APPEL, ALFRED, JR. *A Season of Dreams: The Fiction of Eudora Welty*. Baton Rouge: Louisiana State Univ. Press, 1965.

6680. BRYANT, J. A., JR. *Eudora Welty*. Minneapolis: Univ. of Minnesota Press, 1968.

6681. ———. "Seeing Double in *The Golden Apples*." *The Sewanee Review*, 82 (1974), 300–15.

6682. BURGER, NASH K. "Eudora Welty's Jackson." *Shenandoah*, 20, no. 3 (1969), 8–15.

6683. CARSON, FRANKLIN D. "Recurring Metaphors: An Aspect of Unity in *The Golden Apples*." *Notes on Contemporary Literature*, 5, no. 4 (1975), 4–7.

6684. COLE, HUNTER M. "Windsor in Spencer and Welty: A Real and an Imaginary Landscape." *Notes on Mississippi Writers*, 7 (1974), 2–11.

6685. COOLEY, JOHN R. "Blacks as Primitives in Eudora Welty's Fiction." *Ball State University Forum*, 14, no. 3 (1973), 20–28.

6686. CURLEY, DANIEL. "Eudora Welty and the Quondam Obstruction." *Studies in Short Fiction*, 5 (1968), 209–24.

6687. DAVIS, CHARLES E. "The South in Eudora Welty's Fiction: A Changing World." *Studies in American Fiction*, 3 (1975), 199–209.

6688. DEVLIN, ALBERT J. "Eudora Welty's Historicism: Method and Vision." *The Mississippi Quarterly*, 30 (1977), 213–33.

6689. EAST, CHARLES. "The Search for Eudora Welty." *The Mississippi Quarterly*, 26 (1973), 477–82.

6690. FLEISCHAUER, JOHN F. "The Focus of Mystery: Eudora Welty's Prose Style." *The Southern Literary Journal*, 5, no. 2 (1973), 64–79.

6691. GRIFFIN, ROBERT J. "Eudora Welty's *A Curtain of Green*." In *The Forties: Fiction, Poetry, Drama*. Ed. Warren French. Deland, FL: Everett/Edwards, 1969. pp. 101–10.

6692. GROSS, SEYMOUR L. "Eudora Welty's Comic Imagination." In *The Comic Imagination in American Literature*. Ed. Louis

D. Rubin, Jr. New Brunswick, NJ: Rutgers Univ. Press, 1973. pp. 319-28.

6693. **HARDY, JOHN EDWARD.** "The Achievement of Eudora Welty." *Southern Humanities Review*, 2 (1968), 269-78.

6694. _____. "Eudora Welty's Negroes." In *Images of the Negro in American Literature*. Ed. Seymour L. Gross and John Edward Hardy. Chicago: Univ. of Chicago Press, 1966. pp. 221-32.

6695. **HARRIS, WENDELL V.** "The Thematic Unity of Welty's *The Golden Apples*." *Texas Studies in Literature and Language*, 6 (1964), 92-95.

6696. **ISAACS, NEIL D.** *Eudora Welty*. Austin, TX: Steck-Vaughn, 1969.

6697. _____. "Four Notes on Eudora Welty." *Notes on Mississippi Writers*, 2 (1969), 42-54.

6698. **JONES, ALUN R.** "A Frail Travelling Coincidence: Three Later Stories of Eudora Welty." *Shenandoah*, 20, no. 3 (1969), 40-53.

6699. _____. "The World of Love: The Fiction of Eudora Welty." In *The Creative Present: Notes on Contemporary American Fiction*. Ed. Nona Balakian and Charles Simmons. Garden City, NY: Doubleday, 1963. pp. 175-92.

6700. **JONES, WILLIAM M.** "Growth of a Symbol: The Sun in Lawrence and Eudora Welty." *The University of Kansas City Review*, 26 (1959), 68-73.

6701. _____. "The Plot as Search." *Studies in Short Fiction*, 5 (1967), 37-43.

6702. **LANDESS, THOMAS H.** "The Function of Taste in the Fiction of Eudora Welty." *The Mississippi Quarterly*, 26 (1973), 543-57.

6703. **McFARLAND, RONALD E.** "Vision and Perception in the Works of Eudora Welty." *The Markham Review*, 2 (1971), 94-99.

6704. **McHANEY, THOMAS L.** "Eudora Welty and the Multitudinous Golden Apples." *The Mississippi Quarterly*, 26 (1973), 589-624.

6705. **MASSERAND, ANNE M.** "Eudora Welty's Travellers: The Journey Theme in Her Short Stories." *The Southern Literary Journal*, 3, no. 2 (1971), 39-48.

6706. **MYERS, SUSAN L.** "Dialogues in Eudora Welty's Short Stories." *Notes on Mississippi Writers*, 8 (1975), 51-57.

6707. **OPITZ, KURT.** "Eudora Welty: The Order of a Captive Soul." *Critique*, 7, no. 2 (1965), 79-91.

6708. **PAWLOWSKI, ROBERT S.** "The Process of Observation: *Winesburg, Ohio* and *The Golden Apples*." *The University Review* (Kansas City), 37 (1971), 292-98.

6709. **Percy, Walker.** "Eudora Welty in Jackson." *Shenandoah*, 20, no. 3 (1969), 37–38.

6710. **Pickett, Nell Ann.** "Colloquialism as a Style in The First-Person-Narrator Fiction of Eudora Welty." *The Mississippi Quarterly*, 26 (1973), 559–76.

6711. **Rubin, Louis D., Jr.** "Everything Brought Out in the Open: Eudora Welty's Losing Battles." *The Hollins Critic*, 7, no. 3 (1970), 1–7, 9–12.

6712. ———. "The Golden Apples of the Sun." In *The Faraway Country: Writers of the Modern South*. Seattle: Univ. of Washington Press, 1963. pp. 131–54.

6713. **Russell, Diarmuid.** "First Work." *Shenandoah*, 20, no. 3 (1969), 16–19.

6714. **Tarbox, Raymond.** "Eudora Welty's Fiction: The Salvation Theme." *American Imago*, 29 (1972), 70–91.

6715. **Vande Kieft, Ruth M.** *Eudora Welty*. New York: Twayne, 1962.

6716. ———. "The Mysteries of Eudora Welty." *The Georgia Review*, 15 (1961), 343–57.

6717. ———. "The Vision of Eudora Welty." *The Mississippi Quarterly*, 26 (1973), 517–42.

6718. **Wages, Jack D.** "Names in Eudora Welty's Fiction: An Onomatological Prologomenon." In *Love and Wrestling, Butch and O. K.*. Ed. Fred Tarpley. Commerce, TX: Names Institute Press, 1973. pp. 65–72.

6719. **Warren, Robert Penn.** "Out of the Strong." *Shenandoah*, 20, no. 3 (1969), 38–39.

6720. **Welty, Eudora.** "Words into Fiction." *The Southern Review*, NS 1 (1965), 543–53.

6721. **Yoshida, Michiko.** "Eudora Welty: The Meaning of Silence." In *American Literature in the 1940's*. Annual Report, 1975. Tokyo: Tokyo Chapter, American Literary Society of Japan, 1976. pp. 58–74.

Interviews

6722. **Buckley, William F., Jr.** "The Southern Imagination: An Interview with Eudora Welty and Walker Percy." *The Mississippi Quarterly*, 26 (1973), 493–516.

6723. **Bunting, Charles T.** " 'The Interior World': An Interview with Eudora Welty." *The Southern Review*, NS 8 (1972), 711–35.

6724. **Clemons, Walter.** "Meeting Miss Welty." *The New York Times Book Review*, 12 Apr. 1970, pp. 2, 46.

6725. **Welty, Eudora.** "The Art of Fiction XLVII." With Linda Kuehl. *The Paris Review*, no. 55 (1972), pp. 73–97.

Bibliography

6726. JORDAN, LEONA. "Eudora Welty: Selected Criticism." *Bulletin of Bibliography and Magazine Notes*, 23 (1960), 14–15.

6727. [McDONALD, W. U., JR.]. "The Clipping File." *Eudora Welty Newsletter*, 1, no. 1 (1977), 9–11; 1, no. 2 (1977), 15.

6728. _____. "Welty in British Periodicals: A Preliminary Checklist." *Eudora Welty Newsletter*, 1, no. 2 (1977), 7–8.

6729. _____. "Works by Welty: A Continuing Checklist." *Eudora Welty Newsletter*, 1, no. 1 (1977), 6–7; 1, no. 2 (1977), 8–9.

6730. POLK, NOEL. "A Checklist of Translations and Foreign-Language Editions of Eudora Welty's Works." *Eudora Welty Newsletter*, 1, no. 2 (1977), 3–7.

6731. _____. "Eudora Welty: A Checklist of Scholarship, 1975–77." *Eudora Welty Newsletter*, 1, no. 2 (1977), 10–15.

6732. _____. "A Eudora Welty Checklist." *The Mississippi Quarterly*, 26 (1973), 663–93.

6733. _____. "An Unknown Printing of *A Curtain of Green*." *Eudora Welty Newsletter*, 1, no. 1 (1977), 2–3.

6734. _____, AND RONALD E. TOMLIN. "Collections and Acquisitions." *Eudora Welty Newsletter*, 1, no. 1 (1977), 5–6.

WESCOTT, GLENWAY

"The Dream of Audubon"

See 6736.

"Hurt Feelings"

See 6735, 6736.

"Like a Lover"

See 6735, 6736.

"The Rescuer"

See 6736.

"The Sight of a Dead Boy"

See 6736.

General Studies

*6735. JOHNSON, IRA. *Glenway Wescott: The Paradox of Voice*. Port Washington, NY: Kennikat, 1971.

6736. RUECKERT, WILLIAM H. *Glenway Wescott*. New York: Twayne, 1965.

6737. WESCOTT, GLENWAY. "Fiction Writing in a Time of Troubles." In *Images of Truth: Remembrances and Criticism.* New York: Harper & Row, 1962. pp. 3–24.

Interviews

6738. **GADO, FRANK.** "Glenway Wescott." In *First Person: Conversations on Writers & Writing.* Ed. Frank Gado. Schenectady, NY: Union College Press, 1973. pp. 3–30.

WEST, DOROTHY

"The Typewriter"

See 283.

WEST, JESSAMYN

"The Lesson"

See 374.

"Love, Death and the Ladies' Drill Team"

6739. **KATOPE, CHRISTOPHER G.** "West's 'Love, Death, and the Ladies' Drill Team.' " *The Explicator,* 23 (1964), item 27. *See* 374, 6740.

General Studies

*6740. **SHIVERS, ALFRED S.** *Jessamyn West.* New York: Twayne, 1972.

Interviews

6741. **TOOKER, DAN, AND ROGER HOFHEINS.** "Jessamyn West." In *Fiction!: Interviews with Northern California Novelists.* New York: Harcourt Brace Jovanovich, 1976. pp. 181–91.

6742. **WEST, JESSAMYN.** "The Art of Fiction LXVII." With Carolyn Doty. *The Paris Review,* no. 71 (1977), pp. 141–59.

Bibliography

6743. **SHIVERS, ALFRED S.** "Jessamyn West." *Bulletin of Bibliography and Magazine Notes,* 28 (1971), 1–3.

WEST, NATHANAEL

"The Adventurer"

See 6746.

"Business Deal"

See 6744, 6745.

"Mr. Potts of Pottstown"

See 6745, 6746.

General Studies

6744. **LIGHT, JAMES F.** *Nathanael West: An Interpretative Study.*
Evanston, IL: Northwestern Univ. Press, 1961.

6745. _____. *Nathanael West: An Interpretative Study.* 2nd ed.
Evanston, IL: Northwestern Univ. Press, 1971.

6746. **MARTIN, JAY.** *Nathanael West: The Art of His Life.* New
York: Farrar, Straus and Giroux, 1970.

Bibliography

6747. **VANNATTA, DENNIS P.** *Nathanael West: An Annotated Bibliography of the Scholarship and Works.* New York: Garland, 1976.

6748. **WHITE, WILLIAM.** "Nathanael West: A Bibliography Addenda (1957-1964)." *The Serif*, 2, no. 1 (1965), 5-18.

6749. _____. *Nathanael West: A Comprehensive Bibliography.*
Kent, OH: Kent State Univ. Press, 1975.

6750. _____. "Nathanael West: A Working Checklist." *Bulletin of Bibliography and Magazine Notes*, 29 (1972), 140-43.

6751. _____. "Nathanael West: Further Bibliographical
Notes." *The Serif*, 2, no. 3 (1965), 28-31.

WESTLAKE, DONALD E.

Bibliography

6752. **KODAKA, NOBUMITSU, AND DONALD E. WESTLAKE.** "Donald E. Westlake: A Checklist." *The Armchair Detective*, 8 (1975),
203-05.

WHARTON, EDITH

"After Holbein"

6753. **McDOWELL, MARGARET B.** "Edith Wharton's 'After Hol-
bein': 'A Paradigm of the Human Condition.' " *The Journal of
Narrative Technique*, 1 (1971), 49-58.
See also 6771, 6774.

"Autres Temps"

See 356.

"Beatrice Palmato"

See 6768, 6776.

"Bewitched"

See 6771, 6772.

"The Blond Beast"

See 6766, 6767.

"Bunner Sisters"

6754. SAUNDERS, JUDITH P. "Ironic Reversal in Edith Wharton's *Bunner Sisters." Studies in Short Fiction*, 14 (1977), 241–45. *See also* 6763, 6775, 6776.

"The Children"

See 6765, 6775.

"The Day of the Funeral"

See 6774.

"Diagnosis"

See 6774.

"The Duchess at Prayer"

See 6765.

"The Eyes"

See 4052, 6766, 6769, 6772, 6776.

"Fast and Loose"

6755. WINNER, VIOLA HOPKINS. "Convention and Prediction in Edith Wharton's *Fast and Loose." American Literature*, 42 (1970), 50–69.

6756. ———. "Introduction." In *Fast and Loose, a Novelette by David Olivieri*, by Edith Wharton. Charlottesville: Univ. Press of Virginia, 1977. pp. xiii–xxix.

"The Fullness of Life"

See 6763, 6776.

"Her Son"

See 6773.

"The Hermit and the Wild Woman"

6757. TINTNER, ADELINE R. " 'The Hermit and the Wild Woman': Edith Wharton's 'Fictioning' of Henry James." *Journal of Modern Literature*, 4 (1974), 32–42. *See also* 6769.

"His Father's Son"

See 6776.

"A Journey"

See 6774.

"A Joy in the House"

See 6774.

"Kerfol"

See 6765, 6772.

"The Last Asset"

See 6766.

"The Letters"

See 6768, 6776.

"The Long Run"

See 356, 6770.

"Madame de Treymes"

See 6761, 6765, 6771.

"Mrs. Manstey's View"

See 454, 6776.

"The Muse's Tragedy"

See 6776.

"Old Maid"

See 6776.

"The Other Two"

See 6766, 6773, 6776.

"The Pelican"

See 6766.

"Permanent Wave"

See 6774.

"Pomegranate Seed"

See 6772.

"The Reckoning"

See 356.

"Roman Fever"

See 267, 6774.

"The Touchstone"

See 6768, 6775, 6776.

"The Triumph of Night"

See 6772.

"Valley of Childish Things, and Other Emblems"

See 6776.

"Xingu"

See 6765, 6773, 6775.

General Studies

6758. AUCHINCLOSS, LOUIS. *Edith Wharton*. Minneapolis: Univ. of Minnesota Press, 1961.

6759. ———. *Edith Wharton: A Woman in Her Time*. New York: Viking, 1971.

6760. BELL, MILLICENT. "Edith Wharton and Henry James: The Literary Relation." *PMLA*, 74 (1959), 619–37.

6761. ———. *Edith Wharton & Henry James: The Story of Their Friendship*. New York: Braziller, 1965.

6762. COARD, ROBERT L. "Names in the Fiction of Edith Wharton." *Names*, 13 (1965), 1–10.

6763. COOLIDGE, OLIVIA. *Edith Wharton, 1862–1937*. New York: Scribner's, 1964.

6764. HOWE, IRVING. "Introduction: The Achievement of Edith Wharton." In *Edith Wharton: A Collection of Critical Essays*. Englewood Cliffs, NJ: Prentice-Hall, 1962. pp. 1–18.

6765. KELLOGG, GRACE. *The Two Lives of Edith Wharton: The Woman and Her Work*. New York: Appleton-Century, 1965.

6766. LAWSON, RICHARD H. *Edith Wharton*. New York: Ungar, 1977.

6767. ———. *Edith Wharton and German Literature*. Bonn: Bouvier, 1975.

6768. LEWIS, R. W. B. *Edith Wharton: A Biography*. New York: Harper & Row, 1975.

6769. ———. "Introduction." In *The Collected Short Stories of Edith Wharton*. 2 vols. New York: Scribner's, 1968. I, vii–xxv.

6770. LYDE, MARILYN JONES. *Edith Wharton: Convention and Morality in the Work of a Novelist.* Norman: Univ. of Oklahoma Press, 1959.

6771. McDOWELL, MARGARET B. *Edith Wharton.* Boston, MA: Twayne, 1976.

6772. ———. "Edith Wharton's Ghost Stories." *Criticism*, 12 (1970), 133–52.

6773. PLANTE, PATRICIA R. "Edith Wharton as Short Story Writer." *The Midwest Quarterly*, 4 (1963), 363–79.

6774. SASAKI, MIYOKO. "The Dance of Death: A Study of Edith Wharton's Short Stories." *Studies in English Literature* (Tokyo), 51 (1974), 67–90.

6775. WALTON, GEOFFREY. *Edith Wharton: A Critical Interpretation.* Rutherford, NJ: Fairleigh Dickinson Univ. Press, 1970.

6776. WOLFF, CYNTHIA GRIFFIN. *A Feast of Words: The Triumph of Edith Wharton.* New York: Oxford Univ. Press, 1977.

Bibliography

6777. BRENNI, VITO J. *Edith Wharton: A Bibliography.* Morgantown: West Virginia Univ. Library, 1966.

6778. SPRINGER, MARLENE. *Edith Wharton and Kate Chopin: A Reference Guide.* Boston, MA: G. K. Hall, 1976.

6779. TUTTLETON, JAMES W. "Edith Wharton: An Essay in Bibliography." *Resources for American Literary Study*, 3 (1973), 163–202.

WHITCHER, FRANCES

General Studies

6780. CURRY, JANE. "Yes, Virginia, There Were Female-Humorists: Frances Whitcher and Her Widow Bedott." *The University of Michigan Papers in Women's Studies*, 1, no. 1 (1974), 74–90.

WHITE, E[LWYN] B[ROOKS]

"The Door"

6781. STEINHOFF, WILLIAM R. "The Door: 'The Professor,' 'My Friend the Poet (Deceased),' 'The Washable House,' and 'The Man Out in Jersey.' " *College English*, 23 (1961), 229–32.

See also 6782.

General Studies

*6782. SAMPSON, EDWARD C. *E. B. White.* New York: Twayne, 1974.

600 E[LWYN] B[ROOKS] WHITE

Interviews

6783. **MITGANG, HERBERT.** "Behind the Best Sellers: E. B. White." *The New York Times Book Review*, 20 Nov. 1977, p. 68.

WHITE, STEWART EDWARD

General Studies

6784. **ALTER, JUDY.** *Stewart Edward White.* Boise, ID: Boise State Univ., 1975.

WHITE, WILLIAM ALLEN

"The Gods Arrive"

See 6785.

"The Regeneration of Colonel Hucks"

See 6786.

General Studies

6785. **GROMAN, GEORGE L.** "W. A. White's Political Fiction: A Study in Emerging Progressivism." *The Midwest Quarterly*, 8 (1966), 79–93.
6786. **MCKEE, JOHN DEWITT.** *William Allen White: Maverick on Main Street.* Westport, CT: Greenwood, 1975.

WHITE, WILLIAM ANTHONY PARKER
(See BOUCHER, ANTHONY)

WHITLOCK, BRAND

"The Pardon of Thomas Whalen"

See 6787.

General Studies

6787. **ANDERSON, DAVID D.** *Brand Whitlock.* New York: Twayne, 1968.

Bibliography

6788. **THORBURN, NEIL.** "Brand Whitlock (1869–1934)." *American Literary Realism, 1870–1910*, 1, no. 3 (1968), 30–35.

WHITMAN, WALT[ER]

"Antoinette the Courtesan"

6789. **WHITE, WILLIAM.** "Whitman as Short Story Writer: Two

Unpublished Manuscripts." *Notes and Queries*, NS 9 (1962), 87-89.

"Death in the School-Room"

6790. THOMPSON, G. R. "An Early Unrecorded Printing of Walt Whitman's 'Death in the School-Room.' " *The Papers of the Bibliographical Society of America*, 67 (1973), 64-65.

"Revenge and Requital: A Tale of a Murderer Escaped"

6791. TANSELLE, G. THOMAS. "Whitman's Short Stories: Another Reprint." *The Papers of the Bibliographical Society of America*, 56 (1962), 115.

Bibliography

6792. WHITE, WILLIAM. "Addenda to Whitman's Short Stories." *The Papers of the Bibliographical Society of America*, 57 (1963), 221-22.

6793. ———. "Whitman's Short Stories: More Addenda." *The Papers of the Bibliographical Society of America*, 69 (1975), 402-03.

WILLIAMS, BEN AMES

"Thrifty Stock"

See 6795.

General Studies

6794. CARY, RICHARD. "Ben Ames Williams and the *Saturday Evening Post*." *Colby Library Quarterly*, 10 (1973), 190-222.

6795. YOKELSON, JOSEPH B. "Ben Ames Williams: Pastoral Moralist." *Colby Library Quarterly*, 6 (1963), 278-93.

Bibliography

6796. CARY, RICHARD. "Ben Ames Williams in Books." *Colby Library Quarterly*, 6 (1963), 293-302.

6797. ———. "Ben Ames Williams in Periodicals and Newspapers." *Colby Library Quarterly*, 9 (1972), 599-615.

6798. ———. "Ben Ames Williams in the *Saturday Evening Post*." *Colby Library Quarterly*, 10 (1973), 223-30.

WILLIAMS, JOHN A.

"Navy Black"

See 511.

"Son in the Afternoon"

6799.　CASH, EARL A. *John A. Williams: The Evolution of a Black Writer*. New York: Third Press, 1975.

6800.　FREESE, PETER. "John A. Williams, 'Son in the Afternoon' (1962)." In *The Black American Short Story in the 20th Century: A Collection of Critical Essays*. Ed. Peter Bruck. Amsterdam: B. R. Grüner, 1977. pp. 141–55.

Interviews

6801.　CASH, EARL A. "Interview—October 25, 1971." In *John A. Williams: The Evolution of a Black Writer*. New York: Third Press, 1975. pp. 131–62.

WILLIAMS, JOHN B[ABINGTON]

General Studies

6802.　BLEILER, E. F. "John B. Williams, M.D., Forgotten Writer of Detective Stories." *The Armchair Detective*, 10 (1977), 353.

WILLIAMS, TENNESSEE

"The Angel in the Alcove"

See 6812.

"Desire and the Black Masseur"

6803.　HURLEY, PAUL J. "Williams' 'Desire and the Black Masseur': An Analysis." *Studies in Short Fiction*, 2 (1964), 51–55.
See also 278, 6806, 6808, 6814.

"The Field of Blue Children"

6804.　SHERRILL, ANNE, AND PAULA ROBERTSON-ROSE. "Discussion-Illustration." In *Four Elements: A Creative Approach to the Short Story*. New York: Holt, Rinehart and Winston, 1975. pp. 125–28.

"Hard Candy"

See 6814.

"The Kingdom of Earth"

See 6811.

"The Knightly Quest"

See 6814.

"Man Bring This Up Road"

See 6811.

"The Mysteries of the Joy Rio"

See 6814.

"The Night of the Iguana"

See 6805, 6807, 6808, 6811.

"One Arm"

See 6806, 6808, 6812, 6814.

"The Resemblance between a Violin Case and a Coffin"

See 6808.

"Three Players of a Summer Game"

See 278, 6811.

"Two on a Party"

See 6814.

"The Vine"

See 6808.

"The Yellow Bird"

See 6811, 6812.

General Studies

6805. DRAYA, REN. "The Fiction of Tennessee Williams." In *Tennessee Williams: A Tribute.* Ed. Jac Tharpe. Jackson: Univ. Press of Mississippi, 1977. pp. 647-62.
6806. FALK, SIGNI LENEA. *Tennessee Williams.* New York: Twayne, 1961.
6807. FEDDER, NORMAN J. "Fiction." In *The Influence of D. H. Lawrence on Tennessee Williams.* The Hague: Mouton, 1966. pp. 27-46.
6808. NELSON, BENJAMIN. *Tennessee Williams: The Man and His Works.* New York: Ivan Obolensky, 1961.
6809. PEDEN, WILLIAM H. "Mad Pilgrimage: The Short Stories of Tennessee Williams." *Studies in Short Fiction,* 1 (1964), 243-50.
6810. RAMASWAMY, S. "The Short Stories of Tennessee Williams." In *Indian Studies in American Fiction.* Ed. M. K. Naik, S. K. Desair, and S. Mokashi-Punekar. Dharwar: Karnatak Univ., 1974. pp. 263-85.

6811. **RECK, TOM S.** "The Short Stories of Tennessee Williams: Nuleus for His Drama." *Tennessee Studies In Literature*, 16 (1971), 141–54.

6812. **RICHARDSON, THOMAS J.** "The City of Day and the City of Night: New Orleans and the Exotic Unreality of Tennessee Williams." In *Tennessee Williams: A Tribute*. Ed. Jac Tharpe. Jackson: Univ. Press of Mississippi, 1977. pp. 631–46.

6813. **ROREM, NED.** "Tennessee Now and Then." *London Magazine*, NS 15, no. 2 (1975), 68–74.

6814. **SKLEPOWICH, EDWARD A.** "In Pursuit of the Lyric Quarry: The Image of the Homosexual in Tennessee Williams' Prose Fiction." In *Tennessee Williams: A Tribute*. Ed. Jac Tharpe. Jackson: Univ. Press of Mississippi, 1977. pp. 525–44.

6815. **TISCHLER, NANCY M.** *Tennessee Williams*. Austin, TX: Steck-Vaughn, 1969.

6816. _____. *Tennessee Williams: Rebellious Puritan*. New York: Citadel Press, 1961.

Interviews

6817. **GAINES, JIM.** "A Talk about Life and Style with Tennessee Williams." *Saturday Review*, 55 (29 Apr. 1972), 25–29.

Bibliography

6818. **BROWN, ANDREAS.** "Tennessee Williams by Another Name." *The Papers of the Bibliographical Society of America*, 57 (1963), 377–78.

6819. **PRESLEY, DELMA E.** "Tennessee Williams: 25 Years of Criticism." *Bulletin of Bibliography and Magazine Notes*, 30 (1973), 21–29.

WILLIAMS, THOMAS

"Goose Pond"

6820. **WILLIAMS, THOMAS.** Introduction to "Goose Pond." In *Writer's Choice*. Ed. Rust Hills. New York: McKay, 1974. pp. 397–98.

WILLIAMS, WILLIAM CARLOS

"The Accident"

See 6832, 6834.

"A Face of Stone"

See 6830.

"The Farmers' Daughters"

See 6834.

"Four Bottles of Beer"

See 6834.

"Jean Beicke"

See 416, 6830, 6832.

"Old Doc Rivers"

See 6832, 6834.

"The Use of Force"

6821. BROWN, LUCIE SCOTT. "A Use of 'The Use of Force.' " *The CEA Critic*, 35, no. 2 (1973), 35.

6822. DAVIS, ROBERT GORHAM. "A Note on 'The Use of Force' and Freud's 'The Dream of Irma's Injection.' " *William Carlos Williams Newsletter*, 2, no. 1 (1976), 9–10.

6823. DIETRICH, R. F. "Connotations of Rape in 'The Use of Force.' " *Studies in Short Fiction*, 3 (1966), 446–50.

6824. ———. " 'The Use of Force' (Williams)." In *Instructor's Manual to Accompany* "The Realities of Literature." Ed. R. F. Dietrich. Waltham, MA: Xerox Publishing, 1971. pp. 59–65.

6825. GALLAGHER, FERGAL. "Further Freudian Implications in William Carlos Williams' 'The Use of Force.' " *The CEA Critic*, 34, no. 4 (1972), 20–21.

6826. HART, PAXTON. "Williams' *Mathilda*—Etymology or Serendipity?" *American Notes & Queries*, 10 (1972), 69–70.

6827. SCHWARTZ, MURRAY M. " 'The Use of Force' and the Dilemma of Violence." *The Psychoanalytic Review*, 59 (1973), 617–25.

6828. WAGNER, LINDA W. "Williams' 'The Use of Force': An Expansion." *Studies in Short Fiction*, 4 (1967), 351–53.

See also 157, 384, 518, 6833.

General Studies

6829. BROOKS, VAN WYCK. "Introduction." In *The Farmers' Daughters: The Collected Stories of William Carlos Williams*. Norfolk, CT: New Directions, 1961. pp. xiii–xix.

6830. COLES, ROBERT. "The Passaic Stories." In *William Carlos Williams: The Knack of Survival in America*. New Brunswick, NJ: Rutgers Univ. Press, 1975. pp. 3–59.

6831. CORMAN, CID. *"The Farmers' Daughters*: A True Story about People." *The Massachusetts Review*, 3 (1962), 319–24.

6832. **GUIMOND, JAMES.** *The Art of William Carlos Williams: A Discovery and Possession of America.* Urbana: Univ. of Illinois Press, 1968.

6833. **SLATE, J. E.** "William Carlos Williams and the Modern Short Story." *The Southern Review,* NS 4 (1968), 647-64.

6834. **TALLMAN, WARREN.** "Bells Break Tower: William Carlos Williams' Stories." *boundary 2,* 1 (1972), 58-70.

Interviews

6835. **WALLACE, EMILY M., ED.** "An Interview with William Carlos Williams." With John Gerber. *The Massachusetts Review,* 14 (1973), 130-48.

Bibliography

6836. **DURST, WILLIAM I.** "William Carlos Williams: A Bibliography." *West Coast Review,* 1, no. 2 (1966), 49-54; 1, no. 3 (1967), 44-49.

6837. **ENGELS, JOHN.** *The Merrill Checklist of William Carlos Williams.* Columbus, OH: Merrill, 1969.

6838. **HARDIE, JACK.** " 'A Celebration of the Light': Selected Checklist of Writings about William Carlos Williams." *Journal of Modern Literature,* 1 (1971), 593-642.

6839. **WAGNER, LINDA W.** "William Carlos Williams." In *Sixteen Modern American Authors: A Survey of Research and Criticism.* Ed. Jackson R. Bryer. Durham, NC: Duke Univ. Press, 1974. pp. 573-85.

6840. ———. "William Carlos Williams: A Review of Research and Criticism." *Resources for American Literary Study,* 1 (1971), 17-29.

6841. **WALLACE, EMILY MITCHELL.** *A Bibliography of William Carlos Williams.* Middleton, CT: Wesleyan Univ. Press, 1968.

6842. **WHITE, WILLIAM.** "William Carlos Williams: Bibliography Review with Addenda." *The American Book Collector,* 19, no. 7 (1969), 9-12.

WILLIAMSON, JACK

"Breakdown"

See 140.

"With Folded Hands . . . "

See 351.

General Studies

6843. STEWART, ALFRED D. "Jack Williamson: The Comedy of Cosmic Evolution." In *Voices for the Future: Essays on Major Science Fiction Writers.* Ed. Thomas D. Clareson. Bowling Green, OH: Bowling Green Univ. Popular Press, 1976. pp. 14–43.

WILLIS, N[ATHANIEL] P[ARKER]

General Studies

6844. AUSER, CORTLAND P. *Nathaniel P. Willis.* New York: Twayne, 1969.

WILNER, HERBERT

"Dovisch in the Wilderness"

6845. WILNER, HERBERT. "Dovisch: Things, Facts, and Rainbows." In *The Art of Writing Fiction.* Ed. Ray B. West, Jr. New York: Crowell, 1968. pp. 110–16.

WINSLOW, ANNE GOODWIN

General Studies

6846. WHITE, HELEN, AND REDDING S. SUGG, JR. "Lady into Artist: The Literary Achievement of Anne Goodwin Winslow." *The Mississippi Quarterly,* 22 (1969), 289–302.

Bibliography

6847. WHITE, HELEN. *Anne Goodwin Winslow: An Annotated Check List of Her Published Works and of Her Papers.* Memphis, TN: John Willard Brister Library, Memphis State Univ., 1969.

WINTHROP, THEODORE

"Love and Skates"

See 6848.

"Saccharissa Mellasys"

See 6848.

General Studies

6848. COLBY, ELBRIDGE. *Theodore Winthrop.* New York: Twayne, 1965.

WISTER, OWEN
"The Gift Horse"
See 439.

"Hank's Woman"
6849. LAMBERT, NEAL. "Owen Wister's 'Hank's Woman': The Writer and His Comment." *Western American Literature*, 4 (1969), 39–50.
See also 6851, 6852.

"How Lin McLean Went East"
See 6851.

"How Lin McLean Went West"
See 6852.

"Padre Ignazio"
See 6851.

"The Right Honorable the Strawberries"
6850. LAMBERT, NEAL. "The Values of the Frontier: Owen Wister's Final Assessment." *South Dakota Review*, 9, no. 1 (1971), 76–87.
See also 6851.

"The Winning of the Biscuit Shooter"
See 6852.

General Studies
6851. ETULAIN, RICHARD W. *Owen Wister*. Boise, ID: Boise State College, 1973.
6852. LAMBERT, NEAL. "Owen Wister's Lin McLean: The Failure of the Vernacular Hero." *Western American Literature*, 5 (1970), 219–32.

Bibliography
6853. MAROVITZ, SANFORD E. "Owen Wister: An Annotated Bibliography of Secondary Material." *American Literary Realism, 1870–1910*, 7 (1974), 1–110.

WOLFE, THOMAS
"Chickamauga"
See 6869.

"The Child by Tiger"

6854. **WILHELM, ALBERT E.** "Borrowings from *Macbeth* in Wolfe's 'The Child by Tiger.' " *Studies in Short Fiction*, 14 (1977), 179–80.
See also 535, 6868, 6873.

"Death the Proud Brother"

See 6868, 6876.

"The Hills Beyond"

See 6869, 6878.

" 'I Have a Thing to Tell You' "

See 6867, 6868, 6872.

"In the Park"

See 6864.

"The Lion at Morning"

See 6860.

"The Lost Boy"

6855. **FORSSBERG, WILLIAM.** "Part Two of 'The Lost Boy': Theme and Intention." *Studies in Short Fiction*, 4 (1967), 167–69.
6856. **HARTLEY, LOIS.** "Theme in Thomas Wolfe's 'The Lost Boy' and 'God's Lonely Man.' " *The Georgia Review*, 15 (1961), 230–35.
See also 6243, 6864, 6875.

"No Door"

6857. **DOTEN, SHAUN.** "Thomas Wolfe's 'No Door': Some Textual Questions." *The Papers of the Bibliographical Society of America*, 68 (1974), 45–52.
6858. **EICHELBERGER, CLAYTON L.** "Wolfe's 'No Door' and the Brink of Discovery." *The Georgia Review*, 21 (1967), 319–27.
See also 6865, 6867, 6875.

"A Note on Experts"

6859. **IDOL, JOHN.** "Thomas Wolfe's 'A Note on Experts.' " *Studies in Short Fiction*, 11 (1974), 395–98.

"Oktoberfest"

See 6872.

"Old Man Rivers"

6860. **IDOL, JOHN L., JR.** "Wolfe's 'The Lion at Morning' and 'Old Man Rivers.' " *The Thomas Wolfe Newsletter*, 1, no. 2 (1977), 21–24.

"The Party at Jack's"

See 6865, 6867, 6868.

"A Portrait of Bascom Hawke"

See 6866–6868.

"The Web of Earth"

See 185, 6867–6869.

General Studies

6861. **AUSTIN, NEAL F.** *A Biography of Thomas Wolfe*. Austin, TX: Roger Beacham, 1968.

6862. **FIELD, LESLIE A.** "Introduction." In *Thomas Wolfe: Three Decades of Criticism*. New York: New York Univ. Press, 1968. pp. xi–xxi.

6863. **GOULD, ELAINE WESTALL.** *Look Beyond You, Thomas Wolfe: Ghosts of a Common Tribal Heritage*. Hicksville, NY: Exposition Press, 1976.

6864. **GURKO, LEO.** *Thomas Wolfe: Beyond the Romantic Ego*. New York: Crowell, 1975.

6865. **HOLMAN, C. HUGH.** *The Loneliness at the Core: Studies in Thomas Wolfe*. Baton Rouge: Louisiana State Univ. Press, 1975.

6866. _____. "Thomas Wolfe, *Scribner's Magazine*, and 'The Blest *Nouvelle*.' " In *Essays Mostly on Periodical Publishing in America: A Collection in Honor of Clarence Gohdes*. Ed. James Woodress, et al. Durham, NC: Duke Univ. Press, 1973. pp. 205–20.

6867. _____, ED. WITH INTROS. *The Short Novels of Thomas Wolfe*. New York: Scribner's, 1961.

6868. **KENNEDY, RICHARD S.** *The Window of Memory: The Literary Career of Thomas Wolfe*. Chapel Hill: Univ. of North Carolina Press, 1962.

6869. **McELDERRY, B. R., JR.** *Thomas Wolfe*. New York: Twayne, 1964.

6870. **NOWELL, ELIZABETH.** *Thomas Wolfe: A Biography*. Garden City, NY: Doubleday, 1960.

6871. **PAYNE, LADELL.** *Thomas Wolfe*. Austin, TX: Steck-Vaughn, 1969.

6872. **REEVES, PASCHAL.** "The Second Homeland of His Spirit:

Germany in the Fiction of Thomas Wolfe." In *Americana-Austriaca: Beiträge zur Amerikakunde*, Vol. 2. Ed. Klaus Lanzinger. Vienna: Braumüller, 1970. pp. 53-60.

6873. _____. *Thomas Wolfe's Albatross: Race and Nationality in America*. Athens: Univ. of Georgia Press, 1968.

6874. RYSSEL, FRITZ HEINRICH. *Thomas Wolfe*. Trans. Helen Sebba. New York: Ungar, 1972.

6875. SCHNEIDER, DUANE. "Thomas Wolfe and the Quest for Language." *The Ohio University Review*, 11 (1969), 5-18.

6876. SNYDER, WILLIAM U. *Thomas Wolfe: Ulysses and Narcissus*. Athens: Ohio Univ. Press, 1971.

6877. TURNBULL, ANDREW. *Thomas Wolfe*. New York: Scribner's, 1967.

6878. WALSER, RICHARD. *Thomas Wolfe: An Introduction and Interpretation*. New York: Barnes & Noble, 1961.

6879. _____. "The Transformation of Thomas Wolfe." In *The Thirties: Fiction, Poetry, Drama*. Ed. Warren French. Deland, FL: Everett/Edwards, 1967. pp. 39-45.

6880. WHEATON, MABEL WOLFE, AND LEGETTE BLYTHE. *Thomas Wolfe and His Family*. Garden City, NY: Doubleday, 1961.

Bibliography

6881. ANON. "The Wolfe Pack: Bibliography." *The Thomas Wolfe Newsletter*, 1, no. 1 (1977), 27-29; 1, no. 2 (1977), 40-43.

6882. BEEBE, MAURICE, AND LESLIE A. FIELD. "Criticism of Thomas Wolfe: A Selected Checklist." *Modern Fiction Studies*, 11 (1965), 315-328.

6883. HOLMAN, C. HUGH. "Thomas Wolfe." In *Fifteen Modern American Authors: A Survey of Research and Criticism*. Ed. Jackson R. Bryer. Durham, NC: Duke Univ. Press, 1969. pp. 425-56.

6884. _____. "Thomas Wolfe." In *Sixteen Modern American Authors: A Survey of Research and Criticism*. Ed. Jackson R. Bryer. Durham, NC: Duke Univ. Press, 1974. pp. 587-624.

6885. _____. "Thomas Wolfe: A Bibliographical Study." *Texas Studies in Literature and Language*, 1 (1959), 427-45.

6886. JOHNSON, ELMER D. *Of Time and Thomas Wolfe: A Bibliography with a Character Index of His Works*. New York: Scarecrow, 1959.

6887. _____. *Thomas Wolfe: A Checklist*. Kent, OH: Kent State Univ. Press, 1970.

6888. PHILLIPSON, JOHN S. *Thomas Wolfe: A Reference Guide*. Boston, MA: G. K. Hall, 1977.

6889. REEVES, PASCHAL. *The Merrill Checklist of Thomas Wolfe*. Columbus, OH: Merrill, 1969.

WOOLRICH, CORNELL
"The Loophole"
See 6890.

General Studies

6890. **NEVINS, FRANCIS M., JR.** "Cornell Woolrich." *The Arm-chair Detective*, 2 (1968), 25–28; 2 (1969), 99–102, 180–82.
6891. _____. "A Woolrich Preview." *The Armchair Detective*, 4 (1971), 145–46.

Bibliography

6892. **KNOTT, HAROLD, FRANCIS M. NEVINS, JR., AND WILLIAM THAILING.** "Cornell Woolrich: A Bibliography." *The Armchair Detective*, 2 (1969), 237–50.

WOOLSON, CONSTANCE FENIMORE
"For the Major"
See 6893, 6894.

"The Front Yard"
See 6893–6895.

"In Venice"
See 6893, 6895.

"King David"
See 6894.

" 'Miss Grief' "
See 6894.

"Old Gardiston"
See 6894.

General Studies

*6893. **MOORE, RAYBURN S.** *Constance Fenimore Woolson.* New York: Twayne, 1963.
6894. _____. "Editor's Introduction." In *For the Major and Se-lected Short Stories*, by Constance Fenimore Woolson. New Haven, CT: College & University Press, 1967. pp. 7–22.
6895. **WHITE, ROBERT L.** "Cultural Ambivalence in Constance Fenimore Woolson's Italian Tales." *Tennessee Studies In Literature*, 12 (1967), 121–29.

Bibliography

6896. **MOORE, RAYBURN S.** "Constance Fenimore Woolson (1840–1894)." *American Literary Realism, 1870–1910,* 1, no. 3 (1968), 36–38.

WRIGHT, RICHARD

"Big Black Good Man"

See 6926.

"Big Boy Leaves Home"

6897. **JACKSON, BLYDEN.** "Richard Wright in a Moment of Truth." *The Southern Literary Journal,* 3, no. 2 (1971), 3–17.
6898. **SCHRAUFNAGEL, NOEL.** *From Apology to Protest: The Black American Novel.* Deland FL: Everett/Edwards, 1973.
See also 192, 196, 225, 268, 296, 333, 475, 6910, 6912, 6915, 6917, 6922, 6925, 6926, 6933, 6935.

"Bright and Morning Star"

6899. **OLESON, CAROLE W.** "The Symbolic Richness of Richard Wright's 'Bright and Morning Star.' " *Negro American Literature Forum,* 6 (1972), 110–12.
See also 6910, 6912, 6915, 6922, 6926, 6933, 6934.

"Down By the Riverside"

See 6912, 6915, 6922, 6926, 6931–6933, 6935.

"Fire and Cloud"

6900. **KARRER, WOLFGANG.** "Richard Wright, 'Fire and Cloud' (1938)." In *The Black American Short Story in the 20th Century: A Collection of Critical Essays.* Ed. Peter Bruck. Amsterdam: B. R. Grüner, 1977. pp. 99–110.
See also 6910, 6912, 6915, 6922, 6924–6926, 6933, 6935.

"Long Black Song"

6901. **TIMMERMAN, JOHN.** "Symbolism as a Syndetic Device in Richard Wright's 'Long Black Song.' " *CLA Journal,* 14 (1971), 291–97.
See also 6910, 6912, 6915, 6919, 6921–6923, 6926, 6931, 6933–6935.

"Man, God Ain't Like That . . . "

See 6912, 6926.

"Man of All Work"

See 6912, 6925.

"The Man Who Lived Underground"

6902. **BAKISH, DAVID.** "Underground in an Ambiguous Dream-world." *Studies in Black Literature*, 2, no. 3 (1971), 18–23.
6903. **EVERETTE, MILDRED W.** "The Death of Richard Wright's American Dream: 'The Man Who Lived Underground.'" *CLA Journal*, 16 (1974), 318–26.
6904. **FABRE, MICHEL.** "Richard Wright: The Man Who Lived Underground." *Studies in the Novel*, 3 (1971), 165–79.
6905. **GOEDE, WILLIAM.** "On Lower Frequencies: The Buried Men in Wright and Ellison." *Modern Fiction Studies*, 15 (1969), 483–501.
6906. **MEYER, SHIRLEY.** "The Identity of 'The Man Who Lived Underground.'" *Negro American Literature Forum*, 4 (1970), 52–55.
6907. **REILLY, JOHN M.** "Self-Portraits by Richard Wright." *The Colorado Quarterly*, 20 (1971), 31–45.
See also 192, 209, 240, 360, 484, 6910–6914, 6917–6919, 6924–6926, 6928.

"The Man Who Saw the Flood"

See 6912, 6931.

"The Man Who Was Almost a Man"

6908. **STOCKING, FRED.** "On Richard Wright and 'Almos' a Man.'" In *The American Short Story*. Ed. Calvin Skaggs. New York: Dell, 1977. pp. 275–80.
See 399, 6926.

"The Man Who Was Almost a Shadow"

See 6926.

"Superstition"

6909. **FABRE, MICHEL.** "Black Cat and White Cat: Richard Wright's Debt to Edgar Allan Poe." *Poe Studies*, 4 (1971), 17–19.
See also 6912.

"The Voodoo of Hell's Half-Acre"

See 6936.

General Studies

6910. **BAKISH, DAVID.** *Richard Wright.* New York: Ungar, 1973.
6911. **BONE, ROBERT.** *Richard Wright.* Minneapolis: Univ. of Minnesota Press, 1969.
6912. **BRIGNANO, RUSSELL CARL.** *Richard Wright: An Introduction*

to the Man and His Works. Pittsburgh, PA: Univ. of Pittsburgh Press, 1970.
6913. **BROWN, CECIL.** "Richard Wright's Complexes and Black Writing Today." *Negro Digest*, 18, no. 2 (1968), 45–50, 78–82.
6914. **CAULEY, ANNE O.** "A Definition of Freedom in the Fiction of Richard Wright." *CLA Journal*, 19 (1976), 327–46.
6915. **DELMAR, P. JAY.** "Tragic Patterns in Richard Wright's *Uncle Tom's Children.*" *Negro American Literature Forum*, 10 (1976), 3–12.
6916. **FABRE, MICHEL.** "Richard Wright: Beyond Naturalism?" In *American Literary Naturalism: A Reassessment.* Ed. Yoshinobu Hakutani and Lewis Fried. Heidelberg: Carl Winter, 1975. pp. 136–53.
6917. _____. *The Unfinished Quest of Richard Wright.* Trans. Isabel Barzun. New York: Morrow, 1973.
6918. **FISHBURN, KATHERINE.** *Richard Wright's Hero: The Faces of a Rebel-Victim.* Metuchen, NJ: Scarecrow, 1977.
6919. **GIBSON, DONALD B.** "Richard Wright and the Tyranny of Convention." *CLA Journal*, 12 (1969), 344–57.
6920. **HAND, CLIFFORD.** "The Struggle to Create Life in the Fiction of Richard Wright." In *The Thirties: Fiction, Poetry, Drama.* Ed. Warren French. Deland, FL: Everett/Edwards, 1967. pp. 81–87.
6921. **KENT, GEORGE E.** "Richard Wright: Blackness and the Adventure of Western Culture." *CLA Journal*, 12 (1969), 322–43.
6922. **KINNAMON, KENETH.** *The Emergence of Richard Wright: A Study in Literature and Society.* Urbana: Univ. of Illinois Press, 1972.
6923. _____. "The Pastoral Impulse in Richard Wright." *Midcontinent American Studies Journal*, 10, no. 1 (1969), 41–47.
6924. **KOSTELANETZ, RICHARD.** "The Politics of Unresolved Quests in the Novels of Richard Wright." *Xavier University Studies*, 8, no. 1 (1969), 31–64.
6925. **McCALL, DAN.** *The Example of Richard Wright.* New York: Harcourt, Brace & World, 1969.
6926. **MARGOLIES, EDWARD.** *The Art of Richard Wright.* Carbondale and Edwardsville: Southern Illinois Univ. Press, 1969.
6927. **NYANG'AYA, ELIJAH M.** "Richard Wright's Commitment." In *Standpoints on African Literature: A Critical Anthology.* Ed. Chris L. Wanjala. Nairobi: East African Literature Bureau, 1973. pp. 374–89.
6928. **ORLOVA, R.** "Richard Wright: Writer and Prophet." In *20th Century American Literature: A Soviet View.* Trans. Ronald Vroon. Moscow: Progress, 1976. pp. 384–410.

6929.   SANDERS, RONALD. "Richard Wright Then & Now." *Negro Digest*, 18, no. 2 (1968), 83–98.
6930.   SINGH, RAMAN K. "Christian Heroes and Anti-Heroes in Richard Wright's Fiction." *Negro American Literature Forum*, 6 (1972), 99–104.
6931.   ———. "Marxism in Richard Wright's Fiction." *Indian Journal of American Studies*, 4, nos. 1–2 (1974), 21–35.
6932.   STEPHENS, MARTHA. "Richard Wright's Fiction: A Reassessment." *The Georgia Review*, 25 (1971), 450–70.
6933.   TATHAM, CAMPBELL. "Vision and Value in *Uncle Tom's Children*." *Studies in Black Literature*, 3, no. 1 (1972), 14–23.
6934.   TIMMERMAN, JOHN. "Trust and Mistrust: The Role of the Black Woman in Three Works by Richard Wright." *Studies in the Twentieth Century*, no. 10 (1972), pp. 33–45.
6935.   WEBB, CONSTANCE. *Richard Wright: A Biography*. New York: Putnam's, 1968.
6936.   WILLIAMS, JOHN A. *The Most Native of Sons: A Biography of Richard Wright*. Garden City, NY: Doubleday, 1970.

Bibliography

6937.   BRIGNANO, RUSSELL C. "Richard Wright: A Bibliography of Secondary Sources." *Studies in Black Literature*, 2, no. 2 (1971), 19–25.
6938.   BRYER, JACKSON R. "Richard Wright (1908–1960): A Selected Checklist of Criticism." *Wisconsin Studies in Contemporary Literature*, 1, no. 3 (1960), 22–33.
6939.   FABRE, MICHEL, AND EDWARD MARGOLIES. "A Bibliography of Richard Wright's Works." *New Letters*, 38, no. 2 (1971), 155–69.
6940.   ———, AND ———. "Richard Wright (1908–1960): A Bibliography." *Bulletin of Bibliography and Magazine Notes*, 24 (1965), 131–33, 137.
6941.   GIBSON, DONALD B. "Richard Wright: A Bibliographical Essay." *CLA Journal*, 12 (1969), 360–65.
6942.   McBRIDE, REBECCA AND DAVID. "Corrections of a Richard Wright Bibliography." *CLA Journal*, 20 (1977), 422–23.
6943.   REILLY, JOHN M. "Richard Wright: An Essay in Bibliography." *Resources for American Literary Study*, 1 (1971), 131–80.

WYLIE, PHILIP

General Studies

6944.   KEEFER, TRUMAN FREDERICK. *Philip Wylie*. Boston, MA: Twayne, 1977.

YELLEN, SAMUEL

"The Passionate Shepherd"

See 564.

YERBY, FRANK

"Health Card"

See 511.

Bibliography

6945. **HILL, JAMES LEE.** "Bibliography of the Works of Chester Himes, Ann Petry and Frank Yerby." *Black Books Bulletin,* 3, no. 3 (1975), 60–72.

YEZIERSKA, ANZIA

General Studies

6946. **INGLEHART, BABBETTE.** "Daughters of Loneliness: Anzia Yezierska and the Immigrant Woman Writer." *Studies in American Jewish Literature,* 1, no. 2 (1975), 1–10.

LIST OF SERIAL PUBLICATIONS INDEXED

[*Note*: A dagger (†) precedes those serials coverage of which has been continued from Jarvis Thurston, O. B. Emerson, Carl Hartman, and Elizabeth V. Wright's *Short Fiction Criticism*.]

†*Accent*
Adena
Afro-American Studies
The American Book Collector
American Humor
†*American Imago*
American Indian Quarterly
†*American Journal of Philology*
American Literary Realism, 1870–1910
†*American Literature*
American Notes & Queries
†*American Quarterly*
American Review (formerly *New American Review*)
†*The American Scholar*
†*American Speech*
American Studies (formerly *Midcontinent American Studies Journal*)
American Transcendental Quarterly
Amerikastudien/American Studies (formerly *Jahrbuch für Amerikastudien*)
Amistad
Analytical & Enumerative Bibliography
Anglia
†*The Antioch Review*
Aphra
Approach
Archiv für das Studium der neueren Sprachen und Literaturen
Ariel: A Review of International English Literature
†*The Arizona Quarterly*
The Arlington Quarterly
The Armchair Detective
The Atlantic Monthly
Aztlan
Ball State University Forum (formerly *Ball State Teachers College Forum*)
Black American Literature Forum (formerly *Negro American Literature Forum*)
Black Books Bulletin

Black Creation
Black Images
Black Lines
Black Review
The Black Scholar
Black World (formerly *Negro Digest*)
The Book Collector
Books at Brown
Books at Iowa
Boston University Journal (formerly *Boston University Graduate Journal*)
†*Boston University Studies in English*
boundary 2
Brigham Young University Studies
Bucknell Review
Bulletin of Bibliography & Magazine Notes
Bulletin of The New York Public Library
†*The CEA Critic*
CLA Journal
The Cabellian
Cairo Studies in English
Caliban (University of Toulouse)
Callaloo
The Canadian Review of American Studies
The Centennial Review (formerly *The Centennial Review of Arts & Sciences*)
†*Chicago Review*
Chrysalis: A Magazine of Women's Culture
Cimarron Review
Claremont Quarterly
Clio
Colby Library Quarterly
†*College English*
College Literature
†*The Colorado Quarterly*
†*Commentary*
†*Comparative Literature*
Comparative Literature Studies
The Connecticut Review
Contemporary Literature (formerly *Wisconsin Studies in Contemporary Literature*)
Critical Inquiry
Critical Quarterly
The Critical Review (formerly *The Melbourne Critical Review*)

Criticism
†*Critique: Studies in Modern Fiction*
Dalhousie Review
De Colores
The Denver Quarterly (formerly *The University of Denver Quarterly*)
Descant
The Dreiser Newsletter
†*ELH*
ESQ (formerly *The Emerson Society Quarterly*)
Early American Literature (formerly *Early American Literature Newsletter*)
The East-West Review
The Ellen Glasgow Newsletter
The Emporia State Research Studies
†*Encounter*
†*English*
†*English Institute Essays*
†*English Journal*
The English Language and Literature
English Language Notes
The English Quarterly
†*English Studies*
English Studies in Africa
English Studies in Canada
Essays in Arts and Sciences
†*Essays in Criticism*
Essays in Literature (University of Denver)
Essays in Literature (Western Illinois University)
Études Anglaises
Eudora Welty Newsletter
†*Evergreen Review*
†*The Explicator*
Exploration
Extrapolation
Far-Western Forum
Feminist Studies
Fiction: A Magazine for the Arts of Storytelling
fiction international
First World
Fitzgerald/Hemingway Annual
Fitzgerald Newsletter
The Flannery O'Connor Bulletin
Forum (University of Houston)
The Frederic Herald

Frontiers: A Journal of Women's Studies
Genre
†*The Georgia Review*
Glyph
The Great Lakes Review
Grito del Sol
Harper's Magazine
Hartford Studies in Literature
Harvard Library Bulletin
The Hebrew University Studies in Literature
Hemingway Notes
The Hollins Critic
†*The Hudson Review*
The Huntington Library Quarterly
ICarbS
Illinois Quarterly (formerly *Teacher Education; Illinois State University Journal*)
†*Illinois Studies in Language and Literature*
The Indian Historian
Indian Journal of American Studies
The Indian Journal of English Studies
The International Fiction Review
Interpretations
Iowa English Bulletin: Yearbook
Iowa English Yearbook
The Iowa Review
Jack London Newsletter
Journal of American Folklore
Journal of American Studies
†*Journal of English and Germanic Philology*
The Journal of Ethnic Studies
Journal of Modern Literature
The Journal of Narrative Technique
Journal of Popular Culture
†*Journal of the History of Ideas*
The Journal of the Rutgers University Libraries (formerly *The Journal of the Rutgers University Library*)
Kalki: Studies in James Branch Cabell
Kansas Quarterly
†*The Kenyon Review*
Language and Style
The Library
The Library Chronicle
The Library Chronicle of the University of Texas at Austin

Litera
The Literary Criterion
The Literary Half-Yearly
Literary Monographs
†*The Literary Review*
Literatur in Wissenschaft und Unterricht
Literature and History
†*Literature and Psychology*
Literature East & West
†*London Magazine*
Lost Generation Journal
The Lovingood Papers
The Malahat Review
Manuscripts
†*The Mark Twain Journal*
The Markham Review
The Massachusetts Review
Massachusetts Studies in English
The Michigan Quarterly Review
Midamerica
The Midwest Quarterly
The Minnesota Review
Minority Voices
The Mississippi Quarterly
†*Modern Fiction Studies*
†*Modern Language Quarterly*
†*The Modern Language Review*
Modern Occasions
†*Modern Philology*
Modernist Studies
Mosaic
Moving Out
Names
The Nathaniel Hawthorne Journal
The Nathaniel Hawthorne Society Newsletter
†*The Nation*
Die Neueren Sprachen
†*The New England Quarterly*
New England Review
†*New Letters* (formerly *The University of Kansas City Review; The University Review*)
New Literary History
New Literature & Ideology (formerly *Literature & Ideology*)
†*New Mexico Quarterly*
The New Orleans Review

†*The New Republic*
The New Review
The New Scholar
†*New World Writing*
The New York Times Book Review
The Newberry Library Bulletin
†*Nineteenth-Century Fiction*
The North American Review (New Series)
†*Notes & Queries*
Notes on Contemporary Literature
Notes on Mississippi Writers
Notes on Modern American Literature
Notre Dame English Journal
Novel
Obsidian
The Occasional Review
The Ohio Review (formerly *The Ohio University Review*)
The Old Northwest
†*PMLA*
The Papers of the Bibliographical Society of America
Papers on Language & Literature (formerly *Papers on English Language & Literature*)
The Paris Review
†*Partisan Review*
†*The Personalist*
†*Philological Quarterly*
Philosophy and Literature
Poe Studies (formerly *Poe Newsletter*)
†*Prairie Schooner*
The Princeton University Library Chronicle
Proof
Prospects
The Psychoanalytical Review (formerly *Psychoanalysis and the Psychoanalytical Review*)
Psychocultural Review
Publication of the American Dialect Society
†*Queen's Quarterly*
Quest: A Feminist Quarterly
Rackham Literary Studies
RE: Artes Liberales
RE: Arts & Letters
Regionalism and the Female Imagination (formerly *The Kate Chopin Newsletter*)
Renaissance and Modern Studies
Renascence

Sydney Studies in English
†*Tennessee Studies In Literature*
†*The Texas Quarterly*
†*Texas Studies in English*
Texas Studies in Literature and Language
The Thomas Wolfe Newsletter
Thoth
†*The Times* (London) *Literary Supplement*
TriQuarterly
†*Tulane Studies in English*
†*The Twentieth Century*
†*Twentieth Century Literature*
20th Century Studies
UCT Studies in English (formerly *University of Cape Town Studies in English*)
Under the Sign of Pisces: Anaïs Nin and Her Circle
The University of Dayton Review
The University of Michigan Papers in Women's Studies
The University of Mississippi Studies in English
†*University of Toronto Quarterly*
†*Victorian Studies*
†*The Virginia Quarterly Review*
West Coast Review
Western American Literature
†*Western Humanities Review*
†*The Western Review* (State University of Iowa)
Western Review (Western New Mexico University)
Wichita State University Bulletin (formerly *University of Wichita Bulletin*)
†*The William and Mary Quarterly*
William Carlos Williams Newsletter
The Winesburg Eagle
Women & Literature (formerly *Mary Wollstonecraft Newsletter; Mary Wollstonecraft Journal*)
Women's Studies
Works
World
†*World Literature Today* (formerly *Books Abroad*)
Xavier University Studies
†*The Yale Review*
The Yale University Library Gazette
Yardbird Reader
Y'bird
Yearbook of Comparative and General Literature
Zeitschrift für Anglistik und Amerikanistik